THE MEMORIES OF A RUSSIAN YESTERYEAR

Volume 2

Compiled & Presented by

TONY ABBOTT

AUTHOR OF
'NICHOLAS II - TSAR TO SAINT'
'THE MEMORIES OF A RUSSIAN YESTERYEAR VOLUME 1'

65 ILLUSTRATIONS

New Angle Publishing

Copyright © Tony Abbott 2023
First Published October 2023
email@tonyabbott.co.uk

INDEPENDENT PUBLISHING NETWORK
ISBN 978-1-80517-207-9
Hardback Edition (cream paper)

CONTENTS

SECTION		PAGE
01	PUBLIC DOMAIN BOOKS	3
02	INTRODUCTION	4
	I Catherine Radziwill	6
	II Lily Dehn	9
	III Anna Viroubova	11
03	BOOK ONE	17

CONFESSIONS OF THE CZARINA
By PAUL VASSILI
(The pseudonym of Catherine Radziwill)

04	BOOK TWO	193

THE REAL TSARITSA
CLOSE FRIEND OF THE LATE
EMPRESS OF RUSSIA
By LILI DEHN

05	BOOK THREE	354

MEMORIES OF THE RUSSIAN COURT
By ANNA VIROUBOVA
LADY IN WAITING TO THE TSARINA

06	LIST OF ILLUSTRATIONS	626
07	INDEX OF NAMES	629
08	VOLUME INFORMATION	634
09	OTHER BOOKS BY THIS AUTHOR	635

PUBLIC DOMAIN BOOKS

Copyright applies for a further seventy years after the death of the originating author, this means that the rights to publish can be passed on. For some parts of the world the time length differs. It is also different for corporate rights such as in the United States of America, for Mickey Mouse for example, which is in place for 120 years; since the Sonny Bono Copyright Term Extension Act of 1998, which amended the duration of copyright. For non-corporate works published between 1923 and 1977, these enter the public domain 95 years after their creation (publication date), under the amendment act of 1998.

This means that the prolific memoirs coming out of Russia after the Russian Revolution 1917, mostly written in the 1920s and early 1930s, have been entering the public domain since 1 January 2019, when thousands of titles became available to download, reprint and repurpose, such as The Murder on the Links by Agatha Christie, Jacob's Room by Virginia Woolf, Kangaroo by D.H. Lawrence, and The Inimitable Jeeves by P.G. Wodehouse.

In 2023, those publications from 1927 that were protected by publishing enterprises, entered the public domain. This would include The Big Four by Agatha Christie, first published in the UK by William Collins & Sons on 27 January 1927 and in America by Dodd, Mead and Company later in the same year. This craze for books of old saw the rise of digital libraries such as the HathiTrust Digital Library which includes much of the content digitised by other repositories such as Google Books and Internet Archive.

It's hard to see why anyone would purchase a Public Domain ebook or hard copy version when almost any work out of copyright has been digitised and is freely available. For this to be viable, the new work must have added value, not just editorial by simply typesetting a work so that it looks neater, but reflected in the additional content; has updated news been provided about things that were not known about at the time? Have photographs been added to further explain the issues? In this volume, the three books are presented unabridged with very little added due to the bulging page count, although sharper images and the soothing cream and groundwood papers used, are reason enough to add this to the shelf.

* * *

INTRODUCTION

THE importance of the works within these covers is truly significant in the understanding of life in and around the court of Nicholas II. They share a commonality that they are centric to the Empress Alexandra Feodorovna. In the first book, the author's ties to the Russian court are through her aristocratic family. Her marriage to a Prussian officer developed further social circles in the European courts which she wrote about and during which time she had no less than seven children before returning to St Petersburg. We are talking about the aristocratic Catherine Radziwill whose maternal grandfather had served as Justice Minister to Emperor Nicholas I. Her connections to Alexander III and the inner circles were attained, in part, by her friendship with the Emperor's advisor Konstantin Petrovich Pobedonostsev and the affair she was having (some describing it as a civil marriage,) with the Emperor's court affiliate to the Okhrana police, Lieutenant-General Peter Alexander Aleksandrovich Cherevin. She is the professional author among the three books of memoirs herein, and therefore much higher expectations are held, but in truth her penmanship is matched by the compelling and sincere accounts of the Empress's closest friends as demonstrated in the other two books. These three prominent women make the revelations designed to sell their books which together hone down to a very intimate portrait of the Empress herself, told by those women who knew her best, at her best.

In comparison with Volume 1, there were hardly any typos at all found in the accounts of these authors. The only nuances are the rather long paragraph lengths. It appears that Victorian women did not appreciate that men require information to be spoon-fed in smaller chunks for the comprehension mechanism to activate. In this book format, 6,14" x 9.21", we can just about endure it but in their original format would have been rather taxing; Book III, for example, has a paragraph that begins on page 201 and ends on page 204. There's an underlying cloying erudition in the first two books, perhaps aiming for the erudite reader, which in fairness, doesn't take that long to get used to once acclimatised to the writing style. If we look behind the marketing mechanics these wonderful memories shine through as intended by their illustrious guardians.

Radziwill (Book I) was a contentious character and there can be no doubt that her motive for writing was solely for profit and fame.

INTRODUCTION

On the other hand, Lili Dehn (Book II) was a lucky survivor of the Bolshevik Revolution 1917 who came to live in England with her husband and son and wrote her book of memories. She had no official position at Court and was brought in to the Empress's close proximity by friendship; she writes from the unique perspective of an impartial confidant of the Empress and was making her case for publication as an eye-witness of the events in contrast to the less than well founded versions being circulated by the press. Madame Dehn was the first person to whom the Empress came in her grief with the news of the Emperor's abdication and she saw him return to his wife and face the supreme humiliation.

> "There must surely be friends and relations in England who would welcome facts which proved that the Empress had been true to her English upbringing and to the traditional right living of the descendants of Queen Victoria. English people seem to have forgotten, when the Empress was vilified on the screen and in cold type, that she was the daughter of Princess Alice, a name which is associated with all that is noblest and best in a woman." — The World's News, 1 July 1922, Sydney

In Book III, Anna Viroubova promises the definitive version of the Empress's day to day life. It is certainly the lengthier and more detailed book, and like Dehn she defends the Empress without criticism of any sort, and disposes of the Rasputin legend. In a way, one gets the sense that it is an apologetic work, written as much to set the record straight, as to lay camouflage over her true role in much of the unfortunate events surrounding Rasputin. She was evidently in need of finances seeing that she sold six of her seven large photographic collections as well, nonetheless the extent of her work is a most significant first hand account. The Sun, on 13 January 1924, stated that "her book is politically insignificant, but it has a deep personal interest from the faithful picture which it gives of the Russian Imperial Family in the last years of Nicholas II's unhappy reign."

In *Nicholas II - Tsar to Saint*, I showed the parallelisms with the lives of Nicholas II and Alexandra to Louis XVI and Marie Antoinette; these authors strengthen that comparison. Succinctly, the essence of the Empress is given by Viroubova, "She was quick-tempered, and passionately devoted to her husband and to her children."

INTRODUCTION

I - CATHERINE RADZIWILL (b.1858-1941)

This first book of memoirs in Volume 2 is from a woman using a male pseudonym, certainly a talented literary agent of the time, who conjured interest over the author's true identity and perhaps some trepidation also around her obvious intimate knowledge of the inner workings of the European courts. Unlike many accounts from the 20s and 30s, Catherine Radziwill has not attracted the same scrutiny perhaps because of her mastery in the art of storytelling and her love for the written word - of which at times in her life she had come to depend on for her sole income, despite being a high noble.

She was born in St Petersburg, the only daughter of a tsarist General, Adam Adamowicz Rzewuski, from a Polish House of note. Her father was born and died in Kiev, and saw active service in the Crimean War. After the death of his first wife in 1853, he married Anna Dashkov and produced his only daughter, Catherine. On the maternal side therefore, Catherine Radziwill descended from the illustrious Russian Dashkov-Vorontsov House, among them Count Illarion Ivanovich, in the direct service of Alexander III and Nicholas II, until his death in 1916. Her mother died giving birth to her and her father returned to Kiev where they now lived together.

Catherine Maria Adamevna grew up in the Russian province of Ukraine and therefore considered herself to be Russian, despite her Polish/Lithuanian father. She was left alone to study and received a fair education. However, in 1873, when she was just fifteen years old, she married Wilhelm Radziwill, a Polish prince and Prussian officer, of whom little is known about, except that the couple circulated at the Prussian court in Berlin where they had moved to live with Wilhelm's family. They had seven children before their divorce in 1906, that did not all survive to adulthood. She continued to work as a secretary to the Empress consort Queen Victoria (the eldest daughter of Queen Victoria of Great Britain and mother to Wilhelm II,) after the divorce and also during her second marriage in 1909, until her first husband died in 1910.

The House of Radziwill had expanded their sphere of influence in to Poland and became a powerful House. The recent generations sought out English and American shores. Prince Stanisław Albrecht Radziwill, for example, was established in London, founded the Sikorski Museum for Polish immigrants there, and in 1959 married his third wife Caroline Lee Bouvier, the sister of former First Lady

INTRODUCTION

Jacqueline Kennedy. It was the surname that Catherine remained the proudest to hold up until her own death in 1941, notwithstanding her second marriage to Karl Emile Kolb-Danvin in 1909.

Both marriages exposed her directly to court life and the body of work she subsequently produced was a remarkable feat. Her second husband was of German birth but living in Stockholm when they married; where he exported engineering equipment between the English and Dutch. It was further exposure for her to yet another European court. As far as her extensive knowledge of the English court, she explains it in detail in her later book *Memories of Forty Years* (1915) in which the whole of Part I is devoted to describing, "the numerous journeys I have made to England."

These were dangerous times in Europe and loose talk amid the powerful families could see one removed from the four realms of existence. It was for her own safety that Catherine Radziwell used several pseudonyms. Letters from Count Paul Vasilli first appeared in a French magazine criticising the German court, which were also released in the book *La Société de Berlin: augmenté de lettres inédites* (1884). It drew speculation as to the identity of the true author, as there was no real Count Paul Vassili to account for. Under Vassili, as well as exposing the German court, she also produced *France From Behind The Veil* (1913), *Behind the Veil at the Russian Court* (1914) and *The Austrian Court From Within* (1916). Her sheer output during World War I is staggering, including a work of fiction and the book which is included in this volume: *Confessions of the Czarina* (1918). Her later works concentrated mainly on royal biographies with her autobiography, *It Really Happened,* following in 1932, ten years after the divorce from her second husband in 1922.

From 1915 when she released *The Royal Marriage Market of Europe*, her real name as the author appeared as; Princess Catherine Radziwill (Catherine Kolb-Danvin), acknowledging her current and former matrimonial surnames. But it wasn't until 1918, that she finally admitted that she was also the one and only Count Paul Vasilli - that revelation being made in the book *Confessions of the Czarina* - Book I of this volume - in which the credited author reverts to Count Paul Vassili to cement her claim to it, as it was the case that several works had sprung up using that author byline.

In this regard the reader will note on the title page that the book is by Count Paul Vassili but note also what is said in the 'Publishers'

INTRODUCTION

Note' at the start, and how straight away in the Introduction she admits to having written *La Société de Berlin* and *Behind the Veil of the Russian Court* – she is saying "I am Paul Vassili."

> *"Just before the war, when, indignant at the manner in which Nicholas II. was compromising the work of his great father, I wrote the book Behind the Veil of the Russian Court, I bethought myself of assuming once more the old pseudonym."*

In Volume 1, I stated that Alexender Mossolov's memories were the perfect place to start as he began with a description of Nicholas II's parents . . . Likewise, Paul Vassili was publishing a full decade before Nicholas II became Tsar. Radziwill's view is comprehensive and in *Confessions of the Czarina* she brings the reader close and personal in to the workings of the Russian court where she was active for a time; estranged from her first husband before their divorce, in an affair with Peter Cherevin, a man who held Russia's highest military decoration, the Order of Saint George for bravery. He was described by the historian Alexander Polovtsov as being constantly drunk up until his death in 1896, encompassing the time Radziwill spent in St Petersburg. His passing meant she could not make ends meet and the mounting debts were more than her writing energies could cover. So, in 1899 she left everything and everyone behind and set out for South Africa to meet Cecil Rhodes, whom she eventually persuaded to pay off her debts. That expedition cost her sixteen months in a South African prison for various infractions, among them forging Rhodes' signature to obtain funds. But that's another leaf in the life of the woman who had seven children and exposed the workings of the European courts before she became 'bored' and headed out for an extramarital affair and an African adventure from which she was lucky to return, even if with scandal.

Here in Book I, she starts with, "The former Empress of All the Russias is to-day a prisoner, condemned to a horrible exile." It sets the timeframe perfectly as her book was also published whilst the ex-royal family were imprisoned in Siberia, (at Tobolsk before April and at Ekaterinburg from April 1918). How could she have suspected that in just a few months all of the prisoners would have been disposed of. She managed to escape the Bolsheviks and emigrated to America. She makes it clear in her book that she had not been impressed with the German court and indeed would have been glad to have been kicked out of Berlin had she been identified as the author of *La Société de Berlin*. Her experiences in the Prussian capital evidently had negative effects on her, not least as her son, Prince Vladislaw Radziwill was killed in action in East Prussia during World War I.

One might suspect when she mentions Marie Antoinette, "..., *she had also met on her path the devotion of a Fersen, ...*" that she is using the Proto-Germanic word 'Fersen', the plural of Ferse, meaning 'heel', to imply a servant – but it is simply an innocent reference to Axel von Fersen (1755-1810), a Swedish aristocrat of her acquaintance. It is one of those books that you need to get one or two chapters in before the brain accepts the rather loquacious style, at times challenging and laborious. Yet it is deserving of its place in this volume of memories.

She was writing right up until a few hours before she died, having been admitted to hospital for a hip fracture and dying less than a month later, still in hospital. As early as 1915, in *Memories of Forty Years*, she had started to see herself as more than a writer, perhaps as a philosopher, considering the valuable knowledge she held of the workings of the European aristocratic society.

> "*People may call me a philosopher; they will never be able to think me a misanthrope, for indeed the faculty of enjoyment exists in me just as intensely as in the days of my youth. And, standing on the threshold of old age, I am glad to say that I have lived and loved, suffered and been merry; that my past has been sweet, though it has known bitter hours; but there is not a single page in it I would care to tear away.*"

II - LILI DEHN

Book II opens with a sonnet from Oswald Norman about the late Empress of Russia, in which he blames the mob and Revolution for her tragic fate and credits her enduring faith in a 'God of love' as the source of the fortitude that sustained her through the suffering. It is an apt opening in defence of the Empress's honour for a book from Lili Dehn, *née* Smolskaia, that aims to do the same. Norman published a book of 36 sonnets in 1897 of which the first one, written in 1884 was a dedication 'To My Father.' He credited his father for, '*The love of letters, and their priceless gain : Oh! would*

INTRODUCTION

my verse did higher flights attain," and similarly Dehn tells us in the briefest ever foreword, that her Empress portrayed for her, the love of life, far removed from the caricatures that have been represented by the historical world record.

As Norman claims the peasant's perspective when noting the peculiarities of life, so too does Dehn make it clear that her notations of the Empress, unbiased by their long and intimate friendship, are not influenced by anything other than the innocent witness of her day to day existence as a kindly and simple-minded woman. In this respect we are fortunate to have an account that is totally devoid of the sensational which seems to have found currency in the lurid representations of the Empress by all other accounts, in which Dehn refutes any notion that the Empress was a hysterical neurotic woman – this, we are told, is the 'real' tsaritsa.

Indeed, it is in her attempt to paint the Empress whiter than white, that criticism of her book arises. It is to be expected that such a close friend would want to address imbalances against the Empress, and emphasise the undisputed facts that she was a loving mother, a deeply religious person and more British in her sympathies than German. But her insistence that Rasputin was an entertainer in the mysteries, a hypnotist, having no undue influence otherwise, reveals her level of ignorance, as it is well known that he condemned the hostilities of World War I directly to the Imperial couple – i.e. political, and he did have some effect on the attitudes of the Government and in the workings of the Church.

It is also well known that the Imperial couple abhorred the Duma. In this regard Dehn ascribes the Revolution to the Duma in that the catalyst for its inertia came from the bread famine of which she states was organised by the Duma and to a degree orchestrated by the Jews within. In the chapters devoted to the Revolution she provides no evidence to support these claims and the argument is therefore unpersuasive and simply a reflection of the Empress's views. Yet another writer of sonnets, the historian Hilaire Belloc, dismissed Jewish involvement in his book, The Jews, published in the same year, 1922. He highlighted that, "The Revolution was a Jewish movement, not not a movement of the Jewish race."

Madame Lili (Yulia) Dehn starts off by introducing her parents. Her father was a military engineer, and her mother in her second marriage. In 1907, she married captain Karl Akimovich von Dehn, an officer of the Emperor's personal guard, which was also during

INTRODUCTION

the time that she first met the Empress. Dehn proved her loyalty during the February Revolution 1917, remaining at Alexander Palace with the royal family, even though her own son was still in Petrograd, until the royal family were moved to Siberia,. There-fore, she is a first hand eye-witness to the harsh treatment accorded them by Mr Kerensky. A major interest of her book are the reproduction of letters received from the Tsaritsa when she was a prisoner in Siberia.

Lili Dehn died in Rome in 1963 and is buried in the Testaccio cemetery, sometimes referred to as the English cemetery; among its occupants are the English writers Keates and Shelley.

> 'The author succeeds in giving the reader more than a passing glimpse of one sort of autocracy, that came to an end with the Revolution. Bolshevism, perhaps, was a still worse autocracy of the other extreme, but it is impossible to read such a book as 'The Real Tsaritsa' without feeling that the Government of the Romanoffs did not crash before its time. Madame Dehn certainly tells a powerful and poignant story, and makes a loyal defence of her friends; but she shows that Russia was dead ripe for a change of a drastic kind.'
> — The Queenslander, 22 July 1922; LITERATURE section

III - ANNA VIROUBOVA

For Book I we discussed the author in detail and for Book II, we acknowledged the author's sincerity but questioned her explanations for the Revolution and over Rasputin. The author of Book III should need no introduction as she is perhaps the best known associate of the inner royal family and was particularly close to the Empress from when they first met in 1905 up until their last days. In the Russian tradition there are variations of the spelling and usually Vyrubova is used, but the rule should be to adopt the spelling used in memoirs, which in this case is 'Viroubova' — Anna Alexandrovna Viroubova *née* Taneyeva.

She was just ten years old when Alexandra Feodorovna married Tsar Nicholas II. Her family were no strangers at court but she was mostly under the patronage of the Empress's sister Elizabeth Feodorovna and her husband Sergei Alexandrovich where she spent some of her childhood at their estate in Moscow. It was there that she also associated with playmate Felix Youssoupoff, the man that was to marry the Tsar's only niece in 1914 and murder Rasputin in 1916. (Chapter II) In 1903, at eighteen years old, she was moved closer to the court as a Maid-of-honour at the Winter Palace. It wasn't until 1905 that she moved to Tsarskoe Selo to replace the Empress's sickly Lady-in-waiting, Princess Orbeliani. As Rasputin had also arrived in St Petersburg in 1903 and appeared at the court in 1905, these were unfortunate coincidences that forever linked Viroubova to Rasputin. She moved in to a small house just opposite the palace gates and was seeing the Empress daily. Yet, the Empress would still visit her from time to time, sometimes with the Emperor.

Viroubova is conscious that she is seen as the person that may have betrayed the Empress under the influence of Rasputin as well as being thought of as having a German origin with an ulterior motive to spy on Russia. She is therefore keen to point out that neither theory were true and that her blood was every bit untainted Russian. This of course is demonstrated by her genealogy; born near St Petersburg to Alexander Taneyev, a high-ranking state official who served for twenty-two years as the head of His Imperial Majesty's Own Chancellery, and her maternal side being the Tolstoy family. It was mostly due to her father's connections that Viroubova drew nearer to the Imperial Court.

Another fallacy she is keen to address is the portrayal of her being a lonely child and the possessor of a rather low intellect, which Rasputin identified, being the reason he was able to easily manipulate her to gain access to the court. Firstly she reveals that she had a brother Serge and three sisters, all receiving an education, "rather more practical than was the average at that time." They were schooled in the arts and well grounded in academic studies, attending many court balls and official functions. She takes pride in explaining her parents' service to the Russian Court and her own introductions, first to the Dowager Empress Maria Feodorovna.

By way of addressing the question of her intellect, she mitigates any prospect of that being remotely true by admitting that when she and her brother were struck with Typhus, Serge had recovered well but she had been "at death's door," and was left with many complications, among them, "an affection of the brain whereby I lost both speech and hearing." Perhaps the quality of her memoirs do cast aside any shadows that would be cast by a wavering intellect and she has succeeded in maintaining her dignity and the reputation that was

INTRODUCTION

wrongfully tainted. She feels the need to attach at the end of the book, as Appendix A, the statement from Vladimir Michailovitch Roudneff, Kerensky's appointed investigator in to concerns around the royal family. In an important paragraph he absolves Viroubova of any wrong doing:

> "Such were the conditions which produced in the minds of persons ignorant of the nature of the intimacy between the Empress and Mme. Viroubova, belief in the exceptional influence of Mme. Viroubova on Court affairs. As has been said, Mme. Viroubova possessed no such influence, nor could she have possessed it. The Empress dominated the intelligence and the will of Mme. Viroubova, but the attachment between the two women was very strong. The religious instincts deeply rooted in their two natures explains the tragedy of their veneration of Rasputine. The relations between the Empress and Mme. Viroubova could be likened to those of a mother and daughter, nothing more."

The memories are notably biased and purposefully absent of any intricate conversation about Rasputin given that Viroubova was an ardent supporter of his. If indeed she had been manipulated to the extent that her actions played a part in the tragedy that befell the royal family, then one can understand why such details would be avoided but that is a scant criticism to consider considering the sheer volume of information she is providing. As a childhood friend of Felix Youssoupoff, had she inadvertently provided him information to assist his plot. Had she realised her role after the fact. Was it guilt and shame that was behind her staunch defence of the Empress.

It is a most loving legacy and written in a soft but commanding tone that leaves no doubt of her love for the royal family. Viroubova brings us in to the presence of the family members, "Every day at the same moment the door opened and the Emperor came in, sat down at the tea table, buttered a piece of bread, and began to sip his tea. He drank every day two glasses, never more, never less, and as he drank he glanced over his telegrams and newspapers." Indeed, up until World War I, Viroubova would have us believing that, "Monotonous though it may have been, the private life of the Emperor and his family was one of cloudless happiness."

At times it may seem she ascribes too much importance to her standing within the inner royal circle or that she is wilfully trying to

INTRODUCTION

right the foibles attributed to the royal family by other authors or attempting to smooth over the public record. For example, the well known tragedy at Khodynka Field during the coronation in 1896 is well documented. Many sources have denounced the royal couple for not reacting to the many deaths and for continuing with the celebrations. This is discussed in detail in *Nicholas II - Tsar to Saint*, in which I note that they could not have failed to be touched by the events, even if they did feel obliged to attend the evening ball. Viroubova attempts to right this by confirming that the royal couple were very severely emotionally affected by the events. The views on this are many, one account has it that the Emperor asked why he should cancel the evening ball; when he was advised to.

> "I think the Emperor liked to walk with me because he had need to talk to someone he trusted of purely personal cares which troubled his mind and which he could share with few. Some of these cares were of old origin, but had never been forgotten. I remember once he began to tell me, almost without any preface, of the dreadful disaster which attended his coronation, a panic, induced by bad management of the police, in the course of which scores of people were crushed to death. At the very hour of this fatal accident the coronation banquet took place, and the Emperor and Empress, despite their grief and horror, were obliged to take part in it exactly as though nothing had happened. The Emperor told me with what difficulty they had concealed their emotions, often having to hold their serviettes to their faces to hide their streaming tears."

Viroubova's memories are also invaluable in the corroboration of other accounts, such as with the often told story of Mlle Sophie Tutcheff, also given by Lili Dehn. And, with things like, "In his book M. Gilliard has recorded that he was never able to teach the Grand Duchesses to speak a fluent French. This is true because the languages used in the family were English and Russian, and the children never became interested in any other languages."

The main revelations the reader expects are about Rasputin. He is mentioned in Chapter V in connection to Mlle Tutcheff and thereafter in dribs and drabs, until Chapters XI and XII. It is more 'righting the record' it seems, and plays down Rasputin's behaviours. Her arguments are openly made and seem genuine enough so the

INTRODUCTION

reader alone is left to determine the validity of her account and that of Lily Dehn, against the many others that do not share their opinions on Rasputin.

Always looking for duplicity is a rule with the Romanov story. For example, there is the rather mysterious book *My Empress* by Madame Marfa Mouchanow, who claimed to have been the 'First Maid in waiting to her former Majesty the Czarina Alexandra of Russia', published in New York and London by John Lane Company. If the book is authentic it offers a new perspective on the royal family, The problem is that the book was published at the same time that the Bolshevik purge on the Romanov's began. It would have required time to write and get to print and it figures that within the aristocracy it may have been known by some that the royal family would perish.

So who was Madame Marfa Mouchanow? One theory is that it was an acquaintance of Princess Gedroitz during their time at the Tsarskoe Selo Infirmary. Despite Gedroitz's exemplary service record during the Russo-Japanese War and World War I, she is known to have turned Red during the Revolution and perhaps that exposé book was already in the making.

> "Alexandra Feodorovna did not make any real friends during the first years that followed upon her marriage. Indeed it was only after the Japanese war that she started the intimacies for which she was so much reproached by her subjects. The most notorious was that for Rasputin, but there were two others just as nefarious—that with Madame Wyroubieva and with the Princess Dondoukoff." — *My Empress*, chapter XVI

Another theory for the author of *My Empress* is given by the clues in Viroubova's book. A letter from Alexei dated 24 November 1917 states that Madeleine and Anna [VIROUBOVA] were still in Petrograd. Viroubova explains who Madeleine was and although there is no aroused suspicion, this trusted English person that Viroubova describes as 'invaluable' with access to the Empress's communique's and personal correspondence, could have been the candidate that was secretly writing the exposé book. Also described by Viroubova as 'tyrannical', Madeleine was 'often critical of her mistress's indolent habits'. This hidden author also appears to have disliked Viroubova:

> "Madame Wyroubieva was the daughter not of the Emperor's private secretary, as she represented herself to be, but of a State

INTRODUCTION

Secretary (which is quite a different thing, being a purely honorific position) called Tanieieff. She had been married to a navy officer with whom she could not agree, and they were divorced, not because he had grown mad, as she declared (divorce for insanity is not allowed in Russia), but because he had found reason to object to her conduct. The Empress, for reasons no one ever understood, took her part and invited her once or twice to the Palace of Czarskoi Selo. Madame Wyroubieva made the most of her opportunities and soon became quite indispensable to Alexandra Feodorovna. She it was who, with the Grand Duchess Elizabeth, introduced Rasputin into the Imperial household, and with him she established such control of the Czarina's actions that soon the latter became simply a tool in their hands."
— *My Empress*

"The chief maid of the Empress was Madeleine Zanotti, of English and Italian parentage, whose home before she came to Tsarskoe Selo was in England. Madeleine was a woman of middle age, very clever, and as usual with one in her position, inclined to be tyrannical. Madeleine had charge of all the gowns and jewels of the Empress, and as I think I have related, she was often critical of, in regard to correspondence, etc.

"Intimate letters, it is true, she answered promptly, but others she often left for weeks untouched. About once a month Madeleine, the principal maid of the Empress, would invade the boudoir and implore her mistress to clear up this heap of neglected correspondence."
— ANNA VIROUBOVA

Unravelling the mysteries is what is so rewarding about reading memoirs. In many cases one senses the answers are known, by someone, somewhere, just waiting for it all to be pieced together, and in this respect the amateur historian is much the same as the many astronomical novices that look up at the sky and now and then discover a galaxy, hitherto unseen by human eyes.

* * *

BOOK ONE

This is a book by the aristocratic writer Catherine Radziwill reprising her pseudonym byline count Paul Vassili. For many years the identity was not known and in this book she finally confirmed her claim to it. Her ambitions in life were matched by her talent in writing, she thought big and thought big of herself. Unfortunately her life choices were less than agreeable with her circumstances and she headed in to several scandals to address her finances.

With this work, Radziwill builds on the earlier interest from her book, *Behind the Veil at the Russian Court* (1914) for a much more intimate examination of the Russian Empress.

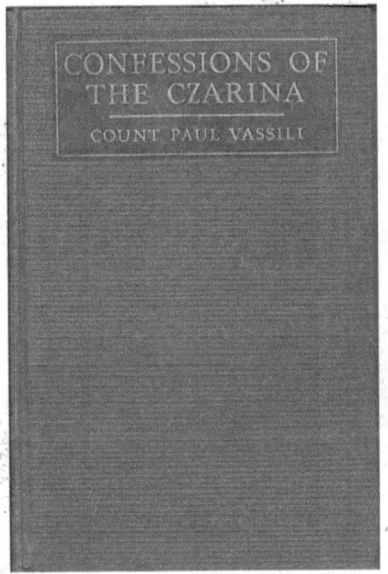

Original book published by Harper & Brothers, in 1918
Published in New York and London
310 printed pages

Confessions of the Czarina

by

COUNT PAUL VASSILI

Author of
"BEHIND THE VEIL AT THE RUSSIAN COURT"
"LA SOCIETE DE BERLIN"

ILLUSTRATED

Copyright, 1918, by Harper & Brothers
Printed in the United States of America
Published April, 1918

HARPER & BROTHERS PUBLISHERS
NEW YORK AND LONDON

CONTENTS

PART I

CHAP	PAGE
PUBLISHERS' NOTE	(ix) 21
INTRODUCTION	(xi) 22
I. BETROTHAL AND MARRIAGE	(1) 25
II. MARRIAGE AND LONELINESS	(18) 34
III. MY COUNTRY, MY BELOVED COUNTRY, WHY AM I PARTED FROM THEE?	(25) 38
IV. A SAD CORONATION	(34) 43
V. DAUGHTERS, DAUGHTERS, AND NO SON	(44) 49
VI. THE EMPRESS'S OPINIONS ABOUT RUSSIA	(53) 54
VII. WHAT THE IMPERIAL FAMILY THOUGHT ABOUT THE EMPRESS	(66) 61
VIII. SORROW AND UNEXPECTED CONSOLATION	(76) 67
IX. PHILIPPE AND HIS WORK	(88) 74
X. ANNA WYRUBEWA APPEARS ON THE SCENE AND HE SAW HER PASS	(99) 80
XI. AND HE SAW HER PASS	(112) 87
XII. LOVED AT LAST	(127) 95
XIII. HE DIED TO SAVE HER HONOR	(137) 100
XIV. A NATION IN REVOLT	(147) 106
XV. A PROPHET OF GOD	(157) 111
XVI. SHE SAW HIM ONCE MORE	(166) 116
XVII. MY SON! I MUST SAVE MY SON!	(177) 122
XVIII. ANOTHER WAR	(188) 129
XIX. MY FATHERLAND, MUST I FORSAKE THEE?	(199) 135
XX. IT IS YOUR HUSBAND WHO IS LOSING THE THRONE OF YOUR SON	(208) 140
XXI. PEACE, WE MUST HAVE PEACE	(219) 146

CHAP	PAGE
XXII. THE REMOVAL OF THE "PROPHET"	(229) 152
XXIII. ANNA COMES TO THE RESCUE	(240) 158
XXIV. YOU MUST BECOME THE EMPRESS	(251) 165
XXV. THE NATION WANTS YOUR HEAD	(261) 171
XXVI. A CROWN IS LOST	(271) 177
XXVII. A PRISONER AFTER HAVING BEEN A QUEEN	(281) 183
XXVIII. THE EXILE	(291) 189

THE CZARINA

From a photograph taken shortly before the Csar's downfall.

PUBLISHERS' NOTE

A FEW months before the great war broke out, there appeared a book, which, under the title *Behind the Veil of the Russian Court*, bearing the signature of Count Paul Vassili, a name that had become famous through the publication of the volume called *La Société de Berlin*. A lively interest was aroused by *Behind the Veil of the Russian Court*, dealing as it did with the intimate existence of four Russian Sovereigns and their respective Courts. The author of this book was declared to be already dead, out of a very natural feeling of precaution for his personal safety. Count Vassili was living in Petrograd at the time, and most certainly would have been banished to Siberia, and perhaps tried for *lèse-majesté*, if that fact had been discovered.

At the present moment the reasons for concealing it exist no longer, and Count Vassili is free to live once more and to publish another work of even greater interest—the life of the former Czarina Alexandra. In relating it, together with some most characteristic incidents which so far are but little known, Count Vassili remarks to the public what a small circle only have known; persons more or less interested in keeping the facts as secret as possible.

Count Vassili had known the Empress personally, in fact was regularly and most exactly informed by numerous friends as to all that went on at the Russian Court, and with all manner of intimate details concerning the existence led by the Czar and by his Consort in their Palace of Tsarskoye Selo. It is interesting to note that in *Behind the Veil of the Russian Court*, written at a time when but few people foresaw the fall of the dynasty of Romanoff, Count Vassili declared the event bound to take place in the then very near future.

INTRODUCTION

I AM not a coward, and it was not out of a feeling of uneasiness in regard to my personal safety, that I had not the courage to publish in my own name the book which, some thirty years ago, produced such a sensation when it appeared in the *Nouvelle Revue* of Madame Adam, under the title of "La Société de Berlin." But I was living in Germany at the time, and though I would have felt delighted had the publication of this volume driven me out of the Prussian capital, from which I was to shake the dust from my shoes with such joy, a few years later, I had there relatives who would most undoubtedly have fared very badly at Bismarck's hands, had my identity been disclosed. And once I am alluding to these distant times, it is just as well to say that the book in question had not at first been written for the benefit of the general public, but consisted of private letters addressed to Madame Adam, who, being happily still in the land of the living, can add many corroborative details. She suggested to me to publish some of these letters; I assented without suspecting the scandal which would follow, and which I do not regret in the very least, now that events have justified the mistrust with which the Prussian monster inspired me. The secret was well kept and one of the victims of it was poor Mr. Gérard, the secretary of Queen Augusta, who was accused of being the author of this book, an accusation that has clung to him ever since, and from which I am happy to relieve him.

The success of *La Société de Berlin* induced Madame Adam to publish other letters in the same style, devoted to other European capitals, with which, however, I had nothing to do, except those dealing with St. Petersburg life. The pseudonym of Count Paul Vassili remained a kind of public property divided between the *Nouvelle Revue* and my poor self. Just before the war, when, indignant at the manner in which Nicholas II. was compromising the work of his great father, I wrote the book *Behind the Veil of the Russian Court*, I bethought myself of assuming once more the old pseudonym. I was living at the time in St. Petersburg, as Petrograd was still called, and my brothers were in the Russian military service. I did not wish them to get into trouble. As it happened, my identity was suspected, and unpleasantness followed; but it is no stigma to have been ostracized by the Russian police under the old régime, so I did not mind or care.

I had not written the book out of any motives of revenge; on the contrary, I had many reasons to be personally grateful to Nicholas II. for various kindnesses I had met with at his hands; but it was impossible for any real Russian patriot to gaze unmoved at the German propaganda that was going on in the Empire, or to forgive its Sovereign Lady for disgracing herself together with the crown she wore, by the superstitious practices that had put her into the power of intriguing persons who ultimately brought about her own destructtion, together with the ruin of the dynasty. It was impossible for any one who had known Russia during the reign of Alexander III., when the whole of Europe had its eyes turned upon her, and was clamoring for her alliance, not to feel deeply grieved in noticing the signs of the coming catastrophe which had been hovering in the air ever since the fatal Japanese war. The Monarch had become estranged from his people and his wife was the person responsible for it; or rather the people who had succeeded in getting hold of her mind. I do not wish here to throw stones at Alexandra Feodorowna, and in relating now what I know concerning her life, I will try not to forget that misfortune has got claims upon human sympathy, and that where a woman is concerned one is bound to be even more careful than in the case of a man.

The former Empress of All the Russias is to-day a prisoner, condemned to a horrible exile. She deserves indulgence; the more so that her follies, errors, and mistakes were partly due to a morbid state of mind, verging if not achieving actual insanity. Her existence, like that of the hero in the beautiful poem of Félix d'Arvers, had its secrets, and her soul its mysteries. The fact that she was a Sovereign did not shield her from feminine weaknesses, and, though she had always remained an innocent woman—a fact upon which one cannot sufficiently insist—in view of all the calumnies which have been heaped upon her, yet, like the unfortunate Marie Antoinette, to whom she has been more than once compared, she had also met on her path the devotion of a Fersen, as accomplished, as brave, and as handsome, as the Swedish officer whose name has gone down to posterity, thanks to his love for the poor Queen who perished on the scaffold of the Champs Elysées. While the latter was spared the sorrow of losing such a faithful friend, Alexandra Feodorowna was destined to be an unwilling witness of a cruel and unexpected tragedy, which ended brutally any dreams she might have nursed in the secret of her heart, and put her good name at the mercy of an infuriated man. Therein lies the drama of her life; a drama the remembrance of which probably haunts her to this day in the solitude of the lonely Siberian town, to which she has been banished by a triumphant Revolution.

This drama, which I am going to relate in the pages about to follow, was made the subject of a shameless exploitation that took advantage of the sorrow and despair to which it gave rise, that neither spared the woman nor respected the Sovereign, and that finally overthrew the Romanoff dynasty, and brought about the ruin of Russia. It seems to me that the revelation of it can harm neither its heroine, nor the country over which she reigned for twenty-two years; while, on the other hand, it may help the public to understand some of the causes of the great Revolution which was to be followed by such momentous consequences, not only for Russia, but also for the whole world.

Before relating it, I must, however, beg my readers to keep always in mind the fact that the Consort of Nicholas II. was not a normal woman; that madness was hereditary in the Hesse-Darmstadt family to which she belonged, twenty-two members of whom had, during the last hundred years or so, been confined in lunatic asylums; that consequently a different standard of criticism must be applied to Alexandra Feodorowna than to an ordinary person in full possession of all her intellectual faculties. The whole course of her history proves the truth of what I have just said, and claims indulgence for her conduct.

As for this history, I think that, such as it really was, few people have so far come to an exact knowledge of it, and that no one yet has related it as I am going to do. The information that has reached me has come almost day by day from sources which I have every reason to know are excellent. I have applied myself to eliminate many facts which appeared to me to be of too sensational a nature. I want also to point out to the reader that, though this book is called the *Confessions of the Czarina*, yet it does not contain one single word which I would like him to believe to have been uttered personally by the former Czarina. It is a story written ONLY by Count Paul Vassili, who accepts its responsibility in signing his name to it.

PAUL VASSILI.

February, 1918.

CONFESSIONS OF THE CZARINA

I

BETROTHAL AND MARRIAGE

TOWARD the close of February in the year 1894 the health of the Czar Alexander III. of Russia began to fail.

Those in the confidence of the inner circle of the Imperial Family, who constituted the small society which used to form the immediate surroundings of the Sovereign, whispered that the Emperor was taking a long time to rally from the attack of influenza which had prostrated him in the beginning of the winter, and that steps ought to be taken to ascertain whether or not he was suffering from something other than the weakness which generally follows upon this perfidious ailment. But they did not dare to mention openly their fears, because it was the tradition at the Russian Court that the Czar ought not, and could not, be ill; whenever any bulletins were public-shed concerning his health or that of any other member of the Imperial Family, it was immediately accepted by the general public as meaning that the end was approaching. In the case of Alexander III., his robust appearance, gigantic height and strength, seemed to exclude the possibility of sickness ever laying its grip upon him. In reality things were very different. The Czar had been suffering for years from a kidney complaint, which had been allowed to develop itself without anything being done to stop, or at least to arrest, its progress. He was by nature and temperament an indefatigable worker, accustommed to spending the best part of the day and a considerable portion of the night, seated at his writing-desk; he rarely allowed himself any vacations, except during his summer trips to Denmark, and he never complained when he felt unwell, or would admit that his strength was no longer what it had been. He had a most wonderful power of self-control and a very high idea of his duties as a Sovereign. On the day of his accession to the Throne, when, on his entering for the first time the Anitchkoff Palace, which was to remain his residence until his death, he was greeted by the members of his household with the traditional bread and salt, which is always offered in Russia upon occasions of the kind. When implored to show himself a father to his subjects, the giant's blue eyes had shone with even more kindness in their expression than was generally the case, and in a very distinct and quiet voice he had replied:

"Yes, I will try to be always a father to my people."

This promise, given in the solemn moment when the weight of his new duties and responsibilities was laid upon him, the late Czar had always kept faithfully, honestly, with a steadfast purpose and an indomitable will. He had put upon his program among other things the resolution never to complain at any personal ailment or misfortune that he might find himself obliged to bear. This resolution he kept up to the last moment, and he went on working at his daily task until at last the pen fell from his weary fingers and he had to own himself beaten. But during the last memorable year of his life he must have more than once felt that the end was drawing near, though he never spoke about it, with the exception of once, when finding himself alone with one of his intimate friends, General Tcherewine, he told him that he did not think he had long to live, adding, sadly:

"And what will happen to this country when I am no longer here?"

The General became so alarmed at this avowal of a state of things he had suspected, without daring to acknowledge, that he tried to open the eyes of Empress Marie as to the state of health of her husband. But the Czarina refused to see that anything was the matter, and angrily reproved the General for daring to suggest such a thing. The latter subsided, and sought one of the doctors who were generally in attendance on the Emperor, asking him to tell him honestly his opinion concerning the Czar. The doctor retrenched himself behind professional secrecy, and only replied vaguely. The truth of the matter was that he did not wish to own that he had been rebuffed by Alexander III. when he had asked the latter to allow him to make an examination of him, and that he had never dared to insist on its necessity.

At this time, when his father's life was trembling in the balance, the heir to the Russian Throne, the General Tcherewine, was twenty-six years old. If the traditions of the House of Romanoff had been adhered to in regard to him, he ought to have been married already, as it had been settled by custom that the eldest son of the Czar ought as early as possible to bring home a bride, so as to insure the succession to the crown. But the Empress Marie had never looked with favor at the possibility of seeing her family circle widened by the advent of a daughter-in-law, and whenever the question of the establishment of her eldest son was raised she always found objections to offer against any princess whose name was mentioned to her as that of a possible wife. The French party at the Imperial Court, which at that moment was in possession of great influence, tried hard to bring about the betrothal of the future Czar with the Princess Hélène of Orléans, and at one time it seemed as if it would be really possible to arrange such a marriage, in spite of the differrence of religion.

But another circumstance interfered; during one of his visits to Germany, where he often repaired as the guest of his aunt, the Grand Duchess Marie Alexandrowna of Coburg, the Grand Duke had fallen in love with the Princess Margaret of Prussia, the youngest daughter of the Empress Frederick, and the sister of William II., and had declared that he would not marry any one else. To this, however, Alexander III. decidedly objected, saying that he would never consent to a Prussian princess wearing again the crown of the Romanoffs. He expressed himself in such positive terms in regard to this matter that the Grand Duke did not dare to push it forward, and it was soon after this that he was sent on a journey round the world, while the Princess Margaret was hurried into a marriage with a Prince of Hesse by her brother, who, furious at her rejection by the Czar, decided to wed her offhand to the first eligible suitor who presented himself. The young girl wept profusely, but had to obey, and the Cesarewitsch for the first time in his life showed some independence, and declared to his friends that since he had not been allowed to marry the woman he loved, he would not marry at all.

Before this, however, there had been made by his aunt, the Grand Duchess Elisabeth, an attempt to betroth him with the latter's sister, the Princess Alix of Hesse, who had spent a winter season in St. Petersburg as her guest, and who was spoken of as likely to be considered an eligible bride for the future Emperor of All the Russias. She was not yet as beautiful as she was to become later on. The awkwardness of her manners had not impressed favorably St. Petersburg society. Smart women had ridiculed her and made fun of her dresses, all "made in Germany," and had objected to the ungraceful way in which she danced, and declared her to be dull and stupid. If one is to believe all that was said at the time, the Grand Duke Nicholas Alexandrowitch shared this opinion, and it was related that, one evening during a supper at the mess of the Hussar regiment of which he was captain, he had declared to his comrades that there was as much likelihood of his marrying the Princess Alix as there was of his uniting himself to the Krzesinska, the dancer who for some years already had been his mistress. But during the spring of the year 1894 things had changed. As the Czar's health became indifferent, his Ministers bethought themselves that it was almost a question of state to marry as soon as possible the Heir to the Throne.

Mr. de Giers, who was in possession of the portfolio of Foreign Affairs, and who (this by the way) had always been pro-German in his sympathies, gathered sufficient courage to mention the subject to Alexander III., saying that the nation wished to see the young Grand Duke married and father of a family. The Emperor understood, and a few days later, in despatching his son to Coburg to attend the nuptials of his cousin, the Princess Victoria Mélita, with the Grand Duke of Hesse, he told him that he would like him to ask for the hand of the Princess Alix, and to offer to the latter the diadem of the Romanoffs.

The Cesarewitsch did not object this time. For one thing, he did not think his father was really ill, and he was becoming very impatient at the state of subjection in which he was being kept by his parents. He imagined that, once he was married, he would be free to live his own life; what he had seen of the Princess Alix had not given him a very high opinion of her mental capacities, and therefore he believed that she would be contented with the grandeur that was being put in her way, and would shut her eyes to any little excursions he might make outside the beaten tracks of holy matrimony. The woman he had loved had been removed from his path, and perhaps in the secret of his soul he was not so very sorry, after all, to show her that he had consoled himself. It seems also that Miss Krzesinska, the Polish dancer by whom he had had two sons, had been won over to the marriage by means about which the less said the better, and had used her influence over her lover to persuade him that the Princess Alix was of so meek and mild a temperament that they would be able to continue their relations after his marriage with her, which perhaps would not be the case were he to wed some one gifted with more independence and more intellect. Nicholas has always been of the same opinion as that of the last person with whom he spoke. He therefore yielded, went dutifully to Coburg, and just as dutifully proposed to the young Princess whose arrival in

Russia was to herald so much misfortune to her new family, as well as to her new country.

The engagement was announced on the 20th of April, 1894, but was not made in Russia the subject of welcome it had been expected. Everybody felt that love had played no part in this union, which politics alone had inspired. The open repugnance which the bride displayed for everything that was Russian, and the hesitation she had shown before consenting to adopt the orthodox faith, had not predisposed in her favor St. Petersburg society. The Empress Marie, whose consent had been a matter of necessity, did not hide the want of sympathy with which this marriage inspired her; the Imperial Family did not care to see put over its head the insignificant Princess it had snubbed two years before; the nation, violently anti-German as it had become, wondered why it had not been possible to find for its future Sovereign a wife in some other country than the one which seemed to consider as its right the privilege of furnishing Russia with its Empresses.

By a curious anomaly, in Darmstadt, and in Berlin, the betrothal was exceedingly unpopular, and the press spoke of it as of an open scandal, on account of the change of religion imposed upon the Princess Alix. The only two people who rejoiced at her good luck were Queen Victoria, who always liked to see her daughters and granddaughters well married; and the Kaiser, who, since his earliest years, had been the particular friend of the future Czarina, and who had succeeded, at the time when she had shown herself reticent in regard to all her other relatives, in winning her confidence and her affection, perhaps out of gratitude, because he had been the only one who had troubled about her in general.

The first weeks which followed upon the engagement of the Cesarewitsch were spent by him in England, whither his fiancée had repaired, and while there he had been very much impressed with the grandeur of Great Britain, and with the kindness which Queen Victoria showed him. He would have liked nothing better than to be allowed to remain where he was for an indefinite time, forgetting all about Russia, which (this is unfortunately an uncontested fact) he never liked nor troubled about.

Events, however, were progressing, and very soon it became evident even to the most indifferent onlooker that the days of Alexander III. were numbered. The dying Sovereign was taken to Livadia in the Crimea, whither his son was hastily recalled. When the latter arrived there took place a small incident which, better, perhaps, than anything else, will give an idea of the young man's utter want of comprehension of the gravity of the events which went on around him. A few hours after he had reached Livadia his father's friend, General Tcherewine, called upon him, to make him a report concerning the health of the Czar. The Grand Duke listened to him in silence, then suddenly inquired:

"What have you been doing the whole time you have been here? Have you been at the theater, and are there any pretty actresses this year?"

The General, surprised, replied:

"But, Sir, I could not possibly go to the theater while the Emperor is so ill."

"Well, what has this got to do with going or not to the theater; one must spend one's evenings somewhere."

Tcherewine, who related to me himself this story a few weeks later, added:

"He will always remain the same; he will never understand anything that goes on around him."

It was during the last days of the useful life of Alexander III. that the plan of marrying immediately his son and future successor to the Princess Alix of Hesse, and of performing the ceremony at Livadia, was suggested, at the instigation, it is said, of the German Ambassador in St. Petersburg, General von Schweinitz, who had received instructions from Berlin to try and hasten the event as much as possible. But the Czar would not hear of it, declaring that the Heir to the Russian Throne could not be married privately. He consented, however, to a telegram being sent to the Princess Alix, inviting her to come at once to Livadia, to be presented to him. She obeyed the summons, but not without reluctance. She did not care for her future husband, and as she elegantly expressed it, to a lady whom she honored with her confidence, she "did not care to find herself in the Crimea at a time when no one would think of her, and when she would be compelled to be the fifth wheel to a coach." She was, however, persuaded, and left for Warsaw, where her sister, the Grand Duchess Elisabeth, was to receive her, and to accompany her farther.

At Berlin she was met by William II., who traveled with her a part of the way, and during a long interview which lasted over five hours gave her his instructions as to what she ought to do in the future. As we shall see, she was to follow them but too well.

The Princess reached Livadia three days before the Czar breathed his last. He found sufficient strength to receive her, bless her, and wish her happiness in her new life. She replied (this must be conceded to her) with great tact to those solemn words of fare-well, and, suddenly surmounting her previous repugnance, she declared herself ready to abjure at once the Protestant faith, and to embrace that of her future husband and subjects. Some people say that she declared she wished to procure this last joy for Alexander III., but this is doubtful, considering the fact that her conversion took place only on the morrow of the death of the latter.

As soon as it had become an accomplished fact, she was given the title of a Russian Grand Duchess and of an Imperial Highness. Her name appeared in the liturgy, and she was treated with all the honors pertaining to a future Empress. But she found herself lonely and forsaken amid her newly acquired grandeur. The Dowager Empress was too entirely taken up by her grief to pay any attention to the haughty girl, who, already during those first few days of her new life, showed herself resentful when she thought that she was not awarded sufficient importance. The young Czar was so absorbed by the many duties and obligations which fell upon his shoulders that he had no time to remain with her as long as she would have wished, perhaps, and his family simply ignored her. Her days were spent in attending the many funeral services which, according to etiquette, took place twice, and sometimes thrice, daily beside the bier of the deceased Monarch. She found herself placed not only in an awkward, but also in an absurd, position, and if she did not realize other things, she understood this one but too well.

When the body of Alexander III. was brought back to St. Petersburg, the Princess Alix accompanied it, together with the other members of the Imperial Family, and one could see her, deeply veiled, during the funeral ceremonies which took place at the fortress, standing beside the Dowager Empress, silent and attentive to all that was going on around her, and making mental notes as to everything that was taking place. She began to assume a Sovereign's attitude, and she tried to take, as if accidentally, precedence over the Grand Duchesses. One of them, the Princess Marie Pawlowna, soon perceived the game, and one afternoon as the future bride was keeping close to her prospective mother-in-law, seeming to dance attendance upon the latter, the Grand Duchess pushed her aside most unceremoniously, saying as she did so:

"Not yet, not yet, Alix; this place belongs still to me."

Affronted, the young girl withdrew; but when she got home to the Palace belonging to her sister, where she had taken up her abode, she declared that she wished to return to Darmstadt because her position was too false in Russia.

Scene followed upon scene; and Nicholas II. was treated for the first time to the hysterics of which he was to see, later on, so many repetitions. At last the Prince of Wales, the future Edward VII., interfered, and it was partly at his instigation, and that of Queen Victoria, who wrote upon the subject to the Empress Marie, that it was at last decided that the marriage of the new Czar with the Princess Alix was to take place immediately after the funeral of the former's father.

I shall never forget that day. In the vast halls of the Winter Palace the whole of Russia was represented, eager to witness this unique ceremony, the marriage of a Reigning Emperor, an event which had never taken place before. The bride was on that day the object of great sympathy. One pitied her for finding herself so suddenly placed in a position for which she had not been at all prepared, and one felt disposed to grant her every indulgence in case she made a mistake of some kind or other, which was almost an unavoidable thing. Some people, whose English sympathies predisposed them in her favor, rejoiced openly to see the Throne occupied by a granddaughter of Queen Victoria, and hoped that the latter's influence and example would induce the new Empress to try and persuade her husband to renounce the principles of the tyrannous autocracy followed by his predecessors. The man in the street, however, remarked that nothing but bad omens surrounded this hurried marriage, and recalled the old Russian proverb, that "wedding-bells ought never to be heard in conjunction with funeral ones."

The most unconcerned person seemed to be the bride herself as, amid the hushed expectation of the crowd assembled on her passage, she entered the chapel of the Winter Palace on the arm of him who since a few days was Nicholas II., Emperor and Autocrat of All the Russias.

A murmur of admiration followed her as she passed. Seldom has anything more beautiful graced human eye than Alexandra Feodorowna in her wedding-dress, as she slowly walked along, with a diamond crown on her head and a long mantle of cloth of gold lined with ermine falling from her shoulders, and carried by Court officials in embroidered uniforms. She was a real vision of lovelyness, "divinely tall and divinely fair," and in the general feeling of admiration excited by her radiant beauty but few people noticed the thin, set lips, pressed together in firm determination, and the hard chin, which gave a disagreeable expression to what otherwise would have been a faultless face. Behind her, also in white attired, walked the Empress Marie, sobbing the whole time, and leaning on the arm of her aged father, the King of Denmark. Every heart went out to her in her widowhood and loneliness; while many wondered whether her successor, on the Throne she had graced so well, would ever become as popular as she had been during her short reign of thirteen years.

An hour later a State carriage with outriders drove the newly wedded couple from the Winter Palace to that of Anitchkoff where they were to take up their residence with the Dowager Empress until their own apartments were made ready for them. The bride was greeted with vociferous cheers by the crowds. It was the one solitary occasion in her life when she could have the illusion of being popular with her newly acquired subjects. Eighteen months later these were to show to her in an unmistakable manner that such was far from being the case, when she was making her entry into that old town of Moscow, where the Imperial Crown was to be put on her brow, to replace the orange flowers which had adorned her head on her wedding morning.

II

MARRIAGE AND LONELINESS

ONE must be fair. The first months of the wedded life of the young Empress Alexandra were not months of unmixed happiness. This, though partly her fault, was also due to circumstances and the people who surrounded her. Though the Consort of one of the mightiest monarchs in Europe, she yet found herself relegated to an absolutely secondary position; she discovered very quickly that no one considered her to be of any importance whatsoever beside her mother-in-law, the Dowager-Empress Marie. The latter had been one of the most popular Sovereigns who ever graced a throne, and from the very first days after her arrival in Russia she had applied herself to the task of pleasing the people. Like her sister, Queen Alexandra, she identified herself completely with the nation that now claimed her as its own, and she entered into all its interests and pursuits, without any exaggeration, but with that quiet, lovely dignity which never failed her, no matter in what position she found herself. Her influence over her husband had been immense, but no one had ever noticed it; on the contrary, she had persistently remained in the background and tried to pass for a pleasant, amiable, and just a little frivolous, woman who cared for balls, pretty clothes, fine jewels, and the pomp which surrounded her at every step she took. She held very properly the idea that it lowers a Sovereign to appear to be under the sway and influence of his wife, and so, though Alexander III. never took any decision of any importance without having first of all discussed it with her, in public she avoided not only talking politics, but even the appearance of being interested in them.

On the other hand, she had always been, not only conscious, but also very jealous, of her power. She did not in the least care to give it up after her widowhood. Her children, strange to say, had always stood in awe of her, much more than of the Czar, who was a most affectionate and loving father, while Marie Feodorowna had always treated them more from the point of view of Sovereign than mother.

This had been especially the case with the Grand Duke Nicholas, who, when he found himself Emperor, discovered that he could not avoid taking the Dowager Empress's opinion, especially in matters concerning his domestic life. He was told by her that the inexperience of his young wife made it imperative she should be guided by the advices of people older than herself.

This, however, did not suit at all Alexandra Feodorowna, and she found an unexpected support in the person of her own Mistress of the Robes, the Princess Galitzyne, who did not like Marie Feodorowna and was but too glad to put spokes in the latter's wheels. That was the cause of much trouble, and brought about strife in the Imperial Family, which might have been avoided by the exercise of a small amount of tact.

The young Empress, compelled to live in two badly furnished, poky little rooms on the ground floor of the Anitchkoff Palace, became impatient and fretful, and did not care to make a secret of the fact. She felt hurt, too, at several incidents which occurred about that time, the first one of which was connected with the introduction of her name in the liturgy. She wished it to figure immediately after that of the Emperor, while Marie Feodorowna pretended that hers ought not to be relegated to a secondary place, but be mentioned before that of her daughter-in-law.

The two ladies quarreled desperately on this subject, and at last the matter was referred to the Synod, which decided, in view of the existent precedents, that the name of the Consort of the Sovereign ought to be called before that of his mother. The Dowager was furious, while Alexandra Feodorowna was triumphant, and not wise enough to hide it from the world, expressing herself quite loudly in regard to the pleasure which she experienced in seeing defeated the attempt made by her mother-in-law to relegate her to an inferior place which she did not in the least wish to occupy.

Another cause of discontent arose in connection with the Crown Jewels. Marie Feodorowna had liked to wear them more often than any of her predecessors on the Throne, and, though her own private collection of pearls and diamonds was one of the most magnificent in Europe, yet she loved to put on the exceptional stones, tiaras, and necklaces which were the property of the State. Her husband, Czar Alexander III., also liked to see them adorn the person of his idolized wife, and in order to spare her the annoyance of going through the long ceremony associated with the demand of any *parure* it pleased her to require from the Treasury, he had had the jewels she cared for the most transferred to the Anitchkoff Palace, where they were kept in a special safe in the Empress's bedroom. After the latter's widowhood, the question arose as to whether she was to be allowed to retain the custody of all these precious stones, or whether, properly speaking, it was only the reigning Empress who had the right to wear them; had they not better be returned to the place which they had occupied before in the Imperial Treasury?

Some Court officials considered that this was the proper thing to do; the more so that, as it happened, the young Empress had not personal diamonds or pearls at all worthy of her new position. She had received some wonderful presents from her husband when they had become engaged, but the usual amount of jewels bestowed upon marriage on all the Grand Duchesses of Russia had not been offered to her, on account of the hurry with which this marriage had been achieved. It was therefore essential that she should be given the opportunity to adorn herself on all State occasions with the brilliants that the Crown held in reserve for the use of the Sovereign's Consorts. No one thought of subjecting the Empress to the ordeal of going to her mother-in-law, to beg from the latter the permission to use the things to which she was legally entitled, and one would have thought that the best way out of the difficulty would be to have the jewels returned to their original place of abode, and reinstated in the Treasury.

But one had not reckoned with the Dowager Empress! She absolutely refused to give up the ornaments she had been so fond of, and when driven out of her last intrenchments, and obliged to capitulate, she protested that it was not usual for an Empress to wear what belonged to the Crown, before that Crown had been officially laid upon her head, and said that she would relinquish the possession of the famous jewels only after the Coronation of her son and daughter-in-law. The Czar, weak as usual, yielded. Alexandra Feodorowna declared that she did not care for the "hateful things," and proceeded to buy out of her allowance the most gorgeous ornaments she could lay her hands upon, getting heavily into debt in consequence, a fact which did not help to make her popular with her subjects.

She had an unpleasant manner that told against her. Not affable by nature, timid to a certain extent, she imagined that her position as Empress of Russia required her to show herself haughty and disdainful with the people who were introduced to her. Her extremely indifferent knowledge of the French language, which was the only one in use in Court circles, also added to her unpopularity. Her mistakes in that respect were repeated every-where and ridiculed by the old ladies whom her want of politeness had con-tributed to offend, and before she had been married three months she found herself not only unpopular, but even disliked by almost every person she had met.

Then, again, Alexandra Feodorowna was possessed of a wonderful, but most unfortunate talent for drawing caricatures, of which she made no secret, but which, on the contrary, used against all those she disliked, and their name was legion! She found herself, of course, extremely lonely, without any friends of her own rank, and deprived of that liberty of going about she had enjoyed so much at Darmstadt. She had taken a violent dislike for all the Princesses belonging to her new family, and even the grace and liveliness of the Grand Duchess Xenia Alexandrowna, her sister-in-law, had failed to win her heart. She did not care for Russia; its climate did not agree with her, its language she could not learn; its religion she despised in those early days which followed upon her marriage, though she was later to become a fanatical adherent of the Greek Orthodox Church; its manners and customs she could not assimilate. All these circumstances put together made her sullen and angry, and added to her general discontent. She at last determined to try and assert herself, and, though secretly despising the weakness of character of her husband, whom she continually chaffed for his blind submission to his mother, she endeavored to supplant the latter in his heart and mind, and to substitute herself for Marie Feodorowna, not only in domestic, but also in political matters.

We shall presently see how this experiment was to be tried, and what were its ultimate consequences.

III

MY COUNTRY, MY BELOVED COUNTRY, WHY AM I PARTED FROM THEE?

THE spring of 1895 brought few changes in the existence of the young Empress.

For one thing, she contrived to influence the Czar to take up his residence in the small Palace of Tsarskoye Selo, which later on they were to inhabit permanently, but which at that time was still badly furnished and rather forlorn in appearance, owing to the fact that no one had ever lived there since the death of Alexander II. It had been a favorite resort of his, and of his morganatic wife, the Princess Youriewsky, and for that reason had been shunned by his successor, who had elected to establish himself in the huge castle of Gatschina. This place was left to the Dowager Empress for life, and thither she repaired in the beginning of the spring, not, however, without having made a feeble attempt to influence her son and daughter-in-law to accompany her. But for once Nicholas II. did not react, and ignored the invitation. His wife was expecting the birth of her first child, and this circumstance gave her more influence, and to her wishes more weight, than would perhaps have been the case under ordinary circumstances.

Though at Tsarskoye Selo Alexandra Feodorowna obtained more liberty than had been the case throughout the weary months of the preceding winter, yet she found that she had to keep in mind the necessity not to give any reason for the criticisms which she knew but too well were directed against her from every side. Needless to say, she might have avoided these criticisms by the display of some elementary notions of tact. In her way she was a very truthful woman; she even carried her love for veracity sometimes too far. She had no experience of the world, and her life at Darmstadt had not prepared her for the responsibilities of her position as Empress. She did not care for St. Petersburg society, which she considered frivolous, and she made no secret of this fact. Of course people resented it.

Her mother-in-law, the Empress Marie, though she had always kept herself very well informed as to all that was going on in the select circles of those privileged beings who were received at Court, yet had taken good care to appear to ignore the many love-affairs which were either known or suspected in regard to these people. She had so much tact that whenever anything she disapproved of occurred, among these Upper Ten Thousand of people, she let them see that such was the case, but never mentioned it in public.

The Empress Alexandra, on the contrary, spoke with acerbity of every small incident which came to her knowledge, and declared loudly that she would refuse to admit in her presence the persons guilty of indiscretions. During the second season which followed upon her marriage, when Court receptions interrupted by the mourning for the late Czar were once more resumed, the Empress struck off from the list of invitations submitted to her the names of some of the most prominent members of St. Petersburg society, giving her reasons for doing so. The result was that nothing but old frumps, or mothers with marriageable daughters, attended this particular ball, and that the Empress in her turn was boycotted by almost everybody of note in the capital, who did not care to have themselves or their relatives publicly branded as not worthy to be admitted within the gates of the Winter Palace. The effects of this ostracism became apparent on the New-Year's reception which followed upon this incident, which only four women attended, wives of Ministers, who, in virtue of their husbands' position, could not well do anything else. The Emperor, surprised at this absence of the feminine element, on an occasion when it was generally very conspicuous, inquired into the matter. When told the story which had given rise to it he forthwith consulted his mother, and the latter, profiting by the occasion, told her son that he had better have the names of the people about to be invited at Court balls submitted to her for inspection, and not to the young Empress. Of course this became known at once, with the result that the popularity of Marie Feodorowna increased, while that of her daughter-in-law, on the contrary, diminished with every day that passed.

Rebuffed on every side, Alexandra Feodorowna first sought comfort and advice from her sister, the Grand Duchess Elisabeth, who, by reason of her residing in Moscow, where her husband, the Grand Duke Sergius, occupied the position of Governor-General, did not often see her. The Grand Duchess, in response to an invitation which she received to come to Tsarskoye Selo, took the first train. When consulted by the Empress in regard to the difficulties with which she found her path beset, she could not find a solution for them, perhaps because she did not honestly seek it. Elisabeth, as well as her husband, was very ambitious, and they would not have been sorry to see Alexandra Feodorowna estranged from all her new family, in order to have her entirely under their influence and control, and to dominate through her the weak Nicholas II., whose character was already beginning to be known, with all its faults and defects, by his near relatives, as well as by his Ministers and advisers. Elisabeth, therefore, advised her sister to try and keep at arm's-length from her mother-in-law, uncles, aunts, and cousins, and especially to be suspicious of her two brothers-in-law, who were represented to her as being her natural enemies, notwithstanding the fact that one of them, the Grand Duke George, was consumptive and did not live in St. Petersburg, the climate of which he could not endure, while the second, the Grand Duke Michael, was a youth of sixteen, hardly out of school.

Alexandra Feodorowna, however, became suspicious of this advice, perhaps because she distrusted the Grand Duke Sergius just as much as her other relatives. Yet advice she felt she must have. It would have been natural for her to seek that of her brother, the Grand Duke of Hesse, and of her other sisters, the Princess Victoria of Battenberg and the Princess Henry of Prussia, but while the former had never been her favorite, the latter refused—at the instigation of her husband, most probably—to be mixed up in things which did not concern her, and intrenched herself behind her ignorance of Russian customs and Russian society. The Empress felt frantic, and it was then that she was seized with violent attacks of homesickness, which she did not attempt to conceal. More than once she was heard to say that she wished she were back in Germany, where at least she would find people capable of understanding her and of advising her well and soundly.

Germany has always, as is but too well known to-day, maintained an army of spies in Russia. Very quickly a report of what was going on in Tsarskoye Selo reached the ears of William II. He saw his opportunity and forthwith wrote to his cousin, reminding her of their former friendship and telling her that he was entirely at her disposal to help her, by his knowledge of Russian affairs, which he professed was very great, and by his experience of the world.

The Empress caught at the opportunity, and from that day there was established between them relations of the closest intimacy, linking the Empress and the Lord of Potsdam. She took the habit of sending him a kind of diary of what she was doing and of what went on at the Russian Court—a diary in which she did not spare her mother-in-law, or her husband, whom she reproached with not taking her part more openly.

Of course it was not easy to carry on such a correspondence. The young Empress was closely watched, a fact of which she was but too well aware. She tried the medium of the German Embassy, but apart from the fact that it would have seemed a suspicious thing to send there letters in a regular way, the Ambassador, Prince Radolin, refused to be the means of forwarding messages of which he did not know the import, and did not care to be involved in an intrigue that would inevitably have brought him to grief if discovered. Some other way, therefore, had to be devised, and for a time it seemed as if it would be next to impossible to find any. Once or twice the Princess Hohenlohe, wife of the Imperial Chancellor, who, through the fact that she was the owner of large estates in Lithuania, often visited St. Petersburg, brought with her messages from the Kaiser to the Empress Alexandra, and took back with her to Berlin the latter's replies. But this was not sufficient, and during the first visit paid by the Czar and his Consort to the German Court William and the young Czarina came to an understanding, after which their correspondence continued through the medium of friends of the Kaiser, who somehow appeared regularly in Russia whenever this was considered necessary.

People, and there were some, who happened to be in the secret of this intercourse pretended that one of the things which William II. urged upon his cousin was the necessity of getting rid of the influence of the Empress Marie, who, by reason of her avowed French sympathies, constituted a danger to German expansion and to German progress in the Muscovite Empire. The fact that for the present Alexandra Feodorowna was still considered a nonentity at the Russian Court was not of much importance because it was thought that if she were once to become the mother of a son she would immediately be raised to the position of an important personage in her husband's house and country. And it must not be forgotten that in the course of the summer of 1895 the Empress was known to be about to give birth to her first child, who of course had to be a boy and an Heir to the Russian Throne.

Alas, alas for these hopes!

It was a Grand Duchess, Olga Nicholaiewna, who saw the light of day on a November morning in the Imperial Palace of Tsarskoye Selo. The disappointment was intense and extended to all classes of the nation, except among the members of the Imperial Family, who made no secret of the fact that they were delighted the little Hessian Princess they all disliked so intensely had not fulfilled her husband's and her subjects' expectations. The news of their joy reached the ears of Alexandra Feodorowna through the channel of the Kaiser, and added to her bitterness against her Russian relatives, which made itself felt in the affected manner with which she continually made allusions in their presence to her regrets at having accepted the position of Empress of All the Russias. She openly spoke of her contempt for this "land of savages" as she called it, and more than once her attendants heard her give vent to the exclamation of "My country, my beloved country, why am I parted from Thee?"

THE CZARINA
When she was Princess Alix of Hesse Darmstadt, before her betrothal to the Czar, 1894.

IV

A SAD CORONATION

CONTRARY to the custom observed at the Imperial Court of Russia, the young Empress insisted herself on nursing her baby. This met with general disapproval, not only from Marie Feodorowna, who, never having thought of the possibility of such an infraction of the traditions of the House of Romanoff, felt considerably affronted at this piece of independence on the part of her daughter-in-law; also from all the dowagers of St. Petersburg, who considered the innovation as *infra dig.* and declared that such a breach of etiquette constituted a public scandal.

Some enterprising ladies, who, by virtue of their own unimpeachable positions, thought themselves entitled to express their opinions, ventured to say so to Alexandra Feodorowna herself. She was indignant at what she termed an insult, turned her back on those voluntary advisers, and flatly declared that she would refuse henceforward to admit into her presence people who had forgotten to such an extent the respect due to her and to her position as the wife of their Sovereign.

Matters assumed an acute form, and during the first ball which took place that season in the Winter Palace the incident was discussed most vehemently. One wondered what would happen later on, and how the Empress would behave in regard to those givers of unsought advice in the future. But Providence interfered in favor of Alexandra Feodorowna, because she suddenly was taken with an attack of the measles, not the German ones this time, but the real, authentic thing, and the Court festivities about to take place were immediately postponed in spite of the protestations of different Court officials, who urged that they could very well take place in the absence of the Empress, and that their abandonment would be a serious blow to trade, which already was very bad, and which had discounted the profits it generally made during a winter season when the gates of the Winter Palace were thrown open with the usual lavishness and luxury displayed there on such occasions. Trade and its requirements were about the last thing which troubled the mind of Alexandra Feodorowna. She was of the opinion prevalent in

Poland at the time of the Saxon dynasty that when Augustus was intoxicated the whole nation had to get drunk, and though she detested or pretended she detested Court balls and festivities, yet she was adverse to others enjoying them while she herself was debarred from doing so. Girls in their first season eager for showing off their pretty frocks, and lively young married women in quest of gaiety, were told to forego expectations of such pleasure, and the gates of the Palace remained closed for the first time in many years, to the general disappointment of St. Petersburg society and of its prominent members.

This disappointment, however, was soon forgotten in the expectation of the Coronation about to take place, the date of which had been fixed for the 15th of May. Great preparations were made for it. Those who remembered the pomp which had attended that of Alexander III., thirteen years before, wondered whether the ceremony about to be repeated would be as brilliant as the one which they had not yet forgotten. The whole of St. Petersburg society, with few exceptions, repaired to Moscow for the solemn occasion, and all the Foreign Courts sent representatives to attend the festival. One tried to guess how the young Empress would carry herself through the trying ordeal, and whether she would conde-scend for once to show herself amiable toward her subjects in the ancient capital of Muscovy, the population of which had always professed far more independence of opinions than that of St. Petersburg, where conversations were more restrained and guarded, in view of the constant presence of the Imperial Family within its walls. The one thing which everybody was looking forward to was the public entry of the young Sovereigns in the old town, an entry which was to be made with unusual pomp and solemnity.

I remember very well the day of the ceremony. I had a seat in a house situated on the great square opposite the residence of the Governor-General of the town, a position which was still occupied by the Grand Duke Sergius. Together with some friends, we watched the long line of troops, followed by representatives from all classes in the country; by Court officials on horseback, in gold-embroidered uniforms, behind whom rode, surrounded by a brilliant staff, the Czar himself, mounted on a gray charger; a small, slight figure, contrasting vividly with his father thirteen years before. Nicholas II. had already acquired the expression of utter impass-ebility which was never to change in the future. He surveyed with a grim look the vast crowds massed in the streets, who cheered him vociferously, but he did so with a look that expressed neither pleasure nor disappointment, but simply indifference mixed with tediousness.

Behind him came a long row of State carriages all gold and precious stones, the diamonds which glittered on them being valued at several millions of rubles. In the foremost, the carriage of Catherine the Great, with an immense Imperial Crown on its top, rode the Dowager Empress dressed in white and looking as young almost as she had done on the day of her own Coronation. Hurrahs without end greeted her appearance; the people cheered her with an enthusiasm such as had rarely been seen in Russia, while, pale and trembling, she bowed incessantly from right to left, with tears streaming down her cheeks. These hurrahs followed her all along her way from the distant Petrowsky Palace to the gates of the Kremlin, which she entered at last, amid the acclamations of the multitude assembled to see her pass.

Immediately behind her, divided only by a squadron of cavalry, drove her daughter-in-law, also dressed in a white gown, and sparkling with all the jewels belonging to the Crown, which she had assumed for the first time on that solemn day. A dead silence, contrasting painfully with the frenzied reception awarded to Marie Feodorowna, greeted her successor on the Throne of Russia. This contrast was so evident that everybody present was struck with it, and something like a presentiment of evil passed through the mind of most of the assistants of this strange scene. One remembered Marie Antoinette at Rheims during the Coronation of Louis XVI. when she also had been received with silence and contempt by the French nation, who a few years later was to send her to the scaffold.

Perhaps something of the kind crossed the mind of Alexandra Feodorowna herself, because it was evident that she was suffering from a violent desire to give vent to tears and rage. I saw her from the place where I stood, through the open large windows of the State carriage in which she sat quite alone, according to the requirements of etiquette, immovable like an Indian goddess, looking neither right nor left, but straight before her, her haughty head thrown back, two red spots on her cheeks, and a set expression on her thin lips closely joined together. She understood but too well the meaning of this strange reception she was awarded; too proud to complain, she seemed to ignore it. Once and once only did I see her start, and that was when, amid the profound silence which prevailed around her, a voice, that of a child, was heard exclaiming:

"Show me the German, mamma, show me the German!"

And with this cry in her ears and in those of other listeners, the big coach with Alexandra Feodorowna sitting in it, in all the splendor of her white dress and glorious jewels, vanished in the distance within the walls of that old fortress called the Kremlin, which, seen in the glamour of dusk already falling, looked more like a prison than a palace.

THE DOWAGER EMPRESS MARIE FEODOROWNA

Three days later I was to look once more on the slight and erect figure of the Consort of Nicholas II. as she emerged out of the bronze gates of the Cathedral of the Assumption walking under a canopy of cloth of gold and ermine, with ostrich plumes towering on its top, the Crown of the Russian Empresses standing high upon her small head and the long mantle of brocade embroidered with the black eagles of the Romanoffs trailing from her shoulders. She looked magnificent, but there was something in the expression of her haughty features which reminded one of the prophecy of the Italian sculptor in regard to Charles Stuart: "Something evil will befall that man; he has got misfortune written on his face."

Beside his wife, Nicholas II. looked the insignificant personage he was to remain until the end of his reign and very probably of his life. He could no more bear the weight of his Crown physically than he was able later on to carry the burden of his responsibilities. As he walked, he staggered and trembled; and one could distinctly notice the signs of the extreme fatigue under which he labored. Supported on either side by two attendants, who carried the folds of his Imperial mantle, he tried to keep erect the scepter which he held in his right hand, and the orb which reposed in his left.

And then occurred the memorable incident of that memorable day.

When the long procession reached the doors of the Cathedral of the Archangels where, according to custom, the newly crowned Czar was obliged to repair for a short service of thanksgiving, I saw Nicholas II. reel from right to left as would have done a drunken man, and suddenly the scepter which he grasped fell heavily from his hand to the stone floor, before the altar of the church.

It would be difficult to describe the emotion produced by this untoward incident, which was at once interpreted by the superstitious Russian people as a bad omen for the reign which had just begun. Strange though this may seem, yet it is absolutely true, that the faith of the Russian nation in Nicholas II. was shattered from that day when it had found him unable to carry the symbol of his supreme power and Imperial might and not strong enough to bear its weight.

This was not, however, the only unlucky incident which was connected with this sad Coronation, which in so many respects reminded one of several others that had marked the marriage festivities of Marie Antoinette, and the anointing of Louis XVI. at Rheims. I will not describe here the horrors which were enacted on the Khodinka field, when more than twenty thousand people were crushed to death during a popular festival given in honor of the Czar's assuming the Crown of his ancestors; I shall only mention the part played by Alexandra Feodorowna in the gruesome tragedy. As everybody knows, unfortunately for her reputation in history, she danced the night which followed upon it, at the French Embassy.

But what is not so well known is the fact that when she and the Emperor were asked by Count de Montebello, the French Ambassador, whether the ball which they had promised to attend had not better be postponed until the next day, which would have been an easy matter, Alexandra Feodorowna had exclaimed that she could not understand why such a fuss was made because "a few peasants had been victims of an accident likely to happen anywhere," while Nicholas II. had replied that he did not see any necessity to make any alteration in the program which had been officially sanctioned and adopted since a long time.

It was only on the third day following upon the catastrophe, when the clamors of public opinion reached even the deaf ears of the Czar and of his Consort, that they decided themselves at last to pay a visit to the various hospitals where the victims of the tragedy had been carried. They went there in great state and ceremony, the Empress dressed in lace and satin, holding in her hands a large bouquet of flowers which had been presented to her by the officials to whom had been deputed the charge of receiving her at the gates of the houses of suffering and death, whither her duties had called her, much against her will. It was related later on that a little girl ten years old or so, perceiving the roses held by the Sovereign, had exclaimed:

"Oh, the pretty roses!"

"Give them to her," said the Emperor.

"Certainly not. Flowers are most unwholesome in a sick-room," replied Alexandra Feodorowna, and she turned away without another word.

V

DAUGHTERS, DAUGHTERS, AND NO SON

IT was not generally known at the time of the Coronation that the Empress was about to become a mother for the second time. She had not mentioned the fact to her family and not to her mother-in-law, not wishing to be bothered with advice as to the manner in which she should take care of herself—advice which she was beforehand determined not to follow. But the strain of the Coronation festivities, with their attendant emotions and unavoidable fatigue, told upon her, and this was the principal reason which induced the Emperor to repair with her to Illinskoye, the country-seat of the Grand Duke Sergius, close to Moscow, immediately after the departure of the Foreign Envoys, who had been sent to Russia to represent their respective Governments.

The public wondered at this decision, the more so that it was openly said that the responsibility for the disaster of Khodinka rested with the Grand Duke, who had not known how to take the necessary precautions, which, if resorted to, would have prevented the catastrophe. No one suspected that the real reason for this determination of Nicholas II. to spend a few quiet weeks with his uncle and brother-in-law was due to the state of health of Alexandra Feodorowna.

The measure, however, was not to prove successful, because a very few days after the arrival of the Imperial pair at Illinskoye its hopes of an increase in the family were dashed to the ground, and an unlucky accident deprived the Empress of a son and the country of an heir, it having been proved that the child born too early was of the male sex. The fact was kept a close secret, as those in authority did not care for the nation to become aware of the disappointment which had overtaken its Monarch, and even Alexandra Feodorowna was not told of the full extent of the misfortune. She learned of it much later, after the birth of the only boy she ever had. To her anxious questions concerning the sex of the prematurely born infant she never got any satisfactory reply, and though she might have suspected the truth, yet it was not revealed to her at the time. She was only adjured to take care of herself and to avoid every kind of fatigue, a difficult thing to do, considering the fact that the Russian Sovereigns were about to start for a tour of visits at the different European Courts. These visits, with the exception of the stay in Paris where they were received with a burst of the most extraordinary enthusiasm ever witnessed in the French capital, did not turn out so successfully as had been hoped and expected. For one thing, Prince Lobanoff, who held the portfolio of Foreign Affairs and was by common consent considered as the ablest statesman in Russia and one of the cleverest in Europe, died suddenly on the Imperial train at a little station of the Southwestern Railway line, called Schepétowka, almost in the arms of the Emperor. Nicholas, seeing him stagger, rushed to his help. This sad event gave rise to many comments, and it was then that people began to whisper in Russia that the young Empress had got the evil eye and brought bad luck to all those who came into too close contact with her.

Nicholas and his Consort first proceeded to Breslau, where William II. with the Empress came to meet them and received them with the greatest cordiality. It was at that time that arrangements for his correspondence with the Czarina were made, much to the joy of the latter, who, as time went on, felt more and more in need of the help and advice of members of her own family. From Breslau, the Emperor and Empress proceeded to Vienna, but there a succession of unpleasant small incidents, insignificant in themselves, but destined in the course of time to bring about totally unexpected results, took place. Francis Joseph had decided to receive his Russian guests with all the pomp and splendor for which the Austrian Court had always been famous, and the Empress Elisabeth, after much pleading, had at last been persuaded to come to Vienna and to do the honors of the Hofburg to them. At the State banquet which was given there, she appeared, regal and magnificent, clothed in that deep mourning which she never gave up after the tragic death of her only son, the Archduke Rudolph, and she was far more observed and looked at than the young wife of Nicholas II., who resented the fact deeply. It is not generally known that at that time (later she outlived the feeling) Alexandra Feodorowna had a very high opinion of her own beauty and could not bear to play second fiddle in that respect to any one. She always hated pretty women whenever she saw them in a position to rival her, and the fact that Elisabeth of Bavaria, in spite of her fifty-seven years, eclipsed in many respects her own young and radiant beauty did not help to put the Czarina into a good temper. The interview, therefore, passed according to the rules of strict courtesy, but no cordiality permeated it. Wise politicians and diplomats began shaking their heads and murmuring that after this experiment it would become hard indeed to bring about pleasant relations between the Court of the Hofburg and that of Tsarskoye Selo.

From Vienna, the Russian Sovereigns went on to Copenhagen to pay to the aged King and Queen of Denmark their respects, but there also things did not go smoothly. The Russian Imperial Family had always been popular in Denmark, which the late Czar Alexander III. liked extremely, and where he used to spend happy weeks every summer. One had hoped that this tradition would continue, but after having seen Alexandra Feodorowna for three days Queen Louise had remarked that it would be just as well if she did not visit too often.

But what everybody in Russia looked forward to was the visits which Nicholas II. and his wife were about to pay to Balmoral and to Paris. In the first of these places they were made the objects of a warm and entirely homelike reception on the part of Queen Victoria. The latter had always been interested in the children of her favorite daughter, the Princess Alice, and had immensely rejoiced to see her youngest grandchild ascend the Throne of Russia. The Queen, however, was beginning to feel some misgivings as to the latter's fitness for the high position that she had been thrust into. She was perhaps the best informed person in Europe as to all that went on in Foreign Courts, and she had heard, not without serious apprehensions, of the growing unpopularity of Alexandra Feodorowna. She took the first opportunity which presented itself to talk seriously to her granddaughter and to try and persuade her that she ought to make some effort to win the respect and the affection of her subjects. To Victoria's surprise, the old lady never having been thwarted or contradicted, the Czarina replied that she did not know in the least what she was talking about, and that what Russians required was not amiable words but a sound administration of the whip. Under these circumstances the conversation very quickly came to an end, though the Queen, astounded as she was at Alexandra's impertinence, tried, nevertheless, to renew it with the Czar. The latter simply replied that his grandmother must have been misinformed, because everybody loved the Empress. After that Victoria gave up the subject, and she would probably never have mentioned it to any one had it not subsequently reached her ears that the Empress boasted among her friends about the way in which she had snubbed her grandmother. This was rather more than the equanimity of the Queen could stand, and in her turn she related her unsuccessful attempts to make the young Czarina listen to reason, not making any secret of the fact that the future of the latter filled her with the greatest apprehensions.

In Paris, the Empress found herself more at her ease. Flattery was poured down upon her in buckets. All the newspapers praised her looks, her jewels, her general demeanor, and it was only here and there that a dissenting voice was raised, as in the person of a dressmaker who remarked on the want of taste which had presided at the confection of the dresses with which Alexandra Feodorowna tried to astonish the Parisian natives. On the whole the visit was a success, and it inspired with new zeal all the promoters of the Franco-Russian alliance, among whom the Empress was most certainly not to be reckoned.

Very soon after this triumphal journey, a second child was born to Nicholas II. and his wife; another girl, to the intense disappointment of everybody. I am informed that the first words of Alexandra Feodorowna upon being told of the sex of the infant were:

"What will the nation say, what will it say?"

As a fact the nation said nothing; it had already begun to lose interest in the family affairs of its rulers.

As time went on this indifference to the joys and the woes of the Reigning House grew and grew, until at last it became a recognized fact in the whole of Russia that, as far as Nicholas II. was concerned, whatever happened to him or to his relatives was an object which presented no interest whatever to the millions of Russian men and women, who all of them were looking forward for a change in the destinies and the Government of their country. When he had ascended the Throne, any amount of expectations had been connected with him and with his name. These were very quickly dashed to the ground by his first public speech—the one which he made in reply to the congratulations of the zemstvos, or Russian local assemblies, on his accession and marriage, when he told the representatives of these institutions that they must not indulge "in senseless dreams" or hope that he would ever sacrifice the least little bit of his Imperial prerogatives or autocratic leanings. The Revolutionary committees, which had begun at that time and from the very day of the death of Alexander III. to renew their political activity, addressed to him a letter which, read to-day in the light of the events which have happened during the last twelvemonth, seems almost prophetic. They warned him that the struggle begun by him would only come to an end with his downfall, and the whole tone of this remarkable epistle, which I have reproduced in my volume, *Behind the Veil of the Russian Court*, reminds one at present that the prophesied blow has fallen, of the writing on the wall which appeared during the banquet of the Persian King, warning him of his approaching ruin.

Neither the Czar nor his Consort thought about these things. As time went on, the attention of the latter became more and more concentrated on the one fixed idea of having a son. She imagined that the secret of her unpopularity, which she had at last discovered, lay in the fact that she had not been able to give an Heir to the Russian Throne. Four times in succession daughters were born to her, each one received with increased disappointment, as the years went on, bringing into prominence the youngest brother of Nicholas II., the Grand Duke Michael, whom the Empress began hating with all her heart and soul. She imagined that wherever she went she was greeted with reproaches for having failed to fulfil the first duty of a Sovereign's Consort, that of assuring his succession in the direct line. The hysterical part of her temperament rose to the surface more and more with each day that passed. She locked herself up in her private apartments, refusing to see the members of her family and denying herself to all visitors, until at last it began to be whispered in Court circles that Alexandra Feodorowna's mind was getting unhinged and that she was suffering from religious mania, mixed up with the dread of persecution from her relatives. She used to sob for hours at a stretch, when no one could comfort her, and during those attacks of despair one cry continually escaped her lips, and was repeated until she could utter it no longer, out of sheer excitement and fatigue:

"Why, *why* will God not grant me a son?"

VI

THE EMPRESS'S OPINIONS ABOUT RUSSIA

ONE of the points about which there has been the most discussion in Russia is as to whether the Empress Alexandra had ever cared for the country which had become her own. Her friends have repeatedly asserted that she had become an ardent Russian patriot, and that her great, particular misfortune was that every action, word, or thought of hers had been misunderstood and this willingly.

As for her enemies, they declared, from the very first days which followed upon her unlucky marriage, that she had arrived in Russia imbued with the feelings of the deepest contempt for the country and its people, and that all her efforts had been applied toward making out of the Empire over which she reigned a vassal of her own native land.

It seems to me, who have had the opportunity to approach her personally, as well as that of hearing about her from persons who nourished no animosity against her, that neither the one nor the other of these two opinions was absolutely correct, though both were right, each in its way. When one attempts to judge the personality and the character of Alexandra Feodorowna, one must first of all take into account the fact that she belonged to that class of individuals who, while being fools, nevertheless think themselves clever. To this must be added a highly strung, hysterical temperament and the fact which was unknown in Russia at the time of her marriage, that madness was a family disease in the House of Hesse, to which she belonged by birth. The circumstances attending her rearing and education also had a good deal to do with the strangeness of her conduct after she had reached the years of discretion. She had been a mere baby, five or six years old, when she had lost her mother, the charming, clever, and accomplished Princess Alice of Great Britain, and she had been brought up partly at Windsor by Queen Victoria and partly at Darmstadt, where, however, she had not found any of the good examples its Court might have afforded her had her mother remained alive. She was the youngest member of her family, and as such treated with negligence and made to give way to her elder sisters, who were neither kind nor affectionate in regard to her—a fact which must have helped her a good deal to develop the haughty, disagreeable temper which was later on to play her so many bad tricks in life. On the other hand, the person who had charge of her education, as well as of that of the other Princesses, had conceived a great and most ill-advised affection for her; ill-advised in so far that she used to repeat to her that she was handsomer and cleverer than her sisters, and that she ought not to mind any slights which the latter might try to put upon her, because she was sure to make a better marriage than they.

When she was about twelve years old there occurred in the Grand-Ducal Palace of Darmstadt the tragedy or romance, call it as one likes, of the Grand Duke's morganatic union with a lovely Russian, Madame Kolémine, which came to such a sad end, owing to the interference of Queen Victoria and to the stupidity of the Grand Duke himself, who, in any case, ought first of all to have made careful inquiries as to the past life and conduct of his intended bride, and then—once he had plighted his troth to her—to have held the promises which he had made to her. He allowed her to be sent away from his Court and country in disgrace; the lady herself would have been but too willing to come to honorable terms with a man for whom she could no longer feel any esteem or affection, because in the whole long story of his intercourse with her Grand Duke Louis never showed himself otherwise than the true German he really was. Of course, the object of his transient affections was represented to his children as being merely an intriguing, base woman who had tried to make a great marriage and to supplant their mother. Whether the elder Darmstadt Princesses believed this calumny to have been the truth remains a matter of doubt. Judging impartially, this would seem to be hardly likely if one takes into consideration the fact that their ages hovered between eighteen and twenty-two, and that consequently one could reasonably assume that they knew what they were about when they showered one proof of affection after another on Madame Kolémine, and when they declared to her in many letters that there was nothing they wished for more than to see her become their father's wife.

This whole story, together with its heroine, is about one of the most perplexing affairs that ever occurred in any Royal House, and everything connected with it is to this very day shrouded in mystery. Madame Kolémine, who (this by the way) married again, after her divorce from the Grand Duke, a Russian diplomat, may or may not have been a bad woman. I hold no brief for or against her. Many people assert that in regard to certain scandals connected with the time of her early married life she was more sinned against than sinning, and that she became the victim of calumnies launched against her by unscrupulous enemies. But, true or not, the breath of suspicion had hovered around her good name to a sufficiently strong degree to have absolutely justified the objections of Queen Victoria to her becoming even the morganatic wife of the Grand Duke of Hesse.

It ought also to have influenced the latter into not admitting the fascinating Russian into the intimacy of his young daughters, which was precisely what he did. The girls could not be told every kind of gossip going about in the world, but they ought to have been shielded from the possibility of contracting friendships likely to lead them into unpleasantnesses in the future. On the other hand, considering the fact that this intimacy had once been established, one does not very well see how any of the Darmstadt Princesses could have been led to believe, after the three years or more that it had lasted, that Madame Kolémine was base and intriguing and cared only for a great marriage. Because this last accusation, leaving aside all others, was absolutely false, a fact no one was better able to know than themselves, who had repeatedly begged and implored her to accept their father's offer and to make him, together with themselves, happy people.

I have had some of these letters in my hands, and can therefore vouch for the truth of this last assertion, and to put an end to the questions of a suspicious public that may wonder how it came that such a correspondence was ever communicated to me, I will say at once that the reason for it was that I am a blood relation of Madame Kolémine, who after her divorce had thought I might be of some help to her in her troubles, and had herself asked me to read them. The impossibility in which I found myself to be of any use to the poor woman, whom I had never seen in my life before, and of interfering in a business which did not concern me in the very least, led her to take a most bitter attitude in regard to me and to become my enemy, so that in trying to take her part to-day I am doing so out of a feeling of justice and nothing else.

I have mentioned the story in general only because it explains to a certain degree the undisguised aversion of the Empress Alexandra for everything that was Russian or that had anything to do with Russia.

She had never shared her sisters' admiration for Madame Kolémine; on the contrary, she had always nourished a pronounced antipathy for the lady, and whatever the three other Darmstadt Princesses may have felt in regard to the woman whom their father was to marry and divorce on the same day, she, at least, had made no secret of her hatred for her. One of the first remarks which she made after she had become acquainted with St. Petersburg society was:

"I shall never like it; all the women remind me of Madame Kolémine."

This episode in the career of the Grand Duke of Hesse brought about, as might have been expected, a change in his relations with Queen Victoria, and he was no longer such a desired guest at Windsor or Balmoral as had been the case. His elder daughters married in quick succession, the second one wedding the Grand Duke Sergius of Russia. The little Alice was left alone at home, and though she was often requested by her grandmother to join her in England, she did not care so much for these invitations as formerly. The fact was that she was gradually acquiring a considerable influence over her father's mind, whose weakness of intellect rendered him an easy tool in his enterprising daughter's hands. She became the virtual mistress of his house, and developed during those years, where she remained absolutely without any feminine control over her, the imperious, disagreeable temper which was to play her such sorry tricks in the future. Small as was the Hessian Court, it yet was administered with that strict respect for etiquette always in vogue in Germany, and it pleased the Princess Alix to find herself the first lady in the land in her father's Dukedom. She preferred it to being the second in Rome.

It was during those years that she was taken on a visit to the Russian Court. This did not turn out a success, because no one in St. Petersburg was in the very least impressed by the beauty of the young girl. Russia, being celebrated for the loveliness of its women, would have required something more than she possessed to fall on its knees and worship her. Then, again, she was dressed with bad taste, her manners left much to be desired, and the rumor which began to circulate at the time of the possibility of her wedding the Heir to the Russian Throne did not appeal to public feeling. Alice thought herself slighted, and returned to her beloved Darmstadt more anti-Russian than she had ever been.

Two years went by, and the Grand Duke of Hesse died, carried off by a disease of the brain, difficult to account for if one takes into consideration the fact that he had never had any brains to lose. His son succeeded him, and, together with his sister, continued to inhabit the Darmstadt Palace, where nothing was changed except the master of the house, whom no one missed. For eighteen months Princess Alice reigned supreme, as she had done before; then one fine morning her brother announced to her that he was about to ask their cousin, the Princess Victoria Mélita of Coburg, to become his wife. A fit of hysterics followed upon this announcement. Alice could not resign herself to the necessity of playing second fiddle at her brother's Court, where she had been the center of attraction for such a long time. The fact that her future sister-in-law was just as young and more beautiful than she did not help her to get over her mortification. She was of a terribly jealous character and temperament, and she began from that very day to hate, with a ferocious hatred which went on increasing as time passed, the innocent girl for whom this Hessian marriage was to prove the source of so much sorrow. But about this I shall speak later on.

It was at this precise moment that talk about a Russian marriage for her began again. Many people wished for it. The Berlin Court was actively intriguing in favor of it, and during the whole of that winter of 1893-94 the newspapers were busy with it. The chancelleries of the different European capitals were very much preoccupied as to whether or not it would take place.

Perhaps few people will believe me when I say that had it not been for her brother's engagement nothing in the world would have ever decided the Princess Alice to give her consent to a union for which she did not feel the least sympathy. She was not at all dazzled by the prospect of becoming the Empress of Russia, because in her vanity and with her ideas of German grandeur she thought herself far superior to the Romanoffs, thanks to her long and unbroken line of ancestry. Her unimpeachable quarterings seemed to her to be so immeasurably above their doubtful ones that she considered it would be she who would do him an incommensurable honor by accepting as her wedded husband the Heir to the Throne of All the Russias. She would have infinitely preferred going on queening it in Darmstadt, or in any other small German town, than to have been chosen as the bride of the future Nicholas II., for whom she felt neither sympathy, affection, nor esteem.

But her brother's prospective marriage changed considerably her position. She would no longer occupy the position of the first lady of her beloved Hesse; she would find installed in the place which had been her own for so many happy years a woman younger than herself, with an independent character, a determined mind, a woman who would most probably grow very quickly to impose herself and her ways of thinking, not only on the whole Hessian Court, but also on the Grand Duke, whose sister was condemned beforehand to be neglected and treated as a negligible quantity.

This was gall and wormwood to the passionate, selfish girl, and this feeling of hers, which she allowed her cousin the Kaiser to guess, was very cleverly exploited by the latter in view of a marriage which none desired more ardently than himself. Next to his own sister, there was no one in the whole world whom he would have more ardently wished to become Empress of Russia than his cousin Alix. He invited himself to Darmstadt for a short visit, and while there took the first opportunity to discuss the subject with her. He told her what very few people knew at the time, and what the general public was entirely ignorant of—the serious nature of the illness with which Alexander III. was attacked, an illness which gave no hope whatever of recovery. By marrying the young Grand Duke Nicholas the Princess would find herself but for a short time in a so to say subordinate position. A few months would see her raised to one of the greatest thrones in Europe, from the height of which she would be enabled to look down with contempt and pity on the cousin who was about to take at the Darmstadt Court the place she had occupied so long she had grown to consider it as her very own.

Moreover, she would be able to win back Russia and its ruler to the cause of the German alliance, and thus accomplish one of her duties as a loyal German woman. He appealed to her worst instincts while seeming to call on her noblest ones to assert themselves, and once more he won the day.

In St. Petersburg, too, Hohenzollern influence and intrigues had worked actively, until at last the Czar, feeling perhaps that his days were numbered and perhaps also no longer strong enough to resist perfidious advice given to him by interested people, yielded the point, and when his eldest son started for Coburg to attend there the Princess Victoria Mélita's wedding, he authorized him to ask for the hand of Alix of Hesse.

As I have related, the marriage was at once announced, and we have seen already its first results. The reason why I have once more returned to its subject was to explain some of the causes which led the Empress Alexandra to conceive such a bad opinion about Russia, and to detest so cordially the Russian people. Her early dislike for Madame Kolémine had given her a natural antipathy for everything connected with the latter country; her visits there had strengthened this feeling; her vanity had been hurt by finding that St. Petersburg's society had paid absolutely no attention to her; and her slow, commonplace mind had been utterly unable to understand the refinement and high breeding of the Russian upper classes. Her natural coldness and ignorance had been repulsed instead of attracted by the simplicity but genuine kind-heartedness of the lower ones. She thought the nation one of savages and she made no secret whatever of that opinion, expressing her intention of correcting those "awful Russian manners," which had seemed to her young and inexperienced eyes so very dreadful when she had first become acquainted with them.

It is most likely that if she had married a small German Prince or Potentate she would have put herself out of the way to please his subjects. But she did not think the Russians worth her while. She considered that they ought to feel themselves highly honored by the fact that she had consented to come and reign over them, and in her own mind she did not attach any more importance to the judgments they might be inclined to bestow in regard to her person than she would have done to the criticisms of the first beggar in the street. She arrived in her new country despising it, together with its people, determined to ignore the wishes it might have or the necessities it might require. She arrived there prejudiced and bigoted, and so full of contempt for the land that hailed her as its Queen that she did not admit the possibility of treating it as one inhabited by human beings, but determined to apply to it some of the methods used by the Germans in their treatment of their Colonies.

For the opinion held by Alix of Hesse-Darmstadt in regard to Russia was simply that it ought to be nothing else but a Colony of the vast German Empire, and she felt more pride at the thought that she might reduce it to this condition than at the idea that she had been chosen out of so many other women to become the Empress of that Realm.

VII

WHAT THE IMPERIAL FAMILY THOUGHT ABOUT THE EMPRESS

IT would not have been human on the part of the Imperial Family to like the young wife of Nicholas II. in those early days which followed upon her marriage. The feminine portion of it especially could have been expected, before even the wedding of Alexandra Feodorowna had been solemnized, to look upon her with eyes full of criticism and with the desire to find fault with whatever she might say or do. Here she was, a young, lovely girl, in the full bloom of her beauty, put into the place of the first lady in the Realm, at a moment's notice, before even she had gone through that period of probation which falls as a general rule to the lot of every Consort of a Sovereign when she is but the wife of the Heir to the Throne. Had the haughty Imperial ladies, who for so many years had ruled according to their fancies St. Petersburg society, found themselves in presence of a Grand Duchess Czarevna whom they would have been able to advise, scold, or pet, according to their fancy, they might have taken, from the height of their own unassail-able positions, a more indulgent view of her unavoidable mistakes. They would have thought of her as of a young niece who owed them respect and submission, and whom it was their duty to train according to the exigencies of Russian etiquette. It must be remembered that Nicholas II. to the very day of his accession had been treated by his family like a mere boy without any importance. All of a sudden he found himself a Sovereign and, what was even worse, his wife, the little Hessian Princess, upon whom everybody had looked down with pity mixed with contempt, was the Empress of All the Russias. This was more than the Romanoffs could endure, especially when they remembered the cool, authoritative manner which the late Czar Alexander III. had always adopted in regard to them, and when they thought it might be possible his successor would imitate him in that respect at least, if not in others.

They need not have been in any apprehension as to this last point. Nicholas II., though he detested his uncles, yet stood in such awe of them that he would never have dared assert himself in their presence, far less contradict them. But the Empress had a different character, and she very quickly realized that all her relatives were furious at the fact of her being placed so far above them in rank and position. Fully conscious as she was of that rank, she determined that she would use its advantages to crush those in whom she saw but enemies, which in some cases was not quite exact, because there were then still some persons who, had she only appealed to them, would have responded to her call for sympathy and put themselves at her disposal, if only out of the motive that in rallying around her they were at the same time establishing their own influence.

Alexandra had no tact, and she never could hide her feelings in regard to the people who surrounded her. This explains the number of her enemies and the antagonism to which her mere presence anywhere gave rise. She knew very well that it would be very hard, if not impossible, for her to overcome certain prejudices existing against her. Instead, however, of trying to make for herself friends in other circles than purely aristocratic ones, she applied herself to wound those in whom she saw adversaries, and to discourage her friends by her utter disregard of the warnings that the latter sometimes thought it their duty to give to her. Her relations with the Empress Dowager had begun by being very cordial and affectionate, and it was she who had proposed to the Czar to take their abode in the Anitchkoff Palace with his mother, until their own apartments in the Winter Palace had been got ready for them. The arrangement had not been a successful one, and it is probable that Marie Feodorowna would have got on better later on with her daughter-in-law had the two ladies not lived under the same roof for about half a year. As it was they grew to know each other "not wisely, but too well," and the result was profound contempt on one side and sullen anger on the other. Servants' gossip did the rest; and the two incidents which I have already described, concerning the Crown Jewels and the liturgy, added the last drop of venom in a cup already full to overflowing. The Dowager began to criticize discreetly the young Empress, together with some of her intimate friends. These did not scruple to repeat what they had heard to their own near chums, and soon it became common property. The Grand Duchesses took their cue from Marie Feodorowna, and in an underhand way lamented over the failings of "dear Alexandra," her coldness, her want of politeness, and so forth, helping her in the meanwhile as much as they could to accentuate the shortcomings of an attitude which very soon came to displease everybody, even the people who had been the most enthusiastic about the young Empress.

As a proof of this fact I will relate a little incident which, at the time it occurred, proved the subject of much gossip in some select circles of St. Petersburg society. During one of the first receptions held at the Winter Palace, after the marriage of Nicholas II., there made her appearance an old lady who for the sake of convenience we shall call Madame A. She wished to be presented to the new Empress, an honor to which her own position, together with that of her late husband, gave her every right, besides the fact that she was one of the few ladies left in the capital who had adhered to the old Russian custom of keeping open house for her friends, and whose *salon* was a social authority in its way. The Empress, upon being shown the list of the people about to be presented to her, wanted to know who they were, and, seeing near her her aunt, the Grand Duchess Marie Pawlowna, the wife of the Grand Duke Wladimir, asked her whether Madame A. was or was not a person of importance. The Grand Duchess, who for reasons of her own disliked the latter, replied to her niece:

"Oh, she is an old frump. Give her your hand to kiss, and she will be satisfied."

Now this was the one thing which would not have satisfied Madame A. at all, who considered herself entitled to quite special consideration. Alexandra Feodorowna, believing her aunt, executed the latter's advice to the letter. She extended her much-bejeweled fingers to the astonished old lady, and then coolly turned her back upon her and passed on without having said one single word. The scandal was immense, so immense that the whole ballroom rang with it within a few minutes, and one of the Empress's ladies in waiting actually went up to her and tried to enlighten her as to the extent of the enormity which she had committed, advising her at the same time to seek out the irate Madame A. and to make her some kind of apology, under the pretext that she had not heard her name when it had been mentioned to her.

Alexandra Feodorowna in her turn, and with a certain amount of reason, became furious against the Grand Duchess Marie Pawlowna for having thus led her into a snare, and, boiling with rage, she crossed the room, went up to where Madame A. was discussing with volubility, together with some of her friends, the slight to which she had been subjected, and told her quite loudly:

"I am sorry, Madame, not to have treated you with the respect to which you are entitled, but it was the Grand Duchess Marie Pawlowna, my aunt, who had advised me to do it."

One may imagine the effect produced by this short sentence, which, instead of soothing the ruffled feelings of Madame A., added to her indignation. She turned round and replied quite distinctly, so that all the people standing near her heard her plainly:

"*Ce n'est pas à l'aide d'une trahison, Madame, que l'on excuse une impolitesse!*" ("It is not with the help of a treachery, Madame, that one can excuse a rudeness").

And making a deep courtesy to the discomfited Sovereign, Madame A. proudly retired and drove away from the Palace, leaving the Empress with the consciousness that in the space of five short minutes she had contrived to make for herself two mortal enemies.

The whole of the Imperial Family took up the cause of the Grand Duchess Marie Pawlowna. The latter's husband, the Grand Duke Wladimir, went to the Emperor and complained bitterly of the conduct of Alexandra Feodorowna. The other Grand Duchesses declared that, dating from that day, they would have nothing to do with her, except when the necessities of etiquette compelled them to appear at Court, but that personal relations with a person capable of such a grave piece of indiscretion were quite out of the question. The Grand Duchess Marie swore that she had never meant to advise her niece to show herself rude to such a respectable personage as Madame A.; that her words had been a mere joke, to which she had never imagined that any importance could be attached, and that it had been a cruel thing to denounce her in such a ruthless way to the worst gossip and most malicious tongue in St. Petersburg.

Even the Dowager Empress expressed herself as shocked beyond words at her daughter-in-law's behavior, but when she had tried to speak with the latter on the subject Alexandra Feodorowna had ex-claim-med that she recognized the right of no one to criticize her actions, and forthwith produced for her mother-in-law's edification a caricature which she had drawn of the Emperor in swaddling-clothes, seated at a dinner-table in a high-backed chair, with his uncles and aunts standing around him, and threatening him with their fingers, adding that she was not going to follow the example of her spouse, and that if he chose to forget before his relatives that he was the Emperor of All the Russias, she would not do so for one single minute. After this the conversation came to an end, as was to be expected, but its consequences survived, with a vengeance into the bargain.

Of course incidents of the kind could not be productive of good relations. It did not take a long while before the general public, which, at that time, looked very much for its inspirations toward the Imperial Family, had come to the conclusion that the young Empress was a capricious, rude, and most disagreeable kind of person to whom it was preferable to give a wide berth. Once this legend had been transferred into the domain of history, every action, every word, every gesture of Alexandra Feodorowna was watched with attentive and critical eyes, always ready to make capital out of all her mistakes and to amplify all her errors into crimes. The fact of her having no son added to the resentful feelings of the nation against her, and that of her undisguised German sympathies did not contribute to make her popular. She in her turn, angry with her family, furious with St. Petersburg society, unable to seek friends among the Russian people, all of whom seemed in her inexperienced and prejudiced eyes to be more or less savage, set herself a task to show her contempt and dislike to those persons whom she had found so ready to throw stones against her on occasions when her conscience had told her that she did not deserve the insult. She retired more and more into the seclusion and privacy of her home at Tsarskoye Selo, and she announced to whoever wished to hear her that she did not see why she should spend her money in giving balls and entertaining a society that seemed to have made up its mind to insult her on every possible occasion. The words were repeated, and immediately taken up by the public in the light of another affront. One declared that for a penniless Hessian Princess to talk about "her money" was, to say the least, ridiculous, and one added that she ought to remember that it was part of the duties of a Russian Empress to entertain her subjects and to give them some pleasures in return for their fidelity.

Such was the position after Alexandra Feodorowna had been married three or four years. She might still at that time, had she attempted it in earnest, won back at least the respect if not the sympathies of the Russian nation. But to do so she would have had to bend down from the height of the Throne upon which she was seated, and to make some efforts to clear the misunderstandings which had arisen between her, her family, and her subjects. Unfortunately for her, the haughty Princess believed so firmly that she had been sinned against without having the least sin to her own credit that this "injustice," as she called it, in the world's judgments of her personality made her rebellious, and, not being clever enough either to forgive or to disdain it, she could find nothing else to do but to seek to revenge herself upon imaginary wrongs by making herself guilty of real ones.

GRAND DUCHESS MARIE PAWLOWNA
THE ELDER

Born Duchess Marie of Mecklenburg-Schwerin in 1854, she was the eldest daughter of a Prussian officer, the Grand Duke of Mecklenburg-Schwerin, by his first of three wives Princess Augusta Reuss of Köstritz. She married Alexander II's brother Vladimir and they produced six children; their second child and son, Kirill (aka Cyril), made himself pretender to the Russian throne after the death of Nicholas II was confirmed.

VIII

SORROW AND UNEXPECTED CONSOLATION

IT was not only her family and St. Petersburg society with whom the Empress could not agree. Her relations with her husband were also not of the best during the first years of her married life. Later on, when Alexandra Feodorowna had fallen into the hands of the clever gang of adventurers whose tool she was to remain until the final catastrophe which drove her from her Throne had taken place, she contrived to get hold of the feeble mind of Nicholas II., and to influence him absolutely, thanks to his love for his children, especially for his son.

During the first five years or so that followed upon his marriage the Czar, though he never quarreled with his wife, yet thought far less about her than he did about his mistress, the dancer Mathilde Krzesinska, a Pole of extreme intelligence, little beauty, but enormous attraction. Their friendship had begun when Nicholas was but a boy, or about that, rumor would have it, though I have reason for knowing that in this rumor was mistaken, as happens so often to the old lady, that the dancer had been chosen by the Empress Marie herself as a fit friend for her eldest son. The fact was that this liaison had started almost immediately after the Grand Duke's return from his journey round the world, which had had such a dramatic incident to enliven it in Japan, when a fanatic had attempted to take the life of the Heir to the Russian Throne, inflicting upon him a deep wound with his sword.

The Cesarewitsch had seen Mademoiselle Krzesinska on the stage of the Marinsky Theater, and had been very much impressed by her talent and grace. He had asked to be introduced to her, and had forthwith carried her off to supper at a fashionable restaurant called Cubat, where all the *jeunesse dorée* of St. Petersburg used to meet, eat, drink, and be merry. This supper, in which had taken part several of Nicholas's friends, officers in the same Hussar regiment where he was a captain, as well as one or two ladies of great beauty and doubtful reputation, had ended in a scandal, which for several weeks had been almost the only subject of discussion in the aristocratic *salons* of the capital. The company had been enjoying itself so much that glasses and plates had been broken; when, at two o'clock in the morning, the owner of the restaurant had ventured to suggest that it would be high time the entertainment came to an end, he had been sent to mind his own business. This the poor man would have been but too glad to do, but police regulations were very strict at that time, and he knew that if a patrol should see light in his windows from the outside that he would be fined heavily, no matter who had elected to remain in his establishment after the curfew had sounded.

This was precisely what happened.

A police officer walked up and knocked at the door of the private room where the Heir to the Russian Throne and his companions were disporting themselves, and ordered them to get out. The Grand Duke's aide-de-camp did not care to disclose the identity of his master, so he came out alone and tried to remonstrate with the man, asking him to give them another half-hour to finish their supper and pay for it. The officer refused and tried to force his way into the room, but was violently thrust aside. He had not the right to enforce his authority against a colonel in the army, which was the rank of the aide-de-camp, so he withdrew and telephoned to the Prefect of the town, General Wahl. The latter, who was an officious busybody, thought it a splendid occasion to assert his authority. He immediately proceeded himself to Cubat, where, in spite of the efforts made by the companions of the Grand Duke to keep him out, he rushed into the room, to find himself confronted by the Heir to the Throne. Nicholas became very angry and asked the General how he dared intrude upon his privacy. Wahl, furious in his turn, retorted that it was his duty to see that order was maintained in the capital, no matter who was troubling it, upon which, in one of the uncontrollable fits of rage to which he was sometimes subject, the Cesarewitsch seized hold of a dish full of caviar which stood on the table and threw its contents in the face of Wahl. A scene of indescribable disorder followed. At last Prince Bariatinsky, one of the generals in waiting on the Czar, who had accompanied the young Grand Duke during the latter's journey round the world, was sent for. He succeeded in putting an end to an incident which reflected credit upon none of those who had taken part in it.

The next day Alexander III. was apprised of what had taken place. History does not say what he told his son, but it was supposed that it had not been anything in the way of praise, because there was nothing that the Emperor hated more than a drunken brawl, and it must have been very painful for him to find that his Heir had become involved in one. But when General Wahl arrived, full of complaints and indignation at the treatment to which he had been subjected, the Monarch expressed to him his entire disapproval of his conduct, saying that he had had no right to intrude upon the privacy of the Grand Duke, and that he ought not to have forgotten the immense difference of rank which existed between him and the future Emperor of Russia. Wahl did not require to be told twice the same thing, and in the future he never attempted to interfere with the pleasures of any member of the Imperial Family.

People who were present at this ill-fated supper told afterward, when relating all the incidents which had made it a memorable one, that Nicholas wished to do something worse than pour the contents of a caviar-dish on General Wahl's head, but that Mademoiselle Krzesinska had thrown herself between them. True or not, it is certain that after this night the Grand Duke took to visiting the beautiful dancer in her home, and very soon their relations became an established fact. She bore him two sons, which gave her distinct advantages over all the other flirtations in which her Imperial lover indulged from time to time, flirtations which she was far too clever and careful to notice. What she aspired to afterward was to become a power in the land, a *Maîtresse de Roi*, such as had been seen at the French Court during the reigns of the last Bourbons. Her Polish propensity for intrigue coming to her help, she very soon contrived to make for herself an excellent position in the world as well as to earn a considerable fortune. She was a very reasonable, matter-of-fact woman; she knew very well that Nicholas had to marry, whether he liked it or not, and her only preoccupation, if we are to believe all that was related in St. Petersburg at the time, was whether he should marry a clever or a stupid woman. It is not difficult to guess the one she would have preferred had the choice been left to her discretion.

When the betrothal of the Cesarewitsch with the Princess Alix of Hesse was announced Mademoiselle Krzesinska, far from objecting to it, applied herself, on the contrary, to persuading him that he had done quite right and that he could not have chosen a better wife. She imagined that the placid German temperament of the bride-to-be would look with innocent eyes on the continuation of her intrigue with Nicholas, in which supposition she was vastly mistaken, because Alice, though she did not care for the husband she had been compelled to marry, did not mean to let him wander away from the conjugal home in search of a happiness she believed herself quite capable of alone procuring for him. She tried to separate the Grand Duke from the clever dancer who held him in her bondage, and of course she failed.

Nicholas kept up his former habits of going to see Mademoiselle Krzesinska whenever he had the time to do so; what was even worse, he continued to consult her on many matters which he never discussed with his wife. The latter became very unhappy, and it was then that even her affection for her children was not sufficient to prevent her from uttering aloud her despair at having been obliged to leave her dear Darmstadt for a country where everything and everybody conspired against her and her peace of mind, and where she could not even win the love of the husband who had been imposed upon her.

Among the few people whom she used to see more frequently than others was the Montenegrin Princess Stana, who had been married to Duke George of Leuchtenberg, with whom she had led a most unhappy, uncanny sort of existence. Stana, like all the Montenegrin daughters of King Nicholas, was a charming and attractive woman, clever into the bargain. In spite of her unhappy conjugal experiences she had grown very fond of Russia, and especially of her position as a member of the Russian Imperial Family. She was very willing to divorce the miserable husband to whom she had been united, who had insulted and outraged her without the least compunction from the very first day of their marriage; but she would have liked to find another one whose affection, and especially whose worldly situation, were such that her future would be assured on even more brilliant lines than the present. Her elder sister, Princess Militza, was the wife of the Grand Duke Peter Nicholaievitch, whose brother was that Grand Duke Nicholas who was later on to acquire such a reputation as Commander-in-chief of the Russian armies during the first months of the present war. Grand Duke Nicholas was not considered as a marriageable man, being bound by ties of close friendship since a good number of years with an attractive woman, Madame Bourénine. Nevertheless, Princess Stana made up her mind to marry him, an enterprise which seemed the more hopeless that it was against the canons of the Greek Orthodox Church for two sisters to marry two brothers. As we have seen, her sister was Grand Duke Nicholas's sister-in-law.

This, however, did not much trouble the determined Stana, but she knew very well that it would be quite impossible for her to succeed in her designs unless she managed to enlist on her side the sympathies of somebody strong enough to protect her and to lend her the support which she needed. It was useless to think of the Empress Dowager, because the latter had never looked kindly upon the Montenegrin Princesses, to whom she had been very good at the time that they were being brought up in the Smolny Convent in St. Petersburg, and who had rewarded her with the basest ingratitude later on. The Emperor was a mere puppet in the hands of his advisers, and these, Stana knew but too well, would be against any idea of her becoming the wife of Nicholas Nicholaievitch. Remained the young Empress, to whom no one to that day had ever dared to apply for anything, who had been considered by general consent as not being worthy of any attention or consideration. Stana imagined that any proofs of respect which she might give to her were bound to be more appreciated than they would have been under different circumstances. She forthwith proceeded to lay siege with great care and tact to the heart and the sympathies of Alexandra Feodorowna.

At first her advances were met with rebuff; then gradually, seeing how attentive and full of deference her cousin showed herself in respect to her person, the young Empress began to thaw; and soon a friendship, the more surprising that the two ladies did not seem to have anything whatever in common in their respective characters—even a close friendship—established itself between them, and the miserable wife of Nicholas II. poured out the sorrows which racked her heart to the willing ears of Stana Leuchtenberg, who, in her turn, related all her own misfortunes. At last Alexandra interested herself so much in the welfare of this other victim of an unhappy marriage that she exerted all her influence to persuade the Emperor to grant her the permission to sue for a divorce. At the same time she applied herself to invite the Grand Duke Nicholas as often as possible either at Tsarskoye Selo or at Livadia, and to make him meet there the beautiful Stana Leuchtenberg. The expected happened, and soon poor Madame Bourénine was forgotten, and the betrothal of the Empress's two protégés was announced, much to the indignation of the man in the street, who did not approve of it by any means.

The Grand Duke Nicholas was in his way just as ambitious a man as the fair Montenegrin he had married. To the Crimea they both repaired as soon as the divorce of the Princess had been pronounced. He knew very well the weakness which characterized his nephew, the Czar, and he would have dearly liked to become the latter's chief adviser and even his Prime Minister. He therefore favored his new wife's intimacy with the Empress, so that the couple were often seen at Tsarskoye Selo, much more so, in fact, than any other members of the Imperial Family.

Now the Grand Duke had one weakness. He believed in spiritualism, in turning tables, and all kinds of superstitious extravagances. The Empress's leanings had also since some time been directed toward the same subject, but she had felt afraid to speak about it, knowing very well that this would not be looked upon with lenient eyes by the Czar or by his mother. When she discovered, however, that Nicholas Nicholaievitch did not feel in the least ashamed if he were caught trying to communicate, through the medium of a table or of a pencil, with the inhabitants of the other world, she confided to him her great desire to do the same thing. The Grand Duke replied that nothing could be easier. They held several séances to which the Emperor also came, attracted by the descriptions which his cousin had made to him. Nicholas Nicholaievitch promised the Empress that he would bring to her a famous French medium called Philippe, who would most certainly make her witness most extraordinary performances in regard to the evocation of the spirits of people dead long before.

Alexandra Feodorowna was delighted. She had already derived great comfort from her intercourse with her cousins, and her feeling of affection for Stana had acquired considerable warmth since the beginning of their friendship. Moreover, she knew that the Grand Duke Nicholas was considered the strong man in the Romanoff family, and she realized that to have him on her side would be a distinct advantage for her, and that his support might help her to overcome many difficulties. Therefore she appreciated very much all the acts of attention which both Stana and her husband were fond of pouring upon her. When Nicholas told her that he would gratify her wish to see a real medium she was more than delighted. She did not foresee whither this fatal introduction was to lead her, nor realize the ill turn that her cousin was doing her by giving her an opportunity of indulging her tastes for the supernatural, to which she was to owe so many of the misfortunes which were to assail her in later years, and which were to play such an important part in the tragedy that ended with her downfall. She was looking for the consolation of the moment without thinking of the possibility of the catastrophe of the morrow. [imgage *Nicholas Nicholaievitch p101*]

THE CZAR

IX

PHILIPPE AND HIS WORK

THE Grand Duke Nicholas kept his word, and one afternoon he brought to Tsarskoye Selo the famous Philippe, about whom his wife had spoken so often and with such enthusiasm to the young Empress. Before relating what followed upon this hasty and ill-advised introduction of an adventurer in the family circle of the Czar, it may not be out of place to say a few words concerning this personage, as well as to give a short description of his person.

Philippe was a Frenchman who, if all that has been related about him is true, had come to grief in his native land, to which he had thought it wiser to bid good-by for a time at least. He had spent several years in Germany, studying at German universities (at least he said so) and had given a great deal of attention to occultism and everything connected with it. Why he came to St. Petersburg no one ever knew, and though he has been accused of having tried from the very first months of his arrival in Russia to get introduced to the Sovereigns, yet I do not personally believe in this part of the story, because at that time no one suspected Alexandra Feodorowna or Nicholas II. of being interested in the supernatural. What is more likely is that he only attempted to get acquainted with the aristocratic circles of the capital, some of which were known to be attracted by these manifestations which begin by turning tables and end in more or less genuine hysteria. Later on when it became known that the Emperor and Empress themselves had given a welcome to the spiritualistic doctrines which Philippe preached, it is probable that the idea was suggested to him, by people who realized what capital might be made out of this circumstance, that he might come to acquire political influence, if he would but make use of his science to enslave the weak persons who had come to believe in him.

Personal ambition and vanity did the rest, combined with a good deal of German money, cleverly and judiciously spent in the furtherance of deep schemes, the real purport of which he was never allowed to suspect. He was encouraged to consider himself as a personage of great importance, and one upon whose shoulders rested some of the responsibilities which, properly speaking, belonged to the Czar alone. He was clever, bright, and assimilated very quickly all that he heard or saw, and knew how to turn to the best advantage every possible circumstance with which his personal welfare or interest was connected. As soon as he found himself in the presence of Alexandra Feodorowna he understood how easy it would be for him to get hold of a mind which he judged at once, and this quite rightly, not to be well balanced. He therefore played upon it; he ministered to it; he took advantage of it and of its vagaries; and he soon acquired over the young Sovereign an influence such as no one before him had ever wielded, and such as no one in the future was to have, with the exception of the famous Raspoutine of evil memory.

At first Philippe proceeded with great caution—so great, indeed, as to elude even the suspicious eyes of the Grand Duke Nicholas, who, though he had been instrumental in bringing this impostor to Court, yet would not at all have liked to see him become influential there, and who watched him very carefully during the séances which were held every Saturday evening at Tsarskoye Selo. Even the suspicious eyes of the Grand Duke Nicholas could not detect anything the least dangerous in his manner of proceeding. Philippe acted the medium to perfection. He used to go into regular trances, during which he replied to the various questions put to him with more or less accuracy; he never could be detected, once he was awake again, as having the slightest knowledge or remembrance of what had taken place while he had been asleep. Several times he prophesied with such exactitude that it seemed marvelous.

On one of these occasions he announced to the small circle assembled to listen to him in the Empress's boudoir that a serious misfortune was threatening the State through the death of one of its most important functionaries. He was still plunged in the hypnotic sleep during which he made this startling announcement when Count Lamsdorff, who occupied the position of Under Secretary of State for Foreign Affairs, arrived at Tsarskoye Selo and asked to be received by the Emperor on urgent and important business. He had come to communicate to the Monarch the news of the sudden death that same evening of the Minister for Foreign Affairs, Count Mourawieff. Of course this set the seal to Philippe's reputation as a prophet. Afterward some meddlesome people assumed that he had become aware of the sad event before he had left St. Petersburg to proceed to the Imperial country Palace by one of those singular accidents which happen sometimes in life, and that he had very intelligently made use of this knowledge during the trance in which he had pretended to be plunged. True or not, the story circulated freely, and was repeated everywhere, but the people who ought to have been the most interested in it did not, of course, hear it. On the contrary, the influence of the impostor was considerably strengthened by the incident, even in regard to the Grand Duke Nicholas, who from that moment began himself to consult Philippe in various matters. Then the Grand Duke had to leave for the Crimea, where he usually spent part of the year, on account of the health of the Grand Duchess, which had never been of the strongest, and he left Philippe in possession of the field.

In spite of Nicholas Nicholaievitch's absence, the séances with the medium continued, and they became even longer and more frequent than had been the case before. The Empress developed more and more interest in their progress, and at last one day, when Philippe asked her whether she would not try to be sent to sleep by him in order to get rid of the cruel headaches from which she suffered, she did not object; on the contrary, expressed herself as quite willing to make the experiment. Philippe, however, insisted on one condition, which was that he should be left alone with her while it proceeded.

Here comes the surprising part of this singular business. Instead of protesting against this pretension of the adventurer, Alexandra Feodorowna accepted it as a matter of course, and, what is more surprising even, she induced the Czar to give his consent. Philippe sent her to sleep, with the result that her headaches really improved and that she began to get into the habit of talking with him, either willingly or unwillingly, about all the events of her daily life and of consulting him whenever she thought that she found herself confronted by any difficulty.

She confided to him—what he knew already—her passionate desire to become the mother of a son, as well as the many disillusions of her married life. Philippe encouraged her, and he was the first one who suggested to her the advisability of taking an interest in public affairs, instead of holding herself aloof from them, and to point out to her the necessity which existed for her, in order to consolidate her personal position, to try and acquire some influence over her husband's mind, and in this way to eliminate that of the Empress Dowager. When Alexandra Feodorowna protested, the adventurer declared to her that he had been sent from heaven to come to her help, that it had been suggested to him by the invisible spirits which always inspired him to go to Russia and to give her the benefit of his experience so as to deliver her from her numerous enemies.

When she declared that she understood nothing about politics, he replied that it was her duty to learn, and that if she did not find any one in Russia willing to teach her, there was her own family in Germany who would be but too glad to come to her rescue, together with their knowledge of the art of government and of handling men and facts. He added that this was the more indispensable that she was about to give birth at last to the son she had been longing for since so many years, and that this son would grow to be an honor to her, as well as the greatest Sovereign Russia had ever known.

Poor infatuated Alexandra believed the adventurer, believed in him so thoroughly that she imagined that she was really about to become a mother once more, and solemnly announced the fact to the Emperor and to the Imperial Family.

Great preparations were made for the auspicious event, and once more the hopes that Nicholas II. might have at last an Heir to his Throne and Crown were awakened. It is related that everything had been got ready, that even the guns which were to announce the birth of a new member of the Romanoff dynasty had been placed on the ramparts of the fortress of SS. Peter and Paul to be fired as soon as the event had taken place, when the suspicions of the Empress Dowager were awakened by the attitude of her daughter-in-law as well as by her physical appearance. She began to watch her, and to do so with the more care. The time for the latter's presumed confinement had passed without that confinement having occurred. Alexandra Feodorowna was observed to be in tears, and her nervous condition became almost alarming, but she refused to see a doctor, and declared that she felt sure she would be better as soon as the suspense under which she was laboring was over. She remained long hours closeted alone with Philippe, who seemed to be the only man capable of bringing some calm to her over-excited system.

Some member of the Court took upon himself the task of writing to the Grand Duke Nicholas Nicholaievitch in the Crimea, advising him that something had gone wrong with the Empress, and that Philippe was concerned in it. One must give the Grand Duke his due. He had never meant any harm to his cousin's wife when he had brought the impostor to Court. As we have seen, the latter had been most careful in his whole demeanor while the Grand Duke had remained at hand to control his conduct and his actions. This did not prevent him from rushing back to St. Petersburg as soon as he heard of the strange doings which were shaking the equanimity of the inhabitants of Tsarskoye Selo. He had no sooner seen the Emperor and the Empress than he guessed what had really occurred. He forthwith proceeded to tell the Monarch that the medical attendants of Alexandra Feodorowna must see and examine her, whether she liked it or not, because her state of health was a question which did not interest her alone, but was of the utmost importance to the whole country as well as to the dynasty. He hinted at certain gossip which was going about, to the effect that it was the intention of the Empress to palm off a supposed son on her husband and on his family. Altogether he spoke so strongly that Nicholas II. became seriously alarmed, and for once in his life asserted his authority and compelled his wife to submit to a medical examination.

The result stupefied him as well as other people, because it was ascertained that the hopes of motherhood of Alexandra Feodorowna had only existed in her imagination; that there was no prospect whatever of her giving to Russia that Heir for whose advent the whole country was so eager. Of course the scandal was great, though an attempt was made to soften it by the publication of an official bulletin stating that an unfortunate accident had destroyed the hopes of the Imperial Family. For those who had perforce to become aware of the true circumstances of this whole adventure, the Empress remained under the shadow of a ridicule which was to cling to her for a long time and was not forgotten even when the present war broke out.

The Grand Duke Nicholas had a stormy interview with Philippe. The impostor pretended that he was not to blame, that the Empress had misunderstood him altogether, and that he, together with the rest of the world, had honestly believed in her supposed hopes of maternity. But in the mean while it had been discovered that during the séances which he had held at Tsarskoye Selo he had mesmerized Alexandra Feodorowna, and abused the confidence she had reposed in him by trying to worm out of her State secrets she was believed to know. The Grand Duke kicked the man out of the Palace, and told him that if he ever dared to set his foot in it again he would have him sent to Siberia under escort. He proceeded to acquaint the Emperor with all that he had discovered and to request the latter to issue orders for the expulsion from Russia of the impostor who had thrown so much ridicule on him as well as on the whole dynasty, who had acquired, thanks to his underhand man-euvers, such a disastrous influence over the mind of his Imperial Consort.

Philippe disappeared and was never seen any more. No one knew what happened to him, or where he was sent, and no one troubled. He had been a nine days' wonder and he sank into oblivion, but the Empress's mad infatuation for him was not forgotten so easily. The more so because she did not attempt to hide her grief at his removal, and bitterly reproached the Grand Duke Nicholas for his interference in a matter which, as she declared, did not concern him. Angry words were exchanged and the old intimacy which had existed between the Grand Duchess Stana, her husband, and Alexandra Feodorowna not only came to an end, but was replaced by a hatred the more bitter that it had perforce to be concealed under the veil of politeness and amiability. The Empress's nature, as we know already, was essentially a vindictive one, and the insult, as she considered it, to which she had been subjected on the part of Nicholas Nicholaievitch was to be avenged by her many years later on the day when, thanks to her and to her new favorite, Raspoutine, he was deprived of his position as Commander-in-chief of the Russian armies in the field.

X

ANNA WYRUBEWA APPEARS ON THE SCENE AND HE SAW HER PASS

AFTER the disastrous Philippe incident, the character of the Empress Alexandra changed considerably. She became a sullen, morose, melancholy woman, with a grudge against the world in general and the people with whom she lived in particular. Her sisters-in-law, the Grand Duchess Xenia Alexandrowna and the Grand Duchess Olga of Oldenburg, tried to come to her help and to enliven her by attempting to bring her out of the solitude in which she shut herself up, and if she would only have responded to these efforts it is possible that the whole course of her life might have run differently. But the Empress persisted in seeing enemies in everyone of her relatives, and, instead of trying to break through this wall of hostility with which she believed herself surrounded, she used all her powers of persuasion to induce her husband to take the same attitude of antagonism in regard to his family which she had adopted herself. Of course this was not forgiven her.

Nicholas II.'s sisters, who loved him dearly, were affronted when they discovered that their former intimate relations with their brother had come to an end, and that for some reason or other he looked upon them with suspicious eyes. Xenia simply shrugged her shoulders, and, being very wisely advised by her husband, the Grand Duke Alexander Michaylovitch, who, like all the members of that branch of the Romanoff family, was exceedingly intelligent, refrained from saying anything. But Olga, who was of a more enter-prising turn of mind, accosted the Czar one day and talked to him quite seriously about the conduct of the Empress, pointing out to him the harm which she was doing him by her rudeness toward the members of the Imperial Family, and expressing the conviction that times were sufficiently serious. This was during the Japanese war. The Emperor listened to her, as he listened to everybody who spoke to him, with courtesy and attention, but the only reply which she could obtain from him was to the effect that the Empress was in a bad state of health, that her nerves were quite unstrung, and that it would be wrong to take anything she said or did too seriously.

"But you are not nervous or ill," exclaimed the Grand Duchess. "How does it come, then, that you avoid us, your sisters, and even our mother just as much as does your wife. What have we done to you, except to love you, for you to treat us as if we were strangers?"

Nicholas II. pulled his mustache, but would not explain himself further, and Olga Alexandrowna had to own herself baffled.

The Empress heard of this conversation and it did not reconcile her to her sisters-in-law. She was in that morbid state of mind which gives an undue importance to the smallest incident which would not arrest for five minutes the attention of any normal person. The predisposition to insanity which existed in the Hesse-Darmstadt family had probably something to do with her condition, because she most certainly suffered from the mania of persecution; being a Sovereign, and a powerful one into the bargain, she imagined that the best use she could make of her unlimited power was to crush those in whom she persisted in seeing enemies bent on her destruction.

Rumors had reached her ears that some members of the Imperial Family (it had been the Grand Duke Nicholas Nicholaievitch, in fact) had said that her place ought to be in a convent rather than on the Throne, and she had immediately made out of the remark a desire on the part of her kinsman to shut her up in a monastery, as had been done in the Middle Ages with other Russian Czarinas, so as to give the Emperor the possibility to marry another woman who could bear him a son.

The supposition was a preposterous one, because such an idea had never crossed the Grand Duke's mind, but it could not be driven away out of the imagination of Alexandra Feodorowna. Hence her continual efforts to estrange her husband from his people, and to keep him entirely in her own hands, far away from any influence hostile to herself or to her daughters. There was, after all, some method in her madness. As things turned out, she was given several opportunities to exert her vengeful feelings in regard to the Imperial Family by the conduct of a few of its members.

I will here mention briefly two or three occasions when her intervention caused any amount of trouble and brought upon her head storms of abuse and indignation. The first one was the morganatic marriage of the Grand Duke Paul, the Emperor's uncle. This event was brought about principally through the want of tact and the stupidity of the people concerned in it, and it would have been far better for the Empress not to have interested herself in it at all, considering the fact that the personages concerned in this affair were certainly beneath her notice.

The Grand Duke had been upon terms of intimate friendship with a lady very well known in social circles of St. Petersburg, the wife of one of the officers of the regiment of which he was the commander. The thing had been going on for a number of years, and society had turned away its head and affected not to notice it; the more so that the husband of the lady in question seemed to ignore it, and to keep his eyes firmly closed as to her indiscretions. But one fine day the Grand Duke thought to make to Madame Pistolkors a present of some jewels which had belonged to his mother first, and to his wife afterward, and which had been locked up in a safe since the latter's death. This again might have passed unnoticed, had Madame Pistolkors not thought to put them on at a Court reception to which she was bidden. The Empress Dowager, who was present, recognized the unlucky ornaments, and, burning with wrath, forgot for once her strained relations with her daughter-in-law, and went up to her to draw her notice to the "scandal," as she termed it. Alexandra Feodorowna, as we know, had never been a tactful woman. She called a chamberlain and ordered him to invite Madame Pistolkors to leave the Palace immediately, and to escort her to her carriage. The next day Colonel Pistolkors, finding that matters had gone too far, introduced an action for divorce against his wife, and the latter, shunned by all her former friends, utterly disgraced before the world, had to flee abroad to hide her diminished head and her lost social prestige, in the solitude of a small Italian town. But then the unexpected, or rather the expected, occurred. The Grand Duke Paul took the only course left to him compatible with his honor as a gentleman. He followed the lady to Italy and married her there without asking anybody's leave, to the general scandal of St. Petersburg society, who declared that the incident with the diamond necklace that had been the primary cause of the catastrophe had been artfully engineered by its heroine in view of the result which was ultimately achieved.

The Emperor was furious; his mother equally so, but it is not likely that anything would have been done, or in general any notice taken of the action of the Grand Duke, had it not been for the intervention of the young Empress, who insisted on her uncle-by-marriage being deprived of his rank in the army and exiled abroad.

It was the first time that she had the opportunity to satisfy her instincts of hatred and of revenge in regard to a member of her husband's family, and she took a special delight, not only in doing so, but also in letting the world know that such was the case. Fate, for once kind to her, had delivered one of her enemies into her hands, and she was but too ready to seize this occasion for scoring her personal real or imaginary wrongs.

A few years later another incident of the same kind afforded her a second opportunity of exercising her powers of retaliation in regard to a Romanoff. The eldest son of the Grand Duke Wladimir, the young Grand Duke Cyril, the same who had nearly perished during the Japanese war in the catastrophe of the ship *Pétropawlosk*, married also without law or leave his first cousin, the divorced Grand Duchess of Hesse, the former sister-in-law of the Empress. The latter had always hated her, ever since the day that she had been obliged to play second fiddle to her at Darmstadt, and she had done her best to bring about an estrangement between her and her husband. This had not been difficult, because anything more brutal than the Grand Duke of Hesse had never existed. His young wife had had more to bear than the public knew, or that she cared herself to relate, but her own conduct had always been beyond reproach, and she had carried herself with remarkable tact and dignity. When at last she obtained her divorce, her only child, a little girl, was not even left entirely in her custody, but had to spend half of the year with the father. The latter did not well know what to do with the baby and most probably would never have availed himself of his rights had not his sister, the Empress Alexandra, interfered and persuaded him to confide to her own care the small Elisabeth, knowing very well that this would be about the most painful thing that could happen to the divorced Grand Duchess.

In accordance with this wish, the Grand Duke of Hesse brought his daughter to Spala in Poland, where the Russian Imperial Family were spending the autumn. The child sickened a few days later, and soon her condition became desperate. The doctors declared that the mother ought to be warned and asked to come, the more so that the little girl kept continually crying for her. But to this the Empress would never agree, until she knew it was positively too late. At last a telegram was sent to the Grand Duchess Victoria Mélita; it preceded but by a few hours the one advising her that her journey would be useless, as the end had come. One may imagine the feelings of the heartbroken mother and the natural resentment she must have felt at this piece of heartlessness on the part of her former sister-in-law. For a long time she would not be comforted, but at last she was induced to listen to her cousin, the Grand Duke Cyril, and she married him at Tegernsee in Bavaria, without the Czar's consent to this union having been so much as asked.

The rage of the Empress would be difficult to describe. Here was the sister-in-law whom she had hated for so many years the wife of a Russian Grand Duke, and of one, too, whose position put him very near to the succession to the Throne. One of those fits of hysterics to which Alexandra used to give way whenever she was crossed followed upon the news, and she insisted on the Czar declaring that he would never recognize the marriage and exiling the young couple. But here she met with an unexpected rebuff. Cyril's father, the Grand Duke Wladimir, was still alive at the time, and he was not a man to endure any slight offered either to him or to his children. He sought the Emperor and in a stormy interview reminded the latter that his new daughter-in-law was also the granddaughter of the Czar Alexander II., and asked him what he thought the latter would have said had he seen a Princess with Romanoff blood in her veins banished from the Russian Court. Nicholas was scared, and revoked the orders he had issued a few hours before, insisting only on the newly married pair not coming back to Russia for a few months, after which he left them free to do what they liked.

Alexandra Feodorowna was defeated, and this did not improve by any means her temper nor her feelings in regard to the Imperial Family. She then bethought herself to win over to her side that same Grand Duke Paul against whom she had been so incensed at the time he had married Madame Pistolkors. It must here be added that one of the reasons for her change of opinion in that respect lay in the fact that she had by that time struck up the extraordinary intimacy with Madame Wyrubewa which was to have such sinister consequences later on, and that this lady had always been one of the closest friends of the morganatic wife of Paul Alexandrowitch. The latter was therefore invited to return to Russia and given to understand that it depended on him to be reinstated in favor, if only he would take the Empress's part against their other relatives. Of course he promised he would do so, and we shall see presently what resulted of this intrigue in the years which followed.

Cyril and his wife returned to Tsarskoye Selo and to St. Petersburg in due course. They were received by both the Czar and Czarina coldly but civilly. Alexandra, however, persisted in her determination to keep her former sister-in-law at arm's-length, and the relations between the two ladies remained official, without the least attempt at any intimacy, until the Revolution sent the Empress into exile and threw into the arms of its leaders both Cyril Wladimirowitch and Victoria Mélita.

It was known already at the time that one of the persons who had the most contributed to excite Alexandra Feodorowna against her cousins had been Madame Wyrubewa. The latter was a new importation at Court, who, thanks to a very clever piece of strategy, had won the good graces of the Empress, whom she had met under rather peculiar circumstances. She was the daughter of a certain Mr. Tanieiew, who occupied important official functions at Court, and she had contrived to let the Czarina hear, through her father, that she was engaged in the occupation of writing a history of Hesse, which she meant to present to a public-school library or other institution of the same kind. Alexandra was immediately interested and asked to see the work. She sent for Madame Wyrubewa and soon the latter became her friend and confidante.

Madame Wyrubewa knew very well what she was about, even before circumstances turned out favorably in regard to her views and designs. She fully meant to become the Gray Eminence of the Empress, and, like the famous Père Joseph of Richelieu, to rule her, and through her the whole of Russia. We shall presently see how she proceeded to reach her aim, which in the mean while she knew very well she could never attain so long as there were near the Czar people whose close relationship with him allowed them to speak quite frankly with him on all subjects, even on that of the caprices and extraordinary behavior of his wife.

Anna Wyrubewa contrived to create a deadly feud between the Imperial pair and the whole clan of the Grand Duke Wladimir's family, who in a certain way was most powerful. The other members of the family were not dangerous in so far that the only thing they aspired to was to be left severely alone, and that they never cared to trouble with their presence the Emperor and Empress, for whom their dislike was only equaled by their contempt. There was only to be feared the Grand Duke Michael, the only brother of Nicholas II. and his Heir so long as the Empress had not given birth to a son. It was therefore against him that the new favorite turned her attention and against him that she excited the revengeful feelings of Alexandra Feodorowna.

What I wish to point out at present is that one of the secrets of the extraordinary influence which Anna Wyrubewa acquired over the mind of her Imperial mistress lay in the extreme ability which she displayed in appealing to all the bad sentiments of the latter, under the pretext of pitying her, and condoling with her on all the real or imaginary troubles of her life. She soon made herself indispensable to the Sovereign, who liked to visit her in her house, where she knew that no one would interfere with her and where she could meet the few people with whom she thoroughly sympathized, who in their turn were but too glad to have an opportunity of seeing almost in tête-à-tête the otherwise unapproachable Empress of Russia.

The small drawing-room full of flowers, where Alexandra Feodorowna was to spend so many happy and peaceful hours, and which was to witness in time such memorable events, filled itself with all manner of people, who, by common accord, never spoke of having been admitted within its precincts, or of having met one another there. It became also the meeting-place of a party, small at first, important later on; not, perhaps, on account of its number, but by the character of those who constituted it; a party that came to be known by the name of the "Empress's Party." It was to number among its adherents men like Mr. Sturmer, the latter's secretary, the too-famous Manassavitch-Maniuloff, Mr. Protopopoff, and, last but not least, the vagrant preacher who for a short time was to be the dominant figure in Russian politics, Grigory Raspoutine.

XI

AND HE SAW HER PASS

MADAME WYRUBEWA was a very clever woman, and an ambitious one into the bargain. Her ambition, however, was absolutely different from what might have been expected of a person brought up in the atmosphere of a Court and having been, if not actually mixed up, at least well posted, thanks to the position occupied by her father and family. She knew all the intrigues which always flourished and made the Court of St. Petersburg such a slippery ground for those who did not possess sufficient support to hold their own amid the rivalries and gossip which constituted the daily existence of the Imperial Family and of their friends. She did not care in the least for money, having got enough for her wants, nor for rank or position, which she knew too well could be lost or obtained according to circumstances, and which, besides, were never sufficient in Russia to make or mar an individual whose social worth depended only on the manner in which he was viewed by the Sovereign—the words of Paul I., when he said that the only persons deserving of any notice in his Empire were those "to whom he spoke, and only while he spoke with them." These words, about which one had laughed all through the three preceding reigns, had come to be absolutely true during that of Nicholas II., when favoritism assumed hitherto unknown proportions, as none knew better than Anna Wyrubewa, whose quick wit and ever-alert intelligence discovered very soon that she would become a far more important personage if she remained in the background content with being the Empress's friend, if she did not work toward obtaining for herself or for her husband a Court appointment or a lucrative official post. She aspired to something much more tangible, and at the same time much more amusing. She wanted to rule the Empress, and through her the whole of the vast Russian Empire. This young and delicate woman had the head of a statesman, and she might have risen to unheard-of might if she had not allowed those superstitious leanings which are inherent in the Russian character in so many cases to get the upper hand of her reason and lead her, together with her Imperial mistress, into the manifold mistakes which culminated in the catastrophe that destroyed the Throne of the Romanoffs.

At the same time Madame Wyrubewa sincerely loved the Empress. About this there is no doubt. She began by feeling sorry for the sad, miserable woman, so lonely amid her luxury and splendor, who stood friendless and defenseless among implacable enemies. She did not stop to consider whether this situation had arisen out of the personal fault of Alexandra Feodorowna, or out of other circumstances. She simply saw the fact, and hearing, as she did, all the different rumors concerning the Czarina which were going about in St. Petersburg society, she conceived the idea of coming to her help, and trying to be to her that friend in need she had never found since she came to Russia in quest of a Crown. This latter had certainly turned out to be, for her, one of thorns!

When her relations with the unfortunate Sovereign in whose life she was to play such an important part began, Anna Wyrubewa did not look beyond this simple fact, finding out how she could best be useful to her. The whole of St. Petersburg was discussing the question of a possible divorce which would send Alexandra Feodorowna into a convent, and bets had been made in select circles of Court society as to whether or not this would really take place. It was known that her relations with the Emperor were anything but tender, and that numerous quarrels had taken place between them.

Nicholas II., after an interval of several years, had resumed his former relations with Mademoiselle Krzesinska, and the dancer was contributing perhaps more than she herself suspected to sow dissentsion in the Imperial *ménage*. The Empress, as we know, was exceedingly proud, and as soon as she perceived, which did not take very long, that her husband was seeking amusement outside his home, she retired once more in haughty silence into the solitude of her own apartments and refused to fulfil the social duties required from her by her position, to the disgust of her friends and the joy of her numerous enemies. Matters had got to such a pass that sometimes days used to go by without the Czar and Czarina exchanging one single word beyond what was absolutely necessary during meals, and even these were not always taken together, Alexandra Feodorowna often putting forward her health as an excuse for having her dinner or lunch served in her own apartments. She was simply playing into her enemies' hands, and, whether consciously or unconsciously, herself tightening around her neck the rope which had been put within her reach.

It was this that made Anna Wyrubewa determined to come to the help of the unfortunate Sovereign whom she saw going with rapid steps toward ultimate destruction. She tried to reason with her, to speak to her of the necessity of not giving up the game, and of her imperative duty to remain upon good terms with her husband, so as to be able to bear him the son whose absence contributed so much to the bad relations that had taken the place of the affectionate ones which had undoubtedly existed at one time between her and Nicholas II. But the Empress would not listen, declaring that she was tired of always giving birth to girls, whose advent into the world only added to her unhappiness, and that, besides, she was sick of a husband whose deplorable weakness of character made him an easy prey for the first intriguing person who approached him. The only thing which she wished was to return to Darmstadt, together with her daughters; but as she knew very well that she would never be allowed to take them out of Russia, she preferred to be sent to a convent, where she could end her days in prayer, and where she could bring up her children without any interference from the outside world. The Emperor could divorce her and marry again; she did not care; all she wished for was a quiet life, far from those detestable Court intrigues that had wrecked all the hopes of happiness she had ever had.

Anna Wyrubewa listened, and very gently applied herself to reason with the sorely tried woman. She told her that it would be unworthy to throw up the game, but, on the contrary, that her duty toward her daughters required her to fight vigorously against destiny represented by the Empress Dowager, the Grand Dukes, the Court, and the nation, who judged her according to what it had been told of her. She repeated to her that if once she had a son her position would change immediately, and the affection of her husband would return to her, together with the popularity she had lost in the country. Alexandra only replied by floods of tears and complaints that she did not know how such a desirable event could happen. She loathed the Emperor and she knew that he did not care for her; that, in fact, no one cared for her; and that was the calamity which to her sensitive heart appeared the most terrible one among all those that had befallen her.

Madame Wyrubewa was at her wits' end, but she did not despair.

She felt, however, that she could not cope alone with the many difficulties which she found in her way, and so she looked round her to see whether she could not find any one in whom she could confide, and from whom she might, in her turn, seek advice.

I don't know whether I have related that the lady had always been a favorite in society. At that time she was going out a great deal, which was not the case later on, when her whole position changed and when she became the Empress's principal confidante, and had perforce to live in retirement. But twelve or fifteen years ago her house in Tsarskoye Selo was the meeting-place of a select circle, and especially of the officers of the regiments constituting the garrison of the Imperial Residence, who liked to drop in of an evening, and find a pleasant hostess, together with an excellent supper which was always waiting for them. Mr. Wyrubew, too, was a general favorite, and altogether the little house occupied by the young couple was very popular with the inhabitants of the Imperial Borough.

Among the special friends of Anna Wyrubewa was a dashing officer called Colonel Orloff. He had a commission in the regiment of Lancers of the Guard, the chief of whom was the Empress Alexandra. A wonderfully handsome man, he was also clever, brave, chivalrous, and altogether different from his comrades in so far that he had never cared for the boisterous pleasures which made up their daily existence. One day as he was going to call on Madame Wyrubewa he saw the Czarina leave her house in a state of evident agitation. Alexandra was alone and on foot, having walked from the Palace to her friend's house, and the Colonel, who, on recognizing the Sovereign, had respectfully stood aside, was much surprised to notice her red eyes and her general attitude of dejection. He waited until she had disappeared among the trees in the park and then rang the door-bell of Madame Wyrubewa.

He found her just as agitated as the Empress, and when he asked her what was the matter he was much surprised to see her begin to weep.

She related to him that she was terribly anxious about the fate of the unlucky Consort of Nicholas II., whose safety and person were threatened as much by her own stupidity as by the intrigues of her numerous enemies. Colonel Orloff listened in silence. He, too, was troubled by this unexpected revelation; the more so that for years he had nourished a secret adoration and worship for Alexandra Feodorowna, which he had hoped no one had, or would ever discover, and the news of her danger was terrible for him. His emotion was so evident that Anna noticed it at once, and an idea which was yet vague and misty began to take shape in her active brain, and induced her to seek the help of this unexpected ally whom circumstances and accident had brought to her. She started to discuss the situation seriously with the young officer, and together they determined to try and save the Empress, even against her own will, from the snares into which she was walking with an unconsciousness which was almost too pitiful to look upon otherwise than with a wild desire to snatch her away from the abyss whither she was sinking with what promised to become rapidity.

Colonel Orloff had a wonderful talent for music. On the very next day following upon the conversation which I have related, Madame Wyrubewa asked him to call on her in the afternoon, and to perform for her some melodies of Chopin which she knew were the favorite ones of the Empress. She also begged the latter to allow the Colonel to play for them, saying that it might interest her to hear him. Alexandra consented and, as in the case of David and Saul, she found a solace in listening to the wonderful music. Very soon she got into the habit of dropping in at her friend's whenever she had a spare moment, and then Orloff would be telephoned for, and he used to come and hold the two ladies under the spell of his rare talent. Of course no one was admitted to these meetings and no one knew anything about them. At that time people did not trouble about the Empress of All the Russias, and her actions did not offer the slightest interest to any one, to the Emperor least of all.

Colonel Orloff was something in character like the famous Count Fersen, the admirer and devoted friend of Marie Antoinette. He, too, had conceived a passion for his Sovereign, in whom he only saw the unfortunate, ill-treated, and misunderstood woman, and he conceived the thought to sacrifice everything for her service, to try and save her from the perils with which he saw her surrounded. And gradually, when his relations with her became more real and intimate, he, too, began to speak to her in the same sense as Anna Wyrubewa had done, of the necessity of trying to reconcile herself with her husband so as to be able to bring into the world that Heir after whom the whole of Russia had been longing for the last nine years or so.

One day Madame Wyrubewa, whether accidentally or intentionally, left the Colonel alone with the Czarina. He saw his opportunity, and began more seriously than he had ever done before to implore her to make an effort to save herself. The young man grew quite eloquent, until Alexandra, moved beyond words, started weeping in real earnest and asked him how he could suggest the possibility of a reconciliation between her and the Czar, in view of his own feelings for her, the nature of which she had guessed for some time. To her surprise, the Colonel fell on his knees before her and told her that it was because of these very feelings that he had felt himself justified in speaking to her as he had done. He was nothing beside her, and all he could do was to worship her from afar, and to try to come to her help, both for her own sake and for that of their country, that required from them both the supreme sacrifice he was asking of her. For once the cold and haughty Czarina was startled out of her usual indifference, and when they parted she had promised her devoted knight and admirer that, though she might not make an effort to win back the love of her husband, yet she would not repulse him, as she had done lately, if he made any attempt to return to her. She promised that on the love she owned to him that she felt for him, and on that of the one which they both had for this great Russia, which Orloff had never forgotten even amid the fervor of his passion. When Madame Wyrubewa came back to the room where she had left her two friends, she saw that something had happened, but she was far too clever to question them, and when the Empress said it was time for her to go home she simply offered to accompany her, hoping that something might be told to her during their walk back to the Palace. For once Alexandra was silent, and parted from Anna without betraying anything of what had passed during that half-hour when she had been left alone with the first man who had aroused some interest in her otherwise impassible heart.

Colonel Orloff was not so discreet, in the sense that he related to his friend all that had taken place between him and the Czarina—related it with such agitation and poignant regret that she saw at once that she was in the presence of a feeling capable of driving the man who was under its influence to any heights of personal sacrifice. She then communicated to him a plan out of which she hoped to find the solution of the troubles against which the Empress was struggling so bravely, but apparently so uselessly. It was a daring plan and it required much daring to accomplish it; but the future of the woman they both loved was at stake, and she thought they ought to risk it.

Nicholas II. was fond of Colonel Orloff, whom he had recently appointed one of his aides-de-camp. The Sovereign liked from time to time to go and dine or have supper at the mess of some regiment or other of the Guards, either at Tsarskoye Selo, Peterhof, or St. Petersburg. These entertainments used to last generally into the small hours of the morning, and ill-natured people said that the Czar when in this company of young men, which was more congenial to him than the one he was compelled to see generally, allowed himself to have more glasses of wine than were good for him, and to indulge in subjects of conversation he would have done better to avoid. Whether this was true or not, it is of course difficult to say, but the fact remains that Nicholas liked these "family festivities," as he used to call them, and that he always returned home in a good temper after having attended them. Colonel Orloff was aware of this weakness of the Sovereign, and one day he proposed to him to go and hear some regimental singers at the mess of his own Lancer regiment, stationed at Peterhof, the same regiment of which the Empress was Colonel-in-chief. Nicholas II. consented and a day was fixed. On the morning of that day Colonel Orloff sought Madame Wyrubewa; the two had a long conversation, the result of which was their reading together a certain page in French history relating how Louis XIII. had been compelled to seek the hospitality of his wife, Anne of Austria, on a stormy night when it had not been possible for him to return from Paris to St.-Germain, where he resided, an incident that had had world-wide consequences in the birth of the child who was to become in time Louis XIV. After that the Colonel returned to the Palace, where he was on duty that day, and his friend went to seek the Empress and to try to induce her to lend a helping hand to the plot which they had both engineered.

 The supper took place, and it was nearly dawn when the Czar left the mess of the Lancers of the Guard, where he declared that he had spent a most pleasant evening. He drove in a motor-car back to Tsarskoye Selo in a very enjoyable frame of mind, which did not require the encouragement of his aide-de-camp, who sat next to him, to become a boisterous one. Lots of champagne had been drunk during the meal, and even after, and when some one in the gay assembly had ventured to say that the only pity of the whole thing was that no representatives of the fair sex had been invited to enliven the party with their presence, Nicholas II. had heartily echoed the regret expressed by the officer in question. Orloff, when alone with the Sovereign, had very cleverly turned the conversation into the same channel, and at last had wormed out of his Imperial Master the confession that he was very unhappy at the extreme coldness of character of his Consort, whose beauty he admired just as much as on the day he had married her. The Colonel, upon this, had ventured to express the conviction that this coldness was only assumed, and proceeded perhaps from jealousy more than from anything else. When at last Tsarskoye Selo was reached, instead of accompanying Nicholas to his own apartments, as it was part of his duties to do, he brought him to the door of the Empress's room, which he opened and closed upon him.

The next day a pale and haggard woman appeared in Anna Wyrubewa's house, coming to seek consolation in what she considered an overwhelming misfortune, and while she was sobbing out the agony of her soul with her head hidden in her friend's lap, a strong man who had borne many a misfortune without flinching, and who had stood calm and unmoved while his heart had been breaking, was sitting alone in his room, his head hidden in his hands, and hot tears dropping one by one between his fingers on the table over which he was leaning, in his overwhelming despair.

THE GRAND DUKE NICHOLAS

XII

LOVED AT LAST

AFTER a storm there comes, generally, so they say, at least, a great calm. And in a certain sense this happened in regard to the troubled mind of the Empress Alexandra. As time went on, she recognized the value of the good advice which she had received from Madame Wyrubewa as well as from Colonel Orloff. Her relations with the Czar, which had been more than strained for long months, became gradually better when she could at last tell him that she had once again, and this time without any mistake, the hope of giving him the Heir for which they had been longing. She saw his former confidence in her return, together with his affection; an affection to which she did not perhaps respond, but which she nevertheless appreciated, perhaps because she was told she ought to do so.

The fact was that her two friends were doing their best to get her to take a healthier view of her own position than had been the case until then. Intrigues at the Court were getting worse and worse, as the various events which finally brought about the Japanese war were slowly unfolding themselves, and it became every day more important for the security of the Empress that she should not disinterest herself from all that was going on around her, as had been her wont, since she had allowed disappointment and sorrow to overpower her.

It was an anxious and a critical time for the dynasty as well as for the country that was coming on, and Anna Wyrubewa with her clear mind was very well aware that such was the case. She used to hear all the gossip in the various circles of St. Petersburg society, and she knew very well that a war was wished for by the enemies of the existing order of things. They saw in it the possibility of overthrowing the dynasty, as the mistakes inevitable in dealing with such a corrupt administration as the Russian one would appear in a new, bold light before the horrified eyes of the public. She was also perfectly aware of the growing unpopularity of Nicholas II., and of the way in which he was daily losing what still remained of the former short-lived affection his subjects had felt for him. She would have liked the Empress to assert herself, and to claim as her right to be initiated in what was going on in the domain of public affairs, but it was still too early for Alexandra to avail herself of this advice. The Czarina did not feel sure of her ground as yet, and she only replied to her friend's adjurations that, if she were lucky enough to give birth to a son, she would follow her advice to the letter; in the mean while she felt afraid of being snubbed by the Emperor, who, though he treated her with far more consideration than he had done for a long time, still kept her in total ignorance of all questions relating to the affairs of the State. On the other hand, he did not hesitate to discuss them with his mother, the Dowager Empress, and even occasionally with his sisters and his brother-in-law, the Grand Duke Alexander Michaylovitch, who had always been his great friend and favorite.

The delicate condition of health of Alexandra Feodorowna furnished her with the pretext she required to isolate herself more than ever from her family, and she used to spend long hours with Madame Wyrubewa in the latter's small house, and whenever she went there she met, as if accidentally, Colonel Orloff, whose faithful, devoted eyes followed her with a love which she could not have helped noticing, even if she had not been aware of its existence. She was a woman gifted with a very pure mind, given to idealize the people she cared for and her own feelings in regard to them. She soon grew to think of the young officer as of a kind of guardian angel sent by Providence to help her in the various difficulties of her daily existence, and with a selfishness almost touching in its unconsciousness she took to confiding to him her various doubts and perplexities, and to initiate him into all the details of her married life, together with the constant disgust and struggles which attended it, not suspecting that by doing so she was breaking the heart of this one faithful friend who had sacrificed himself so entirely to her welfare.

In the mean while events had been rapidly unfolding themselves. The war with Japan had begun and was progressing, together with its long series of appalling disasters coming one on top of the other. Mukden had been fought, the *Pétropawlosk* had gone down in the waves of the Pacific, with brave Admiral Makharoff and its whole crew of officers and men, and the catastrophe of Tsu Shima had also taken place. These had been met by the utter indifference of Nicholas II., who had not even thought it worth while to interrupt the game of tennis he had been playing when the telegram with the news of this unprecedented misfortune had been brought to him. In the interior of the country trouble was also brewing. The Grand Duke Sergius, the uncle of the Czar and the husband of the Empress's eldest sister, Elisabeth, had fallen under the bomb of an assassin in Moscow, and the famous Minister of the Interior, Von Plehwe, whose very name was a horror to all the liberal elements in the land, had met with the same fate.

It was evident that grave events were at hand, and that unless something was attempted to meet them the very foundations of the Throne might come to be shaken by this rising tide of discontent which threatened to engulf the dynasty in its waves. It was high time something were done, and that some one should interfere to save Nicholas II. from impending calamity. Who could do so better than his wife and the mother of his children? Thus reasoned Anna Wyrubewa, and it was also what her friend, Colonel Orloff, thought; but that was not at all what was wished by the various other forces at work trying to dictate to the weak-minded Czar the conduct he ought to hold in the presence of these unexpected difficulties with which he found himself confronted, to his dismay and surprise. There had got about among the public an inkling as to the possibility of the Empress becoming all at once a factor to be reckoned with in the general situation. Immediately the efforts of all her enemies became concentrated on that one point—how best to eliminate this new element, which they understood but too well would necessarily counteract their own influence.

A careful watch was set on the person and the conduct of the young Sovereign. It did not bring any of the hoped-for results, because both Anna Wyrubewa and Colonel Orloff were prudent people, who contrived to arrange matters in such a way, that no one suspected they used to see Alexandra Feodorowna every day, and who had persuaded the latter to resort to all kinds of precautions whenever she visited her friend.

One day, however, an officer who was serving in that very same regiment of Laners to which Colonel Orloff belonged made a playful remark to the effect that he was believed to be a favorite with the lovely and cold Czarina, who had never hitherto allowed her glances to fall on any man whatsoever. The young Colonel became immediately alarmed, the more so that he could not discover the source whence this piece of gossip had arisen. He sought Madame Wyrubewa and told her that he had made up his mind to ask to be transferred to a regiment at the front, so as to put a quick end to any possible unpleasantness. She heartily agreed with him in the opinion that this was the best thing he could do, for the sake of everybody, and especially for that of the Empress.

The latter had to be told of Orloff's resolution. But when he broke to her his intention to request the favor of risking his life in distant Manchuria, she gave way to a fit of despair that absolutely frightened her two devoted friends, and implored him not to leave her, at least not until her child had been born, saying with sobs and tears that she would never be able to undergo the trial which awaited her if she did not know that he was there, as near to her as possible, and that she could see him after all was over, to wish her joy, if the expected babe were a son, and to comfort her if it turned out to be another girl, the one thing which she feared above all others.

At first the Colonel protested. He tried to explain to the despairing and over-excited woman that it was for her sake he wished to go away, at least for a while, and that it cost him more than he could say to come to such a resolution, but that he loved her far too much to let her run any risk. The Empress would not listen to anything, and at last she told him that if he went away she would consider it as a proof that he did not love her, and that all he had said to her had been nothing but empty phrases, such as no doubt he had repeated already to many more women than he even cared to remember. Orloff was stung to the quick, but he remained, nevertheless, firm until Alexandra Feodorowna exclaimed that unless he promised her to remain by her side she would make a scandal and depart for Darmstadt, whether the Emperor allowed her to do so or not. Man-like, he yielded, without suspecting whither this weakness was to lead him sooner than he could imagine.

While this drama was going on in the pretty little house whither Anna Wyrubewa received the Empress of All the Russias, unknown to the rest of the world, so she believed, at least, speculations were rife as to the eventual sex of the child expected by the Czar and Czarina. Everybody, with few exceptions, hoped that it would be another daughter, none more ardently than the Dowager Empress, who would have infinitely preferred the Throne passing to her youngest son than to any boy born to a daughter-in-law whom she made no secret of disliking, and whom she distrusted even more than she disliked. She realized very well that Alexandra Feodorowna, if she was the mother of an Heir to the Imperial Crown, would become a most important personage in the State, as well as in the eyes of her husband. This was not to be desired, in view of her strong German sympathies, which she had lately exhibited more than she had ever dared to do before.

The French alliance was very popular at the time I am talking about, and the Empress was considered as its principal and most bitter adversary. This was one more reason for not wishing her to acquire suddenly an importance that had never been awarded to her by the nation since she had become its Sovereign.

For months this kind of thing went on. Alexandra Feodorowna knew herself to be watched with anything but kind eyes, and this consciousness of the ill-will of which she was the object added to her anxiety and moral sufferings. As the weary months dragged on, she thought more and more of Orloff, and suddenly she realized that she loved him more than any one in the world, and she began to understand all that she must have cost him, in pain and vain regret.

But for her, at least, consolation was at hand. One July morning the Imperial Family were called together with the principal Court and State functionaries in all haste to Peterhof. The long-expected event was at hand, and a few hours would decide as to the future of the Romanoff dynasty. People with anxious faces thronged the vast halls of the Palace, waiting for news which seemed to be very long in coming.

At last, just as the clock struck noon, a doctor entered the room, and told the assistants that Nicholas II. was the father of a son.

There was one person present who listened to this announcement with an impassible face but with a breaking heart, and who could barely find sufficient strength to reach the little cottage where Anna Wyrubewa was sitting pale and anxious, in expectation of—she did not know well herself what. When she saw Colonel Orloff she extended toward him her two hands in a gesture of passionate greeting. But what was her surprise to see him fall on the sofa beside her and bury his head in the silk cushions, with such sobs as rarely shake the frame of a strong man. He had had the courage to sacrifice his personal happiness at the shrine of the woman whom he adored with such religious fervor, but it was more than he could bear to find how thoroughly this sacrifice had been accepted by Providence, and for just a few minutes he had hated this new-born child, whom he knew but too well was going to usurp the place he had hoped to keep forever in the heart and the affections of Alexandra Feodorowna.

XIII

HE DIED TO SAVE HER HONOR

THE christening of the little Grand Duke Alexis was solemnized with great pomp at Peterhof, and there is no doubt but that the position of his mother became, after his birth, quite different from what it had been before this much-wished-for baby had appeared. For one thing, the talk of a divorce between her and the Czar, which had been so frequently indulged in, came to an end, and it was felt, even by the most bitter enemies of the Empress, that it would be waste of time to think about the possibility of its ever taking place.

Nicholas II., in his joy at having at last an Heir, seemed to have returned to his former allegiance in regard to his wife, and he began to confide in her far more than he had done formerly, even consulting her on different occasions. She was the mother of the future Sovereign, and as such entitled to a consideration a childless Empress Dowager could never aspire to in the case of widowhood. It became, therefore, necessary to initiate her in matters concerning the government of the country, and the Czar did this the more willingly that at heart he distrusted his brother, and his numerous uncles and cousins, and feared that in case he died before the small Cesarewitsch had reached his majority the interests of the latter would not be looked after as well as would be necessary, unless his mother were there to protect them.

Alexandra Feodorowna, on the other hand, urged by her two friends, Madame Wyrubewa and Colonel Orloff, began to show far more interest in public affairs than she had ever done since her marriage, and she tried to establish between herself and her husband more intimate relations than she had cared to do formerly, when she used to spend her days lamenting over sorrows, imaginary most of the time, but sufficiently acute to render her intensely miserable. Her son became the principal preoccupation of her existence, and she would not intrust his care to any one, but transformed herself into his nurse, governess, and constant attendant, forgetting everything else, even the care of her daughters, in her nervous solicitude for him. Unfortunately the child was born excessively delicate, and had a curious and rare disease, a weakness of the blood-vessels, which were affected in such a way that he was attacked with hemorrhage at the slightest touch; the smallest of knocks or wounds would endanger his life. He might bleed to death from an ordinary bruise. An unfortunate accident which occurred when he was two years old, and which brought about a rupture that necessitated an operation from which he recovered only by a kind of miracle, only aggravated the chronic ailment with which he was afflicted.

One may imagine how terrible this state of things proved for the Empress, who very stupidly, as it seemed to some people, applied herself to hide from the public the state of physical health of her son, which had, among other results, that of people supposing him to be even more dangerously ill than was the case. The truth was that Alexandra feared that if it were known the boy was afflicted with an incurable disease, it might add to her own unpopularity. Her friends hoped that she might bear another son in time, but after the birth of Alexis she never had any more hopes of maternity, and so there remained nothing else to do but to try and rear this weak, frail, and puny infant, in whom were centered all the future hopes of the proud Romanoff dynasty.

Anna Wyrubewa did her best to comfort the sorrowing mother, and both she and Colonel Orloff agreed that the only thing to do in order to turn her thoughts into another channel than that of her child's state of health, over which she brooded until she had become absolutely morbid in her constant preoccupation of the painful subject, was to speak to her of the necessity of becoming the Czar's principal adviser and counselor. They tried to induce her to assert herself in the interest of Alexis, who they assured her would one day outgrow his native weakness and require her help in the numerous duties entailed upon him by his position as Heir to the Throne. In a certain sense they succeeded, and the Empress began to develop an independence of opinions and views in which she had never dared to indulge before. Ministers were surprised to hear the Czar say to them, when they pressed him for a reply to some decision or order they presented to him for confirmation, that he first wished to discuss the subject with his wife. Somehow there arose among the public, and especially among the Imperial Family, an impression that Alexandra had at last completely subjugated her husband, and that she was henceforward a factor to be reckoned with in every important

State affair which might arise in regard to foreign or home politics.

Of course people did not like it. One had been used for such a long time to consider the Czarina as a nonentity that it seemed a strange thing to have suddenly to take her into account; one began to wonder what could have brought about such an unexpected change in her whole conduct and demeanor. Maternal love was not sufficient to explain it, and the cause of it had to be looked for elsewhere, and one fine day her constant intercourse with Anna Wyrubewa was noticed. Once people were started on that path, there was but one step to take—to try and find out whether or not these suspicions were founded on anything tangible. Some inquisitive persons took to watching the actions of Anna Wyrubewa, and they were not long in discovering that her house served as a meeting-place for several people in whom Alexandra Feodorowna was interested, among others Colonel Orloff, whose hopeless passion for his Sovereign had been already suspected at different times.

Foremost among these voluntary observers, not to give them another name, figured members of the Imperial Family who had never taken kindly to the Consort of Nicholas II., and who hated the idea of her becoming a power in the State. They tried to find out something to her detriment, and who also attempted to enroll among their number the Dowager-Empress Marie, who, however, refused to listen to them, and whose affection for her eldest son induced her to make an effort to warn her daughter-in-law of the dangers which were threatening her. But the young Czarina would not hear anything, and haughtily refused the hand that was extended to her in sincere friendship. She snubbed Marie Feodorowna in such a manner that the latter, wounded to the quick in finding her good intentions misunderstood, swore that she would never again attempt to come to the help of a person who was so prejudiced against her.

In the mean while, ignorant of the conspiracy which was being engineered against her, Alexandra continued to spend her afternoons with Madame Wyrubewa, often taking her little boy with her. The two women watched the child sleeping in his cradle, and often Colonel Orloff shared their vigil with a bleeding heart, the baby reminding him of all that he had suffered for the sake of its mother, but with the consciousness of having done his duty to both. But one day rumors again reached his ears that his name had once more become associated with that of the Empress. This time he made up his mind to go away definitely, no matter how much she might ask him to stay. He realized, if neither she nor Anna Wyrubewa did so, that the position was becoming threatening, and that he ought to put an end to it in some way or other. Unfortunately, when he came to this conclusion it was already too late.

Madame Wyrubewa's husband was a naval officer, not gifted with a superabundance of brains, but honest in his way, and incapable of intrigues of any kind. He had troubled very little about his wife, and was perhaps the only man in St. Petersburg and in Tsarskoye Selo who was not aware of the high favor in which she stood with the Empress. His duties generally kept him far from his home most of the year, and when he was there he rarely troubled Anna with his presence. But he was known to be of a violent disposition, and as a fellow who would not suffer any stain to rest upon his honor. It was of this man that the enemies of Alexandra Feodorowna determined to make use in order to ruin her.

Anonymous letters were sent to him accusing his wife of carrying on a guilty intrigue with Colonel Orloff, intrigue which he was assured the Empress knew and favored. He was advised to return home unexpectedly any afternoon between four and five o'clock, when he would find proofs of the information vouchsafed to him by his unknown friend. The young man, instead of putting these denunciations in the fire, became so enraged that he determined to follow the advice of his anonymous correspondent. After having advised Anna that he was going away on a few days' cruise, he waited until the hour that had been indicated to him, and boldly walked back to his house.

He was met at the door by the Cossack in personal attendance on the Empress, who informed him that he could not get in. Wyrubew protested, and was quietly told that the Sovereign was visiting his wife, and that according to etiquette no one could be allowed to enter a place where she was unless by her special permission. The officer became furious, brushed the Cossack aside, and penetrated into the sitting-room, after having noticed that a military overcoat was hanging in his hall. He found the apartment empty, but in the adjoining one, which was Anna's boudoir, he could hear voices, one of which was distinctly masculine. He did not hesitate, but made his way inside, to find that his wife was not there, but that the Empress, pale and lovely, was standing by the mantelpiece, while Colonel Orloff, on his knees before her, was kissing passionately the hem of her skirt.

Alexandra Feodorowna gave one cry, which echoed through the whole building and brought Madame Wyrubewa to her help. Wyrubew himself remained silent and dazed by the unexpected sight. The only one not to lose presence of mind was Colonel Orloff, who, starting to his feet, went up to the intruder with the stern words:

"You are going to give me your word of honor to remain silent."

Wyrubew passed his hand over his eyes. He could hardly believe his own senses, and the terrible idea crossed his mind that his wife had been helping the Czarina in an amorous intrigue, and that very probably he would have to pay the penalty for this piece of complaisance, which he did not in the least care to do. He thought that insolence was the best way to get out of an impossible position with flying colors, and so he simply sneered in the face of Orloff, with the remark:

"Not I. If you have chosen to abuse my confidence, together with my wife, you cannot expect me to help you in your villainy."

Anna rushed to the Empress and took her in her arms, trying to lead her out of the room. Orloff made a movement forward as if he wanted to strangle Wyrubew; then he contained himself and said in a low voice:

"You know that you are not speaking the truth. Once more I implore you not to mention to any one what has taken place here, and I give you my word of honor to meet you whenever and wherever you like."

"You are not a man from whom one can expect satisfaction," replied Wyrubew, "and I will not claim it from you. There are other means at my disposal to punish you," and he turned away contemptuously.

The young Colonel's face became by turns deadly pale and fiery red. It was evident that he could hardly contain the tumultuous feelings which were racking him. Before him stood the Czarina looking at him with haggard eyes and trying to free herself from the encircling arms of her friend. Anna was weeping profusely and vainly struggling with an emotion she absolutely could not control. Orloff went up to the two women, and once more knelt before the Empress.

"Forgive me," he said. "I ought to have known better, but believe me, I shall atone."

He kissed once more the hem of her garment and went out of the room, without looking round, brushing past Wyrubew as if he had not seen him, and went back to his own house, calm and determined, but probably with the feelings of a man about to be taken to the scaffold.

Madame Wyrubewa seized her husband by the arm.

"Go now," she cried. "You have done enough evil for to-day, but remember that henceforth everything is at end between us."

He laughed sardonically, but obeyed her, and the couple never set eyes upon each other again after that terrible afternoon. The next day St. Petersburg was electrified by hearing that the popular Colonel Orloff had been found dead in his room, shot through the temple. He had atoned.

And two months later the Synod pronounced the decree of divorce between Anna Wyrubewa and her husband. The tragedy, like so many others of the same kind, had come to an end, by breaking two women's hearts.

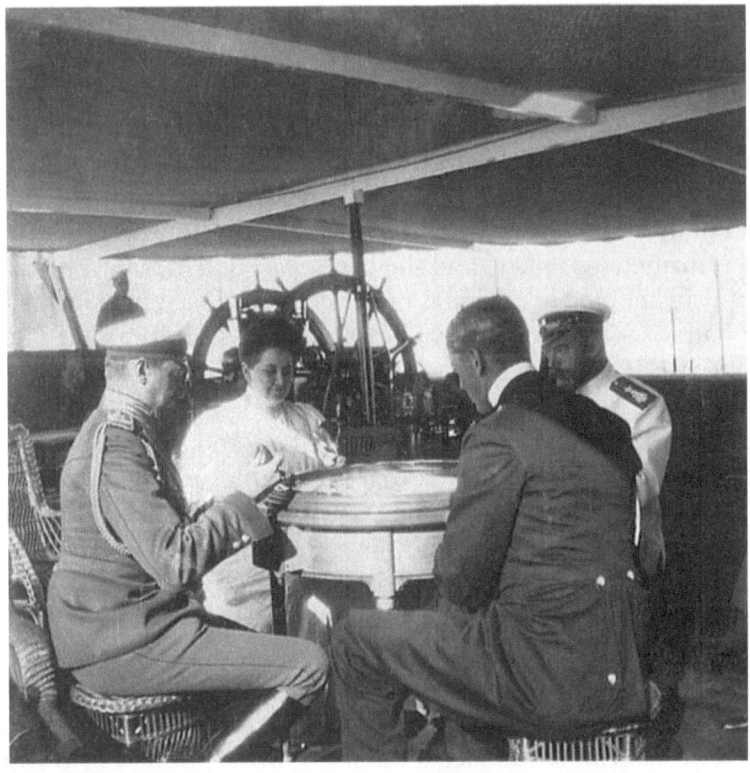

GENERAL ALEXANDER ORLOFF and ANNA VIROUBOVA sit to the left, relaxing with the Czar onboard Standart. (September 1906)

XIV

A NATION IN REVOLT

THE suicide of Colonel Orloff was perhaps one of the events which provoked the most sensation in St. Petersburg in recent years. Everybody had known him, and he had been a general favorite, not only in his regiment, but also among all the circles of society which he had frequented. The Czar, who had also liked him very much, was deeply affected by the catastrophe, and everybody kept wondering what could have induced a man who apparently had not a single thing in the world to trouble him to take his own life in such an unexpected manner.

The Empress alone said nothing. She was present at all the funeral services which were celebrated over the coffin of the young officer, but so was Nicholas II. Her attendance could not be considered as an extraordinary thing. No one, with the exception of Anna Wyrubewa, who had accompanied her, knew that on the night preceding the funeral of her friend Alexandra Feodorowna had proceeded alone and unattended, save for her, to the house where his mortal remains lay in state, and had spent an hour praying beside his dead body and weeping bitter tears. Outwardly, however, her calm had remained unshaken; and she had succeeded in quite a wonderful way in keeping her feelings under control. The only thing which she had insisted upon was to have Colonel Orloff buried in the cemetery of Tsarskoye Selo, where she had a simple monument, con-sis-ting of a large white marble cross, erected. She used to go every day to pray there, and to leave flowers on this tomb which represented for her so many hopes, and perhaps something else besides.

Of course these visits became known, but by a wonderful miracle they were not commented upon in the way they might have been. The reputation for eccentricity of Alexandra Feodorowna had by that time become so well established that people had left off wondering at anything she might attempt to do, and, besides, every one believed that the Colonel's death had been somehow connected with a love intrigue he had carried on with Anna Wyrubewa, whose divorce lent ground for such a theory. It was suspected or guessed that something had taken place in her house, but no one could exactly ascertain what this something had been, and Wyrubew himself had been for once thoroughly frightened, and had come to the conclusion that the best thing he could do for his own sake as well as for that of others was to hold his tongue, and to accept the divorce upon which his wife insisted. Later on, however, he unburdened his soul to some of his particular friends, but that happened at a time when people were thinking of other things than the tragical death of an officer whose existence was already forgotten by most of those who had known him.

As for the Empress, she had, as we have seen, borne herself wonderfully well in the first moments which had followed upon the tragedy, but afterward her nerves gave way entirely, and it was then that she had to be kept in strict seclusion, and under the care of trained nurses. It was said that her reason had given way under the load of her anxiety for her small son, and that the thought of his serious condition had weighed down so thoroughly on her mind that she had grown melancholy to an alarming extent. The story was believed perhaps because it suited so many people to think that it was true, and, besides, the political situation in Russia was becoming so alarming that it entirely absorbed public attention. The war with Japan had come to an ignominious end, and shown the many failings, as well as the thorough insufficiency, of the Government. The first symptoms of the Revolution were clearly appearing on the horizon, with its attendant horrors. Everybody felt that something had to be done in order to avert a catastrophe the extent of which it was impossible to foresee, but which was generally considered as being inevitable, unless the Czar made up his mind to grant the reforms for which his whole Empire was clamoring.

During those years, which were the prelude of other even more eventful ones that were later on to sweep away the Throne of the Romanoffs, Nicholas II. might still have regained the popularity which he had lost. If he had only bravely and courageously faced his people, and tried to get into direct contact with them, he could have secured for his dynasty a new lease of life. He was not liked, it is true, and he was not trusted, which was still worse; but nations are sometimes apt to be led by impulse, and it is certain that Russia would have felt grateful to him if he had only made an appeal to its loyalty for his person, and asked of her to help him in the task of repairing the wounds caused by the disastrous campaign that had come to an end with the signature of the Treaty of Portsmouth.

But the Czar ignored the wishes of his subjects and refused to acknowledge the justice of their claims to be taken into his confidence. He was narrow-minded, cruel by disposition, and though not at all an autocrat, yet every inch a tyrant. He was even something worse than that; he was a coward, and this is a defect which neither nations nor women forgive in those to whom they find their destinies intrusted.

The remembrance of that dreadful Sunday when a crowd of peaceful workmen, under the leadership of the afterward notorious priest, Gapone, marched toward the Winter Palace, to be met with the firing of machine-guns that laid them low by hundreds on the pavement—the remembrance of this bloody deed has never been effaced from the mind of the Russian nation. It traced between itself and its Czar a line of demarcation which could never be removed later on.

Many versions exist as to the conduct of Nicholas II. on that awful day. Some people have said that it was the Empress who had entreated him to fly to Tsarskoye Selo, where she thought that they would be in greater safety than in St. Petersburg; others have asserted that it was he who of his own accord had decided that it would be better for him to leave the capital and to abandon to his uncle, the Grand Duke Wladimir, the task of drowning in blood this attempt of his subjects to enter into direct communication with him. Probably both versions are right, in a sense, at least, because it is certain that Alexandra Feodorowna was always in fear something might happen to her son, and very likely she tried to induce her husband to consider how best to insure the safety of their only boy; on the other hand, the Emperor might, had he only come himself to take a sane view of the situation such as it presented itself at the time, have been able to reassure his wife and to explain to her that neither she nor their children were in any danger. Nicholas II., however, had only one thought in his small mind, and that was how to punish this "insolence," as he termed it, of his people. For him a mob was always a mob, except when it was ordered to cheer him, and lately he had had to acknowledge that, in regard to St. Petersburg, cheering had become rather a rare event.

I am not trying to relate here any of the numerous episodes which have made the unsuccessful Revolution of 1905 memorable. I am not writing the history of Nicholas II. Others have done so, and will do so, better than I could. What I only want to point out is the utter callousness shown by both the Czar and the Czarina in presence of the abominable repression which the police, together with some military commanders, inaugurated in regard to the people compromised even in a slight degree in the movement of emancipation which had shaken the existence of the dynasty. It was in vain that some wise people, like Count Witte, for instance, had tried to explain to Nicholas II. that unless he frankly granted some reforms without which it would be impossible to govern Russia in the future he might expect an explosion of wrath on the part of the nation which it would be almost impossible to subdue or to destroy. The Czar refused to listen, and when at last he yielded to the demands of his Ministry and signed the famous Manifest of the 17th of October, with its "simulacre" of constitution, it was with the firm intention not to keep any of the promises which it contained, and to try, on the contrary, to reduce to absolute powerlessness the National Assembly, or Duma, as it was called, the election of which he had allowed only because he could not help it, but not at all because he believed or hoped it might prove useful to him in the solution of the many problems which were waiting to be unraveled.

What followed upon the first convocation of the first Parliament Russia was to know is already a matter of history. It did not live for more than a few weeks, and very probably the Czar had never intended it to exist for any length of time. What he wished was to appear before the eyes of Europe as a Sovereign who had been willing to make any amount of sacrifices in order to insure the welfare of his subjects, who, instead of showing themselves grateful to him for his good intentions, had rewarded him with the basest ingratitude. He thought this a clever piece of policy, forgetting that any politician worthy of the name could see at once through his game, and that this game could have only one result—that of inspiring an utter contempt for his person as well as for his moral character.

Therein lies the great, the supreme, fault of Nicholas II. He never could bring himself to act frankly in regard to any serious matter in which his people were concerned. The Empress, in her strange way, was far more honest, because she did not hesitate to follow the instincts of her heart, and in her most mistaken actions she was at least sincere.

During the years that followed upon the insurrectionary movement of 1905 Alexandra Feodorowna was in such a state of health that it was almost impossible for her to take any part in what went on around her. Her reason had been seriously compromised by the shock caused by the tragical ending of the only romance she had known in her life, and she used to spend hours weeping in her room, absorbed in the contemplation of her own grief. It was in vain that Anna Wyrubewa, who had become more intimate with her than had even been the case before, had tried to induce her to fight the morbid ideas which were torturing her. The Empress would not listen to her friend, and insisted on secluding herself from the world and even from her own daughters, whose presence irritated her and made her give way to fits of impatience that were very nearly akin to madness. The girls were perfectly charming and had the luck to have an excellent governess, who tried to give them the love their own mother refused or was unable to award them; nevertheless their lives were blighted by the illness of the Empress, and it is not extraordinary that they came to care for their father more than for her, whom they were always more or less afraid to approach, whom they were constantly told they must not bother by questions of any kind or manifestations of affection.

It was only the little Cesarewitsch who was allowed to share his mother's solitude, whom she would never let out of her sight. He was the only preoccupation her diseased mind would admit, and when she saw that his state of health did not improve she became more and more desperate, until one day she confided to Anna Wyrubewa that she was sure God was punishing her for the affection which she acknowledged now that she had borne for Orloff, and that her boy would never get well. Her despair was so evident, and her mind was getting so unhinged, that at last the question of putting her in some retreat where she could be under a doctor's continual care was seriously considered by her medical attendants, who even informed the Czar of their fears in regard to the sanity of his Consort. Of course the fact that they had done so reached the knowledge of Madame Wyrubewa, and it was then that the latter began to consider whether it would not be possible to restore by some way or other the equanimity of Alexandra Feodorowna and to procure for her some kind of consolation for the seemingly incurable grief which was destroying her life and her reason. Unfortunately for all parties concerned, she was to make at that time the acquaintance of the notorious Raspoutine, whom she introduced, under the circumstances which I am going presently to relate, to the miserable, half-demented Empress, an introduction which was to prove so fatal not only to the unhappy Sovereign, but also through her to the whole of Russia.

XV

A PROPHET OF GOD

ANNA WYRUBEWA had always been inclined toward religious exaggeration, and this was perhaps one of the reasons why the Empress, who for years had buried herself in the exercise of all kinds of devotional practices, had taken to her so quickly. They were both of a mystical turn of mind, and never so happy as when enabled to spend long hours absorbed in prayer before some icon or other. And besides this, Anna was in the habit of frequenting certain circles of St. Petersburg society that were considered as the supporters of orthodoxy in its most rigid form, where all questions concerning the discipline of the Church were discussed and in some cases decided.

Such, for instance, was the house of the Countess Sophy Ignatieff, where the higher clergy used to meet at weekly assemblies, during which the laxity of the younger generation in regard to religious matters was discussed with many a sigh and many a shaking of wise heads, disposed to admit that this religious indifference, which was getting stronger and stronger every day, was bound to bring Russia to the brink of terrible misfortunes. Countess Ignatieff had traveled all over her native country in search of its sacred shrines and places, and was very well known personally in almost all the principal convents in the Empire. She had been suspected at one time of sympathies with dissenters, but this has never been proved; on the contrary, in her old age she gained the reputation of being fanatically orthodox, one who saw no salvation outside the fold of her own creed, who favored persecution of all others on account of her conviction that people ought to be brought back to the bosom of the Greek Church by any means, even through violence if other ones failed.

During one of the yearly pilgrimages in which so much of her time was spent she had had occasion to meet a kind of vagrant preacher whose wild eloquence had captivated her fancy and her imagination, and she had been partly instrumental in his coming to St. Petersburg, where she had arranged for him to hold religious meetings in her house, to which she had invited prominent church dignitaries, together with a few ladies of an enthusiastic turn of mind whom she believed would be inclined to listen to the wild ravings, for they were nothing else, of her new *protégé*.

At first people laughed at her, as well as at the uncouth appearance of the "Prophet of God," as she called him, who, while not blessed with the eloquence of a Savonarola, yet possessed sufficient persuasive gifts and talents to shake the equanimity of the hysterically inclined women who listened to him. This "Prophet" was none other than Grigory Raspoutine, who later on was to become such an important personage in Russia.

Madame Wyrubewa had heard about Raspoutine a long time before she ever came to hear him. But after she had had the opportunity of meeting him she thought that it would not be a bad thing to bring him to Tsarskoye Selo, where the poor Empress was eating away her heart in her grief at the loss of all that she had cared for in life, and to try to induce Alexandra to listen to him, and to pray together with him. He was supposed to perform wonders by the intensity and the fervor of his prayers, and it might just be possible that the very fact of his being a complete stranger to her, and moreover a man totally outside Court circles and Court intrigues, would influence the Czarina to give him her confidence and to permit him to cheer her up. At all events, she spoke about him several times, and pleaded hard with the Empress to allow him to be brought to her. This Alexandra Feodorowna absolutely refused, but she was induced at last to consent to see him at the house of Anna Wyrubewa, and thither came one winter evening the adventurer who was in time to become the Cagliostro of a reign which was not even worthy to have any one else but a common, uncouth peasant for its jester.

Now, as has been ultimately proved, Raspoutine was far from being the saintly man his admirers thought he was, but he was endowed with an unusual amount of cunning, and far more spirit of observation than he was credited with. When he was told that he would have the honor of meeting the Empress of Russia, and to pray in her presence for the health of her delicate little boy, he had at once perceived the advantages which might result for him out of this introduction, if only in regard to his personal prestige before his disciples and followers. He was above everything else a man who cared for his enjoyment as well as for the good things of life, and who, in the way of Paradise, only admitted the one described by Mohammed in his Koran. He had led a licentious, godless kind of existence, which he had contrived to persuade the weak women who had succumbed to his exhortations was in accord with the spirit of the doctrine which he preached, the principal points of which consisted in blind submission to his will and to his fancies. He had told them that they would be cleansed of their sins by a complete union with him, which he meant in the physical as well as in the moral sense of the word. It is probable that in his dealings with all the people who had grown to believe in him he had had recourse to his incontestable hypnotical powers and to practices of magnetic influence which he had learned amid some wild tribes of Siberia, where he had spent his childhood and early youth, who are to this day adepts in the art of witchcraft as well as in all kinds of magical rites and customs. At the same time the crafty adventurer knew very well that it would be unwise of him at the beginning of his intercourse with the Consort of his Sovereign, an intercourse which he was fully determined should be continued and not be limited to a single interview, to do aught else but assume the attitude of a man entirely absorbed in God and in the practices of religion. When he was introduced to Alexandra Feodorowna at the house of Anna Wyrubewa, he therefore remained standing before her, in an attitude of apparent humility, and he waited quietly until she should begin talking with him, which she immediately did, saying that she had heard so much about him that she had wished to see him and to ask him to pray for her little boy, whose state of health gave rise to so much anxiety and worry.

Raspoutine looked at her, then replied quietly that he would be happy to pray for the child, but that he thought she was just as much in need of prayer as her son because her state of moral health was far more alarming than Alexis's physical one.

The Empress was so amazed that she could not find a reply to what appeared to her in the first moment to be an unsurpassed piece of insolence. Anna Wyrubewa saw what was taking place in her mind, and, addressing her in English, a language which they always spoke together, implored her not to feel offended, as the man really did not know what he was saying, sometimes being urged by a strength superior to his own to give utterance to thoughts he would never have dared to express otherwise. She then urged the Czarina not to carry on the conversation further, but to ask Raspoutine to begin at once praying for her welfare, and also for that of Russia and of the Imperial Family.

Alexandra acquiesced, and the preacher proceeded to set himself before the icon which, as is usual in all Russian houses, was hanging in a corner of the room. He began long litanies which he recited in a peculiar deep tone of voice, that rose up louder and louder as gradually he worked himself up into a state of religious frenzy akin to the one displayed by the dancing and howling dervishes in Turkey. But whether or not his manner or the tone of his supplications or his personal influence was the cause of it, the Empress as she listened to him felt calmer and quieter than she had done for years. It seemed to her as if a great peace was stealing upon her after the despair and the sadness in which her days had been spent during the last months. When at last Raspoutine's orisons came to an end she was weeping silently, but all the nervous excitement under which she had been laboring at the beginning of the interview seemed to have disappeared and she looked more like a normal woman than she had done since the day when Orloff had said his last good-by to her in the boudoir of Anna Wyrubewa.

She silently extended her hand to the "Prophet," saying as she did so:

"You have done me a great deal of good, and I thank you with all my heart. I shall ask you again to pray for me."

It was thus that Alexandra Feodorowna met the man who was to have such a baneful influence over her whole life, whose fatal influence was to estrange her, still deeper than was already the case, from her subjects, and to give rise to the flood of calumnies in which she was ultimately to be drowned; and to perish, dragging along with her this mighty Russian Empire whose Crown she wore and whose people she had never understood nor even tried to understand.

Anna Wyrubewa was delighted to see that her beloved Czarina had really found some comfort in listening to Raspoutine's prayers. She believed in the "Prophet" who had found favor in the eyes of the Lord, and whose intercession in regard to the little Alexis would be crowned with success. The woman was superstitious to the backbone, and perhaps more mystically inclined even than most Russians are, which is saying a good deal. She thought, at all events, that, once the Empress got to be persuaded that she had to look to God alone for the recovery of her son from a disease that had been pronounced to be incurable by the best medical authorities, she would no longer fret as she had done, but begin to look at things from a religiously fatalistic point of view. She hoped also for another thing, and that was that the Czarina, once she had been taught to look above for comfort and consolation, would cease to lament over the "might have been" that has already caused so much heartburnings in this world, and that she would leave off reproaching herself, as she was constantly doing, for the death of the one man she had cared for, whom in all innocence she had sent to his destruction, and who had bravely preferred to disappear rather than allow a stain to rest upon her honor. She had guessed the agony of the self-reproach under which the soul of Alexandra Feodorowna had almost collapsed, and the remorse which had racked it until her intelligence had almost snapped, through the moral as well as through the physical pain which had clouded all her faculties. She hoped, therefore, seriously and earnestly, that the prayers of Raspoutine might ease this mental distress which had transformed the Empress of All the Russias into a half-demented woman. When she saw that his prayers had over the latter the beneficent influence she had expected, she determined to do her best to induce her to give her confidence to this man in whom her exalted imagination saw a savior as well as a friend.

This was the real beginning of the Raspoutine intrigue, and it would have been a lucky thing for all those who came afterward to be concerned in it if it had stopped at this stage, and not been transferred to a more dangerous one, the stage upon which European politics had to be played and, unfortunately for Russia, played by utterly unskilful hands. The comedy of Raspoutine did not last longer than a few months. Its drama dragged on for years, and is not yet over by a long way.

XVI

SHE SAW HIM ONCE MORE

AFTER she had made the acquaintance of Raspoutine the Empress changed considerably. For one thing, she became more cheerful and seemed once more to interest herself in what went on around her. She tried also to keep her mind away from the one morbid thought which had been haunting her, the thought that her son's bad health was a punishment which God had sent her on account of her conduct in regard to Colonel Orloff. She had most undoubtedly loved the young officer, and she realized with a painful but clear perspicacity that if she had allowed him to go away when he wished to do so the tragedy which had culminated with his suicide would never have taken place. Her mind, which was dimmed as to so many other points, was quite awake to the terrible one that the man to whom her whole heart had belonged had died to save her honor and to prevent her good name from being compromised. This was quite sufficient to fill her soul with acute remorse, but apart from this she missed the companionship of this faithful friend before whom she could allow herself to speak about her sorrows and her trials just as if she had been an ordinary woman and not an Empress.

There were times when her grandeur oppressed her, and then it was that she longed for a confidant and friend before whom she would not be ashamed to bare her heart and unburden it. She felt so lonely amid the pomp and splendor which surrounded her, so solitary in her great Palace which was so very different from the simple house in which her childhood and youth had been spent, and she was such a stranger in a land she had not learned to love and where she had found herself confronted with hostility from the very first day that she had set her foot in it. Of course her children, and especially her son, constituted a great interest and a great preoccupation in her life, but their existence was not sufficient to fill it entirely. In moments when she thought herself forsaken by the world she would have given ten years of her future existence to be able to see once more the man who had died for her because he had found it impossible to consecrate his whole life to her service.

Raspoutine was a keen observer of human nature. Lurking behind his hopeless ignorance there were immense cunning and a natural intuition of what was going on in other people's minds. Apart from this faculty, he always made it a point to try and find out as much as he could concerning the past of all persons with whom he happened to have dealings. He understood quite admirably the art of "drawing out" those with whom he conversed, and he could put together quite nicely the tangled threads which another man would never have gone to the trouble of trying to untwine. As soon as he had looked upon the Empress he had understood that she must have gone through some great grief which was not concerned with the state of health of her child alone, but which had deeper foundations. In the fashionable drawing-rooms where he was a welcome guest he had heard discussed more than once the personality as well as the conduct of Alexandra Feodorowna; he had come to the conclusion that the mystery which surrounded the death of Colonel Orloff was in some way connected with her, and not with Madame Wyrubewa alone. He applied himself, therefore, to dis-cover what had really taken place.

For some time he could learn nothing, as no one seemed to know anything more than the bare fact of the suicide of the young officer. It is true that when he had asked Anna for the true version the latter had angrily denied any connection implying guilt, but Raspoutine, peasant though he was, understood sufficiently the character of a woman of the world to know that such denials were not worth much. Altogether he was puzzled, but continued, however, to put in an appearance at Tsarskoye Selo whenever he was asked to do so, and he was shown several times the little Heir to the Throne. The Empress had brought the babe to Madame Wyrubewa's cottage several times for him to pray over. The "Prophet" had at once declared that the child would not die, and that there was every likelihood he would outgrow his weakness, a prophecy it had been relatively easy for him to make, considering the fact that before doing so he had taken good care to talk with a doctor of his acquaintance about the illness of Alexis, and had heard from him all that there was to hear on the subject, which was not much. The boy might live with care, and even get strong, once he had reached the years of adolescence; he might die from the effect of a hemorrhage, which the slightest accident might bring about. The whole thing was a matter of chance, and nothing else.

The Empress, however, became full of hope when Raspoutine told her not to worry unnecessarily, but to trust more to Providence than she had been doing. It happened just at that time that the little boy got stronger and better than he had been since his birth, and this fact inspired her with a hope such as she had never allowed herself to nurse since the day when she had realized to what a weak and frail piece of humanity she had given birth in the person of the only son and Heir of Nicholas II. She began to speak of the future, which she had hitherto not dared to do, and she seemed suddenly to think that this future might still hold some joys for her in reserve. As was but natural, she attributed this change in her feelings and mind to the influence of Raspoutine's prayers, and as was also natural she felt grateful to him for having brought it about.

The crafty peasant, however, was not so satisfied as the Empress. He had begun to make great plans concerning her and the influence he meant to acquire over her person. Somehow he could not bring them to realization. He might have gone on for a long time in this state of uncertainty if he had not made just at that moment the acquaintance of one of the cleverest secret police agents the Russian Government had in its pay, Manassavitch-Maniuloff. This personage, whom I have described at length in another book, knew more about what went on in the Imperial Palace of Tsarskoye Selo than any one else in the world. During the time when the famous Plehwe occupied the post of Minister of the Interior he had had the Palace watched just as much as the houses of the people whom he suspected of not favoring his views and policy. Among the agents whom he had intrusted with this task Manassavitch-Maniuloff had occupied a foremost place. He was one of the most unscrupulous men alive, and, as the future proved, had but one aim in his existence, that of enriching himself, thanks to all kinds of shady speculations and blackmail he practised on a large scale. He knew, if others did not, all that had taken place in the house of Anna Wyrubewa on the day when Colonel Orloff had left it for the last time, but he had never divulged this secret, and had been content with waiting patiently until the day when he might be able to turn it into account and to make capital out of it. Always on the alert, and just as keen an observer as Raspoutine himself of the weaknesses of human nature, with the additional advantage of being a very well educated and cultured man, he very quickly grasped the importance of what the "Prophet" confided to him when he started to relate to his friend the details of his first interview with the Empress of All the Russias.

Maniuloff was very well posted as to all the details of the Philippe incident, together with its ridiculous end. When he had heard how much Alexandra Feodorowna had been impressed by the fervor of Raspoutine's prayers, he suggested to the latter that he make use of the hypnotic faculties which he possessed in order to get the inexperienced and weak-minded Sovereign to become a tool in the hands of both. He gave him very detailed instructions as to how he was to proceed.

Armed with these instructions, Raspoutine started upon a campaign which brought Mr. Maniuloff to penal servitude, sent the Czarina to exile in Siberia, and himself to an untimely and bloody grave.

At the meetings at Anna Wyrubewa's house, during which the "Prophet" not only prayed himself for the prosperity of the House of Romanoff, he also persuaded the Empress to pray, too, in accordance with the particular rites which he declared were indispensable to a perfect communion of the human spirit with God, and which consisted in numerous genuflexions, and other things of the same kind; in long fasts and hours spent in meditation with the face on the floor, in what grew in time to be a hysterical state of ecstasy. These meetings went on undisturbed for a consider-able length of time, until one day Raspoutine informed Alexandra Feodorowna that he thought it wiser to discontinue them because certain things had been revealed to him by the Holy Ghost which had caused him to think that it would be better if he went away; otherwise he would be compelled to try and take her spiritually with him into regions whither perhaps she would not care to follow him. The Empress, of course, eagerly asked what he meant, upon which he replied that to perfect people such as he and she the Lord could grant the privilege of entering into relations with dead and gone people whom they had loved in this world; he did not know whether she would be able to go through this ordeal; therefore he thought it better to discontinue their meetings for the present.

The Czarina went home brooding upon what she had heard and with all her superstitious curiosity awakened. At first she tried not to think of what the "Prophet" had told her. Then she wondered whether she would be strong enough to face the ordeal of entering into communion with the other world, that world for which she had been longing, where had gone the one man she had loved beyond every other earthly thing. For some weeks she struggled against the temptation as it had been presented to her by Raspoutine; then at last she yielded to it, and asked Anna Wyrubewa to bring the "Prophet" once more to her house, as she wanted to speak with him again.

The adventurer demurred at first, finding one obstacle after another in order to decline the invitation which had been extended to him. At last he consented to an interview, but declared that he would insist that no one else be present at it, as the things which the "spirit" had commanded him to say to Alexandra Feodorowna were of such a secret nature that no one but herself could hear them. When he was introduced into the presence of the Sovereign he began by falling on his knees and praying with a fervor such as she had never seen him display before. At last he told the miserable, deluded woman that he had been commanded to say to her that there was one pure spirit now in another world who had been allowed to communicate with her through his medium; that he did not know who it was, but that if she wished to try the experiment she must, before attempting it, prepare herself for it, with long prayers and fastings, so as to be in a complete state of grace; otherwise the favor about to be conferred on her could not be awarded. By that time the Czarina had reached a nervous condition where anything Raspoutine told her would have been acceptable to her over-excited brain. She promised to conform herself to all the directions given to her, and three days later she met again the impostor in a place which he indicated to her, whither she went, accompanied by the faithful Anna. Madame Wyrubewa, however, was not admitted to the room where Raspoutine was waiting for the Empress. He stood before several holy images, with lamps burning before them.

The Empress had scarcely touched any food for three days; she had spent the time in long and almost continual orisons. She was just in a condition when any appeal to her superstition would be sure to meet with response. When she prostrated herself beside the "Prophet," she had reached a state of exhaustion and excitement which made her an easy prey to any imposture practised by the unscrupulous. For about an hour Raspoutine kept praying aloud, invoking the spirits of heaven in an impressive voice, every word of which went deep into the heart of Alexandra Feodorowna. Suddenly he seized her by the arm, exclaiming as he did so: "Look! look! and then believe!"

She raised her eyes, and saw distinctly on the white wall the image of Colonel Orloff, which, by a clever trick had been flashed on it by a magic lantern held for the purpose by Manassavitch-Maniuloff. The Empress gave one terrible cry and fell in a dead faint on the floor. Anna Wyrubewa, hearing her scream of agony, rushed into the room to find nothing but Raspoutine absorbed in deep prayer beside the inanimate form of his victim.

This was but the first scene of many of the same character. The Czarina recovered her scared senses with the full conviction that she had really seen the spirit of the man she had loved so dearly; she was very soon persuaded that he had been allowed to show himself to her and that he would henceforward watch over her and guide her with advice and encouragement in her future life. She quite believed that Raspoutine, whom she sincerely thought to be in total ignorance as to that episode in her life, was a real Prophet of God, and that, thanks to him, she would be able to communicate with the dead. Whether Anna Wyrubewa shared this conviction or not it is difficult to say, but it is not likely that either Raspoutine or Maniuloff confided in her. They knew too well the small reliance that, as a rule, can be placed upon feminine secrecy, and the game they were playing was far too serious for them to run the risk of compromising it by an indiscretion. It is therefore far more probable that they also played upon the superstitious feelings of the Empress's friend, and that they used both ladies for the furtherance of their own nefarious schemes with as much unscrupulousness as consummate art.

XVII

MY SON! I MUST SAVE MY SON!

AFTER the episode which I have just related, there was no longer any question of Raspoutine being allowed to leave the proximity of the Imperial Court. The Empress came to have such utter confidence in him that she even tried to induce the Czar to consult him; this he refused to do, but, seeing how much brighter his wife had become since her acquaintance with the "Prophet," he made no objection to her seeing him.

One must here remark that both Raspoutine and his chief adviser, Manassavitch-Maniuloff, played their cards wonderfully well by avoiding every appearance of mixing themselves up with politics. The "Prophet" talked with the Empress when he had the opportunity to do so, which, by the way, was not so frequent as might have been supposed. His conversations were always confined to religious subjects. He was very carefully coached by his accomplice every time he had to meet Alexandra Feodorowna, and he used to relate to her some sensational supernatural stories, which a man of his ignorance could not possibly have learned if he had not been inspired by the Almighty, as she fondly imagined. Her superstitious feelings had entirely taken the upper hand of her reason in all matters where Raspoutine was concerned, and she truly believed him to be a Prophet of God, whose every word was inspired by Heaven, whose intercession in her behalf had decided the Almighty to cure her son of a disease which all the doctors who had seen him had pronounced to be quite incurable.

In the mean while, although the relations of the Czarina with the crafty adventurer who had succeeded in captivating her confidence remained restricted to the purely religious ground, people were talking about them, trying to turn them into a vast agency where everything in the world could be bought and sold, providing the necessary money was forthcoming to do it. Manassavitch-Maniuloff, thanks to the numerous spies whose services he could command for a consideration, started to spread the rumor that Raspoutine had become all powerful in Court circles, and that if only one applied to him one could bring through the most difficult kind of business. It must be remembered that at the time I am referring to (the five years or so immediately preceding the war) Russia had been transformed into a vast stock-exchange, thanks to the mania for speculation which, since the Japanese war, had seized hold of the public. Industry always more or less neglected had suddenly taken a new and unexpected lease of life, and banks did a roaring business in selling and buying for the account of the innumerable speculators who rushed to invest their money. Nothing mattered in that respect save the quotation of yesterday and the one expected or hoped for to-morrow.

Government contracts for all kinds of things, especially contracts connected with the railway business and with factories of every sort, were eagerly sought for. In the fight which was taking place to obtain them every possible argument was employed. The art of Maniuloff and of his friends, because he was not alone in this detestable business, consisted in persuading others, even men in power who ought to have known better, that Raspoutine, through his connection with the powers who ruled at Tsarskoye Selo, could get for them such contracts that he expected in return a solid commission, which, of course, was never refused to him.

How long this kind of thing would have gone on it is difficult to say if Mr. Stolypine, who was at the time Prime Minister, had not had his attention drawn toward the activity of the "Prophet." Not knowing very well what to make of the conflicting reports which were brought to him, he expressed one day the desire to meet Raspoutine. After the interview he uttered his famous phrase:

"The only use the man could be put to was to light the furnace of the house he was living in."

The words were repeated, of course, to the person whom they concerned, and they proved the death sentence of Stolypine, because his "removal" by fair or by foul means was decided immediately after he had uttered them. Stolypine, however, in spite of his apparent disdain for the strange personality of Raspoutine, was far too clever not to realize that the constant presence of this man by the side of the Empress of Russia was likely to lead to gossip of a dangerous kind, if not to various complications. He tried at first to get rid of him by diplomatic means, and enrolled the sympathies of the Grand Duchess Elisabeth, the eldest sister of Alexandra Feodorowna, who, by reason of her having embraced a religious life, was in possession of great respect everywhere and could say what she liked to the Czar as well as to the Czarina. The Prime Minister explained to her that it was to the highest degree harmful for the reputation of the Imperial dynasty in general to see its heads give way to a superstition which only evoked ridicule on the part of reasonable people. Elisabeth Feodorowna promised that she would try what she could do, but after a while she had to acknowledge that at the first words she had spoken concerning the advisability of sending Raspoutine back to his native village of Pokrowskoye in Siberia the Empress had interrupted her so angrily that she had not been able to go on with the conversation.

Stolypine was not a man to stop at half-measures. He asked no one's law or leave, and in virtue of his powers as Prime Minister he had the "Prophet" exiled from the capital at twenty-four hours' notice.

Raspoutine wished to communicate with the Empress as soon as the order to leave St. Petersburg was signified to him, but he was prevented from doing so by his friend, Manassavitch-Maniuloff, who assured him that it would be far wiser not to murmur, and to accept the decree of banishment issued against him; because in that way he would acquire far more sympathy than would be the case if he rebelled; besides, in his absence it would be relatively easy to play upon the nervous temperament of the Empress to such an extent that after he had been recalled he would never stand again the risk of a second dismissal. This was accordingly done and Alexandra Feodorowna found herself alone, deprived of the possibility of going on with religious practices that had gradually assumed the character of those indulged in by that sect of the Khlystys to which Raspoutine belonged.

By a strange coincidence, which was nothing but a coincidence because, weak and foolish as was Anna Wyrubewa, she did not lend herself to the conspiracy which was so falsely attributed to her, which in reality did not exist, the conspiracy of drugging the little Cesarewitsch for the purpose of proving to his mother that he could not be well so long as Raspoutine was not there to pray for him—the child suddenly sickened in a more dangerous manner than ever before. The poor Empress again went out of her mind. She used to cry aloud that God was punishing her for not having known how to protect His "Prophet," and things of the same kind. At last the baby grew better, and the Court could remove to the Crimea, where it was hoped he would more rapidly recover than in the damp climate of St. Petersburg.

It was during this journey that Stolypine was murdered by secret police agents, a crime in which it was generally believed that Raspoutine, together with his accomplices, had been mixed up. The Empress, who had hated the Prime Minister ever since she had ascertained that it was he who had banished her favorite, did not disarm even in the presence of death, and it was related that she publicly prided herself upon having persuaded the Emperor not to attend the funeral of the man who had died for him, but to leave Kieff for Livadia on the eve of the day when it was to take place.

She had become very bitter just then, and she never missed any opportunity which presented itself to show her want of affection for the Imperial Family, as well as her contempt for the Russian people. The morganatic marriage of the only brother of Nicholas II., the Grand Duke Michael, which took place at about that time, procured her a new occasion to prove the unbounded influence which since the birth of her son she had acquired over the mind of the weak Emperor, and to exercise her revengeful feelings in an unexpected manner. This marriage, so much must be conceded, was of a nature to give rise to unpleasantness, and could not in any case have been viewed with favorable eyes either by the Czar or by the Imperial Family.

The lady had already been divorced twice, and the fact of her last husband having been an officer in the same regiment as the Grand Duke was also a reason why the match would have been disapproved of in any case. But, on the other hand, Michael Alexandrowitch, in uniting himself to the woman who had captivated his heart and his fancy, was acting as a man of honor, considering several facts which made it almost imperative for him not to forsake a person who had sacrificed much for his sake. It would certainly have been sufficient to oblige him to leave the army and to reside for some time abroad as a punishment, and no one imagined that worse could befall him.

The Empress had always intensely disliked her brother-in-law, who would have been Regent of the Empire in case the Czar had died before the Heir to the Throne had reached his majority, and she determined to make use of the opportunity which had arisen to vent her bad feelings on a man in whom she saw a rival to the claims of her own son. She induced Nicholas II. to deprive the Grand Duke of his fortune as well as of his civil rights, and to make out of him a ward in chancery. The scandal was immense, and it did not procure any friends for Alexandra Feodorowna.

In the mean while the Cesarewitsch sickened again, and the frantic mother implored Anna Wyrubewa to write to Raspoutine and to implore the latter to work a miracle of some kind in favor of her son. The "Prophet" replied that he would pray with all his heart for the child, but that he doubted very much whether this would avail, because the Empress had neglected her duties in regard to the Almighty and forgotten to continue the practices of mortification and of devotion she had been wrapped up in the whole time he had been near her to urge her to go on with them. Alexandra Feodorowna could not stand this last reproach, and she forthwith tarted to implore the Czar to recall the "Prophet." But Nicholas II. had been warned against him quite recently and refused to grant her request. This brought about a renewal of tears and hysterics on the part of the Czarina, and at last, one day that she was alone with Anna, she unburdened her soul to the latter, exclaiming that she knew her beloved boy was going to die and that it would be her fault, ending her confession with the agonized cry:

"My son! I must save my son!"

Madame Wyrubewa saw that the poor creature was in such an over-excited state that she might really be facing a collapse of her reason. She then proposed to the infatuated Alexandra to have recourse to a bold measure, which consisted in bringing back Raspoutine quite secretly to St. Petersburg, where he could stay at her house without any one getting to hear of it. If, then, his prayers brought about the amelioration required in the state of health of the little Alexis, the Empress would be able to tell the Czar what she had done, and perhaps to convince the latter of the efficacy of the holy man's intervention and intercession on behalf of their boy.

The Czarina caught eagerly at the idea, and after long negotiations, which very nearly failed because Raspoutine did not yield at once to the entreaties sent to him, he at last consented to return to St. Petersburg. He was secretly introduced into the room where the Heir to the Russian Throne was lying, in what every one thought were already the throes of death. He prayed for the child, he prayed for the Empress, and he urged the latter to submit to certain mysterious passes which he proceeded to perform over her head. A few days after this secret interview Alexis suddenly began to improve; not only this, but he became stronger and brighter than he had been for a long time.

Alexandra Feodorowna was radiant, and one day when Nicholas

II. was rejoicing at the happy change which had taken place in the condition of their son she informed him of what she had done and begged from him permission to bring Raspoutine to him and to allow him to remain in the vicinity of the Court in the future. Nicholas II. was convinced and granted the necessary authorization. After this the question of Raspoutine's return to Siberia was not raised again, and he never left, except for short vacations, the Sovereigns who had at last been persuaded to give to him their complete confidence.

He refused, however, to take up his abode in Tsarskoye Selo, and showed himself very discreet in his demeanor. He was admirably advised, and he prepared himself in silence for the part it was intended for him to play in the future. But at stated intervals, and upon stated days, he used to see the Empress, either in her own rooms or, most frequently, at the house of Anna Wyrubewa, when he evoked for her the spirit of Colonel Orloff and transmitted messages which he was supposed to have received.

Alexandra Feodorowna believed him, and this new understanding, which she firmly thought had, thanks to the prayers of the "Prophet," established itself between her and the man who had possessed her heart, proved to her the greatest consolation she had known. It induced her to come out of her retirement and to begin to take part in the management of public affairs, which she insisted upon the Czar communicating to her. The time was coming when it would become known in Russia that if the Sovereign was a weak man his Consort was trying to show herself a strong woman, and comparisons between Alexandra Feodorowna and Catherine the Great began to be heard in the yet small circle which affected to admire the new qualities it prided itself upon having discovered in the young Empress.

. . . .

THE PALACE OF TSARSKOYE SELO

XVIII

ANOTHER WAR

THE years which followed upon Raspoutine's triumphant return to Tsarskoye Selo were most eventful ones for Russia as well as for the Imperial Family. Europe, too, went through political convulsions which were the preliminary of the disaster that was to sweep over it in 1914, but in which very few people in 1912 were able to discern danger. I am referring to the annexation by Austria of Bosnia and Herzegovina and to the two Balkan wars. When Servia was threatened by Bulgarian ambition there existed a powerful party in Russia which would have liked the Czar to interfere on her behalf, and to lend her his aid against King Ferdinand, on one side, and the Austrian spirit of conquest, on the other. Popular feeling was very much in favor of a Russian demonstration, and for some weeks St. Petersburg was the scene of a violent agitation which, in the opinion of many people, was destined to end in a war with the Austro-Hungarian monarchy. It was not a secret that the Servian Government would not have objected, had such a contingency presented itself, and during the whole of the summer and autumn of 1913 different Servian politicians came to Russia to discuss the situation. In Moscow, as well as in St. Petersburg, they applied themselves to the task of awakening in favor of their country the sympathies of all the Russian Slavophils. At one time it seemed as if they were going to succeed and as if the Czar would be compelled to yield to the general wishes of his subjects.

Here Raspoutine interfered, and, thanks to his influence over the Empress, he contrived to prevent the spread of a conflagration which threatened to extend itself far beyond the Balkan Peninsula. It must not be assumed, however, that in doing so he was actuated by any patriotic motives. He was a man for whom the word "patriotism" had absolutely no meaning. But his friends, as well as himself, were plunged head foremost in financial schemes which a war would in all probability have wrecked, and therefore he applied himself with all his energy to set hindrances in the path of the chauvinists who tried to induce the Emperor to assert the might of his Empire, to rush to the rescue of those Slav nationalities that had refused to conform themselves to the anti-Russian policy which Bulgaria had been pursuing ever since King Ferdinand had been put in control of her destinies.

This interference on the part of the "Prophet" in matters which did not concern him in the least became known very quickly, not only in Russia, but also abroad, and one of the most active members of the German Embassy in St. Petersburg, who was *persona grata* in the Wilhelmstrasse, wrote a whole report on the subject, raising at the same time the question as to whether it would not be worth while to try, with the help of substantial arguments, to win Raspoutine over to the idea of a *rapprochement* between Russia and Germany. The latter was steadily making preparations for the war which she was quite determined to provoke within a very few months. She had always worked toward the destruction of the Franco-Russian understanding, which stood in her way, which she feared might come to endanger her dreams of a world-wide Empire. Every effort had been made on the part of the Berlin Court to win over the Czar to the idea of renewing the intimate bonds which, during the whole time of his grandfather's reign, had united the Hohenzollerns and the Romanoffs. When Nicholas II. had repaired to Berlin for the marriage of the Kaiser's only daughter with the son of the Duke of Cumberland he had been made the object of one of the warmest welcomes he had ever received in his life, a welcome which had touched him so much that he had come back to Tsarskoye Selo full of enthusiasm for his Prussian relatives. If the truth need be told, he was also slightly disillusioned as to the advantages which his country might obtain through its alliance with the French Republic. This feeling of distrust which had thus been sown in his mind in regard to the good intentions of his Latin ally was of course at once reported to the Kaiser by the many friends which the latter had in St. Petersburg, and it made him doubly anxious to win over to his side the good-will as well as the sympathies of Nicholas II. At the same time William was very well aware that it was most difficult to rely on anything promised by a man with such a weak character, or rather with such a lack of character, as his Russian cousin. An ally who would continually whisper in the latter's ear all the advantages which a friendly treaty and understanding with Germany could bring to him, as well as to the whole Russian Empire, was indispensable; of course, when it was suggested to those who controlled the actions and the politics of the Wilhelmstrasse that he might be found in the person of the Empress Alexandra's favorite, the Kaiser came very quickly to the conclusion it would be worth while to obtain the good offices of this remarkable man.

This, however, would have proved difficult, even for the experienced spies which Prussia maintained in all circles of Russian society, as it was not easy to discover means of getting into contact with the formidable adventurer whose name had already become one of the most powerful to conjure with in the vast Russian Empire. At this juncture Mr. Manassavitch-Maniuloff interfered and volunteered his services to William II. The crafty fox had heard that the Czar's confidence in France was slightly shaken. Maniuloff at once bethought himself of the possibility of turning his knowledge to his personal advantage, and he managed, no one knows how, to impart to the German Ambassador in St. Petersburg, Count Pourtalès, his willingness to persuade Nicholas II., through Raspoutine, that he would do well to throw France overboard and to conclude a treaty with the Prussian Government, which eventually might prove of immense advantage to himself by assuring him of German protection in the not improbable case of a new Revolution taking place in his Empire.

This sort of thing went on for some time, and it is quite likely that if events had not precipitated themselves one upon the other with the most startling rapidity, the policy of Raspoutine and his friend might have borne fruit in some way or other, and the relations between the Cabinet of St. Petersburg and that of Paris, which had already sensibly cooled down, would have become even fresher than was already the case. In fact, the announced visit of President Poincaré had not appealed to the Czar, who, while unable to decline it, yet had expressed himself quite loudly as to the small amount of pleasure which he expected to get out of it. Of course Berlin heard about the remarks that had escaped the lips of the Russian Sovereign, and it was not slow to draw its own conclusions from them. In fact, if we are to believe all that was related at the time by persons well up as to what went on in European politics, it was confidently expected by the Kaiser that instead of drawing France and Russia closer together the journey of the French President, thanks to personal frictions he felt sure would arise, would, on the contrary, irritate Nicholas II. and make him look with more favorable eyes than he had done before on the possibility of a change in the conduct of

Russian Foreign Affairs.

Whether this would have taken place or not it is difficult to say, because at the last moment Germany lost her most devoted ally, and the influence of the man who had, more than any one else, worked in its interests was eliminated for the time being. A woman, who had just reasons for feeling revengeful against Raspoutine, stabbed him as he was coming out of church in his native village of Pokrowskoye in Siberia, whither he had gone on a short visit. He was ill for a long time, and during the weeks that he was laid up, to the intense consternation of the Empress, who was only with great difficulty prevented from going herself to nurse him, the Austrian ultimatum consequent on the assassination of the Heir to Francis Joseph's Throne was presented to Servia, and followed by the declaration of war launched by Germany almost simultaneously against Russia and France.

This proved for Alexandra Feodorowna the most terrible blow that had yet befallen her since the day when she had plighted her troth to the mighty Czar of All the Russias. During the eventful hours that preceded the initial act of the tragedy which was to change the face of the whole world she went about like a demented woman, crying and praying in turns, and imploring her husband to pause before he allowed the accomplishment of a calamity which she vaguely guessed would claim her for one of its first victims. But this time there was no Raspoutine at her side to play on the feelings of humanity of the weak-minded Nicholas, to persuade him that he ought rather to submit to the humiliation of Russian prestige than to allow another war to throw its shadow on his already too unfortunate reign. On the contrary, all the advisers of the Emperor, all his Ministers, public opinion, the press, and the army, eager to wipe out the remembrance of the Japanese disaster, poured into his ears their conviction that if he did not rush to the help of poor threatened Servia he would not only lose the last fragments of popularity which were left to him, but also put Russia before the whole world in a most shameful and dishonorable position.

As usual, the Czar yielded, with the results which we know and have seen. He could hardly have done anything else, if we take into consideration that Germany was absolutely determined to start the abominable war, from which she hoped to obtain the realization of her schemes of domination of the whole earth. But—and this must be told here—the Kaiser in letters far more authentic than the famous

Willy and Nicky correspondence, which personally I consider as subject to much doubt, in view of certain improbabilities which it contains, the Kaiser did propose at that time to his cousin to conclude with him a defensive and offensive alliance against France and England. In return for which he engaged himself to uphold any designs which Russia might nurse in regard to the Balkans and the Straits.

It may not be to the advantage of his intellectual faculties that Nicholas failed to see the vast political scheme which lay behind this offer; it is certainly to the honor of his moral character that he refused it, and this in spite of the supplications of his wife, who entreated him not to plunge their country into a war which, as she repeated, could only prove disastrous for its future, as well as for that of the dynasty. In spite of his natural defects, of his cruelty, harshness of heart, and utter disregard of the rights of others, the Czar was still a gentleman and he could not be induced to do anything capable of dishonoring him as a gentleman, though he may have lent himself to actions degrading for a Sovereign. During the terribly responsible days which preceded the declaration of war he behaved quite irreproachably. It was later on that he was influenced by Raspoutine and by the Empress to lend himself to political schemes unworthy of him, as well as of the nation over which he ruled.

On the 1st of August, 1914, twelve hours after Germany had thrown her gauntlet into his face, he showed himself for the last time to his people on the balcony of the Winter Palace. An immense crowd had gathered together in the big square which it faces, and for the last time, too, cheered him vociferously, forgetting in this solemn moment all the follies, mistakes, and errors which had saddened his reign and raised a barrier between him and this great Russia that his father had made so prosperous and so mighty. If in that supreme moment he had been able to find words capable of electrifying this crowd into believing in him again, who knows but that the reverses which were to crowd upon him could not have been avoided, or at least diminished! But Nicholas II. never knew how to speak to his subjects or how to touch their hearts. He remained impassible and indifferent in the most critical hours of his life and of theirs, and this incapacity to rise to the height of the situation of the moment was perhaps one of the things which contributed the most to his fall.

I remember him so well on that August afternoon, facing the multitude assembled to greet him as its Czar and leader, and I remember, too, the thought which swept through my mind, that it was a thousand pities it was not his father who stood there in his place. Alexander III. would have known how to address Russia in an hour of national danger. He was neither a brilliant nor an extremely intelligent man, but he was a man and a Sovereign, who realized the duties of a Monarch and of a man. He was, moreover, a Russian who thought and who felt as a Russian alone could think and feel, in questions where the honor and the future of the country were involved. Nicholas II. was simply an Emperor who wished to be an autocrat. It was too much and not enough at the same time, and many among those who looked upon him, as he appeared before his people on that historical balcony whence it was the custom to announce to the population of the capital the death of a Sovereign whenever it took place, many wondered whether they were not going to hear that another one had started on the long journey whence there is no return. His presence seemed to herald a funeral rather than the hope of a triumph, and this impression which he produced was so vivid that more than one acknowledged having experienced it when talking about this famous day which, though we knew it not, proved to be the last upon which a Russian Czar faced the Russian people before the latter overthrew the chief of the House of Romanoff from the Throne which he had disgraced.

XIX

MY FATHERLAND, MUST I FORSAKE THEE?

IT would not have been human on the part of the Empress Alexandra if she had not felt deeply aggrieved at the war which had so unexpectedly broken out between the country of her birth and that of her adoption. She had never really become a Russian at heart and her sympathies had remained exclusively German all through her married life. Apart from this, she had experienced from the intercourse which she had kept up with her own family the only pleasure which she had frankly enjoyed since the Crown of the Russian Czarinas had been put upon her head. She dearly loved her two sisters, the Princess Victoria of Battenberg and the Princess Irene of Prussia, far more, indeed, than she did her other one, the Grand Duchess Elisabeth, whom she considered more or less as a rival and whom in the secret of her heart she could not forgive for having won in Russia a popularity which had always been denied to her own self.

Then there was her brother, the Grand Duke of Hesse, with whom she had remained in correspondence, who paid her frequent visits in Tsarskoye Selo; there was also her cousin, the Kaiser, who had been the first person to point out to her the responsibilities which were inseparable from the exalted position she occupied as Empress of All the Russias, who had applied himself to persuade her that she had great political talents, and that she could undoubtedly, if she only wished it, become a most important factor in European politics. Strange to say, though she had been brought up partly in England, though her mother had been an English Princess, though she was the grandchild of Queen Victoria, she intensely disliked everything that was English, and had for English customs, English ambitions, and English politics the same hatred which characterized William II. Perhaps this common aversion was one of the reasons why they had always got on so well together, and why they had been able to be of so much use to each other. At all events, the fact that it existed in an equal degree in both of them had drawn them together, and at last, after she had contrived to eliminate the influence of her anti-German mother-in-law, Alexandra Feodorowna had been able to give herself up body and soul to the task of drawing together her husband and her own kindred. She had tried to persuade the former that the only means to insure the prosperity and the welfare of the Russian Empire in the future consisted in a closer union with Germany, with whom there existed absolutely no reason to quarrel, because there were no interests capable of clashing between the two people. She had represented to the weak-minded Nicholas that Russia had obtained from France all that she could hope to get, and that the latter had become weary of always being called upon to invest money in Russian bonds without any return being made for her generosity.

Nicholas II. had always detested republics, and though he had been made much of during his visits to Paris, which he had thoroughly enjoyed, he yet had never felt quite at home amid the Republican society he had been called upon to get acquainted with; in the secret of his heart he despised all French political men, whom he considered as much inferior to himself. But a natural inclination to dissimulation, which he carried so far that many people called it by quite another name, had made him carefully conceal the real state of his feelings in regard to his French ally. It is, however, quite certain that if the war had not broken out the Franco-Russian alliance would have died a natural death. As things occurred, it was for a short space of time to appear more complete than ever; this was not the merit of Nicholas, but the result of the honesty which the French Government brought to bear in all that happened in 1914. In Russian Court circles, which were all of them, more or less, given up to Germany, the news that the country was going to war was received with consternation, and there were many people who declared that it was a shame for Russia to be drawn into a struggle which was essentially a personal quarrel between France and Germany, with which she had nothing to do.

At first and before the anti-German feeling became fierce in St. Petersburg, the Empress, in spite of political complications, remained in private correspondence with her brother, and through him with the Kaiser, to whom she promised that she would spare no efforts to induce the Czar to conclude peace as soon as it became practicable. She had never been able to form an idea of the power which public opinion, especially in times of national danger, can exercise over a nation. She imagined that the authority wielded by the Crown would be sufficient to put an end to any manifestations of sympathy in regard to France on the part of the Russian people. She therefore felt confident that the struggle which had just begun would not last long, and that Russia could come out of it, if not with flying colors, at least without any serious losses.

No one during those early days of the war admitted for one moment the possibility that Warsaw and the line of fortresses which defended the Russian frontier on the side of the Niemen could fall into the hands of the enemy; all that the Empress expected was a defeat of the Russian armies which would not seriously compromise their prestige, but at the same time convince the country that an advantageous peace was, after all, the best way of getting out of a situation where all the time one adversary had either willingly or unwillingly misunderstood the good intentions of the other.

She was consequently working along this line when Raspoutine returned to Tsarskoye Selo. He did this as soon as the doctors had pronounced him fit to travel. She began once more to pray with him and to ask him to put her again into communication with that other world where she imagined that Colonel Orloff was waiting to advise her as to what she ought to do in regard to the war and to the necessity of putting an end to it as soon as possible. But while she believed that none outside the few people she had admitted into her confidence—one of whom was Anna Wyrubewa, and another Sturmer, who was later on to play such an important part in the tragedy of her fall—could guess what she was about, Sazonoff began to suspect that it was due to her influence that the Emperor was no longer so amenable to the advice which he ventured to offer. It was partly to put an obstacle in the way of any independent act of the Sovereign that might have been interpreted as not quite loyal in regard to Russia's Allies, that he had suggested the drawing up of the document known by the name of the Treaty of London, in which the Allied Powers engaged themselves not to conclude any individual or separate peace with Germany. He thought, and others did the same, that this would prove the best means to hold together the Entente without exposing it to mutual suspicion. He concluded this pact of his own authority, only acquainting the Czar with what he had done after it had become an accomplished fact.

Nicholas understood for once the significance of his Minister's bold action, but he could not disavow it; therefore he had to make the best of it. But he refrained from telling the Empress of this new complication which would surely interfere with her hopes of a prompt peace, and it was through a letter from her brother that she heard at last what had taken place in London. Her wrath was intense, the more so that her German relatives blamed her for a thing she had known nothing about and for which they tried to make her responsible. Alexandra Feodorowna had never under-stood what self-control meant, and she gave public vent to her indignation, accusing Sazonoff of having betrayed his Imperial Master's confidence, and vowing that he would be made to repent for this piece of audacity.

The Empress was still smarting under the sense of her personal defeat in a struggle against the people who were trying to control Russian politics and to lead them in a road she strongly objected taking, when the news of the defeat of the Russian army at Tannenberg came like a thunderbolt out of the blue, to stir up all the patriotic feelings of the Russian nation and to put an end to any idea of peace which may have existed in some timorous minds. The Empress had perforce to appear to share the general indignation against the ruthless conduct of Germany, and she had to acknowledge her momentary helplessness to speak what she considered to be the language of reason, and to try to persuade her subjects that it would be to their advantage to abandon their Allies to their fate, and to apply themselves to withdraw their own pawns out of the game.

In these days of suspense Raspoutine turned out to be the greatest comfort in the world to her. For one thing, he made it possible for her to begin again seeking in Berlin inspirations as to the course of conduct she ought to pursue. Thanks to him, Mr. Manassavitch-Maniuloff was persuaded to undertake a journey abroad, during which he was to see the leading political men in Europe and to ascertain their views on the subject of the conduct of the war in general, as well as of its chances of success. Ostensibly it was a newspaper on which he was assistant editor, the *Nowoie Wrémia*, that sent him on this perilous mission. In reality, he started as the agent of the Empress, and he saw several German officials in Stockholm, as well as in Copenhagen, where he spent a few days. He proceeded to London and to Paris, only to lend coloring to what otherwise would have been an impossible trip. When he returned to Russia he brought along with him a whole program drawn out by the Kaiser, which Alexandra Feodorowna proceeded at once to execute.

But here again she found obstacles in her path, the principal of which was the stubbornness of the Grand Duke Nicholas, who, in spite of the fact that he had to acknowledge that Russia had neither guns nor ammunition in sufficient quantity to be able to hold her own against the hordes of William II., yet refused to consider his country as beaten. The Grand Duke was popular in the army. The fact that it began to be known that he represented at Court the Russian party, in opposition to the hated Empress, who was supposed to head the German one, gave him considerable prestige. When the Czar had consulted him as to what ought to be done, he had replied:

"Do anything you like except conclude peace, because if you do I shall be the first one to lead the army against you, and to compel you to go on with the struggle."

Nicholas had repeated to the Czarina the threat of his cousin, and this had been sufficient to incense the latter, even more than she had been before, against a man whom she considered, perhaps not quite without reason, as her most formidable enemy.

Nevertheless, she tried to persuade him to change his mind, and made an appeal to his feelings of humanity, asking him whether it was right to go on with a war in which hundreds of thousands of Russian soldiers had already fallen, which would probably entail more sacrifices in the future than the country could afford. She spoke eloquently, but the Grand Duke remained unmoved, and at last Alexandra Feodorowna, worn out by the supreme effort which she had made, gave way to her uncontrollable grief, exclaiming in her deep distress:

"My country, my poor country, must I forsake thee?"

Nicholas Nicholaievitch turned round and said, with a withering contempt:

"To what country do you allude, Madam—to Russia or to Germany?"

The Empress jumped up, her eyes blazing with rage. She rang the bell, and told the lady in waiting who came in response to her call:

"Show the Grand Duke out. He must never be allowed to enter this room any more."

And Nicholas Nicholaievitch never did so again.

XX

IT IS YOUR HUSBAND WHO IS LOSING THE THRONE OF YOUR SON

THIS interview with the Grand Duke, Commander-in-chief of the armies in the field, could not fail to produce a deep impression on the troubled mind of the Empress. Her proud and unforgiving character had been goaded to the extreme by the irony with which her husband's cousin had received the overtures which she had made to him, and she could not bring herself to forgive him for the calm disdain with which he had asked her whether she considered Russia or Germany as her Fatherland.

Of course she flew to Anna Wyrubewa to seek consolation, but when the latter advised her to ask Raspoutine to pray for her in this crisis of her life, Alexandra Feodorowna for once did not accept this suggestion, saying that a man absorbed in religious practices like the "Prophet" could not be expected to take a sane view of a position which was getting so intricate that it would require a statesman of unusual ability to unravel it. But she expressed herself willing to talk to Mr. Sturmer about it, and to ask him what he thought of the Grand Duke's insolence, as she termed it, and what he would suggest as to the means of putting it down.

It is time here to say a word concerning Mr. Sturmer, who was so soon to play a prominent part in the drama of the Romanoffs' fate. He was a man of moderate intelligence, great ambition, and above everything else an opportunist—a perfect type of the class called in Russian Tchinownikis, who always and in everything it does approves the government of the day. He had for years paraded ultra-conservative opinions, and while he had performed the functions of Master of the Ceremonies at the Imperial Court, he had professed great sympathies for England and for everything British, playing the European, while at heart he was the personification of the Tartar hidden under the Russian flag. He was, moreover, an excellent talker and a well-read, well-educated man. His German origin had imbued him, as was to be expected, with considerable admiration for the Kultur, such as it was understood at the time I am referring to. The late

Czar Alexander III. had always abominated him and shown him that such was the case in an unmistakable manner. But Mr. Sturmer had the happy knack never to notice what it was inconvenient for him to be caught looking at; he stuck to his post until he contrived to get another appointment, that of President of the zemstwo of the province of Twer, where he possessed a large estate. This position, however, he had to abandon soon, because his colleagues happened all of them to be very ardent liberals who refused to accept his monarchical views.

Sturmer retired to private life, but at the time of the accession to the Throne of Nicholas II. he came to St. Petersburg, and managed to convey to the new Czar a detailed report as to the wave of liberalism that, to use his words, "infected" the province of Twer. If we are to believe a rumor which was persistently circulated in the capital, this had a good deal to do with the famous speech in which the Emperor told the deputies of the zemstwos (come to congratulate him on his marriage) that they need not in the future indulge in "senseless dreams," as it was his firm intention to uphold intact the principles of autocracy.

Sturmer was clever enough to conceal his extreme delight at the Sovereign's attitude, and he went on with his attempt to worm himself into the latter's favor. Very soon afterward he re-entered public life, was appointed Governor of that same province of Twer where he had met with such unsuccess, and proceeded steadily to work out for himself the reputation of being a first-rate statesman. He was shrewd enough to see what others had failed to perceive, and this was that, with the weak character of Nicholas II., it would require very little trouble on the part of the Empress to obtain complete mastery over his mind. He therefore applied himself to persuade the latter that it was her duty to make the attempt. He had always been a fanatical orthodox, perhaps because he had not been born one, and he was in great favor with several high Church dignitaries, including the new confessor of the Imperial Family, Father Schabelsky, whom the Czarina liked very much, and in whom she had great confidence. This made it relatively easy for him to carry to the ears of Alexandra Feodorowna his opinions on the current events of the day, and he did not fail to do so during the troubled times of the Revolution of 1905, and of the repression which followed upon it, in which he took an active part. He occupied then a post in the Ministry. However, he had to give up this upon his appointment as a member of the Council of State, which promotion had covered an attempt on the part of his colleagues to get rid of him. He took an important share in the deliberations of this Assembly, and very soon was recognized as one of the leaders of the ultra-conservative party there, and as a strong supporter of an alliance with Germany.

This attitude alone would have been sufficient to win for him the good-will of the Czarina, and when the war broke out she often talked with him over the sad consequences it was sure to bring; she discussed with this faithful friend the possibility of putting an end to it, in a sense favorable to Russian interests, not likely to harm Russian prestige abroad nor the dynasty at home.

Sturmer had been introduced to Raspoutine by the good offices of Manassavitch-Maniuloff, whose services he had had the opportunity to appreciate when they were both in the employ of the Government, and he soon played a prominent part in all the designs of these two sinister personages. It has even been related that it was due to his special suggestion that the comedy of the Empress being put into direct communication with the spirit of Colonel Orloff had been engineered; of this there exists so far no proof, and we must therefore accept the tale under the reserve that, according to the French proverb, it is only the rich to whom one lends money.

When Sturmer heard about the conversation which had terminated with such violence between Alexandra Feodorowna and the Grand Duke Nicholas he saw at once the capital that could be made out of the incident. He also disliked the Grand Duke; it was therefore easy for him to enter with alacrity and zeal into the plans of revenge that were being harbored by the Czarina, to whom he reported that Nicholas Nicholaievitch was trying to supplant the Czar, to get himself appointed Dictator of the Empire; that he had, moreover, the most sinister designs against the little Cesarewitsch, as well as against her, who, as he had openly declared, ought to be locked up in a convent. He pointed out further to the distracted Empress that the weakness of character of her husband might easily make him a prey to the ambitions of his cousin and cause him to lend himself to the latter's schemes. Besides this, it was against all the traditions of autocracy for a member of the Imperial Family to aspire to make for himself an independent position outside the Czar, and if the Grand Duke was allowed to work out the consolidation of his popularity among the army and the military party a Palace revolution could easily follow, which would overthrow Nicholas II. and dethrone him in favor of some other Romanoff, willing to become an easy tool in the hands of the Grand Duke Commander-in-chief.

After this it became the one object of Alexandra Feodorowna's ambition to deprive her cousin of his command, to have him exiled somewhere far from St. Petersburg, which by this time had been renamed Petrograd.

This, however, was a difficult piece of work to perform, precisely on account of the weakness of temperament of Nicholas II. and of the awe with which any violent decision to be taken in regard to any one whom he knew to be stronger than himself inspired him. Religious superstition was therefore brought to bear upon him; he was told by his wife, by a few people who were devoted to her, and last but not least by Raspoutine, that it was part of the duties of a Russian Czar to lead his nation in times of peril; that the enthusiasm which his presence at the head of the army would be sure to provoke would prove a great element in the achievement of a complete victory against a formidable foe, the strength of which had never been properly appreciated. At first Nicholas grew impatient and would not listen. At heart he had the vague consciousness of his own incapacity to command a big army in the field; he feared to take such a perilous responsibility upon his shoulders. He also knew that it was not the fault of the Grand Duke that he had been compelled to retreat before the invading German forces, but of the men who had failed to supply him with the necessary ammunition, artillery, and provisions. The Emperor did not care to make out of his cousin the scapegoat for all the sins of Israel. On the other hand, he dreaded the ascendency which Nicholas Nicholaievitch was undoubtedly acquiring in public opinion, and he did not care for any member of his family to become popular at his own expense. Still, he would not come to a decision. Even when the Grand Duke Commander-in-chief had objected to the presence of the Empress at headquarters, which she had wished to visit, he had refrained from insisting on the point. He had, on the contrary, applied himself to soothe his wife's ruffled feelings.

This hesitation on the part of the Sovereign did not please at all the small group of men who had entered into the schemes of the Empress. They knew very well that so long as Nicholas Nicholaievitch remained in power it would be impossible to bring to the front the question of a separate peace with Germany for which they were steadily working. It was therefore determined to force the Empress to extort from her husband the decision they wished for; consequently Raspoutine asked her to attend a prayer-meeting he wanted to hold, during which he said that it had been revealed to him that she would come to learn many things hitherto kept from her knowledge, but which it was time she should hear. What occurred at this meeting no one ever could ascertain exactly. It seems pretty certain that Raspoutine evoked the spirit of Colonel Orloff, and that the customary game of making a pencil write by itself was resorted to, with the result that Alexandra Feodorowna returned to the Palace fully convinced that, in resisting her demand for the removal of the Grand Duke Nicholas from his position as Commander-in-chief of the army, the Czar was endangering not only his own life, but also the Throne, and the chances of succession to it of his only son.

The Empress implored her husband to listen to her, telling him that if he really felt alarmed about taking any violent measures against the Grand Duke, he ought at least to dismiss the latter's head of the staff, General Januchevitch, to whose blunders all the disasters that had overpowered the Russian armies were due. She representted to her bewildered spouse that public opinion claimed some one should be punished for all the unsuccesses which had attended the war, and that it would be satisfied to a small degree if the General were removed from his command.

This was a compromise which Nicholas II. seized hold of with alacrity. It had been proposed to him because it was known very well that the Grand Duke would not consent to be parted from his faithful adviser with whom he had shared all the anxieties of the disastrous campaign that had been carried on amid such terrible difficulties, that he would rather resign his own command than give him up. The surmise proved quite correct. When Nicholas Nicholaievitch was informed of the change that had been made in the direction of the staff, without his having been consulted, he telegraphed to the Emperor, asking him to be also relieved as soon as possible from the duties of his responsible position. The Empress, Sturmer, and Raspoutine were jubilant. It was easy to persuade the Czar that his cousin, in thus resisting his orders, had rendered himself guilty of insubordination. It was decided not to accept his resignation, but simply to dismiss him and to appoint him at the same time Viceroy in the Caucasus, a position that had just been rendered vacant by the departure of Count Worontzoff-Daschkoff for reasons of health. This they thought would be a courteous way of getting rid once for all of a personality so strong and so encumbering at the same time as that of the Grand Duke, and of doing it in a manner to which no one could raise any objections.

The Emperor said yes to everything. He had been thoroughly frightened, and was no longer in a condition of mind capable of judging impartially of the events taking place around him. A solemn religious service was celebrated in the private chapel of the Imperial Palace of Tsarskoye Selo, to implore the protection of Heaven on the new Commander-in-chief of the Russian troops, after which Nicholas II. started for the headquarters of the army. He was received with great pomp and ceremony by the Grand Duke, and at once assumed the supreme command over demoralized regiments who were full of regret at the departure of their former leader.

Nicholas Nicholaievitch behaved with immense dignity. In this crisis of his life he only remembered that he was a Romanoff, and he showed an absolute submission to the decisions of the head of his dynasty. In words of incomparable nobility he issued an army order in which he thanked his soldiers for their good services, and expressed the hope that the presence of their Sovereign at their head would inspire them with a new energy in the struggle that lay before them. Then he left for his new post, accompanied to the railway station by the Czar himself, from whom he parted solemnly and respectfully, and whom he was never to see again, at least not as Emperor of All the Russias.

XXI

PEACE, WE MUST HAVE PEACE

THE removal of the Grand Duke Nicholas from the position of Commander-in-chief of the army did not meet with the general satisfaction that his enemies had hoped it would provoke. The sane elements of the nation understood quite well that, whatever mistakes he had been guilty of, they had proceeded more from the many difficulties which he had found in his way than from his own incapacity. No one liked the thought of his place having been taken by the Czar himself, who had long ago lost his personal prestige, whom no political party in the country trusted. The influence of the Empress was also dreaded, and the fact of her German leanings was openly discussed. The demand for a responsible Cabinet, from whom explanations could be demanded by the nation, was already to be heard everywhere. The Duma, when it had met, had been the scene of furious discussions during which the conduct of the Government had been severely censured. Russia was beginning to get tired of the tyrannous hand which was weighing it down and crushing every attempt at independence on the part of those who were in possession of her confidence.

The Ministry was neither respected nor considered, the Sovereign was despised, and his wife was hated. Dissatisfaction was spreading even in the spheres which out of old traditions and principles had kept it within bounds. The aristocracy had become weary of finding all its good intentions disdained or misconstrued; in all classes of society people were cursing the hidden "dark powers," as they were called, that disposed of the fate of the nation and that ruled the feeble and weak-minded Monarch who had been con-verted into a figurehead for whom no one cared except the un-scrupulous people who were abusing his credulity and who had contrived to get hold of his confidence.

The Czarina was openly accused of working hand in hand with her cousin, the Kaiser, and of assisting him in his dreams of a world-wide Empire into whose power the Russian one was to be delivered. And when the old, feeble, opinionated, but at any rate honest,

Gorémykine had been replaced as Prime Minister by the hated Sturmer, who by this time had risen to the position of leader of the ultra-conservative and reactionary party in the Council of State, the general indignation against the weakness of Nicholas II. could no longer be repressed, and the possibility of a Palace revolution came to be spoken of as the next thing likely to happen.

In the mean while Raspoutine and his friends were daily becoming more powerful. The "Prophet" had by that time completely mastered the details of the intrigue into which he had been drawn by the clever people of whom he had been the tool. These had been at first Count Witte, who in his hatred of the men who had driven him out of power had willingly lent himself to the conspiracy which transformed the Empress into one of the most active agents the Kaiser had ever had at his disposal in Russia. When this much-discussed statesman died at the very moment he might have been called again to play a part in the history of his country, his place had been taken by Sturmer, Manassavitch-Maniuloff, and other adventurers of the same kind, all eager to enrich themselves at the expense of their own Fatherland, all of them men who only looked for their personal financial advantage, who remained perfectly indifferent to the disasters which one after the other were crowding upon unfortunate Russia. Germany was clever enough to see through the game played by these sharks and she did not hesitate an instant in buying their services for all that they were worth.

Raspoutine had very accurately taken stock of the mental caliber of the half-demented Czarina, and while carefully avoiding discussing or even touching upon the subject of politics with her, he had contrived to persuade her to trust those so-called statesmen of whom he was but the instrument. As time went on she became more and more anxious to communicate with these spirits of the other world, in whose existence she had been led to believe as firmly as in that of the Divinity itself. Raspoutine, whenever he prayed in her presence, pretended to get into trances during which he told her things which he assured her he did not remember later on, but which he persuaded her he had been inspired by the celestial powers to tell. She was kept by him and by Anna Wyrubewa in a state of semi-hypnotism, which went so far that sometimes she was herself seized with attacks of convulsions bordering on epilepsy, during the long prayers in which she used to spend half of her days and most of her nights. The superstitious fears which had always haunted her were played upon by these clever adventurers whom she had admitted into the secret of her thoughts. She was finally convinced that her duty as a Russian Empress required of her to sacrifice herself for the welfare of her subjects, and to induce her husband to sign a peace that would put an end to the useless and terrible slaughter that had transformed the whole of Russia into one vast churchyard.

She still labored under the illusion that the dynasty was popular and that every decision of the Czar would be received with respect and gratitude by the nation. Though she knew that she was personally disliked, she did not imagine that this dislike extended itself to the Emperor, and she never supposed that, even in regard to her own person, the hatred of which she was the object existed anywhere else than among the aristocratic circles of Petrograd society. In one word, she believed in the power of autocracy, and she worked as hard as she could to consolidate it by getting Nicholas II. to appoint as his Ministers and advisers men who shared her opinions on this point, and who were ready to crush with the greatest vigor and the utmost severity every attempt to shake the prestige and the authority of the Crown.

Of course, the fact that the country was at war made her path most difficult; for this very reason she thought it was indispensable for the safety of the dynasty and of her son that peace should be concluded. She did not care in the least for the secret treaties or obligations Russia had assumed. To her, honor was but a question of opportunism. She set the existence of the Romanoffs before their self-respect. Her German blood made her lose sight of the real interests of her husband and of her children.

Here we must pause a moment and touch upon a point that has been as much discussed as it has remained mysterious to this day. Was Raspoutine a German agent directly employed by the Kaiser to persuade the half-demented Czarina that it was her duty to put an end to the war? Or was he simply the instrument of other people more in possession of the secret of Germany's schemes than himself? Personally I am inclined to believe this second version of his activity. Raspoutine was far too ignorant and uncouth to have been taken into the confidence of William II., but Mr. Sturmer, Mr. Manassavitch-Maniuloff, and Mr. Protopopoff undoubtedly were confidants of the Kaiser. They had been promised, most likely, large sums of money for their co-operation in this vile intrigue, which even after their fall was to be renewed and, as we have unfortunately seen, renewed with success.

I shall not repeat here the story of Mr. Protopopoff's famous journey to Sweden, where he got into direct touch with agents of the German Government. I shall not even return to the subject of the negotiations begun by him and continued by Mr. Sturmer. All this is now a matter of history, and what I am writing here only concerns the personal part played by the Empress in this dark plot, directed against all the Allies of Russia in the war as well as against Russia herself. I am only concerned with Alexandra Feodorowna and her share in the catastrophe which was to send her a captive and an exile to that distant Siberia whither so many innocent people had been banished by her husband.

I wish to explain how it could have become possible for her to be transformed into an active agent of German ambition on the Russian Throne. She was, as we have seen, only half-responsible for her actions. Her intelligence had never been properly balanced and self-control had never been taught her. She had, however, principles, and very strong ones, too, which had stood between her and temptation in the serious sentimental crisis of her life. But this resistance to what perhaps had been the one passion she had known, except her love for her son, had helped to overthrow her mental balance. She had given to God, represented by a Divinity of her own created by her imagination, all the affection she had not been allowed to expend on earth, and full of a spirit of self-sacrifice as stupid as it was devoid of any ground to stand upon. She had fancied that she could work out her personal salvation, together with that of her family and subjects, in restoring to the country whose Empress she happened to be the blessings of a peace that would stop the effusion of blood the thought of which robbed her of sleep at night and repose by day.

She was living in a state which most certainly was bordering on insanity, and she had entirely lost the faculty of discriminating between what was reality and what was a dream. Raspoutine held her in a kind of trance, which was further aggravated by the long fasts to which he obliged her to submit. She was told that she was the victim chosen by the Almighty to expiate all the sins of the Russian Empire, that it was only through constant prayer, combined with all kinds of other mortifications, that she could hope to see restored the peace of her mind and the health of her son. It is probable that she suffered from hallucinations during which she saw, as in a cloud, the rising shapes of soldiers killed in battle, clamoring to her to stop the useless massacres going on in the Polish plains where they had fallen. Is it a wonder that, unconscious of aught else than this condition of self-reproach to which she had been reduced, she tried to end her own sufferings, as well as the misery which had fallen upon her country, by disregarding all the advice she received from her real friends and making the most frantic efforts to induce her husband to accept the peace terms which the Kaiser had more than once caused to be secretly conveyed to him?

Nicholas II. was also weary of the struggle, but he realized better than his wife the impossibility which existed for him of acting independently of his Allies. He had Ministers who, in spite of their respect for his person and authority, would not have hesitated to point out to him the grave consequences which a defection of Russia would mean for the whole cause of the Allied nations, who, after all, had been entangled in this disastrous war because they had rushed to his help and to that of his people.

Sturmer, who had for a short time taken the conduct of Foreign Affairs in his hands, had been compelled to resign, owing to the opposition which he had encountered in the Duma, and especially owing to the masterful speech in which Professor Miliukoff had exposed all the vices and all the crimes of his administration. His retreat had not had for consequence a diminution of his favor or of his influence; he still remained the trusted adviser of both Czar and Czarina. Together with him were working Protopopoff, who pretended that he would be strong enough, with the help of the hundreds, nay thousands of police agents he had at his disposal, to crush every attempt at a revolution; Madame Wyrubewa; and, last but not least, the formidable Raspoutine, whose influence had proved wide enough to cause the postponement of the trial for blackmail of his confederate, Manassavitch-Maniuloff. A bank director from whom he had tried to extort 25,000 rubles had denounced the latter to the military authorities, and, in spite of the angry protest of Mr. Sturmer, whose confidential adviser he had become, he had been imprisoned and sent before a jury.

But even the efforts of these people combined could not move Nicholas II. to act in accordance with their wishes, because, as I have said, he still had Ministers unwilling to betray the country into the hands of its enemies. The head of the Cabinet was Mr. Trepoff, an honest man credited with liberal sympathies, who, at all events, would not lend himself to anything that could be interpreted into the light of a treason of Russia in regard to her Allies. Unfortunately, he could not hold out against the attacks that were directed against him by all the pro-German party, and after he had fallen the latter felt at last free to act as it liked, because Prince Galitzyne, who had accepted the difficult position of Prime Minister in a country already standing on the brink of ruin, was far too timid a man to dare express an opinion of his own, after the Sovereign had once spoken and signified his will to him.

RASPOUTINE

XXII

THE REMOVAL OF THE "PROPHET"

THERE is a well-known Latin proverb which says that the gods begin by depriving of their reason those whom they mean to destroy.

Never was its truth more forcibly illustrated than in the tragedy which brought about the fall of the autocratic system of government under which Russia had been suffering for centuries. Its last representative had incarnated in his person all the follies, the crimes, the mistakes, and the ruthless cruelty of his predecessors. Unlike them, he had not known how to temper them by personal authority or personal sympathy. He was an effeminate, degenerate descendant of strong ancestors; the whole atavism of a doomed race seemed to have become embodied in his weak individuality. If outside catastrophes had not occurred in his reign, it is still likely that he would have been compelled by a revolution of some kind or other to step back into an obscurity out of which he ought never to have emerged, because he was most certainly not able to bear the rays of the "fierce light which beats upon a throne." It is, however, possible that none of those supreme calamities which destroy the independence and self-respect of nations as well as of individuals would have been connected with his name and history. But destiny condemned him to remain forever, in the annals of the world, a living proof of the degeneracy which threatens all royal houses who do not possess sufficient energy to stand in perfect union with their people whenever a trial of some kind comes to threaten their mutual existence.

It would have been hard enough to be branded by the centuries to come as the last of the Romanoffs and as an unworthy Heir of Peter the Great. It was worse than hard for Russia, even more than for Nicholas II., to have to realize that, through stupidity, weakness of character, and an exaggerated opinion of his own power and might, he had been the direct cause of the ruin of his country and the means of plunging it into an abyss of distress and of anarchy from which it will take the work of several generations to redeem it.

His wife was the instrument of his destruction. About this last point there cannot exist any doubt whatever. She had a character stronger than his and she could speak to him in the name of the son to whom they were both so completely devoted. She could also appeal to his religious and superstitious feelings, which, though not as exaggerated as her own and not quite so foolishly carried to extremes, were yet also devoid of sound common sense. They were connected with the conviction that he had a mission to perform in regard to the future of his subjects, and to their welfare both in this world and in the next. Nicholas II. had in his character something of the traits of Caligula and other Roman emperors—a mixture of cruelty and theatrical sentimentality combined with cowardice in presence of danger and indecision before immediate peril. He never knew what it meant to play the game, and he perished because he refused to fight it out on the day that he discovered his adversary held all the trumps.

In the mean while the war was going on, claiming every day new victims. The insufficiency of the Government to face its various problems became more patent. Instead of applying himself to the task of coping with them, the Czar became absorbed, thanks to the remonstrances of his wife, in the one thought of how to consolidate his own authority, reduce to silence the protestations of the country and those of its representatives in the Duma, and conclude a peace with Germany which would allow him to make an appeal to his troops to help him to crush once more the Revolution which was hammering at his door, which he imagined he could subdue as easily as he had annihilated the one that had broken out after the Japanese campaign.

These were splendid plans indeed, and the Empress was already rejoicing at their success, in ignorance of the revolt which was shaking public opinion out of its previous apathy, a revolt which had extended itself to her own family. Bad as were most of the Grand Dukes, dissolute as their conduct had ever been, yet they had in their veins the blood of Catherine the Great and of all the dead and gone Romanoffs. They rose in rebellion against the gang of adventurers who were dishonoring the chief of their race and of their dynasty.

By that time the name of the Empress was being dragged in the dirt by every street boy, and open comments were made in public places in regard to her friendship, not to call it by another name, for Raspoutine—comments which were devoid of truth, because there was never any immorality in their relations, but which were generally believed, perhaps, because it would have been impossible for any one to guess that it was through superstitious practices that the "Prophet" had contrived to get absolute hold of her mind.

The Imperial Family felt the degradation to which this common peasant had reduced it, and though they had no reason in the world to like Nicholas II., yet they resented the humiliation which any slur upon the reputation of his wife conferred upon him as well. After all, Alexandra Feodorowna was the mother of the future Czar, and as such she ought to inspire respect in the Russian nation. If she did not realize this fact herself, others had to do it for her and rid her of a contact which was a slur. Besides, there was the hope that if once the adventurer was removed she could be brought to look upon the world from a more reasonable point of view. The principal thing was to deliver her from this evil adviser who was fast leading her, as well as the dynasty, to inevitable destruction and ruin.

The story of Raspoutine's assassination is too well known to be repeated here. At any time it would have broken the heart of the poor, misguided Czarina. But coming at the moment it took place, it did something more—it deprived her of what she considered to be her only moral support amid the troubles of her life, the possibility of communicating with the spirit of the man whom she had loved, who she felt sure was watching over her and over her child, from the heavens.

In the weeks preceding the murder of the "Prophet" he had subjected the Empress almost every evening to the agony of these prayer-meetings during which he communicated to her the so-called wishes of her dead friend, who, as he said, advised her, through his medium, as to what she ought to do to avert the dangers which were hovering over her head. The miserable woman used to listen to these revelations with anxious eagerness, and pray, pray, with a fervor she had never known before, for the strength to obey the commandments of a spirit who in death, as well as in life, had proved to be her best, and indeed her only, friend. Is it a wonder that the last remnants of sanity which were still left to her snapped under this terrible strain, and that at last she became the mere shadow of her former self, a fit subject for a lunatic asylum, where, indeed, she ought, for the good of everybody, to have been confined?

Her conduct after she had been told of the murder of the creature whom she revered as a Prophet of God was quite in accord with her character, such as it had developed itself through all the years during which she had allowed her mind to be invaded with superstitious notions, which would have been laughable if they had not been so pathetic. Her only thought was that of vengeance. She exercised it with a relentlessness which set against her the few people left in Petrograd who might have felt inclined to take her part and to pity her in this tragedy of her life. She left no peace for the Czar until he had exiled the persons whom she knew to have been the authors of the deed. When she was implored to take pity on the young Grand Duke Dmitry, and not have him sent to the Persian front, where there existed so many epidemics that it was hardly likely he would ever come back again, she had merely smiled and coldly said:

"Why should I pity him? He did not pity others."

And yet public feeling was so strong against her, and so entirely in favor of those who had had the courage to rid Russia of a man who had proved so fatal to it, that the schemes of revenge of Alexandra Feodorowna suffered a collapse. Mighty and powerful as Nicholas II. believed himself to be, yet he understood that the best thing he could do would be to let silence and oblivion fall over a crime that was eminently popular in the whole country. He had heard of the telegrams of congratulation, and of the flowers which had been sent to both his cousin Dmitry Pawlowitch and to the husband of his niece, young Prince Youssoupoff, as well as the joy to which the population of Petrograd had given way when it had become aware of the fate of the adventurer whose name had been so prominently and so sadly associated with that of the Empress of All the Russias. Perhaps at heart he was not so very sorry at an event which had certainly rid him of a great incumbrance.

Nicholas II. had always practised dissimulation to a considerable extent, and he had never allowed outsiders to guess what was going on in his mind. During the days which followed upon the disappearance of Raspoutine he certainly expressed great sympathy for the grief of his wife, but at the same time he did not, as she expected, cause the perpetrators of the murder of this low adventurer to be prosecuted publicly for their daring action. This apathy exasperated Alexandra Feodorowna.

During the last weeks of Raspoutine's life he had been working, conjointly with Sturmer and Protopopoff, toward convincing her to lend herself to a Palace revolution which would have overturned her husband and made little Alexis Czar under her own Regency. She had been told over and over again that she possessed all the great talents of Catherine II., that the Emperor was not a better man than Peter III. She had been made acquainted with his unpopularity, but at the same time persuaded that this unpopularity was a purely personal thing and that it did not extend itself to the person of the Heir to the Throne, nor even to her own. As Regent she could do any amount of good, and conclude peace with Germany the more easily that she was not bound by the terms of the agreement entered into by Mr. Sazonoff with the Entente, in the name of Nicholas II.

The foolish woman believed absolutely all the nonsense which was being constantly poured into her ears. Her ambition and lust for revenge over her enemies also played a part in this whole tragedy. She therefore began wondering whether, after all, she ought not to follow the advice which she had received from Heaven, as she fondly imagined, through the mouth of Raspoutine. She would have liked to be able to consult once again the spirit of Colonel Orloff so as to relieve her perplexity, because she had still sufficient scruples to hesitate before allowing those whom she considered to be her friends to use her name for the execution of a Palace revolution directed against her own husband, whom she may not have loved, but whom she still respected as the Czar of All the Russias.

It is at this juncture that a new incident occurred, the real details of which have never yet transpired. Raspoutine, just before he had been murdered, had introduced to the Empress a Tibetan doctor with whom he was on terms of intimate friendship, telling her that he was a man of great ability, devoted to occult sciences, had studied them in the convents of his country, and who was quite able to perform miracles. This man, whose name was Badmaieff, certainly saw Alexandra Feodorowna several times, and it was reported that he gave her certain drugs which he told her she ought to administer to the Emperor in secret, drugs which would make him quite subservient to her will. Whether she used them or not it is impossible to say. Young Prince Youssoupoff declared immediately after the Revolution that she had done so, and that in consequence of this experiment Nicholas II.'s will, which had always been a weak one, had completely disappeared, until he had been reduced to the condition of a puppet in the strong hands of his wife. But this assertion, coming as it did from a personage who could not have nursed kind feelings in regard to the Empress, must be accepted with caution.

It is a fact, however, that those in attendance on the Sovereign remarked more than once that he seemed at times to have lost the real consciousness of what was going on around him, that his eyes had acquired a vague, dazed look they had never worn before.

It is out of this introduction of Badmaieff into the intimacy of the Czarina that the rumor arose that Raspoutine, together with Anna Wyrubewa, had tried to administer slow poison to the small Grand Duke Alexis. Such a thing had never taken place, and indeed it could never have occurred if one considers the fact that the strongest trump in the game played by the pro-German agents who were leading Russia to its ruin was precisely the little Cesarewitsch, without whose existence it would have been impossible for them to think of making out of Alexandra Feodorowna a Regent of the Russian Empire. They had, therefore, the greatest interest in keeping the child in as good a state of health as possible, and he was far too delicate for them to try any experiment upon him. On the other hand, the necessity of getting rid by natural means of the Czar himself was so evident that it would not be surprising if the superstitious mind of his Consort had been influenced so as to persuade her to lend herself to what she had been told was nothing but a religious practice, but which in reality was an attempt to accomplish by this means what it would perhaps not have proved wise to try and bring about in another way.

PETER BADMAIEFF

XXIII

ANNA COMES TO THE RESCUE

IN the course of an interview which Anna Wyrubewa gave to a foreign newspaper correspondent a short while after she had been released from the fortress of SS. Peter and Paul, where she was confined for about three months following the outbreak of the Revolution, she said that the Empress Alexandra had never been so near to insanity as during the weeks which followed upon the murder of Raspoutine. What she failed to relate, however, was the manner in which she succeeded in preventing the half-balanced mind of the miserable woman from snapping altogether under the strain put upon it by circumstances.

When the outsider tries to form an opinion as to all the events which preceded the rebellion that destroyed the Throne of the Romanoffs, it is essential he should remember the state of mind of the Czarina at this particular time, as well as the condition of her nerves—a condition which was very nearly akin to the one into which a man falls when, after having been the victim of a pernicious drug habit, he finds himself unexpectedly and suddenly deprived of his favorite morphia or cocaine. The Empress had been living for months under the influence of these mysterious night sittings during which Raspoutine evoked for her, as she firmly believed, spirits of another world from whom she sought inspiration and in whom she found comfort. All at once this moral aid, which had helped her to live, was denied to her, and she did not know any longer what she was to do, surrounded as she felt herself to be by ever-increasing dangers which threatened not only her own person, but that of her beloved child, that son in whom she firmly believed Russia would find its salvation and who was destined to become one of the greatest and mightiest Sovereigns the country had ever seen reign over it since the days of Peter the Great. She felt absolutely at sea, like a ship deprived of its pilot and abandoned to inexperienced hands, ignorant of the first principles of navigation. Neither her husband, whom at heart she despised, nor her friend, Anna Wyrubewa, whom she had never entirely initiated into all the details of her secret intercourse with the dead, nor her faithful advisers, Sturmer and Protopopoff, could make up to her for the irreparable loss of the companionship which, thanks to Raspoutine, she believed she had succeeded in establishing between herself and the soul of the only man she had ever truly loved.

It is only after having grasped these essential facts in the life of the misguided Empress of Russia that it is possible to come to a reasonable appreciation of her person, character, and intrigues.

Once this has been done, it becomes relatively easy to understand the influence which Raspoutine had acquired over her mind, and not to share the general opinion that there existed something immoral in her relations with him. Immorality alone could not explain this entire submission on the part of a cultured, well-educated, elegant woman to the will of a dirty, uncouth, ignorant peasant. Besides that, Alexandra Feodorowna was far too proud to forget for one moment the social difference which separated her from the "Prophet." In her intercourse with him she remained the Empress, and on his side he was far too shrewd not to remember it also. He knew very well that one indiscreet word, one imprudent gesture, would have put an end at once to his influence, and the man as well as his accomplices were working for far too great and far too important an object to compromise its success by anything which might have savored of immoral intrigue.

The state of health of the little Cesarewitsch also was not the real reason why the latter's mother would not allow Raspoutine to leave her. She believed in the efficacy of his prayers for her son, but this belief alone would not have been sufficient to make her so entirely submissive to his will and to reduce her to the state of slavery into which she had been entranced. No, the secret of Raspoutine's influence lay in the simple fact that, thanks to the hypnotic faculties which he undoubtedly possessed, he had contrived to acquire an absolute dominion over her mind, and to persuade her that every time she prayed with him she was put into direct communication with her dead lover; that this lover had been allowed by the Almighty to come to her help in the troubles and perplexities of her life, to guide her in her conduct as a woman and a mother and in her duties as a Sovereign.

During the hours of agony which followed upon the news of the murder of that man whom she had considered as a holy creature and a real Prophet of God, Alexandra Feodorowna blurted out something of what lay on her mind to her devoted friend and companion, Anna Wyrubewa. The latter had removed from her own house to the Palace of Tsarskoye Selo, so as to be able to remain in constant attendance on the miserable Empress. Seeing her so forlorn and desolate, she bethought herself of rousing her faculties, and tried to persuade her that, though she had lost her advisers and counselors, she had yet a duty to perform, which consisted in going on with the work they had suggested to her to start. Peace was more than ever necessary to Russia, as well as to the dynasty, against which such fierce attacks were being launched. The sacred principles of autocracy that were being everywhere challenged ought to be

THE CESAREWITSCH

maintained, and how could this be done when the army which was the only force on which the Czar could rely was being kept at the frontier and uselessly butchered in battles it could not by any possibility win? There were other mothers besides herself in Russia who were crying over their dead sons and appealing to her to spare those who were still left to them. This war was a monstrous crime against humanity, as well as against the whole of the Russian nation. It must be stopped because otherwise worse calamities even than those that had already fallen on the country would occur. The performance of a duty was sometimes painful, but this ought not to prevent any right-minded person from trying to accomplish it. It was quite evident that the duty of the Empress required her to work toward the conclusion of peace with Germany, and this had been already suggested to her not only by the devoted friends she still had in the world, but by the spirit of the dead ones who had loved and honored her while they had been alive on earth.

Whether Anna Wyrubewa was sincere or not in thus pleading a cause which she knew her Imperial mistress had but too much at heart even without her interference, I shall not attempt to guess. Russia was most certainly going through a terrible crisis, and those who thought that the quick conclusion of a peace after which so many were secretly longing and sighing was indispensable were by no means a small minority in the country. It is quite likely that the Empress's confidante was sincere in her conduct, and it seems pretty certain that she had no pecuniary or material advantages in view when she lent herself to the dangerous scheme suggested to her by Sturmer and the latter's accomplices. *They* were not disinter-ested; they had decidedly ambitious views as to their own future, and they were most certainly in the employ of Germany, to which they had promised their co-operation. Protopopoff was a man who, in regard to the large fortune he was credited with possessing, was entirely self-made; he had never shown any hesitation as to the choice of the means by which he had acquired it. Sturmer thought himself endowed with the genius of a Bismarck or of a Richelieu, and dreamed of the glory of a peace that would leave Russia in appearance as strong as ever, but united by the closest of ties to the German Empire, of which he had been all through his political career a devoted admirer and servant. He had always preached the necessity of the renewal of the former alliance that in bygone times had united the Hohenzollerns and the Romanoffs. His vanity felt deeply flattered upon hearing from his friends in Berlin that the Kaiser, as well as the latter's Government, considered him the one great Minister Russia had ever possessed and were looking up to him to heal all the evils and all the miseries which the war had brought about. He did not care for the treaties that had been signed between Russia and her Allies, and probably shared the opinion of Mr. von Bethmann-Hollweg that all such documents were nothing but scraps of paper, not worthy of any notice on the part of intelligent people. He cared only for success, for titles, decorations, power, and a crowd of flatterers about him. Russia had ceased to be for him a matter for consideration. She would always fare well, in his opinion, if only he were allowed to direct her destinies. The war itself, with all the terrible breakage it had brought about, did not trouble him. It had begun with broken treaties and broken faith, broken honor and broken word; its result had been broken houses in broken lands, broken men, and broken hearts, but about these last Mr. Sturmer did not think at all.

And what about the third personage in this sinister tragedy? What about Manassavitch-Maniuloff, who had been all along the *Deus ex machina* of this dark intrigue, and the chief spy and accomplice of William II.? It was he who had engineered the conspiracy for peace which was being carried on by the Empress under his supervision. It was he who had been the real creator of the Raspoutine legend, and he was perhaps the one who at first suffered the most through the collapse of the adventurer. When the "Prophet" was murdered, Maniuloff was in prison under the accusation of blackmail. Once before he had escaped a trial that had been post-poned on the personal order of Nicholas II. addressed to the president of the court. But after Raspoutine's disappearance the influence of Sturmer alone had not been able to help him. He was sent before a jury and sentenced to two years' penal servitude, which, however, he was never to undergo. The man had more than one arrow to his bow, and when the Revolution broke out he contrived to let Kerensky know that he could put at his disposal most incriminating documents in regard to the part played by the Empress in the peace negotiations which had taken place in the preceding February between Petrograd and Berlin. The bait probably took, because the spy who had for a long number of years cheated everybody was sent across the frontier to expiate his sins and most probably to go on for the benefit of the new masters of Russia with the nefarious game he had been playing in regard to all those who had had the misfortune to employ him.

After Sturmer had been compelled to resign his position of Prime Minister and leader of the Foreign Office he had, nevertheless, remained, as I have had already the occasion to tell, in close relations with the Court and with the Emperor and Empress. He had acquired a new ally in the person of the Metropolitan of Petrograd, Monseigneur Pitirim, a friend and favorite of Raspoutine, who now came to offer his consolations to the half-distracted Alexandra, and who also told her that it was henceforward her duty to go on doing all that the dead "Prophet" had suggested to her, no matter how much it might cost her. Between his preachings, the advice of Sturmer and Protopopoff, and the adjurations of Anna Wyrubewa, the Empress was at last persuaded to forget for a while the deep grief into which she had allowed herself to fall and to resume her political activity. But when she attempted to influence the Czar to approve of what she was about to do she found, to her surprise, that he did not show the same enthusiasm for her schemes as he had done before.

What had happened was this: The Imperial Family had once more tried to open the eyes of the Sovereign as to the folly of his wife's conduct. Nearly all the Grand Dukes and Grand Duchesses in Petrograd had sought his presence in succession, implored him to save the dynasty before it was too late, and to call together a responsible Ministry, chosen from among the men who had the confidence of the country and who represented it in the Duma. Their remonstrances had not convinced Nicholas II., but they had caused him to pause before consenting to the conclusion of a peace with Germany, which he began to fear he would not have the power or the strength to impose upon public opinion in Russia. He believed in his wife, and he felt convinced that she was the only disinter-rested friend left to him; at the same time he could not make up his mind to take a decision which—this much he knew—would be deeply resented by his Allies as well as by his own subjects. In his perplexity he preferred to wait for events to develop themselves in one sense or in the other, totally oblivious of the fact that there are periods in the life of nations when waiting is also a crime.

And while this struggle was going on in his mind, that of his wife was becoming more and more the prey of the evil advisers who had secured her sympathies and were abusing her confidence. They were becoming bolder and bolder as time went on, and at last they suggested to her to urge upon the Czar the necessity of returning to the front, where, they told her, he could come to a better understand-ding of the feelings of the army and be at last convinced that it was, like the rest of Russia, only longing for peace. Nicholas caught eagerly at the suggestion and departed, leaving the Empress mistress of the field and free to do what she liked, together with her friends.

METROPOLITAN PITIRIM (OKNOV PAVEL VASILIEVICH)
17th Metropolitan of Petrograd and Ladoga
b.1958 - d.1920

Rasputin's influence on the Russian Orthodox Church through the Imperial Court meant that he controlled the Holy Synod. The Bishops opposed him but to no avail and this led to the exile of several bishops to Crimea or Siberia. It was in this way that the existing Metropolitan of Petrograd and Ladoga from 1912 to 1915, Vladimir Bogoyavlensky, who had been criticising Rasputin, found himself extricated to Kiev and replaced with Pitirim, a Rasputin supporter. Bogoyavlensky was killed by the advancing Bolsheviks in to Crimea in 1918.

XXIV

YOU MUST BECOME THE EMPRESS

WHEN the Czar left Tsarskoye Selo—for the last time, as it turned out, as a powerful, dreaded Sovereign—the Empress had not yet made up her mind as to what she ought to do. She was being urged by Sturmer and Protopopoff to come to a decision in regard to the future of the dynasty, which they declared to her was entirely in her hands; at the same time she lacked the moral courage to put herself boldly at the head of a movement to dethrone her husband. She had not the audacity of Catherine the Great, nor the latter's unscrupulousness, and, moreover, her mind was so weakened by the superstitious practices in which she had become absorbed that it is to be questioned whether or not she was given a true account of what was going on around her. She was entirely at the mercy of the first determined man who came along, audacious enough to compel her to sing according to his tune. But neither Sturmer nor Protopopoff were clever enough to be that. And they had no political party on whom they could rely to help them execute any plans they might form. They depended for their inspiration on the directions which they received from Berlin. By a lucky accident this inspiration failed them at the very moment they most needed it.

What had happened was this: The Allies had begun to get some inkling as to the intrigue which was going on under the Czar's own roof, an intrigue in which his wife held the foremost rôle. They contrived to put obstacles in the way of Mr. Protopopoff and of his friends, and to stop for a while the active correspondence which he was carrying on with the German Government *via* Stockholm. At the same time they arranged matters in such a way that the liberal leaders in the Duma became apprised of the negotiations pending between the Kaiser and his kinswoman at Tsarskoye Selo.

The story of the eventful days which preceded the Revolution have nothing to do with the present book, and I shall refer to them only in so far as they concern the Empress. She was mostly responsible for the rapidity with which rebellion spread and for the unexpected way in which it broke out. Had she remained quiet, it is likely that things might have dragged on for a few weeks, perhaps even for a few months, longer, because no one at this particular moment cared to see a change in the Government. But when it was ascertained that she had become a danger to the nation in general there was no longer any question of a delay, and events had to be forced on in some way or other.

What Sturmer proposed to the Czarina was to provoke a movement against the war in the garrisons of Petrograd and the towns in its neighborhood; this to be further accentuated by false news concerning the Czar, who would be represented as having died suddenly. The Government had at its disposal all the telegraph and telephone wires. It was, therefore, an easy matter to cut off the capital from all communication with the headquarters of the army. In the confusion inseparable from the consternation caused by the news of the Sovereign's demise it would have been but a matter of a few hours to get the little Grand Duke Alexis proclaimed Emperor under the Regency of his mother, who would thus have been left free to sign a peace which nothing and no treaty prevented *her* from concluding. Nicholas would be easily persuaded to accept accomplished facts and most likely would surrender with pleasure, or at least with absolute indifference, a Throne he had never cared for. So they thought that an act of formal abdication would not be difficult to obtain from him.

The country also would not feel sorry to be rid of a Monarch who had never been in possession of its affection or respect, and the army, glad to return to its homes, would most likely rally with alacrity around the Regent and the little Czar. The very fact that it was a woman and a delicate child upon whom the whole burden of an immense responsibility had fallen would predispose public opinion in their favor, and most likely this Palace revolution would end with complete success.

The Empress allowed herself to be won over to the conspiracy, and it was decided to put it into execution about the middle of the month of February. Protopopoff declared that he required that much time to gather together a sufficient number of police agents in Petrograd, without whom he did not dare to risk the adventure. Alexandra Feodorowna assented to everything that was proposed to her. She went about like one in a dream, unconscious of the abominable plot in which she had been induced to participate, thinking only of the time when she would be able at last to renew with her own family and with her own people the tender and intimate relations which the war had forcibly interrupted.

In the mean time the Emperor remained at the front, and if we are to believe all that was subsequently related about his conduct there, he changed considerably his opinion and point of view after having resumed direct contact with his troops. He convinced himself that they were not at all as anxious for peace as he had been led to expect, and that the feelings of the men in regard to Germany were revengeful more than anything else. His generals, and especially Aléxieieff, who was Head of the Staff, kept urging upon him the necessity of preparing a formidable offensive, this time on the Riga front. The General gave him hopes that it would turn out to be a successful one, provided (and this was the one everlasting and burning question) that the War Office sent sufficient ammunition to the front. The Emperor was persuaded that this could be done, but Aléxieieff was not so sanguine, and he started a private inquiry of his own as to what was going on in Petrograd in that respect. The result of it was that he was convinced that the Ministry had lately completely neglected this important item and had spent its time in arresting workmen whom it suspected of harboring democratic opinions, as well as in curtailing the hours of labor at the different factories where ammunition was manufactured. Protopopoff wanted the war to end, and he hoped that in limiting the output of shells and guns he would be able to place the country in such a position that a cessation of hostilities would become unavoidable.

A report to the Emperor, in which the situation such as it presented itself was exposed with great details, was brought to him by the Staff. As usual, it left him unmoved. He merely said that he would give orders to the War Office to take henceforward its orders from the Commander-in-chief of the Armies in the Field, meaning himself, but he refused to blame Protopopoff or to hear anything concerning the appointment of a liberal and responsible Cabinet from whom the Duma could require accounts. He did not mean to lessen his own prerogatives by the merest fraction, and he still thought that Russia might hold its own against her formidable foes without arms, provisions, shells, or big guns, and in general without means of defense capable of stopping the progress of the invaders in their triumphal march through his Empire.

The commanders of the different fronts held a consultation, and one of them, whose name I cannot mention at the present moment, first suggested the idea that it would not be a bad thing to try and bring about a military conspiracy which would overthrow the weak Monarch whom it was impossible to bring to take a sane view of the position in which the army found itself placed. Another general suggested that such an upheaval would only bring to the foreground the personality of the Empress, who would insist on being consulted in all matters in which the welfare of her son might be concerned. And no one wanted Alexandra Feodorowna to be raised to a position in which her voice might come to exercise an influence of any kind on the destinies of the country. It was by far preferable to let Nicholas II. remain where he was, and try to persuade him to allow the Staff, instead of the Cabinet, to have the last word to say in all questions connected with the national defense.

This secret, or rather not secret, conference, because its purport became known on the very same day it took place, thus accomplished nothing. In the mean while the object of its deliberations was communicated to the Ministry in Petrograd, and Protopopoff triumphantly informed the Empress of the fact that it had come to almost the same conclusions which he and his friends had arrived at long before. It was necessary to change the person of the Sovereign. He carefully refrained, however, from acquainting her with the knowledge of the opposition that the idea of a Regency had provoked.

It is a curious but certain fact that at this very time large sums of money were distributed to the troops quartered in Petrograd, Tsarskoye Selo, Peterhof, and Gatschina by unknown people in the name of the Empress. The latter declared, later on, when questioned on the subject by the Provisional Government, that she had known nothing about it; certainly it had not been her money which had been scattered about with such reckless generosity. I believe that in saying so she spoke the absolute truth. But then the question arises, by whose orders was this money thrown into the arena of the battle-field, where the fate of a nation and of a dynasty was about to be decided? Some people have declared that it was Protopopoff together with Sturmer who had hit upon the idea of making Alexandra Feodorowna popular among the army by appearances of a generosity with which no one had credited her before. But against this theory comes the probability that if either of the above mentioned gentlemen had been able to draw from the Treasury several millions of rubles to be applied to secret purposes, they would have begun by putting them into their own pockets and trusting to the future and to Providence for the success of any enterprise they embarked upon. Therefore the question arises again as to the origin of this money which was circulated with such a generous hand among the regiments considered as likely to lend themselves to a Palace revolution in favor of the delicate little boy who was the sole Heir to all the glory and the splendor of the Romanoffs.

I think that very few people, among those who knew how vital was Germany's interest at this particular moment to see a peace concluded, will doubt whence came these funds. They were certainly spent to favor the appointment of the Czarina as Regent of the Russian Empire. Who had procured them for the benefit of a vast conspiracy, the object of which was to deliver Russia, bound hand and foot, to the tender mercies of her formidable neighbor and enemy?

On the other hand, the liberal parties, now thoroughly awakened to the dangers of the situation, were also working earnestly toward the defeat of the plans conceived by Messrs. Sturmer, Protopopoff & Co. Several meetings of the leaders of the different factions in the Duma took place at the Tauride Palace, but none seemed to come to anything serious in the way of a revolution, which had been by that time recognized as absolutely inevitable.

The Cabinet saw this hesitation, and would undoubtedly have struck a serious blow at its adversaries if, just at the time, the children of the Empress had not sickened from the measles in a serious form. The mother forgot all her political intrigues in her anxiety; the plot about to be executed had perforce to be put off until a more favorable day. It must be here remarked that the Czar, when he heard about his son's and daughters' illness, telegraphed to his wife asking her whether she wished him to come back to Tsarskoye Selo. This did not suit in the least the people who were only waiting for a favorable opportunity to dethrone their Sovereign. Alexandra Feodorowna was easily persuaded to oppose herself to this desire of her husband and to wire back to him not to return. By a singular coincidence the presence of Nicholas II. at Tsarskoye Selo, which would without doubt have given quite another coloring to events which were going to happen within a few days, was desired neither by his friends nor by his foes nor even by his family. They all of them knew that something terrible was about to take place, but they also felt that, for the sake of everybody, it would be better he should be absent.

And in the silence of his study at Potsdam the Kaiser was secretly discounting this Russian Revolution which he saw quite clearly was approaching with quickening strides. He knew what he was about, and little did it matter to him if those whom he had used as pawns in the difficult game he had been playing would perish or not in the storm which his efforts had contributed to let loose.

ALEXANDER DMITRIEVICH PROTOPOPOFF
INTERIOR MINISTER (September 1916 – February 1917)

XXV

THE NATION WANTS YOUR HEAD

I FEEL personally sure—and others who were in Petrograd at the time of the fall of the Romanoffs told me the same thing—that in this whole history of the overthrow of one of the most formidable powers the world had ever known there are yet details which we do not know. In fact, no one knows them, but perhaps they will be explained to us later on. The catastrophe occurred with such startling rapidity that even those who were the most concerned in it were hardly able to realize its importance, even while recognizing its seriousness.

There is also another curious feature connected with the tragedy. All its principal actors, the men who were really instrumental in bringing about the change which transformed Russia from an autocratic—the most autocratic Government in the world, in fact—into a democratic Republic disappeared before even their task was done. It was the Duma in the person of its president, Mr. Rodzianko, it was the zemstwos who had taken up the cause of the liberal movement from the very beginning of the war, who really were responsible for the abdication of Nicholas II. And yet the Duma disappeared, melted into space with an unbelievable rapidity; Mr. Rodzianko has hardly been heard of since the activity of the zemstwos was suddenly interrupted.

How did all this happen? Who was responsible for the chaos into which Russia is plunged at the present moment? It is next to impossible to say to-day, though one may easily guess. All that the world knows is that chaos has supervened, and that, thanks to this chaos, Germans have once more re-entered Petrograd, by the back door, perhaps, but still re-entered it, and what does this detail matter to them! What they wanted was only to get there again; the rest would adjust itself as time went on, and the general confusion became even more complete than it was at the beginning.

Another feature in this extraordinary Revolution was the swiftness with which the country accepted it and accommodated itself to its consequences. In the space of a few hours the portraits of the Czar had disappeared from all public places, the Imperial arms, wherever these had graced a shop or concern of some kind, had followed suit. Ushers in the former Imperial theaters had discarded their liveries, sentinels at the Winter Palace had been removed, and the Red flag had taken the place of the Romanoff standard on top of the Imperial Residence. All this had been performed quietly, joyously, and in a perfectly orderly manner. It seemed almost as if people had been prepared for a long time for what was to come and had practised beforehand the various manifestations of their joy to which they gave vent as soon as it became known that the Guard regiments quartered in the capital had gone over to the Duma and sworn allegiance to Mr. Rodzianko, its president.

Of the war there was no longer any question. It seemed to be forgotten in the excitement of the hour, and somehow a general impression prevailed that, once the Czar had been overturned, peace was but a question of days. By one of those strange anomalies such as happen so often in life, the Czar had been accused of wishing to bring this peace about; yet when he was no longer there the world rejoiced at the thought that peace would surely be concluded before any unreasonable quantity of water had run through the Neva. It is also a singular feature of this singular time that while Petrograd was in the throes of revolution, while Ministers with Mr. Protopopoff at their head were being arrested and transferred to the fortress, the Czar at headquarters and the Empress at Tsarskoye Selo did not in the least suspect what was taking place in the capital. It was said later that the Grand Duke Paul had forced his way into the apartments of Alexandra Feodorowna and had acquainted her with the details of the upheaval which was to carry away her Throne.

I can hardly bring myself to believe this. For one thing, no one in the Imperial Family cared sufficiently for the Czarina to take the trouble to warn her of any peril in which she might find herself. And then she had not been upon good terms with the Grand Duke Paul in particular; it is to be questioned if she would, in view of the fact that it was his son who had helped to slay Raspoutine, have consented to receive him in general. I think it far more likely that it was only through the indiscretion of some of her attendants that the Empress heard of what was taking place. It is probable her first thought was that her friends had been working in her behalf, and that the insurrectionary movement which was shaking Petrograd was distinctly in her favor; that its aim was to make out of her the Regent of the Russian Empire.

It would be difficult, otherwise, to understand her apathy in the presence of this overwhelming catastrophe, or the resistance which she opposed to the advice which the few attendants who were still faithful to her and who had remained at Tsarskoye Selo, gave to her—to telegraph immediately to the Czar to return home. Up to the last minute she refused to do so, saying that she felt quite capable of resisting the mob in case it chose to invade the Imperial Residence. And at last it was not she, but the officer in command of the troops quartered in the town, who took it upon himself to inform General Woyeikoff, head of the Okhrana, or personal police service of the Czar, that it was high time for the Sovereign to return home, as he could no longer guarantee the safety of the Empress and of her children. All the regiments under his orders had gone over to the enemy.

Alexandra Feodorowna was waiting the whole time for Protopopoff and Sturmer; she was only wondering why they were so long in coming to her. When at last she was informed that they had been arrested by the mob and taken to the fortress, whither they had sent so many innocent people, she began to realize that things were not going so smoothly as she had fondly imagined, that something quite out of the common had taken place. Then she remembered certain words which Raspoutine had told her: so long as he was at her side no harm would befall her, but that, if he were once removed, misfortune upon misfortune would crowd on the House of Romanoff and sweep away the Crown to which she had become so attached.

In that acute moment when there flashed across her mind this prediction of a man in whom she had seen a Prophet of the Almighty, and the Empress realized the tragedy of her destiny, all the courage of which she had boasted earlier fell flat to the ground. She no longer thought of struggling against an implacable fate, and a complete indifference as to her possible future took the place of her previous energy and determination. The game was lost, absolutely lost, and she had better confess herself beaten before any more harm was done.

News of her husband's abdication reached her, and did not even rouse her sentiments of revolt at a piece of weakness which, under different circumstances, would have brought on one of those hysterical attacks to which she had been subject. She understood that she was alone, quite alone with the burden of her past sins and mistakes.

She accepted with stoical resignation the decrees of Destiny. Not one single feeling of pity for the miserable Monarch for whose fall she was so responsible, or for the children about to lose a glorious inheritance, moved her heart. She was thinking the whole time of the dead man who had loved her and of the murder-ed adventurer who had comforted her in the hours of her greatest moral agony.

Nothing seemed to make any impression on her blurred mind—not even the angry crowd when it appeared in the courtyard of the Palace where she was still staying, carrying before it great banners upon which were written the ominous words:

"Give us the head of Alexandra Feodorowna! We want the head of that German woman, Alexandra Feodorowna!"

When asked to leave the window and not to appear before this multitude clamoring for her blood, she merely shrugged her shoulders and remained where she was. She certainly was not courageous, but she did not lack bravery—the bravery born of fatalism or of indifference, which renders those who are endowed with it impassible before danger, because they fail to realize its importance or its imminence. This woman is a historical riddle which only history will be able to unravel, but not so soon as one imagines, because it is likely that she has not yet come to the end of her sinister and mischiefvous career.

While the life of his wife was threatened, while his Ministers were imprisoned, and while the nation was preparing to claim his abdication, Nicholas II., at Mohilew, where headquarters were stationed, remained just as indifferent to the convulsions which were shaking his country as the Empress watching by the bedside of her sick children. He also did not understand; he also failed to realize that what was taking place in Petrograd was the first act of a big game the stakes of which might easily come to be his own head and those of his family. The thought of Louis XVI. never once crossed his mind. At least it is allowed one to suppose so, because, when some officers of his suite remarked to him that the rebellion (the news of which had by that time reached him) bore many traits of resemblance to the premonitory riots that had heralded the introduction of the Terror in France, he simply replied:

"Oh, it is not at all the same thing. Russians are not Frenchmen—and the Romanoffs are not the Bourbons."

The Czar might at this early stage of the Revolution have returned to Tsarskoye Selo if he had only energetically insisted upon doing so. But he spent three days in complete indecision, and when at last he made up his mind to go home it was too late. By that time General Aléxieieff had been won over to the cause of the Duma, which was supposed to represent the only responsible authority in Russia; he put every possible obstacle in his way, going so far as to interfere with the arrangements made by General Woyeikoff for the departure of the Imperial train. It seems also that he sent telegrams asking for this train to be either stopped or at least delayed on its way.

No one at this stage wished Nicholas II. to go back to Petrograd, where it was feared his presence would prevent, if not stop, the establishment of the new Government; a useless fear, because, even if he had reached his former capital, he would never have found sufficient courage or energy to fight against an adverse fate or to do aught else but submit to the will of the multitude eager for his fall. The man who signed without one word of protest an abdication against which his whole soul ought to have protested, such a man was not to be feared, he could only be despised.

This was also the feeling which the whole nation began to entertain for him. People had pitied him in the beginning, but as the details of his conduct at Pskow became known, contempt took the place of any commiseration which the tragedy of his fate might have provoked. This opinion was so general that a friend of mine happening to discuss with one of the Deputies of the Workmen in those Soviets which were being organized just then the conduct of the former Czar, asked if he thought it likely the life of the deposed ruler was in danger. He received this characteristic reply:

"In danger? No. He is not worth a shot."

It is likely that the Empress, if she had been asked her opinion, would have agreed with this judgment. Though she had also thrown up her hands and renounced the game, she would not have given up her rights to the Crown that had been put upon her brow with such pomp and ceremony at Moscow twenty-one years before. She would have fought against the insolence of those who had come to demand it from her. Here I must say that, according to the words of one of the two Deputies sent by the Duma to interview Nicholas II. at Pskow, the prestige of the latter's personality as the anointed Czar of All the Russias was still so great that if he had mustered sufficient energy to throw out of the railway carriage the men audacious enough to claim his abdication, this gesture of Imperial rage would have brought back to him the allegiance of the troops. He was living through a terrible drama, and he was accepting it like a comedy. After having disgraced himself, he was dishonoring by his attitude the misfortunes which had fallen on his country, on his dynasty, and on his race.

MIKHAIL VLADIMIROVICH RODZIANKO
CHAIRMAN OF THE FIFTH DUMA

XXVI

A CROWN IS LOST

THE Monarchy of the Romanoffs had fallen like a house of cards which crumbles on the ground at the slightest touch. It had been considered one of the strongest, one of the most powerful, in Europe; yet its collapse had come with an amazing promptitude and there had not been found in the whole vast Empire over which it had ruled one single man or woman willing to arrest its downward course toward the abyss into which it finally disappeared. What the tyranny of Nicholas I., the selfishness of Alexander II., and the iron rule of Alexander III. had failed to produce, the weakness, indecision, and incapacity of Nicholas II. had made easy. What a German Princess, Catherine II., had maintained, another German Princess compromised and lost forever.

Without wishing to add to the faults and mistakes of Alexandra Feodorowna, it is nevertheless quite impossible to acquit her of blame in the catastrophe which finally wrecked poor, unfortunate Russia. Without her it is likely that the Crown would have kept some prestige, at least in the eyes of those whose family traditions were linked with the fate of the Monarchy in their country. She destroyed this prestige by the singularity of her conduct, the want of balance of her mind, and her proud, haughty, and totally false conception of the Russian character. She firmly believed that nothing she could do would be criticized and that even those who disliked her, whose number was legion, as she knew very well, would never dare to question her right to do whatever she pleased, or to choose her friends no matter in what circles or among what kind of people.

This woman, whom misfortune associated with the fate of the House of Romanoff at the very time when the latter ought to have had the aid of an intelligent, well-intentioned, and unselfish Princess to help it face the dangers which were threatening it, had never known how to put herself at the level of the persons by whom she found herself surrounded. She lacked not only tact, but also generosity, and she never could hold broad views about anything or about anybody. She was as scathing as she was hasty in her judgments.

From the very first day she was raised to the Throne of Russia she abused the privileges which her position conferred upon her, and either through stupidity—or willingly—because of her dislike for the nation whose Crown she wore, she applied herself to wound those whom she ought to have spared and to propitiate persons whom it would have been imperative for her to keep away as far as possible from her person and from that of her husband.

Of course she was in a certain sense a strong character, in so far, at least, as she never would yield to reason or accept any compromise. She had principles of her own, which, however, did not help her to win respect for herself or esteem for her conduct. Without ever allowing herself to be led by impulse, she failed to perceive that in most of her actions she was influenced by superstition of a most foolish kind. The fact that insanity existed in her family may excuse her to a certain point, but should not blind us to faults which might easily have been corrected had she only realized their existence.

She was a blameless wife; about this there cannot be any doubt. But she never loved her husband and she only cared for his position. She was a tender mother, at least to her son, whatever may have been her feelings in regard to her daughters, whom she most unjustly blamed for their sex, if we are to believe all that we have been told on the subject. But she lacked sympathy, which she never could give to others or win for herself. She was a cold, ambitious, stern creature, so convinced of her own perfection that she never could be brought to see good in anything with which she was not connected in some way or other. Her life certainly had tragedy entwined with its course. Perhaps the most cruel blow, until the final catastrophe that wrecked all her hopes, had been her unfortunate affection for the dashing officer, Colonel Orloff, who had died to save her honor and good name, whose post-mortem influence had been so cleverly made use of by unscrupulous adventurers in order to win her confidence. Alexandra had always at heart despised the weak man to whom she was married, but she had loved the high position which, thanks to her union with him, she had acquired; she would have liked to remain alone in control of it and to revenge her supposed wrongs at the hands of the Russian nation, by delivering it into the power of that German Fatherland of hers to which she had always remained attached. Her desire for peace was sincere (at least we must hope so), and everything we know about her and about her conduct during that momentous time when she kept working toward its conclusion points to the truth of this supposition. It had all along been a terrible trial for her to find the land of her birth at war with that of her adoption, and to this initial agony was added the superstitious terror which Raspoutine had inspired in her, thanks to the hypnotic practices in which he had induced her to participate—terror which ended by completely wrecking her already badly balanced mind.

But the supreme misfortune of the last Empress of Russia, a misfortune for which she was not responsible, was the fact of her having been married to a being who was too weak to lead her, too selfish to understand her, too cruelly inclined to sympathize with her; who at the same time did not acquire sufficient authority over her to inspire her with respect for his individuality as a man and for his position as a Sovereign. Had she been the wife of Alexander III., it is likely that she would have turned out entirely another woman from the one which she ultimately became; on the other hand, had Nicholas II. had for Consort a person different from the one to whom destiny had linked him, it is also probable that he would have contrived to avoid some of the mistakes into which he fell. He might have shown himself more plucky and more human in the different moments of crisis which made his reign such a sad and such an unfortunate one.

One of the most tragical things with which a student of history finds himself confronted when he analyzes any of the great catastrophes that come to change the fate of nations is the total insufficiency of the people who have to meet them or to handle them. There is no more pitiful spectacle than the vacillations of Louis XVI. during the first days of the great Revolution which sent him to the scaffold. Witness the want of character of the miserable Czar who is meditating at present in Tobolsk over the misfortunes that have landed him into exile; it is another of those sights one should have liked to see spared to posterity. During the twenty-two years he occupied the Russian Throne Nicholas II. constantly opposed himself to the wishes of his people, even the most reasonable ones, when he thought that they implied any diminution of his personal prerogatives or power. He sent hundreds of thousands of innocent people to the gallows or to horrible Siberian prisons under the slightest of pretexts. He had no hesitation at spilling the blood of his subjects either on the battle-field or on the scaffold. He allowed the detestable police system, which became, under his rule, stronger than it had ever been before, to interfere with private liberty and private opinions to an extent that had never been witnessed in his country even in the times of Nicholas I. or of Paul. While he reigned no one felt secure in his home or could go to bed with the consciousness that he would not be wakened in the middle of the night by an army of police agents come to search his drawers, or to arrest him under the most futile of pretexts or simply because he had refused to pay a bribe. And yet that man in whose name the most terrible injustices had been committed, who did not admit any resistance to his will, who believed in his unlimited power over one hundred and eighty millions of human beings—that man did not find sufficient courage to resist the only demand, among the many which were addressed to him during the course of his nefarious reign, that he ought never to have granted; and without one single thought of the future of his country or of his son he gave up without a murmur the Crown of which he was the bearer, when two determined men came to claim it from him, and he did so without even noticing that they were far more awed by the solemnity of the scene in which they found themselves unwilling actors than he was himself.

There never was a Throne relinquished with less dignity, there never was an act of abdication accomplished with less consciousness of the importance of its meaning. When one recapitulates all the details of the drama which was performed at Pskow, one can, when one is a Russian, feel but one passionate regret—that no one was found by the side of the last crowned Romanoff to drive a knife into his heart or put a bullet through his brain, and thus spare this haughty dynasty the shame of having been dragged into the gutter by its Head.

It is scarcely to be doubted that if Nicholas II. had only given more thought to the importance of the act he was invited to perform he might at least have saved his dynasty, if not himself. His brother, the Grand Duke Michael, who could easily renounce the Crown for himself, would hardly have been able to refuse the Regency on behalf of his little nephew. A man with the slightest political knowledge would have put the interests of his country before his own selfish feelings of paternal affection, and the Czar ought to have abdicated in favor of his son, and not have put forward this stupid pretext of lacking the courage to part from him. This very remark proves how little he understood the situation in which he found himself. It also shows us how utterly helpless he was when confronted by any difficulties of an overpowering and potential character. When one considers his whole conduct during those eventful hours when he lost not only his own, but his posterity's, Crown, it is impossible not to wonder as to whether or not there was any truth in the rumor that the Empress had been giving him drugs of some kind with the purpose of annihilating his will. It seems almost incredible that any man should have so quietly and so spontaneously lent a hand to his own degradation.

It is to be doubted, also, whether he regretted what he had done. Certainly he never imagined to what it would lead him. The idea that his people would have the courage to make him a prisoner does not seem to have crossed his mind, any more than did the fact that, once he had lost his position, he had become not only a useless, but an embarrassing factor in Russian politics. He went back to Mohilew, to the headquarters of that army of which he had been the Commander-in-chief as well as the Sovereign, quite naturally and in the same quiet manner he might have done in the days gone by. He did not even seem to yearn after his wife and children, and never once did he suggest the advisability of returning to Tsarskoye Selo. Of all the people assembled around him he appeared the most unconcerned. This indifference lasted even when he found himself faced with captivity and when the former Head of his Staff, General Aléxieieff, came to acquaint him with the decision of the Provisional Government to arrest him.

His wife, left alone in the Palace where she had spent so many happy days, did not perhaps share his indifference; she certainly displayed the same apathy. Alexandra Feodorowna, from the moment that she saw her schemes of personal grandeur frustrated, gave up the game; she gave it up with more dignity than her husband had ever shown—this much must be conceded to her. She never flinched before the insults that were poured down upon her; she never gave a sign that she was moved to anything else but disdain when General Korniloff read to her the orders of the Government in regard to her person, and acquainted her with the fact that she was a prisoner. She declared to the few people left with her that she considered herself only as a Sister of Charity in attendance on her sick children. The Empress had disappeared, outwardly at least, and perhaps it was just as well that she accepted the situation in this way, rather than attempt a useless resistance, which could only have added to her unpopularity.

But still the fact remained that the whole Russian Revolution had been conducted after the style of a comic opera of Offenbach. No one at first had recognized its serious character. No one had seemed to realize that it constituted the most portentous event of the last hundred years or so. Those who had carried it out had done it on the spur of the moment, without thinking of what would follow; and the Monarch who had bowed his head under its decrees also had not suspected that a morrow was there, waiting for the results of what was being done to-day. The historical stick that had been wielded by Peter the Great had been transformed into the ridiculous sword of the Grand Duchess of Gerolstein.

LA GRANDE DUCHESSE DE GÉROLSTEIN
An opéra bouffe in three acts and the greatest success of Offenbach's career. Originally banned in France after the Franco-Prussian War.

XXVII

A PRISONER AFTER HAVING BEEN A QUEEN

A NEW life began for Alexandra Feodorowna. Until that fatal day when she was taken into captivity her existence had been one of ease and luxury. She had been the Empress of All the Russias, being revered by some as almost a divinity, the absolute mistress of all her surroundings, with servants in attendance on her, eager to execute any commands it might please her to lay upon them. She had not a wish which was not instantly gratified; the misfortunes that had assailed her (I am not speaking now of those that fell upon Russia) had always left her indifferent; they had existed more in her imagination than in reality. Suddenly without warning and, what was even worse, at the very moment when she had expected to reach even loftier heights than the one upon which she was placed, she had been hurled down into an abyss of sorrow, of misery, and of pain such as she had never imagined she could ever know. She was no longer a Sovereign; her courtiers, servants, attendants, had all vanished with the exception of a very few, and those she had never cared for much, in the days of her prosperity. Her children were sick and she could not even obtain for them a doctor's help. Her friends had fled or were in prison; her Crown had been wrested from her; she was a prisoner, deprived of the means of communicating with her own people and relatives; the guards who surrounded her Palace were no longer placed there to protect her safety; they were intrusted with another mission, that of watching over every one of her movements and of preventing her from getting any news from the outside world. Instead of crowds gathered to cheer her, she saw assembled under her windows an angry multitude asking for her blood and calling out to her that she ought to be punished as a traitor. She had no friends, no money, no influence any longer. The dream had come to an end, and she found herself facing stern reality, a reality against which it was useless to struggle.

Her husband came back to her, a prisoner, likewise, but with perhaps less consciousness of the horror of their position than she had. They had to settle down to a new life entirely different from the previous one—a life of idleness, of inaction; an existence which made them realize with every step they took the awful change that had overtaken them. When they wished to go out they had to ask permission to do so from an officer who often refused it out of pure malice. They had to pass before sentinels who no longer presented arms to them, who only sneered in their faces as they saw them hurry through a room or a corridor, anxious to escape insult or outrage. No one was allowed to come near them. They were condemned to a solitude in which they were continually reminded of the days gone by forever.

A few faithful attendants had been left them, it is true, but these last friends were just as badly off as themselves, and could do but very little to alleviate the miseries of a position which was an illustration of the famous verses of Dante, that there is nothing more dreadful during days of misery than to remember the past joyful ones. Even religion, which for such a long period of years had consoled the Empress in many sad and troubled hours, had ceased to be a comfort to her; divine service, during which her name and that of her husband were carefully omitted from the liturgy, was only one new source of torment for her. It seemed to her as if the Church as well as the Russian nation repulsed her and treated her as a pariah and an outcast. Another woman, with higher, loftier views, would have looked with more philosophy on these small sides in a great tragedy, might perhaps even have failed to notice them. But for Alexandra Feodorowna they constituted something far more tangible and real than the fact that the House of Romanoff had lost its Throne.

She would most probably have wished to discuss with the Czar all the events which had brought about the catastrophe, but even this comfort was denied to her. The Provisional Government had issued orders that husband and wife should not be permitted to communicate with or see each other, except in presence of witnesses. Some people have said that this was an unnecessary cruelty, but it seems that there was some reason for this decision. A strong party at that time was clamoring for repressive measures in regard to the ex-Empress. Papers had been found in which her negotiations with the Kaiser had been revealed, and the question of bringing her to trial had been seriously discussed. But no one wished to see the former Czar mixed up with this business, as it was generally felt it would be a great political mistake to make a martyr out of him.

There was, however, ground to fear that if he were permitted to speak with his wife alone, she would contrive in some way or other to entangle him in her personal intrigues. This Mr. Miliukoff, then Minister for Foreign Affairs, wished to avoid, for reasons of a general political order, and Mr. Kerensky for other ones of a purely personal character. It seems that this leader of the Socialist party in the Duma had, before events had transformed him into a Minister, spoken also with certain agents of the Kaiser who had contrived to remain in the Russian capital. Nicholas II. had friends who, knowing this fact, warned the radical chief that if any harm was done to the former Sovereign his own participation in eventual peace negotiations with the enemy would be exposed. Can one imagine that when Nicholas was told of this fact he only blamed those who had thus attempted to save him, saying that he did not like blackmail of any kind, even when it was performed for his advantage? That man who had been one of the most important political factors of his time was not even shrewd enough to see that it was only politics which could save his life after they had dispossessed him of his Throne.

The Provisional Government, so long as decent men composed it, would have been willing to spare any unnecessary humiliations to the former Czar and his family. Unfortunately, the military men who had been put in charge of the Palace of Tsarskoye Selo and of its inhabitants did not share this opinion, and there is no doubt but that the deposed Monarch was subjected to insult, as well as to all kinds of small and petty annoyances calculated to make him feel bitterly the change in his position. I do not believe personally in the tales which were put into circulation as to his having been hustled about by the soldiers on guard at the castle the day he had returned there a State prisoner from Mohilew, a few short weeks after he had left it a powerful Sovereign. For one thing, his devoted aide-de-camp, Prince Dolgoroukoff, was with him, and he would most certainly have interfered had any violence been used in regard to his master. But the unfortunate Nicholas was made in other ways to drink the cup of humiliation to the dregs.

The troops were told not to salute him; the sentries were forbidden to present arms to him; he was addressed as Colonel Romanoff by his jailers; his letters were opened and his expenses controlled in a searching, insulting manner which must have been terribly bitter for him to bear. Every kind of newspaper containing insults addressed to him or to the Empress were sent to him or put in his way. When

THE ROYAL FAMILY

Seated, from left to right: The Grand-Duchess Marie; the Czarina, with the little Grand-Duke Alexis at her knee; the Czar; the Grand-Duchess Anastasia, the youngest of the four girls. Standing, from left to right: The Grand-Duchess Tatiana, and the Grand-Duchess Olga immediately behind her father.

he went out in the park he was often accosted by people who upbraided him for all the misfortunes that had fallen upon Russia, for which they made him responsible. I do not mention insignificant daily worries, such as the shutting off of the electric light, or of the water-pipes, so that the unfortunate Imperial Family was left without baths, and other small unpleasantnesses of the same kind. These would perhaps not have been noticed if the other ones had not been there to remind the once powerful Czar of All the Russias that he was at the mercy of the subjects whose rights he had not respected and whose cries for freedom he had quenched in blood.

But Nicholas, in the midst of all these miseries, preserved the same impassibility he had displayed when the news of the disasters of Mukden and Tsu Shima had been brought to him, or when he had heard that Warsaw and the long line of fortresses that had defended the Russian frontier on the Niemen and the Vistula had fallen into German hands. He accepted everything with stoicism; he expressed no surprise at the blows which were being hurled at his head. He simply remained indifferent, perhaps because he was too much of a fatalist to rebel, but most probably because he had not yet grasped the real significance of all that was happening to him.

The Empress was not so resigned, in spite of her apparent apathy. She had more reasons to fear for her personal safety than her husband, and she knew very well that in case of a rising of the anarchists in Petrograd she would be the first victim they would claim. This dread led her into another of the mistakes which she was continually perpetrating, the mistake of trying to call to her rescue her German cousin.

According to people whom I have reason to believe exceptionally well informed, she caused certain information to be carried to the Kaiser. In return for this she implored him to try and save her, together with her children. Of course this became known to the Provisional Government, but the latter wished to spare her, partly because it feared that if her new misdeeds were published nothing could save her from the wrath of the public, and it did not wish the Revolution to be dishonored by the murder of a defenseless woman, whatever that woman might have done. But the question of the transfer of Nicholas II. and of his family to a place where he could be guarded more closely than at Tsarskoye Selo was discussed seriously. It is likely that this would have been executed already during the first six weeks which followed upon his abdication if other things had not interfered, and if in rapid succession the men who had taken up the task he had been unable to fulfil had not in their turn disappeared one after the other, making room for Ministers more advanced in their opinions and more devoid of scruples as to the punishment which they believed ought to be inflicted on the former Emperor.

Alexandra Feodorowna had been subjected to a strict examination of her political activity by the military authorities in charge of the district of Petrograd, and particularly by General Korniloff, who had a personal grudge against her and who did not spare her in the scathing reproaches which he addressed to her. But nothing could shake the equanimity of the haughty Czarina. She sneered at the General, she scorned his threats, and proudly declared to him that she would not reply to any of his questions, as she did not recognize his right to address them to her. While her husband showed no sign of impatience under the affronts which were showered down upon him (on the contrary, he exhibited absolute submission to the will of those who had taken him captive), the Empress remembered the position which she had occupied a few days before, and simply smiled at her persecutors with a disdain that had certainly something exasperating about it if one considers the intellectual and moral standard of the people to whom this proof of her contempt was addressed.

Alexandra refused to show that she suffered from the change that had taken place in her position, while her husband hardly knew whether he was suffering from it or not. There lay the difference in their two characters and in their way of meeting the catastrophe which had changed their whole lives and destinies.

There came, however, a day when the composure of the Consort of Nicholas II. failed, when she at last gave way to despair. It was during the afternoon when her friend and the confidante of all her thoughts, Anna Wyrubewa, was taken away from her, and carried off to the fortress of SS. Peter and Paul in Petrograd. Until that day the Empress had not felt quite alone in her misery. There was at least near her one person with whom she could speak about all those dear dead ones whose memory she either cherished or worshiped. So long as that friend was there the miserable Empress could talk about Orloff, Raspoutine, and the prayer-meetings during which the latter evoked for her the spirit of the former. When Anna was taken away from her this last consolation came also to an end. Henceforward the solitude of Alexandra Feodorowna was to be complete; and nothing was left to her except her eyes to weep, and her memory to remind her of those whom she had loved and lost. The horrors which were to follow, the Siberian exile whither she was to be sent, were to leave her unmoved. She had inwardly died in that terrible hour when the last friend and the sharer of all the secrets of her life had been snatched away from her arms.

XXVIII

THE EXILE

THESE days in Tsarskoye Selo which seemed so hard to bear were Paradise compared with what awaited the previous masters of this Imperial place.

Soon there came one August morning when a man who a few months before had been known only as one of the leaders of that Socialist party which the Government of Nicholas II. had taken such trouble to suppress, and whom the tide of events had transformed into one of the Ministers of the new Russian Republic, Alexander Feodorovitch Kerensky, entered, uncalled for and unannounced, into the private apartments of the former Czar, and acquainted him with the new decision to which the Government of the day had come in regard to his person and to the fate of his family. How he did it, how he mustered the courage to inform the fallen Monarch that he was about to be exiled to that distant Siberia, where so many people had been sent during his reign and had gone cursing his name, no one knows. None of the actors in this scene ever revealed its details.

It is probable, however, that Kerensky had experienced far more emotion in signifying to the deposed Sovereign the horrible punishment to which he had been condemned than the latter had displayed when receiving the terrible news, the nature of which must have completely bewildered him. Of all the things he had expected, this was certainly the last. The possibility of a public trial, in imitation of the one of Louis XVI. in France, had been discussed between the Emperor and the Empress, and they had in a certain sense both schooled themselves for such a supreme ordeal. But exile in cold, bleak Siberia, in that land of mystery and of crime, of heroic deeds and ignoble deaths—this solution of the difficulties of a position which was daily growing more threatening had never presented itself to the mind of the last Russian Autocrat. Tobolsk, too! This dreariest spot in a dreary country; this accursed place from which all those who could do so fled away with alacrity! What could have been more awful than to have chosen it as the future residence of a Monarch who, if all was well considered, had by his own act rendered himself impossible as a ruler in the future? No political necessity required his being sent so far and there were many other places where he might have been just as safe, and not quite so unhappy, as in that small Siberian town. Can one wonder if despair took hold of the souls of the unhappy Czar and of his wife? Can one wonder if he exclaimed that he would have preferred to die rather than have to meet such an atrocious fate?

There were his children, too; his innocent children, who had done no harm and who were to share this miserable destiny to which he was condemned. Kerensky had told him that the young Grand Duchesses and their brother would be left free to follow their parents in that distant land whither they were to depart, or to remain in Russia if they preferred. But this was almost adding insult to an abominable injury, because the children could hardly do anything else than decide to accompany their father and mother. Verily nothing was to be spared to Nicholas II., not even the knowledge that his daughters and his idolized boy were about to be exposed to hardships which it was hardly likely they could survive.

Nevertheless, he took the news bravely, and neither he nor Alexandra Feodorowna murmured. The latter is credited with having remarked that the new Government had evidently wanted to please her by sending them to a place that could only be dear to her on account of its associations with Raspoutine, who had been born there. Whether this is exact or not I will not undertake to say. What is true, however, is that she left with dry eyes the place where she had spent so many happy years, and that not even during the religious service, which was celebrated in the private chapel of the Palace, when the blessings of Heaven were invoked in favor of people about to start on a long journey, did she shed a tear. All the other assistants, including her daughters, sobbed passionately and bitterly the whole time that it lasted.

Though the hour of the departure of Nicholas had been kept as secret as possible, the whole town of Tsarskoye Selo knew that he was about to leave it forever. The population for once was awed before the immensity of the disaster. One was used in Russia to people being sent to Siberia; one had seen a Menschikoff, a Biren, a Dolgorouky, and more recently a Prince Troubetskoy, and a Mourawieff-Apostol, start on this dreaded journey whence so few ever returned. But here was something different. Here was a

Romanoff about to go there where his ancestors and himself had deported so many, so many, entirely innocent people. Here was the dreaded Sovereign, whose name had been for such a long time mentioned only with reverence and with fear, exiled like one of those persons whom he had sent to Siberia with a mere stroke of his pen. Here was Nicholas II., formerly Emperor and Autocrat of All the Russias, here was the mighty Czar who had been crowned at Moscow, reduced to the condition of a common criminal by the subjects whose rights he had violated, whose consciences he had trampled upon, whose liberty he had taken away, and whose lives he had in so many instances tried to destroy. Truly the sight was appalling, and there were but few among those who in the early twilight of a summer morning looked at that mournful train which was carrying away toward the distant north so much dead grandeur and such awful misfortune, there were but few who did not realize that they were witnessing something more tragic and more solemn even than a funeral, that they were looking upon the end of a great chapter in Russian history, and that it was not only a Czar who lay buried under all these ruins, but also something of the past glories of the country.

They had been, after all, together with the future of the Romanoff dynasty, a great race that had produced great men and they deserved to have, as their last crowned descendant, some one better than Nicholas II. had proved to be. They had often been cruel, more frequently even unjust; they had never respected what the world is used to venerate and to esteem; they had shown themselves hard in regard to their subjects; but they had made out of dark, ignorant Russia an immense Empire on which even more immense hopes had been built. They had exercised on several occasions a restraining influence over the exaggerations of half-educated and half-instructed men with all the instincts of the savage and but few of the qualities of the civilized being. They had led their people through danger, through war, through many momentous days of rejoicing as well as of anguish. They had been a part of the Russian nation, and with their disgrace and fall something in that nation, too, had been dishonored and had perished.

With the personal failure of Nicholas II. this book has nothing to do. From the very first day that he had ascended the Throne of Russia it had been evident to any person gifted with the talent of observation that his reign was bound to end in disaster and in ruin;

that all the work performed by his late father, who, after all, when things are well considered, had been a great man and a wise Sovereign, would very soon be destroyed by his want of character and of principle and by his abominable selfishness. People, however, had hoped that during the years supreme power remained concentrated in his hands at least blood would not flow. No one's imagination had conceived the horrors of Mukden and of Tsu Shima, nor the massacres which took place at Tannenberg and in the Polish plains. No one had suspected that the rivers would be dyed red while he went on living unconscious and unconcerned about all the misery which would remain forever associated with his name. When destiny was at last fulfilled in regard to him, it was discovered that it had also been fulfilled in regard to Russia, and this was what the country could not bring itself to forgive him; this is what his ancestors also would not have pardoned him had they been able to arise out of their graves, and to

> Rend the gold brocade
> Whereof their shroud was made*

in horror at all the evil perpetrated by their unworthy descendant.

Yes, in the past they had been a strong race, these Romanoffs, about whom no one thinks any longer to-day in the vast realm that owned them once as its masters and lords. But it would be useless to deny that crimes without number were committed by them and that injustice flourished during the centuries when they could dispose absolutely of the fate of millions and millions of human creatures whom they killed and tortured at their will and according to their fancies. Perhaps it was a just punishment for the ruthless cruelty of some of them that the glories of their race came to an end and perished, together with all the traditions that had surrounded them for such a long time, because of the follies, sins, mistakes, blunderings, iniquities, and indecisions of a weak, characterless, and half-witted man and of a superstitious, intriguing, and half-demented woman.

* Longfellow, "The White Czar."

END OF BOOK I

BOOK TWO

Yulia Alexandrovna von Dehn, known as Madame Lily Dehn

> There are some listings for this book published in 1919 but the widely available versions were published in London (April 1922) by Thornton Butterworth; the same publisher of *The Last Days of the Romanovs* by Robert Wilton in 1920 and The World Crisis 1911-1914 by Winston Churchill, in 1923. The other edition, *The Last Tsarista* was published in New York (September 1922) by Boston, Little, Brown, and Company.

— *The English edition was published by Thornton Butterworth Limited, London, 1922.*
— *Pages: 249 total pages*

THE
REAL TSARITSA

BY

MADAME LILI DEHN

CLOSE FRIEND OF THE
LATE EMPRESS OF RUSSIA

THORNTON BUTTERWORTH LTD.
15 BEDFORD STREET, LONDON, W.C.2

First Published – April, 1922

TSARKOE SELO

To

H.I.M. ALEXANDRA

THE LATE EMPRESS OF RUSSIA

Adieu, c'est pour un autre monde

The fate which destined thee for lofty power,
And crowned thee Sovereign o'er an Empire wide,
Placed too the cup of suffering by thy side
And sorrow gave thee for imperial dower :
How little did'st thou dream in Fortune's hour
Thy barque would founder on such tragic tide
Of blood as wrecks a mighty nation's pride,
While black the clouds of Revolution lower!
What force sustained thee in those days of stress
When death and ruin held their sombre court,
And frenzied mob set might all right above ?
What made thee still thy prayers to Heav'n address,
And solace to thy stricken spirit brought ?
'Twas faith unshaken in a God of love.

OSWALD NORMAN.

N.B. This list is from the London edition and varies from the U.S. edition published September 1922. It's included her for completion with the corresponding page numbers listed for this volume where applicable.

LIST OF ILLUSTRATIONS

H.I.M. Alexandra	(Frontispiece)	n/a
Anna (Ania) Virouboff	(to face page 48)	219
Her Imperial Majesty with the Tsarevitch	(56)	207
H.I.M. The Tsar with Officers of the Royal Yacht "Standart"	(96)	250
The Empress on board the "Standart"	(96)	250
H.I.M. on board the tender of the "Standart"	(96)	250
Grand Duchess Olga	(104)	n/a
Grand Duchess Tatiana	(104)	n/a
The Imperial Family	(152)	186
Royal Shooting Party	(160)	291
The Tsarevitch at G.H.Q.	(160)	291
The Tsarevitch and his Spaniel "Joy"	(160)	291
His Imperial Majesty and the Tsarevitch	(184)	308
H.I.M. Alexandra (end of 1915)	(184)	308
The Empress at Tobolsk	(208)	n/a
The Empress with Tatiana at Tsarkoe Selo	(208)	n/a
The Grand Duchesses Marie and Anastasie	(208)	n/a

FACSIMILIA

Part of letter of June 5/18, 1917	(to face page 240)	
Part of letter of March 2/15, 1918	(245)	350
Note from the Empress	(208)	n/a
Part of letter on day of departure for Siberia	(234)	n/a
Letter from the Empress (1916)	(235)	340
Part of letter of 30th July, 1917	(241)	n/a
Christmas Card drawn by the Empress	(242)	346

FOREWORD

IN giving to the world my memories of the Empress Alexandra of Russia, I do not wish to pose as one who is biased by a long and intimate friendship. I write of the Tsaritsa as I knew her: the real Tsaritsa. I was not acquainted with the heroine of the films, the hysterical devotee, or the pro-German who, it is asserted, betrayed both her country by adoption and the country which knew her as a granddaughter of Queen Victoria and the daughter of a much loved English Princess.

PART I - Old Russia

CHAPTER I

I WAS born on the beautiful estates in South Russia which belonged to my grandmother and my uncle. My father was Ismail Selim Bek Smolsky, whose ancestors hailed from Lithuanian Tartary, and my mother, before her marriage, was Mlle Catherine Horvat, whose grandfather had been invited by the Empress Elizabeth Petrovna to come from Hungary and assist in the colonization of South Russia. Colonel Horvat, who was half Serbian and half Hungarian by birth, was appointed general of the armies of the South by the Empress, and there is a story in our family that when he first arrived in Russia he was taken to the summit of a high mountain and told to look at the panorama of fields and forests lying beneath him.

Colonel Horvat dutifully admired the view, but an unexpected surprise awaited him. "Look well around you, M. le Colonel," said his guide, "the country, as far as you can see, is yours; it is the gift of the Empress!" Truly an Imperial gift, but all that remains of those great possessions are the estates where I was born. These properties were situated on the Dnieper, in the country known as "Little Russia," which in former times was the seat of the Ukranian Government. My forefathers became typical Russian noblemen; they were lavishly generous where their inclinations were concerned, and it is asserted that one of them once exchanged a large forest for a sporting dog which he especially coveted!

Revovka, my birthplace, was close to the other estates which came into our possession through Prince Goleniktcheff Koutousoff, the hero who saved Russia from falling into the hands of the French. It was a delightful old house, standing in a wellwooded park, with avenues of lime trees where the nightingales sang, and as I write, I can smell the unforgettable perfume of the limes, and recall the beauty and peace of the surroundings; it was, indeed, a real fairyland. All was prosperity and happiness at Revovka. The village nestled close to the Great House, and my ancestors were buried in the church. There were rows of little cottages which were whitewashed every week; the roofs were thatched with reeds, and the gardens were gay with flowers. A cherry tree stood in every garden (cherry trees are typical of South Russia), it was the country of cherry trees, spotless houses and simple joys.

The peasants were on the best of terms with my family, and they regarded my grandmother Horvat as a beneficent deity who replaced the reed roofs when they were destroyed by fire, and who supplied them with unlimited quantities of fuel. They were quite contented, and my grandmother still employed some of the peasants who had once been given to her as serfs. In the old days, it was customary to include a few serfs in a bride's *corbeille*, and the ten peasants who had been chosen to accompany my grandmother to Revovka adored her. "People say that we were unhappy as serfs," they would often remark, "but we were always well looked after—our landlord and our owner was also our father."

The peasant as master or mistress was invariably a tyrant, and I remember hearing about a beautiful girl who had become the mistress of a great nobleman, and who out-Heroded Herod in her arrogance. She employed her family to do her laundry work, and she always insisted upon her linen being rinsed in running water. If her petticoats were not sufficiently starched, the whole batch of her relatives was flogged. Personally, we did not resent the lack of starch, to this extent, but I suppose that this family flogging may be regarded as typical of the usual procedure of beggars on horseback!

My grandmother, Mme Horvat, *née* Baroness Pilar, was the sweetest of women, and I loved her with a child's passionate devotion. She used to tell me all kinds of stories, and our old nurse ably seconded her. Whenever we walked by the river, and I exclaimed at the beauty of the lilies, I was thrilled anew by hearing how, long ago, when the Tartar hordes descended on Beletskovka, the women and children used to wade into the water, and shelter under the broad green lily-leaves until the marauders had passed. The peasants at

Revovka were extremely superstitious, and they believed implicitly in witches and warlocks. It was common knowledge that certain women possessed tails and bewitched the cows, and woe betide the widow who mourned her husband too much! He would assuredly return in the likeness of a big snake, and make an unwelcome descent down the chimney. I was terribly scared by some of these narratives, and I much preferred the pretty customs prevalent at certain seasons, now vanished, alas! under the Bolshevik regime, since the teaching of Lenin would seemingly only include the ritual of blood in its category.

I chiefly remember the quaint methods of divination practised on New Year's Eve, when the girls of the village went out to listen at the closed doors, and those who heard a man's name mentioned were certain to marry within the year. They varied these proceedings by throwing their slippers over their heads, to see if they fell in the shape of anything that might be construed into an initial letter. Others preferred to try and catch the rays of the moon in a towel; all pretty gay conceits, dear to the heart of girlhood, and, on St. Catharine's Day, cherry tree branches were put in water, and, if the bare wood blossomed by Xmas, then marriage bells were about to ring.

Midsummer Day was sacred to the river, a survival doubtless of those pagan customs which are so difficult to destroy. Large fires were lighted along the river banks, and the village maidens, wearing wreaths, leapt into the water, across the fires, and left the wreaths in the river as an offering, perchance to the God of Streams. The next morning, they set out to look for their wreaths, and those who were lucky enough to find them discovered by the direction in which the wreath had been washed up the way by which marriage would come.

The storks brought luck, and they were invited to sojourn with us by means of wheels placed in the roofs on which they built their nests. The solemn birds were family friends, and, whenever a baby stork fell from its nest, everyone went to enormous trouble to put it back.

My grandmother had a passion for embroidery, and she employed from ten to fifteen girls constantly working for her. She believed that, as a typical industry, the art of embroidery in South Russia ought to be revived, and she spared no pains or expense over her hobby. She proved conclusively that the progress of the nations from East to West had left its traces even in embroidery patterns, as she often saw similar designs in antique carpets and Venetian work.

None of my grandmother's embroideries was ever sold: whenever a piece was finished, it was labelled with the date of its commencement and completion, and packed away in great presses, already nearly full of exquisite work. She presented a quantity of this embroidery to the Grand Duchess Elizabeth, the Tsaritsa's sister, when she was received into the Greek Church. My grandmother had the honour of acting as godmother to the Grand Duchess, and I believe her "christening" present was much appreciated. The embroideries were really wonderful: the designs were never drawn, the threads only were counted, and the pattern was evolved in this painstaking manner. Some of my grandmother's favourite designs were taken from Easter eggs, which were first covered with pinked-out wax, and colour inserted in them. Snow crystals formed another inspiration; my grandmother never tired of utilising anything decorative, and she was unusually successful. I like to think of those quiet days—the industrious girls, and the good feeling which existed between the employer and the employed. It is difficult to realise that the progress of Revolution has destroyed all this, that the great presses have been broken open and their contents dispersed to the four winds, and that to ask a peasant to pass her time profitably would be accounted a sin.

My grandmother, notwithstanding her patriarchal outlook, could be the "grande dame" when occasion warranted, and my old nurse used to relate how one of her neighbours, a certain Prince, came to ask her in marriage. This gentleman believed in the impressiveness of pomp and circumstance, so he arrived at Beletskovka in a carriage and six horses. He was most courteously received—and refused—by my grandmother, and, when he drove away, his horses, by some preconceived arrangement, cast their shoes in the avenue. These "cast off" shoes were solid silver, a mute testimony to his wealth, and, as he passed through the village, he and his postillions distributed undreamt-of largesse. The Prince was a haughty personage, who lived in a gorgeous mansion boasting fifty rooms. He gave two balls yearly, when an orchestra was specially sent for from Petrograd, a four days' journey from his estate. But in the Prince's opinion nobody, save my grandmother and our family, was good enough to associate (even as a dance partner) with him and his, so the balls were rather tame affairs, a few couples only taking the floor, but those who did were—like Cæsar's wife—entirely above suspicion.

Silver horse-shoes, expensive orchestras, and other unconsidered trifles cost money, and, as the male members of this super-aristocratic family were all in Hussar regiments, financial ruin eventually came as an uninvited and unwelcome guest: it closed the doors of the castle, the orchestra came no more, and the ladies of the house sought refuge in an institution for noble ladies of fallen fortunes!

My great-aunt, the Baroness Nina Pilar, was a romantic figure in my childhood's memories, as her name conjured up the fascination which surrounds those who breathe and have their being in the air of Courts. She was Lady-in-Waiting to the Empress Marie, wife of Alexander II, and she made her appearance at Court when she was sixteen, under the auspices of Countess Tizenhausen (another great-aunt), Grande Maîtresse de la Cour, who brought up Felix Soumarokoff, the grandfather of Prince Felix Yousopoff. There was a great deal of gossip about the paternity of old Soumarokoff, who had been confided, as a baby, to Countess Tizenhausen by an intimate friend, but nobody was ever any the wiser, and Soumarokoff's antecedents remained an unsolved mystery.

The Empress Marie loved Aunt Nina, and the Emperor was very kind to her until my innocent relative was the victim of chance, and a *costumière*. The Emperor had become infatuated with a certain Princess Dolgorouky, and one day, when my aunt was walking on the Quai, looking especially attractive in a new costume, she suddenly heard a voice addressing her in most endearing terms. She turned sharply round, and found to her dismay that the voice was the voice of the Emperor! Explanations followed, and my aunt discovered that Princess Dolgorouky possessed a duplicate of her new costume, and, as their heights and figures were similar, it was a case of mistaken identity.

The Empress was almost always ill, but her Court was distinguished by its elegance and refinement, and my aunt was one of the acknowledged leaders of fashion.

Like most pretty women, Aunt Nina had her love story, but she never married. Her Prince Charming was the Grand Duke Nicholas, to whom she was secretly engaged.

But, when the Grand Duke asked the Emperor's permission to marry his inamorata, the Emperor, who had never forgiven the contretemps on the Quai, refused his consent!

The unhappy lovers met in Switzerland when Aunt Nina was in attendance on the Empress, and there they bade each other farewell, and threw their engagement rings into the lake. The Grand Duke never forgot his broken romance, although he, like most lovers, eventually married someone else! But he was present at my aunt's funeral, and stood silently and sorrowfully looking at the coffin which held many of the dreams and much of the enchantment of his youth.

Aunt Nina practically sacrificed her life to save that of the Empress, although the latter died years later at Petrograd, when, it is asserted, a luminous Cross appeared over the Winter Palace, typical of her physical and mental sufferings.

It so happened that when the Empress and my aunt were driving in Switzerland, their carriage was run into by a cart, and, in order to prevent one of the shafts from striking the Empress, my aunt stood up to protect her, and was badly bruised in the chest. Some time afterwards cancer developed, but my aunt survived her Imperial mistress, and became Lady-in-Waiting to the Empress Dagmar, and Grande Maîtresse de la Cour to the Grand Duchess Elizabeth. The Grand Duchess was very much attached to her, and at her death she begged my grandmother to take her place. My grandmother, for family reasons, declined the honour, but she often used to visit the Grand Duchess and the Grand Duke Serge, and I remember hearing her describe the pathetic figure presented by the Grand Duchess after her husband's assassination, when she had relinquished the spleendours of life and had become a nun at Moscow.

My childhood was chiefly passed on my grandmother's estates. We led a somewhat patriarchal life at Revovka; a simple existence which will, I fear, never again return, and it is exceedingly difficult for me, as a Russian, to recognise the peasants of then and now. The average peasant was kindly by nature, entirely ignorant, and excessively difficult to educate. Whenever my grandmother tried to persuade her tenants to send their children to school, the answer was always the same: "Knowing how to read and write doesn't provide food. Our parents got on very well without education, our sons can do likewise." Their faith in the aristocratic class was boundless, they entirely depended on their landlords, but the Russian peasant has always, unfortunately for himself, been easily influenced by speeches and printed matter—hence the complete success of the Revolutionary Propaganda, and the belief in many of the false statements circulated in order to damage the Imperial family in the eyes of the people. I cannot defend our own attitude in not attempting to combat this danger; we were aware that it existed, but only one section, known as the Black Band, tried to destroy it by counter propaganda. Its efforts were unsuccessful, it received no support, for the very good reason that *nobody believed that the masses would rise*. The Russian aristocrat, secure in his class prejudices, and his optimistic faith in *himself*, was as loth as the French aristocrat of 1789 to realise that his position was, or could ever be, insecure!

The South Russian peasant, as I knew him, was a poetical, simple soul. After dinner we often used to watch the men turning their horses into our meadows for safety, and securing the animals' legs with chains, in order to prevent any inclination to roam. They invariably sang whilst making these nightly preparations, and they danced afterwards in the bright moonlight which flooded meadows and woodland with a white radiance. They had many quaint customs at Revovka, which may not be uninteresting to English readers who only know the Russia of to-day as a strange and poisonous growth, and not as the orchid which had its home in the eternal snows—a curious simile, perhaps, but in my mind a correct one. Our country, in many respects, was an exotic growth; super-refinement walked cheek by jowl with ignorance, and an almost oriental luxury brushed the skirts of poverty. It was a land of extreme contrasts, where emotions and passions either ran riot or else were suppressed to an undreamt-of extent. It was almost inconceivable at one time that the family coachman, who obstinately turned his horses' heads in the direction of home because he met a white dog in the road, could ever become the Bolshevik who would have murdered his employers instead of protecting them from the bad luck attendant on the unwelcome animal!

I must admit that my grandmother was as superstitious as her coachman. She believed implicitly in dreams, and an old woman from the village was always sent for to expound the more exciting ones. I remember that one of her dreams had a disastrous sequel, inasmuch as it involved the dismissal of a very devoted servant who, my grandmother dreamt, had attempted to kill her. She resolutely declined to see him again, and he was sent away to another estate. I supposed she was influenced in this by the knowledge that, on several occasions, she had "dreamed true."

Our peasants confided all their joys and sorrows in my grandmother, and, when any of them married, we were always invited to the wedding. This invitation was issued on set lines; the bride-to-be, dressed in full national costume, plentifully bedecked with flowers and ribbons, came with her bridesmaid to the servants' sitting-room, where she was received by my grandmother. The girl thereupon knelt, and bowed three times, informing my relation what an honour our presence would confer on her family, and, gratified by the assurance that we would promise to come, she withdrew, all smiles! After the ceremony, which always took place on a Sunday, the whole of the wedding party came back to our house and assembled on the terrace, where a village orchestra discoursed strange sweet sounds, and where unwearied dancing enlivened the music and singing. We always gave one kind of present—a cow! When I married, our employees surpassed themselves and gave me, not a cow, but two oxen!

We fasted on Christmas Eve until the first star appeared, when we partook of a heavy supper of which the fifteen courses always included fish. Hay was strewn under the tablecloth to remind us of the humility of the Manger, and it was customary for the children to carry the Christmas supper to their friends and relations. All the windows of the Chateau were darkened, but one was left open, and, when the first star appeared in the serene sky, this window was illuminated in honour of the Christ-Child. It was then that the children arrived "en masse," carrying revolving paper transparencies adorned with pictures of Christ; it was one illuminated stream of little children, and one of the prettiest sights imaginable.

New Year's Day was an occasion for general rejoicing, when the men of the village assembled on the terrace to congratulate us, throwing wheat in our pathway as a sign of prosperity. We then witnessed the procession of our servants, who filed past us, accompanied by their special charges. First, came the stablemen leading the horses, who, in addition to being superlatively well-groomed, were adorned with gilt crowns and many ribbons. Then came the herdsmen with their grave-eyed steers, whose horns were gilded in honour of the New Year; the sheep were accompanied by the shepherds, and the cortège was terminated by the poultry maid, who escorted a turkey smothered in ribbons.

On the first New Year's Day after the Revolution, the crowd came to the Chateau as usual, but there was no procession of animals, no smiling faces, and no wheat-strewn pathway. We were confronted by scowling peasants, who roughly informed us that henceforth nothing belonged to us, since they were masters. But to do our own people justice, the better minded amongst them absented themselves, and only the worst characters were in evidence—and these, in their turn, were under the evil influences rampant in towns. I have no hesitation in stating that the motive power in the destructtion of Russia emanated, and still emanates, from the Jews.

When the snows began to melt, the children and young people heralded the approach of Spring with song. Joining hands, they wandered singing in the twilight, a lovely, living chain of Youth in its Spring-time. They repeated these songs at Easter, that wonderful festival of Resurrection and the rebirth of Nature. On Holy Thursday the Gospels were read in the churches until midnight, and everyone carried a taper. My mother's estates were situated in the mountains, and it was a picturesque sight when the peasants wended their way churchwards at Easter. The church was half-way up a steep ascent, and the procession of taper-bearers could be traced by hundreds of lights, as two villages participated in the ceremony.

Revovka was an entrancing home for a child blessed, as I was, with an imaginative temperament. We had our particular White Lady, a tragic phantom who haunted the Park, and who used to swing in the branches of the lime trees. She had been the mistress of one of my great-uncles, and she was buried in the Park. No one seemed to know her fate, but it was said that she was beautiful and unhappy. Her grave was marked with a flat stone, without any inscription, as the poor little creature had sought refuge from love and life in self-destruction. But Nature was kinder to her than Man, and an enormous bush of wild roses threw out caressing arms towards the cold stones, and showered pink petal-tears on the unhonoured dead.

There was a similar forgotten grave on my father's property, formerly a huntingbox of the Kings of Poland. The occupant of this grave had been the mistress of a king, and, like the beauty of Revovka, she had killed herself; but she was a restless spirit, and she used to haunt the Park and the house in the summer, running swiftly across the greensward, wearing little scarlet slippers and darting up the staircase, her scarlet heels tap-tapping as she went her way, unsubstantial and fantastic as the morning mist.

I used to dream all kinds of dreams, but I never anticipated what Destiny held in store for me. I was, by nature, timid; I was to become courageous through force of another's shining example. I was to see and experience the real meaning of selfless love, and I was to know the comfort and beauty of religion. I do not say that I was irreligious—few Russians are really irreligious—our Belief is too deeply rooted—but I did not yet understand the meaning of the word Faith.

I always looked forward to our yearly pilgrimage to the Convent of Tchigrin, twenty-five miles away from Revovka. Custom ordained that we should proceed thither on foot, but the carriage invariably went with us! The convent contained a miraculous Virgin which, when the Turks pillaged Tchigrin, had been taken away by them. One day a disconsolate nun walking on the river's bank saw something floating on the surface of the water. The Virgin had returned to her convent, and from that time it became the scene of wonderful miracles, and many pilgrimages. I liked Tchigrin; it breathed an atmosphere of calm, standing alone in the midst of dense pine woods. But the wind, which respects neither convents nor humanity, was occasionally unkind to Tchigrin, as it swept away the sand which filled the crevices of the walls, almost like natural mortar, and the nuns daily brought bags of sand wherewith to repair the damage. This sand-carrying was an especial duty connected with Tchigrin, and occasionally it was a penance—but I think those simple creatures rarely deserved punishment.

I have perhaps devoted too much time to the festivals, ghosts and unexciting incidents of a country life. But I have done this in order to explain many subsequent happenings which would be otherwise incomprehensible to an English public. These events cannot, and must not, be judged entirely from an English standpoint. We are a race apart, our country is one of extreme mysticism and superstition. It is a land of miracles, where the holy pictures are believed to shed tears, and where every village possesses its seer and its saint. It would be possible to cover the length and breadth of England in a week's motoring tour, thus England is of necessity more circumscribed. One could not see Russia in such a manner. It is a country of vast distances, of densely populated cities, and lonely tracts which extend for thousands of miles. You cannot contrast the mode of life prevalent at Tooting with that of Tobolsk, or compare the customs of Moscow with those of Manchester. Our upbringing is entirely un-English. True, we are citizens of the world, we are indeed cosmopolitan, but—once a Russian, always a Russian. The Tsaritsa told me that, when she first came to Russia, she was greatly surprised to find that Russian servants did not understand the art of blackleading grates. She had always been accustomed to see shining grates in England when she stayed with her grandmother at Windsor—in Petrograd, shining grates were non-existent. We are miles apart from English ways in little things like these, and no Englishwoman worthy of the name has ever been known to be ignorant of the use of blacklead. But *we* ought not to be condemned for the non-recognition of its virtue. It is merely a question of outlook. In connection with these differences of outlook, I cannot do better than quote the words of a contributor to the "Daily Mail"; they will plead for my opinions, as the writer possesses the peculiar gift of racial and temperamental understanding:

"We have," he writes, "in England a cold fish-minded way of affecting to laugh at what we are prone to call local superstition. Let me tell you that this point of view will not work in Africa." (He is dealing, I fancy, with Morocco.) "What is obviously a childish hallucination in Hampstead or Newcastle is sober reality under this immense blue sky. You can disbelieve a lot of truths you do not understand as you strap-hang homewards, but you will learn to believe everything in Africa."

Might not this also apply to Russia?

HER IMPERIAL MAJESTY AND THE TSAREVITCH

CHAPTER II

MY childhood and early girlhood were passed quietly at Revovka and the Crimea. But I loved Revovka, and, whenever I went to stay with my uncle at Livadia, I took with me a little earth from the place which, to me, represented home. The great event at Revovka was the visit of my uncle Horvat, who came from Siberia to see my grandmother once a year. He was head of the Siberian railways, and occupied a political position which corresponded with that of a Viceroy of Ireland. He was a typical Horvat, tall, with deep, kind eyes, and he was also a very clever man. On the night of his arrival I never went to bed, and I remember that we saw the dawn together; he did not reach Revovka until 3 a.m. It was touching to witness his meeting with my grandmother. They were entirely "en rapport," and he was my greatest friend as well as my much loved uncle.

I never went to school. My first tutor was a priest, but, as I hardly knew Russian (we always spoke French at home) and he knew no French, I made little progress; afterwards Miss Ripe, an English governess, took me in hand, but I think she looked upon us as very much behind the times. The old house was protected at night by a watchman, and I regarded his intermittent coughing and his heavy tread somewhat as a lullaby. Whenever he went to the next town by boat, the watchman "called" my grandmother's maid in a very curious manner. He was an illiterate peasant, and time, as time, conveyed no meaning to him, so he would occasionally tap on the maid's window and tell her that such and such a star was in the sky. By this simple calculation she was enabled to judge how much longer it was permissible for her to remain in bed. Winter was a delightful season at Revovka, and I always wanted to be decorative, and drive out in the antique sledges which were painted with trails of flowers, and magnificently gilded. The modern sledges, covered with carpet, and piled up with bear skins, were not nearly so pretty. English people always associate sledges with wolves, and imagine that a winter's drive in Russia is fraught with desperate danger. The wolf terror is fast becoming a legend; wolves are now only found in districts far from the haunts of men, although an old custom at

Revovka ordained that lanterns were hung outside the stables at night to scare away the wolves! But I met a wolf unawares one evening when I was crossing the park. I had never seen one of our national animals face to face, so I thought that the big grey creature was a dog. I called it, and ran towards it, desirous of its better acquaintance, but it merely regarded me with furtive, unfriendly, green eyes, and then turned and trotted away in the opposite direction. When I reached the house, I described my encounter with the strange dog, but, greatly to my surprise, my story produced general excitement, and a search-party set forth to look for the footprints in the snow. These proved to be typical wolf marks, exactly like the print of a thumb, but our visitor had, by this time, completely disappeared.

When I was a young girl the disaffection in Russia was already well on the way to Revolution. In 1905, when I was staying with one of my uncles in Livadia who had charge of the Emperor's estates at Yalta, we were not left long in ignorance as to the methods which were employed by the Revolutionary Agents. It is now well known that most of the seeds of Revolution were sown at Yalta, but it was dreadful to see the boats smothered in red flags and to hear the Marseillaise sung defiantly from the water, since my uncle had prohibited all political meetings on land. One day, it was discovered that the golden eagles which marked the boundaries of the Emperor's estate had been broken and overthrown, but this act of vandalism was always attributed to the Jews and the more hot-headed of the students. There was general excitement in the Crimea at this time, and a few of the Revolutionary printing presses were secretly set up at the Grand Duke Constantine's Castle of Orianda, which for some reason had fallen into decay. It had always been my ambition to visit the ruins of Orianda, so one day I persuaded my cousins to accompany me thither. It was a forbidden expedition, but we considered the possible results of our disobedience would be amply compensated for by the mysteries of the underground passages, which we at once began to explore. As we neared the end of one of these the sound of distant voices broke the stillness, and, terrified out of our wits, we did not know whether to beat a retreat or to dare all and discover whence the sound proceeded. Curiosity eventually conquered cowardice, and we crept cautiously along until the darkness was lit up by a glow of a large fire. Thinking that we had now reached the entrance to the infernal regions we turned and fled precipitately, and, risking punishment, described the whereabouts of Hell to my uncle. And Hell, in a way, it proved to be, as it was discovered that secret printing presses existed underground, and that most of the evil propaganda had emanated from Orianda.

Although the Jews instigated much of the prevalent sedition, the biter was occasionally bit, and in 1905 there was serious trouble. Many people assert that the actual Revolution began by beating the Jews, as some of the soldiers returning from the war became very unruly, and set about the Jews most unmercifully.

My mother, who had married as her second husband an officer in a regiment stationed near us, received news of the trouble just at the moment when we were starting to drive into town. But she rather pooh-poohed the warning, until she saw for herself that the report was not exaggerated. We first encountered people fleeing through the fields, and, when at last we reached civilisation, we found the town in a state of confusion. Windows were broken, Jewish shops pillaged, and the leaders, regardless of the protesting Hebrews, seized their goods and distributed them broadcast to the mob. The black and white praying robes peculiar to the Jews were in special request, as pieces of these, worn next to the skin, were supposed to render the wearer immune from marsh fever.

Next day, when I was walking in the Park, I found myself close to the walled-in right of way which traversed it, and, to my surprise and horror, I heard the passers-by giving vent to most undreamt-of declarations. "It's the Jews *now*," said someone, uttering a curse, "but wait until the next time. We have our orders: soon it will be the turn of the landed proprietors!"

The speaker spoke the truth. Some days later fires and pillage broke out around my home, and, from the terrace at Revovka, we could see an ever widening circle of flame, and our peasants informed us that, most assuredly, Revovka would suffer next. But we escaped, although the house of Madame Tchebotaiff, a great landowner and Revolutionist, was one of the first to be destroyed. She was afterwards sent to Siberia, a rather ironical form of justice, I am inclined to think!

When all was calm, the Duma came into existence, in which representatives of every class met in Parliament for the first time. Troops were sent to punish the peasants, and many of them were flogged by the soldiers. Our peasants were not included amongst the offenders. The idea of whipping human beings was repellent to me, and, girl though I was, I felt that we, as a class, were responsible for the existence of many evils, and that it lay with us to try and remedy them. But whipping was applied to the guilty as the most effectual and the most easily understood antidote against rebellion: it is a barbarous punishment—in English eyes it must seem *utterly* so; but these whippings were as naught compared with the savagery and super-refinement of torture inflicted later by the whipped upon the whippers.

But my attention was soon to be diverted from rebellion and punishment. Shortly afterwards I went with my grandmother to Petrograd, where my marriage was arranged; in fact, I was already engaged when I was presented at Court. My fiancé was Captain Charles Dehn, of Swedish descent, whose ancestors had come into the northern provinces at the time of the Crusades, and the members of whose family were mostly generals or officers in the service of the State. Captain Dehn had taken part in quelling the Boxer Rebellion, and at the siege of Pekin he was the first officer to scale the walls of the Forbidden City in defence of the embassies. For this service he received the Order of St. George (the Russian Victoria Cross), and the Order of the Legion of Honour was awarded him by the ambassadors of the various nations represented in Pekin.

On his arrival at Petrograd he was presented to the Emperor, who appointed him an officer on the "Standart," and an officer of the Mixed Guard, whose members were chosen from various regiments, and many of whom were honoured by the personal friendship of the Emperor.

Captain Dehn was a great favourite with the little Tsarevitch and the Grand Duchesses, and he used to play with them in their nurseries, his nickname with the children being "Pekin Dehn." Both the Emperor and the Empress manifested the greatest interest in his engagement, and the Empress intimated to my grandmother that she wished to make my personal acquaintance.

My engagement was formally announced in 1907, but we waited in Petrograd for a month before we were received by the Empress. The Grand Duchess Anastasie was ill with diphtheria, and the Empress was nursing her at the Alexandria Palace, Peterhof, where, until all danger of infection had passed, she had isolated herself from the other members of the Imperial family.

How well I remember that first meeting with one whom I was to love so devotedly, and whose constant friendship has been one of my greatest joys. One summer morning in July, my grandmother and I arrived at the station at Peterhof, where my fiancé and a Court carriage were awaiting us. I was literally trembling with terror, and I was too excited to even notice Charles!

We duly reached the Alexandria Palace, but, as the Empress was still nervous about infection, it had been arranged that my presentation should take place in the Winter Garden attached to the Palace. We were received at the Palace by the Mistress of the Household, Princess Golitzin, who was exactly like an old picture, and whose adherence to regime made everyone dread being guilty of the smallest lapse of etiquette. But she was very kind and gracious to us, and I felt somehow that my simple white gown from Bressac's, and my rose-trimmed hat had met with her approval. As we walked through the Park to the Winter Garden I noticed a lady in one of the avenues, who stopped and looked at me intently. She was "petite," with an innocent baby face, and great appealing eyes, and so childish-looking in fact that she seemed only fit for boarding school. This lady was Anna Virouboff whose name was later to become associated with that of Rasputin, and whose friendship with the Empress has given rise to so many unwarrantable statements and scandalous stories.

I returned her scrutiny with interest, and we passed on with the Princess to the Winter Garden, a lovely tropical place, full of flowers and palms. It was exactly like a Garden of Dreams, at least I thought so until I saw the prosaically comfortable garden chairs, and noticed some toys and a child's dolls'-house. Then I decided that this beautiful garden must be real!

At last, advancing slowly through the masses of greenery, came a tall and slender figure. It was the Empress! I looked at her, admiration in my heart and in my eyes. I had never imagined her half so fair. And I shall never forget her beauty as I saw her on that July morning, although the Empress of many sorrows remains with me more as a pathetic and holy memory.

The Empress was dressed entirely in white, with a thin white veil draped round her hat. Her complexion was delicately fair, but when she was excited her cheeks were suffused with a faint rose flush. Her hair was reddish gold, her eyes—those infinitely tragic eyes—were dark blue, and her figure was as supple as a willow wand. I remember that her pearls were magnificent, and that diamond ear-rings flashed coloured fires whenever she moved her head. She wore a simple little ring bearing the emblem of the Swastika, her favourite symbol, and one which has given rise to so many conjectures, and been quoted triumphantly as proof positive of her leanings towards the occult by those who are ignorant of what it really meant to her.

Directly Princess Golitzin had left us alone, the Empress extended her hand for my grandmother and me to kiss; then, with a sweet smile, and a world of kindness in her eyes, "Sit down," she said, and, turning to Captain Dehn: "When is the marriage to take place?" she enquired.

My nervousness had vanished. I was no longer afraid; in fact it was the Empress who seemed shy, but she was, I found later, always shy with strangers, a trait peculiar to her and to her cousin, the Princess Royal, Duchess of Fife. However, this excessive shyness was not accounted as shyness in Petrograd, it was called German superciliousness! and as such it has even been described by some English writers.

The Empress talked to my grandmother for quite a long time, as she was anxious to hear the latest news of the Grand Duchess Elizabeth; she then chatted to my fiancé, and I noticed that she spoke Russian with a strong English accent. She afterwards addressed me as the blushing heroine of the morning, and she seemed quite pleased at the interest which I had displayed in the dolls'-house.

"Where are you going to spend your honeymoon?" she said, her blue eyes now mischievous. We told her. "Ah! . . . I do hope that I shall see you again very soon. I am quite alone, I cannot see my husband or my children, I shall be so glad when this tiresome quarantine is over, and we can be together again."

Our interview lasted well over half an hour. The Empress spoke French to my grandmother and me, she made no attempt to converse in German; then she rose to say good-bye, and we kissed hands. "I shall see you again very soon," she repeated. "Be sure you let me know when you return."

I went back to Petrograd almost beside myself with happiness. Mine was not the worldly pleasure of one who had been presented to an Empress. My happiness had its origin in another source. I felt instinctively that I had found a friend, someone I could love, and who, I dared hope, might love me! I was so tired out with my emotions that, on arriving home, I threw myself on my bed, regardless of my Bressac dress and my rose-wreathed hat, and I slept the sleep of exhaustion until four in the afternoon.

I was married two months later from my aunt's house in Livadia.

The Emperor received Captain Dehn before he left for the Crimea, blessed him, and gave him a beautiful ikon in a carved silver and gold frame. The Empress also presented him with an ikon, and, on our wedding day, we received a "wireless" from them, wishing us every happiness. This "wireless," so we heard afterwards, caused endless talk and many petty jealousies, as "wireless," then in its infancy, was only supposed to be used for important official communications.

We went to the Caucasus for our honeymoon and stayed three weeks in the mountains among the vines. It was the season of Autumn, and he had cast his flaming many-coloured mantle over everything. The wildness and luxuriance of that mountain region entranced me. I insisted upon being told all the legends connected with the locality, and I believed, with the peasants, that it was possible to hear the hoofs of the Centaurs, as they thundered down the passes in the silence of night. Gagree was an ideal place for a honeymoon, and I was actually sorry to return to my beloved Revovka, although we received a right royal welcome from my grandmother and her tenants.

Revovka was fifteen miles from the nearest railway station, but the whole of the way to our estate was illuminated with blazing tar barrels, and at every turn of the road we were offered bread and salt. Needless to say, the drive was a little protracted, and the *pièce de résistance* consisted in the two oxen which were presented to us at the journey's end.

My married life began under the most auspicious circumstances. Charles had promised me that he would always remain in the Emperor's Personal Guard, and I possessed a subconscious intuittion that my future was to be closely connected with that of the Imperial family. This feeling did not arise from any worldly outlook, I never had any idea of the material benefits which might accrue to us through the Emperor's regard for my husband. My first meeting with the Empress had influenced me in an undreamt of manner. Although I felt it was ridiculous to associate any idea of sorrow with that radiant vision of the Winter Garden, I had, nevertheless, a strong feeling of fatality in connection with her. Time was destined to prove that my presentiment was right.

Our first home was in the Anitchkoff Palace, the residence of the

Dowager Empress Marie, where the Guards had their quarters, but afterwards we moved to Tsarkoe Selo. Our house was immediately opposite the Palace, and close to the barracks. The officers of the Personal Guard were most picturesque individuals, since each wore the uniform of the regiment from which he had been selected. There was no distinctive uniform; to be a member of the Guard was, in itself, an honour.

I used often to walk in the great Park of Tsarkoe Selo when my husband was on duty. The Palace dates from the time of Catherine the Great, and all the important receptions were held there. The Imperial family lived in the Alexander Palace, a white building in the style of the First Empire; the Palace had four entrances, the first was exclusively used by Their Majesties, two others were used for receptions, and the fourth was the entrance by which the Suite went to and fro. The Palace was entirely surrounded by the Park, in which was some beautiful ornamental water, a Chinese pavilion, and a bridge which connected the smaller park with that of the more important Palace.

As a young married woman, blessed with many kind relations and friends, it was not long before I took my place in Petrograd society. In 1907, one year after the Japanese war, life was not gay as many families were still in mourning, so those who looked for Court gaieties were disappointed—none being forthcoming. The Empress felt that the war was of too recent a date to warrant much entertaining; she was entirely sincere in this conviction, but her attitude did not meet with general approval. It was argued by the anti-Tsaritsa clique that an Empress of Russia belonged to Society, and not to herself. Her duty was merely to pose as a magnificent figure-head on the barque of pleasure—the war was over, and the world of Society wanted its ceaseless round of empty pleasures once again.

Petrograd Society was divided into many sets; each Grand Ducal Court had its own particular clique, and that of the Grand Duchess Marie, wife of the Grand Duke Vladimir, was perhaps specially joyous. The Grand Dukes, taken as a whole, led amusing lives; they were usually very handsome men—quite heroes of romance, many of them possessing a great admiration for the Imperial Ballet, in which they had various fair friends.

It was an expensive existence even in 1907, when Petrograd was supposed to be dull! People went every Sunday to the Ballet, and on Saturdays to the Théatre Français—this, a most fashionable rendezvous, where extremely decolleté toilettes were compensated for by an abundance of jewels! After the play, it was customary to adjourn to the Restaurant Cuba, or to that of L'ours, where a wonderful Roumanian orchestra enlivened supper; nobody thought of leaving the restaurants until three in the morning, and the officers usually remained until five! Occasionally, when I returned home in the early hours, I contrasted the dawn at Revovka with that of Petrograd; the same pearl, rose and silver tints painted the sky, but the dawn in South Russia witnessed no flight of human butterflies whose wings had been singed in the flame of pleasure. I was young enough to enjoy life, but at times our restless gaiety seemed to hold a hidden menace.

English was the medium of conversation in Society at Petrograd; it was invariably spoken at Court, and, although once fashionable to have German nurses, the fashion in 1907 was to have only English ones, and many Russians who could not speak English spoke French with an English accent! The great shopping centre was "Druce's" where one met one's friends, and bought English soaps, perfumery and dresses. The "Druce habit" primarily emanated from Court where everything English was in special favour—Jewish Society and that of the "haute finance" existed in Petrograd, but neither touched us.

The great enlivenments of the Season after the Japanese war were the Charity Bazaars. The Grand Duchess Marie always organised one in the Assemblée de la Noblesse, a huge building where an ultra-smart throng of Society leaders sold all kinds of pretty and expensive trifles. The Grand Duchess Marie (who was a German Princess) occupied the centre of the room, and sold at her own table. She was a tall, striking-looking woman, but not so handsome as the Grand Duchess Cyril at whose table I occasionally assisted. All the Grand Duchesses had tables, as was the case with the greater and lesser lights of Society. In fact the position of one's table was the index to one's position in Society. The bazaars were brilliant functions, the toilettes were wonderful, and it was quite the usual thing to change one's gown three times during the day. The air was heavy with perfume, flowers were lavishly displayed, and the tired vendors occasionally refreshed themselves with the best brands of champagne.

The Empress had her own table at the Assemblée de la Noblesse, and I sold at it once. She made quantities of things herself, instead of sending haphazard orders to Paris or London. The homely intimacy of her nature was very evident in this habit, nothing at her table was useless; she was true to type, the type of Queen Victoria's descendants, the Empress shared Queen Mary of England's love for needlework, and, like her, crocheted many pretty "woollies" for bazaars.

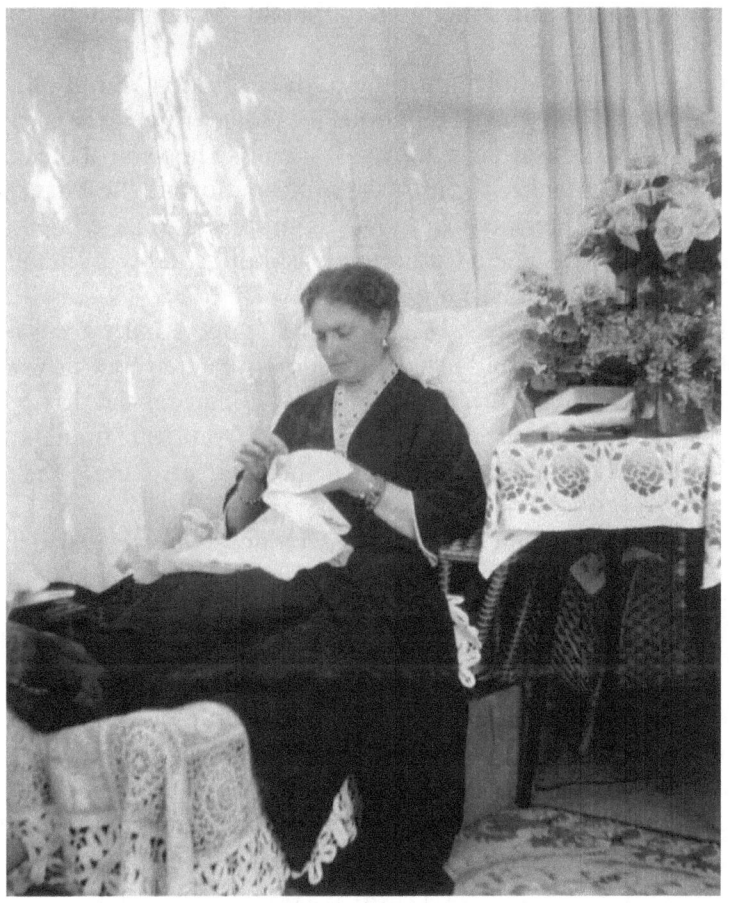

EMPRESS ALEXANDRA FEODOROVNA
Regularly worked on her needle point work

CHAPTER III

ALMOST immediately after my arrival at Tsarkoe Selo, I made the acquaintance of Anna Virouboff, the Lady of the Avenue, and my distant cousin, as her grandfather and my grandmother were related.

It is exceedingly difficult for me to discuss Anna Virouboff, as I am confronted with the tremendous prejudice which exists against her. In England she appears to be a Borgia-like heroine of the films, an hysterical sensualist, the mistress of Rasputin, and the evil genius of the Empress. Her political power is supposed to have been that of a Sarah Jennings and a Catherine Dashkoff, and her influence at Court paramount.

If I deny these charges, I shall lay myself open to the accusation of blind partisanship, and I shall be deemed an utterly untrustworthy chronicler; but, notwithstanding these possibilities, I can do no less than speak of Anna Virouboff as I knew her from 1907 until the day in March, 1917, when we were both removed from Tsarkoe Selo by order of Kerensky.

Anna's father, General Tanief, was Honorary Secretary of State, and all her family were connected with officers in the Imperial House. She married the same year as myself, but before her marriage she was deeply in love with General Orloff, who commanded the Lancers, and who was a great friend of the Empress. Rightly or wrongly, Her Majesty thought that General Orloff would be too old a husband for Anna, and, although the General loved her, and desired nothing better than to marry her, Anna yielded her will to that of the Empress, and accepted Lieutenant Virouboff, to whom she was married in the Palace Chapel at Tsarkoe Selo. The union turned out a complete failure, and I believe that the Empress's original interest in Anna was intensified by the fact that she was indirectly responsible for this unhappy marriage. The Empress accepted what she considered to be her responsibilities very seriously, as her salient characteristics were thoroughness and a fine sense of justice. It was not difficult for her to show more kindness to one whom she already loved, and whose unhappiness was now so poignant. Anna was one of those beings who always look as if someone has hurt them; one wanted to "mother" Anna, to amuse her, to hear her confidences, and to laugh at her exaggerated joys and sorrows.

This photograph of Anna Alexandrovna was used in *Nicholas II – Tsar to Saint*, on page 313. A different image is used here, of a slightly younger Anna.

ANNA ('ANIA') VIROUBOFF

In appearance, Anna is a person entirely different from the Anna Virouboff of the films and the novel, and she even dares to differ from more serious descriptions of her. She is of middle height, with brownish hair, large, appealing, long-lashed, grey-blue eyes, and a little turned-up nose. She has a baby face, all pink and white, and, alas for the Vampire the Anna of romance, she was then very fat. But her smile was charming, and her mouth pretty; she was weak as water, as clinging as the most obstinate ivy, and the Empress treated her much in the way that one treats a helpless child. Anna was excessively good-natured, always ready to help others, in whom she was never able to see evil. This virtue (for I suppose it is accounted a virtue) was the ultimate downfall of Anna. She was too credulous, and, therefore, too easily imposed on. She adored the Imperial Family with the devotion of an adherent of the Stuarts, but—and now I am about to make a statement which will be probably treated with derision—*she possessed no political influence whatever*, she could not influence the Empress one hair's breadth; the Empress petted her, teased her, and scolded her, but she never sought Anna's advice, save in questions of charity.

The Empress and her former Lady-in-Waiting were, however, one where religion was concerned; they shared the same religious sympathies in the midst of an unsympathetic and jealous entourage, and, as Anna did not get on well with the entourage, this fact gave the Empress an additional reason to protect her friend. Anna told me that some of the Ladies-in-Waiting disliked the Empress solely on account of her friendship with her, and, although she had told the Empress that, were she given an official position, all jealousies and comments would be silenced, the Empress had refused to entertain the suggestion.

Later on, when I became on intimate terms with the Empress, she gave me the reason for her refusal.

"I will never give Anna an official position," she said. "She is my friend, I wish to retain her as such. Surely an Empress is allowed the right of a woman to choose her friends. I assure you, Lili, I value my few real friends more than many of the persons in my entourage."

Four years after her marriage, Anna met with a train accident. She never again walked without crutches, her body was completely deformed, but even then slander did not spare her, and evil tongues in Petrograd asserted that, as well as being the friend of the Empress, Anna Virouboff was the mistress of the Emperor!! After her accident, the Empress gave Anna a carriage and pair, and often drove out with her. She lived in a pretty little house which had once belonged to Alexander I, and she usually lunched at home, after spending the morning at the Palace. "The children" liked her, everyone who really knew her liked her, and the best proof of her absolute harmlessness lies in the fact that after the Revolution she was never condemned to death. Surely, if she had been such an evil creature, the first action of those in authority would have been to destroy her? But Anna Virouboff lives, and perhaps one day she will defend herself.

One Monday, shortly after my marriage, I received a note from Anna, asking me to dine with her that evening. Captain Dehn had been in Petrograd for several days, and, as I was rather lonely, I was glad to accept. The dinner was very gay, several officers had been invited, and Emma Fredericks, the daughter of the Minister of the Court, was also a guest. At half-past nine, we heard the sound of wheels, and a carriage stopped outside the house. Anna instantly left the salon, and, a few minutes after, the door opened, and, to our great astonishment, the Emperor, the Empress and the Grand Duchesses entered. They were all laughing, as this surprise visit had been arranged by the Empress, who, seating herself, told us to do likewise, and motioned me to come to her.

"I told you that I should see you again very soon," she said, smiling, and thereupon she began to talk in the most friendly and simple manner.

Once again I had that curious, inexplicable foreboding of tragedy, but no tragedy lurked in that bright, gay room, and my gloomy thoughts were soon dispelled when I was presented to the Emperor.

This was the first occasion on which I had spoken to His Majesty, and I found him as charming and friendly as the Empress. His kind eyes, and his smile, struck me at once, he seemed to move in an aura of goodwill, and his peculiar fascinating charm of manner has been admitted even by his enemies, as M. Kerensky acknowledged that the Emperor possessed one of the noblest natures he ever met!

The Emperor, who bore a striking likeness to his cousin, King George of England, was a very amusing conversationalist, and blessed with a keen sense of humour. He instantly put me at my ease, and I made the acquaintance also of the Grand Duchesses, then quite girls, with whom I was later to become on terms of the closest friendship.

The Empress, having expressed a wish to play Halma, we had two or three games; she was greatly addicted to Halma, but she had one little lovable weakness in connection with it. She never liked to lose! The Emperor played dominoes in the next room, and afterwards Emma Fredericks sang, the Empress accompanying her. Her

Majesty was a very good pianist, and played with rare feeling, but her excessive shyness often precluded her from playing in the presence of others. At midnight the Imperial family took their departure, and the Empress whispered to me: "Au revoir, we shall meet to-morrow."

She did not forget. I was commanded to go to the Palace on the morrow. It was Tuesday, and I remember how pleased I was. "Everything nice happens on a Tuesday," I kept saying, for this was an old belief of mine.

After my meeting with the Empress at Anna's house, I often went to Tsarkoe Selo, and the Grand Duchesses and I used to ride on the wooden switchback, which was set up in one part of the Palace. It was tremendous fun, and we slid and played together for hours, but I quite forgot that I was a married woman and that I had hopes of becoming a mother in some months' time. However, the Empress had some idea of my condition, and one day, after she and Anna had been watching our performance on the switchback, Anna drew me aside.

"Lili," she said, "I've a message for you. The Empress wants you to be very careful just now." She held up a playful finger. "So no more switchback!"

During the months that followed, the Empress manifested the greatest kindness towards me. She insisted upon her own doctor attending me, and, when the Imperial family went yachting about a fortnight before the birth of my baby, my husband received orders to absent himself from the "Standart," and to remain with me instead.

This act of consideration was due to the Empress, and it caused, like the "wireless," much petty jealousy and a good deal of comment.

But the expected baby delayed his arrival, and, when the Imperial family returned to Tsarkoe Selo, the Emperor's first words to my husband were:

"Has the baby come?"

"No, Sire, not yet."

"Well, well, don't worry, Dehn, these things will happen, you know."

However, the baby arrived next morning, and shortly afterwards Anna Virouboff came to make enquiries on behalf of the Empress, bringing with her two lovely ikons, and a package done up in tissue paper and covered with masses of rambler roses. The package contained a thin, fleecy shawl, and my happiness was complete when Anna told me that the Empress wished to be my son's godmother.

This was a great honour, but it presented difficulties, inasmuch as the Dehns, in order to benefit from certain family monies, were obliged to be baptized as Lutherans. The Empress was told about this, and, although she made no objection at the time, I was to discover later how deeply she was imbued with the faith of her adopted country. At the first christening, the Empress attended in person, and held the baby, now known as Alexander Leonide. She gave me a beautiful sapphire and diamond brooch, and all kinds of presents, and for seven years the question of the child's religion was never mooted between us. But, at the end of that time, the Empress told me that her dearest wish was that "Titi" (as she called him) should be received into the Greek Church.

"It is more than a wish, Lili," she said earnestly, "it is a command. I insist upon my godson being Orthodox. He must be baptized before Christmas."

This quiet persistency seems to me to afford one of the most conclusive proofs of how Russian the Empress had become. It may be argued that most converts are usually fanatics, but this was not so in her case. With that "thoroughness" which I have mentioned as one of her chief characteristics, the Empress was now more Russian than most Russians, more Orthodox than the most Orthodox. She was intensely religious. Her love of God and her belief in His mercy came before her love of her husband and her children, and she found her greatest happiness in religion at a time when she was surrounded by the panoply of Imperial splendour. She was to derive consolation from her religion throughout the Via Dolorosa of the saddened years, and, if it is indeed true that she met death in the noisome cellar-room at Ekaterinburg, I am sure that the same ardent faith sustained her in that last moment of agony. She told me that she had hesitated to accept the Emperor's offer of marriage until she felt that her conscience would allow her to do so and she could say with truth: "Thy country shall be my country, thy people my people, and thy God my God."

Titi's second baptism took place during the war at the St. Theodor Cathedral. I had come to Tsarkoe Selo from Reval, and the ceremony took place at 8 in the morning. The Grand Duchesses Marie and Anastasie were present at the first service, but the Empress, previously indisposed, came with the Emperor and the suite to the second service, and afterwards took Holy Communion. Titi was obliged to remain during both services, but he was a good little boy, and he held his lighted candle carefully and firmly the whole time.

After the service we went back to the Palace, and the Empress displayed more emotion than she had done at the first christening. I could see how deeply the religious question had affected her all these years. She told me how relieved she was, how pleased, how she felt now that all was well with the child, and she gave her godson a wonderful ikon of St. Alexander and a Cross engraved with her initials.

But I must return to the earlier days—I have wandered from my narrative to give this example of how Russian the Empress was at heart; hers was no eye-service—to know her made it impossible to doubt her genuineness.

The Empress was always sweet with Titi. She adored children, and she often came to my house, when she nursed the baby and whistled to him. This amused her, and she declared that Titi knew her whistle and always opened his eyes whenever he heard it. I remember that on the morning after the "Lutheran" baptism the Empress paid me a surprise visit.

"I've come to see the baby," she said. "Let me go to the nursery and fetch him."

I followed her upstairs, and she took Titi out of his cot and carried him to the drawing-room, where she played with him for an hour, sitting on the carpet to do so.

I think I am right in saying that our affectionate friendship began from the birth of Titi. It was then that the Empress first called me "Lili," and as "Lili" I caused much mystification during the Revolution, when this signature was supposed to possess some cryptic meaning.

The Imperial Family spent part of that year in Finland, whither my husband accompanied them, and I and the baby went to stay with his parents. I was at Petrograd during the winter, and I saw a great deal of the Imperial Family, and learned to love them all. They led the simplest of lives; the Emperor often amused himself during the evening with a game of dominoes, and I worked with the Empress and her daughters. It was a real "vie de famille," the life which appealed to them as individuals, but not the life which appeals to the smart world, with which the Empress had so little in common. This was my first Christmas at Petrograd, and I deter-mined to have a little tree in Titi's honour. I came in from my shopping late in the afternoon of Christmas Eve, and at 6 o'clock a courier arrived with a large box full of all kinds of "surprises." This was a present from the Empress—she always sent a similar box at Easter, and it always arrived at 6 o'clock. Indeed, so punctual was this present, that my husband often used to hide the box and pretend that it had been forgotten—but I knew better!

We were invited to spend Christmas Day with the Imperial Family. There was a gigantic Christmas tree, the Grand Duchesses and the Tsarevitch thoroughly enjoyed themselves, and busied themselves in the distribution of friendship's offerings. The Empress had one curious fancy in connection with her Christmas trees: she always insisted upon blowing out the candles herself, and she was quite proud because she was able to extinguish the topmost candle by some extraordinary effort of breathing.

And now I feel I must speak of the real Tsaritsa, the Empress whose personality is known to so few—the Tsaritsa who was the most misjudged and unfortunate of human beings. I know in my heart that Time, the best historian, will make clear much that is dark. Even now, slowly, it is true, but none the less surely, people are beginning to wonder whether the Empress was in reality the pro-German and the hysterical *exaltée* she is supposed to have been. She did not deign to defend herself from the calumnies and lies which were scattered broadcast in Russia; to such a nature, these trials were sent by God—all that *she* had to do was to *endure*. But I saw her tears when she and the Emperor received the news of the loss of the "Hampshire" and the death of Kitchener. These were no Judas tears—hers was the grief of the woman and the Sovereign at the death of a brave soldier, and yet, whenever her name is mentioned in England, people say carelessly: "Oh, she saw to the torpedoing of the 'Hampshire,' and wasn't she the mistress of Rasputin?"

A pro-German, and the mistress of Rasputin!! Must this then, be the epitaph of the friend whom I knew, and the Empress to whom I owed the respect of a subject? I am not blind to the knowledge that any vehement defence may do her memory still more harm, but, nevertheless, I am impelled to write of her as she existed in her home, and in our hearts.

I have read and heard almost all that has been laid to her charge; I am no skilled writer, I know little or nothing of politics, but I can lay claim to some knowledge of my own sex. During the awful days of the Revolution, the Empress spoke to me as woman to woman. Her mind constantly dwelt on the days of her girlhood, her life with her grandmother, and the unhappiness of her childhood at Hesse

Darmstadt.

The Emperor was the love of her life. She told me herself that he was her first love, but, the greater her love, the greater her fear lest she would prove unworthy. She gave herself to Russia when she married, and she accepted Russia as a sacred trust; but she and the Emperor were always more husband and wife than Emperor and Empress— they lived the intimate life of happily married people, they liked simplicity, they shrank from publicity, and this love of retirement was the source of many of the evil reports which assailed the Imperial Family.

The Empress told me that when she cried at the marriage of her brother her tears were said to be tears of jealous rage at seeing herself dispossessed of authority.

"But, Lili, I was *not* jealous. I cried when I thought of my mother; this was the first festival since her death. I seemed to see her everywhere."

She described the dull Palace, its strict regime, her father's intermittent kindness, and how much she had looked forward to her visits to Windsor. I think that the intimacy with her grandmother unconsciously brought out the Early Victorian strain in the Empress's character. She undoubtedly possessed this strain, as in many ways she was a typical Victorian; she shared her grandmother's love of law and order, her faithful adherence to family duty, her dislike of modernity, and she also possessed the "homeliness" of the Coburgs, which annoyed Society so much. The Russian aristocracy could not understand why on all the earth their Empress knitted scarves and shawls as presents for her friends, or gave them dress-lengths. Their conception of an Imperial gift was totally different, and they were oblivious of the love which had been crocheted into the despised scarf or the useful shawl—but the Empress, with her Victorian ideas as to the value of friendship, would not, or could not, see that she was a failure in this sense. The Empress was in many ways as thrifty as her grandmother, but she did not share the miserly proclivities of her uncle, the late Duke of Saxe-Coburg. Her father was not a wealthy man, in fact life at Darmstadt was occasion-ally a question of ways and means. The Empress had been taught to be careful. She *was* careful.

"When I was engaged, Lili, I showed my grandmother some of the jewels which the Emperor had given me. What do you think she said?"

"I cannot imagine, Madame."

"Well . . . she looked at my diamonds and remarked: 'Now, Alix, don't get too proud!' The Queen was a tiny creature, and she wore such long trains . . . but she was very forceful." Then, reminiscently, "My sister Elizabeth and I always loved the little houses in England . . . dear little houses set in their pretty gardens. You'll see them one day, but I never shall."

Queen Victoria had instilled in the mind of her granddaughter the entire duties of a *Hausfrau*. In her persistent regard for these Martha-like cares, the Empress was entirely German and entirely English—certainly not Russian. I have mentioned her horror when she arrived at Petrograd and discovered that the servants were unaware of the use of blacklead. This was an actual worry to the Empress.

"I wanted my grates blackleaded every day," she said. "They were in a very bad condition, so I called one of my maids and told her to do the grate, only to discover that it was not within her province. Eventually a man-servant was sent for, but imagine, Lili, I had actually to show him how to blacklead a grate *myself*."

This practical side of the Empress was entirely distasteful to the entourage—they laughed at it equally as much as they criticised her friendships with people whom they did not consider in any way worthy of the friendship of an Empress of Russia. I and Anna came under the category of the unworthy, for, although we were well born, we were not of the "sang azur" of certain noble ladies who were desirous of admittance into the charmed circle. The Empress was accused of not being true to class, but on one point she was inflexible; she allowed no interference with her friendships. I sometimes wondered why she preferred "homely" friends to the more brilliant variety—I ventured to ask her this question, and she told me that she was, as I knew, painfully shy, and that strangers were almost repellent to her.

"I don't mind whether a person is rich or poor. Once my friend, always my friend." Yes, her loyalty was indeed worthy of the name of a friend, but she put friendship and its claims before material considerations. As a woman she was right, as an Empress perhaps she was wrong.

The aristocracy never tried to understand the real Tsaritsa. Their pride was up in arms against her—she found no favour in their eyes. I remember an incident which went to prove this, and which was widely discussed at the time.

Princess Bariatinsky, who then happened to be one of the Maids of Honour to the Empress, was a charming woman, but, like most of the aristocracy, she was excessively proud. One day, hearing that the Empress was about to go out, the Princess held herself in readiness to accompany her, but the Empress left the Palace by another entrance, accompanied by Mlle. Schneider, a Russian lady who gave the Empress lessons in Russian.

This unintentional slight was too much for the Princess. She, metaphorically and literally, put on her hat, and departed never to return, remarking as she did so: "*Quand une Bariatinsky met son chapeau, c'est pour sortir.*" The Empress detested any form of snobbism. One day, during the Japanese war, she was busy at one of her working parties at the Winter Palace; the windows of the salon opened on to the Neva Quai, and from where she sat the Empress could see the soldiers and officers passing to and fro. Suddenly she looked intently out of the window—an expression of distaste on her countenance—and she sighed impatiently. An officer ventured to ask her what was the matter. The Empress pointed to the Quai:

"*That* is the matter," she said, indicating an officer who had just been saluted by some soldiers, but who had not returned the salute. "Why cannot an officer recognise the men by whose side he may one day fall? I detest such snobbism," she added, coldly.

The scandals about the Empress, circulated by propaganda and rumour, will be believed, alas! for many years. She is credited with dabbling in occult practices, with a belief in Spiritualism, and of even attempting to call up the illustrious dead in order to influence the Emperor, who is supposed to have indulged in various dramatic séances at the Winter Palace. Perhaps these stories originated in the more or less retired life led by the Empress. This retirement was often enforced—she was a delicate woman, but, although many writers state that she suffered from the hereditary malady of her father's family, she never mentioned its existence to me. Her heart was weak, owing to rapid child-bearing, and at times she experienced great difficulty in breathing. I never saw the slightest trace of hysteria. The Empress was apt to get suddenly cross, but she usually kept her feelings well under control. Apart from her delicate health, there was another reason for these periods of retirement. The Tsarevitch and the Grand Duchesses were often ailing, the Empress was a devoted mother, and she insisted upon being with her children and sharing the duties of a nurse. The maternal element was strongly developed in her; the Empress was never so happy as when she was "mothering" somebody, and, whenever a person had gained her affection and her trust, she never failed to interest herself in the smallest details connected with him and his.

Her occultism has been grossly exaggerated. Her superstitions were of the most trivial description: she thought that a bright day was propitious for a journey, that the gift of an ikon to her was not propitious, but her fancy for the sign of the Swastika was not for the Swastika as a *charm*, only as a symbol. She told me that the ancients believed in the Swastika as the source of motion, the emblem of Divinity. The significance of it as a "luck bringer" never crossed her mind. "Faith, Love and Hope are *all* that matter," she would say. I will readily admit that she possessed a strong element of mysticism which coloured much of her life; this was akin to the "dreaming" propensities of her grandfather, the Prince Consort, and environment, and the Faith of her adoption fostered this mystic sense. English writers condemn this trait. I have before me a book in which the author quoted the opinion of one of the most bitter enemies of the Empress. "Alexandra Feodorovna," he says, "is an interesting type for future psychologists, historians and dramatic authors . . . a German Princess educated in England, on the Russian Throne, a convert to a peasant's religious sect, and an adept at occultism. She is made of the substance that those terrible, tyrannical Princesses of the XV-XVII centuries in the western countries of Europe were made of; those Princesses who united in their personality the despot Sovereign, bordering on the witch, and skirting the fanatical visionary, who were completely in the hands of their reactionary advisers, and their insinuating wily confessors."

I had read the book containing this extract before I began to write my memories of the real Tsaritsa. I read many passages with eyes half blinded with tears, sometimes I felt mine would be an impossible task. How could I, an unknown name in England, attempt to combat such statements? I am not assuming for one moment that the writer of the book was ill-disposed towards the Empress; he wrote for posterity, setting down his own opinion and that of others. But I am curious to know if he ever knew the Empress personally, and if he ever shared the intimate life of the Imperial Family. I did *both*—not only in the days before and during the war, but also in the days of despair, when murder and sudden death faced us at every turn. It was then no time for pretence—but the Empress never changed; she was the same unselfish soul, the same devoted mother and wife, the same loyal friend.

The material for another book which was largely circulated in England was supposed to have been "given" to the author by a lady well known, and in great favour at Court. This novel—for it was, in many respects, fiction pure and simple—was mentioned to me, and, upon reading it, I was amazed to find the names of persons who never existed, and who were, therefore, never at Court. There was no attempt to hide names under pseudonyms or initials—these imaginary beings lived, moved and had their being in the book as real individuals!

I was so much interested in the creative genius of the "Court Lady" that a friend of mine wrote to the part-author and asked him, on my behalf, to disclose her name. My request was refused: the part-author said that he was under an honourable vow of secrecy not to disclose the name of his collaborator!

But was this sporting? The book contained certain damning statements against the Empress, it bristled with inaccuracies; truly, anonymous Court histories cover a multitude of untruths! But surely those who profit thereby should have courage enough to come out in the open when certain questions arise. You either make a statement, or you do not. If you believe in its truth, you should not be ashamed to say why, and wherefore, and to acknowledge the source of its origin, but I am inclined to think that the words, "I gave my word not to say who told me," place little value on malicious gossip, either in books or in everyday life.

CHAPTER IV

THE Empress was an early riser. She had six dressers, of whom the chief, Madeleine Zanoty, was an Italian by birth, whose family had long been in the service of the Hesses. Louise Toutelberg, known as "Toutel," the second in authority, came from the Baltic, and there were four others. The dressers had three days' service, but none of them ever saw the Empress undressed or in her bath. She rose and went to her bath unassisted, and slipped on a Japanese kimono of silk or printed cotton over her undergarments when she was ready to have her hair arranged. The Empress was extraordinarily modest in her disarray, and in this the Victorian influence was again discernible, as her conception of the bedroom was à-la-mode de Windsor and Buckingham Palace in 1840. She did not countenance the filmy and theatrical, either in her lingerie or in her sleeping apartment; her underwear was of the finest linen, beautifully embroidered, but otherwise plain. Her red-gold hair was never touched with curling irons, and it was usually very simply dressed, except when great State functions called for a more elaborate coiffure.

The bedroom of the Emperor and the Empress was a large room with two tall windows opening on to the Park. It was on the ground floor, as, owing to the Empress's heart complaint, she found the exertion of ascending any stairs very exhausting. A lift in the corridor communicated with the nurseries, but during the Revolution the water supply was cut off, and the lift stopped working. Nevertheless the Empress insisted upon mounting the stairs to visit the invalid Grand Duchesses, and I always accompanied her, going behind her, and propping her up at each step. It brought tears to my eyes when I saw how ill she was, but she was determined not to miss a single chance of seeing her beloved children.

A large double bed made of lightish wood was near the windows, between which stood the Empress's dressing-table. At the right of the bed was a little door in the wall, leading to a tiny dark chapel lighted by hanging lamps, where the Empress was wont to pray. This chapel contained a table, and a praying-stand on which were a Bible and an ikon of Christ. This ikon was afterwards given to me by Her Majesty, in memory of the days which we spent together at Tsarkoe

Selo, and is one of my most treasured possessions to-day.

The furniture in the Imperial bedroom was in flowered tapestry, and the carpet was a plain coloured soft pile. The Emperor's dressing-room was separated from the bedroom by the corridor, and on the other side were the Empress's dressing-room and bathroom—but, alas! for her rumoured extravagances and her "odd" fancies! The bathroom was no luxurious place of silver and marble, but an old-fashioned bath set in a dark recess, and the Empress, with her Victorian love of neatness, insisted that the bath was hidden during the day under a loose cretonne cover. There was a fireplace in the dressing-room, and the dressers waited in the next room until the Empress required their services. The Empress's gowns were kept here, and another room full of large cupboards (half-way up the staircase leading to the nurseries) was given over to the use of those maids whose especial duty it was to iron and renovate Her Majesty's clothes.

The Empress favoured long, pointed footgear with very low heels: she usually wore suède, bronze or white shoes, never satin. "I can't bear satin shoes, they worry me," she would say. Her gowns, except those worn by her on State occasions, were very simple; she liked blouses and skirts, and she was greatly addicted to tea-gowns: her taste in dress was as refined as that of Queen Mary of England; like her she disapproved strongly of exaggerated fashions, and I shall not easily forget her condemnation when I once came to see her wearing a "hobble" skirt. "Do you really like this skirt, Lili?" asked the Empress.

"Well . . . Madame," I said helplessly, "c'est la mode."

"It is no use whatever as a skirt," she answered. "Now, Lili, prove to me that it is comfortable—run, Lili, run, and let me see how fast you can cover the ground in it."

Needless to say, I never wore a "hobble" skirt again.

The Empress has been accused of a mania for precious stones. I never saw any signs of it: true, she had quantities of magnificent jewels, but these possessions were consequent upon her position as Empress. She was fond of rings and bracelets, and she always wore a certain ring set with one immense pearl, and a jewelled cross. Some writers assert that this cross was set with emeralds, but I do not agree. I am sure that the stones were sapphires, and, as I saw it every day, I fancy I am correct. The Empress had soft, well-shaped hands, but they were neither small nor useless hands, and she never had her nails polished, as the Emperor detested highly polished and supermanicured nails.

At nine o'clock the Empress breakfasted with the Emperor; it was a simple meal à l'Anglaise, and after breakfast she went upstairs to see the children. Then Anna Virouboff arrived, and, if certain interviews were imperative, these were usually given during the morning, but, if the Empress found herself "free," she went to inspect her training college for domestic nurses, which was arranged entirely on English lines. She had great faith in the value of English-trained nurses for children, and she put all her usual "thoroughness" into the working and management of this institution.

Lunch was at one o'clock, and at twelve-thirty on Sundays; but when, as it often happened, the Empress was indisposed, she either lunched in her boudoir or alone with the Tsarevitch. After lunch the Empress walked, or drove herself in a little open carriage. Tea was at five, but sometimes receptions were held between lunch and tea. The Imperial Family all met at tea, which was quite "en famille"; and dinner, which was at 8 o'clock, was often a movable feast in the literal sense of the word. The Emperor disliked dining in one special room, so a table was carried to whichever room he happened to fancy that evening. Dinner over (and it was a very simple dinner) the Imperial Family spent the remainder of the evening together, and the Grand Duchesses, who had a *flair* for puzzles, usually indulged in puzzle-making: sometimes the Emperor read aloud whilst his daughters and their mother worked. It was the homely life of a united family—but a life with which the great world was not in sympathy; in fact a Russian writer did not hesitate to state openly that "it would have been better for Russia's felicity if the Empress had succumbed to the many frailties which were attributed to Catherine II." It is ironical to dwell on such an opinion when one remembers how the newspapers and the general public condemned her association with Rasputin. But had she been Catherine II, it is possible that this "frailty" might have been considered necessary for the "felicity" of Russia!

The Empress's boudoir, known as "Le Cabinet Mauve de l'Imperatrice," was a lovely room, in which the Empress's partiality for all shades of mauve was apparent. In spring-time and winter the air was fragrant with masses of lilac and lilies of the valley, which were sent daily from the Riviera. Lovely pictures adorned the walls—and one of the Annunciation, and another of St. Cecilia, faced a portrait of the Empress's mother, the late Princess Alice of England, Grand Duchess of HesseDarmstadt.

The furniture was mauve and white, Heppelwaite in style, and there were various "cosy corners." On a large table stood many family photographs, that of Queen Victoria occupying the place of honour.

The other private drawing-room was a large room, decorated and upholstered in shades of green, and the Empress had arranged in one corner a sort of tiny staircase and a balcony, which was always full of violets in the spring. In this room were pictures of herself and the Emperor, and some exquisite miniatures of the Grand Duchesses by Kaulbach, that of Marie being especially beautiful.

Books were everywhere; the Empress was a prolific reader, but she was chiefly addicted to serious literature, and she knew the Bible from cover to cover. The library was next the green drawing-room, and here all the newest books and magazines were placed on a round table, and constantly changed for others in the order of their publication.

The Empress was a great letter-writer, and she wrote her letters wherever she fancied. Her writing-table proper was in the room next her bedroom, but I have often seen her writing letters on a pad in her lap, and she invariably used a fountain-pen. Before the war she wrote daily to a great friend in Germany, and she always read this lady's letters to me. Her stationery, like her lingerie, was plain, but stamped with her cypher and the Imperial Crown.

Apropos of her fondness for lilac and lilies of the valley, I may mention that the Empress loved all flowers, her especial favourites being lilies, magnolias, wistaria, rhododendrons, freesias and violets. A love of flowers is usually akin to a love of perfumes, and the Empress was no exception to the rule. She generally used Atkinson's White Rose; it was, she said, "clean" as a perfume, and "infinitely sweet"—as an eau-de-toilette, she favoured Verveine.

When I first knew the Empress, she did not smoke, but during the Revolution she smoked cigarettes: I fancy they soothed her overwrought nerves.

The Empress always kept a diary, but I shall presently relate how it became my duty to burn her diaries, also those of Princess Sofia Orbeliani and Anna Virouboff; and last, but not least in sentimental interest, all the letters which the Emperor had sent her during their engagement and married life.

Dr. Botkin, the devoted friend and physician to the family, was introduced to me by Anna Virouboff, and I liked him exceedingly. He was a clever, liberal-minded man, and, although his political views were opposed to those of the Imperialists, he became so devoted to the Emperor that his once cherished views mattered little to him.

I think, from my description, which possesses the merit of accuracy, that it will be recognised what simplicity of life surrounded the rulers of one of the greatest Empires the world has ever known. Simplicity characterised all their doings, the simplicity which was to prove their undoing. The Imperial pair wished to lead the lives of private individuals; they imagined that it was possible. In Russia it has never been popular or possible for a Tsar to be human; he was an emblem, a representative of crystallised traditions; he united in himself the rôles of the Father of his people and the splendid, all-conquering, unapproachable Tsar. An Emperor or an Empress in mufti, so to speak, never yet appealed to popular imagination, and, just as the English cottager preserved and venerated the horrible "royal" oleographs of Queen Victoria, so did the Russian peasant venerate similar oleographs of the Emperor and his Consort. Neither cottager nor peasant would have understood or cared to possess "family" photographs of their rulers. Popular imagination has ever been appealed to by scarlet and ermine, golden crowns, and kingly sceptres. It doesn't understand or value anything else.

In the March following the birth of Titi, the Empress wrote and told me that she was anxious to see her godson, then nine months old. So I went with him to Tsarkoe Selo, where the Grand Duchesses made much of him, and used to take it in turns to bath him. We took up our quarters in Anna's house, where the Empress had personally superintended the arrangement of the baby's room, and she sent his cot, of which she crocheted the hangings and coverlet herself. She spent hours with the child, playing with him, "snap-shotting" him, and, after our first visit, I was constantly "commanded" to "come and bring the baby." I remember that, when I once missed the train, and arrived too late for lunch, the Empress, who was waiting for me, noticed my fatigue, and ordered tea. She took Titi on her lap, and saying, "Well . . . Lili, you do look hungry and tired," she fed me with pieces of sandwiches, pressing them on me much in the same way that a mother soothes a tired child. But she was ever "plus mère que mère, plus Russe que Russe," but her love of country was only for Russia and England. She had, and I say it with absolute conviction, no love for Germany as her "Motherland." She liked Darmstadt, because to her it represented home, but she manifested no interest in any other part of Germany.

My friendship with the Empress increased as the months passed. That autumn the Imperial Family went to Livadia, and I stayed with my uncle, going constantly to and from the Palace. The first day I saw the Empress in Livadia she gave me an entire layette for Titi which she had made herself. I had wondered why she had telegraphed for his measurements—now I knew! She would often call at my uncle's and take the baby with her for a drive. The little thing got to know her well, and one day, looking at her photograph, he said "Baby"; so after this the Empress of Russia was known to Titi by her own wish, *tout simplement*, in English, as "Aunt Baby." He always called her "Aunt Baby," and in many of her letters she alludes to herself by this pet name, but, needless to say, the favour shown to me and my child by the Imperial Family was the source of much comment at Court.

On one point my mind was made up. I determined never to allow any ideas of preferment or material advantage to spoil what was to me a condition of great happiness. My husband entirely agreed, and he declined to consider any mention of the posts which were from time to time spoken of in connection with him. As for myself, the Empress understood and appreciated my outlook. "You can always be my *friend* if matters remain as they are," she said. "I don't want to lose my Lili in an official personage."

We were very happy in those days. The Grand Duchesses were fast leaving childhood behind them and blossoming into charming girls; they did not greatly resemble one another, each was a type apart, but all were equally lovely in disposition. I cannot believe that any men so inhuman existed as those who, it is said, shot and stabbed those defenceless creatures in the house of death at Ekaterinburg. Apart from their beauty, their sweetness should have pleaded for them, but, if it is true that they have "passed," then surely no better epitaph could be theirs than the immortal words,

"Lovely and pleasant were they in their lives, and in their death they were not divided."

The Grand Duchess Olga was the eldest of these four fair sisters. She was a most amiable girl, and people loved her from the moment they set eyes on her. As a child she was plain, at fifteen she was beautiful. She was slightly above middle height, with a fresh complexion, deep blue eyes, quantities of light chestnut hair, and pretty hands and feet. She took life seriously, and she was a clever girl with a sweet disposition. I think she possessed unusual strength of character, and at one time she was mentioned as a possible bride for the Crown Prince of Roumania. But the Grand Duchess did not like him, and, as the Crown Prince liked the Grand Duchess Marie better than her sister, nothing came of the project. The sisters loved each other, and united in a passionate adoration for the Tsarevitch. In a recent book published in England, the Grand Duchesses have been described as Cinderellas, who were entirely subservient in family life owing to the attention paid the Tsarevitch. This is untrue. It is a fact that the Empress ardently desired a son, and that the birth of four daughters in succession was a disappointment to her, but she loved her daughters, they were her inseparable companions, and their plain and rather strict upbringing had nothing whatever of the Cinderella element.

The Grand Duchess Tatiana was as charming as her sister Olga, but in a different way. She has been described as proud, but I never knew anyone less so. With her, as with her mother, shyness and reserve were accounted as pride, but, once you knew her and had gained her affection, this reserve disappeared, and the real Tatiana became apparent. She was a poetical creature, always yearning for the ideal, and dreaming of great friendships which might be hers. The Emperor loved her devotedly, they had much in common, and the sisters used to laugh, and say that, if a favour were required, "Tatiana must ask Papa to grant it." She was very tall, and excessively thin, with a cameo-like profile, deep blue eyes, and dark chestnut hair . . . a lovely "Rose" maiden, fragile and pure as a flower.

All the Grand Duchesses were innocent children in their souls. Nothing impure was ever allowed to come into their lives—the Empress was very strict over the books which they read, which were mostly by English authors. They had no idea of the ugly side of life, although, poor girls, they were destined to see the worst side of it and to come in contact with the most debased passions of humanity! And yet it has been stated that the Empress, in her neurotic, religious exaltation, gave each of her daughters to Rasputin. Knowing her, knowing the Emperor, and knowing the daughters as I did, such an assertion savours of the monstrous; it has even been circulated that Mlle. Tutcheff objected to Rasputin being admitted to the Grand Duchesses' bedchamber to give them his nightly blessing after they had retired to bed, and that, as her protest was disregarded, she sent in her resignation. Mlle. Tutcheff was never governess to the Grand Duchesses, and she never witnessed Rasputin's nightly blessing, inasmuch as it never took place. The Emperor would never have permitted such a thing, even had the Empress wished it, and she certainly did not consider such a proceeding necessary for her daughters' salvation. Mlle. Tutcheff was the victim of her own spite and jealousy. She was not a very pleasant person, and, whenever the Imperial Family went to Livadia, she usually made herself very disagreeable, as she thoroughly disliked the Crimea. Continual grumbling wears away the patience of most people; the Empress was only human, and Mlle. Tutcheff was first given a holiday and then dismissed by the Grande Maîtresse de la Cour.

Mlle. Tutcheff did not hesitate to spread all kinds of vindictive rumours to account for her dismissal. She was too small-minded to state the real facts, and, as l'affaire Rasputin was generally spoken about, she decided to vent her spite on the Empress through this medium. I again assert that there is no truth in the legend of Rasputin's nightly blessing.

When I first knew the Grand Duchess Marie, she was quite a child, but during the Revolution she became very devoted to me, and I to her, and we spent most of our time together—she was a wonderful girl, possessed of tremendous reserve force, and I never realised her unselfish nature until those dreadful days. She too was exceeding fair, dowered with the classic beauty of the Romanoffs; her eyes were dark blue, shaded by long lashes, and she had masses of dark brown hair. Marie was plump, and the Empress often teased her about this; she was not so lively as her sisters, but she was much more decided in her outlook. The Grand Duchess Marie knew at once what she wanted, and why she wanted it.

Anastasie, the youngest Grand Duchess, might have been composed of quicksilver, instead of flesh and blood; she was most amusing, and she was a very clever mimic. She saw the humorous side of everything, and she was very fond of acting; indeed, Anastasie would have made an excellent comedy actress. She was always in mischief, a regular tom-boy, but she was not backward in her development, as M. Gilliard once stated. Anastasie was only sixteen at the time of the Revolution—no great age after all! She was pretty, but hers was more of a clever face, and her eyes were wells of intelligence.

All the sisters were utterly devoid of pride, and, when they nursed the wounded during the war, they were known as the Sisters Romanoff, and thus answered to the numbers 1, 2, 3 and 4.

The Grand Duchesses occupied two bedrooms; Olga and Tatiana shared one, Marie and Anastasie the other. These apartments were large and light, decorated and furnished in green and white. The sisters slept on camp beds—a custom dating back to the reign of Alexander I, who decreed that the daughters of the Emperor were not to sleep on more comfortable beds until they married. Ikons hung in the corners of the rooms, and there were pretty dressing-tables, and couches with embroidered cushions. The Grand Duchesses were fond of pictures and photographs—there were endless snapshots taken by themselves, those from their beloved Crimea being especially in evidence.

A large room, divided by a curtain, served as dressing-room and bathroom for the Grand Duchesses. One half of the room was full of cupboards, and in the other half stood the large bath of solid silver. The Grand Duchesses had departed from their mother's simple ideas, and, when they bathed at night, the water was perfumed and softened with almond bran. Like their mother, they were addicted to perfumes, and always used those of Coty. Tatiana favoured "Jasmin de Corse"; Olga, "Rose Thé"; Marie constantly changed her perfumes, but was more or less faithful to lilac, and Anastasie never deviated from violette.

The Grand Duchesses' attendants were a compromise between dressers, maids and nurses. They were all girls of good family, the most favoured being Mlle. Tegeleff, known as "Shoura"; the other two were "Elizabeth" and "Neouta." The Empress—once again Victorian—was very desirous for these girls to wear caps, but they declined respectfully but firmly to do so, and she did not press the matter. The Grand Duchesses liked their attendants, and often used to help them tidy the rooms and make the beds! Unlike their mother, but like most Russians, the four sisters showed a predilection for dress, but the Empress had her own ideas on the subject, and she chose and ordered all their clothes. As children, the girls were dressed alike, but later the two eldest wore similar gowns, and the next two were dressed, so to speak, "to match." The only frivolity which the Empress tolerated lay in her daughters' dressing-gowns, which carried out the colours of the regiments of which they were colonels, and the Grand Duchesses were very proud of their dressing-gowns and their regiments. They were always present at parades, when they wore the uniform of their regiments, and this excitement was one of their chief pleasures.

The sisters led most ordinary, uneventful lives; their exalted station never troubled them. With true courtesy they always made me pass out of a room before them, there was no ceremony, no fuss—they were the dearest, most affectionate girls, and I loved them all. The Grand Duchesses rose early, and were soon occupied with their lessons. After morning lessons they walked with the Emperor, and between lunch and tea they again went out with him. They spoke Russian, English or a little French, *never* German, and, although they danced well, they had not much chance to do so, unless the Imperial Family went to the Crimea, then Princess Marie Bariatinsky always arranged a series of dances for them.

The motive power in the lives of these charming children was family love. They had no thought apart from their home. Their affection was lavished on their father and mother, their brother and a few friends. Their parents were their paramount consideration. With the "children," as we called them, it was always a question of "Would Papa like it?" "Do you think this or that would please Mama?"—and they always alluded to their father and mother by the simple Russian words of Mama and Papa.

The Tsarevitch, that Child of many Prayers, one of the most pathetic figures in this tragedy of innocence, was born in 1904, and he was a healthy baby weighing eleven pounds at the time of his birth; many of the stories about his delicacy of constitution which have been given to the world are very exaggerated, especially the one which insists that the Nihilists mutilated the child when he was on the Imperial yacht. No such mutilation ever took place. The Tsarevitch certainly suffered from the hereditary trouble of thin blood-vessels, which first became apparent after a fall in Spala, but he was otherwise a normally healthy boy, and at the time of the Revolution he was really getting much stronger and much freer from the complaint. I know he was ailing at Tobolsk and Ekaterinburg, but that is hardly to be wondered at!

In appearance he resembled his sister Tatiana: he had the same fine features, and her beautiful blue eyes; he loved his sisters, and they adored him, and patiently submitted to his teasing. The Tsarevitch was a lively, amusing boy, with a wonderful ear for music, and he played well on the *balalika*: like Tatiana he was shy, but, once he knew and liked anyone, this shyness vanished.

The Empress insisted upon her son being brought up, like his sisters, in a perfectly natural way. There was no ceremonial in the daily life of the Tsarevitch: he was merely a son, and a brother to his family, although it was sometimes quaint to see him assume "grown up" airs. One day, when he was indulging in a romp with the Grand Duchesses, he was told that some officers of his regiment had arrived at the Palace and begged permission to be received by him.

The Tsarevitch instantly ceased his game, and, calling his sisters, he said very gravely: "Now, girls, run away. I am busy. Someone has just called to see me on business."

He adored his mother, and her passionate devotion to him is world-known, although, like many other things, this devotion has been used as a weapon against her. To the Empress, the Tsarevitch represented the direct result of prayer, the Divine condescension of God, the crowning joy of her marriage. Surely, if she manifested undue anxiety over him, she only did what all mothers have done, and will do until the end of time. There was certainly some subtle sympathy between mother and son: she was all that was lovely and beloved to him, and I especially remember one typical instance of this devotion:

My husband and I had been dining with the Imperial Family, and after dinner the Emperor suggested that we should accompany them to the Tsarevitch's bedroom, as the Empress always went thither to bid him good night and hear him say his prayers. It was a pretty sight to watch the child and his mother, and listen to his simple prayers, but, when the Empress rose to go, we suddenly found ourselves in complete darkness— the Tsarevitch had switched off the electric light over his bed!

"Why have you done this, Baby?" asked the Empress. "Oh," answered the child, "it's only light for me, Mama, when you are here. It's always quite dark when you have gone."

He loved his father, and the Emperor's great wish in the "happy days" was to undertake his son's education himself: this, for many reasons, was impossible, and Mr. Gibbs and M. Gilliard were his first tutors. Later, under very different conditions, the Emperor was enabled to carry out his wish. In the gloomy house at Tobolsk, he taught the Tsarevitch, and in the squalor and misery of Ekaterinburg the lessons still continued; but perhaps the greatest lesson learnt by the Tsarevitch and the other members of the unfortunate family was that of Faith: for faith sustained them, and strengthened them at a time when riches and friends had fled and they found themselves betrayed by the very country which had been all in all to them.

The Tsarevitch had various playmates—all sorts and conditions of boys shared his games: there were the two sons of his sailor-servant, two peasant boys with whom he was on friendly and affectionate terms, and my "Titi," who ran about with him, upsetting everything, and thoroughly enjoying himself. The Heir to the Throne was as courteous as his sisters. One day the Empress and I were sitting in the mauve boudoir, when we heard the excited voices of the Tsarevitch and Titi in the next room.

"I believe they're quarrelling," said the Empress, and she went to the door and listened to what the children were saying. Then she turned to me laughing. "Why they're not quarrelling, Lili. Alexis is insisting that Titi shall come into the mauve room first, and the good Titi won't hear of it!"

If the Tsarevitch had any peculiarities, I think the most striking was a decided penchant for hoarding. Many descendants of the Coburgs have been unusually thrifty, and perhaps the Tsarevitch inherited this trait. While thrifty he was really a most generous child, although he hoarded his things to such an extent that the Emperor often teased him unmercifully. During the sugar shortage he saved his allowance of sugar, which he gravely distributed among his friends. He was fond of animals, and his spaniel, "Joy," has happily found a home in England: his chief pet at Tsarkoe was an ugly sandy and white kitten, which he once brought from G.H.Q. This kitten he christened Zoubrovka, and bestowed a collar and a bell on it as a signal mark of affection. "Zoubrovka" was no respecter of palaces, and he used to wage war with the Grand Duchess Tatiana's bulldog "Artipo," and light-heartedly overthrow all the family photographs in the Tsaritsa's boudoir. But "Zoubrovka" was a privileged kitten, and I have often wondered what became of him when the Imperial Family were taken to Tobolsk.

All the children were fond of animals. The Grand Duchess Tatiana's pet was a bulldog called "Artipo," who slept in her bedroom, much to the annoyance of the Grand Duchess Olga, who disliked its propensity for snoring. The Grand Duchess Marie favoured a Siamese cat, and, the year before the Revolution, Anna Virouboff gave a little Pekinese dog to the Grand Duchess Anastasie.

This little creature had a tragic history. Curiously enough many people said that "Jimmi" seemed an unlucky dog; but he was a sweet little creature, whose tiny legs were so short that he could not walk up or down stairs. The Grand Duchess Anastasie always carried him, and "Jimmi" lavished a Pekinese devotion on her and her sisters. "Jimmi" went with the family to Tobolsk, and he is now identified in history with their fate. According to one account, his corpse was found, preserved in ice, at the top of the disused mine shaft; another writer has it that "Jimmi" defended his friends in the cellar at Ekaterinburg, barking defiance at the murderers, and guarding Tatiana's fainting body until they were both killed. His skeleton is said to have been discovered later in a clump of undergrowth, and subsequently identified by its size and by a bullet hole in the skull.

He was a dear little dog, and probably, could he have spoken, he would have desired no better fate than to perish with those in whose fortunes and affections he had equally participated.

The Emperor greatly resembled King George V in appearance, but his eyes were unforgettable; and those of his cousin, although fine, do not possess the expression peculiar to the eyes of the Emperor. It was a combination of melancholy, sweetness, resignation and tragedy: Nicholas II seemed as if he saw into the tragic future, but he also seemed to see the Heaven that lies beyond this earth. He was "God's good man." I can give no higher praise, render him no more fitting homage.

He was essentially charming: when you were with him you forgot the Emperor in the individual; he made formality impossible. He loved to tease people, and I came in for my full share of this propensity. One day when I was out walking at Livadia, several carriages passed me, but I did not especially notice their occupants. The next evening when I was dining at the Palace, the Emperor addressed me in grave tones: "*Lili—ce n'est pas bien, vous comprenez, mais ne pas reconnaitre vos amis.*"

"*Mais, Votre Majesté, qu'est que vous voulez dire?*"

"Well," said the Emperor, "you *cut* me yesterday."

"Votre Majesté, it's impossible!"

"Ah . . . it's quite possible, Lili. I drove past you, and bowed to you many times, but you wouldn't recognise me. Tell me in what I've offended you." And he continued to tease me until I felt ready to die with confusion. He loved his wife: no one has ever dared dispute the quality of the affection which existed between them; theirs was an ideal love-marriage, and when their love was tried in the furnace of affliction it was not found wanting.

Nicholas II had been reproached for his weakness of character, but this weakness was not weakness in the literal sense. The Empress, who was fully aware of what was said concerning the Emperor and herself, once told me how utterly people misunderstood her husband. "He is accused of weakness," she said bitterly. "He is the strongest—not the weakest. I assure you, Lili, that it cost the Emperor a tremendous effort to subdue the attacks of rage to which the Romanoffs are subject. He has learnt the hard lesson of self-control, only to be called weak; people forget that the greatest conqueror is he who conquers himself."

On another occasion she remarked that she knew that the Emperor and herself were blamed for not surrounding themselves with genuine people.

"It's an extraordinary thing, Lili," she said, "we've tried to find genuine advisers for the last twenty years, but we've never found them. I wonder whether any exist!"

The Empress always resented the cruel slanders which were circulated about the Emperor. "I wonder they don't accuse him of being too good: that, at least, would be true!" she cried.

As for herself, she troubled little.

"Why do people want to discuss me," she said. "Why *can't* they leave me alone!" Again: "Why will people insist that I am pro-German? I have spent twenty years in Germany, and twenty years in Russia. My interests, and my son's future lie in Russia:

how, therefore, can I be anything but Russian?"

The Empress has been censured for exerting undue influence over her husband, and this "pernicious" influence has made her the scapegoat for all the ills which have befallen Russia. But her "influence" was merely that of a good woman over a man. If she influenced the Emperor in any other way, it was done unconsciously. I will never believe otherwise, although, in making this assertion, I shall perhaps be confronted with all kinds of hostile criticism. It will be asked by what right I dare defend a woman who has been tried and found guilty. But I dare to do so. True, I am a person whose name is entirely unknown to the general public, but it cannot be disputed by those who knew life at Tsarkoe Selo and Petrograd that I was honoured by the Empress's friendship and confidence.

The Emperor shared his wife's "thoroughness"; he never believed anything until (were it possible) he had tried it for himself.

During the war, a new uniform was submitted for the Emperor's approval; he determined to test its qualities, and he walked for twenty miles wearing it, in order to see what weight was possible to carry with it. The sentinels failed to recognise the Emperor when he passed them wearing the sample "Tommy's" kit, a fact which greatly amused him; but, as a result of his practical experiment, the uniform (with certain alterations suggested by the Emperor) was "passed."

The Empress put her husband first in everything—it was always "The Emperor wishes it," "The Emperor says so"; she was very tender towards him, the maternal element was apparent in her love even for her husband: she took care of him, but perhaps this arose chiefly from a feeling that he suffered by reason of his love for her.

As husband and wife they were indeed one. They only asked happiness of life. The Emperor's tastes were of the simplest, the Empress was shy and retiring—both their dispositions were similar—and this similarity of tastes, ideal in the usual walks of life, was fatal to both of them as rulers. By this I do not for one moment wish to infer that they shirked their responsibilities: far from it, they were always ready to assume them, but they forgot that the times were out of joint, that it was their duty always to live in the fierce light that beats upon a throne. I do not think that by so doing they could have saved Russia. The case of Nicholas II and Alexandra of Russia is almost parallel with that of Louis XVI and Marie Antoinette. The Russian monarchs, like their French prototypes, were called upon to reign over a country ripe for Revolution, whose dragon's teeth had been sown by the vicious hands of their predecessors. France boasted as extravagant and exotic a society as that of Russia: the writing was already to be seen on the walls of Versailles and the Winter Palace, but the Sovereigns of Then and Now heeded it not. Louis XVI wanted to be left alone in his workroom, to make locks and to mend watches, and Marie Antoinette sighed for the simple pleasures of the Trianon and the pastoral joys of a farmer's wife.

Nicholas II did not care to be a locksmith, he merely wished to live the quiet life of a well-bred gentleman: chivalrous by nature, he (and here an English writer is correct) came nearer the British public-school idea than any other. The Empress did not require a Trianon, she wanted a home; but, although she loved Russia, Russia was always antagonistic to her. This she never realised, any more than she recognised the fact that the peasant class never wanted her to try and understand them.

The Emperor was a clever man, and he possessed that wonderful memory for faces peculiar to his uncle, King Edward VII. On one occasion when my husband was presented to the Emperor after receiving some special decoration, a colonel of a Siberian regiment also attended the Levée. The Emperor stretched out his hand to the colonel. "Surely I've seen you before?" he enquired. "Yes, Your Majesty." "Well, but *where*?" continued the Emperor, in puzzled tones; then brightening, "Ah, I know," he said, "I met you twelve years ago when I passed through Saratof."

The chief pleasures of the Emperor were those appertaining to an outdoor life. He was a good shot, fond of all kinds of sport, and his hands were exceptionally powerful. Boating was a favourite amusement; he liked to row in a small boat, or paddle a canoe, and the Emperor passed hours and hours on the water when the Imperial Family were staying at Shker, in Finland.

Both the Emperor and the Empress disliked the Kaiser. I say this with perfect sincerity, and in all truth. They rarely mentioned his name before the war, and I know that his love of theatrical displays appealed to neither of them. In 1903 the Emperor William arrived in his yacht at Reval to witness a military review. The "Standart" with the Emperor of Russia aboard was also at Reval. After the Kaiser had paid a formal call on the Emperor, signals passed between the two yachts.

"What's all this?" asked the Emperor. An officer enlightened him.

"Your Majesty," said he, "the signal from the 'Hohenzollern' says: 'The Emperor of the Atlantic salutes the Emperor of the Pacific.'" The Emperor looked cross.

"Oh, that's it—well reply 'Thank you'—that's quite enough."

The Kaiser did not shine as a visitor to the "Standart"; the first thing he did was to shake hands indiscriminately, a proceeding which caused much amusement and confusion, and everyone was heartily glad when the "Emperor of the Atlantic" took his departure.

The Grand Duchesses disliked any mention of the Kaiser, but some of the officers used to tease them about him. The usual question of any privileged arrival at Tsarkoe Selo was: "Well, how is Uncle Willie to-day?" And the invariable answer was: "No— no— he's not our Uncle Willie—we don't want to hear his name."

Russia has been described as a country of tears and misery during the war, but this is incorrect. The peasants were never so rich as at this time, and there was no discontent in the country districts;

the wives received big allowances, and they earned extra money for themselves without any difficulty. Every boy indulged in high patent-leather boots, every girl spent money on dress. There were certainly tears for the fallen, but there was no material misery in Russia.

The Emperor had made great plans to help those disabled in the service of their country. His idea was to give all wounded, disabled or decorated soldiers gifts of Crown Lands at the end of the war. He planned various land reforms, but the Revolutionaries incited the landlords against him by telling them that the Emperor was going to be generous at their expense, and not at his own!

It is impossible for an English public to realise the plots and counter-plots which existed in Russia. The Empress, on many occasions, barely escaped with her life; she was unpopular with all classes, but she was unable, mercifully, to estimate the quality of the hatred meted out to her. I do not think there is a single charge that has not been laid at her door; she is credited with hysteria, religious mania, pro-Germanism, the qualities of a Judas, the morals of a Messalina; she has been described as the intriguing, strong-minded consort of a weak man, a willing tool of an infamous sensualist, as well as being a half-witch, and a half-mystic. The real Tsaritsa, firm in her convictions, the devoted wife, mother and friend, is unknown. Her acts of charity have been misconstrued, her religion has been made her shame, the very nationality which she so willingly relinquished has become an unmerited reproach. She knew and read all the reports concerning her, but, although anonymous letters sought to vilify her, and journalism bespattered her with filth, nothing touched her serenity of soul.

I have seen her grow pale, and I have watched her eyes slowly fill with tears when something exceptionally vile came under her notice. But Alexandra Feodrovna was able to see the stars shining far above the mud of the streets.

CHAPTER V

I AM going to write of Gregory Rasputin as I knew him. My personal acquaintance with him lasted from 1910 to 1916, but I know that I might as well attempt to cleanse the Augean stables single-handed, as to be believed if I say one word in his defence. As a man, and as an infamous figure in history, he matters little to me, and, knowing the popular prejudice against him, I hesitated to mention his name in these pages. But I was urged to do so; it was represented to me that my silence might be equivalent to an acknowledgment, not only of his guilt, but also of that of the Empress. This last consideration decided me to forgo my resolution, and to write a faithful record of the man who was supposed to play such an important rôle during the last few years of the Russian Empire.

If I say that I never saw the evil side of Gregory Rasputin I shall be called a liar or a fool—perhaps, more chivalrously, the latter. It is, however, the truth when I say that we never saw the evil side of him. May I, therefore, plead for a hearing on the grounds that some men possess dual natures, and that they adapt these to the company in which they find themselves? I have heard of men who at home have led most moral lives, leading elsewhere existences before which an up-to-date French novel is as naught. Yet they never betrayed themselves to their nearest and dearest. Their friends were likewise deceived. Perhaps this dark side was never discovered, and they died and were buried as undefiled Christians. But even if something unforeseen had disclosed the man's secret orchard, his inner life, and his frailities (sic), their existence even then would most probably have been disbelieved by those who had known him intimately for years.

A person tells you that your dearest friend is a liar and a sensualist. Do you believe him? Rarely, I think, if you are worthy to call yourself a friend. You advise the traducer to make himself or herself scarce, and, if you allow your mind to become poisoned by slow dropping venom, you place yourself at once on a level with the slanderer.

The Empress refused to believe ill of Rasputin because she had never seen the evil side of him, and also because both she and the Emperor had extended the hand of friendship to him. There was no question of affection in her continual refusal to disown him, no phase of the passing passions which distinguished Catherine the Great, and which were so kindly tolerated by her subjects. The Empress inherited much of her illustrious grandmother's tenacity of purpose, and she refused to be dictated to. In this, she was the woman of character who resembled Queen Victoria. I do not wish to compare Rasputin with John Brown—they are as the poles apart—but what I wish to point out in connection with both of these persons, is that Queen Victoria and the Empress called John Brown and Gregory Rasputin their friends, and neither family disapproval nor public censure was a sufficient reason in their eyes to merit the sacrifice of a friend. There the similarity ends.

Gregory Rasputin arrived in Petrograd from Siberia on a pilgrimage, walking the entire way with irons on his body in order to make his progress more painful and difficult. If a pilgrim were to arrive in London from Edinburgh in similar circumstances he would be taken before a magistrate, and most probably sent to a lunatic asylum; these things do not happen in England, but they were of daily occurrence in Russia. We were so accustomed to the miraculous that I do not think the average Russian would have manifested any surprise if he had been accosted in the street by the Angel Gabriel! Rasputin had been introduced by certain people to Germogen, a priest and a friend of Elidor, who possessed great influence in the region of the Volga. Elidor's dominant idea was to found a particular sect of his own, but he failed to do so, and he was ultimately dismissed from authority. This, he attributed, rightly or wrongly, to Rasputin. Germogen was a firm believer in Rasputin's spiritual powers, and he was also much interested in his arduous pilgrimage. In fact, so greatly was he impressed that he decided to introduce the "staretz" to the Grand Duchess Peter, formerly Princess Meliza of Montenegro, and to her sister the Grand Duchess Anastasia, the wife of the Grand Duke Nicholas. Both these Princesses were addicted to mysticism; I may describe them as "soulful." Rasputin impressed them equally as much as he had impressed Germogen, and they talked everywhere about their wonderful "discovery."

At this time the two Grand Duchesses were on very friendly terms with the Empress, and it is not to be wondered that, little by little, her curiosity was aroused, and at last she and the Emperor expressed a wish to see Rasputin.

H.I.M. THE TSAR
Surrounded by the Officers of
The Royal Yacht 'Standart'

THE EMPRESS On board the Royal Yacht 'Standart'

H.I.M. THE TSAR WITH THE TSAREVITCH
On board the Tender going out to the Royal Yacht 'Standart'

The "staretz" was in due course presented to Their Majesties. Once again I repeat that such things could only happen in Russia, and it is therefore impossible to judge the Rasputin affair from an English standpoint. This uncouth peasant who came into the presence of Their Majesties barefooted, wearing the clumsy irons of penance, was in nowise impressed by his surroundings—he spoke freely to the Emperor, who was struck, like many others, by Rasputin's sincerity. The interview was not productive of any notable result, so far as Rasputin was concerned; it was merely an interesting incident, and when I first knew the Empress she never mentioned the name of Rasputin. In my opinion, and I speak in all sincerity, I believe that Rasputin was the unconscious tool of the Revolution. If John of Cronstadt had lived in 1910 to 1916, he would have been called another Rasputin. It was necessary for the Revolutionaries to find someone whose name they could couple with that of the Empress—a name whose connection with the Imperial Family would destroy their prestige with the higher classes, as well as nullifying the veneration of the peasant class. A member of the Duma once heckled one of the Revolutionary party on the question of Rasputin:

"Why," said he, "don't you kill Rasputin if you are so against him?" He received this surprising but wholly truthful reply:

"Kill Rasputin! Why, we should like him to live for ever! He represents our salvation!"

Rasputin's position was many-sided. One section of Society looked upon him as a "cult," and I have no doubt that there was a certain pathological interest in this. Another group formed a mystical conception of him as a "teacher," and a more material clique courted him, hoping thereby to gain influence with the Empress. The shame lies not so much with Rasputin as with those who "exploited" him.

At one time Rasputin was the guest of a well-known general, but, when this gentleman discovered that there was nothing to be gained by his hospitality, he quickly dropped his one-time acquaintance, and Rasputin took up his quarters in a small flat where he was supported by voluntary contributions. It was a humble abode, the "staretz" lived on the meanest food, and it was only during the last year of his life that he received presents of wine.

Anna Virouboff met Rasputin for the first time when she had just made up her mind to leave her husband. As I have said, her marriage with Lieutenant Virouboff had turned out disastrously, and their relations terminated in a most distressing manner. It so happened that once, when Anna was entertaining the Empress and General Orloff, Lieutenant Virouboff arrived unexpectedly from sea, and, as the police did not recognise him, he was refused admittance to his own house. There was a terrible scene between him and his wife after the Empress left, and Anna was beaten unmercifully. Anna then refused to live with him any longer, and returned to her parents. This affair created a great scandal, and, in order to console Anna, the "Montenegrin" Grand Duchesses took her to see Rasputin.

I cannot say whether or no this was a mistake. I am inclined to think that it was a well-meant error, as Anna Virouboff was a super-sensitive, rather neurotic person, easily impressed by an effective *mise en scène*. And this *mise en scène* was amply provided for her. The heart-broken and insulted young wife was received at the Palace of the Grand Duchess Anastasia with immense ceremony, and what took place is best described as an emotional prayer meeting.

Suddenly a door opened and Gregory Rasputin made his appearance. He walked into the midst of the overwrought worshippers, untouched by their exaltation. He radiated peace, and he personified the Strong Man beloved as an ideal by the majority of women. To Anna, the shattered and the disillusioned, Rasputin typified the calm that comes after a great storm; he prayed with her, he consoled her, she felt that she could confide in him. She was utterly oblivious of the social gulf which separated them. Rasputin was something to lean on, and Anna always leant on somebody; this weak, lovable, credulous creature was unable to stand alone. And in this way their intimacy began. I am sure that Anna was never in love with the *man* (although she was always in love with someone), but his chief influence over her was that of the priest.

I believe that at this time the Empress saw Rasputin occasionally, but he was chiefly to be found in the company of the two Grand Duchesses who had "discovered" him, and who now reported that Rasputin was undoubtedly a "seer." This annoyed the Emperor, and, the next time he saw Rasputin, he asked him to tell him *how* he "saw" true. "Your Majesty, I know nothing of clairvoyancy," said Rasputin.

"Then why have the Grand Duchesses asserted that you possess clairvoyant gifts?" replied the Emperor, crossly; and, when the Empress put the same question to Rasputin, she received the same reply.

The real reason for this report will never be known. It was in all probability political, but, after Rasputin had disowned clairvoyancy, the two Grand Duchesses disowned their protegé and sided with Germogen against him. The commencement of endless intrigues dates from this period, as Elidor and Germogen were afraid that Rasputin would become more important than themselves.

I must now deal with Rasputin's alleged influence over the Empress. There is no doubt that her subconscious belief in his spiritual powers was confirmed by the long arm of coincidence. The Tsarevitch fell ill, the attack was severe and his parents were frantic. If any mother with an only son reads these pages, she will admit that the word "frantic" best describes the feelings of a mother at such a crisis. The Empress was literally beside herself; it was then that someone suggested that Rasputin should be sent for. When he arrived he bade the despairing parents hope. He prayed by the bedside of the Tsarevitch, and it seemed that directly he did so the child began to get better. There is not the slightest truth in the film and "novel" versions of the incident; coincidence, and coincidence alone, was responsible for the Tsarevitch's recovery at the moment of Rasputin's impassioned prayers.

I met Rasputin just before the Germogen scandals. My husband had gone to Copenhagen to escort the Empress Marie thither on the "Pole Star," and he was anxious for me to join him. To do this would have entailed leaving Titi with my mother, and I was reluctant to do so, although naturally desirous of acceding to my husband's wishes. Thus I was in somewhat of a dilemma. Anna noticed I was worried and unhappy.

"Look here, Lili, there's someone who can help you," she said.

"Who?" I asked.

"Gregory Rasputin," she answered.

I was not anxious to meet Rasputin—I did not possess the boundless belief in him which characterised Anna, but I agreed, to humour her, and she took me to Rasputin's eyrie (I say eyrie, since his flat was high up under the roof), and then left me.

I waited for some time alone in a little study until a man came in so noiselessly that I was almost unaware of his presence. It was Rasputin! Our eyes met, and I was instantly struck by his uncanny appearance. At a first glance, he appeared to be a typical peasant from the frozen North, but his eyes held mine, those shining steel-like eyes which seemed to read one's inmost thoughts. His face was pale and thin, his hair long, and his beard a lighter chestnut. Rasputin was not tall, but he gave one the impression of being so; he was dressed as a Russian peasant, and wore the high boots, loose shirt and long, black coat of the moujik. He came forward and took my hand.

"Ah . . . I see. Thou art worried." (He "tutoyed" everybody). "Well—nothing in life is worth worrying over—'tout passe'—you understand—that's the best outlook." He became serious.

"It is necessary to have Faith. God alone is thy help. Thou art torn between thy husband and thy child. Which of them is the weaker? Thou think'st that thy child is the more helpless. This is not so. A child can do nothing in his weakness—a man can do much."

Rasputin advised me to go to Copenhagen, but I did not go. I left Petrograd next day for the country—perhaps out of bravado! But the impression which Rasputin had produced on me was very vivid. I was at once attracted, repelled, disquieted and reassured; nevertheless, his eyes were productive of a feeling of terror and repugnance, and I made no answer when the Empress greeted me with the words: "So, Lili, you've seen our friend? He'll always help you."

My second meeting with Rasputin took place in the winter. Titi was seriously ill, it was thought that diphtheric conditions would set in, and the poor little boy lay tossing from side to side in delirium. Anna, who made constant enquiries, at last 'phoned. "Lili," she said, "my advice is—ask Gregory to come and pray." I hesitated—I knew my husband's distaste for anything touching the supernatural. But, when I saw how ill Titi was, I hesitated no longer. At any rate, no one could possibly condemn the prayers offered for a sick child. Rasputin promised to come at once, and he arrived in company with an old woman who was dressed as a nun. This quaint creature refused to enter the boy's bedroom, and sat on the stairs, praying.

"Don't wake Titi," I whispered, as we entered the nursery, for I was afraid that the sudden appearance of this strange peasant might frighten the child. Rasputin made no reply, but sat down by the bedside and looked long and intently at the sleeper. He then knelt and prayed. When he rose from his knees he bent over Titi.

"Don't wake him," I repeated.

"Silence—I *must.*"

Rasputin placed a finger on either side of Titi's nose. The child instantly awoke, looked at the stranger unafraid, and addressed him by the playful name which Russian children give to old people. Rasputin talked to him, and Titi told him that his head ached "ever so badly."

"Never mind," said Rasputin, his steel eyes full of strange lights. Then, addressing me: "To-morrow thy child will be well. Let me know if this is not so." And, bidding us farewell, he departed with his odd escort.

Directly Rasputin had gone the child fell asleep, and the next morning the threatened symptoms had disappeared, and his temperature was normal. In a few days, greatly to the doctor's amazement, he was quite well. After this, I could hardly dispute Rasputin's peculiar powers, and I always saw him whenever he came to the Palace— this, on an average, about once a month.

It is only fair to Rasputin to say that he derived no material benefits from these visits, in fact, he once complained to me that he was never even given his cab-fares! Rasputin's influence over the Empress was purely mystical. She had always believed in the power of prayer—Rasputin strengthened her in this belief, and I am sure that her perplexed soul was soothed by his ministrations. There was absolutely no sensual attraction. It gives me intense pain to touch on this subject, but I must not shrink from what I consider to be my duty. I have heard the most dreadful stories of the Empress—how, in the spirit of sacrifice she gave herself, and those dear children to Rasputin, in order to prove that the sacrifice of the body was acceptable to God. Such a monstrous thing never happened. But when I have defended her, and said that Rasputin was a common man, unpleasing to look on, dirty in his habits and uncouth in every respect, I have been told that these defects matter nothing in certain types of sensualism. I have put forward the indisputable fact that the Empress was an intensely fastidious woman, that she possessed no "animal" propensities, that her morals were the ultra-strict morals of her grandmother. The answer to this has been that many fastidious and super-moral women have been guilty of incomprehensible lapses, solely by reason of their fastidious and moral qualities. If such examples exist, why should not the Empress have done likewise?

I am confronted at every turn by these reports, and people say pityingly: "Well, of course, you *loved* the Empress." That is so ... but *I also knew* the Empress. The Emperor's attitude in the Rasputin scandal ought alone to destroy these accusations, as the Empress never saw Rasputin without the knowledge and consent of her husband. Even assuming Nicholas II to be a weak man, entirely under the domination of his wife, he would certainly have been man enough, husband enough, and father enough, never to have countenanced any immoral relations between Rasputin and his family. The Emperor was primarily a Christian and a gentleman, but he was likewise a Romanoff and an Emperor. In these capacities he would have meted out the only possible punishment for such an offence. When he was told the "outside" scandals concerning Rasputin, he would not credit them. And why not? *Simply because they were so bad*, had they been less so, the Emperor might have listened. It is a great mistake for anyone to attempt to destroy any friendship by describing the person whose ruin is contemplated as being entirely worthless. The desired result is obtained far more easily by damning him or her with faint praise!

When various people reproached the Empress for being on terms of friendship with a common peasant, and for believing that he was endowed with the attributes of holiness, she replied that Our Lord did not choose well-born members of Jewish society for His followers. All His disciples except St. Luke were men of humble origin. I am inclined to think that she placed Rasputin on a level with St. John . . . both were, in her opinion, mystics.

She was perfectly frank in her belief in Rasputin's powers of healing. The Empress was convinced that certain individuals possess this gift, and that Rasputin was one. When it was urged that the services of the most skilled physicians were at her disposal, she gave the invariable answer: "I believe in Rasputin." As for the stories that Rasputin and Anna Virouboff gave the Tsarevitch poisons and antidotes, I dismiss these with contempt—they belong solely to sensational fiction. Anna Virouboff would have been too frightened to give a kitten a dose of medicine, much less would she have tampered with the medicines given to the Tsarevitch.

The first grave scandal which assailed the Empress in connection with Rasputin was the discovery and publication of a letter written by her, in which she made use of the expression: "*Je veux reposer mon âme auprès de vous.*" The enemies of Rasputin were fully aware that he was guilty of the fatal habit of keeping interesting letters, so Rasputin (always desirous of popularity) was invited to meet certain influential people, and, on his way to the rendezvous, he was attacked and robbed, and all the correspondence which he carried on him was stolen.

In due time the contents of the Empress's letter were published, and this did her tremendous harm. Even the Duma took the worst view of the much quoted sentence, "*Je veux reposer mon âme auprès de vous.*" But that expression was not used at all in the physical meaning. The Empress merely wished to tell her friend that her soul was desirous of spiritual consolation.

Since I have lived in England, I have constantly met women who pin their faith in certain spiritual and physical advisers. Most Catholics have a special confessor to whom they invariably repair, just as most people have one particular doctor in whom they trust—most representatives of any denomination have their especial following. It is solely a question of one individual meeting the requirements of another.

The Emperor was very much troubled over the attacks which were made on the Empress. But both he and the Empress possessed a mistaken sense of their responsibilities in connection with Rasputin, and this mistaken sense of responsibility was to prove the ultimate destruction of both Rasputin and themselves. The Imperial couple resolutely refused to throw him over. In this decision the Emperor was as one with the Empress; perhaps they "humanly" declined to admit the right of anyone to dictate to them . . . but, be that as it may, Rasputin's position remained undisturbed.

It is well known that Rasputin condemned hostilities, but it is not equally well known that he tried to stop the declaration of war. Nevertheless, when mobilization began, he wired to Anna, saying: "The war must be stopped—war must *not* be declared; it will be the end of all things." No notice whatever was taken of this telegram, for the excellent reason that Rasputin's political influence was *nil*; he had, in fact, no influence in material matters, although many have thought otherwise.

General Beletsky once asked Rasputin to speak to the Emperor and suggest his name as Governor-General of Finland. Rasputin promised to do so, and mentioned the matter to the Emperor, in the presence of the Empress. The Emperor listened, but made no comment. General Beletsky was never appointed.

It seems impossible to obtain a logical hearing on behalf of either the Empress or Rasputin. All kinds of reports have been circulated in connection with the latter's excesses and debaucheries. There may have been some truth that Rasputin's private life was not all that it should have been, but I assert most solemnly that we never saw the slightest trace of impropriety in word, manner or behaviour when he was with us at Tsarkoe Selo.

Prince Orloff, the head of the Chancellerie Militaire, never made any pretence of liking or even tolerating the Empress. He experienced a sort of nervous repugnance to meeting her, and it was common knowledge that he took quantities of valerian in order to steady his nerves, whenever it was necessary for him to see her. The Empress was aware of this.

"I saw Prince Orloff to-day," she said to me, "he was reeking of valerian. Poor man, what an effort it must cost him to speak to me."

The Prince exercised no discretion whatever in his statements about the Empress and Rasputin; he seemed impelled to disparage her—his hatred amounted almost to a 'phobia—and at last the Emperor lost patience with him and sent him to the Caucasus. Princess Olga Orloff was received shortly afterwards by the Empress. The Empress was very fond of Olga, but it was a very unpleasant interview, as the Princess tried to explain that her husband had been grossly maligned. The Empress described the interview to me:

"I've had a dreadful time, Lili," she said, "Olga Orloff has just been. I'm very, very sorry for her, she's in a terrible state. When I rose, she began to speak most wildly, and to insist that her husband was devoted to me and to our interests. I knew that, if I were to sit down, I should burst into tears; so I kept standing. It was an awful moment."

Rasputin always had a presentiment of a violent death. He often remarked, with an air of profound conviction: "Whilst I'm alive all will be well, but, after my death, rivers of blood will flow. Nothing, however, will happen to 'Father' and 'Mother'"—this was his way of alluding to the Emperor and Empress. About this time an old woman, a disciple of Elidor's, came to see Rasputin one night, wearing a white dress plentifully trimmed with scarlet ribbons.

Rasputin reproved her for this display.

"How awful of you to wear these red ribbons," he said.

"Ah," replied the old woman. "I *know* why I wear red."

"And she knew full well," said Rasputin, gloomily, when describing the incident to me. "Red is the colour of blood—and blood will soon be as plentiful as her scarlet ribbons."

Everyone who loved the Imperial Family was horrified at the ever increasing scandals; the wildest reports, mostly lies, with a substratum of truth were current, and Rasputin was even said to have been sinning in Petrograd when he was actually in Siberia. It was impossible to persuade the Empress that popular feeling was against her. True, she heard what was said, and she occasionally read what was imputed to her, but she paid no attention to gossip or to mendacious paragraphs. She was obsessed by her religion, and she sent me and Anna Virouboff on a pilgrimage to Tobolsk in the summer of 1916. A new saint had been recently canonized at Tobolsk, and the Empress had made a vow to go thither herself, or to send a substitute. Anna asked me to consent, as she was afraid to travel alone, and, as the Empress begged me to go, I could do no less than prove my devotion to her wishes.

When I arrived at Petrograd I discovered that Rasputin was to travel with us. I could not help thinking that, in view of popular feeling, it was most ill-advised to advertise the expedition, but I dared not suggest this. We left Petrograd in the greatest publicity. ... A special saloon carriage was attached to the train . . . it was a progress of publicity, wires were sent in advance all along the line to announce our advent, and crowds thronged the stations to catch a glimpse of us.

At last, late in the evening, we arrived at Tumen, and from thence we took the steamer to Tobolsk. Little did I dream that, in a year's time, the Imperial Family were to make the same pilgrimage—of which the whole journey was to prove indeed a Via Dolorosa! They, too, were to see the black and swiftly flowing river, and the wild Tartar villages on its banks, and, like myself, they were to see the city on the mountain, with its churches and houses sharply silhouetted against the fast darkening sky.

We were received at Tobolsk by the Governor, the chief officials, and the Church dignitary, Varnava, and we were afterwards taken to our quarters in the Governor's house, where I slept in the little room which the Emperor, a year later, used as his study. The next day we visited the saint's grave, and attended a very impressive service in the Cathedral. Rasputin stayed with the priest, but, unfortunately, he quarrelled with Varnava, so matters became some-what strained, and I was not sorry when our two days' visit came to an end.

On the way back to Tumen, Rasputin made a point of us stopping at his village and seeing his wife. I was rather intrigued at this, as I had always wondered how and where he lived, and I felt quite interested when I saw the dark grey, carved wooden house which was the home of Rasputin. The village consisted of a group of small wooden houses built on two floors. Rasputin's house was, perhaps, a little larger than the others, and he said that he hoped one day

Their Majesties would visit him.

"But it's too far," I said—aghast at the proposal.

Rasputin was angry. "They *must*," he declared, and, a few minutes afterwards, he added the prophetic words: "Willing or unwilling, they will come to Tobolsk, and they will see my village before they die."

We remained one day at Rasputin's house. His wife was a charming, sensible woman, and the peasants were a fine type—honest, simple folk, who cultivated the fields belonging to Rasputin, and accepted no payment for so doing—working absolutely in the spirit of holiness.

Rasputin had three children—the two girls were being educated in Petrograd, but the boy was quite a peasant. Everyone was friendly, but most of the villagers were strongly against Rasputin's returning to Petrograd.

As we had decided to go on to Ekaterinburg, and from thence to the Convent of Verchoutouria, I thought it would be a good idea to persuade Rasputin to remain with his people. This he refused to do; I told Anna that there must be no more gossip, and that she must persuade Rasputin to leave us. She promised to do so, but at the last moment he went with us to Ekaterinburg.

I shall never forget my first impression of this fatal town. Directly we got out of the train, I felt a sense of calamity—we were all affected; Rasputin was ill at ease, Anna perceptibly nervous, and I was heartily glad when we reached the Convent of Verchoutouria, which is situated on the left bank of the river Toura. We stayed a night in the guest house attached to the Convent, and then Rasputin asked us to go into the woods with him and visit a hermit who was locally supposed to be a very holy man.

This pilgrimage must appear entirely foolish in the eyes of English readers. I try and put myself in their place, and imagine what the English public would think if the "Daily Mail" announced that Queen Mary had sent two of her friends on such an expedition. "This couldn't happen—Queen Mary is far too sensible," you will say.

No doubt Queen Mary *is* far too sensible . . . such a thing could never happen in England, and I am only relating it in order to prove that, once again, it is impossible to judge Russia from an English standpoint.

The hermit lived in the heart of the forest and his hermitage might easily have been taken for a poultry farm. He was surrounded by fowls of all sizes and descriptions. Perhaps he considered fowls akin to holiness; he gave quantities of eggs to the Convent, but we supped frugally off cold water and black bread. The hermit had no use for beds, so we slept miserably on the hard, unyielding floor of dried mud, and I must confess that I was glad when we returned to Verchoutouria and we were able to sleep and bath in comfort.

Rasputin decided to take leave of us at Verchoutouria, so we went on alone to Perm, where our saloon carriage was coupled to another train. Crowds came to stare at Anna, and some of their comments made me feel very uneasy. There was much dissatisfaction, and, when our saloon was uncoupled, it was done so forcibly that the carriage was almost derailed, and I was thrown from one end to the other. But we returned to Petrograd safely, there to be welcomed and thanked by the Empress.

"After all, Lili," said Anna, now prostrate with nerves and a heart attack, "we must believe that God *likes* us to endure."

I do not know whether this remark was reminiscent of the hermitage, or of the saloon carriage, but I was able honestly to thank God that I was once more within a civilized area.

Rasputin did not stay long in his village; he returned to Petrograd, and the brazen voice of scandal was again heard. One day, in 1916, when I was at Reval, the Empress telegraphed asking me to come and see her.

I obeyed, and found her alone, looking sad, and obviously much troubled in her mind. She did not, at first, touch on the subject nearest her heart; then, all at once, she told me how hard she thought it of people to speak against her so bitterly.

"I know *all*, Lili," she said. "Why does Gregory stop in Petrograd? The Emperor doesn't wish it. I don't. And yet we can't possibly discard him—he's done no wrong. Oh, why won't he see his folly?"

"I'll do all in my power, Madame, to make him do so," I replied. My heart overflowed with love for the Empress, she seemed so utterly broken, so tragically sad.

"I've already reproached Anna for not helping me in the matter," continued the Empress, and she gave me her permission to go at once to the house in Gorohovaya Street where Rasputin lived. I went with Anna.

We did not find Rasputin alone. It was tea time and he was surrounded by a little crowd of admirers. Next to him sat his *âme damnée*, Akilina Laptinsky, the secret agent, under whose skilful tutelage Rasputin unconsciously played the well-planned game of the Revolutionaries. Akilina posed as a Sister of Charity, and many people believed in her; she possessed great influence with Rasputin, and in his unguarded moments he made many deplorable confidences in Akilina, who used everything she heard in a way detrimental to the Imperial Family.

Akilina disliked me: she thought Anna was a weak fool, but I imagine that she regarded me as a foe more worthy of her steel. I acknowledged her presence, and I asked Rasputin if I could speak to him in private.

"But certainly," he answered, and we went into the next room, Akilina following us.

"And now?" enquired Rasputin, seating himself. I did not mince matters.

"Gregory," I said bluntly, "you must leave Petrograd at once. You can pray for Their Majesties equally well in Siberia. You *must* go— for their sakes, I implore you. Go—You know what is said—if you insist upon remaining, it will only mean danger for us all."

Rasputin considered me gravely—he did not speak. I could see Anna's "hurt child" look, I could feel Akilina's sinister scrutiny. Then Rasputin uttered these unexpected words:

"Perhaps thou art right. I'm sick and tired of it all. I'll go."

But a surprising interruption occurred. Akilina banged her clenched fist on the table, and confronted me with rage in her eyes.

"How *dare* you try and control the Father's spirit?" she screamed. "I say that he *must* stay. Who are you?—why, a nobody— you are too insignificant to judge what is best for anyone."

Silence, pregnant with meaning, fell in the little room. Anna was crying, Rasputin said nothing, but I still defied Akilina: the thought of the Empress gave me courage.

"Are you going to listen to the Sister?" I demanded coldly. Akilina recommenced her table-banging.

"If you leave Petrograd, Father, you'll have bad luck—you are *not* to go." "Well—well—" said Rasputin helplessly, "perhaps thou art right. I shall stay."

My efforts were unavailing. Rasputin could be as obstinate as a mule; and so, greatly distressed, I returned to the Palace. The Empress was very disappointed.

"I wonder why the Sister was so against my wishes," she said.

Later on we understood. I think that, despite her plotting and contriving, Akilina really had some affection for Rasputin, and she was occasionally ashamed of her Judaslike rôle. I remember that once, when Rasputin left Petrograd on a visit to his family, I went to see him off, and there, naturally, I encountered Akilina. As the train steamed out of the station she burst into tears—genuine tears; I saw there was no hypocrisy in her grief. Although I disliked Akilina, I felt sorry for her.

"You'd better let me drive you home," I said.

She accepted my offer, but in the car her tears recommenced.

"Whatever is the matter?" I enquired. "You'll see the Father again." Akilina raised her tear-drenched eyes.

"Ah—you know *nothing*—if you only knew—if you only knew what I know."

Surely this remark must have implied that she possessed some inner knowledge which terrified her, and which may have made her conscience-stricken.

Akilina nursed Anna at Tsarkoe Selo when she was ill with the measles, but on the second day of the Revolution she sent me a note, asking me to come over to the left wing of the Palace. She then informed me that Anna was delirious. . . .

"However, I can't do much for her. Will you tell Her Majesty that I must go into town for a day. I want to see Gregory's family."

I promised to deliver the message, but we never saw Akilina again. A fortnight later we were told that she was living in the family of one of the most prominent Revolutionaries.

Another "Sister," Voskoboinikova, equally associated with Rasputin, was head matron of Anna's hospital. She was, likewise, a great friend of M. Protopopoff, the Minister of the Interior, who used to spend hours in her company. Voskoboinikova possessed a certain fascination, but she was very inquisitive, and we equally disliked each other. Following the example of Akilina, she left Tsarkoe on the second day of the Revolution, but, the night before relinquishing her position at the hospital, she gave a dinner to the convalescent soldiers, when wine flowed freely and all sorts of seditious speeches were made. The soldiers were told to look to Petrograd for freedom, and that revolvers and bullets were fine things. Truly women had their uses during the Revolution!

But to return to Rasputin. The feeling against him daily assumed larger proportions. Elidor once sent a woman to kill him, and the Father was badly wounded in the stomach, but it is untrue to say that

Anna Virouboff nursed him during the illness which ensued. She never attempted to do so.

Prince Felix Yousopoff, whose name will always be connected with the tragedy of Rasputin, first met him at the house of Mme Golovina, a sister-in-law of the Grand Duke Paul. The demoiselle Golovina greatly admired Felix Yousopoff, in fact her "flamme" for him was well known. Some considerable time elapsed between the first meeting of Prince Felix and Rasputin: I spent the next two years chiefly in Reval, but I used to pay a fortnightly visit to the Empress, and, after my husband was sent to England, I went to Petrograd, where I saw the Empress daily. I was very surprised when she told me that Felix Yousopoff was a constant visitor at Rasputin's house; in fact I was so incredulous that I asked Rasputin whether this was true.

"Yes—it's quite true," he answered, "I have a great affection for Prince Yousopoff, I never call him anything else but 'Little One.'"

Mary Golovina, to whom also I expressed my astonishment, said that Prince Yousopoff declared that Rasputin's prayers benefited him: so there was nothing more to be said.

On December 16th, when I was at Tsarkoe Selo, I told the Empress that I wanted to see Rasputin on the morrow, but just before starting for his house—about five o'clock on the afternoon of December 17th—I was rung up from Tsarkoe Selo—the Empress wished to speak to me. Her voice seemed agitated.

"Lili," she said, "don't go to Father Gregory's to-day. Something strange has happened. He disappeared last night—nothing has been heard of him, but I'm sure it will be all right. Will you come to the Palace at once?"

Thoroughly startled by this disturbing news, I lost no time in taking the train to Tsarkoe Selo. An Imperial carriage was waiting for me, and I soon found myself at the Palace.

The Empress was in her mauve boudoir; once again I felt the premonition of coming disaster, but I endeavoured to disregard it. Never did the "cabinet mauve" look so home-like. The air was sweet with the fragrance of many flowers and the clean odour of burning wood; the Empress was lying down, the Grand Duchesses sat near her, and Anna Virouboff was sitting on a footstool close to the couch. The Empress was very pale—her blue eyes were full of trouble, the young girls were silent, and Anna had evidently been weeping. I heard all there was to tell me; Gregory had disappeared, but I believe the Empress never imagined for one moment that he was dead. She discountenanced any sinister conjectures; she soothed the ever weeping Anna, and then she told me what she wished me to do.

"You will sleep in Anna's house to-night," she said. "I want you to see people for me to-morrow—I am advised that it will be better for me not to do so."

I told the Empress that I was only too happy to be of service to her, and, after dinner, I went to Anna's house, which I was astonished to find in the occupation of the Secret Police!

The pretty little dining-room was full of police agents, who received me most courteously, explaining that their presence was accounted for by the fact that a plot to kill the Empress and Anna Virouboff had just been discovered. This was not reassuring, but I decided not to be nervous, and, bidding good night to the officers of justice, I went into Anna's bedroom.

The familiar room looked strangely unfamiliar—terror lurked in the shadows, and death seemed in the air. I am not by nature superstitious, but I must confess that I felt so when an ikon suddenly fell down with a crash, carrying a portrait of Rasputin with it in its fall. I hastily undressed and got into bed—I could not sleep; I lay awake for hours, and when, towards dawn, I dropped off in an uneasy slumber, I was suddenly aroused by what seemed a great noise outside. I heard in the distance the tread of countless feet, the sound of many voices; a mighty multitude was marching towards Tsarkoe Selo—and the dreadful thought flashed across my mind that perhaps there had been a rising at Petrograd. I jumped out of bed, threw on a wrapper, and rushed to the dining-room. There all was quiet; the police officers were sleeping on the floor. My entrance awakened them. "Why, madame, what's the matter?" they enquired.

"Cannot you hear for yourselves?" I said, impatiently, "the noise—the crowd— I'm sure something dreadful has happened at Petrograd."

"We have heard nothing. . . ."

"Oh, but I assure you it's correct."

The police opened the shutters, then the windows . . . outside all was still with the intense stillness of a winter's night. The officers made no comment, and closed the windows.

"Madame has perhaps been dreaming," said one, sympathetically. "She has had much to try her nerves."

But I knew differently. I had certainly experienced much to try my nerves, but what I heard was neither a nightmare nor a delusion. When I re-entered the sombre bedroom, with its fallen ikon and its fallen saint, I shuddered, for, although I knew it not, the veil had been lifted, and I had heard the fast approaching footsteps of Revolution and murder.

I was an early arrival at the Palace, but the Empress was already up and she greeted me most affectionately. She told me that M. Protopopoff had strongly urged her to receive no one: there was evidence of a plot to murder her, and, for the first time, she seemed to feel some misgivings concerning the fate of Rasputin. She manifested no anxiety about her own danger; she was utterly serene and fearless: I was so struck by this that I could not help saying:

"Oh, Madame, you don't seem afraid to die. I always dread death—I'm a horrible coward."

The Empress looked at me in astonishment.

"Surely, Lili, you are not *really* afraid to die?"

"Yes, Madame, I am."

"I cannot understand anyone being afraid to die," she said, quietly. "I have always looked upon Death as such a friend, such a *rest*. You mustn't be afraid to die, Lili."

I passed an anxious and exciting morning. I was besieged with visitors for Anna, and people who desired to see the Empress. I think my position gave rise to a great deal of jealousy in the Palace, as at this time the Empress made me the sole medium of her wishes and no official etiquette was observed.

Nothing was heard of Rasputin, but all kinds of disturbing rumours were current. A certain person paid twenty-two visits to Tsarkoe Selo in one day, hopeful to see the Empress, but, acting on the advice of Protopopoff, she absolutely declined to receive him.

Two days later, Rasputin's body was discovered under the ice in the Neva. It was taken to a hospital close by, where an autopsy was performed. Rasputin had been wounded in the face and side, and there was a bullet wound in his back. His expression was peaceful, and the stiff fingers of one hand were raised in a gesture of benediction; it was impossible to arrange the hand in a natural position! The autopsy proved without a doubt that Rasputin was alive when he was thrown into the Neva!

The news of the murder caused the greatest consternation at the Palace—Anna Virouboff was prostrated with grief, and the Imperial Family were deeply concerned. The reports that the Empress gave way to violent hysterics are incorrect. It would be untrue to say that she was not inexpressibly shocked and grieved, but she displayed no untoward emotion. The Emperor was troubled, but his feelings arose more from the significance of Rasputin's death than from the actual death of the man: he realised that this murder was the first definite blow against the hitherto absolute power of the Tsar!

Akilina Laptinsky came to the Palace immediately after the autopsy had been performed: she wished, so she said, to discuss the question of Rasputin's burial. She was received by the Empress; Anna and I were also present. The "Sister" first asked the Empress if she did not wish to see the corpse.

"Certainly not," replied the Empress—in a tone which admitted of no argument.

"But there is the question of the burial," said Akilina. "Gregory always wished to be buried at Tsarkoe Selo."

"Impossible . . . impossible . . ." cried the Empress. "The body had better be taken to Siberia and buried in the 'Father's' village."

Akilina wept. . . . She declared that Rasputin's spirit would never rest were he to be buried so far away from the Palace. The Empress hesitated. . . . I could see she was thinking that it would be equally as unfriendly to discard the dead as to discard the living. Anna, however, settled the question by proposing that Rasputin should be interred in the centre aisle of the new church adjoining her hospital for convalescents. The church and the hospital were being built on Anna's own property. . . . There could be no question of any scandal touching the Imperial Family. . . . This proceeding would only enable people to cast another stone at Anna's already shattered reputation.

"And . . . I care little for the opinion of the world," whimpered Anna, looking more than ever like a hurt baby.

So it was settled that Rasputin should be buried in Anna's church, and, as I attended the burial, I may say with absolute conviction that mine is a true account of the proceedings. I have been told, and I have read various wholly inaccurate reports—the most prevalent being that Rasputin was buried secretly at dead of night in the Park at Tsarkoe Selo. Nothing of the kind. Rasputin's burial took place at 8 o'clock on the morning of December 22nd. The Empress asked me, on the preceding evening, to meet the Imperial Family by the graveside, and I promised to do so.

It was a glorious morning, the sky was a deep blue, the sun was shining, and the hard snow sparkled like masses of diamonds; everything spoke of peace, and I could hardly believe that I was about to witness the closing scene of one of the greatest scandals and tragedies in history. My carriage stopped on the road some distance from the Observatory, and I was directed to walk across a frozen field towards the unfinished church. Planks had been placed on the snow to serve as a footpath, and when I arrived at the church I noticed that a police motor-van was drawn up near the open grave. After waiting several moments, I heard the sound of sleigh-bells, and Anna Virouboff came slowly across the field. Almost immediately afterwards, a closed automobile stopped, and the Imperial Family joined us. They were dressed in mourning, and the Empress carried some white flowers; she was very pale but quite composed, although I saw her tears fall when the oak coffin was taken out of the police van. The coffin was perfectly plain. It bore no inscription, and only a cross outside it testified to the faith of the departed.

The ceremony proceeded—the burial service was read by the chaplain to the hospital, and, after the Emperor and Empress had thrown earth on the coffin, the Empress distributed her flowers between the Grand Duchesses and ourselves, and we scattered them on the coffin.

When the last solemn words had been uttered, the Imperial Family left the church. Anna and I followed them. . . . Anna got into her sledge, I into my carriage. It was barely nine o'clock.

I looked back at the snowy fields, the bare walls of the unfinished church, and I thought of the murdered man who was sleeping there. I felt an immense pity for his fate, but, above all, I felt an immense pity and love for those who had believed in him and befriended him in defiance of the world, and on whose innocent shoulders the burden of his follies was destined to rest.

I have not attempted to introduce any picturesque imagery in my description of Rasputin's burial. I have stated the facts exactly as they occurred, and it now devolves upon me to contradict one of the most unjust accusations which have been made against the Empress in connection with the burial of Rasputin.

Several writers have asserted that, when Rasputin's remains were dug up after the Revolution, a holy image bearing the signatures of the Empress and the Grand Duchesses was discovered resting under the cheek of the dead man. The Empress has been credited with placing this image there herself, but this is not the case. The image (that of the Miraculous Virgin of Pskov) was one of several which the Empress brought back from Pskov when she and her daughters visited her hospital. The Empress purchased these images much in the same manner that visitors to Lourdes purchase souvenirs of Our Lady of Lourdes. The Imperial Family wrote their names and the date in pencil on the base of all these souvenirs, which were given to various friends. Rasputin received one, and, when his body was placed in the coffin, Akilina, with some sinister motive, insisted upon the image being placed under his cheek, and she was, doubt-less, responsible for the story that this was done by order of the Empress.

After Rasputin's death, his son and daughters came to Tsarkoe Selo and were received by the Empress. They related how, on the night of the murder, their father had received a message from Prince Yousopoff, asking him to come and see him. It appeared that Rasputin's daughters had some vague presentiment of ill, and begged their father to remain at home. He, however, insisted upon going to the "little one," and the finding of one of the goloshes which he wore on account of the deep snow was partly the means of discovering that foul play had taken place.

The family begged the Empress to avenge their father's death. She replied:

"I can promise you nothing. All rests with justice; we cannot possibly interfere in any way for or against that which has taken place."

These were her actual words, and they must surely discredit the story that Prince Yousopoff and the Grand Duke Dmitry were victims of the vindictive spirit of the Empress.

Rasputin, as I knew him, was, I repeat, not the villain of the novel and the films. In my eyes he was an uneducated man with a mission; he spoke an almost incomprehensible Siberian dialect, he could hardly read, he wrote like a child of four, and his manners were unspeakable. But he possessed both hypnotic and spiritual forces, he believed in himself and he made others do so. I am not ignorant of what has been said concerning his abnormal animalism, his satyr-like sensualities, the nameless orgies in which young women and young girls gave themselves as willing victims to his lust.

An English saying states that there is "no smoke without fire"— this may, perhaps, apply to Rasputin's sensual side, but never to the alleged extent. One woman in twenty may lose her sense of fitness and seek to mate with a man in an inferior station of life, but it is not an everyday occurrence. The reports about his dress and his extravagance are also very much exaggerated. Rasputin lived, and died, a poor man. He usually wore the dress of a peasant, and his wonderful jewelled cross only exists in the brains of novelists and journalists. Rasputin at first wore a simple copper cross, later he wore one of gold which he afterwards sent to the Emperor at the Stavka. This gift in Russia is usually unwelcome, as it signifies that you present with it the sorrows and sufferings synonymous with the Cross. The Emperor thought that Rasputin's cross was unlucky, so he gave it back to me, and asked me to give it to Anna. But Anna stubbornly refused to accept it, and I was at my wits' end to know what to do. I could not tell the Emperor that Anna would have none of Rasputin's cross—so I mislaid it, and I do not know what became of it. But I only saw the moral side of this apparently immoral man, and I was not alone in my conception of Rasputin's character. I know for a fact that many women of my world who had "affairs" and many demi-mondaines were not dragged further into the mire by Rasputin, for—incredible as it may appear—his influence in such cases was often for the best.

I remember that I once met Rasputin when I was walking on the Morskaya with a brother-officer of Captain Dehn's. He eyed me severely, and, when I returned home, I found a message telling me to come and see him. Partly out of curiosity I obeyed, and, when I saw Rasputin, he demanded an explanation.

"Of what?" I asked.

"Oh . . . thou know'st well enough. Art *thou* going to follow the example of these frivolous Society women? Why art thou not walking with thy husband?" He repeatedly said to women who sought his advice:

"If you mean to do wrong, first come and tell me."

So I can do no more than speak of Rasputin as I found him. If I had been a Rasputinière, or the victim of an abnormal passion, I should not be living happily with my husband, and Captain Dehn would never have countenanced any association with Rasputin if the latter had been guilty of immoralities at Tsarkoe Selo. His duty as a husband would have been greater than his devotion to the Imperial Family.

I cannot entirely defend the Empress's attitude. I love her, I reverence her memory, but I think she was, in many ways, perhaps, mistaken in her outlook. She argued, very rightly, that, even if she belonged to Russia, her soul belonged to God, and she had a perfect right to worship Him exactly in what manner most appealed to her.

I have mentioned her views as to position being no ban where the instruments of God were concerned. In a worldly sense this was impossible, especially in Russia, where humility appealed neither to the peasant nor to the higher classes. The religious "communism" of the Empress outraged their sense of fitness . . . the peasants could not understand one of their own class being on intimate terms with the Sovereigns . . . the higher classes were bitterly contemptuous.

Knowing the strong religious convictions of the Empress and the inborn characteristics of both classes, the Revolutionaries found in Rasputin a fitting agent of Imperial destruction.

The Greek Church is the most mediæval of religions . . . it is quite harmless, so to speak, when modern conditions are not introduced into its practice; but modernity, ever a fatal element in religion, is especially fatal to the Greek Church. The Empress would not understand this . . . her faith taught her to credit the existence of holy men, hermits, and seers—so, when Rasputin appeared in the character of one of these, she was not surprised, and she accepted the actuality of his heaven-sent mission, as the teachings of her Church bade her.

As I have stated, coincidence was largely responsible for the belief of the Empress in Rasputin's gift of healing. His prayers coincided with the recovery of the Tsarevitch—that child of many prayers. In her love for her son the Empress was *plus mère que mère*. I am likewise assured that there was no theatrical clap-trap in Rasputin's association with Anna Virouboff. Had Anna possessed the brains of Akilina, I might not be so positive—but Anna was no *intrigante*; in the face of possible denunciation as a Russian Sapphira, I repeat my estimate of Anna Virouboff, i.e., *childish, harmless, weak*.

If the Empress were guilty of any glaring weakness, it was, paradoxically, that of stubbornness. She did not allow any interference in what she considered her own province. Her grand-mother and the Prince Albert had tolerated none; her distant connection, Princess Clementine of Coburg, was ultra-obstinate; another of her connections, Ferdinand of Bulgaria, has also manifested the Coburg peculiarity. It is an interesting psychological study: in some of the family this trait is manifest in their undeviating pursuit of worldly ambition, in others it is apparent in their views of morality and domesticity. In the case of the Empress, morality, domesticity and religion were subjects in which she brooked no contradiction.

Had the Emperor been less religious, he might have (from a

worldly point of view) influenced his wife to have seen less of Rasputin. But he made no attempt to interfere with her on religious questions, remembering perhaps how wholly she had relinquished the faith of her fathers to embrace his own. The Empress has been accused of contributing to the downfall of Russia through her association with Rasputin. The finger of scorn and hatred has pointed at her, and an almost universal voice has cried, "Thou art the Woman." But history, if not always just, is at least generous, and it may be that Alexandra Feodorovna will one day be given the benefit of the doubt, and allowed to appeal against the sentence which has been passed on her. For many years prior to her advent as Empress of Russia, the movement for Freedom had been slowly but surely spreading over the entire country, and the creation of the Duma strengthened public opinion. But certain Revolutionaries—themselves as evil as their prototypes in the French Revolution—did not scorn to employ base agents in order to attain their base ends. These men used Rasputin—with what result is now apparent. But have the murders of Rasputin and the Empress cleansed Russia and enabled it to be rechristened Utopia?

The ashes of Rasputin are scattered to the four winds, the blood of the innocent cries aloud to Heaven for vengeance; but Russia—drunken with carnage, liberated from her ancient yoke, and delivered of her rulers—has as yet only produced Robespierres.

CHAPTER VI

I HAVE dealt with the subject of Rasputin before touching on that of the War, but his name is also connected with the War, as he is supposed to have been a German spy, and to have encouraged the alleged pro-German leanings of the Empress. Although I shall always adhere to my original belief that Rasputin was an unconscious agent of the Revolutionaries, I cannot deny that he was against the War, and always desirous of peace, but this attitude was due to his own wishes and convictions. I asked Rasputin in 1915 when he thought the war would be over. "Not yet. . . . Don't expect the war to be over yet," he answered; and in 1916, when I returned from Reval, I asked the Empress the same question. "Not yet, Lili, not yet," she said. Both these replies might serve to show how little was the political influence either of the Empress or of Rasputin. As an individual, doubtless the Empress desired peace: as a Russian, she could not possibly have desired the victory of Germany.

There was great excitement in 1914 throughout Russia; everyone hoped that England would come in, especially in naval circles, who were well aware of the weakness of the Russian fleet.

The excitement increased when Russia became the ally of France. The Imperial band played the hymns of the Allies daily; there was no question of pro-Germanism at Court—Russia, as befitting her great traditions, was fighting the good fight!

My husband was ordered to escort the Imperial Family to sea on the "Standart," and I knew that I must therefore spend my birthday without him. One evening, when we were sitting in the Park making plans for a belated celebration, my husband was accosted by one of the heads of his Department. "Dehn . . ." said he . . . "go at once to the Commander of the Port . . . you're wanted."

Upon his return my husband was very excited. "Lili," he cried, "I have received orders to join Admiral Essen's fleet. I must leave almost immediately." It was, indeed, "almost immediately," for at 3 a.m. my husband bade me good-bye.

The Empress sent me a note directly she knew that Charles had left. "I hope everything will be all right," she wrote. "Poor Lili, don't despair."

I tried *not* to despair, and, like most wives at this time, I kept a smiling face, although I was perilously near tears. Every day the Military Council was in consultation with the Emperor, and, on the evening before the declaration of war, I knew that mobilization had been decided upon.

The Emperor firmly believed that Russia was amply supplied with munitions. He had been assured on this point by the Grand Duke Nicholas and General Soukhomlinoff. Soukhomlinoff knew that the ammunition of the Russian army was insufficient, but he still continued to reassure the Emperor and the Allies. The Grand Duke Nicholas, who was far from blameless . . . instigated a Special Commission under the presidency of the Grand Duke Serge, with the declared object of providing the army with the requisite munitions. But three months passed, and nothing was done. Even when certain supplies of munitions arrived at the Front, these were useless, as they would not fit the guns and musketry which required them! The Emperor was most unjustly blamed for these calamities—but he was guiltless—the real offenders were the Grand Duke Nicholas, General Soukhomlinoff and their agents.

On the day following my husband's departure the Empress sent me a message asking me to go with her to the church usually attended by the Lancers (the Empress's Own). The service was very impressive; I stood behind the Empress, who was praying ardently, and, at the conclusion, she turned to me: "Don't look sad, Lili," she whispered. "This war *had* to be."

Whenever the regiments of which the Empress was colonel left for the front, she saw the officers and soldiers, and blessed them and spoke to them. A great deal has been said and written about the Empress's unpopularity with the soldiers. I have hardly heard a good word on her behalf, and yet I know how devotedly she was loved by many of the officers and men. It will be my privilege to show how, during the Revolution, she received many touching evidences of their affection, and I am determined not to allow the Sisyphus weight of calumny to deter me from telling what I know of the truth. After the declaration of hostilities the Empress at once instituted her own hospitals, and both she and her daughters went in for a medical course to qualify as Sisters of Charity. Princess Gedroits, herself a professor of surgery, instructed them, and the Imperial Family gave up most of their time to lectures and demonstrations.

Directly they had passed the necessary examinations, the Empress and "the four sisters Romanoff" started nursing, spending hours with the wounded and almost invariably being present at operations.

Society at once began to criticise this procedure. It argued that it was not the duty of an Empress of Russia to become a nurse. It failed to remember that at this time the illustrated papers were full of pictures of various crowned heads who were doing precisely the same thing for which they condemned the Empress! But she wore her rue with a difference. What was praiseworthy in others constituted a sin in her case. Without being accused of bitterness, I think I may be allowed to say that it makes me sad when I realise the persistent animosity displayed towards the Empress by all classes, from the prince to the peasant . . . "the evil that men do lives after them, the good is oft interred with their bones." In the case of the Empress, the good she undoubtedly did during her life was not only interred with her but it was never recognised during her life. Her innocent fault consisted (to quote the words of an English writer) in not being able to understand "that in the eyes of her subjects she must shine and be ornamental, but not useful in the trivial acceptance of the word." Perhaps the Empress erred in her conception of the mentality of the Russian peasant. As an impartial critic, I fear this was the case. When she wore the Red Cross, the sign of a universal Brotherhood of Pity, the average soldier only saw in the Red Cross an emblem of her lost dignity as Empress of Russia. He was shocked and embarrassed when she attended to his wounds and performed almost menial duties. His idea of an Empress was never as a woman, but only as an imposing and resplendent Sovereign.

The pro-German tendencies of the Empress were mentioned after our reverse at Brest, when the Emperor assumed command. Everyone was suspicious of her, and, when she spoke English at the hospitals to her daughters and her ladies-in-waiting, the soldiers declared she was speaking German, and this report once started was magnified exceedingly.

The actual dawn of Revolution occurred before the death of Rasputin, but during the war it was openly stated that the end of Tsardom was at hand. All our defeats were attributed to the pro-German influence of the Empress, who was spitefully alluded to as "The Colonel" in certain salons.

Protopopoff, the Minister of the Interior, was always reporting plots against the life of the Empress. One, it was said, had been disclosed in an intercepted letter from a Society woman to a friend in Moscow. The writer lamented that the murder of the Empress had not been a "fait accompli," and declared that, failing murder, the next best remedy was incarceration in a madhouse. Princess Vasiltchikoff sent a letter to the Empress, in the name of the women of Russia, telling her that all classes were against her, and daring her to mix further in Russian affairs.

It has been said that the Empress was equally furious at the contents of the letter, and the fact that it was written on paper torn off a letter-pad! But it was *not* the question of the breach of etiquette which writing to the Sovereign on a letter-pad implied, it was the horrible accusations, the virulent animosity of the missive which at first angered the Empress, and afterwards grieved her. She cried bitterly when she told me. "Of what am I accused?" she said. "Gregory is dead. Surely people might leave me alone!"

Princess Vasiltchikoff's letter gave rise to much excitement; her portrait was in all the newspapers, and public opinion was divided for and against her.

Another letter was sent to the Empress, this time anonymously, but it was equally reprehensible, and this letter and the preceding one caused the greatest indignation in the hospitals, as the officers who knew the Empress as she really was were very angry. Life in general was excessively difficult and painful, so much so that, when my husband arrived from Mourmansk, and asked Count Kapnist how things were going, the Count replied: "You'll soon see for yourself, and you'll be horrified. We have gone back to the days of Paul I. Ruin lies ahead of us."

The Empress saw a good many people at this time. Every Thursday there were musical evenings, where I met various friends—officers in the Artillery, the Emperor's A.D.C., Linavitch, Count Rabindar and his wife (who was a faulty likeness of the Empress), the officers of the "Standart," Prince Dolgouroki (who was after-wards murdered), Madame Voeikoff, the wife of the Commandant du Palais, Colonel Grotten, and many others.

A Roumanian orchestra, under the direction of the famous Goulesko, played on these Thursdays, and the Empress derived great pleasure in listening to the really exquisite music. A huge fire was always burning in the salon; the Empress sat near it, and a little seat immediately behind her was arranged for my exclusive use. If I happened to arrive after the Empress was seated, she always indicated the vacant place with a gesture and a sweet smile.

One evening, about a fortnight before the Revolution, when I was sitting in my usual place, listening to the Roumanian orchestra, I noticed that the Empress seemed unusually sad. So I ventured to bend forward and whisper, anxiously, "Oh, Madame, why are you so sad to-night?" The Empress turned and looked at me.... "Why am I sad, Lili?... I can't really say, but the music depresses me.... I think my heart is broken."

The same evening, Anna childishly observed: "We all seem out of sorts. What fun it would be to have some champagne!" The Empress was angry at the suggestion. "No . . ." she said, "the Emperor hates wine, he can't bear women to drink wine—but what matter his likes or his dislikes, when people will have it that he's a drunkard himself?" The Empress was in very indifferent health; mental worry had increased her heart trouble, but she endeavoured never to let her health interfere with her public duties. At an official reception following the departure of the Guards, the Empress told me that she hardly knew how to endure the strain. "Veronal is keeping me up. I'm literally saturated with it," she said.

When my husband came home on a few days' leave, the Emperor sent for him, and listened attentively to all that he had to say, questioning him very closely on certain subjects. We had never thought of or mentioned the subject of his preferment; he had now spent two strenuous years in the mine-fields, and the Emperor noticed how ill he looked. "Dehn must have a rest," remarked His Majesty. "I shall give him a post near my person."

But this kindly thought never matured. My husband was sent for by the Minister of the Marine, and left for England at twenty-four hours' notice, in company with General Meller-Zakomelsky, taking with them decorations destined by the Emperor for certain English officers. The news of the Revolution was not known by them or in England when they arrived, so an elaborate official reception was given them. Almost immediately afterwards the news was public property and it was impossible to use the Emperor's decorations. I often wonder what became of them.

Before leaving for England, my husband asked me to join him there. I could not promise. I loved him very dearly, but I felt that my duty lay with the Empress.

"No, Charles," I said, "I cannot promise anything at present, but, if things become better, I'll come."

When he had gone, I felt utterly unhappy, but I did not regret any sacrifice I was called upon to make for the Imperial Family. I loved them all far too much.

At this time the Emperor had every intention of remaining with his family, but, one morning, after having received General Gourko in audience, he suddenly announced:

"I'm going to G.H.Q. to-morrow." The Empress was surprised.

"Cannot you possibly stay with us?" she enquired.

"No," said the Emperor, "I must go."

Almost immediately after the Emperor's departure, the Tsarevitch fell ill with measles, and I used to spend every evening with the Empress, who was naturally much worried over her son's illness. In these days, our intimacy had increased so much that my time was mostly devoted to the Empress, and I saw few of my friends and relations. But my aunt, the Countess Kotzebue-Pilar, was a great Society leader, and I heard all that transpired in her salon. One evening before dinner my aunt (who was always furious at the rumours current about the Empress) 'phoned me to come to her house at once. I found her in an excessively agitated condition. . . .

"It's awful what people are saying, Lili," she cried. . . . "And I must tell you—you *must* warn the Empress."

In somewhat calmer tones my aunt continued: "Yesterday I was at the Kotzebues'. . . . Many officers were present, and it was openly asserted that His Majesty will never return from G.H.Q. What are you going to do? You are constantly in the society of the Empress—you cannot allow her to remain in ignorance of these reports."

"She will not believe them," I said.

"Nevertheless," said my aunt, "it is your duty to warn her."

I returned to the Palace feeling very unhappy. I hardly knew what to do for the best. At last, after a struggle, I decided to tell the Empress. As I had anticipated, she made light of the story.

"It's all nonsense, Lili, I can't believe such a thing—it's nothing but malicious gossip. However, as you seem so apprehensive, send for Grotten (the Commandant du Palais) and tell him."

"Don't pay any attention to such a canard," cried Grotten angrily, when he heard my story. "It's a lie which stamps itself as the worst kind of lie."

"Well, General," I retorted, now thoroughly vexed with myself for having apparently made a mountain out of a molehill, "if God ordains my aunt's report to be a lie, so much the better."

"Don't be cross. . . . I'll most certainly get in touch with G.H.Q.," said Grotten reassuringly. THREE DAYS AFTER CAME THE REVOLUTION.

And now the funeral knell of Russia began to sound, at first muffled, but always insistently. Disorders broke out in Petrograd. The strikes began on February 21st (Old Style), and crowds clamoured for bread, of which the supplies had suddenly stopped.

No one could understand this, as Protopopoff's last words to the Emperor were: "There is plenty of flour, I'll pledge my word that we have enough flour to last us for a month, and after that fresh supplies will be coming in." The bread shortage was in reality due to the action of the Duma—it was an organised arrangement!!

Each day matters grew worse. Fighting took place in the streets, drunkards indulged in indescribable orgies, the police were murdered much in the same manner as they have been in Ireland. It was bitterly cold—snow lay in deep drifts, and Petrograd was in the iron grip of a black frost.

Protopopoff, the Minister of the Interior, was always ultra-optimistic—I never liked or trusted him; he did not seem the man to handle any great crisis. He was appreciated by the Duma until his deplorable interview in Stockholm, when he discussed the war in a very indiscreet manner; but, when the Emperor appointed Protopopoff Minister of the Interior, he was universally hated, and everyone blamed the Emperor for appointing a man so singularly devoid of merit. Protopopoff promised everything, without considering whether his promises were possible. It was the same with his statements: he disliked telling unpleasant truths, so he took refuge in pleasant evasions. He was the man who continually told the Imperial Family that nothing could possibly happen. "Trust in me," said Protopopoff, striking an attitude. And, whenever someone meekly remarked that the working classes were undoubtedly restive, Protopopoff struck another attitude which implied, "Did I fancy I heard you say '*restive*'?" and, aloud, in pained but hearty tones: "What? Are you actually troubling yourself about a little unrest? We'll soon crush them—Labour cannot stand up against *Me*."

It may be asked: Why did the Imperial Family, and especially the Empress, place so much reliance in M. Protopopoff's statements, as, since the Empress knew all that was written concerning her, she, at least, could have possessed no illusions? The answer is simple: The Empress knew that she was unpopular, but she never would believe that this unpopularity lay with the people—she attributed the scandals and calumnies to class-hatred, and to that craving for sensation without which a certain section of the Press would be unable to exist. When, made bold by my ever growing apprehendsions, I ventured to tell the Empress that in these days the "people" were not paragons of fidelity, she bade me remember the afternoon, not long distant, when we drove out to a little "Lett" village near Peterhof. I *did* remember. The automobile had stopped near the church, and, the moment the Empress alighted, she was surrounded by a crowd of peasants, who knelt before her, and, with tears in their eyes, prayed aloud for her happiness. After this the Empress was offered bread and salt, and it was with great difficulty that a passage was cleared to her waiting automobile. This incident occurred two years before the Revolution. "And yet you tell me, Lili, that these people wish me ill!"

"Madame, many things have happened during the last two years."

"*Nothing* has happened, Lili, to touch the real heart of Russia."

I do not profess to have any knowledge of politics, and I never wished to meddle in them, so it is impossible for me to attempt to discuss the so-called political influence of the Empress. We hardly ever spoke of politics, but I can truthfully state that I never once heard her utter one sentiment that might be described as even faintly pro-German. Her letters written after her arrest, which are reproduced for the first time, ought to plead for her more strongly than any words of mine. When the Empress wrote to me, neither she nor I had any idea that part of her correspondence would be read by the English public. The letters might never have reached *me*: they were smuggled out of the Palace and sent from Tobolsk in circumstances of much difficulty and danger. But they breathe sincerity of purpose in every line: they were written when the shadow of death was falling on the Imperial Family. . . . There is no trace of the hysterical, intriguing woman in any of them. The letter which contains the passage relating to the fleet will perhaps serve to vindicate the memory of the Empress more than anything else, at least so far as her alleged pro-Germanism is affected. Even now, Justice, blind, but nevertheless all-seeing, has decreed that Germany should acknowledge having laid the mines which destroyed the "Hampshire": Germany, brought to book, would not have scrupled to lay the guilt to the charge of the Empress, especially since she cannot defend herself. But Germany has not availed herself of the universal detestation which surrounds the name of Alexandra Feodorovna: so she has, at least, been spared *one* degradation.

Part II—The Revolution

CHAPTER I

ON Saturday, February 25th, 1917, the Empress told me that she wished me to come to Tsarkoe Selo on the following Monday, and I was (let me confess it) still in bed when the telephone rang at 10 a.m. I suppose my delay in answering must have amused the Empress, for her first words were: "I believe you have only just got out of bed, Lili. Listen, I want you to come to Tsarkoe by the 10.45 train. It's a lovely morning. We'll go for a run in the car, so I'll meet you at the station. You can see the girls and Anna, and return to Petrograd at 4 p.m. I'm certain you won't catch the train, but anyhow I'll be at the station to meet it."

I dressed at express speed, and, snatching up my gloves, a few rings, and a bracelet, I ran into the street in search of a fiacre. I had quite forgotten that there was a strike, and no conveyances were available! At this moment I saw M. Sablin's carriage: I hailed him, and begged for a lift to the station. On the way I questioned him.

"What news, Monsieur . . . ?"

"There's nothing fresh," he replied, "but everything is quite all right, although I must admit it is very strange about the bread shortage."

The train for Tsarkoe was just moving out of the station when I arrived on the platform, but I scrambled in, and found myself in the company of Madame Tanieff, Anna's mother, who was going to see her daughter, now ill, like the Grand Duchesses Olga and Tatiana, with the measles. Madame Tanieff, like M. Sablin, knew nothing fresh; she was chiefly concerned about Anna's illness; but the first words of the Empress, who, true to her promise, was awaiting me, were:

"Well, how is it in Petrograd? I hear things are very serious."

We said that there was apparently nothing alarming, and the Empress told Madame Tanieff to get into the car with us, and she would take her to the Palace.

It was a glorious morning: I remembered the splendour of the day long afterwards; the sky was an Italian blue, and snow lay everywhere. We were not able to drive in the Park on account of the drifts! On the way back, we met Captain Hvostchinsky, one of the Garde Equipage. The Empress intimated her wish to speak to him, and the car stopped.

Captain Hvostchinsky smiled at the notion of danger. "There is no danger, Your Majesty" he said; so, reassured, the Empress and I returned to the Palace. I went at once to see the Grand Duchesses. They were certainly very ill, suffering from bad pains in the ears; but they were pleased to see me, and I sat between the two camp beds, talking to them. After lunch I went up again, and presently the Empress joined us.

She beckoned me into the next room: I could see that she was agitated. "Lili," she said, breathlessly, "it is *very* bad. I have just seen Colonel Grotten, and General Resin, and they report that the Litovsky Regiment has mutinied, murdered the officers, and left barracks: the Volinsky Regiment has followed suit. I can't understand it. I'll never believe in the possibility of Revolution—why, only yesterday, everyone said it was impossible! The peasants love us . . . they adore Alexis! I'm sure that the trouble is confined to Petrograd alone. But I want you to go and see Anna . . . she may also have been told this, and you know how easily she is frightened!"

I found Anna ill, and light-headed, and, as I entered her bedroom, I thought what a contrast it presented to the cool, darkened room which I had just left. Olga and Tatiana were so patient, they lay so still, and were grateful for any attention. *This* sick room resembled a "lever du Roi" in the days of Louis XIV. Anna was surrounded by a crowd of "sisters" and three doctors were in attendance. Madame Tanieff was there, looking the picture of misery, and Anna's sister, who was almost hysterical, kept on exclaiming, "All is lost." They had expected General Tanieff to lunch, but he had not arrived . . . there was no news of him. What were they to do? General Tanieff entered in the midst of this confusion, breathless, and scarlet in the face. "Petrograd is in the hands of the mob," he exclaimed, "they are stopping all cars . . . they commandeered mine, and I've had to walk every step of the way."

At this intelligence, Allie Pistolkors (she had married the Grand Duke Paul's stepson) burst into tears and begged me to ask the Empress what she had better do. I promised to see the Empress at once, and, as the Grand Duchesses Anastasie and Marie had just come to fetch me, I returned to the private apartments with them.

The winter afternoon was fast drawing in, and I found the Empress alone in her boudoir. She could give me no message for Mme Pistolkors. "I don't *know* what to advise," she said, sadly. Then, turning to me, "What are *you* going to do, Lili? Titi is in Petrograd . . . had you not better return to him this evening?"

At the sight of the Empress, so tragically alone, so helpless in the midst of the signs and splendour of temporal power, I could hardly restrain my tears. Controlling myself with an effort, I tried to steady my voice:

"Permit me to remain with *you*, Madame," I entreated.

The Empress looked at me without speaking. Then she took me in her arms and held me close, and kissed me many times, saying as she did so:

"I *cannot* ask you to do this, Lili."

"But I must, Madame," I answered. . . . "Please, please let me stay. I can't go back to Petrograd and leave you here."

The Empress told me that she had tried to 'phone the Emperor, and that she had been unable to do so. "But I have wired him, asking him to return immediately. He'll be here on Wednesday morning."

After this conversation we went to see the Grand Duchesses, and the Empress lay down on a couch in their bedroom. I sat beside her, and we conversed in low tones so as not to awaken the sleeping girls. The Empress was still unable to believe in the reports, and she expressed a wish to see the Grand Duke Paul. "How I wish he would come," she said. She then asked me to go over to Anna's apartments, and say that she felt too unwell to come herself.

Anna's room still looked like a "lever du Roi"; Allie had taken her departure, so Mme Tanieff told me, and had gone to the Palace of the Grand Duke Paul. I lost no time in delivering the Empress's message, and quickly returned to her. The evening wore on. . . . News came that Petrograd was in a state of upheaval, and that crowds of mutineers were everywhere. The Empress begged me to 'phone Linavitch, the A.D.C. to the Emperor, and ask him to tell us what was happening. Linavitch was in command of a company of Horse Artillery at Pavlosk, two miles from Tsarkoe Selo, so it was not difficult to "get" him. "Tell Her Majesty," he said, "that I am here with my company, and that all will be well."

I spent the evening with the Empress in the mauve boudoir, and she told me how glad she was to have me near her. "I know the

Grand Duchesses want you to be somewhere close to their room, so I've decided that the red drawing-room will be the best place for you to sleep.* Come with me. Anastasie is waiting for us," she said.

The red drawing-room was a fine room; everything in it was upholstered in scarlet, and scarlet and white chintz covered the easy chairs. A bed had been arranged on one of the couches, and the two Grand Duchesses, with tender solicitude, had seen to the minor details themselves. Anastasie's nightgown lay outside the coverlet, Marie had put a lamp and an ikon on the table by the bed; and a snapshot of Titi, taken from their collection of photographs, had been hastily framed, and occupied a place next to the holy ikon. How dearly I loved them all . . . how glad I was that I was privileged to share their danger!

The Empress left me with Anastasie, as she wished to see Count Benckendorff, so Anastasie and I sat down comfortably on the red carpet, and amused ourselves with jigsaw puzzles until she returned.

The Empress came back from her interview with Count Benckendorff in a state of painful agitation, and, directly Anastasie had gone to bed, she told me that the reports were worse. "I don't want the girls to know anything until it is impossible to keep the truth from them . . ." she said, "but people are drinking to excess, and there is indiscriminate shooting in the streets. Oh, Lili, what a blessing that we have here the most devoted troops . . . there is the Garde Equipage . . . they are all our personal friends, and I place implicit faith in the tirailleurs of Tsarkoe."

I think that this thought comforted her: she seemed happier when she bade me good night.

I woke early on Tuesday morning. . . . Sleep had been almost impossible, but I had dropped into an uneasy slumber soon after dawn. I dressed at once, hoping to be ready for the Empress, but she was before me, and at half-past eight she entered the red drawing-room. We went at once to the Grand Duchesses, and drank our *café au lait* in their room. The Empress told me that she had wired repeatedly to the Tsar, but had received no reply. Later in the morning she received Count Benckendorff and Colonel Grotten, who informed her that matters were becoming more alarming and that the Garde Equipage had better remain inside the Palace, as there

---

* The apartments at Tsarkoe Selo reserved for guests and the suite were situated over the third and fourth entrances to the Palace. The red drawing-room was in the private apartments.—L. D.

THE REAL TSARITSA

was a report that the mob, supported by the Duma, was even now marching on Tsarkoe.

[*For the image that is inserted here, please see a very similar one already included in Book I on page 186.*]

THE IMPERIAL FAMILY
BACK ROW left to right: Grand Duchesses Marie, Olga, and Tatiana
CENTRE left to right: H.I.M. The Tsaritsa, Tsar Nicholas II. Grand Duchess Anastasia
FRONT The Tsarevitch

The Empress immediately consented; she was really delighted at the thought of having the Garde Equipage at the Palace, and the Grand Duchesses were frankly overjoyed. "It's just like being on the yacht again," they said. The Garde Equipage, which was now augmentted by the Mixed Guard, and by sentinels taken from the Cossack Convoi, took up its quarters outside the Palace and in the vast souterrains. One part of the Palace was arranged as an ambulance station. We were very busy, but the Grand Duchesses made light of danger and showed none of our agitation. The Empress was always awaiting a reply to her telegrams. None came.

Tuesday was a day of general unrest. It seemed as if the weather were in sympathy with man's savage mood. The blue sky of Monday had vanished, an icy blizzard swept around the Palace, and a north wind drove the deep snow into still deeper drifts. In the afternoon, on my way back from seeing Anna, I encountered Baroness Ysa Büxhoevgen on one of the corridors. She was almost running and she seemed very much disturbed. "I must see the Empress," she said. "I've just come from Tsarkoe Selo (the town): everything is awful—they say there is mutiny and dissatisfaction amongst the troops." Ysa's terror was general: panic seized the dwellers in the

Palace, but none of the servants left us. Mlle Schneider's maids, it is true, fled, but they came back again the next day.

The Empress was very anxious to see the Grand Duke Paul, but I believe that at first there was some misunderstanding, as the Grand Duke thought that etiquette demanded that the Empress should ask *him*, and he declared that he would not come unless she did. I had received a hint of this, so, when next I saw the Empress, I suggested that perhaps the Grand Duke was waiting for her invitation. . . . This had not occurred to the Empress; she told me to 'phone at once and ask the Grand Duke to come and see her after dinner.

I was placed, unwillingly, in a very awkward predicament. I had no official position at Court, but the Empress seemed to think that my duty was to act as her mouthpiece, and to assume an authority which I was far from desiring.

However, I 'phoned to the Palace of the Grand Duke, and, in the name of the

Empress, I asked him to come to Tsarkoe Selo. His son answerred the 'phone, and rather brusquely demanded to know who on all the earth was speaking.

"Lili Dehn," I said.

His "*Oh!*" was more eloquent than words!

During the afternoon the Empress called me into her boudoir. "Lili," she said, "they say that a hostile crowd of 300,000 persons is marching on the Palace. We shall not be, we *must* not be afraid. Everything is in the hands of God. To-morrow the Emperor is sure to come. . . . I *know* that, when he does, all will be well." She then asked me to 'phone to Petrograd, and get in touch with my aunt, Countess Pilar, and other friends. I 'phoned to several, but the news grew worse and worse. At last I 'phoned to my flat. The Emperor's A.D.C., Sablin, who lived in the same building, answered my ring. I begged him to take care of Titi, and, if it were possible, to join us at Tsarkoe, as the Imperial Family needed protection; but he replied that a ring of flames practically surrounded the building, which was well watched by hostile sailors. He managed, however, to bring Titi to the 'phone—and my heart ached when I heard my child's anxious voice:

"Mamma, when are you coming back?"

"Darling, I'll come very soon."

"Oh, *please* come; it's so dreadful here."

I felt torn between love and duty, but I had long since decided where my duty lay. I told the Empress what Sablin had reported; she listened in silence, and then, by some tremendous effort of will, she regained her usual composure. Her strength strengthened me. We had, indeed, every need for courage. The poor "children" were lying desperately ill. . . . They looked almost like corpses. . . . Anna was in high fever, the Palace was terror-stricken, and outside brooded the dread spectre of Revolution!

All at once the Empress was seized with an idea to talk to the soldiers. I begged to accompany her, in case of any unforeseen treachery, but she refused. "Why, Lili," she said, reproachfully, "they're all friends!" Marie and Anastasie went with her, and I watched them from a window. It was quite dark, and the great courtyard was illuminated with what appeared to be exceptionally powerful electric lights. The distant sound of guns was audible . . . the night was bitterly cold. From where I stood, I could see the Empress, wrapped in furs, walking from one man to another, utterly fearless of her safety. She was the calm, dignified Tsaritsa—the typical consort of the Tsar of all the Russias. Here was no hysterical religious maniac, no abandoned heroine of the novel! The Empress moved in this tragic *mise en scène*, protected by her own goodness; but, when the light fell on her fair, pale face, I trembled. I knew her weak heart, her delicacy of physique—suppose she were to faint?

When the Empress came back, she was apparently possessed by some inward exaltation. She was radiant; her trust in the "people" was complete, she was sustained by that, often, alas, broken reed of friendship. "They are our friends," she kept on repeating, "they are so devoted to us." She was, alas, presently to discover that the name of Judas is often synonymous with that of a friend.

One thing troubled her fleeting happiness. "I haven't seen a company in the basement. . . . It is such a pity, but I didn't feel well enough. Perhaps I can manage it tomorrow."

After her visit to the soldiers, the Empress received Count and Countess Benckendorff, who asked to be permitted to remain at the Palace. Their request was gladly granted, and rooms were arranged for them.

The Grand Duke Paul arrived later in the evening. He was a tall, imposing man, who was considered to be very fascinating, and, what was more to his credit, excessively kind at heart. He had a long conversation with the Empress, and we could hear their agitated voices in the next room. The Empress told me afterwards that almost her first words had been:

"What of the Guards?"

And the Grand Duke had replied in tones of fatality:

"I can do nothing. Nearly all of them are at the Front."

When we went to bid the Grand Duchesses good night, I was distressed to find that the firing was distinctly to be heard from their room. Olga and Tatiana did not appear to notice it, but, when their mother had gone, Olga asked me what the noise signified.

"Darling, I don't know—it's nothing. The hard frost makes everything sound much more," I said lightly.

"But are you *sure*, Lili?" persisted the Grand Duchess. "Even Mamma seems nervous, we're so worried about her heart; she's most certainly overtiring herself—*do* ask her to rest."

The Empress decided that Marie should sleep with her. "You, Lili, will sleep in the room with Anastasie, and have Marie's bed. Don't take off your corsets . . . one doesn't know what may happen. The Emperor arrives between 5 and 7 to-morrow morning, and we must be ready to meet him. Come to my room early, and then I'll tell you the train."

Neither the Grand Duchess nor I could sleep, and we lay awake in the darkness talking in low tones. Occasionally I was silent, but, when this was so, Anastasie never failed to ask: "Lili, are you asleep?"

During the night we got up and looked out of the windows. A huge gun had been placed in the courtyard. "How astonished Papa will be!" whispered Anastasie. We stood for a few minutes watching the weird scene. It was so bitterly cold that the sentinels were dancing round the gun in order to keep warm. Their figures were sharply defined against the arc-lights—it seemed like some new Carmagnole; in the distance we heard shouts of drunken voices and occasional shots—and so the night passed.

At 5 a.m. on Wednesday morning we went downstairs to the Empress's bedroom. She was awake, and as she opened the door she whispered: "Hush . . . Marie is asleep: the train is late. . . . Most probably the Emperor won't come until ten." The Empress was fully dressed, and she looked so sad that I could not help saying impulsively: "Oh, Madame, *why* is the train late?"

She smiled wanly, but did not reply. As we went back to our bedroom, Anastasie said in agitated tones: "Lili, the train is *never* late. Oh, if Papa would only come quickly. . . . I'm beginning to feel ill. What shall I do if I get ill? I can't be useful to Mamma. . . . Oh,

Lili, say I'm not going to be ill."

I tried to calm her, and I persuaded her to lie down on her bed and sleep; but the poor child was actually sickening for the measles. Anastasie was the sweetest-natured girl: she adored her mother, and delighted in running hither and thither on her errands.

The Empress always alluded to Anastasie as "my legs!"

When the Empress joined me in Olga's room a little before nine, she still hoped for the 10 o'clock train. "Perhaps the blizzard detains him," she said. She lay down on the couch, and I sat on the floor beside her; we spoke in undertones; but her chief anxiety was concerning my want of sleep. "Sit on a chair, Lili, and put your feet up on the couch," she said.

"No—no—Madame," I replied, "it is not to be thought of." But, at her request, I compromised matters by resting the tips of my shoes on the end of the couch.

Ten o'clock came, but we still heard nothing. It was the first of March, a month fatal to the Romanoffs—well might they "beware the Ides of March!" The Emperor Paul was suffocated on the first of March, and, thirty-six years previously, on this date, the Emperor's grandfather, Alexander II, was killed by a bomb. The March of 1917 is destined to be associated with the downfall of the dynasty.

We were living in a state of continual and unrelieved anxiety. Dr. Botkin and Dr. Direvenko were in constant attendance on the three Grand Duchesses, but the Tsarevitch was, fortunately, much better. Poor Anastasie could not reconcile herself to the idea of being ill: she cried and cried, and kept on repeating, "Please don't keep me in bed."

Service in the Palace was quite normal, but the water supply which worked the private lift used by the Empress had been cut off, and in consequence she was now obliged to walk upstairs. This sounds a trivial incident, but it entailed a great deal of suffering on the Empress, who was already overtired and overstrung. Her heart, always affected, now became much worse, owing to her having to go up and down stairs so often, but she insisted upon seeing her children, and she used to go up the staircase at times almost on the verge of fainting. I supported her—walking behind her and holding her underneath the arms.

We could not understand what had become of the Emperor: the Empress thought that the delay arose owing to the confusion on the railways, which were now in the hands of the Revolutionaries.

The dreary afternoon of March 1st was signalised by an unhappy occurrence. The Empress and I were standing at the window overlooking the courtyard, when we noticed that many of the soldiers had bound white handkerchiefs on their wrists. An enquiry as to the reason elicited the reply that the white handkerchiefs signified that upon the representation of a Member (who had come to Tsarkoe Selo) the troops had consented to act in unison with the Duma.

The Empress turned to me. "Well . . . so everything is in the hands of the Duma," she said, with a certain degree of bitterness. "Let us hope that it will bestir itself, and do something to remedy the disaffection."

She moved away from the window. I could see she was hurt and disappointed . . . but this was not destined to be the last of her many disillusions!

Count Appraxin, Secretary to the Empress, arrived later in the day: he had experienced the greatest difficulty in reaching Tsarkoe— and his news was not reassuring. We sat up late that evening—dinner had been a mere farce—our minds were too anxious and too preoccupied to think of food. The children were dangerously ill, the whereabouts of the Emperor were unknown, and the Revolution was at our gates. When at last I bade the Empress good night, she told me not to undress. "I'm not going to do so," she said, and her quiet tones were significant that she anticipated the worst!

DOCTOR DIREVENKO

SHOOTING PARTY IN FINLAND, AUTUMN, 1910
Centre—the Emperor: Right—Lieut.-Com. Dehn

THE TSAREVITCH AT G.H.Q.

THE TSAREVITCH AND HIS SPANIEL 'JOY'

CHAPTER II

EARLY on the morning of March 2nd the Empress came into the Grand Duchesses' bedroom. She was deathly pale—she seemed hardly alive. As I ran towards her I heard her agitated whisper: "Lili—the troops have deserted!"

I found no words with which to answer. I was stupefied. At last I managed to stammer:

"Why, Madame? In the name of God, why?"

"Their Commander-in-Chief, the Grand Duke Cyril, has sent for them." Then, unable to contain herself, the Empress said brokenly, "My sailors—my *own* sailors—I can't believe it."

But it was too true. The Garde Equipage had left the Palace at 1 a.m. and 5 a.m.—the "faithful friends," the "devoted subjects," were with us no longer. The officers of the Garde were received by the Empress in the mauve boudoir during the morning: I was present, and I heard from one of my husband's friends that the duty of taking the Garde to Petrograd had been carried out by a "temporary gentleman," Lieutenant Kouzmine. The officers were furious, especially their commandant, MiasocdoffIvanof, a big, burly sailor, whose kind eyes were full of tears. . . . One and all begged to be allowed to remain with the Empress, who, almost overcome by emotion, thanked them, saying: "Yes—yes—I beg you to remain: this has been a terrible blow, what *will* the Emperor say when he hears about it!" She then sent for General Resin, the Commander of the Mixed Guard, and instructed him to make room for the loyal officers in his regiment.

General Resin told me long afterwards that he was relieved when he knew that the cowardly Garde had actually left the Palace, as orders had been given for a detachment to go on one of the church towers which commanded a view of the courtyard, and if, by a certain time, the troops had not joined the Duma, to train two enormous field-guns on to the Palace!

There was still no news of the Emperor, although the Empress constantly telegraphed. It was reported that his train was returning to G.H.Q., and at the time many people thought that if it reached there the troops would have followed the Emperor. We 'phoned to the hospitals for news, and the Empress received a good many people. To all these she was her usual calm, dignified self. When I marvelled at her fortitude, she replied: "Lili, I must *not* give way. I keep on saying, '*I must not*'—it helps me."

In the late afternoon, Rita Hitrowo (one of the younger ladies-in-waiting, and a friend of the Grand Duchesses) arrived from Petrograd with the worst possible tidings, and, after the Empress had spoken to Rita, she received two officers of the Mixed Guard, who proposed to try and get a letter from her through to the Emperor: it was arranged that they should leave Tsarkoe the next evening. The Empress was always willing to hope. But the night passed, and still never a word came from the Emperor.

On March 3rd I took my *café au lait* with Marie, and we were joined by the Empress. It was a day of agony. The Grand Duchesses grew worse: their ears were badly inflamed, it seemed as if they might not recover. The Empress tried to snatch a little rest by occasionally lying on a couch: her feet had now become very painful, and her heart affection was, at times, alarming. Meals were silent and horrible affairs: I felt as though each morsel would choke me. But, as I had now grown desperate with anxiety, I conceived the notion of communicating with the Emperor by aeroplane. Might not his whereabouts be discovered in this way? The Empress welcomed the idea, and she sent for General Resin, and asked for an aeroplane to be despatched at once. He agreed, but even the weather was against us. . . . A blizzard set in; the dark sky was blotted out with scudding snow, and the wind howled dismally round the Palace.

The Grand Duke Paul arrived about 7 o'clock in the evening. The Empress was engaged in writing letters for the officers to convey to the Emperor, but she received the Grand Duke without a moment's delay.

The interview took place in the red drawing-room. Marie and I were in the adjoining study, and from time to time we heard the loud voice of the Grand Duke and the agitated replies of the Empress. Marie began to get apprehensive.

"Why is he shouting at Mamma?" she asked. "Don't you think I had better see what's the matter, Lili?"

"No, no," I said, "we had better remain here quietly."

"*You* can remain, but I'll go to my room," she answered. "I can't bear to think Mamma is worried."

Hardly had the Grand Duchess left the study when the door

opened and the Empress appeared. Her face was distorted with agony, her eyes were full of tears. She tottered rather than walked, and I rushed forward and supported her until she reached the writing-table between the windows. She leant heavily against it, and, taking my hands in hers, she said brokenly:

"*Abdiqué!*"

I could not believe my ears. I waited for her next words. They were hardly audible.

At last: "*Le pauvre . . . tout seul là bas . . . et passé . . . oh, mon Dieu, par quoi il a passé! Et je ne puis pas être près de lui pour le consoler.*"

"*Madame, très chère Madame, il faut avoir du courage.*"

She paid no attention to me, and kept on repeating, "*Mon Dieu, que c'est pénible. . . . Tout seul là bas!*" I put my arms around her and we walked slowly up and down the long room. At last, fearing for her reason, I cried: "*Mais Madame—au nom de Dieu— il vit!!*"

"Yes, Lili," she replied, as if new hope inspired her. "Yes, he lives."

"I entreat you, Madame, don't lose your courage, don't give way: think of your children and of the Emperor."

The Empress considered me with almost painful scrutiny. "And you, Lili, what of you?"

"Madame, I love you more than anything in this world."

"I know it—I see it, Lili."

"Well, Madame, *write* to him. Think how pleased he will be." I drew the Empress towards the writing-table, and she sank on a chair. . . . "Write, dear Madame, write," I repeated.

She obeyed almost like a child, murmuring, "Yes, Lili . . . how glad he'll be."

Feeling that I might venture to leave the Empress for a few minutes, I went in search of Dr. Botkin, who gave me a composing draught for her. . . . But the Empress did not wish to take it, and it was only when I said: "For *his* sake, Madame," that she complied.

The sound of bitter weeping now attracted my attention. In one corner of the room crouched the Grand Duchess Marie. She was as pale as her mother. She *knew* all! At this moment Volkoff, that faithful servant, entered, and in trembling tones announced that dinner was served. The Empress rose and endeavoured to regain her composure. . . .

I followed her into the next room. She looked round. "Where is Marie?" she said.

I went back to the red drawing-room. Marie was still crouching in the corner. She was so young, so helpless, so hurt, that I felt I must comfort her as one comforts a child. I knelt beside her, her head rested on my shoulder. I kissed her tear-stained face.

"Darling," I said, "don't cry. . . . You will make Mamma so unhappy. Think of *her*." At the words, "Think of *her*," the Grand Duchess remembered the unswerving devotion of the children towards their parents. Every thing was always subservient to Mamma and Papa.

"Ah . . . I'd forgotten, Lili. Yes, I must think of Mamma," she answered. Little by little her sobs ceased, her composure returned, and she went with me to her mother.

That night the Empress and I sat up very late: she had paid her usual visit to the Grand Duchesses, when she had tried outwardly to appear calm. But alone with me it was a different matter. The Empress told me that the Emperor had abdicated in favour of the Tsarevitch. "Now *he'll* be taken from me," she cried. "The people are to assume the Regency. What shall I do?" She started at every footfall; she trembled at the mere sound of a voice. . . . One idea obsessed her—someone might come at any moment to take away her son!

"But, Madame, nothing can be done until the Emperor returns."

"No, surely they will not dare; and he'll be with us very soon," she said. Then, with her usual unselfishness, the Empress insisted upon seeing Count Benckendorff. "I must console him and strengthen him. I can imagine his state of mind."

It was an affecting interview. . . . I do not know what actually transpired, but, when the Empress returned, she was crying. "*Le pauvre vieux*," she murmured, as if to herself.

I did not allow the Empress to see how apprehensive I was, how utterly despairing. I did not share her optimism. . . . The position was most precarious, and the desperate condition of the Grand Duch-esses augmented the general unhappiness. Our only hope lay in the Emperor's return—at any rate, his presence would afford us some moral protection! That night Marie and I slept in the red drawing-room. We lay awake for hours talking about the new developments. But one thought consoled us. The Emperor was still alive!

When the Empress paid her usual visit to the Grand Duchesses, she told us that her first idea was to see all those in the Palace, and console them as much as possible. Countess Gendrinkoff, her devoted lady-in-waiting, who was away visiting a sick relative, returned to Tsarkoe directly she heard of the Emperor's abdication, and her meeting with the Empress was most touching. At first neither of them spoke; and then the Countess, usually a most self-contained individual, broke into bitter weeping.

It was a tragic morning. Towards noon the Empress sent for me. "Lili," she said, "the Duma is losing no time. M. Rodziansko[*] has intimated that we must make our preparations for departure. He says we are to meet the Emperor somewhere *en route.* But we can't possibly go; how can we move the children? I've spoken to the doctors, and they say it would be fatal! I've told Rodziansko this, and he is returning later to acquaint me with the decision of the Duma."

Rodziansko and his colleagues returned at the time appointed. They were at once taken to the Empress.

"The decision of the Duma is unalterable," said Rodziansko curtly.

"But my children—my daughters . . ." pleaded the Empress.

"When a house is on fire, it is best to leave it," answered Rodziansko, with a sardonic smile.

There was apparently nothing to be done. We were at the mercy of Tiberius, and we commenced our preparations for departure. The Empress asked me if I would like to accompany them. I begged to be permitted to do so. "I *cannot* leave you, Madame," I said.

We endeavoured to 'phone to certain friends, but it was impossible. At last the operator, in frightened tones, whispered, "I can't give you the number; the telephone is not in our hands. I beg you, don't talk—I'll ring you up directly it is safe."

In the course of the afternoon a servant informed us that an officer of one of the Tartar regiments begged the Empress to receive him. The Empress asked me to interview him, as she felt too ill to do so, and accordingly I went over to the fourth wing of the Palace, where the officer was waiting. As I traversed the long corridors, I heard the sound of rough voices. I stopped, terrified, at the entrance of one of the salons—the Mixed Guards were just about to change the guard; but "changing the guard" was no longer the decorous proceeding of yester-year! When the fresh detachment entered the salon, they threw themselves literally into the arms of the other soldiers, shouting, "New-born citizens of freedom, we congratulate you."

I passed the "new-born citizens of freedom," and I found Lieu-

---

[*] M. Rodziansko, the President of the Duma, was an aristocrat who had turned Revolutionary: he was always antagonistic to the Imperial Family.

tenant Markoff, to whom I explained the reason of my "deputising." The poor boy had been wounded, he could scarcely stand; but his spirit was unconquerable. "Madame," he said, "I've fought my way through the mob in order to see the Empress, and assure her of my devotion.

The assassins wanted to tear off my epaulettes with HER cypher. I told them that the Empress had given them to me, and that it was her right alone to deprive me of them.

I've arrived here at last. . . . I entreat you to ask the Empress to allow me to remain somewhere near her. . . . I don't care if I wash up the dirty plates. I'll do anything—only let me stay!"

I promised Markoff to deliver his message, and on my way back I heard the soldiers laughing and singing. Sick at heart, and utterly disgusted at their behaviour, I reported it to the Empress. "*Les malheureux*," she said, "*ce n'est pas leur faute, c'est la faute à ceux qui les trompent.*" She granted poor young Markoff's request, and told me to see General Resin, and arrange for Markoff to be included in his detachment.

I suppose the first idea of most people in the position of the Empress, faced with hurried flight, would have been to save their jewels. But jewels were a secondary consideration with the Empress; her chief treasures were those of sentiment, and, as I watched her collecting her favourite books and photographs, I thought that in this instance, as in all others, she was more of the woman than the Empress. And the idea of leaving the scene of many of her happiest associations must have been heart-rending to her. She had transformed the Palace into a home; here she had watched the beautiful growth of her four fair daughters and her adored son. And here she was destined to drink the uttermost dregs of the Cup of Sorrow.

Whilst she was gathering together her personal treasures, the Empress, recalled in imagination to Petrograd, by the sight of a photograph, asked me to telephone to Prince Ratief, the Commandant of the Winter Palace, and tell him that her thoughts were with them all. Fortunately I was enabled to do so; the Prince himself answered my call. "I thank Her Majesty from my heart. We are still alive, but crowds surround the Palace," he said.

After dinner, we went to see the Grand Duchesses, and then to the mauve boudoir—there was no news from the Emperor; all sorts of rumours were current, the most insistent being that he had returned to G.H.Q.

Sunday, the 5th of March, was for us another hopeless dawn. The Empress gave orders for a Te Deum to be sung, and the miraculous ikon from Znaminie* brought to the Palace and taken to the sick-rooms. The procession bearing the ikon passed through the Palace; the Empress walked in it, and, as I looked at the lovely representation of the Virgin and Child, the expression of the eyes seemed the same which I had often seen in those of the Empress—a combination of Faith, Hope and Tragedy!

It was a strange sight to witness the solemn little procession as it traversed the almost deserted splendours of the Palace. Incense wafted wreaths of perfume towards Heaven, the solemn chant rose and fell, the gold and blues of the Virgin's draperies glowed when the ikon passed one of the windows, the sacred symbol of the Cross raised its head above the tumult of Revolution. It seemed to me as if this were some last appeal to God, Who, we are told, is a God of Love and Pity.

The Empress was anxious that the ikon should be taken to Anna's room, so the procession wended its way thither. There, as usual, were the fuss and overcrowding which seemed inseparable from Anna's attack of measles; doctors, nurses and sisters took up all the available space, so, whilst the Empress was praying by the bedside, I stood by the door. One of the doctors from Anna's hospital was near, and, recognising me, he whispered: "I say, Madame Dehn, I think I shall say good-bye to the Palace. Things are getting too hot for *my* comfort." But, if he expected an answer, he received *none*. I simply stared at him.

The Empress was still kneeling by Anna's bed, and Anna, now thoroughly hysterical and *exaltée* by reason of much incense and many prayers, was crying and kissing the Empress's folded hands. It is quite impossible for English readers to imagine such a scene, but these religious processions in the case of illness were of common occurrence with us.

I went back to see Anna later in the evening, and, when I entered the bedroom, I was surprised to see the matron of Anna's hospital, who was praying—a taper in her hand. Directly she saw me, her prayers took unto themselves wings; we had always disliked each other, so our conversation was short and to the point.

"What, are *you* still here?" she exclaimed, meaningly.

---

* Znaminie is a little church adjacent to the Palace.

"Yes . . . I'm *here*," I replied, with equal emphasis.

Anna said nothing; she looked more childish than ever, and very ill at ease. The impression which I received was a bad one, and, when I related to the Empress what I had seen, she wrote to the doctor at the hospital, and asked him to send for the matron, as her presence was not required. Soon after this she resigned, and, like many others of her kind, she left Tsarkoe for an unknown destination.

On Monday, March 6th, all was in readiness for our departure. But one thing yet remained for us to do, and this was, in my eyes, of the utmost importance. During one of my restless nights, I suddenly remembered that the Empress had always kept a diary and that she possessed the diaries of her friend, Princess Orbelliany, which had been bequeathed to her by the Princess.

These contained most intimate accounts of various people, and events connected with the Court. I likewise remembered the Empress's sentimental habit of preserving correspondence with associations, and I dreaded the possibility of either letters or diaries falling into the hands of the Revolutionaries. I knew that the worst construction would be placed by the "Sons of Freedom" on anything unusual which these papers might contain. Even the Empress's habit of calling people by pet names might be construed as sensualism or treason!

I hardly dared suggest the wisdom of destroying this personal property, but my devotion triumphed over my nervousness. To my intense surprise, the Empress at once agreed to do as I proposed.

It may be argued that I was guilty of the worst Vandalism in persuading the Empress to destroy her diaries and correspondence. I may have been, in an historical and artistic sense—but I was right on the score of friendship. We had already experienced the misconstruction which had been put on *one* sentence in a letter: What might not be the fate of the contents of the Imperial diaries if they fell into the hands of censorious and "pure-minded" Revolutionaries?

Princess Orbelliany's diaries were burned first. They consisted of nine leatherbound volumes, and we experienced much difficulty in destroying them. This *auto-dafé* of sentiment took place in the red drawing-room, but we did not attempt to finish burning the diaries and correspondence in one day. It was at best a melancholy task, and we decided to spread it over a week—especially as the Grand Duchesses were very ill, and we had to be with them constantly. Olga was now suffering with inflammation in the head, and Anastasie made little or no progress.

After lunch, when the Empress and I were sitting in the mauve boudoir, we were startled by the sudden entrance of Volkoff. He was very agitated, his face was pale, he trembled in every limb. Without waiting to be addressed by the Empress, and utterly oblivious of etiquette, he cried: "The Emperor is on the 'phone!"

The Empress looked at Volkoff as if he had taken leave of his senses; then, as she realised the full import of his words, she jumped up with the alacrity of a girl of sixteen, and rushed out of the room.

I waited anxiously. I kept on praying that a little happiness might yet be hers . . . perhaps, for all we knew, the danger had passed.

When the Empress returned, her face was like an April day—all smiles and tears! "Lili," she exclaimed, "imagine what were his first words . . . he said: 'I thought that I might have come back to you, but they keep me here. However, I'll be with you all very soon.'" The Emperor added that the Dowager Empress was coming from Kieff to be with him, and that he had only received the Empress's wires *after* the abdication.

"The poor one!" said the Empress. "How much he has suffered! how pleased he'll be to see his mother!"

Thus the day which had begun so sadly ended happily . . . we went at once to tell the glad news to the Grand Duchesses and the Tsarevitch, who was much better, and greatly excited at the prospect of his father's return. M. Gilliard, a charming Swiss, who taught the children French, was with him, but Mr. Gibbs, his English tutor, was in Petrograd. I always remember Mr. Gibbs and his kindness to me. On one occasion upon going to Petrograd he put himself to great inconvenience to get news of Titi, and procure clothes for myself. Notwithstanding innumerable difficulties, he returned with reassuring tidings of Titi, and a clean nurse's uniform and lingerie for myself.*

---

* During this time the Empress and I wore nurses' uniforms. It has been erroneously stated that the Empress wore ordinary dress. This is not the case.

CHAPTER III

AFTER our usual visit to the children (March 7th) the Empress and I went into the red drawing-room, where a fierce fire was burning in the huge grate, and we recommenced our work of destruction.

A large oaken coffer had been placed on the table; this coffer contained all the letters written to the Empress by the Emperor during her engagement and married life. I dared not look at her as she sat gazing at the letters which meant so much. I think she re-read some of them, for at intervals I heard stifled sobs, and those sighs which have their origin in the heart's bitterness. Many of the letters had been written before she was a wife and a mother. They were the love-letters of a man who had loved her wholly and devotedly, who still loved her with the affection of that bygone Springtime. Little dreamt either the lover or the beloved that these letters were afterwards destined to be wet with tears.

The Empress rose from her chair, and, still weeping, laid her love-letters one by one on the heart of the fire. The writing glowed for an instant, as if desirous of burning itself into her very soul, then it faded, and the paper became a little heap of white ash. . . . Alas for Youth! Alas for Love!

When the Empress had destroyed her correspondence, she handed me her diaries to burn. Some of the earlier volumes were gay little books bound in white satin; others were bound in leather. She smiled bravely as I took them, and an immense disgust seized me when I thought that the country of my birth was responsible for her misery and the injustice meted out to her. "I can't bear Russia," I cried. "I hate it."

"Don't dare say such things, Lili," said the Empress. "You hurt me. . . . If you love me, don't ever say you hate Russia. The people are not to blame; they don't understand what they are doing."

A coloured post-card of South Russia fell out of one of the diaries. I picked it up. It was a pretty picture of young girls standing in a flower-starred meadow . . . and it brought Revovka back to me. "That's *home*," I murmured. But the Empress heard my words.

"What did you say? Repeat it, Lili. You said, 'That's *home*.' Now you must never say you hate Russia."

At this time, I am proud to say, the Empress relied on me as woman to woman. To her, I was always "Lili," or "My brave girl." I was her friend in trouble. The fact that I possessed no official position mattered nothing to her; every moment I was writing letters, taking messages, and seeing people on her behalf. I obeyed her absolutely, and her gentle influence gave me fresh strength to hope and to endure.

The burning of the diaries extended over Wednesday and Thursday ... but on Thursday one of the Empress's dressers came to the red drawing-room and begged us to discontinue. "Your Majesty," said she, "the sweepers are searching for the half-charred pieces of paper, some of which have been carried up the chimney. I beg of you to cease.... These men are talking among themselves. ... They are utterly disloyal." But our task was completed—at any rate we had checkmated the curiosity of the Revolutionaries!

At 7 o'clock the Empress asked me to telephone again to the Winter Palace. As on the previous occasion, Prince Retief answered me.

"How are things with you?" I enquired.

"The mob is even now at the gates of the Palace," he replied with absolute unconcern. "I beg you, Madame, to present my assurances of fidelity and devotion to the Empress.... I may not be able to do so again.... Ah!... I thought as much. Madame, it distresses me to appear discourteous, but I fear I am about to be killed.... The doors of this room are being forced!" His voice ceased—there was a terrible crash.... I could bear no more, and the receiver slipped from my nerveless hands.

We remained in the mauve boudoir until quite late, but, just as we were about to go to bed, Volkoff entered in a state of painful agitation. He managed to tell us that M. Goutchkoff had arrived, and insisted upon seeing the Empress. It was then 11 o'clock.

"But, at this hour—it's impossible," said the Empress.

"Your Majesty, he *insists*," stammered Volkoff. The Empress turned to me—terror and pathos in her eyes. "He has come to arrest me, Lili," she exclaimed. "Telephone to the Grand Duke Paul, and ask him to come at once." Regaining her composure, the Empress rearranged the Red Cross head-dress which she had taken off, and stood waiting in silence for the Grand Duke. Neither Marie nor myself dared speak. At length, after what seemed an interminable agony of suspense, the Grand Duke entered, and the Empress told him in a few words about her ominous summons. The next moment, loud voices in the corridor, and the banging of a door, announced Goutchkoff's arrival in the adjoining room.

Goutchkoff, the Minister of War during the Revolution, was an openly avowed personal enemy of the Emperor, whom he had never forgiven for not having accepted him at his own valuation as the uncrowned king of Moscow. He had compelled the Emperor to abdicate through revenge; spiteful curiosity now urged him to gloat over the sufferings of a defenceless woman! He was a hideous creature, who wore big spectacles with yellow glasses, which partially disguised the fact that he was unable to look anyone straight in the face.

Marie and I clung desperately to the Empress; we were certain that all was now finished. She kissed us both tenderly, and passed out with the Grand Duke Paul, an infinitely tragic figure, recalling to my mind a vision of Marie Antoinette, whose troubles possessed so many similarities with those of the Empress. Volkoff, that loyal servant, true to the traditions of Imperial regime, informed us that Goutchkoff had brought two A.D.C.'s with him, and that one of these men had accosted him with the words: "Ha, ha! Here we are. You didn't expect us to-night, eh? But *we* are masters of the Palace *now*!"

Marie and I sat side by side on the sofa, the young girl shook with fear, but her terror was not for herself—Marie, like all the children, thought only of her beloved mother.

In this crisis of their fortunes, the Imperial Family manifested no sorrow at the loss of their rank and prestige. The only anxiety shown by them was the fear of parting one from the other. Theirs might have been the words inscribed upon the wall of a certain old prison in Italy: "Better death than life without you." And, if the report of their death be true, they most mercifully never knew the pain of separation.

At last footsteps sounded in the corridor—the door of the boudoir opened—and, to our unspeakable relief, we saw the Empress!

Marie ran towards her mother, half crying, and half laughing, and the Empress quickly reassured us.

"I am not to be arrested this time," she said. "But, oh! the humiliation of the interview! Goutchkoff was impossible—I could *not* give him my hand. He told me that he merely wanted to see how I was supporting my trials, and whether or no I was frightened." Her pale cheeks were rose-flushed, her eyes sparkled—at this moment the Empress was terrible in her anger. But she soon regained her calm dignity, and we bade her good night, thankful that she was spared to us.

Wednesday, March 8th, is a day momentous in the annals of new-born Russia, inasmuch as it witnessed the arrest of a woman and five sick children, and of those adherents who knew the meaning of the words Friendship and Duty.

In the morning Count Benckendorff came to inform us that the Emperor would arrive at Tsarkoe on the 9th, and that the Revolutionary authorities had decided to arrest everyone in the Palace by noon. The Count asked the Empress to give him a list of those of her suite who would be willing to remain, and the Empress at once addressed me: "Lili . . . do you understand what this order means? After it is enforced, nobody will be allowed to leave the Palace, all news from outside will be stopped. What do you wish to do? Think of Titi . . . Can you bear to be without tidings of him?" I did not hesitate. "My greatest wish is to remain with you, Madame," I replied. "I knew it!" exclaimed the Empress. "But . . . it will, I fear, be a terrible experience for you."

"Don't worry on my account, Madame," I answered. "We will share the danger together."

At noon, General Korniloff made his appearance at the Palace with the order for the arrest of the Imperial Family. The Empress received him wearing her Red Cross uniform, and she was genuinely pleased to see him, since she laboured under the mistaken idea that he was well disposed towards herself and the family. She was entirely mistaken, as Korniloff, thinking that the Empress disliked him, never lost an opportunity of spreading the most malicious reports concerning her.

Korniloff told the Empress that the Palace troops were to be replaced with those of the Revolution; there was no use for the Mixed Guard and the Cossack Convoi; the Palace was now thronged with Revolutionaries, who were walking about everywhere. When the officers of the Mixed Guard bade farewell to the Empress, many of them broke down and sobbed. She afterwards told me that it was also for her a most painful moment. The officers asked the Empress for a handkerchief, as a souvenir of her and the Grand Duchesses. . . . This handkerchief they proposed to tear in pieces, and divide between them; and later, to their great joy, we sent them some "initial" handkerchiefs.

It was a day of good-byes; many officers came in from Petrograd to bid farewell to the Imperial Family; the Tanieffs left, as the Empress had insisted upon them returning to the Palace of the Grand Duke

Michael, where they might reasonably hope to be in safety.

At last the Empress decided to tell the Grand Duchesses about the abdication . . . she could not bear this painful task to devolve upon her husband. She therefore made her way to their apartments, and was with them alone for a long time. Anantasie seemed to sense what had happened . . . and after her mother had left them she looked at me, and said, very quietly, "Mamma has told us everything, Lili; but, as Papa is coming, nothing else matters. However, you have known what was going on . . . how could you keep it from us? Why, you're usually so nervous . . . how is it you are so calm?"

I kissed her, and said that I owed all my fortitude to her mother. She had set such an example of courage that it was impossible for me not to follow it.

When the Empress broke the news to the Tsarevitch, the following conversation took place: "Shall I never go to G.H.Q. again with Papa?" asked the child.

"No, my darling—never again," replied his mother.

"Shan't I see my regiments and my soldiers?" he said anxiously.

"No . . . I fear not."

"Oh dear! And the yacht, and all my friends on board—shall we never go yachting any more?" He was almost on the verge of tears.

"No . . . we shall never see the 'Standart.' . . . It doesn't belong to us now."

The Empress and I took tea together, and she told me how glad she felt that the Garde Equipage had left their colours in the Palace. "I should be so sorry to think that the colours were in the possession of the Duma," she remarked. At that moment we heard the sound of voices, and a noise of singing and shouting. The Empress sprang off the couch on which she was lying, and rushed across to the window. "Oh, Madame, don't look, I implore you," I said, fearing the worst. But she did not hear me. Then I saw her grow pale, and she fell back half fainting on the couch. The sailors were leaving the Palace with the colours!

The Grand Duchess Marie was seized with measles late that evening. Like her sister, Anastasie, she dreaded being ill. "Oh, I did so want to be up when Papa comes," she kept on repeating, until high fever set in, and she lost consciousness . . . her last comprehensible words being, "Lili, can't you sleep with Mamma to-night?"

"Yes, darling," I told her. "I won't leave Mamma alone—I'll be somewhere near her, even if I have to sleep in the bath."

I went to the Empress. "Madame," I said, "will you permit me to remain near you to-night?"

"No, Lili, certainly not. If anything should happen, why should you be obliged to witness a tragedy?" she replied.

I returned to Olga and Tatiana, who, like Marie, were very anxious about their mother. "Lili, you *must* not leave Mamma alone. One of us has always slept with her*—she's not strong. Promise, promise us that you won't leave her alone;" and, when the Empress came to pay her last visit to the sick-room, the Grand Duchesses reiterated their request.

The Empress at first demurred . . . but, when she realised how much the Grand Duchesses dreaded her being left alone, she consented. "Well, Lili," she said reluctantly, "you see that the children must have their own way. But I will not allow anyone to think I am frightened. Undress upstairs, and, when my maids have left me, slip down the private staircase, bring your sheets and blankets, and you can make up a bed on the couch in my boudoir."

It was a bright moonlight night. Outside, the snow lay like a pall on the frost-bound Park. The cold was intense. The silence of the great Palace was occasionally broken by snatches of drunken songs and the coarse laughter of the soldiers. The intermittent firing of guns was audible. It was a night of beauty, defiled by the base passions of men.

I went quietly downstairs to the mauve boudoir. The Empress was waiting for me, and as she stood there I thought how girlish she looked. Her long hair fell in a heavy plait down her back, and she wore a loose silk dressing-gown over her night clothes. She was very pale, very ethereal, but unutterably pathetic.

As I stumbled into the boudoir with my draperies of sheets and blankets she smiled—a little affectionate, mocking smile, which deepened as she watched me trying to arrange my bed on the couch. She came forward, still smiling. "Oh, Lili . . . you Russian ladies don't know how to be useful. When I was a girl, my grandmother, Queen Victoria, showed me how to make a bed. I'll teach *you*." And she deftly arranged the bedding, saying, as she did so: "Take care not to lie on this broken spring. I always had an idea *something* was amiss with this couch."

* From the time that the Emperor left for the Front, one of the Grand Duchesses always slept with the Empress.

The bed-making "à la mode de Windsor" was soon finished, and the Empress kissed me affectionately and bade me good night. "I'll leave my bedroom door open," she said; "then you won't feel lonely."

Sleep for me was impossible. I lay on the mauve couch—*her* couch—unable to realise that this strange happening was a part of ordinary life. Surely I must be dreaming; surely I should suddenly awake in my own bed at Petrograd, and find that the Revolution and its attendant horrors were only a nightmare! But the sound of coughing in the Empress's bedroom told me that, alas! it was no dream. . . . She was moving about, unable, like myself, to sleep. The light above the sacred ikon made a luminous pathway between the bedroom and the boudoir, and presently the Empress came back to me, carrying an eiderdown. "It's bitterly cold," she said. "I want you to be comfortable, Lili, so I've brought you another quilt." She tucked the quilt well round my shoulders, regardless of my protestations, and again bade me good night.

The mauve boudoir was flooded with moonlight, which fell directly on the portrait of the Empress's mother, and on the picture of the Annunciation. Both seemed alive. . . . The sad eyes of the dead woman watched the gradually unfolding tragedy of her daughter's life, whilst the radiant Virgin, overcome with divine condescension, welcomed the angel who hailed her as blessed among women.

Masses of lilac were arranged in front of the tall windows. It was customary for a fresh supply of lilac for the mauve boudoir to be sent daily to Tsarkoe Selo from the south of France; but, owing to the troublous times, no flowers had reached the Palace for a couple of days. Just before dawn, the dying lilac seemed to expire in a last breath of perfume . . . the boudoir was suddenly redolent of the perfume of Spring . . . tears filled my eyes. The poignant sweetness hurt me—winter was around us, and within our hearts. Should we ever know the joys of blue skies, and the glory of a world new-born? All was silent, save for the footsteps of the "Red" sentry as he passed and repassed up and down the corridor. At first the Revolutionaries had celebrated their sojourn in a Palace by singing seditious and obscene songs, but little by little these had ceased . . . the soldiers slept. My mind reverted constantly to the sick girls and to their brother, who, happily, unlike them, did not share their apprehendsions. What a contrast this night presented to the quiet, happy nights of long ago! I confess it was difficult to see the hand of God in this—to me—unnecessary suffering, and to accept all in the spirit of humility which the Empress manifested.

At seven o'clock the Empress told me I had better return to the red drawing-room, so I gathered my bedclothes together and slipped unperceived and unheard up the staircase.*

H.I.M. AND THE
TSAREVITCH, 1913

THE EMPRESS
(End of 1915)

* The remaining members of the suite occupied apartments in the fourth wing of the Palace. The Empress, who was afraid of infection for others, only saw them occasionally. I was quite alone with her and the children.

CHAPTER IV

ON the morning of Thursday, March 9th, the Empress came into the Grand Duchesses' bedroom; she was agitated and anxious, as she had been informed that the Emperor would arrive at the Palace between eleven and twelve. I went with her to see the Tsarevitch, and we sat by his bed talking to him. The little boy was very excited, and he kept on looking at his watch, and counting the seconds which must pass before his father's arrival.

Presently we heard the sound of an automobile, and Volkoff entered. The faithful servant had refused to accept the fact of the Emperor's abdication, and, in a manner worthy of Imperial traditions, he announced:

"His Majesty The Emperor!"

The Empress sprang from her chair, and ran out of the room. I, too, rose. The meeting between the reunited family must not, surely, be witnessed by any outsider! But the Tsarevitch seized my hand. "No, no, Lili, you're not to leave me," he insisted, so I sat down by him for five minutes, and eventually I managed to slip away and take refuge in Anna's room—where I remained until after lunch, when I was summoned to the Imperial presence.

Following my instructions, I went into the Grand Duchesses' room; the Empress was not there. Suddenly I heard the sound of footsteps. I knew to whom they belonged—but they were no longer the footsteps of a confident and happy man. They sounded as if the person who was advancing was very, very tired.

I trembled from head to foot—I dared not at first raise my eyes. When I did so, I encountered the tragic, weary eyes of the Emperor.

He advanced to where I was standing, and took my hands in his, saying, very simply:

"Thank you, Lili, for all you have done for us . . . and I? . . . what have I done for you?

Absolutely nothing! Why, I have not even kept Dehn near you."

"Your Majesty," I answered, now unable to speak without crying . . . "it is for me to thank you for the privilege of being allowed to remain with you."

As we went into the red salon, and the light fell on the Emperor's face, I started. In the darkened bedroom I could not see clearly, but I now realised how greatly he had altered. The Emperor was deathly pale, his face was covered with innumerable wrinkles, his hair was quite grey at the temples, and blue shadows encircled his eyes. He looked like an old man; the Emperor smiled sadly when he saw my horrified expression, and he was about to speak, when the Empress joined us; he then tried to appear the light-hearted husband and father of the happy years; he sat with us and chatted on trivial matters, but I could see that he was inwardly ill at ease, and at last the effort was too much for him. "I think I'll go for a walk—walking always does me good," he said.

We passed through the corridors to Anna's apartments, where the Emperor left us, and went downstairs. The Empress and I entered the bedroom, and stood by one of the windows which looked out over the Park. Anna was very excited; she kept talking and crying, but we had eyes only for the Emperor, who by this time was outside the Palace. He walked briskly towards the Grande Allée, but suddenly a sentinel appeared from nowhere, so to speak, and intimated to the Emperor that he was not allowed to go in that direction. The Emperor made a nervous movement with his hand, but he obeyed, and retraced his steps; but the same thing occurred— another sentinel barred his passage, and an officer told the Emperor that, as he was now to all intents and purposes a prisoner, his exercise must be of the prison-yard description! . . . We watched the beloved figure turn the corner . . . his steps flagged, his head was bent, his whole aspect was significant of utter dejection; his spirit seemed completely broken. I do not think that until this moment we had realised the crushing grip of the Revolution, nor what it signified. But it was brought home to us most forcibly when we saw the passage of the Lord of All the Russias, the Emperor whose domains extended over millions of miles, now restricted to a few yards in his own Park.

The Empress said nothing, but I felt her hand grasp mine; it was, for her, an agonizing experience. After an interval, she spoke. . . . "We'll go back to the children, Lili; at any rate we can be together there."

The Grand Duchesses were delighted to know that their father had returned, and I think the knowledge of his safety acted on them like a tonic. Poor Marie, who had so longed to be the first to welcome the Emperor, was now delirious, with intervals of consciousness.

When I entered her room, she recognised me. "Well, Lili, where have you been?" she exclaimed. "I've been waiting and waiting for you. Papa is really *here*, isn't he?" The next moment she was back in the fantastic and terrible kingdom of fever. "Crowds of people . . . dreadful people . . . they're coming to kill Mamma!! Why are they doing these things?" Alas, poor child, others have since asked the same question.

That day the Emperor and the Empress dined and spent the evening together. The Empress told me afterwards that the Emperor lost his self-control when he was alone with her in the mauve boudoir; he wept bitterly. It was excessively difficult for her to console him, and to assure him that the husband and father was of more value in her eyes than the Emperor whose throne she had shared.

. . . . .

I cannot say that the Revolutionaries treated us with excessive discourtesy, but some of their methods were reprehensible. For instance, when certain complications ensued with Marie, it became necessary to have another medical opinion. This request was at first refused, but afterwards the authorities agreed, on condition that an officer and two soldiers were present at the medical examination! Colonel Kotzebue, the first Revolutionary commandant, had formerly been an officer in the Lancers, and, as he was a distant cousin of mine, I could hardly believe my eyes when I saw him in this official capacity, and I asked him to come and talk to me in Anna's room, as I considered he owed our family some explanation of his conduct.

"I can't imagine why I was nominated for the post," said Kotzebue. "All I can tell you, Lili, is that I was awakened in the middle of the night, and told to report myself at Tsarkoe Selo. Will you assure Their Majesties that there is nothing I will not try and do for them. This is really the happiest moment of my life, since it enables me to be of service to them."

When the Empress sent for me on the morning of March 10th, I found her lying on the couch in her boudoir. The Emperor was with her; she motioned me to come and sit beside her, and the Emperor talked to us.* (*footnote on next page*). He first described an incident which had impressed him most strongly that very morning.

"When I got up," he said, "I put on my dressing-gown and looked through the window which gives on the courtyard.† I noticed that the sentinel who was usually stationed there was now sitting on the steps—his rifle had slipped out of his hand—he was dozing! I called my valet, and showed him the unusual sight, and I couldn't help laughing—it was really absurd. At the sound of my laughter the soldier awoke, but he did not attempt to move—he scowled at us, and we withdrew. But what a conclusive proof of the general demoralisation! All must indeed be at an end for Russia, as without law, obedience and respect no empire can exist."

The Empress then questioned the Emperor about certain doings at G.H.Q. "Some occurrences were exceptionally painful," replied the Emperor. "My mother drove with me through the town, which was profusely decorated with red flags and a profusion of bunting. My poor mother couldn't bear to look at the flags . . . but the sight of them did not affect me; it seemed such a stupid and useless display! The behaviour of the crowd was in curious contrast to this exhibition of Revolutionary power, as they all knelt, as of yore, when our automobile passed."

"I could not bear to say good-bye to Voeikoff, Niloff and Fredericks. They didn't want to leave me. I had to insist at last. The Revolutionaries promised most faithfully not to harm them."‡

"One thing especially touched me," continued the Emperor. "When I got into the train, I noticed five or six schoolgirls who were standing on the platform trying to attract my attention. I went to the window, and, when they saw me, they began to cry, and made signs for me to write something for them. So I signed my name on a piece of paper, and sent it to the children. But they still lingered on the platform, and, as it was bitterly cold, I tried to make them understand that they had better go home. However, when my train left, two hours later, they were still there. They blessed me, poor children," said the Emperor, greatly moved by the recollection. "I hope their pure blessing will bring us happiness."

* (previous page) In all my descriptions of the conversations between the Emperor, the Empress and myself, I have endeavoured to describe what took place, almost word for word. I have not attempted to elaborate any of the statements, and my record may therefore be considered accurate.—L. D.
† The sleeping apartments of the Emperor and the Empress were situated on the ground floor of the Palace.—L. D.
‡ These faithful adherents were arrested at the next station and sent to Petrograd, where they were incarcerated in the Fortress of Peter and Paul.—L. D.

The Emperor told us that he had received countless telegrams after the news of his abdication was generally known. Many were abusive, but others breathed the concentrated spirit of loyalty. Count Keller sent a telegram informing the Emperor that he declined to recognise the existence of the Revolution.* The Count afterwards refused to sign the documents of allegiance, and he broke his sword and threw the pieces down.

"General Rousky was the first to broach the subject of my abdication," said the Emperor. "He boarded the train *en route*, and came into my saloon unannounced. 'Goutchkoff and Shoulgine are also coming to talk to you,' he informed me. These gentlemen made their appearance at the next station, and they were excessively impertinent. Rousky told them that he had already discussed matters with me. But I refused to be ignored. I struck the table with my fist. 'I'm going to speak, I *will* speak,' I cried.

"'You must abdicate in favour of the Tsarevitch, and the people will nominate a Regent,' said Goutchkoff and Shoulgine.

"'But,' I replied, 'are you sure—can you promise that my abdication will benefit Russia?' 'Your Majesty, it is the only thing to save Russia at the present crisis,' they replied.

"'But I must think it over. . . . I'll give you my answer in a couple of hours.'" "The delegates consented. I knew," continued the Emperor, looking with affection at his wife, "that their first idea was to separate Alexis from the Empress, so I spoke to Dr. Fedoroff, who was in the train, and I asked him whether he considered it advisable to allow the Tsarevitch to be taken from her.

"'It will shorten the Tsarevitch's life,' said Fedoroff bluntly.

"When Goutchkoff and Shoulgine returned, I intimated plainly that I would not part with my son. 'I am ready to abdicate,' I said, 'but not in favour of my son, only of my brother.'

"My decision appeared to trouble them: they asked me to think Better of it, but I was firm. Afterwards I signed the Act of Abdication. The train was then sent back to G.H.Q."

Such is the bare narrative of the abdication, related as nearly as possible in the Emperor's own words. Baron Stackelberg, a cousin of my husband's, who was travelling with the Emperor, afterwards told me that he and M. Voeikoff, the Commandant du Palais, met Rousky on the platform of the station where he joined the train. The

* Count Keller was killed at Kieff later.

two gentlemen were about to send some telegrams from the Emperor to Rodziansko, in which the Emperor replied to the former's request to give Russia a constitutional government. In the opinion of the Emperor, the moment had not arrived.

"Whose telegrams are these?" said Rousky.

"His Majesty's," answered Baron Stackelberg coldly.

Rousky snatched the telegrams from Baron Stackelberg, and put them in his pocket, remarking as he did so, "Useless!" So Rodziansko never received the Emperor's telegrams, and Baron Stackelberg, who is now in Finland, can confirm the truth of the story. M. Voeikoff and the Baron looked at each other, neither spoke, but each read in the other's eyes the unspoken thought—to kill Rousky then and there, and so avenge the insult to the Emperor. But Rousky had disappeared—the moment for righteous murder had passed!

. . . . .

Life at first went on much as usual after the Emperor's return: he always insisted upon reading the daily papers, but the filth of the gutter press sickened and pained him. One evening I happened to come into the library where the Emperor was reading a newspaper: his expression showed that something had seriously displeased him. "Just look here, Lili," he said, showing me the portraits of the new Cabinet. "Look at these men. . . . Their faces are the real criminal type. And yet I was asked to approve of this Cabinet, and to agree to the Constitution," he added with a touch of bitterness. My time was now fully occupied. The Grand Duchess Marie was seriously ill, and I relieved the Empress in nursing her. . . . I had taken upon myself the task, formerly performed by the Empress, of sponging poor Marie's body, and, when the child was conscious, she liked me to brush and comb her lovely hair, which became sadly tangled as she tossed to and fro in her delirium. Marie was the first unmarried Grand Duchess to sleep on a "real" bed of her own, but, as she was so ill, we moved her from the narrow camp-bed to a more comfortable resting-place.

The Empress was a skilful nurse; she was especially expert in changing sheets and night-clothes in a few minutes without disturbing the patients. When I showed my surprise, she said quite simply: "I learnt to do useful things in England. . . . I've never forgotten what I owe to my English upbringing."

One day my cousin, Kotzebue, told me that an English gentleman, Mr. A. Stopford,* a friend of the Grand Duchess Marie Paul, was desirous of being of use to the Empress. He had, it appeared, a cult for the Imperial Family, and, as he was about to return to England, he asked Kotzebue whether the Empress would not like to send some letters by him to her relations. I told the Empress at once. It seemed such a wonderful chance.... Her first cousin, King George V, and his devoted consort, would surely welcome news from the Imperial Family!

The Empress was deeply touched by Mr. Stopford's offer. "I'll think about it, Lili," she said. But the next day she told me that she had decided not to communicate with King George and the Queen. "I *can't* write. What can I say? I'm too hurt and wounded by my country's behaviour.... But even with this I can't speak against Russia.... Besides, the Emperor is more worried than ever; he is so fearful that his abdication, and the unrest, may spoil the Great Offensive.... No ... we can't communicate with our cousins."

Both the Emperor and the Empress constantly referred to England. The first idea of the Duma had been to induce the Imperial Family to go to England, but certain powers there were antagonistic to the proposition, as it was considered likely to be unfavourably received by the Labour Party. But those who were fearful of sheltering a defenceless family, whose only crime consisted in being defenceless, need have had no apprehensions.

The Emperor and the Empress did not wish to leave Russia. "I'd rather go to the uttermost ends of Siberia," said the Emperor. Neither he nor the Empress could face the prospect of wandering about the Continent, and living at Swiss hotels as exRoyalties, snapshotted and paragraphed by representatives of the picture papers, and interviewed by amazing American journalists. Their retiring spirits shrank from cheap publicity; they considered that it was the duty of every Russian to stand by Russia, and face the common danger together.

Apart from their personal disinclination to go to England, the Soviets were opposed to the suggestion, and it was stated that, if any train left Tsarkoe with the Imperial fugitives, it would be stopped, and everyone murdered, as the Emperor knew too much to be allowed to leave Russia.

The Emperor brought me the newspaper which contained this statement. He was in a terrible rage.... He could scarcely contain

* If Mr. A. Stopford (1a St. James's Square) ever reads these lines, he may be glad to know that the Empress greatly appreciated his kindness.—L. D.

himself, and he almost threw the paper at me.

"Read this, Lili," he exclaimed, his face white with passion. "*Beasts!* How dare they say such things. . . . They judge others by themselves."

"Oh, Your Majesty," I answered, greatly troubled, "please don't read these horrible papers."

"I must, I must, Lili. I feel that I must know all," said the Emperor.

Occasionally he was in better spirits, and more like his old cheerful self. The Emperor was generally able to see the humour of any situation, and he would sometimes laugh at the idea of being, what he called, "an Ex." Everything was then "Ex." "Don't call me an Empress any more—I'm only an Ex," laughed the Empress; and one day, when some especially unpalatable ham was served at lunch, the Emperor remarked, "Well, this may have once been ham, but now it's nothing but an 'ex-ham.'" He was always amused by the likeness between him and his cousin, King George. One day he showed me a photograph of the latter, saying, "Have you seen my last photograph, Lili? Doesn't it flatter me?"

He had a great admiration for his cousin, and the Empress often spoke of Queen Alexandra, . . . her beauty, her sympathetic nature, and her boundless charity. "I would so much like to see my married sister in England," she invariably added, whenever she discussed her family. "Darmstadt is only a little spot in the garden of my memories," she would say, "but my mother died there, so I can't really be blamed for liking Darmstadt. . . . Isn't 'Home sweet Home' typically English?

"None of my daughters shall marry German Princes," she said on one occasion. It was suggested that Anastasie's future home might be in England, and the Empress welcomed the idea. . . . An English marriage would have been very near her heart. But "*l'homme propose, et Dieu dispose.*" If Russia had not betrayed herself, or if she had remained as solidly united as France, nothing would ever have been heard of the pro-Germanism attributed to the Empress. She was essentially English—English in her dress, her personal habits, her absolutely Victorian outlook; some of her ideas respecting a *ménage* were akin to those of the *Hausfrau*, but even these were English, as domesticity has always been a British attribute.

The Empress showed no special marks of favour to Germans who had settled in Russia. The reports of her having done so are untrue, or greatly exaggerated. There is no doubt that German agents were very active in Russia, and that the octopus of espionage put forth its tentacles in every direction. But in justice to a much defamed woman, surely it is unfair to credit her with being the instigator of this. Every European country was riddled with Germans, England more so than any other, and, although it was more intimately connected with Germany by marriage and consanguinity, no stones were ever hurled at the various personages, Royal and otherwise, who were really not as English as was the Empress. I remember, in connection with her impartial outlook, that, in 1910, a wealthy German named Faltsfein, was obsessed with the idea of becoming a Russian nobleman. A friend of his, an officer named Masloff, asked the Empress to make it possible for Herr Faltsfein to change his skin, but she was very disgusted, and told Masloff that nothing would induce her to put such a proposal before the Emperor!

One awful day a lorry full of soldiers, in charge of an excessively ill-favoured officer, arrived at the Palace. Kotzebue interviewed him.

"I've come to fetch the Emperor," said the officer, with an unprintable oath. "He's going to be imprisoned in 'Peter and Paul.'"

"You cannot remove the Emperor," answered Kotzebue. "I am commandant here. I refuse to give up the Emperor at your orders."

"Ah... ah... I knew it," shouted the officer. "The Emperor has fled!... we were told so in Petrograd. Let's search the Palace."

Kotzebue almost came to blows with the man. "I tell you the Emperor is *here* . . . I'll prove it." He then sent for Count Benckendorff and told him to ask the Emperor to pass through the corridor whilst the soldiers were looking. In a few moments the Emperor came slowly down the corridor ... the officer rushed threateningly towards him, but Kotzebue restrained him, saying, "Well, you——, now you've seen the Emperor. Go back to the Soviet, tell them he's still here, and don't come again on a fool's errand."

The Emperor now walked in the Park every day, and each time he returned greatly depressed at some fresh mark of disrespect. "But," he said, "it's very foolish to think that this behaviour can affect my soul—how petty of them to seek to humiliate me by calling me 'Colonel' ... after all, it's a very worthy appellation."

The Empress was a tragic figure, and, in her invariable Red Cross uniform, she symbolised Pity, in a world which knew not the meaning of the word. Every hour that I knew her, I loved her more.

One day, Kotzebue told me that Titi was ill; in fact, *very* ill, but I did not like to agitate the Empress until Kotzebue came to ask her to permit me to go with him and telephone from the basement of the Palace. She was greatly distressed to hear that her godson was ill, and equally concerned at not having been told before. "My poor girl, what you must have suffered!" she said.

Kotzebue and I descended into the basement: two soldiers guarded the telephone, and I was informed that I could only be allowed five minutes' conversation.

"How is the child?" was my first question. "Very ill, Madame," answered my maid.

"Please, please bring him to the 'phone.'" I waited impatiently, and then a little feeble voice whispered: "*Maman . . . c'est vraiment toi! quand viendras-tu?*" At that moment a soldier interposed.

"Your five minutes is up!"

I returned to the Empress, almost heart-broken, but I endeavoured to appear cheerful. The interminable day wore away, evening fell, and I assisted at what had now become a sort of nightly routine. Every evening the Emperor wheeled the Empress in her invalid-chair across the Palace in order to visit the suite. It was a melancholy pilgrimage. She first stopped to talk with the Benckendorffs, and afterwards passed from group to group of her faithful adherents, taking Anna's room on the way back— Anna, so to speak, representing the last word in dejection, as she was ever full of terrors and presentiments.

That night I was glad to seek refuge in the red drawing-room and find myself alone, and able to indulge in what is described as "a good cry." As I left the mauve boudoir, the Emperor and the Empress kissed me, and made the Sign of the Cross. I felt instinctively that they loved me, and were sorry for me.

A bright fire was burning in the red drawing-room, but I did not undress—I sat in front of the fire thinking of Titi. Yet even the knowledge that my son was seriously ill did not suffice to make me feel that my place was not here. I knew in my soul that the Empress came first, and would always be first where my duty was in question. I was well aware that I might never see my husband or my child again . . . but I knew that I should follow the Imperial Family wherever Destiny might beckon me. I confess I had my moments of weakness, when I longed for the security of home, and the peaceful existence which had hitherto been mine. To-night I felt more than usually despondent. The fire burnt low, and I sought to read the future in the red embers, just as I had done at Revovka in the long ago. Suddenly I heard the door of the salon open very softly, and a line of light pierced the darkness . . . someone was coming in!

I turned quickly to face the person who dared intrude upon the privacy of the apartments occupied by the Imperial Family. . . . Was it some fresh assumption of power on the part of the Revolutionaries?

But my visitor was no emissary of the Revolution—the slender figure standing in the doorway was that of the Empress. She looked more than usually fragile . . . she breathed with difficulty, her face was pale with fatigue, and, when I remembered the arduous ascent of the stairs, I was terrified lest a heart attack would ensue.

"Madame, Madame," I cried, "is anything amiss? Are you in danger?"

"Hush, Lili," said the Empress. "The Emperor and I are quite safe. But I couldn't rest without coming to see you. I know all about Titi, I quite realise what you feel." She took me in her arms just as a tender mother might have done, and she soothed me and caressed me. "My poor, dear child," she said. "Only God can help you. Trust in Him, as I do, Lili."

We mingled our tears, and she stayed with me for some considerable time. It was a strange scene, but I wish that those who revile the memory of the Empress could have seen her then, and experienced the pity, love and understanding which were so essentially her prerogatives. She strengthened and consoled me as no other could have done, and her last words of comfort before she left me were: "Perhaps they'll let us bring Titi from Petrograd to the Red Cross Hospital opposite the Palace, then you could always see him through one of the windows."

CHAPTER V

THE Tsarevitch was now almost well, and running about the Palace much as usual. I do not think he noticed many changes, the Revolution conveyed nothing to him except when he missed certain of his soldiers and his friends. He was still a happy, light-hearted child.

The Imperial Family had no presentiment of disaster for themselves, but they suffered untold agonies of mind over the fate of Russia. "Can you imagine what it means to the Emperor to know that he is cut off from active life?" said the Empress.

Soon after the episode of telephoning from the basement, Kotzebue went to Petrograd. I was anxious for his return, as he had promised to go and see Titi, and bring me the latest news from home. Days passed . . . I became apprehensive, and made enquiries, only to be told that we should not see him again at Tsarkoe! I saw in this an omen of coming trouble, so I went at once to the Emperor and acquainted him with what I had heard. The Emperor and the Empress were watching some of the ladies-in-waiting who were walking in the Park, followed by sentinels; the Empress noticed my agitation.

"Why, Lili, whatever is the matter?" she enquired.

"Madame . . . I hear that Kotzebue is to be replaced."

The Emperor looked at me. Then, shrugging his shoulders, he remarked: "Well— it can't be helped" and straightway changed the conversation . . . possibly to calm our fears, or more probably to show how unaffected he was by the mandates of the Revolutionaries.

The long, monotonous days passed—we endured them alternately with the calmness of despair and with gratitude for their dullness. Once we witnessed a sight of horror. Hearing a sound of military music, and the tramp, tramp of many people, we went to the windows, and saw a funeral procession wending its way across the snow-covered Park. But this was no ordinary funeral; the dead were some of the soldiers who had been killed at Tsarkoe Selo on the first day of the Revolution. It was a red burial—the coffins were covered in scarlet, the mourners were dressed in scarlet, and scarlet flags waved everywhere. Seen in the distance the procession looked like a river of blood flowing slowly through the Park. Everything was red and white, and the superstitious might have inferred from this a presage of the innocent blood so soon to be outpoured . . . since the snow was not whiter than the souls of the young and beautiful who are now safe in the keeping of a God of Justice, who most surely will repay!

None of us could forget the impression produced by this funeral; blood seemed everywhere, and terror lurked in the shadows. The soldiers were buried in the Park, within sight of the Palace—another refinement of torture for those whose imaginations were already overexcited. Our nerves were frayed, although I do not think that we were guilty of giving way to our emotions. But it was difficult to maintain our composure when insolent officers treated us in a shameful manner, or a soldier called the Empress by some filthy epithet. One soldier, however, was a Bayard. He possessed an English name, and his father taught in a school at Riga. This man was really extraordinary. He was not only polite, but he invariably tried to show us that he did not share the Revolutionary outlook. The two regiments which were at the Palace distinguished themselves by a series of petty thefts; not even the spoons were safe. I suppose they would have described these articles as "Souvenir spoons"!

. . . . .

We were no longer to complain of monotony. Even then, events unknown to us were moving quickly, and in my case definitely.

The Grand Duchess Marie was still very ill, and Anna, who knew this, decided to go and see her. The Empress was against the idea; Anna was ill, she said, and it was better for her health and her safety to keep as quiet as possible, and not to draw any undue attention to her presence in the Palace. So strongly did the Empress disapprove, that she was taken in her wheeled chair to see Anna, but she returned more nervous and apprehensive than before.

I spent the morning with the Empress, and I lunched with Anna, in the apparently forlorn hope of dissuading her from attempting to see Marie. After luncheon we discussed the burning question of Kotzebue's disappearance. Suddenly we were startled by hearing a noise in the corridor. . . . Anna instantly rang the bell. A servant answered it.

"Who is outside?" demanded Anna.

"I don't know," replied the man, who was evidently much disturbed; "the soldiers are here." At this moment a *skorohod** entered, and handed me a tiny folded note. I opened it. . . . Written in pencil, in the Empress's handwriting, were these ominous words:

"*Kerensky passe par toutes nos chambres, pas avoir peur—Dieu est là. Vous embrasse toutes les deux.*"†

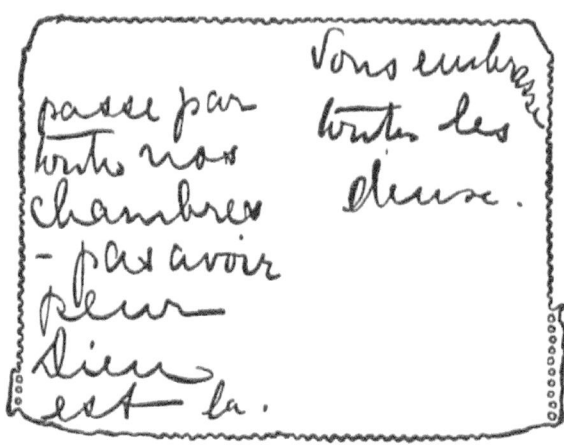

Heavy footsteps sounded in the corridor. I had barely time to slip the precious note inside my bodice when the door was flung open, and a man, followed by two others, came in. I stood up at once and looked at our visitor—it was Kerensky himself!

I saw a slight man with a pale face, thin lips, shifty eyes, seen under lowered lids, and a nondescript nose. Kerensky gave one the impression of being *mal soigné*. . . . He was not tall, but slight in figure, and his head drooped in a curious manner: he wore the blue jacket of an ordinary workman. Kerensky slowly considered us.

"Are you Madame Anna Virouboff?" he said, addressing Anna.

"Yes," replied Anna, faintly.

"Well, put on your clothes immediately and be ready to follow me." Anna made no answer.

"Why the devil are you in bed?" he demanded, staring at Anna's invalid *déshabillée*. "Because I'm ill," whimpered Anna, looking more childish than ever.

"Well" . . . said Kerensky, turning to an officer, "perhaps we had

---

* The skorohod were the confidential messengers of the Imperial Family. They wore a distinctive livery, and wonderful hats adorned with black and yellow ostrich feathers.

† The actual note is reproduced in these pages. Translation: "Kerensky is passing through all our rooms—Do not be afraid—God is present. I kiss you both."

better not move her. I'll have a chat with the doctors. In the meantime, isolate Madame Virouboff. Place sentinels before the door—she's to hold no communication with anyone. Nobody is to come into this bedroom or to leave it until I give the order."

He went out of the room, followed by the officers. Anna and I looked at each other, speechless with dismay. My first collected thought was for the Empress. I would not be separated from her.

"I *must* try and see Their Majesties," I said wildly.

"Yes, Lili, do. For God's sake see them," sobbed Anna.

I opened the bedroom door very softly: the sentinels had not yet arrived. I caught a glimpse of Kerensky entering the room occupied by the doctors; then, impelled by some desperate courage, I ran down the corridors, and arrived breathless in the Grand Duchesses' apartments. I found the Empress with Olga. I told her, in a few words, what had happened. Then distant footsteps warned us of Kerensky's approach.

"Run . . . Lili—hide in Marie's room—it's dark *there*," whispered the Empress.

I had barely time to crouch down behind a screen in Marie's room when Kerensky came in. He took no notice of the sick girl, but went in search of the Empress, who, with the Emperor, had now gone into the schoolroom. From where I was hiding I could hear Kerensky shouting. In a few moments the Empress entered; she was trembling visibly. . . . The Grand Duchesses Olga and Tatiana (now convalescent) rushed forward. "Mamma, Mamma, what is the matter?"

"Kerensky has insisted upon my leaving him alone with the Emperor," answered the Empress. . . . "They'll most probably arrest me."

The two girls clung to their mother, and slowly made their way back to Marie. I had now emerged from behind the screen, and I went into the schoolroom, where I determined to remain until I saw the Emperor.

After what seemed a very long time the Emperor came out—alone.

"Your Majesty," I cried, "tell me, I implore you, if there is anything dreadful in store for Her Majesty?"

The Emperor was painfully nervous. "No, no, Lili, and if Kerensky had uttered one word against Her Majesty, you would have heard me strike the table—thus—" and he struck the writing-table with his fist. "But I hear they've arrested Anna. Poor unfortunate woman, what will become of *her*?" At the sound of her husband's voice the Empress came out of Marie's bedroom. The Emperor told her that Kerensky had arrested Anna because he suspected that she was implicated in political plots. "If it's true, it's an awful thing," said Kerensky; "but I suppose everything will now be disclosed."

Their Majesties then related the particulars of their interview with Kerensky.

"His first words," said the Empress, "were, 'I am Kerensky. You probably know my name.'

"We made no answer.

"'But you must have heard of me?' he persisted.

"Still no reply.

"'Well,' said Kerensky, 'I'm sure I don't know why we are standing. Let's sit down—it's far more comfortable!'

"He seated himself," continued the Empress. "The Emperor and I slowly followed his example, and, finding that I still declined to speak, Kerensky insisted upon being left alone with the Emperor."

Shortly afterwards, to our great relief, we were informed that Kerensky had left the Palace and gone to the Town Hall. The new commandant, Colonel Korovichenko, was then presented to the Empress, who begged him to allow her to say good-bye to Anna. Korovichenko consented, and the Empress went, unaccompanied, to Anna's room. She sat very silent when she returned: she felt the parting keenly, as both the friends knew that, in all probability, it might be for ever!

The Emperor, the Grand Duchesses and myself now took up our position in "Orchie's room,"* from which the windows commanded a view of the entrance to Anna's apartments. I was sitting by the Empress near the window. . . . All at once she took my hand, and said in a voice choked with emotion:

"At least, God will allow you to remain, and. . . ."

Her sentence remained unfinished. . . . At this moment someone knocked at the door; it was Count Benckendorff, who had hurried along to tell the Empress that he still hoped better things for Anna. This was only a temporary respite. A little later we heard the sound of an automobile in the courtyard. I looked down, and saw two automobiles drawn up in front of the Imperial entrance to the Palace. Another knock! This time it was a servant who announced:

* Orchie was a pet name for Miss Orchard, the Empress's old governess, who had died at the Palace. Her room had been left undisturbed since her death.

"The new Commandant wishes to speak to Madame Dehn."

I went out; Korovitchenko, a fair-haired, common-looking man with a hard mouth, was standing at the end of the corridor.

"Madame Dehn?" he enquired brusquely.

"Yes . . . I am Madame Dehn."

"Well . . . get ready. Take as little as possible with you; you are going with Kerensky to Petrograd."

I nearly fainted, but I managed to run back to "Orchie's room." In a few hurried words I acquainted the Empress with Korovitchenko's orders. . . . I could not look at any of them. I tried to be calm, but at the sound of Tatiana's uncontrollable sobbing I broke down and wept in the arms of the Empress.

"*Eh bien . . .*" she said, releasing me gently from her embrace, "*il n'y rien à faire.*"

"Is Madame Dehn ready?" shouted someone outside.

The Empress called Zanoty (one of her dressers) and told her to put some things together in a suit-case. She did not speak to me—or I to her—our hearts were too full. It was like some terrible nightmare. At length I managed to go into Anastasie's room. . . . She was in bed. I kissed her many times, and told her that I would never forsake them. Poor Marie lay asleep in her darkened room. . . . I kissed her flushed cheek, blessed her, and went out quietly. There was no time to say good-bye to the Tsarevitch.

. . . . .

Zanoty had packed my suit-case, and the Empress now sent her to fetch a sacred medal, which she hung round my neck, blessing me as she did so. At the last moment Tatiana ran out of the room, and returned with a little leather case containing portraits of the Emperor and the Empress, which had stood on her especial table ever since she was a tiny child. "Lili . . ." she cried, "if Kerensky *is* going to take you away from us, you shall at least have Papa and Mamma to console you."

Another imperative summons told us that the moment of parting was at hand. I put on my hat, and we left "Orchie's room"; the Emperor and the Empress walked on either side of me, and the Grand Duchesses Olga and Tatiana followed us. I had never imagined in the "happy" days that it would ever be my lot to traverse this corridor with a breaking heart, or under such conditions. For ten years I had received nothing but affection from the Imperial

Family—I had watched the children grow up, I had been their playmate and their friend—now I had to leave them in hostile and menacing surroundings.

Russia had already deprived them of their Imperial state, their possessions and their liberty: surely she might not have deprived them of their friends!

We walked slowly towards the head of the great staircase . . . the moment for saying farewell had arrived . . . I tried to be brave . . . the silence was unbroken save by Tatiana's stifled sobbing. Olga and the Empress were quite calm, but Tatiana, who has been described by most contemporary historians as proud and reserved, made no secret of her grief.

Two soldiers were waiting on the staircase . . . the little group of the Imperial Family stopped, and surrounded me . . . then all pretence of self-control vanished. We clung together, but our unavailing tears made no impression on hearts harder than the marble staircase on which we stood.

"Come . . . Madame . . ." said one of the soldiers, seizing me by the arm.

I turned to the Empress. With a tremendous effort of will, she forced herself to smile reassuringly; then, in a voice whose every accent bespoke intense love and deep religious conviction, she said: "Lili, by suffering we are purified for Heaven. This goodbye matters little—we shall meet in another world."

The soldiers hurried me down the staircase, but I stopped halfway, and looked back. The Imperial Family was still where I had left them; with a rough gesture, my guards motioned me to descend. I could see my beloved Empress no longer.

I walked to the door of the second entrance where some officers and soldiers stood, laughing and talking. Two automobiles were waiting outside. It was bitterly cold, and a bleak wind howled round the Palace, and drove the snow in stinging dust against my face as I sat in the open automobile waiting for Anna. At last she appeared; she looked ghastly, and her eyes were swollen with crying. Two officers sat facing us, and a third took his place beside the chauffeur. In this manner we saw the last of Tsarkoe Selo . . . but I had left my heart behind.

We proceeded rapidly towards the private station, where the automobile stopped. I walked quickly inside. I held myself erect . . . I would *not* let our enemies think that I knew the meaning of the word FEAR. As I passed, some of the soldiers sneered . . . "See how haughty she is," they remarked; but I took no notice.

The Imperial train was waiting, and the thought flashed across my mind that the Revolutionaries were surely most inconsistent people, since Kerensky & Co. did not scruple to avail themselves of the luxuries appertaining to Imperial state. Anna and I made our way to the drawing-room compartment, where we seated ourselves—I say "ourselves," but, in reality, Anna was lying half fainting on a chair. I could just see the Palace through the window of the saloon, and I looked at nothing else until the train moved out of the station, and, even then, my straining eyes sought the familiar building which held so much that was dear to me.

Suddenly I became aware that someone was shouting, and thumping on the floor with a stick. I withdrew from the window to see what was the matter, and I encountered the angry gaze of Kerensky.

"Look here . . . you'd better listen when I'm talking to you," he raged.

I simply looked at him. Nobody had ever addressed me in such a manner! I am a tall woman; perhaps my height (I towered above him) and my unspoken contempt made him think better of continuing in this strain.

"I merely wanted to tell you that I am taking you to the prison of the Palais de Justice," said Kerensky. "From there you will be transferred (with deep meaning) *somewhere else*, and *that* will be the actual place of your imprisonment."

I still looked through him, and he beat a retreat into his own compartment. Ten minutes later we were at Petrograd!

The A.D.C.'s made Anna go first; I followed and as we walked down the train we passed through the saloon where Kerensky and another man were stretched out comfortably in the Emperor's easy chairs! When Kerensky saw me he sat up, and looked me up and down with a kind of half-fierce curiosity. I returned his appraising glance with one of disdain . . . the next moment Anna and I were told to get into a closed carriage (another relic of Imperialism), and we drove away in the company of the A.D.C.'s—mere boys—who were evidently keenly interested in us both.

I was horrified at the change which the Revolution had wrought in Petrograd. Its quiet, well-bred look had completely disappeared, it wore the aspect of a person just recovering from a drunken bout. Red flags were everywhere, and crowds of unrestful people were waiting in long queues outside the bakers' shops. This sight roused Anna from her lethargy of grief, and, childish as ever, she remarked, quite happily, "Well, Lili, it's no better *after* the Revolution than it was before." I silenced her further criticisms with a glance at the A.D.C.'s, and I felt quite relieved when our carriage sank first in one, and then in another of the dirty heaps of snow which cumbered the streets, and which had not been removed by the road sweepers. No policemen were visible; law and order had ceased to exist, but groups of odd-looking people hung about at the corners of the streets. These loungers were unmistakably Jews. . . . The Ghetto-like appearance of Petrograd was amply accounted for.

The carriage stopped outside the Palais de Justice, and we were conducted down seemingly endless corridors to a room on the fourth floor. This room was empty, save for two easy chairs, a small chair and a table on which stood a carafe of cold water. The aides-de-camp told us to ask the sentinels for anything we wanted, and they were about to leave us alone when I said to one of them: "Will you try and let my servants know that I'm here?"

"Impossible," he answered, "but in your next prison you'll be allowed to see your friends once a week." The young men then went away, and Anna at once began to cry. I tried to console her, but I was completely worn out—my powers of endurance had snapped, since there was no one to be brave for!

The room was bitterly cold, and we huddled together, wondering what next would happen. Suddenly shots rang out in the corridor ... were they harbingers of death? The firing was followed by coarse laughter, and a soldier ran into our room. "Ah . . . ha! . . . ha!! . . ." he mocked, "were you afraid . . . did you think you were going to be killed?"*

As I sat in the cheerless room, thinking over many things, I suddenly remembered that Anna had a great predilection for carrying letters and photographs about with her—my heart sank—supposing that she had done so now?

"Anna," I said, trying to speak lightly, "what papers have you

---

* General Knox was discussing certain matters with Kerensky at the moment when this shooting occurred, and he asked Kerensky what the shots signified. "Oh, it's only two friends of the Imperial Family who have just been brought here," answered Kerensky. I met General Knox after my escape to England, and when he related the incident I informed him that I was one of the "two friends."—L. D.

brought away with you?"

"Oh, lots, Lili," answered Anna. "I've some letters of the Empress, some letters from Gregory, and two photographs of him."

I suppose my expression must have betrayed me. Anna began to whimper.... "Oh, Lili, why do you look so grave? Surely they won't treat us badly? What *shall* we do?"

"You must give me every paper in your possession."

She demurred. "But *why*, Lili?"

"Because it's dangerous to retain anything connected either with Her Majesty or with Rasputin. The worst construction is likely to be placed on the most innocent expressions... you cannot surely wish to injure the Empress!"

Anna instantly handed over the letters, but the difficulty arose as to how best to destroy them. To burn them was impossible, as we had no stove; I therefore decided to tear the letters up in minute pieces, and throw them down the lavatory which we were permitted to use. In this way, I destroyed what might have been considered "compromising" documents!

After what seemed an interminable time, steps sounded in the corridor, the door was flung open, and Kerensky entered. He deliberately turned his back on Anna, but he surveyed me with the same appraising yet hostile scrutiny. We looked at each other without speaking.... At last, he shrugged his shoulders, and remarked to an officer:

"This place is damnably cold. Have the stove seen to immediately."

He left us without another word, and we heard him speaking at some length outside. The sentinels were then changed, and the soldier who was on duty in our room began to talk to me.

"Well, Mademoiselle," he said, "it's ten thousand pities to see you here... you *do* look sad. Whatever have you done?"

"Nothing."

"It's horrible... they've no right to arrest young ladies like you."

"Perhaps the new regulations are responsible for our arrest."

"The new regulations!" The man laughed loudly. "That's a good idea... I don't think they'll bring much luck. How can we get on without an Emperor? Don't imagine that *we* wanted this. Do you think we joined willingly? Why, they had to use force to get us... we were unarmed, it was no good attempting to resist them."

This kindly soul came from South Russia, and, when I told him who I was and where my estates were situated, he was ready to do anything for me.

"I'm on duty again to-morrow," he said, "so try and write a letter, and I'll see that it's delivered."

Night fell, and we were faint with hunger and fatigue. A little soup was brought us, but we could not swallow it. Every few minutes the door opened, and soldiers came in and made fun of us.

"We've two pretty girls now to look at," they mocked, but their laughter was better than their coarse jokes . . . some of these made me grow scarlet with, shame, and I trembled lest their coarseness might become something unspeakable. We wanted to wash . . . but washing was impossible—we had neither jug nor basin—the only water available was that in the carafe. I opened my suit-case, and as Zanoty had put some cotton-wool and lint with my things I quickly made a pad of some of the wool, and, pouring a little water into the glass, I damped the pad and mopped my face, drying it afterwards with some more cotton wool. At 1 a.m. we were surprised to see the two A.D.C.'s come in with some soldiers. One of the A.D.C.'s addressed Anna.

"Madame . . . we have orders to remove you."

Anna caught hold of my hand. "Oh, Lili, Lili," she moaned, "don't let them take me away. Can't you come with me? . . . I daren't go to another prison without you." "Cannot you let me accompany Madame Virouboff?" I said.

"The order is for *Madame Virouboff*," replied the A.D.C., and at this moment an officer entered.

"What's all the fuss about?" he demanded. The A.D.C. explained. "What . . . is Madame Virouboff really here?" cried the officer. "Well, I've always wanted to have a look at her . . . which one is it?" The A.D.C. indicated Anna, who was gazing from one to the other with frightened eyes.

"Get up," ordered the officer.

Anna meekly obeyed; as she did so, her crutch was visible.

"But . . . what's wrong?" asked the officer, now evidently greatly astonished. "I'm a cripple," faltered Anna.

"Good God," exclaimed the officer. He was silent, but he examined Anna much in the same way that a naturalist surveys a prehistoric beast. He could not reconcile the Anna of reality with the Anna of fiction. In common with many people, not only in Russia, but all the world over, he had imagined a totally different Anna

Viroubolf. Perhaps he had visualised her as an adventuress of melodrama, a passionate *intrigante*, a subtle schemer, the masterful confidante of a weak Empress!

What did he actually see?

Rasputin's reputed *sorcière-en-chef* stood before him, a little trembling creature, with the prettiness and the plaintive voice of a child. The officer could not believe his eyes. "Do you mean to tell me that you are a cripple?" he stammered.

"I've always used a crutch since my railway accident," she said, helplessly, "I couldn't avoid being in an accident, could I?"

"Extraordinary, extraordinary," muttered the officer—he was still looking at her— "now, come along." But Anna threw herself on my neck, and refused to leave me. Her sobs were heart-breaking. To do them justice, the soldiers handled this butterfly broken on the wheel very gently. A group of journalists, male and female, all equally unkempt, were busy taking notes, and they glanced half-scornfully and half-pityingly at the shrinking figure of Anna Viroubolf as she disappeared in the darkness.

CHAPTER VI

THE long days passed in their monotonous progress. I no longer seemed to belong to the outside world. I heard nothing, nobody came near me—I was as one dead. But, if my days were monotonous, my nights were full of horror. When darkness fell, and the authorities relaxed their incessant watchfulness, the soldiers became brutish . . . when I say that I dared not fall asleep, some idea may be gathered of my dread! I had never met the eyes of lust until now . . . but it was impossible not to understand the glances of many of the soldiers. And I was not under any false illusions about the morality of freedom, it might surely be called the Freedom of Immorality! I thought of my husband far away in England, of my child lying ill within a short distance of my prison, and of that dear family for whose sakes I would gladly suffer untold misery. Memory opened her book, and I saw within its pages people and scenes which stirred many bitter-sweet recollections in my heart. Once again I walked under the linden trees at Revovka, and listened to the nightingales. I saw the forgotten grave with the wild rose weeping her petal-tears over *la morte amoureuse*; once again I stood in the Winter Garden waiting to see the Empress, sometimes I played with Titi and the Grand Duchesses and heard the Empress's kind voice. The pale face and hypnotic eyes of Rasputin recalled my pilgrimage. . . . The church towers and houses of Tobolsk rose against the evening sky, the dark and sinister river flowed past me. . . .

Memory turned back more pages of her wonderful book, and I saw the Tsarkoe Selo of yesterday, the sick children, their fragile mother, and the Emperor, to whom Destiny had proved so cruel.

I endeavoured to preserve a calm mental outlook, it was useless. . . . I wondered whether escape might be possible, but my room was situated on the fourth floor, I dared not risk the descent from the window. One idea obsessed me. I *must* see Kerensky, and this idea grew more intense when I heard that I was shortly to be removed to another prison. "They are making enquiries about you," said the A.D.C.

"Well, I want you to do something, and inform the Minister Kerensky that I would like to see him."

The A.D.C. was evidently startled by my request.

"Hm . . . I'll do my best, but—" his gesture was significant of the hopelessness of such a request.

Upon his return, the A.D.C. said tersely:

"I've seen about your affair, but Kerensky sleeps; he has just dined." "Will you ask him to see me when he awakes?" "Yes. . . ." Again the significant gesture.

I waited impatiently. I felt that this interview with Kerensky would prove the critical point in my present desperate situation. I paced up and down the room, and my nervous agitation aroused the pity of one of the soldiers, who remarked kindly:

"Poor young lady! You *do* seem worried!"

Three hours passed. . . . They seemed like centuries, and then the A.D.C. entered.

"The Minister will receive you," he said.

I hastily arranged my sadly crumpled Red Cross uniform, and two soldiers with fixed bayonets stationed themselves on either side of me. The A.D.C. led the way down endless stairs and lengthy corridors. At last we halted before a half-open door, and, as I stood there, I smelt the delicate fragrance of roses. Surely no roses grew in this terrible prison soil? But the perfume was unmistakable, and I was not left long to wonder from whence it proceeded.

I was ushered into a large, well-furnished reception room, formerly occupied by some Minister under the Empire, and on a table stood an enormous basket of blood-red roses. On another table was a basket of scarlet carnations, the warm air was heavy with the mingled odours of roses and clove pinks. So the Ministers of the Revolution were able to indulge their taste for roses in March, whilst the Sons of Freedom clamoured in the snow for bread!

The door at the extreme end of the room was ajar; presently it opened, and Kerensky came in. He glanced at me, walked to the writing-table, where he seated himself, and indicated a place for me.

KERENSKY: "Well, what do you want. You asked to see me?"

MYSELF: "I want to ask you why I am under arrest. I have never meddled in politics, they are the last things that interest me. I can't regard myself as a political prisoner."

KERENSKY (taking a roll of paper off the desk, and perusing it): "Listen. . . . Firstly, you are accused of staying voluntarily with Their Majesties when you had no official position at Court. Can you deny this?"

MYSELF: "Certainly not, I have no wish to do so. I stayed with Their Majesties, as I could not possibly desert them at such a moment. I love the Imperial Family as individuals. Surely this cannot constitute a crime in your eyes."

KERENSKY: "Well . . . let it pass. . . . What is this close friendship between you and the Empress?"

MYSELF: "I am honoured with the friendship of the Empress. She knows my husband, she has been so good to us that we cannot be devoted enough to her."

KERENSKY (impatiently): "Enough of the Empress. What do you want?"

MYSELF: "What I ask is *not* freedom, but imprisonment in my own house. My child is ill. I want to be with him."

KERENSKY (laughing satirically): "You didn't consider your child when you left him alone in Petrograd in order to remain with your beloved Empress."

MYSELF (angrily): "I know best *why* I left him. You call yourself a patriot . . . I suppose you put the love of your country before family ties? I love the Imperial Family, they come before my family ties. You've taken me away from *them*—I haven't gone willingly. Why deprive me of my child?"

KERENSKY (with sinister emphasis): "Listen, Madame Dehn, *you know too much.* You have been constantly with the Empress since the beginning of the Revolution. You can, if you choose, throw quite another light on certain happenings which we have represented in a different aspect. You're DANGEROUS."

A long silence.

KERENSKY: "Can you explain why all orders from the Empress passed through you? You had no official position . . . it's a most suspicious occurrence."

MYSELF: "We were practically isolated in the private apartments through fear of contagion. Besides, what orders could the Empress give without their being known to *you*?"

KERENSKY: "The servants are witnesses that all orders came through you. Enquiries will reveal the truth . . . if you are honest ... well and good. If not . . . that's another matter."

I looked at him. Kerensky seemed absolutely implacable, but I decided to make one last appeal. He apparently loved flowers; this proved that, as his senses could be appealed to, why not his heart? "If *you* had a child of your own, you'd understand my feelings," I said.

Kerensky surveyed me with that now familiar appraising scrutiny. "I don't think much of you as a mother," he replied, smiling coldly, "but—how old is your child?"

"He is seven."

"Well, Madame, it so happens that I *have* a child, and he, too, is seven. I can decide nothing, but I am now going to a Council at which Prince Lvoff will be present. *He* must decide."

I looked him straight in the eyes. This time he met my gaze fully and squarely.

"I'm perfectly certain that you can do anything you like, without consulting anyone," I said. This tribute to his vanity appealed at once to Kerensky. With most men vanity is the most powerful factor. Wound a man's vanity and he will never forgive you; pander to it, and he is your friend for life. Kerensky was no exception: I had discovered the heel of this Russian Achilles.

"You are quite right. Of course I can do what I like. Go back to your room—I'll send you my answer later in the evening." He pressed an electric bell on his table. The A.D.C. entered.

"Has Madame Dehn a bed in her room?" asked Kerensky. "If not, see that one is placed there."

"Oh, I don't want a bed," I interrupted. "Please let me go to my child."

"I've already told you," said Kerensky, "that I'll let you know later. But . . . if I allow you to go home, you must give me your written promise not to act in any way against us."

The A.D.C. made a sign to the soldiers, Kerensky took no further notice of me, and I was hurried out of the warm flower-scented apartment into the icy corridor.

Black despair overcame me when I regained my room. Kerensky had been noncommittal; but I had hopes that my allusion to him as omnipotent might have some favourable effect; so I sat in the corner nearest the door, straining my ears to catch the sound of approaching footsteps.

Shortly after midnight my friend the A.D.C. made his appearance, and, with a theatrical gesture, indicative of boundless space, he advanced, saying:

"The Minister grants you permission to go home."

My feelings are better imagined than described. I sprang up, and made the Sign of the Cross, and my hand sought the beloved medal hidden in my dress. So I was really free! I could hardly believe it, surely I could not have heard aright!

The A.D.C. told me to put on my hat and cloak and follow him. . . . Before I did so he asked me to sign a paper agreeing not to leave Petrograd, and to hold myself in readiness to be interrogated. I did so; then, picking up my suit-case, I went downstairs. He left me in the hall. I had now apparently lost all interest for him, as he did not trouble to bid me farewell. . . . He merely pointed out the door, and disappeared. I looked round, hardly daring to move. I was not able to realize that I was free to go when, and where, I chose. I pushed open the heavy door, and found myself in the cold and darkness outside. Not a single fiacre was in sight; I felt too exhausted to move, but I made a supreme effort to walk. . . . Impossible! My feet slipped in all directions in the melted snow and slush of the road. Suddenly I noticed a man who was regarding me with evident curiosity. . . . My heart sank. What if this scrutiny meant that I was about to be rearrested?

The man made his way to where I was standing. "Are you Madame Dehn?" he enquired civilly.

"I am."

"I thought I recognised you, Madame. I've been at your house several times. I was formerly Madame Kazarinoff's footman. Poor, poor Madame, who would have believed this could happen to you. Let me help you. I know where I can find a fiacre."

He presently returned with a fiacre, and assisted me to get in with all the courtesy and deference of a well-trained servant. I thanked him many times. . . . He gave the direction to the driver, and we drove away.

It was one in the morning before I arrived home. I rang the bell, and after some delay the door was opened by my maid . . . who nearly fainted when she saw me. . . . I couldn't speak. My thoughts were concentrated on Titi. . . . I ran past her upstairs to his room. ... It was empty! What had happened—could he be dead? I hurried across the landing to my bedroom. . . . A light was burning. . . . Someone was in bed. . . . Thank God, I recognised the beloved dark head of my boy—he was safe. I fell on my knees beside him. With a little start, and a smile, which was like balm to my yearning heart, Titi awoke. . . .

"Mother, mother. . . ." He flung his arms round me. I covered his face with kisses.

"Where have you come from?" he enquired. "From prison."

The child began to cry. I realized the tactlessness of my reply. "If they ever take you away again I'll go too," he sobbed. "But where's 'Aunt Baby'? What has happened to her? And where is Papa? They say he's been killed."*

"Darling, darling, I can tell you nothing about Papa."

Hearing the sound of voices, my father now came into the room. He was greatly relieved to know that I was safe, as all sorts of stories were current respecting my fate and that of Anna Virouboff. But my one thought was for my child: he was much better, but the room struck cold, and I asked my father how it was that there was no fire. He shrugged his shoulders. "*Ma chère*," he replied, "the answer is quite simple—we have no wood! The servants manage to steal a little to burn during the day, but at night *c'est bien autre chose*."

I undressed as quickly as possible, and got into bed. I held Titi close. I kissed him passionately. I trembled with mingled joy and fear! . . . No one should separate us. I knew nothing as to our ultimate fate, but I had made up my mind, during these first hours of freedom, to escape as soon as possible to my estates in South Russia, and, if the Imperial Family were removed from Tsarkoe, to join them.

It was a strange home-coming. The whole house was disorganised. The servants were still devoted to my interests, but food and fuel were difficult to obtain. I spent the morning of the next day lying on a couch in my dressing-room. I was really ill; the long strain had told, and Nature was now exacting her toll in the shape of occasional heart attacks. The hours passed peacefully and slowly, but at ten o'clock in the evening the telephone rang, and my maid told me that the Commandant of the Equipage de la Garde wanted to speak to me.

I was surprised and vexed. After the way in which certain officers had treated the Imperial Family, it was not agreeable for me to continue their acquaintance. However, I went to the 'phone.

"Madame Dehn," said a well-known voice, "have you actually come back from the Palace?"

"Yes, I returned to Petrograd a few days ago."

"I heard that you had been placed under arrest. How is it then that you are at home?"

"Kerensky has given me permission to be with Titi. Cannot you,

---

* I heard later that it was reported that my husband had been killed and his body thrown overboard.

for my husband's sake, and as one of his brother-officers, come over and see me?"

"Impossible," answered the voice. "Look here, you can't stay where you are."

"Very well, since you order, I suppose I must obey. I'll try and find somewhere else, as soon as I am rested."

"You must go NOW."

"I haven't anywhere to go, and the child is ill."

"Take him to an hotel. I won't be responsible for your safety. Lots of things may happen during the night. . . . The sailors may come and murder you." The Commandant then rang off, and left me to face this new terror. But my mind was made up. I would not leave home at a moment's notice. If we had to die, we would die together. I was too exhausted, and the child was too ill, to contemplate a midnight flight.

I rang up my husband's nephew, who was in barracks, and he promised to keep me well advised; but fortunately the night passed peacefully. Nobody came near the house.

Weeks elapsed, and Kerensky seemed to have completely forgotten my existence. I led a quiet life, but my heart was torn with anxiety concerning my beloved friends. I received some letters from the Empress, and I wrote constantly to her, and to the Grand Duchesses. It was in connection with this correspondence that I was summoned to Tsarkoe Selo, by order of Commandant Kobilinsky.

I was instructed to leave Petrograd secretly, and to wear my Red Cross uniform. It was early in July, and the trees were bravely apparelled in their young verdure. It was very different to that bleak March afternoon when the snow lay thickly on the ground, and the wind had stung my face with its icy breath. Outwardly, at all events, everything was peaceful, but tears filled my eyes at the recollection of past Julys. . . . Surely God would not permit the innocent to suffer; surely Justice would awaken in the soul of misguided Russia, and all might yet be well.

As I approached the Palace I became sensible of an eerie change, both in it and in its immediate surroundings. I stopped to consider in what the change consisted. Then knowledge dawned upon me. Tsarkoe was a *dead* place. Its windows were almost hidden by the straggling branches of the unclipped trees, grass grew between the stones of its silent courtyard, and I instantly likened it to a famous Russian picture, "Le Chateau Oublié." . . . It was indeed a forgotten castle! I walked to and fro gazing up at the windows, but those within the Palace gave no sign of life. I wanted to call aloud that I was there, but I dared not imperil their safety or my own. I considered even now that I held my life in trust for the service of the Empress.... Who knew when she might require me?

[handwritten letter in Russian]

PART OF LETTER FROM HER IMPERIAL MAJESTY WRITTEN ON THE DAY OF DEPARTURE FOR SIBERIA.
(*The note in centre is in the handwriting of the Tsarevitch.*)

Kobilinsky had taken up his quarters in the large building opposite the Palace, so I repaired thither. There were hardly any people visible, and I was directed to Kobilinsky's private room. He was a dark, shortish, nervous man, wearing military uniform, and, as the Empress had written that he was kind to them, I was naturally anxious to make a good impression. This interview is of some importance as I am enabled to contradict a part of Kobilinsky's deposition which appeared in a recent publication. In this deposition he queries the name of the writer of certain letters which came to Tsarkoe Selo, and attributes them to quite another person. The actual writer was myself, and the confusion respecting the signature

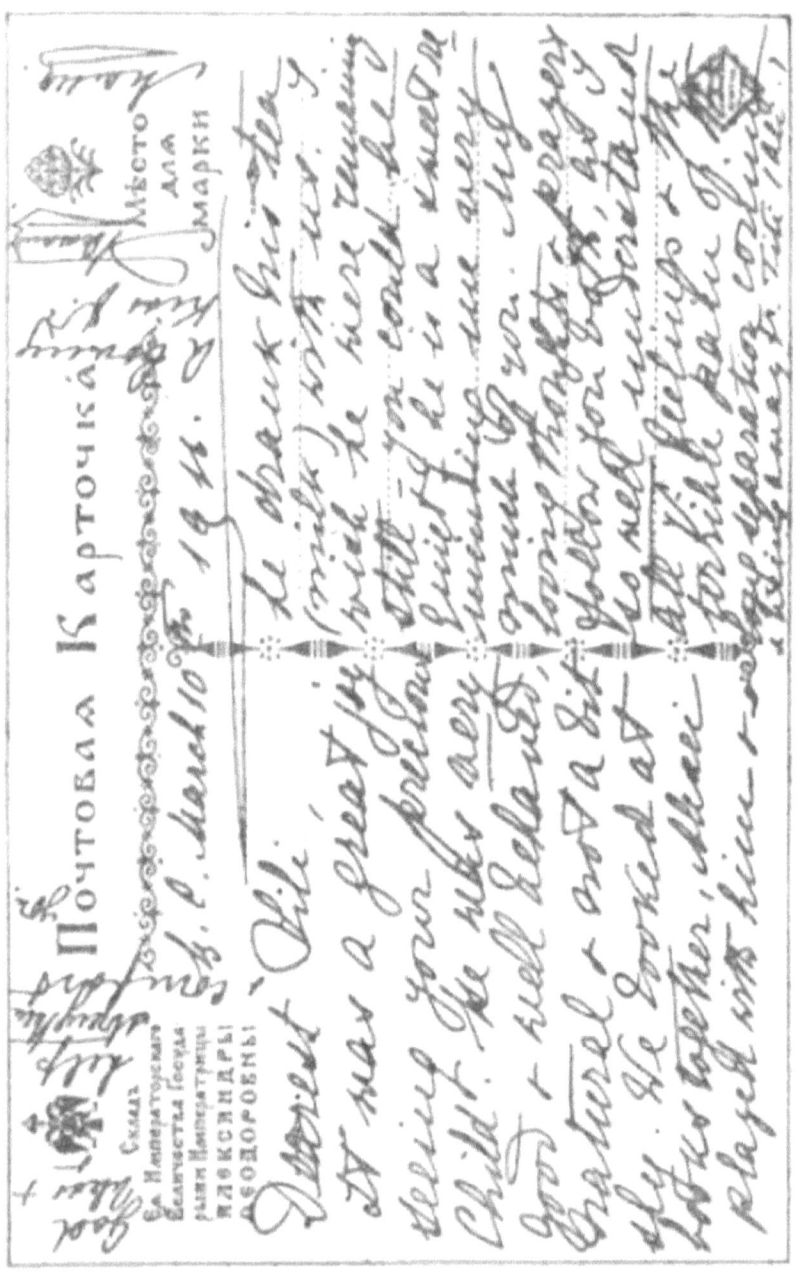

LETTER RECEIVED AT VLADIVOSTOK, IN 1916, WHEN I WAS ON MY WAY TO JAPAN WITH MY HUSBAND. HER IMPERIAL MAJESTY HERE GIVES ME A REPORT OF THE DOINGS OF MY LITTLE SON WHOM I HAD LEFT IN HER CHARGE.

arose from the fact that I had used a fanciful name composed of that of Titi and myself. There was not, and never has been, any "Mysterious Personage" as Kobilinsky's deposition leads one to suppose.

"Are you Madame Dehn?" asked Kobilinsky, eyeing me with some degree of curiosity.

"Yes, Commandant!"

"Are these from you?. . ." he continued, handing me a packet of letters.

"Most certainly. They are all in my handwriting," I said.

"Then why on earth don't you sign your full name when you write?" he queried testily.

"Because I've never been in the habit of doing so. 'Tili' is a fanciful name, a combination of 'Lili' and 'Titi.'"

"I don't believe you," he said bluntly. "It is the name of another lady."

"Why don't you make enquiries if you doubt my word?" I returned. "You'll easily find out that I'm telling the truth."

"Well, well," he grumbled. "I suppose I must believe you. But, see here, Madame, you've got to promise me something. You *must* agree to destroy all the letters which the Empress has sent you. If you don't, I won't allow you to write or to receive any more letters. I suppose," he added, "that such a devoted friend as yourself has not come to-day without bringing some letters for the Family?"

I acknowledged that such was the case. Kobilinsky smiled, and took the letters. He then signified that the interview was over.

Kobilinsky "passed" many letters to and from the Empress after this, but I was always haunted by the fear lest my precious corresponddence might be stolen, or else forcibly destroyed. Fortune favoured me, and an opportunity occurred to send my letters and certain private papers to England under the safe conduct of General Poole. These papers were ultimately deposited in a safe in London belonging to Prince George Shrinsky-Shihmatoff.

The Empress and the Grand Duchesses corresponded with me regularly after they left Tsarkoe, in fact up to a few weeks of their departure for Ekaterinburg. These letters were entrusted to confidential persons and smuggled by them out of the prison. Those who expect startling revelations of political importance will be sadly disappointed in these pathetic little leaves which have drifted from Friendship's tree across a passion-racked country, and, like the song, "have found their home" in the heart of a friend. But, for the student of psychology, the just man or woman, the curious seeker "behind the scenes" of Royalty, they will, I think, possess some interest. They will plead for a hearing far more effectively than any poor words of mine. Not one of them contains a sigh for the splendours of a throne. The woman who longed to be in the Crimea at a time of year when the acacias were like "perfumed clouds" made no allusion to the past glories of the Winter Palace, or the comfortable "English" life at Tsarkoe Selo. Perhaps the words of the writer who "being dead yet speaketh" may serve to efface some of the lies and scandals which have bespattered the name of an Empress who has been condemned so unmercifully.

The Empress and I have never met since that March afternoon when she bade me farewell. I cannot accept the almost overwhelming proofs of the tragedy of Ekaterinburg. From time to time reports of the safety of the Imperial Family have reached us, but the next moment we are faced with evidence that the whole of them have perished. God alone knows the truth, but I still permit myself to hope.

After my interview with Kobilinsky I returned to Petrograd, where I spent some uneventful weeks. Poor Anna was right when she said that things were no better after the Revolution than they were before! Existence was a difficult problem: a period of starvation set in, and we, like others, became familiar with the pangs of hunger. It was impossible to procure nourishing food for Titi; so, almost at my wits' end, I applied for permission to remove him to South Russia.

This permission was most unexpectedly granted. Two weeks later Kerensky's Government fell, and for the moment I was forgotten!

We lived very quietly at Beletskovka, and I was always planning the best way of escape to rejoin my beloved friends. "*L'homme propose, et Dieu dispose.*" A wave of Bolshevism swept over South Russia, and our safety was menaced to such an extent that I was forced to escape with Titi to Odessa, and, as our adventures in no way touch on the subject of this book, I shall refrain from relating them. Suffice it to say that we managed to reach Odessa, and from thence, under the protection of the French, we went to Constantinople.

From Constantinople we made our way to Gibraltar, and from Gibraltar to England, where my husband was awaiting me after a three years' separation.

* * *

EXTRACT FROM THE LETTER OF 5 JUNE, 1917.
TSARKOE SELO.

Oh! how pleased I am that they have appointed a new Commander-in-Chief of the Baltic Fleet (Admiral Raswosoff). I hope to God it will be better now. He is a real sailor and I hope he will succeed in restoring order now. The heart of a soldier's daughter and wife is suffering terribly, in seeing what is going on. Cannot get accustomed and do not wish to. They were such hero soldiers, and how they were spoilt just at a time when it was necessary to start to get rid of the enemy (Germans). It will take many years to fight yet. You will understand how he (Tsar) must suffer. He reads, and tears stand in his eyes (newspapers), but I believe they will yet win (the War). We have so many friends in the fighting line. I can imagine how terribly they must suffer. Of course nobody can write. Yesterday we saw quite new people (new guard)—such a difference. It was at last quite a pleasure to see them. Am writing again what I ought not to, but this does not go by post, or you would not have received it. Of course, I have nothing of interest to write. To-day is a prayer at 12 o'clock. Anastasia is to-day 16 years old. How the time flies. . . .

I am remembering the past. It is necessary to look more calmly on everything. What is to be done? Once He sent us such trials, evidently He thinks we are sufficiently prepared for it. It is a sort of examination—it is necessary to prove that we did not go through it in vain. One can find in everything something good and useful—whatever sufferings we go through—let it be, He will give us force and patience and will not leave us. He is merciful. It is only necessary to bow to His wish without murmur and await—there on the other side He is preparing to all who love Him undescribable joy. You are young and so are our children—how many I have besides my own— you will see better times yet here. I believe strongly the bad will pass and there will be clear and cloudless sky. But the thunder-storm has not passed yet and therefore it is stifling—but I know it will be better afterwards. One must have only a little patience—and is it really so difficult? For every day that passes quietly I thank God. . . .

Three months have passed now (since Revolution)!! The people were promised that they would have more food and fuel, but all has become worse and more expensive. They have deceived everybody—I am so sorry for them. How many we have helped, but now it is all finished. . . .

It is terrible to think about it! How many people depended on us. But now? But one does not speak about such things, but I am writing about it because I feel so sadly about those who will have it more difficult now to live. But it is God's will! My dear own, I must finish now. Am kissing you and Titi most tenderly. Christ be with you.

"Most hearty greetings"—(from the Czar).

Yours loving,
AUNT BABY.

30th July, 1917.
TSARKOE SELO.

MY DEAREST,

Heartiest thanks for letter of the 21st. Cannot write—he has no time to read ("he"—Colonel Kobilinsky, Revolutionary Commandant of the Palace), the poor man is so busy all the time that he is often without lunch and dinner. Am pleased have made his acquaintance. E. S. has seen you ("E. S."—Doctor Botkin). I am so pleased that you know all about us.

Will remember your last year's trip. Do you remember? Have not been quite well lately—often had head and heartache. My heart was enlarged. Am sleeping very badly. But never mind—God gives me His strength. Have brought the ikon of Snameni (of God Mother). How thankful I am that this was possible, at this day dear to me (birthday of Tsarevitch). I prayed hard for you and remembered how we used to pray together before it. How Tina (Anna Virouboff) will now suffer—without anybody in the town and her sister in Finland and her friends going so far away (meaning herself)—how much people have to suffer—the path of life is so hard. Please write to A. W. (Colonel Siroboyarski—one of the wounded officers) and send him heartfelt greetings and blessings ✠—kiss you most tenderly and the darling Titi (my son). God preserve you and the Holy Mother.

Always yours,
AUNT BABY.

Kindest regards (meaning the Czar).

I remember—Faith, Hope, Love—that is all, all in life. You understand my feelings. Be brave. Thank you most heartily. All touched by your little ikons—will just put it on. Ask Rita (Miss Hitrovo) to write to the mother of your countryman (Colonel Siroboyarski).

Added by Tsarevitch:

Kiss you most tenderly. Thanks for congratulations.

ALEXEI.

Added by Grand Duchess Olga:

I also kiss you most tenderly and thank you Lili my heart, for post card, and little ikon. God preserve you.

OLGA.

Added by the Empress:

Thank you for your dear letters—we understand each other. It is hard to be separated. Greetings to R. Gor. ✠ I have learnt only now how you spent the first days (in prison). It is terrible, but God will reward. Am pleased that your husband has written.

PART OF LETTER OF 30TH JULY 1917.
(Day of removal from Tsarkoe Selo to Tobolsk. The upper portion is written by the Grand Duchess Olga, the postscript is in the handwriting of Her Imperial Majesty.)

29th November, 1917.
TOBOLSK.

MY DEAREST,

I am for such a very, very long time without news of you, and I feel sad. Have you received my post card of the 28th October?

CHRISTMAS CARD DRAWN SPECIALLY FOR ME
BY HER IMPERIAL MAJESTY WHILE AT TOBOLSK.

Everybody is well—my heart is not up to much, fit at times, but on the whole it is better. I live very quietly and seldom go out as it is too difficult to breathe in frozen air.

Lessons as usual. (News from Petrograd) "T" is as always. Zina has been to see her and O. V., who is very sad, she is always praying. Father Makari passed on on the 19th July.

Rumours have it that Gariainoff has married, but we do not know whether it is true. (Speaking of herself the Empress writes) Aunt Baby drew this herself. How is Titi?—Granny—I want to know such, such a lot. How is Count Keller? Have you seen him in Kharkoff? The present events are so awful for words, shameful and almost funny, but God is merciful, darling. Soon we shall be thinking of those days you passed with us. My God, what remembrances!

Matresha has married, they are now all in P., but the brother is at the front.

I read a lot, embroider and draw (I have to do it all with my spectacles, am so old). I think of you often and always pray fervently for you and love you tenderly.

I kiss you very, very much.

May Christ protect you.

Your countryman is at Vladivostok and Nicholas Jakovlevitch (one of the wounded) is, I think, also in Siberia. I am so lonely without you all. Where is your husband and his friends? We are still expecting Ysa and the others.

I kiss Titi tenderly. Write, I am waiting so. Verveine (toilet water) always reminds me of you.

2/15 March, 1918.
TOBOLSK.

MY OWN DEAR DARLING,

Best and tender thanks for your dear letter. At last we have received good news from you; it was an anxious time not to hear for so long, knowing that things are bad where you are living. I can imagine though what terrible mental agony you must be going through, and you are alone. My little godchild (Titi) is with you always—what he must see and hear! It is a hard school. My God, how sorry I am for you my little giant one; you have always been so brave. I think of those days of a year ago. I shall never forget that you were everything to me and believe that God will not leave you or forsake you. You left your son for "Mother" (meaning herself) and her family, and great will your reward be for this.

Thank God that your husband is not with you, for it would have been terrible, but not to know anything about him is more than awful. When I did not know for four days where mine was "then" (during the days of the Revolution), but what was that in comparison with you. But for us, in general, it is better and easier than for others—it hurts not to be with all our dear ones and not to be able to share their troubles. Yes, separation is a dreadful thing, but God gives strength to bear even this, and I feel the Father's presence near me and a wonderful sense of peaceful joy thrills and fills my soul (Tina feels the same), and one cannot understand the reason for it, as everything is so unutterably sad, but this comes from Above and is beside ourselves, and one knows that He will not forsake His own, will strengthen and protect.

Have news at last, two received new from K.; poor thing, she has a new sorrow, has buried her beloved father—her mother is with her. It is not easy for her to stay in town, though she has good friends and is not so cut off as you are, dearest. Be careful of certain of your friends—they are dangerous.

If you see dear Count Keller again, tell him that his ex-Chief (meaning herself) sends him her heartiest greeting (to her as well), and tell him that she prays constantly for him. I am anxious to know whether he has any news of his eldest son. Radionoff and his brother are in Kieff I hear that Gariainoff and his wife have been in Gagra and are now—so they say—at Rostoff. Am anxious about them, all last week have been *worrying* over it, and do not know why.

To-day we have 20 degrees of frost, but the sun is warm and we have already had real spring days. Godmother (meaning herself) does all the housekeeping now, looks through books and accounts—a lot to do, quite a real housewife. Everybody is well—only a few colds, and feet ached, not very badly, but enough to keep from walking. They have all grown, Marie is now much thinner, the fourth is stout and small. Tatiana helps everyone and everywhere, as usual; Olga is lazy, but they are all one in spirit. They kiss you tenderly—(stands for the Emperor) sends his hearty greetings. They are already sunburnt, they work hard, sew and cut wood, or we should have none. The court is full of timber, so we shall have enough to last.

We still are not allowed to go to church. A. V.'s mother (one of the Empress's wounded) is very sorry that you have not been to see her. She is living with some relatives of your mother's. Their estate has been taken away from them. The son has returned, he now looks, as they all do, pale and miserable.

They, poor things, can no longer keep M. S., and will probably be obliged soon to leave the house. She hardly ever gets a letter from her son; he too is complaining, so I copy what they write to me and send it on to them.

He is very upset not to hear from you, though he himself has written to you. He is going to Japan to learn English, he learnt more than 900 words in ten days and of course overtired himself and has been feeling ill. He was operated upon in December, in Vladivostok. Rita writes that Nicholas Jakovlevitch (one of the wounded) is at Simferopol with his friend, the brother of little M. Their splendid (good) friend (Alexandre Dumbadze) has been killed there, we loved him very much, he was one of our wounded.

I only write what I dare, for in the present days one never knows in whose hands the letter might fall. We hope to do our devotions next week if we are allowed to do so. I am already looking forward to those beautiful services—such a longing to pray in church. I dream of our church (at Tsarkoe Selo) and of my little cell-like corner near the altar. Nature is beautiful, everything is shining and brilliantly lighted up. The children are singing next door. There are no lessons to-day as it is Friday of Carnival week.

I relive in mind, day by day, through the year that has passed and think of those I saw for the last time. Have been well all along, but for the past week my heart has been bad and I do not feel well, but this is nothing. We cannot complain, we have got everything, we live well, thanks to the touching kindness of the people, who in secret send us bread, fish, pies, etc.

Do not worry about us, darling, dearly beloved one. For you all it is hard and especially for our Country!!! This hurts more than anything else—and the heart is racked with pain—what has been done in one year! God has allowed it to happen—therefore it must be necessary so that they might understand, that eyes might be opened to lies and deceits.

I cannot read the newspapers quietly, those senseless telegrams—and with the German at the door!!!

K. and everyone else looks at "brother" as a saviour—Great God, to what have they come to, to wait for the enemy to come and rid them from the infernal foe. And who is sent as the leader?

Aunt Baby's brother (meaning herself). Do you understand. They wished to act nicely, probably thinking that it would be less painful and humiliating to her—but for her (meaning herself) it is far worse—such an unbearable pain—but everything generally hurts now—all one's feelings have been trampled underfoot—but so it has to be, the soul must grow and rise above all else; that which is most dear and tender in us has been wounded—is it not true? So we too have to understand through it all that God is greater than everything and that He wants to draw us, through our sufferings, closer to Him. Love Him more and better than one and all. But my country—my God—how I love it, with all the power of my being, and her sufferings give me actual physical pain.

And who makes her (Russia) suffer, who causes blood to flow?. . . her own sons. My God, what a ghastly horror it all is. And who is the enemy? This cruel German, and the worst thing for Aunt Baby is that he (the enemy) is taking away everything as in the time of Tsar Alexsei Michailovich (meaning that frontiers of Russia would become again as during the reign of A. M.). But I am convinced that it will not remain so, help will come from Above, people can no longer do anything, but with God all things are possible, and He will show His strength, wisdom and all forgiveness and love—only believe, wait and pray.

This letter will, in all probability, reach you on the day of our parting (one year ago), it seems so near and yet again as if centuries had passed since then.

It is seven months that we have been here. We see Ysa* only through the windows, and Madeleine (the Empress's lady's-maid, Madeleine

Zanotti) too. They have been here for three or four months to-day, I am told. I must give that letter at once.

I kiss you and Titi tenderly, Christ be with you, my dearest ones. Greeting to Mother and Grandmother. The children kiss and love you, and he (the Emperor) sends his very best wishes.

YOUR OLD GODMOTHER.

PART OF LETTER DATED MARCH 2/15, 1918, WHICH REACHED ME THREE YEARS LATER IN ENGLAND

. . . . .

* (previous page) Baroness Büxhoevgen Lady-in-waiting to the Empress.

L'ENVOI

THE first idea of writing this book occurred to me some time after my arrival in England. I had always known that the Empress had been grossly misrepresented in Russia, but I had not attached much importance to the fact, as I had seen the Revolutionary propaganda, and I fully realized the methods of the Revolutionaries in relation to the Imperial Family.

I was, however, astonished and horrified to discover that the same ideas were current in the broad-minded and enlightened country which has afforded me and so many other fugitives such kindly sanctuary.

If possible, I think the Empress has been more universally condemned in England than in Russia. I have scarcely heard her name mentioned without its being coupled with the degrading attributes of treachery, sensualism, hysteria, and religious mania. To one who knew her intimately and who loved her devotedly, such a state of things is unspeakably painful. I accidentally saw a film which was the grossest libel on her character and her personality, the mind of the producer having been apparently bent upon presenting the Empress as a combination of the chief forms of lurid wickedness which appeal to patrons of the cinema. I have also read novels about her which, whilst enraging me as mendacious chronicles, have considerably enlightened me as to the capacity for invention of which the human imagination is capable. More serious works have condemned the Empress in a courteous manner, but they have been none the less scathing in their judgment. Some writers, after the story of Ekaterinburg was authentically given to the world, have been more tolerant and more pitying in their censure, but it has been always censure.

Therefore, in the face of such hatred and contempt for one at whose hands I have received nothing but kindness and love, I determined to write my impressions of the Empress as I knew her, both in the happy days and afterwards in those of war and unrest during the first dark weeks of the Revolution.

I reasoned, I trust with justice, that although the majority of people are always ready to believe the worst of anyone, there must be others who, in the spirit of fair play, would be willing to look on the reverse side of the picture. There must surely be friends and relations in England who would welcome facts which proved that the

Empress had been true to her English upbringing and to the traditional right living of the descendants of Queen Victoria. English people seem to have forgotten, when the Empress was vilified on the screen and in cold type, that she was the daughter of Princess Alice, a name which is associated with all that is noblest and best in woman, a name which alone, one might have thought, would have pleaded for that of her daughter. But nothing protected her, not even the facts that her first cousin was King of England and that one of her sisters was married and living in this country.

I knew the almost impossible task of rehabilitation which lay before me, but, as the task daily assumed greater proportions, love and pity for my beloved friend urged me to attempt it.

I knew that I might be accused of being a Rasputinière, since my photograph taken with him had appeared in one of the English illustrated papers; but my best reply to such a possible charge is that I am living in England with my husband and child, and that my husband has sanctioned my description of Rasputin as I and others knew him. If the Empress's association with Rasputin had been a guilty one, or if I had not been in a position to describe events exactly as they happened, this book would never have been written.

It is both unjust and untrue to ascribe the Revolution as directly consequent upon the Emperor's weakness, or the pro-Germanism and hysteric sensuality of the Empress. I have endeavoured to show that Rasputin was probably one of the unconscious tools of the Revolution against Imperialism: there is no doubt that German intrigues brought Lenin back from Switzerland to overthrow the milder rule of Kerensky, who was not ready to offer the country an efficient substitute for Tsardom, but the Empress was entirely innocent of pro-Germanism. Russia was ripe for Revolution; she had essayed Revolution years before the Empress or Rasputin saw the light. Her political history alone proves my statement, but War hurried the feet of Revolution toward her bloodstained goal. Other European kingdoms have tottered or fallen, but Russia is a land of extremes: hence the extreme methods of her ideas of equality, which are, in many respects, similar to those of the French Revolution.

I am well aware that certain "official" documents relative to the Empress were sent to England, and I know the shameful assertions which they contained. These documents emanated from the Duma, and were "arranged" by the Duma, in order to justify many things which would otherwise have been unjustifiable.

I have not attempted to give to the world any elaborate descripttions of Court festivities, and those happenings which are the common property of all European journalists. Mine is a very simple résumé of the daily life and personality of the Empress as I knew her. I have endeavoured to avoid anything in the nature of exaggeration, in the hope that the public, who have innocently lent a ready ear to those things which are untrue, and which have been exploited by people who never saw or spoke to the Empress, will give equal consideration to the testimony of one who both knew and loved The Real Tsaritsa.

PRINTED BY BURLEIGH LTD.,
AT THE BURLEIGH PRESS BRISTOL ENGLAND

END OF BOOK TWO

BOOK THREE

Anna Aleksandrovna Viroubova is a controversial figure with some painting her as an innocent friend of the Imperial Family and others as the nefarious mole in their camp for Rasputin. Her memories recorded here, are what she decided to leave for us, having had plenty of time, whilst living in Finland following the Revolution, to decide what to include. The reader must ascertain how sincere they are.

ANNA VIROUBOVA

Unlike other royal household staff, Viroubova was not permitted to accompany the royal family in to exile. She was imprisoned for some time in St Petersburg and interrogated by the Cheka police and the Provisional Government, of which she writes about in this book. She also wrote to the former Empress whenever possible, of which some correspondence is reproduced in this book.

She managed to escape Russia and lived out her life in relative safety in Finland where she joined a religious order. While there she wrote her memoirs, passed on her prized photo albums and even was interviewed.

Image: Viroubova stands with the walking cane she required for the rest of her life after a road traffic accident in St Petersburg.

First published in 1923 by the Macmillan Company - London, New York. Published in Australia 26 January 1924. Pages: 400

MEMORIES OF
THE RUSSIAN COURT

THE EMPRESS OF RUSSIA IN HER HAPPY YEARS

TO MY EMPRESS,
WITH LOVE AND FIDELITY ETERNAL

MEMORIES OF THE RUSSIAN COURT

BY

ANNA VIROUBOVA

THE MACMILLAN COMPANY
NEW YORK · BOSTON · CHICAGO · DALLAS
ATLANTA · SAN FRANCISCO

MACMILLAN & CO., LIMITED
LONDON · BOMBAY · CALCUTTA
MELBOURNE

THE MACMILLAN CO. OF CANADA, LTD.
TORONTO

"When you are reproached—bless; when persecuted—be patient; when calumniated—comfort yourself; when slandered—rejoice; this is your road and mine." Words of St. Seraphine.

ALEXANDRA FEODOROVNA, from *Tobolsk*,
March 20, 1918

Yea, though I walk through the valley of the shadow of death I shall not fear. Thy rod and Thy staff shall comfort me.

ILLUSTRATIONS

The Empress of Russia in Her Happy Days	*(Frontispiece)*	355
The Empress Driving Her Pony Chaise	(8)	364
The Empress with Grand Duchess Tatiana in Her Bedroom, Tsarskoe Selo	(8)	364
Alexander Sergievitch Tanieff	(9)	365
The Winter Palace, Petrograd	(20)	n/a
Military Review, Tsarskoe Selo	(21)	n/a
The Emperor and Empress in a Quiet Hour on Board the Imperial Yacht	(32)	382
The Empress Distributing Presents to Sailors at the End of a Cruise	(33)	382
Livadia, the New Palace of the Tsars in the Crimea	(38)	n/a
A Corner of the Court of the Palace of Livadia	(39)	n/a
The Imperial Children Bathing in the Black Sea at Livadia	(39)	n/a
The Imperial Yacht Arrives at Livadia, the Crimea	(50)	393
The Tsar, Grand Duchesses Olga and Tatiana and Mme. Viroubova at Homburg	(51)	394
The Empress Giving Alexei a Lesson on the Terrace	(74)	n/a
Alexei Playing in the Snow at Tsarskoe Selo	(74)	n/a
The Empress in Bed with Convalescent Tsarevitch	(75)	n/a
Grand Duchesses Olga and Tatiana on Board the "Standert"	(78)	n/a
The Tsarevitch with His Cousins, Children of Grand Duke Ernest of Hesse	(79)	n/a
Nicholas II and the Tsarevitch on Board the Imperial Yacht "Standert"	(80)	412
The Tsarevitch with His Sailor, Derevanko	(81)	413
The Tsar, Tsarina, and Alexei in the Gardens at Tsarskoe Selo	(81)	413
The Emperor and Empress in Old Slavonic Dress, Jubilee of 1913	(98)	427

The Invalid Empress on the Balcony at Peterhof	(99)	428
The Guest Room in Rasputine's House in Siberia	(169)	472
The Three Children of Rasputine Before Their House in Siberia	(169)	471
The Empress and Young Grand Duke Dmitri, Afterwards One of Rasputine's Assassins	(184)	481
Minister of Court Count Fredericks, the Empress and Tatiana Taking Tea in Finnish Woods	(185)	482
Grand Duchesses Olga, Tatiana, Anastasie, and Marie, Prisoners at Tsarskoe Selo, 1917	(266)	534
Anna Viroubova Shortly After Her Release from the Fortress of Peter and Paul	(267)	535
Letters From Nicholas II to Anna Viroubova, from Tobolsk, 1917	(306)	n/a
Letters from Alexei, Tatiana, and Marie, Smuggled from Siberia in 1917	(307)	n/a
One of the Empress's Last Letters to Mme. Viroubova, Written in Old Slavonic, 1918	(320)	571
Smuggled Letter from the Empress on Birchbark after Paper Gave Out	(321)	572
The Ex-Emperor and Alexei Feeding Turkeys in the Barnyard, Tobolsk, 1918	(342)	n/a
The Last Photograph Taken of the Empress and Her Daughters, Olga and Tatiana, Shortly Before the Murder of the Imperial Family in Siberia	(343)	625

Publisher Note: With very few exceptions all these photographs were taken by members of the Imperial Family and by Mme. Viroubova, all of whom were experts with the camera.

Editing note: This list of illustrations from the London Edition 1923, of which some items are not included in certain versions; you can see n/a alongside these which were either very small or of very bad quality and not worth reproducing here.

CHAPTER I

IT is with a prayerful heart and memories deep and reverent that I begin to write the story of my long and intimate friendship with Alexandra Feodorovna, wife of Nicholas II, Empress of Russia, and of the tragedy of the Revolution, which brought on her and hers such undeserved misery, and on our unhappy country such a black night of oblivion.

But first I feel that I should explain briefly who I am, for though my name has appeared rather prominently in most of the published accounts of the Revolution, few of the writers have taken the trouble to sift facts from fiction even in the comparatively unimportant matter of my genealogy. I have seen it stated that I was born in Germany, and that my marriage to a Russian officer was arranged to conceal my nationality. I have also read that I was a peasant woman brought from my native Siberia to further the ambitions of Rasputine. The truth is that I am unable to produce an ancestor who was not born Russian. My father, Alexander Sergievitch Tanieff, during most of his life, was a functionary of the Russian Court, Secretary of State, and Director of the Private *Chancellerie* of the Emperor, an office held before him by his father and his grandfather. My mother was a daughter of General Tolstoy, aide-de-camp of Alexander II. One of my immediate ancestors was Field Marshal Koutousoff, famous in the Napoleonic Wars. Another, on my mother's side, was Count Kontaisoff, an intimate friend of the eccentric Tsar Paul, son of the great Catherine.

Notwithstanding my family's hereditary connection with the Court our own family life was simple and quiet. My father, aside from his official duties, had no interests apart from his home and his music, for he was a composer and a pianist of more than national fame. My earliest memories are of home evenings, my brother Serge and my sister Alya (Alexandra) studying their lessons under the shaded lamp, my dear mother sitting near with her needlework, and my father at the piano working out one of his compositions, striking the keys softly and noting down his harmonies. I thank God for that happy childhood which gave me strength of soul to bear the sorrows and sufferings of after years.

Six months in every year we spent in the country near Moscow on an estate which had been in the family for nearly two hundred years. For neighbors we had the Princes Galatzine and the Grand

Duke and Grand Duchess Serge, the last named being the older sister of the Empress. I hardly remember when I did not know and love the Grand Duchess Elizabeth, as she was familiarly called. As small children she petted and spoiled us all, often inviting us to tea, the feast ending in a grand frolic in which we were allowed to search the rooms for toys which she had ingeniously hidden. It was at one of these children's teas that I first saw the Empress Alexandra. Quite unexpectedly the Tsarina was announced and the beautiful Grand Duchess Elizabeth, leaving her small guests, ran eagerly to greet her. The time was near the beginning of the reign of Nicholas II and Alexandra Feodorovna, and the Tsarina was at the very height of her youthful beauty. My childish impression of her was of a tall, slender, graceful woman, lovely beyond description, with a wealth of golden hair and eyes like stars, the very picture of what an Empress should be.

For my father the young Empress soon conceived a warm liking and confidence and she named him as vice president of the committee of *Assistance par le Travail*. During this time we lived in winter in the Michailovsky Palace in Petrograd, and in summer in a small villa in Peterhof on the Baltic Sea. From conversations between my mother and father I learned a great deal of the life of the Imperial Family. The Empress impressed my father both by her excessive shyness and by her unusual intelligence. She was above all a motherly woman and often combined baby-tending with serious business affairs. With the little Grand Duchess Olga in her arms she discussed all kinds of business with my father, and while with one hand rocking the cradle where lay the baby Tatiana she signed letters and papers of consequence. Sometimes while thus engaged there would come a clear, musical whistle, like a bird call. It was the Emperor's special summons to his wife, and at the first sound her cheek would turn to rose, and, regard less of everything, she would fly to answer it. That birdlike whistle of the Emperor I became very familiar with in later years, calling the children, signaling to me. It had a curious, appealing, resistless quality, peculiar to himself.

Perhaps it was a common love of music which first drew the Empress and our family into a bond of friendship. All of us children received a thorough musical education. From childhood we were taken regularly to concerts and the opera, and our home, especially on Wednesday evenings, was a rendezvous for all the musicians and composers of the capital. The great Tschaikovsky was a friend of my father, and I remember many others of note who were frequent guests at tea or dinner.

Apart from music we received an education rather more practical than was the average at that time. In the Russia of my childhood a girl of good family was supposed to acquire a few pretty accomplishments and nothing much besides. Accomplishments I and my sister were given, but besides music and painting, for which my sister had considerable talent, we were well grounded in academic studies, and we finished by taking examinations leading to teachers' diplomas. I may say also that even in our drawing-room accomplish-ments we were obliged to be thorough, and when my father ventured to show some of our work to the Empress she expressed warm approval. "Most Russian girls," she said, "seem to have nothing in their heads but officers."

The Empress, coming from a small German Court where everyone at least tried to occupy themselves usefully, found the idle and listless atmosphere of Russia little to her taste. In her first enthusiasm of power she thought to change things a little for the better. One of her early projects was a society of handwork com-posed of ladies of the Court and society circles, each one of whom should make with her own hands three garments a year to be given to the poor. The society, I am sorry to say, did not long flourish. The idea was too foreign to the soil. Nevertheless the Empress persisted in creating throughout Russia industrial centers, *maisons de travail*, where the unemployed, both men and women, and especially unfortunate women who, through errors of conduct, lost their positions, could find work.

Life at Court was by no means serious. In fact it was at that time very gay. At seventeen I was presented, first to the Empress Dowager who lived in a palace in Peterhof known as the Cottage. Extremely shy at first, I soon accustomed myself to the many brilliant Court functions to which my mother chaperoned my sister and myself. We danced that first winter, I remember, at no less than twenty-two balls besides attending many receptions, teas, and dinners. Perhaps it was partly the fatigue of all this social dissipation which made so serious the illness with which in the ensuing summer I was stricken. Typhus, that scourge of Russia, struck down at the same time my brother Serge and myself. My brother's illness ran a normal course and he made a rapid recovery, but for three months I lay at death's door. After the fever succeeded many complications, inflammation of the lungs and kidneys, and an affection of the brain whereby I lost both speech and hearing. In the midst of my suffering I had a vivid dream in which the saintly Father John of Kronstadt appeared to me and told me to have courage and that all would finally be well.

This Father John of Kronstadt, whom all true Russians reverence as a saint, I remembered as having thrice been at our house in my early childhood. The gentle majesty of his presence, the beauty of his benign countenance had so deeply impressed me that now, in my desperate illness, it seemed to me that he, more than the skilled physicians and the devoted sisters who attended me, had power of help and healing. In some way I managed to convey to my parents that I wanted Father John, and they immediately telegraphed begging him to come. It was some days before the message reached him, as he was away from home on a mission, but as soon as he received word of our need he hastened to Peterhof. As in a vision I sensed his coming long before he reached the house, and when he came I greeted him without astonishment with a feeble movement of my hand. Father John knelt down beside my bed, praying quietly, a corner of his long stole laid over my burning head. At length he rose, took a glass of holy water, and to the consternation of the nurses sprinkled it freely over me and bade me sleep. Almost instantly I fell into a deep sleep, and when I awoke next day I was so much better that all could see that I was on the road to recovery.

In September of that year I went with my mother first to Baden and afterwards to Naples. We lived in the same hotel with the Grand Duke and Grand Duchess Serge who were very much amused to see me in a wig, my long illness having rendered me temporarily almost bald. After a quiet but happy season in southern Italy I returned to Russia quite restored to health. The winter of 1903 I remember as a round of gaieties and dissipations. In January of that year I received from the Empress the diamond-studded *chiffre* of maid of honor, which meant that, following my marriage, I would have permanent entry to all Court functions. Not immediately but very soon afterwards I was called to duty to the person of the Empress, and there began then that close and intimate friendship which I know lasted with her always and which will remain with me as long as God permits me to live.

I would that I could paint a picture of the Empress Alexandra Feodorovna as I knew her before the first shadow of doom and disaster fell upon unhappy Russia. No photograph ever did her justice because it could reproduce neither her lovely color nor her graceful movements. Tall she was, and delicately, beautifully shaped, with exquisitely white neck and shoulders. Her abundant hair, red gold, was so long that she could easily sit upon it when it was unbound. Her complexion was clear and as rosy as a little child's. The Empress had large eyes, deep gray and very lustrous. It was only in later life that sorrow and anxiety gave her eyes the melancholy with which they are usually associated. In youth they wore an expression of constant merriment which explained her family nickname of "Sunny," a name by the way nearly always used by the Emperor. I began almost from the first day of our association to love and admire her, as I have loved her ever since and always shall.

The winter of 1903 was very brilliant, the season culminating in a famous ball in costumes of Tsar Alexis Michailovitch, who reigned in the seventeenth century. The ball was given first in the Hermitage, the great art gallery adjoining the Winter Palace, but so immense was its success that it had to be twice repeated, once in the *Salle de Concert* of the palace and again in the large ballroom of the Schermetieff Palace. My sister and I were two of twenty young girls selected to dance with twenty youthful cavaliers in an ancient Russian dance which required almost as much rehearsal as a ballet. The rehearsals were quite important society events, all the mothers attending, and the Empress often looking on as interested as any of us.

That summer I again fell ill in our villa in Peterhof, and I remember particularly that this was the first time the Empress ever visited our house. She drove in a low pony chaise, coming up to my sickroom all in white with a big white hat and in the best of spirits. Needless to say, her unexpected visit did me a world of good, as did her second visit at our home in the country when she left me a gift of holy water from Saroff, a place greatly venerated by Russians. That winter with its artless pleasures, and the pleasant summer which followed, marked the end of an era in Russia. Immediately afterwards came the catastrophe of the Japanese War, so needlessly entered into. This war was the beginning of a long line of disasters which ended in the supreme disaster of 1917.

I must confess that at the time the Japanese War made no very deep impression on young girls who, like myself, faced life lightly like happy children. We resigned ourselves to an almost complete cessation of balls and parties, and we put aside our pretty gowns for

THE EMPRESS DRIVING IN HER PONY CHAISE. PETERHOF, 1909.

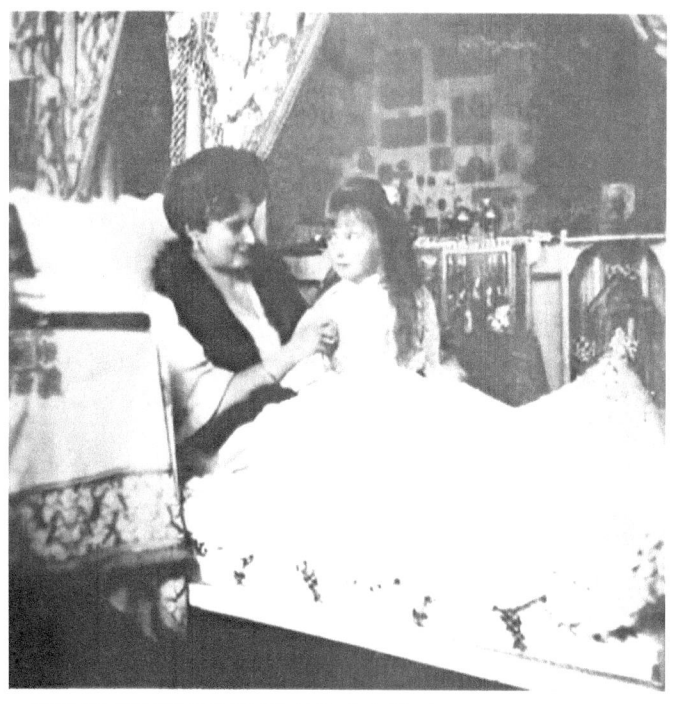

THE EMPRESS WITH GRAND DUCHESS TATIANA IN HER
BEDROOM, TSARSKOE SELO. FAVORITE IKONS IN BACKGROUND

the sober dress of working sisters. The great salons of the Winter Palace were turned into workrooms and there every day society flocked to sew and knit for our soldiers and sailors fighting such incredible distances away, as well as for the wounded in hospitals at home and abroad. My mother, who was one of the heads of committees giving out work to be done at home, was constantly busy, and we obediently followed her example.

ALEXANDER SERGIEVITCH TANIEFF,
Director of the Tsar's Private Chancellerie, Father of Anna Viroubova.

Every day the Empress came to inspect the work, often sitting down at a table and sewing diligently with the others. This was shortly before the birth of the Tsarevitch and I have a clear picture in my mind of the Empress looking more than ever fine and delicate, her tall figure clad in a loose robe of dark velvet trimmed in fur. Behind her chair, bringing into splendid relief her bright gold hair, stood a huge negro servant, gorgeous in scarlet trousers, gold-embroidered jacket, and white turban. This negro, Jim, was one of four Abyssinians who stood guard before the doors of the private apartments. They were not soldiers and they had no functions except to open and close the doors, and to signify by a sudden, noiseless entrance into a state apartment that one of their Majesties was about to appear. The Abyssinians were in fact simply one of the left-overs from the days of Catherine the Great, in whose times dwarfs and negroes and other exotics figured as a part of Court ceremonials. They remained not because Nicholas II or the Empress wanted them, but because, as I shall later explain, it was practically impossible to change any detail of Russian Court life.

The following summer the heir was born amid the wildest rejoicings all over the Empire. I remember the Empress telling me with what extraordinary ease the child was brought into the world. Scarcely half an hour after the Empress had left her boudoir for her bedroom the baby was born and it was known that, after many prayers, there was an heir to the throne of the Romanoffs. The Emperor, in spite of the desperate sorrow brought upon him by a disastrous war, was quite mad with joy. His happiness and the mother's, however, was of short duration, for almost at once they learned that the poor child was afflicted with a dread disease, rather rare except in royal families where it is only too common. The victims of this malady are known in medicine as haemophiliacs, or bleeders. Frequently they die soon after birth, and those who survive are subject to frightful suffering, if not to sudden death, from slight injuries to blood vessels, internal as well as external.

The whole short life of the Tsarevitch, the loveliest and most amiable child imaginable, was a succession of agonizing illnesses due to this congenital affliction. The sufferings of the child were more than equaled by those of his parents, especially of his mother, who hardly knew a day of real happiness after she realized her boy's fate. Her health and spirits began to decline, and she developed a chronic heart trouble. Although the boy's affliction was in no conceivable way her fault, she dwelt morbidly on the fact that the disease is transmitted through the mother and that it was common in her family. One of her younger brothers suffered from it, also her uncle Leopold, Queen Victoria's youngest son, while all three sons of her sister, Princess Henry of Prussia, were similarly afflicted. One of these boys died young and the other two were lifelong invalids.

Everything possible, everything known to medical science, was done for the child Alexei. The Empress nursed him herself, as indeed, with the assistance of professional women, she had nursed all her children. Three trained Russian nurses were in attendance, with the Empress always superintending. She bathed the babe herself, and was with him so much that the Court, ever censorious of her, complained that she was more of a nurse than an Empress.

The Court, of course, did not immediately understand the serious condition of the infant heir. No parents, be their estate high or low, are ready all at once to reveal a misfortune such as that one. It is always human to hope that things are not as desperate as they seem, and that in time some remedy for the illness will be found. The Emperor and Empress guarded their secret from all except relatives and most intimate friends, closing their eyes and their ears to the growing unpopularity of the Empress. She was ill and she was suffering, but to the Court she appeared merely cold, haughty, and indifferent. From this false impression she never fully recovered even after the explanation of her suddenly acquired silence and melancholy became generally known.

CHAPTER II

IN one of the earliest days of 1905 my mother received a telegram from Princess Galatzine, first lady in waiting, saying that my immediate presence at Court was required. The Princess Orbeliani, also a lady in waiting, was seriously ill, and some one was needed to replace her in attendance on Her Majesty. I left at once for Tsarskoe Selo, then, as always, the favorite home of the Imperial Family, and on my arrival was conducted to the apartments in the palace known as the Lyceum. The rooms were small and dark with windows looking out on a little church. It was the first time I had ever been away from home, and in any surroundings I should have been homesick and forlorn, but in these unfriendly surroundings my spirits were with some excuse depressed.

The time of my coming to Court was unpropitious, the Imperial Family and all connections being in deep mourning for the Grand Duke Serge who, on the morning of February 4, had been barbarously assassinated. The Grand Duke Serge, uncle of Nicholas II, had been Governor of Moscow. He was undoubtedly a reactionary, and his rule was said to have been harsh. Certain it is that his administrative methods earned him the intense enmity of the Social Revolutionaries and he had long lived in danger of assassination. His wife, the Grand Duchess Elizabeth, was devoted to him in spite of his somewhat difficult temperament, and she never willingly allowed him to leave the palace of the Kremlin unaccompanied. Usually she went with him herself, but on this fatal February morning he, being in a dark mood, left the palace without her knowledge. Suddenly a great explosion shook all the windows, and the poor Grand Duchess, springing from her chair, cried out in an agonized voice: "It is Serge!"

Rushing out into the court she saw a horrible sight, the body of her husband scattered in a hundred bleeding fragments over the snow. The bomb had literally torn the unfortunate man to pieces, so that in the dismembered mass of flesh and blood there was nothing recognizable of what had been, only a few minutes before, a strong and dominating man.

The terrorist who threw the bomb was promptly arrested, tried, and sentenced to death. It was entirely characteristic of the Grand Duchess Elizabeth that in the midst of her grief and horror she still found room in her heart to pity the misguided wretch sitting in his cell waiting his miserable end. The Grand Duchess insisted on visiting the man in prison, assuring him of her forgiveness, and praying for him on the stone floor of his cell. Whether or not he joined in her prayers I do not know. The Social Revolutionaries prided themselves on being irreligious and very many of them were Jews.

The Court weighed down by this terrible tragedy was a sad enough place for a homesick girl like myself. Like all the other ladies in waiting I wore a black dress with a long veil, and when at length I was received by the Empress I found her, too, dressed in deep mourning. After this first formal reception I saw very little of the Empress, all her time being devoted to her sister, the Grand Duchess Elizabeth, and to Princess Henry of Prussia, who was visiting her. The Empress Dowager also came, so that the suite was thrown together in what for me was not altogether a pleasant association. My special duty, as I discovered, was attendance on the old Princess Orbeliani, whose illness, I am bound to admit, did not sweeten her disposition. But as she was dying of that terribly trying malady, creeping paralysis, I am ashamed, even now, to criticize her. For the other *dames d'honneur*, however, I have no hesitation to say that they were not on their best behavior. Being entirely a stranger at Court and unacquainted with insincerities which afterwards I came to know only too well, I suffered keenly from the cutting remarks of my colleagues. My French, which I own I spoke rather badly, came in for a great deal of ridicule. On the whole it was rather an unhappy period in my young life.

The one bright spot that I remember was a drive with the Empress to which I was summoned by telephone. It was a warm day in early spring and the snow around the tree roots along the road was thawing in the pale sunlight. We drove in an open carriage, a big Cossack, picturesquely uniformed, riding behind. It was my first public appearance with Royalty and I was a little confused as to how to behave in the presence of the low-bowing crowds that lined the way. The Empress, however, soon put me at my ease, chatting of simple things, talking of her children, especially of the infant heir, at that time about eight months old. Our drive was not very long because the Empress had to hurry back to superintend a dancing lesson of the young Grand Duchesses. I remember when I returned to the apartment of the invalid Princess Orbeliani, she commented rather maliciously on the fact that I was not invited to attend the dancing lesson. But by that time, alas! I knew that had I been invited her comment might have been more malicious still. Still I must not speak badly of the poor Princess, for in spite of her illness and approaching death she was very brave and kinder than most people in her circumstances would have been.

Lent came on and in the palace church there were held every Wednesday and Friday special services for the Imperial Family. I asked and was given permission to assist in these services and I found great solace in them. At that time also I became warmly attached to a maid of honor of the Grand Duchess Serge, Princess Senkovsky, a woman of rare character. She had recently lost her mother and was in a sad mood. Almost everyone, in fact, was sad at this time. The Grand Duchess Serge, although she bore her tragedy with dignity and courage, went about with a white face and eyes in which horror still lingered. On religious holidays she laid aside her black robes and appeared all in white like a madonna.

The Princess Irene of Prussia (Princess Henry) was still in mourning for her little son who had died of the same incurable disease which afflicted the Tsarevitch. She spoke to me with emotion of the child, to whom she had been deeply attached.

My duty came to an end in Holy Week, and I went to the private apartments to make my farewell of the Empress. She received me in the nursery, the baby Tsarevitch in her arms, and I cannot forget how beautiful the child appeared or how healthy and normal. He had a wealth of golden hair, large blue eyes, and an expression of intelligence rare in so young a child. The Empress was kindness itself. At parting she kissed me, and gave me as a souvenir of my first service a locket set in diamonds. Yet for all her gracious kindness how gladly I left that night for my beloved home.

The following summer, which as usual we spent at Peterhof, I saw much more of the Empress than in my month of attendance on her. With my mother and sister I again worked daily in the workrooms established for the wounded in the Japanese War, and there almost daily the Empress came to sew with the other women. Once every week she visited the hospitals at Tsarskoe Selo, and twice that summer, at her request, I accompanied her to her foundation hospital for training nurses. The Empress in the military hospitals was at her very best. Passing from bedside to bedside, speaking as tenderly as a mother to the sick and suffering men, sitting down to a game of checkers with convalescent officers, it was difficult to imagine how anyone could ever call her cold or shy. She was altogether charming and as she passed all eyes followed her with love and gratitude. To me she was everything that was good and kind, and into my heart there was born a great emotion of love and loyalty that made me determine that I would devote my whole life to the service of my Sovereigns. Soon after I was to know that they, too, desired that I should be intimately associated with their household. The first intimation came in the form of an invitation to spend two weeks on the Royal yacht which was about to leave for a cruise in Finnish waters. We left on the small yacht *Alexandria*, and at Kronstadt transferred to the larger yacht *Polar Star*. We were a fairly large company on board, among others Prince Obolensky, Naval Minister, Admiral Birileff, Count Tolstoy, Admiral Chagin of the Emperor's staff, and Mademoiselle Schneider and myself in attendance on Her Majesty. A little to my embarrassment I was placed at table next the Emperor with whom I was not at all acquainted. It is true that I had often seen him at Tsarskoe and at Peterhof riding, or walking with his kennel of English collies, eleven magnificent animals in which he took great pride. But this time, on the *Polar Star*, was the first time I had been brought into personal contact with him. With the Empress I felt more at home, and this he knew, for he began almost at once to speak to me of her and of her great help to him in the pain and anxiety of the Japanese War. "Without her," he said with feeling, "I could never have endured the strain."

The war was again recalled by a visit on board the yacht from

Count Witte, fresh from the Portsmouth Conference. As a reward for his work done there he received for the first time his title by which the world now knows him. During dinner he related with great gusto all his experiences in the United States, his triumph over the Japanese delegates, his popularity with the Americans, appearing very happy and satisfied with himself. The Emperor complimented him warmly, but Count Witte for all his talents was never a favorite with the Sovereigns.

Life on board the *Polar Star* was very informal, very lazy and agreeable. We sailed through the quiet waters of the Baltic, every day going ashore for walks, the Emperor and his staff sometimes shooting a little, but more often spending the time climbing rocks, hunting mushrooms and berries in the woods and meadows, and playing with the children to whom this country holiday was heavenly pleasure. Living long hours in the open air and indulging in so much vigorous exercise made me desperately sleepy so that I found myself drowsy at dinner and almost dead for sleep by the time the eleven o'clock tea hour came round. Everyone found my drowsiness a source of never-ending amusement, and once, after I had actually fallen asleep at tea and had nearly pitched out of my chair, the Emperor presented me with a silver matchbox with which he said I might prop my eyes open until bedtime.

There was, of course, a piano in the salon of the yacht, and the Empress and I found a new bond in our common love of music. We spent hours playing four-hand pieces, all our dearly loved classics, Bach, Beethoven, Tschaikovsky, and others. In our quiet hours with our music, and especially before going to bed, the Empress and I had many intimate conversations. As if to relieve a heart too much constrained to silence and solitude the Empress confided in me freely the difficulties of her life. From the first day of her coming to the Russian Court she felt herself disliked, and this was all the more a grief and mortification to her because her marriage with the Emperor was a true love match, and she ardently desired that their union should increase in the Russian people the loyalty and devotion they undoubtedly felt in those days for the House of Romanoff.

All the stories of the reluctance of Alexandra Feodorovna to marry Nicholas II are absurdly untrue. As a small child she had been taken to Petrograd to the marriage of her older sister Elizabeth and the Grand Duke Serge. With the Grand Duchess Xenia, sister of Nicholas, she formed a warm friendship, and with the young heir himself she was on the best of terms. One day he presented her with a pretty little brooch which from very shyness she accepted but afterwards repenting, she returned, squeezing the gift into his hand in the course of a children's party. The young Tsarevitch, much offended, or rather much hurt, passed the brooch on to his sister Xenia who, not knowing its history, cheerfully accepted it.

The attraction so early established increased with years and ripened into romantic love, yet Alexandra Feodorovna hesitated to accept Nicholas as her betrothed because of the change of religion which was necessary. Her home life at this time was not particularly happy. Her mother, Princess Alice of England, had died in her childhood, and now her father, the reigning Grand Duke of Hesse, died suddenly of a stroke of paralysis. Her brother Ernest, who inherited the title and who was of course her guardian, had made an unhappy marriage with Princess Victoria of Coburg, and the home life of the family was not particularly pleasant. Later this marriage was dissolved, and in 1908 Grand Duke Ernest was happily united to Princess Eleanor of Sohmslich. It was at his first marriage that Alexandra Feodorovna again met the Tsarevitch, and from this time on he became a suitor. After their formal betrothal the young pair spent some happy weeks with Queen Victoria in England, where the match met with the approval of all the English relatives.

Emperor Alexander III was at this time lying mortally ill in the Summer Palace Livadia, in the Crimea, and when his condition became hopeless Alexandra Feodorovna, as the future Tsarina, was summoned to join the Imperial Family at his bedside. The dying Tsar rose from his sickbed and, dressed in full uniform, gave her the greeting due her dignity as a royal bride. From the rest of the family, unfortunately, she had a less cordial reception. The Empress and her ladies in waiting, Princess Oblensky and Countess Voronzoff, were distant and formal, and the rest of the Court, as might be expected, followed their example. The whole atmosphere of the palace seemed to the young girl unwholesome and unsympathetic. Upstairs lay the dying Emperor, while below the suite lunched and dined and followed ordinary pursuits very much as though nothing untoward was happening. To Alexandra Feodorovna, accustomed to the intimacy of a small and much less formal Court, this behavior seemed unfeeling and unkind.

The end came suddenly one day when the Emperor, at the

moment almost free from pain or weakness, was sitting in his armchair. The Empress Marie, quite overcome, fainted in the arms of Alexandra, who in that hour of extreme sorrow, prayed sincerely that she and her future mother-in-law might be drawn together in bonds of affection. But this, alas! was never to be.

The days that followed were gray and desolate for the young bride. The funeral procession of Alexander III wound slowly and solemnly from the Crimea to Petrograd, a journey of many days. The young Emperor, absorbed in his new duties, had little time to devote to the lonely, homesick girl, and indeed they hardly met before the morning of their marriage, a few days after the state funeral of the dead Emperor. The marriage took place in the church of the Winter Palace, and those who witnessed it have said that the bride, in her rich satin robes, looked very pale and unhappy. As she herself told me, the wedding seemed only a continuation of the long funeral ceremonies she had so lately attended.

Thus came Alexandra Feodorovna to Russia, nor did the weeks that followed her arrival bring her any happiness. To her friend Countess Rantsau, lady in waiting to Princess Henry of Prussia, she wrote:

> I feel myself completely alone, and I am in despair that those who surround my husband are apparently false and insincere. Here nobody seems to do his duty for duty's sake, or for Russia, but only for his own selfish interests and for his own advancement. I weep and I worry all day long because I feel that my husband is so young and so inexperienced. He does not at all realize how they are all profiting at the expense of the State. What will come of it in the end? I am alone most of the time. My husband is all day occupied and he spends his evenings with his mother.

This was true, as Nicholas was very inexperienced and his mother's influence and, it must be said, her knowledge of affairs were very potent. All during the first year the Emperor and the two Empresses lived together in the Annitchkoff Palace on the Nevski Prospekt. Alexandra Feodorovna comforted herself with the thought that summer would bring her a real honeymoon in the Crimea. Meanwhile she and her young husband went for an occasional sledge ride together, about the only time granted them for confidences. Fortunately the first baby came soon and the second was soon expected. That autumn in the Crimea the Emperor was stricken with typhus and his wife insisted upon nursing him herself, hardly permitting his personal servant to assist her. Christmas was celebrated in his sickroom, his recovery having set in some weeks before. During these days of convalescence they went on solitary walks together, and the Emperor began to read with his wife, to confide in her with affection. When they went back to Petrograd it was with every cloud dispelled, and the Empress a radiantly happy wife. However, the somewhat cold and distant manner acquired in the first unhappy months of her stay in Russia remained with her. Russia seemed to her an unfriendly land, and she was never able to present to it her really sunny and amiable disposition.

Not all of these confidences did the Empress impart to me on that first cruise I was privileged to share with her on the *Polar Star*. Little by little, then and later, I learned the story of her unhappy youth. But what she told me that summer seemed to relieve her mind, and she was more cheerful at the ending of the cruise than at the beginning. The commander of the yacht was good enough to tell me that I had broken down the wall of ice that seemed to surround Her Majesty, and that now she could be more easily approached. At the close of the voyage the Emperor said: "You are to go with us every year after this."

But dearest of all in my memory were the words of the Empress at parting: "Dear Annia, God has sent me a friend in you." And so I remained ever afterwards, not a courtier, not long a lady in waiting, or even a maid of honor, or in any capacity an official member of the Court, but merely a devoted and an intimate friend of Alexandra Feodorovna, Empress of Russia.

CHAPTER III

SHORTLY after our return to Peterhof I went abroad with my family, stopping first at Karlsruhe, Baden, to visit my grandmother, and afterwards going on to Paris. The Empress had given me letters to her brother, the Grand Duke of Hesse, and to her eldest sister, Princess Victoria of Battenberg, both of whom I saw before leaving Germany. The seat of the Grand Duke of Hesse was

Wolfsgarten near Darmstadt, a beautiful place surrounded by extensive gardens laid out according to the Grand Duke's own plans. After my first luncheon at the palace, during which the Grand Duke asked me many questions about the Empress and her life at the Court of Russia, I walked in the gardens with Mme. Grancy, hofmistress of the Court of Hesse, a gracious and charming woman. She showed me the toys and other pathetic relics of the little Princess Elizabeth, only child of the Grand Duke's first marriage, who had died in Russia after an acute illness of a few hours. I also saw the white marble monument which the people of Hesse had raised to the memory of the child.

To the second luncheon I attended at the old Schloss came the Princess Victoria of Battenberg with her lovely daughter Louise. Etiquette at Hesse was of the severest order and I observed with some astonishment that the Princess Victoria curtsied deeply to her sister-in-law, Princess Eleanor, who though much younger than herself, was the wife of the reigning Grand Duke. The old Princess was a very clever woman and a brilliant conversationalist, although, to tell the truth, as she spoke very rapidly I lost a great deal of what she said. I remember her questioning me rather closely about the political situation in Russia, and although I was not very enlightening on the subject she was good enough to invite me and my sister to lunch with her at Jugenheim in the neighborhood of Darmstadt. Both the brother and the sister of the Empress entrusted me with letters to her, and I took them with me to Paris, not knowing that it would be a long time before I should be able to deliver them.

For in the midst of these pleasant days, all unknown to me, the tide of trouble and unrest was rising high in Russia. Beginning with a railroad strike in Finland, a succession of labor troubles and revolutionary demonstrations extending over a large territory brought about a serious crisis which for a time tied up most of the railroads and prevented our return to Russia. Of the cause of the trouble, and above all, of its ultimate consequences, I must say that I remained in complete ignorance. That the situation was grave of course I realized, and my heart went out to the Emperor on whom the responsibility of restoring order largely rested. But that this railroad strike, for that is all it seemed to amount to, was the beginning of a revolution never crossed my mind. I longed to get back to the Empress who I knew would be sharing the anxiety of the Emperor, but as a matter of fact I did not get back until after the manifesto of

October, 1905, had been signed and delivered to a startled world.

This October manifesto, relinquishing the principle of autocracy, creating for the first time a Duma of the Empire, was the result of many councils, some of them dramatic, not to say violent. Count Witte and Grand Duke Nicholas were determined that the Emperor should sign the manifesto, a thing which he was reluctant to do, not because he clung to his privileges as autocrat of all the Russias, though I know that this is the motive still attributed to him by almost all the world. The Tsar hesitated to create a house of popular representation because he knew how ill prepared the Russian people were for self-government. He knew the dense ignorance of the masses, the fanatical and ill-grounded socialism of the intelligentsia, the doctrinaire theories of the Constitutional Democrats. I can say with positive knowledge that Nicholas II fervently desired the progress of his country towards a high civilization, but in 1905 he felt very serious doubts of the wisdom of radical changes in the Russian system of government. At last, however, overborne by his ministers, he signed the manifesto. It is said that the Grand Duke Nicholas, in one of the last councils, lost all control of himself and drawing a revolver threatened to shoot himself on the spot unless the manifesto was signed. Whether this actually occurred or not I do not know, but from what was told me later by the Empress the scenes with the Grand Dukes and the ministers were painful in the extreme. When in one of the final councils the actual form of the national assembly was decided upon the Emperor, with a hand trembling with emotion, signed his name to the fateful document, all in the room rose and bowed to him in token of their continued fidelity.

The Empress told me that while these trying scenes were in progress she sat in her boudoir alone save for her near relative the Grand Duchess Anastasie, both of whom felt that in the stormy council chamber a child was being dangerously brought into the world. Yet all the prayers of the Empress, as well as those of the Emperor, were that the new policy of popular representation would bring peace to troubled Russia.

The Duma was elected, the Socialists alone of political parties repudiating it as too "bourgeois." I was present with all the Empress's household, in the Throne Room of the Winter Palace on the opening day of the Duma when the Tsar welcomed the deputies, and I remember with what a strong, steady voice, and with what clear enunciation, the opening speech was read. Of the proceedings of the first Duma I have no very definite recollections, because they were marked with endless and very wordy discussions rather than with any attempt at constructive action. Everyone knows that the Duma was dissolved by Imperial order after a short life of two months.

Of these momentous political events which rocked Russia and were featured prominently in every newspaper in the world only faint echoes reached the inner circle of the Russian Court. This may sound incredible to readers in republican countries where the press is entirely uncensored and where public opinion is educated in politics. In the Russia of 1906 the reading public was a comparatively small one and the press was poorly representative of the really intelligent people of the Empire. Few men and fewer women of my class attached any particular interest to the Duma, the best we hoped for it being that in time it would become an efficient working agency, like the parliaments of western European countries, adapted, of course, to Russian needs. The first Duma we thought of only as a rather foolish debating society.

The Empress and I were engaged, at that time, with singing lessons, our teacher being Mme. Tretskaia of the Conservatoire. The Empress was gifted with a lovely contralto voice, which, had she been born in other circumstances, might easily have given her a professional standing. My voice being a high soprano we sang many duets. Sometimes my sister joined us and as she also sang well we formed a trio singing many of the lovely arrangements for three voices by Schumann and others. Occasionally came also an English friend of the Empress, a talented violinist, and among us we arranged concerts which gave us the greatest pleasure, although we always had to hold them in another building of the palace called the Farm in order not to disturb the Emperor, who, for some strange reason, did not like to hear his wife sing.

When summer came and while the Duma was talking out its brief existence we again took up our sea life, this time on board the large royal yacht the *Standert*. We cruised for two months, the Emperor frequently going ashore for tennis and other amusements, but occupied two days of each week with papers and state documents brought to him by messenger from Petrograd. The Empress and I were almost constantly together walking on shore, or sitting on deck reading, or watching the joyful play of the children, each of whom had a sailor attendant to keep them from falling overboard or otherwise suffering mishap. The special attendant of the little Alexei was a big, good-natured sailor named Derevanko, a man seemingly devoted to the child. It was in fact Derevanko who taught Alexei to walk, and who during periods of great weakness following severe attacks of his malady carried the boy most tenderly in his arms. All of these sailors at the end of a cruise received watches and other valuable presents from the Emperor, yet most of them, even Derevanko, when the revolution came, turned on their Sovereigns with meanest treachery.

On my days of regular service, Wednesdays and Fridays, for I was then a regularly appointed lady in waiting, I dined with the Imperial Family, and at that time I formed a close friendship with General Alexander Orloff, an old companion in the Royal Hussars with the Emperor. After dinner the Emperor and General Orloff usually played billiards, while the Empress and I read or sewed under the warm lamplight. Those were happy evenings, full of bright talk and laughter, and I came to regard General Orloff as one of my best friends. Already the hateful hand of jealousy and gossip had been directed against me by people who could not understand, or who, from motives of palace politics, deliberately misunderstood the Empress's preference for my society. Practically every monarch has some close personal friend, absolutely disassociated with politics and social intrigue, but I have noticed that these friendships are always misunderstood and frequently bitterly resented. I used to take my small troubles to General Orloff, at least they seem small now after years of real trouble and affliction. But even after these bitter years of sorrow and affliction the kindly counsels of the good old general often come back to me, as they did then, like a friendly hand laid on my hot and resentful heart.

I was then, in 1906, a fully grown and mature young woman and, as I could not help knowing, I was the subject of many conversations in the family circle because of my indifference to marriage. I had, I suppose, the normal amount of attention from men, and the usual number of suitors, but none of the young officers and courtiers with whom I danced and chatted made any special appeal to my imagination. There was one young naval officer, Alexander Virouboff, who after December, 1906, came to our house almost every day, paying me the most marked attentions. One day at luncheon he spoke with pride of the very good service to which he had just been appointed, and very soon afterwards I found myself greeted on all sides as his affianced. In February there was a ball in which I was formally presented as a bride, and in the after whirl of dinners, presents, new gowns and jewels, I began to share the excitement, if not the happiness, of those around me. The Empress approved the match, my parents approved, and no one except my old friend General Orloff expressed even a faint doubt of the wisdom of the marriage. But on the day when he spoke to me frankly, advising me to think seriously before taking such a serious step, the Empress entered the room and said in a decided voice that I had given my word and that therefore I should not be given any discouragement.

I was married on the 30th of April, 1907, in the palace church at Tsarskoe Selo. The night before I slept ill and in the early morning I awoke in a mood of sadness and depression. The events of the day passed more like a dream than a reality. As in a dream I allowed myself to be dressed in my white satin wedding gown and floating veil, and still in a dream I knelt before their Majesties who blessed me, holding over my head a small ikon. Then began the marriage procession through the long corridors to the church. First walked Count Fredericks, master of ceremonies of the Court. Then came their Majesties, arm in arm, with my little boy cousin, Count Karloff, carrying a holy image. Then I, walking with my father. I must have shown by my excessive pallor the anxiety I felt, for on the stairs the Empress looked at me with concern and having caught my eye smiled brightly and glanced upward reassuringly at the bright sky.

During the ceremony I stood quite still like a manikin, gazing at my bridegroom as at some stranger. I had one moment of faint amusement when the officiating priest, who was very near-sighted, mistook the best man for the bridegroom addressing us affectionately as "my dear children." The Empress, as my matron of honor, stood at my left hand with the four young Grand Duchesses, and two others, the children of Grand Duke Paul. One of these was the Grand Duke Dmitri, who was destined to grow up to take part in the assassination of Rasputine. On the day of my marriage he was just a dear little boy, wide-eyed with the excitement of being one of a wedding party. After the ceremony there was tea with the Emperor and the Empress, and as usual when she and I parted there was an affectionate little note pressed into my hand. How like an angel she looked to me that day, and how hard it was for me to turn away from her and to go away with my husband. There was a family dinner that night in our home in Petrograd, and afterwards we went away for a month into the country.

It is a hard thing for a woman to tell of a marriage which from the first proved to be a complete mistake, and I shall say only of my husband that he was the victim of family abnormalities which in more than one instance manifested themselves in madness. My husband's nervous system had suffered severely in the rigors of the Japanese War, and there were many occasions when he was not at all responsible for what he did. Often for days together he kept his bed refusing to speak to anyone. One night things became so threatening that I could not forbear telephoning my fears to the Empress, and she, to my joy, responded by driving instantly to the house in her evening gown and jewels. For an hour she stayed with me comforting me with promises that the situation should, in one way or another, be relieved.

In August the Emperor and Empress invited us both to go for a cruise on the *Standert*, and sailing through the blue Finnish fjords it did seem for a time that I should find peace. But one day a terrible thing happened, possibly an accident, but if so a very strange one, as we had on board an uncommonly able Finnish pilot. We were seated on deck at tea, the band playing, a perfectly calm sea running, when we felt a terrific shock which shook the yacht from stem to stern and sent the tea service crashing to the deck. In great alarm we sprang to our feet only to feel the yacht listing sharply to larboard. In an instant the decks were alive with sailors obeying the harsh commands of the captain, and helping the suite to look to the safety of the women and children. The fleet of torpedo boats which always surrounded the yacht made speed to the rescue and within a few minutes the children and their nurses and attendants were taken off. Not knowing the exact degree of the disaster, the Empress and I hastened to the cabins where we hurriedly tied up in sheets all the valuables we could collect. We were the last to leave the poor *Standert*, which by that time was stationary on the rocks.

We spent the night on a small vessel, the *Asia*, the Empress taking Alexei with her in one cabin and the Emperor occupying a small cabin on deck. The little Grand Duchesses were crowded in a cabin by themselves, their nurses and attendants finding beds where they could. The ship was far from clean and I remember the Emperor, rather disheveled himself, bringing basins of water to the Empress and me in which to wash our faces and hands. We had some kind of a dinner about midnight and none of us passed an especially restful night. The next day came the yacht *Alexandria* on which we spent the next two weeks. A fortnight was required to get the ill-fated *Standert* off the rocks on which she had so mysteriously been driven. From the *Alexandria* and later to the *Polar Star,* to which we had been transferred, we watched the unhappy yacht being carefully removed from her captivity. We had not been very comfortable on the *Alexandria* because there was not nearly enough cabin room for our rather numerous company. The Empress occupied a cabin, the Tsarevitch and his sailor another one adjoining. The four little Grand Duchesses did as well as they could in one small cabin, while the Emperor slept on a couch in the main salon. As for me, I slept in a bathroom. Most of the suite found quarters on a Finnish ship which stood by.

After our return to Peterhof my husband became worse rather than better and his physician advised him to spend some time in a sanatorium for nervous patients in Switzerland. He left, but on coming back to Russia was noticeably in worse condition than before. In the hope that active service would be of benefit to his shattered nerves and disordered brain he was ordered to sea, but even this expedient proved of little benefit. After a year of intense suffering and humiliation my unhappy marriage, with the full approval of their Majesties and of my parents, was dissolved.

I kept my little house in Tsarskoe Selo, its modest furnishings beautified by many gifts from the Empress. Among these gifts were some charming pictures and six exquisitely embroidered antique chairs. A silver-laden tea table helped to make the salon cozy, and I have many happy memories of intimate teas to which the Empress sent fruit and the Emperor the cherry brandy which he especially affected.

The little house, however, was far from being the luxurious palace in which I have often been pictured as living. As a matter of fact, it was frightfully cold in winter because the house had no stone foundation but rested on the frozen earth. Sometimes when the Emperor and Empress came to tea we sat with our feet on the sofa to keep warm. Once the Emperor jokingly told me that after a visit to my house he kept himself from freezing only by going directly to a hot bath.

The summer of 1908 the Emperor and Empress paid an official visit to England, but on their return they sent for me and again I spent a happy holiday on the yacht. Not altogether happy, however, for

THE EMPEROR AND EMPRESS IN A QUIET HOUR ON BOARD THE *STANDERT*. Photograph by Mme. Viroubova.

THE EMPRESS DISTRIBUTING PRESENTS AT THE END OF A CRUISE ON THE IMPERIAL YACHT *STANDERT*.

towards the end of the cruise my poor friend General Orloff, then near his death from tuberculosis, came to say good-bye to his Sovereigns.

Correct in his uniform and all his orders the fine old soldier bade us all a brave farewell before leaving for Egypt, where he well knew that his end awaited him. Peace to his honored ashes. He lies buried at Tsarskoe Selo, where the Emperor and Empress often visited his grave. Poor Orloff, he too suffered from the malicious gossip of the Court where his honest admiration of the Empress was deliberately misinterpreted and assoiled. I can bear witness, and I do, that his greatest devotion was to the Emperor, his old comrade in arms, the friend of his youthful days.

CHAPTER IV

IN the autumn of 1909 I went for the first time to Livadia, the country estate of the Imperial Family in the Crimea. This part of Russia, dearer to all of the Tsars than any other, is a small peninsula, almost an island, surrounded on the west and south by the Black Sea and on the east by the Sea of Asov. A range of high hills protects it from the cold winds of the north and gives it a climate so mild and bland as to be almost sub-tropical. The Imperial estate, which occupies nearly half the peninsula, has always been left as far as possible in its natural condition of unbroken forests, wild mountains, and valleys. There was at the time of which I write but one short railroad in the whole of the Crimea, a short line running from Sevastopol, the principal port of the Black Sea, northward to Moscow. All other journeys had to be taken by carriage, motor cars, or on horseback.

The natural beauties of the Crimea would be difficult to exaggerate. The mountains, dark with pines, snow-covered during most of the year, make an imposing background for the profusion of flowering trees, shrubs and vines, making the valleys and plains one continuous garden. The vineyards of the Crimea are, or were previous to the Revolution, equal to any in Italy or southern France. What they became afterwards God knows. But certainly up to the summer of 1914, when I saw them last, the vine-clad hills and valleys of the Crimea were an earthly Paradise, as lovely and as peaceful as the mind can picture. From the grapes of the Crimea were distilled the best wines in Russia, among others an excellent champagne and a delicious sweet wine of the muscat variety.

Almost every kind of fruit flourished in the valleys, and in spring the wealth of blossoms, pink and white, of apples, cherries, peaches, almonds, made the whole countryside a perfumed garden, while in autumn the masses of golden fruit were a wonder to behold. Flowers bloomed as though they were the very soul of the fair earth. Never have I seen such roses. They spread over every building in great vines as strong as ivy, and they scattered their rich petals over lawns and pathways in fragrance at times almost overpowering. There was another flower, the glycinia, which grew on trailing vines in grapelike clusters, deep mauve in hue, the favorite color of the Empress. This flower, too, was intensely fragrant, as were the violets which in spring literally carpeted the plains. Imagine these valleys and plains, with their vineyards and orchards, their tall cypress trees and trailing roses, sloping down to a sea as blue as the sky and as gentle as a summer day, and you have a picture, imperfectly as I have painted it, of the country retreat of the Romanoffs. Here of all places in Russia they were loved and revered. The natives of the peninsula were Tartars, the men very tall and strong and the women almost invariably handsome. They were Mohammedans, and it was only within late years that the women had discarded their veils. Both men and women wore very picturesque dress, the men wearing round black fur caps and short embroidered coats over tight white trousers. It was the fashion for the women to dye their hair a bright red, over which they wore small caps and floating veils and adorning themselves with a wealth of silver bangles. These Tartars were an honest folk, absolutely loyal to the Tsar. They were wonderful horsemen, comparing favorably with the best of the Cossacks, and their horses, through long breeding and training, were natural pacers. To see a cavalcade of Tartars sweep by was to imagine a race of Centaurs come back to earth, so absolutely one was every horse and man.

The palace, as I saw it in 1909, was a large, old wooden structure surrounded by balconies, the rooms dark, damp, and unattractive. The only really sunny and cheerful room in the whole house was the dining room, where twice a day the suite met for luncheon and dinner. The Emperor usually presided at these meals, but the Empress being in bad health lunched privately with the Tsarevitch. The Empress had been for some time a victim of the most alarming heart attacks which she bravely concealed, not wishing the public to know her condition. Oftentimes when I remarked the blue whiteness of her hands, her quick, gasping breaths, she silenced me with a peremptory "Don't say anything. People need not know."

However, I was intensely relieved when at last she consented to have the daily attention of a special physician, this being the devoted Dr. Botkine, who accompanied the family in their Siberian exile, and shared their fate, whatever that fate may have been. Dr. Botkine, although a very able physician, was not a man of great social prominence, and when, at the Empress's request, I went to apprise him of his appointment as special medical adviser to their Majesties, he received the news with astonishment almost amounting to dismay. He began his administration by greatly curtailing the activities of the Empress, keeping her quietly in bed for long periods, and insisting on the use of a rolling chair in the gardens, and a pony chaise for longer jaunts abroad.

Life at Livadia in 1909 and in after years was simple and informal. We walked, rode, bathed in the sea, and generally led a healthful country life, such as the Tsar, eminently an outdoor man and a lover of nature, enjoyed to the utmost. We roamed the woods gathering wild berries and mushrooms which we ate at our al fresco teas, cooking the mushrooms over little campfires of twigs and dried leaves. The Emperor and his suite hunted a little, rode much, and played very good tennis. In this latter sport I was often the Emperor's partner and a very serious affair I had to make of each game. No conversation was allowed, and we played with all the gravity and intensity of professionals.

We had each year many visitors. In 1909 came sometimes to lunch the Emir of Bokhara, a big, handsome Oriental in a long black coat and a white turban glittering with diamonds and rubies. He seemed intensely interested in the comparative simplicity of Russian royal customs, and when he departed for his own land he distributed presents in true Arabian Nights' profusion, costly diamonds and rubies to their Majesties, and to the suite orders and decorations set with jewels. Nevertheless the souvenir of the Emir's visit to Livadia which I most prized was a photograph of himself for which he obligingly posed in the gardens. This photograph and hundreds of others which I took during the twelve years I spent with the Imperial Family I was obliged to leave behind me when I fled, a hunted refugee, across the Russian frontier. I have no hope of ever seeing any of them again.*

The 20th of October, the anniversary of the death of Alexander III, was always remembered by a solemn religious service held in the room where he died, the armchair in which he breathed his last being draped in heavy black. This death chamber was not in the main palace but in a smaller house adjoining, one which in 1909 was used as a lodging for the suite. The last part of our stay in the Crimea that year was not very gay. The Emperor left us for an official visit to the King of Italy, and on the day of his departure the Empress, greatly depressed, shut herself up in her own room refusing to see anyone, even the children. It was always to her an intolerable burden that she and the Emperor were obliged by etiquette to part from each other in public and to meet again after each absence in full view of the suite and often of the staring multitude.

This autumn was made sad also by one of the all too frequent illnesses of the unfortunate little Tsarevitch. The sufferings of the child on these occasions were so acute that everyone in the palace was rendered perfectly miserable. Nothing much could be done to assuage the poor boy's agony, and nothing except the constant love and devotion of the Empress gave him the slightest relief. We who could do nothing else for him took refuge in prayer and supplication in the little church near the palace. Mlle. Tutcheva, maid of honor to the young Grand Duchesses, read the psalms, while the Empress, the older girls, Olga and Tatiana, two of the Tsar's aides, and myself assisted in the singing. In the midst of our anxiety and distress during this illness of Alexei my father paid us a brief visit, bringing important reports to the Emperor, and this was at least a momentary bright hour in the sorrow of my existence. At Christmas time the Court returned to Tsarskoe Selo, both the Empress and the Tsarevitch by this time much improved in health.

The next time I went with their Majesties to the Crimea we found the estate transformed and greatly beautified by the substitution of a palace of white marble for the ancient and gloomy wooden buildings. The new palace was the work of the eminent architect, Krasnoff, who had also designed the palaces of the Grand Dukes Nicholas and George. In the two years Krasnoff had indeed worked marvels, not only in the palace, which was a gem of Italian Renaissance architecture, but in many smaller buildings, the whole constituting a town in itself, harmonious in material and design.

* Happily many of these photographs were later recovered and appear among illustrations of this volume.

I shall never forget the day we landed in Yalta, and the glorious drive through the bright spring sunshine to the palace. Before the carriage rode an old Tartar of the Crimea, one of the tribe I described earlier in this chapter. To ride before the Tsar's carriage was an ancient prerogative of these honest and loyal people, a prerogative which had to be resigned when carriages gave way to motor cars. No Tartar horse could have kept pace with, much less have preceded, a motor car of Nicholas II, for he always insisted on driving at a terrifying speed. But as late as 1911 he kept up the old custom of driving from Yalta to Livadia.

We drove, as I say, through the dazzling sunshine and under the fresh green trees of springtime until the white palace, set in gardens of blooming flowers and vines, burst on our delighted eyes. Russian fashion we proceeded first to the church, from whence in procession we followed the priests to the anointing and blessing of the new dwelling. The first day I spent with the Empress superintending the hanging of pictures and ikons, placing familiar and homely objects, photographs and souvenirs, so necessary to make a dwelling place out of an empty house, even though it be a royal palace. On the second floor were the private apartments of the family, including a small salon. The apartments of the Empress were furnished in light wood and pink chintzes and many vases and jars always kept full of the pink and mauve flowers she loved. From the windows of her boudoir one looked out on the wooded hills, and from the bedroom there was an enchanting view of the sparkling sea. To the right of the Empress's boudoir was the Emperor's study, furnished in green leather with a large writing table in the center of the room. On this floor also was the family dining room, the bedrooms of the Tsarevitch and of the Grand Duchesses and their attendants, a large day room for the use of the children, and a big white hall or ballroom, seldom used.

Below were the rooms of state, drawing rooms and dining rooms, all in white, the doors and windows opening on a marble courtyard draped with roses and vines which almost covered an antique Italian well in the center of the court. Here the Emperor loved to walk and smoke after luncheon, chatting with his guests or with members of the household. The whole palace, including the rooms of state, were lightly, beautifully furnished in white wood and flowered chintzes, giving the effect of a hospitable summer home rather than a palace.

That autumn was marked by a season of unusual gaiety in honor of the coming of age, at sixteen, of the Grand Duchess Olga, who received for the occasion a beautiful diamond ring and a necklace of diamonds and pearls. This gift of a necklace to the daughter of a Tsar when she became of age was traditional, but the expense of it to Alexandra Feodorovna, the mother of four daughters, was a matter of apprehension. Powerless to change the custom, even had she wished to do so, she tried to ease the burden on the treasury by a gradual accumulation of the jewels. By her request the necklaces, instead of being purchased outright when the young Grand Duchesses reached the age of sixteen, were collected stone by stone on their birthdays and name days. Thus at the coming-out ball of the Grand Duchess Olga she wore a necklace of thirty-two superb jewels which had been accumulating for her from her babyhood.

It was a very charming ball that marked the introduction to society of the oldest daughter of the Tsar. Flushed and fair in her first long gown, something pink and filmy and of course very smart, Olga was as excited over her début as any other young girl. Her hair, blonde and abundant, was worn for the first time coiled up young-lady fashion, and she bore herself as the central figure of the festivities with a modesty and a dignity which greatly pleased her parents. We danced in the great state dining room on the first floor, the glass doors to the courtyard thrown open, the music of the unseen orchestra floating in from the rose garden like a breath of its own wondrous fragrance. It was a perfect night, clear and warm, and the gowns and jewels of the women and the brilliant uniforms of the men made a striking spectacle under the blaze of the electric lights. The ball ended in a cotillion and a sumptuous supper served on small tables in the ballroom.

This was a beginning of a series of festivities which the Grand Duchess Olga and a little later on her sister Tatiana enjoyed to their utmost, for they were not in the least like the conventional idea of princesses, but simple, happy, normal young girls, loving dancing and parties and all the frivolities which make youth bright and memorable. Besides the dances given at Livadia that year, large functions attended by practically everyone in the neighborhood who had Court entrée, there were a number of very brilliant balls given in honor of Olga and Tatiana after the family returned to Tsarskoe Selo. Two of these were given by the Grand Dukes Peter and George and the girls enjoyed them so much that they begged for another before Christmas. This time it was Grand Duke Nicholas who provided a most regal entertainment, preceded by a dinner for the suite, to which I was invited. I went because the Empress wished it, but I went rather unwillingly knowing that the atmosphere was not a friendly one. Their Majesties were at that time particularly friendly with Grand Duke George and his wife who was Princess Marie of Greece, as formerly they had been with Grand Dukes Peter and Nicholas and their wives, the Montenegran princesses, Melitza and Stana, of whom more must be written later on.

In relating the events of the coming of age of Olga and Tatiana I must not forget to mention affairs of almost equal consequence which occurred in the Crimea in that season of 1911. The climate of the Crimea was ideal for tuberculosis patients, and from her earliest married life the Empress had taken the deepest interest in the many hospitals and sanatoria which nestled among the hills, some of them almost within the confines of the Imperial estate. Before the beginning of the reign of Nicholas II and Alexandra Feodorovna these hospitals existed in numbers but they were not of the best modern type. Not satisfied with these institutions the Empress out of her own private fortune built and equipped new and improved hospitals, and one of the first duties laid on me when I first visited the Crimea was to spend hours at a time visiting, inspecting and reporting on the condition of buildings, nursing and care of patients. I was particularly charged with discovering patients who were too poor to pay for the best food and nursing, and one of each summer's activities when the family visited the Crimea was a bazaar or other entertainment for the benefit of these needy ones. Four great bazaars organized and largely managed by the Empress I particularly remember. The first of these was held in 1911 and the others in 1912, 1913, and 1914. For all of these bazaars the Empress and her ladies worked very hard and from the opening day the Empress, however pre-carious the condition of her health, always presided at her own table, disposing of fine needlework, embroidery, and art objects with energy and enthusiasm. The crowds around her booth were enormous, the people pressing forward almost frenziedly to touch her hand, her sleeve, her dress, enchanted to receive their purchases from the hand of the Empress they adored, for she was adored by the real Russian people, whatever the intriguing Court and the jealous political rivals of her husband thought of her. Often the crowd at these bazaars would beg for a sight of Alexei, and smiling with pleasure the Empress would lift him to the table where the child would bow shyly but sweetly, stretching out his hands in friendly greeting to the worshipping crowds. Indeed the people loved all the Imperial Family then, whatever changes were made in the minds of the many by the horrible sufferings of the War, by propaganda, and by the mania of the Revolution. The great mass of the Russian people loved and were loyal to their Sovereigns. No one who knew them at all can ever forget that.

Perhaps they were more universally loved in the Crimea than elsewhere because of the simplicity of their lives and the close touch they were able to keep with the people of the country. We went to Livadia again in 1912, in 1913, and last of all in the spring and summer of 1914. We arrived in 1912 in the last week of Lent, I think the Saturday before Palm Sunday. Already the fruit trees were in full bloom and the air was warm with spring. Twice a day we attended service in the church, and on Thursday of Holy Week, a very solemn day in the orthodox Russian calendar, their Majesties took communion, previously turning from the altar to the congregation and bowing on all sides. After this they approached the holy images and kissed them. The Empress in her white gown and cap looked beautiful if somewhat thin and frail, and it was very sweet to see the little Alexei helping his mother from her knees after each deep reverence. On Easter eve there was a procession with candles all through the courts of the palace and on Easter Sunday for two hours the soldiers, according to old custom, gathered to exchange Easter kisses with the Emperor and to receive each an Easter egg. Children from the schools came to salute in like manner the Empress. For their Majesties it was a long and fatiguing ceremony, but they carried it through with all graciousness, while the Imperial household looked on.

Such was the intimate, the patriarchal relation between the Tsar and his people, and such was the real soul of Russia before the Revolution. I have often read, in books written by Western authors, that the Tsar and all the Imperial Family lived in hourly terror of assassination, that they knew themselves hated by their people and were righteously afraid of them. Nothing could possibly be farther from the truth. Certainly neither Nicholas II nor Alexandra Feodorovna feared their people. The constant police supervision under which they lived annoyed them unspeakably, and never were they happier than when practically unattended they moved freely among the Russian people they loved. In connection with the

Empress's care for the tuberculosis patients in the Crimea there was one day every summer known as White Flower Day, and on that day every member of society, unless she had a very good excuse, went out into the towns and sold white flowers for the benefit of the hospitals. It was a day especially delightful to the Empress and, as they grew old enough to participate in such duties, to all the young Grand Duchesses. The Empress and her daughters worked very hard on White Flower Day, spending practically the whole day driving and walking, mingling with the crowd and vending their flowers as enthusiastically as though their fortunes depended on selling them all. Of course they always did sell them all. The crowds surged around them eager and proud to buy a flower from their full baskets. But the buyers were no whit happier than the sellers, that I can say with assurance.

Of course life in the Crimea was not all simplicity and informality. There were a great many visitors, most of them of rank too exalted to be treated with informality. I remember in particular visits of Grand Duke Ernest of Hesse, brother of the Empress, and his wife, Princess Eleanor. I remember also visits of the widowed Grand Duchess Serge, who had become a nun and was now abbess of a wonderful convent in Moscow, the House of Mary and Martha. When she visited Livadia masses were said daily in the palace church. I ought not, while speaking of visitors, to omit mention of the old Prince Galitzin, a very odd person, but strongly attached to the Tsar, to whom he presented a part of his own estate, some distance to Livadia, and to which we made a special excursion on the royal yacht. Another memorable excursion was to the estates of Prince Oldenbourg on the coast of Caucasia. The sea that day was very rough and by the time we reached our destination the Empress was so prostrated that she could not go ashore. It was a pity because she missed what to all the others was a remarkable spectacle, a grand holiday of the Caucasians who, in their picturesque costumes, crowded down to the shore to greet their Sovereigns. The whole countryside was in festival, great bonfires burning in all the hills and on all the meadows wild music and the most fascinating of native dances.

Such was life in the Crimea in the old, vanished days. Simple, happy, kind, and loyal, all that was best in Russia.

CHAPTER V

THESE yearly visits to the Crimea were diversified with holiday voyages on the *Standert*, and visits to relatives and close friends in various countries. In 1910 their Majesties visited Riga and other Baltic ports where they were royally welcomed, afterwards voyaging to Finnish waters where they received as guests the King and Queen of Sweden. This was an official visit, hence attended with considerable ceremony, exchange visits of the Sovereigns from yacht to warship, state dinners and receptions. At one of these dinners I sat next the admiral of the Swedish fleet, who was much depressed because during the royal salute to the Emperor one of his sailors had accidentally been killed.

In the autumn of 1910 the Emperor and Empress went to Nauheim, hoping that the waters would have a beneficial effect on her failing health. They left on a cold and rainy day and both were in a melancholy state, partly because of separation from the beloved home, and partly because of the quite apparent weakness of the Empress. On her account the Emperor showed himself deeply disturbed. "I would do anything," he said to me, "even to going to prison, if she could only be well again." This anxiety was shared by the whole household, even by the servants who stood in line on the staircase saying their farewells, kissing the shoulder of the Emperor and the gloved hand of the Empress.

I heard almost daily from Frieberg, where the family were stopping, letters from the Emperor, the Empress, and the children, telling me of their daily life. At length came a letter from the Empress suggesting that I join my father at Hombourg, not far distant, that we might have opportunity for occasional meetings. As soon as I arrived I telephoned the château at Frieberg, and the next day a motor car was sent to fetch me. I found the Empress improved in health but looking thin and tired from the rather rigorous cure. The Emperor, in his civilian clothes, looked unfamiliar and strange, but he wore the conventional citizen's garb because he as well as the Empress wished to remain as far as possible private persons. When the health of the Empress permitted she, with Olga and Tatiana, enjoyed going unattended to Nauheim, walking unnoticed through the streets, and gazing admiringly into shop windows like ordinary tourists. Once the Emperor and the young Grand Duchesses motored over to Hombourg and for a short hour walked about quite happily

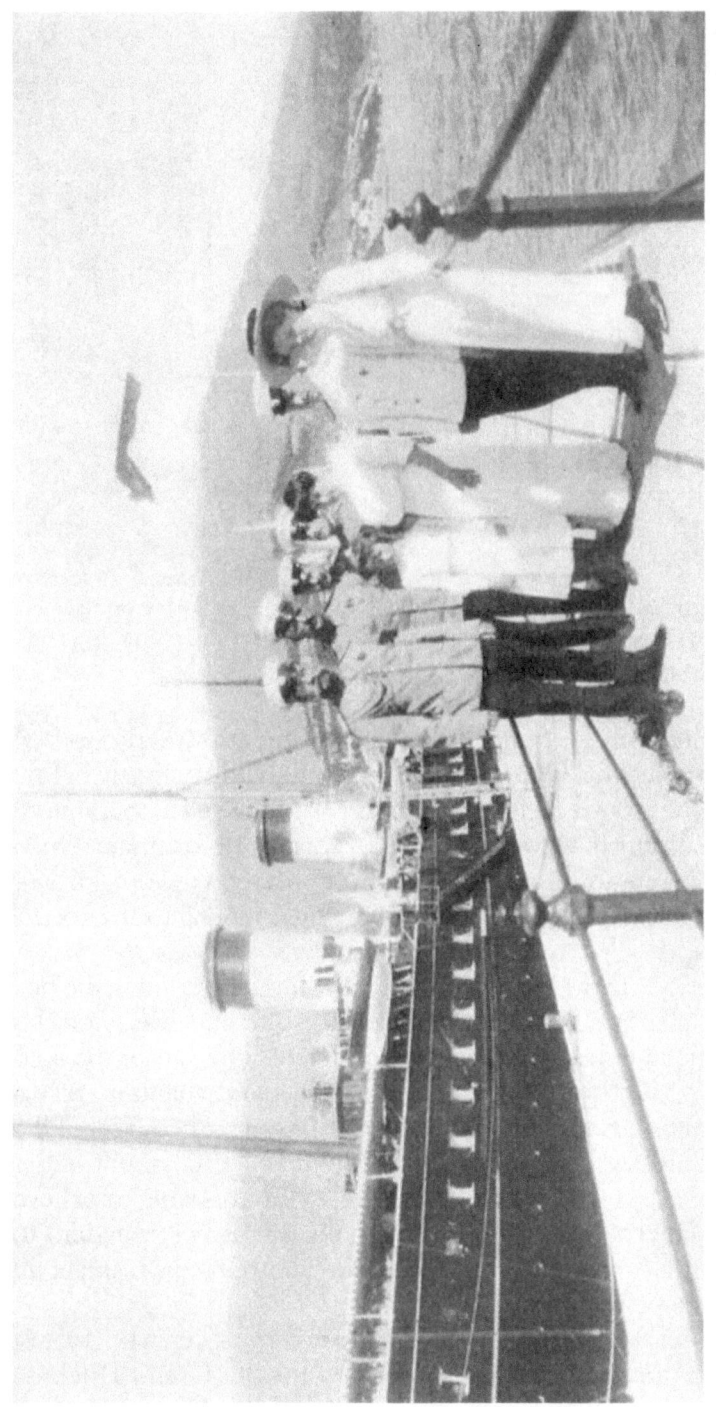

COMING IN AT YALTA, THE CRIMEA, 1911. THE EMPEROR, GRAND DUCHESSES OLGA AND ANASTASIE, MME. VIROUBOVA AND OFFICERS OF THE YACHT STANDERT. Photograph by the Empress.

THE EMPEROR, GRAND DUCHESSES OLGA AND MARIE STROLLING THROUGH HOMBURG IN 1910. THE EMPEROR OUT OF UNIFORM WAS ALMOST SAFE FROM RECOGNITION.

unobserved. Only too soon, however, the Emperor was recognized and our whole small party was obliged to flee precipitously before the gathering crowds and the ever enterprising news photographers. On some of our outings the Emperor was more fortunate. Once when we were wandering along a country road on the outskirts of Hombourg a wagon passing us dropped suddenly into the road a heavy box.

The carrier, try as he would, could not succeed in lifting the box back to its place until the Emperor went forward and, exerting all his strength, helped the man out of his difficulty. The carrier thanked his Majesty with every expression of respect and gratitude, recognizing him as a gentleman but never dreaming, of course, of his exalted station. To my expressions of amused enjoyment of the situation the Emperor said to me gravely: "I have come to believe that the higher a man's station in life the less it becomes him to assume any airs of superiority. I want my children to be brought up in this same belief."

Soon after this I returned to Russia to visit my sister, who had just borne her first baby, a little girl named for the Grand Duchess Tatiana, who acted as godmother for the child. My stay was not long, as letters from the Empress called me to Frankfort in order to be near her. On my arrival at Frankfort a surprise awaited me in the form of an invitation from the Grand Duke Ernest of Hesse to stay with his Imperial guests at his castle. At the castle gates I was welcomed by Mme. Grancy, the charming hofmistress of the Hessian Court, and by Miss Kerr, a bright and clever English girl, maid of honor to Princess Victoria. Miss Kerr took me at once to my apartments, near her own, and I quickly made myself at home. That night at dinner I sat between the Emperor and our host, the Grand Duke of Hesse. The company, which was most distinguished, included Prince Henry of Prussia, who that evening happened to be in rather a disagreeable mood, Princess Irene, Princess Victoria of Battenberg, and her beautiful daughter Princess Louise, Prince George of Greece, and the two semi-invalid sons of Prince and Princess Henry. The Empress was not present, being excused on account of her cure. Besides, it was understood that the Empress almost never appeared at state dinners.

The Grand Duke of Hesse I have always liked extremely both for his amiable disposition and for his many accomplishments. He was, and is still, an unusually gifted musician, a painter, and an artist craftsman seriously interested in the great pottery in Darmstadt, where his own designs are used. He has always been a man of liberal social ideals and his popularity among the people of Hesse not even the German Revolution has been powerful enough to overthrow. His wife, Princess Eleanor, when I knew her, was dignified and gracious and gifted with a genuine talent for dress. Prince Henry of Prussia, brother of the Kaiser and brother-in-law of the Empress, was a tall and handsome man, but inclined to be—let us say—temperamental. At times he was overbearing and very satirical, and at others friendly and charming. His wife was a small woman, simple in manner and of a kindly, unselfish nature. Princess Alice, daughter of Princess Victoria of Battenberg and wife of Prince Andrew of Greece, was a beautiful woman but unhappily quite deaf.

The Castle of Frieberg, which stands on a high hill overlooking a low valley and the little red-roofed town of Nauheim, is an ancient structure not particularly attractive either inside or out. There was nothing much for Grand Duke Ernest's guests to do in the way of amusement except to walk and drive. Of the Empress I saw rather less than we had planned, but sometimes late in the evenings the Emperor, the Empress, and myself met for Russian tea and for familiar talks before bedtime.

In October or November their Majesties returned to Tsarskoe Selo, the Empress greatly benefited by her cure. How happy we were to be once more at home, the Empress in her charming boudoir hung with mauve silk and fragrant with fresh roses and lilacs, I in my own little house which I dearly loved even though the floors were so cold. The opal-hued boudoir of the Empress, where we spent a great deal of our time, was a lovely, quiet place, so quiet that the footsteps of the children and the sound of their pianos in the rooms above were often quite audible. The Empress usually lay on a low couch over which hung her favorite picture, a large painting of the Holy Virgin asleep and surrounded by angels. Beside her couch stood a table, books on the lower shelf, and on the upper a confusion of family photographs, letters, telegrams, and papers. It was undeniably a weakness of the Empress that she was not in the least systematic about her correspondence. Intimate letters, it is true, she answered promptly, but others she often left for weeks un-touched. About once a month Madeleine, the principal maid of the Empress, would invade the boudoir and implore her mistress to clear up this heap of neglected correspondence. The Empress usually began by begging to be left alone, but in the end she always gave in to the importunities of the invaluable Madeleine. The Empress of course had a private secretary, Count Rostovseff, but it was one of her peculiarities that she preferred to handle her letters and telegrams before her secretary, and he seemed to accustom himself with ease to her dilatory ways.

It would be difficult to imagine two people more widely different on points of this kind than Nicholas II and Alexandra Feodorovna. Their private apartments were very close together, the Emperor's study, billiard and sitting room and his dressing room with a fine swimming bath, almost adjoining the apartments of the Empress. The big antechamber to the study, well furnished with chairs and tables and many books and magazines, looked out on a court, and here people who had business with the Emperor waited until they were summoned to his private room. The study was a perfect model of orderliness, the big writing table having every pen and pencil exactly in its place. The large calendar also with appointments written carefully in the Emperor's own hand was always precisely in its proper place. The Emperor often said that he wanted to be able to go into his study in the dark and put his hand at once on any object he knew to be there. The Emperor was equally particular about the appointments of his other rooms. The dressing table in the white-tiled bathroom, separated from the sitting room by a corridor and a small staircase, was as much a model of neatness as the study table, nor could the Emperor have tolerated valets who would not have kept his rooms in a condition of perpetual good order. Of course the ample *garderobes*, where the gowns, wraps, hats, and jewels of the Empress and the innumerable uniforms of the Emperor were kept, were always in order because they were in the care of experienced servants and were rarely if ever visited by others than their responsible guardians.

The Emperor's combined billiard and sitting room was not very much used because the Emperor spent most of his leisure hours in his wife's boudoir. But it was in the billiard room that the Emperor kept his many albums of photographs, records of his reign. These albums bound in green with the Imperial monogram, contained photographs taken over a period of twenty years. The Empress had her own albums full of equally priceless records, priceless from the historian's standpoint at any rate, and each of the children had their own. There was an expert photographer attached to the household whose only duty was to develop and print these photographs, which were, in almost every case, mounted by the royal photographer's own hand. This work used to be done, as a rule, on rainy days, either in the palace or on board the *Standert*. The Emperor, as usual, was neater about this work of pasting photographic prints than any other member of the household. He could not endure the sight of the least drop of glue on a table. As might be expected of so orderly a person the Emperor was slow about almost everything he did. When the Empress wrote a letter she did it very quickly, holding her portfolio on her knees on her *chaise longue*. When the Emperor wrote a letter it was a matter of hours before it was completed. I remember once at Livadia the Emperor retiring to his study at two o'clock to write an important letter to his mother. At five, the Empress afterwards told me, the letter remained unfinished.

The private life of the Imperial Family in these years before the War was quiet and uneventful. The Empress never left her room before noon, it being her custom, since her illness, to read and write propped up on pillows on her bed. Luncheon was at one o'clock, the Emperor, his aide-de-camp for the day, the children, and an occasional guest attending. After luncheon the Emperor went at once to his study to work or to receive visitors. Before tea time he usually went for a brisk walk in the open.

At half past two I came to the Empress, and if the weather was fine and she well enough, we went for a drive or a walk. Otherwise we read or worked until five, when the family tea was served. Tea was a meal in which there was never the slightest variation. Always appeared the same little white-draped table with its silver service, the glasses in their silver standards, and for the rest simply plates of hot bread and butter and a few English biscuits. Never anything new, never any surprises in the way of cakes or sweetmeats. The only difference in the Imperial tea table came in Lent, when butter and even bread made with butter disappeared, and a small dish or two of nuts was substituted. The Empress often used gently to complain, saying that other people had much more interesting teas, but she who was supposed to have almost unlimited power, was in reality quite unable to change a single deadly detail of the routine of the Russian Court, where things had been going on almost exactly the same for generations. The same arrangement of furniture in the state rooms, the same braziers of incense carried by footmen in the long corridors, the same house messengers in archaic costumes of red and gold with ostrich-feathered caps, and for all I know the same plates for hot bread and butter on the same tea table, were traditions going back to Catherine the Great, or Peter, or farther still perhaps.

Every day at the same moment the door opened and the Emperor came in, sat down at the tea table, buttered a piece of bread, and began to sip his tea. He drank every day two glasses, never more, never less, and as he drank he glanced over his telegrams and newspapers. The children were the only ones who found tea time at all exciting. They were dressed for it in fresh white frocks and colored sashes, and spent most of the hour playing on the floor with toys kept especially for them in a corner of the boudoir. As they grew older needlework and embroidery were substituted for the toys, the Empress disliking to see her daughters sitting with idle hands.

From six to eight the Emperor was busy with his ministers, and he usually came directly from his study to the eight o'clock family dinner. This was never a ceremonial meal, the guests, if any, being relatives or intimate friends. At nine the Empress, in the rich dinner gown and jewels she always wore, even on the most informal evenings, went to the bedroom of the Tsarevitch to hear him say his prayers and to tuck him into bed for the night. The Emperor worked until eleven, and until that hour the Empress, the two older Grand Duchesses, and I read, had a little music, or otherwise passed the time. Perhaps it is worth recording that bridge, or in fact any other card games, we never played. Nobody in the family cared at all for cards, and only a little, once in a while, for dominoes. At eleven the evening tea was served, and after that we separated, the Emperor to write his diary for the day, the Empress and the children to bed and I for home. All his life the Emperor kept a daily record of events, but like all the private papers of the Imperial Family, the diaries were seized by the Revolutionary leaders and probably (although I still hope to the contrary) destroyed. The diaries of Nicholas II, apart from any possible sentimental associations, should be possessed of great historical value.

Monotonous though it may have been, the private life of the Emperor and his family was one of cloudless happiness. Never, in all the twelve years of my association with them, did I hear an impatient word or surprise an angry look between the Emperor and the Empress. To him she was always "Sunny" or "Sweetheart," and he came into her quiet room, with its mauve hangings and its fragrant flowers, as into a haven of rest and peace. Politics and cares of state were left outside. Never were we allowed to speak of them. The Empress, on her part, kept her own troubles to herself. Never did she yield to the temptation to confide in him her perplexities, the foolish and spiteful intrigues of her ladies in waiting, nor even lesser troubles concerning the education and upbringing of the children. "He has the whole nation to think about," she often said to me. The only care she brought to the Emperor was the ever precarious health of Alexei, but this the whole family constantly felt, and it had to be spoken of very often. The Imperial Family was absolutely united in love and sympathy. I like to remember of the children, who adored their parents, that they never felt the slightest resentment of their mother's attachment for me. Sometimes I think the little Grand Duchess Marie, who especially worshipped her father, felt a little jealous when he invited me, as he often did, to accompany him on walks in the palace gardens. This may be imagination, and at all events the child's slight jealousy never interfered with our friendship.

I think the Emperor liked to walk with me because he had need to talk to someone he trusted of purely personal cares which troubled his mind and which he could share with few. Some of these cares were of old origin, but had never been forgotten. I remember once he began to tell me, almost without any preface, of the dreadful disaster which attended his coronation, a panic, induced by bad management of the police, in the course of which scores of people were crushed to death. At the very hour of this fatal accident the coronation banquet took place, and the Emperor and Empress, despite their grief and horror, were obliged to take part in it exactly as though nothing had happened. The Emperor told me with what difficulty they had concealed their emotions, often having to hold their serviettes to their faces to hide their streaming tears.

One of the happiest memories of my life at Tsarskoe Selo were the evenings when the Emperor, all cares past and present forgot, sat with us in the Empress's boudoir reading aloud from the work of Tolstoy, Tourgenieff, or his favorite Gogol. The Emperor read extremely well, with a pleasant voice and a remarkably clear enunciation. In the years of the Great War, so full of anguish and apprehension, the Emperor found relief in reading aloud amusing stories of Averchenko and Teffy, Russian humorists who perhaps have not yet been translated into foreign tongues.

Before the War the Emperor was pictured far and wide as a cruel tyrant deliberately opposed to the interests of his people, while the Empress appeared as a cold, proud woman, a *malade imaginaire*, wholly indifferent to the public good. Both of these pictures are cruelly misrepresentative. Nicholas II and his wife were human beings, with human faults and failings like the rest of us. Both had quick tempers, not invariably under perfect control. With the Empress temper was a matter of rapid explosion and equally sudden recovery. She was often for the moment furiously angry with her maids whom too often she discovered in insincerities and deceit. The Emperor's anger was slower to arouse and much slower to pass. Ordinarily he was the kindest and simplest of men, not in the least proud or over-conscious of his exalted position. His self-control was so great that to those who knew him little he often appeared absent-minded and indifferent. The fact is he was so reserved that he seemed to fear any kind of self-revealment. His mind was singularly acute, and he should have used it more accurately to gauge the characters of persons surrounding him. It was entirely within his mental powers to sense the atmosphere of gossip and calumny that surrounded the Court during the last years, and certainly it was within his power to put a stop to idle and malicious talk. But it was rarely possible to arouse him to its importance. "What high-minded person would believe such nonsense?" was his usual comment. Alas! he little realized how few were the really high-minded people who, in the last years of the Empire, surrounded his person or that of the Empress.

Sometimes the Emperor found himself obliged to take cognizance of the malicious gossip which made the Empress desperately unhappy and in the end poisoned the minds of thousands of really well-meaning and loyal Russians. Beginning as far back as 1909 the tide of treachery had begun to rise, and one of the earliest of those responsible for the final disaster, I regret to say, was a woman of the highest aristocracy, one long trusted and affectionately regarded by the Imperial Family. Mlle. Sophie Tutcheff, a protégée of the Grand Duchess Serge, and a lady who was a general over-governess to the children, was perhaps the first of all the intriguing courtiers of whom I have positive knowledge. Mlle. Tutcheff belonged to one of the oldest and most powerful families in Moscow, and she was strongly under the influence of certain bigoted priests, especially that of her cousin, Bishop Vladimir Putiata, who for ten years had lived in Rome as official representative of the Russian Church. It was he, I firmly believe, who inspired in Mlle. Tutcheff her antipathy to the Empress and her evil reports concerning the life of the Imperial Family. Mlle. Tutcheff, either of her own accord or encouraged by her relative, was continually opposed to what she called the English upbringing of the Imperial children. She wished to change the whole system, make it entirely Slav and free from any imported ideas.

Mlle. Tutcheff was, I believe, the first person to create what afterwards became the international Rasputine scandal. At the time of her residence in the palace at Tsarskoe Selo Rasputine's influence had scarcely been felt at all by the Emperor or Empress, although he was an intimate friend of other members of the Romanoff family. But Mlle. Tutcheff spread abroad a series of the most amazing falsehoods in which Rasputine figured as a constant visitor and virtually the spiritual guardian of the Imperial Family. I do not wish to repeat these stories, but merely to give an idea of their preposterous nature I will say that she represented Rasputine as having the freedom of the nurseries and even the bedchambers of the young Grand Duchesses. According to tales purported to have their origin with her, Rasputine was in the habit of bathing the children and afterward talking with them, sitting on their beds.

I do not think the Emperor believed all these rumors, but he did believe that Mlle. Tutcheff was guilty of malicious gossip of his family, and he therefore summoned her to his study and rebuked her severely, asking her how she dared to spread idle and untrue stories about his children. Of course she denied having done anything of the sort, but she admitted that she had spoken ill of Rasputine. "But you do not know the man," protested the Emperor, "and in any case, if you had criticisms to make of anyone known to this household you should have made them to us and not to the public." Mlle. Tutcheff admitted that she did not know Rasputine, and when the Emperor suggested that before she spoke evil of him it might be well for her to meet him she haughtily replied: "Never will I meet him."

For a short time after this Mlle. Tutcheff remained at Court, but being a rather stupid and very obstinate woman, she continued her campaign of intrigue. She managed to influence Princess Oblensky, long a favorite lady in waiting, until she entirely estranged her from the Empress. She even began to speak to the children against their own mother, until the Empress, who felt herself powerless against the woman, actually refused to visit the nurseries, and when she wanted her children near her sent for them to come to her private apartments. Too well she knew the Emperor's extreme reluctance to dismiss any person connected with the Court, and she waited in silent pain until the scandal grew to such proportions that the Emperor could no longer ignore it. Then Mlle. Tutcheff was summarily dismissed and sent back to her home in Moscow.

So powerful was the influence of the Tutcheff family that this incident was magnified beyond all proper proportions, and the former over-governess of the Imperial children was represented as a poor victim of Rasputine, a man whom she had never seen and who probably never knew of her existence. The last I ever heard of Mlle. Tutcheff, who, by the way, was a niece of the esteemed poet Tutcheff, she was living in Moscow, under the special protection of the Bolshevik Government. Her cousin, the former Bishop Vladimir Putiata, I understand has for several years been a great favorite of those Communists who have prosecuted such brave and fearless opponents of church despoilment as the unhappy Patriarch Tikhon and others.

Of the Emperor I think it ought to be said that his education, under his governor, General Bogdanovitch, was calculated to weaken the will of any boy and to encourage in Nicholas II his natural reserve and what might be called indolence of mind. But this I know of him that after his marriage he became much more resolute of temper and much more gentle of manner than other members of his family. It is certain that he loved Russia and the Russian people with his whole soul, and yet, under the political system for centuries in force, he had often to leave to people whom he knew only superficially many important details of government. Unquestionably it was a fault of the Emperor that he was over-confident, and only too ready to believe what was told him by people whom he personally liked. He was impulsive in most of his acts and sometimes made important nominations on the impression of a moment. It goes without saying that many of his officials took advantage of this overconfidence and sometimes acted in his name without his knowledge or authority.

Only too well for her own happiness and peace of mind did the Empress Alexandra Feodorovna understand her husband. She knew his kind heart, his love for his country and his people, but she knew also how easily influenced he could be by men in whom he reposed confidence. She knew that too often his acts were governed by the last person he happened to consult. But for all this I wish to say that the Emperor never appeared to his friends as a weak man. He had qualities of leadership with very limited opportunities to exercise those qualities. In his own domain he was "every inch an Emperor." The whole Court, from the Grand Dukes down to the last petty official and intriguing maid of honor, recognized this and stood in real awe of their Sovereign. I have a keen recollection of an episode at dinner in which a certain young Grand Duke ventured to utter an ill-founded grievance against a distinguished general who had dared to rebuke his Highness in public. The Emperor instantly recognized this as a mere display of temper and egoism, and his contempt and indignation knew no bounds. He literally turned white with anger, and the unfortunate young Grand Duke trembled before him like an offending servant. Afterwards the still indignant Emperor said to me: "He may thank God that the Empress and you were present. Otherwise I could not have held myself in hand." Towards the end of the Russian tragedy in 1917 the Emperor had learned to hold himself almost too well in hand, to subdue and to conceal the commanding personality of which he was naturally possessed. It would have been far better if he had used his personality and his great charm of manner to offset the tide of intrigue and revolution which in the midst of a world war overcame the Empire.

As long as I knew him, whether in the privacy of the palace at Tsarskoe Selo, in the informal life of the Crimea, on the Imperial yacht, in public or in private, I was always conscious of the strong personality of the Emperor. Everybody felt it. I can instance one occasion at a great reception of the Tauride Zemstvo when two men present were deliberately resolved to behave in a disrespectful manner to the Emperor. But the moment he entered the room these men found themselves completely overpowered. Their manner changed and they showed in every subsequent word and action their shame and regret. At one time a group of Social Revolutionaries were able to put on a cruiser which the Emperor was to visit a sailor charged with his Sovereign's assassination. But when the opportunity came the man literally could not do the deed. For his "weakness" this poor wretch was afterwards murdered by members of his party.

The character of the Empress was quite different from that of her husband. She was less lovable to the many, and yet of a stronger fiber. Where he was impulsive she was usually cautious and thoughtful. Where he was over-optimistic she was inclined to be a bit suspicious, especially of the weak and self-indulgent aristocracy. It was generally believed that the Empress was difficult to approach, but this was never true of sincere and disinterested souls. Suffering always made a strong appeal to the Empress, and whenever she knew of anyone sad or in trouble her heart was instantly touched. Few people, even in Russia, ever knew how much the Empress did for the poor, the sick, and the helpless. She was a born nurse, and from her earliest accession took an interest in hospitals and in nursing quite foreign to native Russian ideas. She not only visited the sick herself, in hospitals, in homes, but she enormously increased the efficiency of the hospital system in Russia. Out of her own private funds the Empress founded and supported two excellent schools for training nurses, especially in the care of children. These schools were founded on the best English models, and were under the general supervision of the famous Dr. Rauchfuss and of head nurse Miss Puchkine, a near relative of the great poet Puchkine. I could enlarge at length on the many constructive philanthropies of the Empress, paid for by herself, hospitals, homes, and orphanages, planned in almost every detail by herself, and constantly visited and inspected. After the Japanese War she built a *Hôtel des Invalides*, in which hundreds of disabled men were taught trades. She also built a number of cottages with gardens for wounded soldiers and their families, most of these war philanthropies being under the supervision of a trusted friend, Colonel the Count Shoulenbourg of the Empress's favorite Lancers.

The Empress possessed a heart and a mind utterly incapable of dishonesty or deceit, consequently she could never tolerate either in other people. This naturally got her heartily disliked by people of society to whom deceit was a matter of long practice. Another quality condemned in the Empress because entirely misunderstood, was her care as to expenses. Brought up in the comparative poverty of a small German Court, the Empress never lost the habit of a cautious use of money. Quite as in private families, where economy is an absolute necessity, the clothing of the young Grand Duchesses when outgrown by the elders were handed down to the younger girls. In the matter of selecting gifts for guests, for relatives, or at holidays for the suite, the Emperor simply selected from the rich assortment sent to the palace objects which best pleased him. The Empress, on the other hand, always examined the price cards and considered before choosing whether the jewel or the fur or the bijou, whatever it was, was worth what was asked for it. The difference between the Emperor and the Empress in regard to money was a difference in experience. The Emperor, all his life, had had everything he wanted without ever paying a single ruble for anything. He never had any money, never needed any money. I can recall but one solitary instance in which the Tsar of all the Russias ever even felt the need of touching a kopeck of his illimitable riches. It was in 1911 when their Majesties began to attend services at the Feodorovsky Cathedral at Tsarskoe Selo. In this church it was the custom to pass through the congregations alms basins into which everyone, of course, dropped a contribution, large or small. The Emperor alone was entirely penniless, and embarrassed by his unique situation he made a representation to the proper authorities, after which at exact monthly intervals he was furnished with four gold pieces for the alms basin of the Feodorovsky Cathedral. If he happened to attend an extra service he had to borrow his contribution from the Empress.

But if the Emperor carried no money in his pockets it was well enough known that he commanded vast sums, and it was characteristic of the sycophants who surrounded him that he was constantly importuned for "loans," for money to help out gambling or otherwise impecunious officers who, aware of the Emperor's great love for the army, played on it to their advantage. One day when the Emperor was taking his usual brisk walk through the grounds before tea a young officer who had managed to conceal himself in the shrubbery sprang out, threw himself on his knees, and threatened to kill himself on the spot unless the Emperor granted him a sum of money to clear the desperate wretch of some reckless deed. The Emperor was frightfully enraged—but he sent the man the money demanded.

The Empress had always handled money and knew quite well how to spend it wisely. From the depths of her honest soul she despised the use of money to buy loyalty and devotion. For a long time after my first formal service as maid of honor, with the usual salary, I received from her Majesty literally nothing at all. From my parents I had the income from my dowry, four hundred rubles a month, a sum entirely inadequate to pay the running expenses of my small establishment with its three absolutely indispensable servants, and at the same time to dress myself properly as a member of the Court circle. The Empress's brother, Grand Duke Ernest of Hesse, was one of the first of her intimates to point out to her the difficulties of my position, and to suggest to her that I be given a position at Court. The suggestion was not welcomed by Alexandra Feodorovna. "Is it not possible for the Empress of Russia to have one friend?" she cried bitterly, and she reminded her brother that her relation and mine were not without precedent in Russia. The Empress Dowager had a friend, Princess Oblensky; also the Empress Marie Alexandrovna, wife of Alexander III, had in Mme. Malzoff an intimate associate, and neither of these women had had any Court functions. Why should she not cherish a friendship free from all material considerations? However, after her brother and also Count Fredericks, Minister of the Court, had pointed out to her that it was scarcely proper that the Empress's best friend and confidante should wear made-over gowns and go home from the palace on foot at midnight because she had no money for cabs, the Empress began to relent a little. At first her change of attitude took the form of useful gifts bestowed at Christmas and Easter, dress patterns, furs, gloves, and the like. Finally one day she asked me to discuss with her the whole subject of my expenses. Making me sit down with pencil and paper, she commanded me to set forth a complete budget of my monthly expenditures, exactly what I paid for food, service, light, fire, and clothing. The domestic budget, apart from my small income, came to two hundred and seventy rubles a month, and at the orders of the Empress I was thereafter furnished monthly with the exact sum of two hundred and seventy rubles. It never occurred to her to name the amount in round numbers of three hundred rubles. Nor did it occur to me except as a matter of faint amusement. Of course I was often embarrassed for money even after I became possessed of this regular income, and even later when it was augmented by two thousand rubles a year for rent, and it often wrung my heart to have to say no to appeals for money. I knew that I appeared selfish and hard-hearted. The truth was that I was simply impecunious.

MLLE SOFIA TUTCHEFF

CHAPTER VI

THE year 1912, although destined to end in the almost fatal illness of the Tsarevitch, began happily for the Imperial Family. Peaceful and busy were the winter and spring, the Emperor engaged as usual with the affairs of the Empire, the Empress, as far as her health permitted, superintending the education of her children, and all of them busy with their books and their various tutors. Of the education and upbringing of the children of Nicholas II and the Empress Alexandra Feodorovna it should be said that while nothing was omitted to make them most loyal Russians, the educational methods employed were cosmopolitan. They had French, Swiss, and English tutors, but all their studies were under the superintendence of a Russian, the highly cultured M. Petroff, while for certain branches such as physics and natural science they were privately instructed in the gymnasium of Tsarskoe Selo. The first teacher of the Imperial children, she from whom they received their elementary education, was Miss Schneider, familiarly called "Trina," a native of one of the Baltic states of the Empire. Miss Schneider first came into service, years before the marriage of the Emperor and Empress, as instructor in the Russian language to Elizabeth, Grand Duchess Serge. Afterwards she taught Russian to the young Empress, and was retained at Court as reader to her Majesty. "Trina" was rather a difficult person in some ways, taking every advantage of her privileged position, but she was undeniably valuable and was heart and soul in her devotion to the family. She accompanied them to Siberia and there disappeared with them.

Perhaps the most valued of the instructors was M. Pierre Gilliard, whose book "Thirteen Years at the Russian Court" has been published in several languages and has been very well received. M. Gilliard, a Swiss gentlemen of many accomplishments, came first to Tsarskoe Selo as teacher of French to the young Grand Duchesses. Afterwards he became tutor to the Tsarevitch. M. Gilliard lived in the palace, and enjoyed to the fullest extent the confidence and affection of their Majesties. Mr. Gibbs, the English tutor, was also a great favorite. Both of these men followed the family into exile and remained faithful and devoted friends until forcibly expelled by the Bolsheviki.

In his book M. Gilliard has recorded that he was never able to teach the Grand Duchesses to speak a fluent French. This is true because the languages used in the family were English and Russian, and the children never became interested in any other languages. "Trina" was supposed to teach them German but she had less success with that language than M. Gilliard with French. The Emperor and Empress spoke English almost exclusively, and so did the Empress's brother, the Grand Duke of Hesse and his family. Among themselves the children usually spoke Russian. The Tsarevitch alone, thanks to his constant association with M. Gilliard, mastered the French language.

Every detail of the education of her children was supervised by the Empress, who often sat with them for hours together in the schoolroom. She herself taught them sewing and needlework, her best pupil being Tatiana, who had an extraordinary talent for all kinds of handwork. She not only made beautiful blouses and other garments, embroideries and crochets, but she was able on occasions to arrange her mother's long hair, and to dress her as well as a professional maid. Not that the Empress required as much dressing as the ordinary woman of rank and wealth. She had that kind of Victorian modesty that forbade any intrusion on the privacy of her dressing room. All that her maids were allowed to do was to dress her hair, fasten her boots, and put on her gown and jewels. The Empress had great taste in dress and always chose her jewels to finish rather than to ornament her costumes. "Only rubies to-day," she would command, or "pearls and sapphires with this gown."

The Empress and the children have been represented as surrounded by German servants, but this accusation is absolutely false. The chief woman of the household was Mme. Geringer, a Russian lady who came daily to the palace, ordered gowns, did all necessary shopping, paid bills, and attended to any business required by the Empress. The chief maid of the Empress was Madeleine Zanotti, of English and Italian parentage, whose home before she came to Tsarskoe Selo was in England. Madeleine was a woman of middle age, very clever, and as usual with one in her position, inclined to be tyrannical. Madeleine had charge of all the gowns and jewels of the Empress, and as I think I have related, she was often critical of her mistress's indolent habits in regard to correspondence, etc. A second maid was Tutelberg, "Toodles," a rather slow and quiet girl from the Baltic. She and Madeleine were mortal enemies, but they agreed on one thing at least, and that was that they would not wear caps and aprons. The Empress good-naturedly acquiesced and permitted simple black gowns and ribbon bows in the hair for her chief maids. There were three under maids, all Russians, and all perfectly devoted to the Imperial Family. These girls, who wore the regulation caps and white aprons, cared for the rooms of the Empress and the children. All the maids, when the Revolution came, remained faithful to the family, and one of them, as I shall tell later, performed the dangerous service of smuggling letters in and out of Siberia. One girl, Anna Demidoff, shared the fate of the family in 1918.

The Emperor had three valets, one of whom, Shalferoff, who had served Alexander III, turned spy during the Revolution. Another, old Raziesh, also a former servant of Alexander III, died in the service of Nicholas II, and was replaced by Chemoduroff, a fine and very loyal man. The third valet's name was Katoff. All three, as their names testify, were Russians, as were also the three men in the service of the Empress, Leo and Kondratief, both of whom died during the early days of the Revolution, and Volkoff, who followed the Royal exiles as far into Siberia as he was permitted by the Provisional Government.

The children's nurses were Russians, the head nurse being Marie Vechniakoff. Others I remember well were Alexandra, nicknamed "Shoura," a great favorite with the girls, Anna and Lisa, kind, faithful girls who spoke no word of any language except Russian. There were, of course, hundreds of house servants, and to my knowledge most, if not all of them, were Russians. The chef was a Frenchman, Cubat, a very great man in his profession. Sometimes, when an especially splendid dish had been prepared, Cubat was wont to introduce it, as it were, by standing magnificently in the doorway, clad in immaculate white linen, until the dish was served. Cubat became very wealthy in the Tsar's service, and now lives happily and luxuriously in his native France. He was, I believe, truly loyal to the Imperial Family, which is more than can be said for most of the servants. Their children were educated at the expense of the Emperor, and the majority, instead of choosing useful trades, elected to go to the universities, where they nearly all became Revolutionists.

In my father's opinion this was due to the fact that the Russian universities and higher schools offered little if any technical training. Recognizing this, the Empress created in Petrograd a technical school for boys and girls of the whole Empire. In this school the students were trained to become teachers in many useful handicrafts, and in addition to this normal academy the Empress established in many governments schools where boys and girls were perfected in the beautiful peasant arts of embroidery, dyeing, carving, and painting. I give these details because I think it only just to offset with facts the lying slanders of sensational writers who could not possibly have known anything of the intimate life of the Imperial Family of Russia but who have substituted propaganda for truth.

None of these sensational writers knew or tried to know how simple, not to say rigorous, was the régime followed by the Imperial children. All of them, even the delicate little Tsarevitch, slept in large, well-aired nurseries, on hard camp beds without pillows and with the least possible allowance of bedclothing. They had cold baths every morning and warm ones only at night. As a consequence of this simple life their manners were unassuming and natural without a single trace of *hauteur*. Although in 1912 the four girls were rapidly approaching womanhood—Olga was in her eighteenth year and Tatiana was nearly sixteen—their parents continued to regard them as children. The two older girls were spoken of as "the big ones," and were given many grown-up privileges, as for example, concerts and the theater to which the Emperor himself escorted them. The two younger Grand Duchesses and the Tsarevitch, "the little ones," were still in the nursery.

In the darkness of the mystery which surrounds the fate of these innocent children it is with poignant emotion that I recall them as they appeared, so full of life and joy, in those distant, yet incredibly near, days before the World War and the downfall of Imperial Russia. Of the four girls, Olga and Marie were essentially Russian, altogether Romanoff in their inheritance. Olga was perhaps the cleverest of them all, her mind being so quick to grasp ideas, so absorbent of knowledge that she learned almost without application or close study. Her chief characteristics, I should say, were a strong will and a singularly straightforward habit of thought and action. Admirable qualities in a woman, these same characteristics are often trying in childhood, and Olga as a little girl sometimes showed herself wilful and even disobedient. She had a hot temper which, however, she early learned to keep under control, and had she been allowed to live her natural life she would, I believe, have become a woman of influence and distinction. Extremely pretty, with brilliant blue eyes and a lovely complexion, Olga resembled her father in the fineness of her features, especially in her delicate, slightly tipped nose.

Marie and Anastasie were also blonde types and very attractive girls. Marie had splendid eyes and rose-red cheeks. She was inclined to be stout and she had rather thick lips which detracted a little from her beauty. Marie had a naturally sweet disposition and a very good mind. All three of these girls were more or less of the tomboy type. They had something of the innate brusqueness of their Romanoff ancestors, which displayed itself in a tendency to mischief. Anastasie, a sharp and clever child, was a very monkey for jokes, some of them at times almost too practical for the enjoyment of others. I remember once when the family was in their Polish estate in winter the children were amusing themselves at snowballing. The imp which sometimes seemed to possess Anastasie led her to throw a stone rolled in a snowball straight at her dearly loved sister Tatiana. The missile struck the poor girl fairly in the face with such force that she fell senseless to the ground. The grief and horror of Anastasie lasted for many days and permanently cured her of her worst propensities to practical jokes.

THE EMPEROR AND TSAREVITCH WALKING ON BOARD THE *STANDERT*. Photograph by the Empress.

THE TSAR, TSARINA, AND ALEXEI IN THE GARDENS OF TSARSKOE SELO, 1911.

THE TSAREVITCH IN COSSACK UNIFORM WITH HIS SAILOR, DEREVANKO

Tatiana was almost a perfect reincarnation of her mother. Taller and slenderer than her sisters, she had the soft, refined features and the gentle, reserved manners of her English ancestry. Kindly and sympathetic of disposition, she displayed towards her younger sisters and her brother such a protecting spirit that they, in fun, nicknamed her "the governess." Of all the Grand Duchesses Tatiana was with the people the most popular, and I suspect in their hearts she was the most dearly loved of her parents. Certainly she was a different type from the others even in appearance, her hair being a rich brown and her eyes so darkly gray that in the evening they seemed quite black. Of all the girls Tatiana was most social in her tastes. She liked society and she longed pathetically for friends. But friends for these high born but unfortunate girls were very difficult to find. The Empress dreaded for her daughters the companionship of oversophisticated young women of the aristocracy, whose minds, even in the schoolroom, were fed with the foolish and often vicious gossip of a decadent society. The Empress even discouraged association with cousins and near relatives, many of whom were unwholesomely precocious in their outlook on life.

I would not give the impression that these young daughters of the Emperor and Empress were forced to lead dull and uneventful lives. They were allowed to have their little preferences for this or that handsome young officer with whom they danced, played tennis, walked, or rode. These innocent young romances were in fact a source of amusement to their Majesties, who enjoyed teasing the girls about any dashing officer who seemed to attract them. The Grand Duchess Olga, sister of the Emperor, sympathized with her nieces' love of pleasure and often arranged tea parties and tennis matches for them, the guests, of course, being of their own choice. We had some quite jolly tea parties in my little house also. In the matter of dress, so important to young and pretty girls, the Grand Duchesses were allowed to indulge their own tastes. Mme. Brisac, an accomplished French dressmaker, made gowns for the Imperial Family, and through her the latest Paris models reached the palace. The girls, however, inclined towards simple English fashions, especially for outdoor wear. In summer they dressed almost entirely in white. Jewels they were too young to wear except on very great occasions. Each girl received on her twelfth birthday a slender gold bracelet which was afterwards always worn, day and night, "for good luck." I have described in a previous chapter the Russian custom of presenting each Grand Duchess, on her coming of age, with a pearl and diamond necklace, but this was worn only at state functions or very formal balls.

Alexei, the only son of the Emperor and Empress, a more tragic child than the last Dauphin of France, indeed one of the most tragic figures in history, was, apart from his terrible affliction, the loveliest and most attractive of the whole family. Because of his delicate health Alexei began life as a rather spoiled child. His chief nurse, Marie Vechniakoff, a somewhat over-emotional woman, made the mistake of indulging the child in every whim. It is easy to understand why she did so, because nothing more heart-rending could be imagined than the little boy's moans and cries during his frequent illnesses. If he bumped his head or struck a hand or foot against a chair or table the usual result was a hideous blue swelling indicating a subcutaneous hemorrhage frightfully painful and often enduring for days or even weeks.

At five Alexei was placed in charge of the sailor Derevanko, who for a long term of years remained his constant body servant and companion. Derevanko, while devoted to the boy, did not spoil him as his women nurses had done, and the man was so patient and resourceful that he often did wonders in alleviating the child's pain. I can still in memory hear the plaintive, suffering voice of Alexei begging the big sailor to "lift my arm," "put my leg up," "warm my hands," and I can see the patient, calm-eyed man working for hours on end to give the maximum of comfort to the little pain-racked limbs.

As Alexei grew older his parents carefully explained to him the nature of his illness and impressed on him the necessity of avoiding falls and blows. But Alexei was a child of active mind, loving sports and outdoor play, and it was almost impossible for him to avoid the very things that brought him suffering. "Can't I have a bicycle?" he would beg his mother. "Alexei, you know you can't." "Mayn't I play tennis?" "Dear, you know you mustn't." Often these hard denials of the natural play impulse were followed by a gush of tears as the child cried out: "Why can other boys have everything and I nothing?"

Suffering and self-denial had their effect on the character of Alexei. Knowing what pain and sacrifice meant, he was extraordinarily sympathetic towards other sick people. His thoughtfulness of others was shown in his beautiful courtesy to women and girls and to his elders, and in his interest in the troubles of servants and dependents. It was a failing of the Emperor that even when he sympathized with the troubles of others he was rather slow to take action, unless indeed the matter was really serious. Alexei, on the contrary, was always for immediate action. I remember an instance when a boy in service at the palace was discharged for some reason which I have quite forgotten. The story somehow reached the ears of Alexei, who immediately took sides with the boy and gave his father no rest until the whole case was reviewed and the culprit was forgiven and restored to duty. Alexei usually defended all offenders, yet when the day came when his parents, in deep distress, told him that Father Gregory, that is, Rasputine, had been killed by members of his own family the boy's grief was swallowed up in rage and indignation. "Papa," he exclaimed, "is it possible that you will not punish them? The assassins of Stolypine were hanged."

I ask the reader to remember that the Imperial Family firmly believed that they owed much of Alexei's improving health to the prayers of Rasputine. Alexei himself believed it. Several years before Rasputine had assured the Empress that when the boy was twelve years old he would begin to improve and that by the time he was a man he would be entirely well. The undeniable fact is that after the age of twelve Alexei did begin very materially to improve. His illnesses became farther and farther apart and before 1917 his appearance had changed marvelously for the better. He resembled in no way the invalid sons of his mother's sister, Princess Henry of Prussia, who suffered from his own terrible malady. What the best physicians of Europe had been unable to do in their case some mysterious force had done in the case of the Tsarevitch. His parents to whom the young boy was as their very heart's blood believed that the healing hand of God had wrought the cure, and that it was in answer to the supplication of one whose spirit was able to rise in higher flight than theirs or any other's. They knew of course that the boy was not yet entirely well, but they believed that he was getting well. Alexei believed this also and it is certain that he looked forward to a healthy, normal manhood.

Alexei, like his father, dearly loved the army and all the pageants of military display. He had every kind of toy soldier, toy guns and fortresses, and with these he played for hours, with his sailor companion Derevanko, or "Dina" as the boy called him, and with the few boy companions he was allowed. Two of these boys were sons of "Dina," and a third was the son of one of the family physicians, by coincidence also named Derevanko. In the last years before the

Revolution a few carefully selected boys, cadets from the Military School, were called to the palace to play with Alexei. These boys were warned of the danger of any rough play, and all were extremely mindful of their responsibility. It was because no other type of boy could be trusted to play with Alexei that the Empress did not often invite to the palace the children of the Grand Dukes. They were Romanoffs, brusque and rude in their manners, thoughtless of the feelings of others, and the Empress literally did not dare to leave them alone with her son. But because of her caution she was bitterly assailed by her enemies who spoke sneeringly of her preference for "low born" children over the aristocratic children of the family.

The Emperor and Empress and all the children were passionately fond of pets, especially dogs. The Emperor's inseparable companion for many years was a splendid English collie named Iman, and when in the natural course of time this dog died the Emperor was inconsolable. After that he had a fine kennel of collies but he never made a special pet of any dog. The favorite dog of the Empress was a small, shaggy terrier from Scotland. This dog's name was Eira, and, to tell the truth, I did not like the little animal at all. His dis-agreeable habit of darting from under chairs and snapping at people's heels was a trial to my nerves. Nevertheless the Empress doted on him, carried him under her arm even to the dinner table, and amused herself greatly talking to and playing with the dour little creature. When he fell ill and had to be mercifully killed she wept in real grief and pity. Alexei's pets were two, a silky little spaniel named Joy and a beautiful big gray cat, the gift of General Voyeikoff. It was the only cat in the household and it was a privileged animal, even being allowed to sleep on Alexei's bed. There were two other dogs, Tatiana's French bull and a little King Charlie which I contributed to the menagerie. Both of these dogs went with the family to Siberia, and Jimmie, the King Charles spaniel, was found shot to death in that dreadful deserted house in Ekaterinaburg.

How far, how unbelievably far away now seem those peaceful days of 1912, when we were watching the Tsar's daughters growing towards womanhood, and even in our minds speculating on possible marriages for them. Their prospects as far as marriage was concerned, I must say, were rather vague. Foreign matches, because of religion and even more because of the girls' devotion to home and country, were almost out of the question, and suitable husbands in Russia seemed to be entirely lacking. There was a time in his boyhood when Dmitri, son of the Tsar's uncle, Grand Duke Paul, was a great favorite with the Imperial Family. But Dmitri as he grew older became so dissipated that he quite cut himself off from the prospect of an alliance with any of the Grand Duchesses. There had once been a faint possibility of an engagement between Olga and Crown Prince Carol of Rumania. As early as 1910 the beautiful Queen Marie and her son visited Russia for the purpose of introducing the young people, but nothing came of the visit. In 1914 the family made a return visit to Rumania on the *Standert*, the Rumanian Royal family, including the old Queen, "Carmen Sylva," meeting the yacht at Constanza, on the Black Sea, and making a splendid fête which lasted for three days. This time the matter was seriously broached to Olga who, in her usual quick, straightforward manner, declined the match. In 1916 Prince Carol again visited the Russian Court, and now his young man's fancy rested on Marie. He made a formal proposal for her hand, but the Emperor, declaring that Marie was nothing more than a schoolgirl, good-naturedly laughed the Prince's proposal aside.

Not all these proposals ended so merrily. One day coming as usual to Peterhof, I found the Empress in tears. A formal proposal had just been received from the old Grand Duchess, Marie Pavlovna, aunt of the Emperor, for a marriage between her son Boris Vladimirovitch and Grand Duchess Olga. This young man, Prince Boris, was much better known in questionable circles in Paris than in the Court of Russia and the mere suggestion of a marriage with one of her daughters was enough to reduce the Empress to mortified tears. Of course the proposal was rejected, greatly to the wrath of Grand Duchess Marie Pavlovna, a Russian *grande dame* of the old school in which the debauchery of young men was regarded as a perfectly natural phenomenon. She never forgave the slight, as she chose to consider it, and later became one of the most active of the circle of intriguers which, from the safety of a foreign embassy in Petrograd, plotted the ruin of the Imperial Family and of their country.

In the summer of 1912 the family and their immediate household, including myself, went on another long cruise in Finnish waters. During the cruise the yacht was visited by the Empress Dowager of whom previously I had seen but little. I write with some hesitation about the Empress Dowager, who is still living, and for whom I entertain all due respect. She was, as I remember her then, a small, slender woman, not beautiful certainly, not as attractive as her sister,

Queen Alexandra of England, but with a great deal of presence and, when she chose to exert it, considerable personal charm. The Emperor she apparently loved less than her other children, especially her son, Grand Duke Michail, and the Empress I fear she loved not at all. To the children she was affectionate but a trifle distant. I am sure that she resented the fact that the first four children were girls, and there is little doubt that she felt bitterly the affliction of the heir. Possibly she felt in her secret heart that it should have been her own strong son Michail who was the acknowledged successor of Nicholas II. I say this from my own conjecture and observations and not from positive knowledge. Yet after events, I think, confirmed my opinion.

The Dowager Empress after the death of Alexander III relinquished with rather bad grace her position of reigning Empress. In fact she never did relinquish it altogether, always taking precedence on public occasions of Alexandra Feodorovna. Just why the Tsar consented to this I never knew, but certain it is that always, when the Imperial Family made a state entrance the Tsar appeared first with his mother on his arm, the Empress following on the arm of one of the Grand Dukes. Society generally approved this procedure, the Empress Mother enjoying all the popularity which the Empress lacked. There were actually in Russia two Courts, a large one represented by society and the Grand Dukes, and a small one represented by the intimate circle of the Emperor and Empress. In the one everything done by the Empress Mother was right and by the shy and retiring Empress wrong. In the small Court it was exactly the other way around, except that even in the palace a certain amount of petty intrigue always existed.

The visit to Finnish waters by the Empress Mother in 1912 was marred by no coldness or disharmony. When we went ashore for tennis the Emperor admonished us all to play as well as we could, "because Mama is coming." We lunched aboard her yacht and she dined with us on the *Standert*. On the 22d of July, which was her name day, as well as that of the little Grand Duchess Marie, she spent most of the day on the Emperor's yacht, and after luncheon I took a photograph of her sitting with her arm around the Emperor's shoulders, her two little Japanese spaniels at their feet. She made us dance for her on deck, photographing us as we danced. After tea the children performed for her a little French playlet which seemed to delight her. Yet that evening at dinner I could not help noticing how her fine eyes, so kind and smiling towards most of the company, clouded slightly whenever they were turned to the Emperor or the Empress. Still I must record that later, passing the open door of Alexei's cabin, I saw the Empress Mother sitting on the edge of the child's bed talking gaily and peeling an apple quite like any loving grandmother.

I do not pretend to understand the Empress Dowager or her motives, but, as far as I can judge, her chief weakness was love of power. She carried her insistence on precedence so far that the *chiffres* of the maids of honor of both Empresses bore the initials M. A. instead of A. M., which was the proper order. She wanted to be first in everything and could not bear to abdicate either power or influence. She never, I believe, understood her son's preference for a quiet, family life, or the changed and softened manners he acquired under the influence of his wife.

CHAPTER VII

IN the autumn of 1912 the family went to Skernevizi, their Polish estate, in order to indulge the Emperor's love for big-game hunting. In the vast forests surrounding the estate all kinds of game were preserved and the sport of hunting there was said to be very exciting. During the war these woods and all the game were des-troyed by the Germans, but until after 1914 Skernevizi was a favorite retreat of the Emperor. I had returned to my house in Tsarskoe Selo but I was not allowed long to remain there. A telegram from the Empress conveyed the disquieting news that Alexei, in jumping into a boat, had injured himself and was now in a serious condition. The child had been removed from Skernevizi to Spala, a smaller Polish estate near Warsaw, and to Warsaw I accordingly traveled. Here I was met by one of the Imperial carriages and was driven to Spala. Driving for nearly an hour through deep woods and over a heavy, sandy road I reached my destination, a small wooden house, something like a country inn, in which the suite was lodged. Two rooms had been set apart for me and my maid, and here I found Olga and Tatiana waiting to help me get settled. Their mother, they said, was expecting me, and without any loss of time I went with them to the palace.

I found the Empress greatly agitated. The boy was temporarily improved but was still too delicate to be taken back to Tsarskoe Selo. Meanwhile the family lived in one of the dampest, gloomiest palaces I have ever seen. It was really a large wooden villa very badly planned as far as light and sunshine were concerned. The large dining room on the ground floor was so dark that the electric lights had to be kept on all day. Upstairs to the right of a long corridor were the rooms of the Emperor and Empress, her sitting room in bright English chintzes being one of the few cheerful spots in the house. Here we usually spent our evenings. The bedrooms and dressing rooms were too dark for comfort, but the Emperor's study, also on the right of the corridor, was fairly bright.

As long as the health of little Alexei continued fairly satisfactory the Emperor and his suite went stag hunting daily in the forests of the estate. Every evening after dinner the slain stags were brought to the front of the palace and laid out for inspection on the grass. The huntsmen with their flaring torches and winding horns standing over the day's bag made, I was told, a very picturesque spectacle. The Emperor and his suite and most of the household used to enjoy going out after dinner to enjoy this fine sight. I never went myself, having a foolish love of animals which prevents enjoyment of the royal sport of hunting. I even failed to appreciate, as the head of the estate, kind Count Velepolsky, thought I should, the many trophies of the chase with which the corridors and apartments of the palace were adorned.

What I did enjoy was the beautiful park which surrounded the palace, and the rapid little river Pilitsa that flowed through it. There was one leafy path through which I often walked in the mornings with the Emperor. This was called the Road of Mushrooms because it ended in a wonderful mushroom bench. The whole place was so remote and peaceful that I deeply sympathized with their Majesties' irritation that even there they could never stir abroad without being haunted by the police guard.

Although Alexei's illness was believed to have taken a favorable turn and he was even beginning to walk a little about the house and gardens, I found him pale and decidedly out of condition. He occasionally complained of pain, but the doctors were unable to discover any actual injury. One day the Empress took the child for a drive and before we had gone very far we saw that indeed he was very ill. He cried out with pain in his back and stomach, and the Empress, terribly frightened, gave the order to return to the palace. That return drive stands out in my mind as an experience of horror. Every movement of the carriage, every rough place in the road, caused the child the most exquisite torture, and by the time we reached home he was almost unconscious with pain. The next weeks were endless torment to the boy and to all of us who had to listen to his constant cries of pain. For fully eleven days these dreadful sounds filled the corridors outside his room, and those of us who were obliged to approach had often to stop our ears with our hands in order to go about our duties. During the entire time the Empress never undressed, never went to bed, rarely even lay down for an hour's rest. Hour after hour she sat beside the bed where the half-conscious child lay huddled on one side, his left leg drawn up so sharply that for nearly a year afterwards he could not straighten it out. His face was absolutely bloodless, drawn and seamed with suffering, while his almost expressionless eyes rolled back in his head. Once when the Emperor came into the room, seeing his boy in this agony and hearing his faint screams of pain, the poor father's courage complete-ly gave way and he rushed, weeping bitterly, to his study. Both parents believed the child dying, and Alexei himself, in one of his rare moments of consciousness, said to his mother: "When I am dead build me a little monument of stones in the wood."

The family's most trusted physicians, Dr. Rauchfuss and Professor Fedoroff and his assistant Dr. Derevanko, were in charge of the case and after the first consultations declared the Tsarevitch's condition hopeless. The hemorrhage of the stomach from which he was suffering seemed liable to turn into an abscess which could at any moment prove fatal. We had two terrible moments in which this complication threatened. One day at luncheon a note was brought from the Empress to the Emperor who, pale but collected, made a sign for the physicians to leave the table. Alexei, the Empress had written, was suffering so terribly that she feared the worst was about to happen. This crisis, however, was averted. On the second occasion, on an evening after dinner when we were sitting very quietly in the Empress's boudoir, Princess Henry of Prussia, who had come to be with her sister in her trouble, appeared in the doorway very white and agitated and begged the members of the suite to retire as the child's condition was desperate. At eleven o'clock the Emperor and Empress entered the room, despair written on their faces. Still the Empress declared that she could not believe that God had abandoned them and she asked me to telegraph Rasputine for his prayers.

His reply came quickly. "The little one will not die," it said. "Do not allow the doctors to bother him too much." As a matter of fact the turning point came a few days later, the pain subsided, and the boy lay wasted and utterly spent, but alive.

Curiously enough there was no church on this Polish estate, but during the illness of the Tsarevitch a chapel was installed in a large green tent in the garden. A new confessor, Father Alexander, celebrated mass and after the first celebration he walked in solemn procession from the altar to the sickroom bearing with him holy communion for the sick boy. The Emperor and Empress were very much impressed with Father Alexander and from that time on they retained him in their private chapel at Tsarskoe Selo. He was a good man but not a brave one, for when the Revolution came, and the Emperor and the Empress sent for him to come to them, he confessed himself afraid to go. Poor man! His caution, after all, did not save him. He was shot by the Bolsheviki a year or two afterwards, on what pretext I do not know.

The convalescence of Alexei was slow and wearisome. His nurse, Marie Vechniakoff, had grown so hysterical with fatigue that she had to be relieved, while the Empress was so exhausted that she could hardly move from room to room. The young Grand Duchesses were tireless in their devotion to the poor invalid, as was also M. Gilliard, who read to him and diverted him hours on end. Gradually the distracted household assumed a more normal aspect. The Emperor, in Cossack uniform, began once more to entertain the officers of his Varsovie Lancers, commanded by a splendid soldier, General Mannerheim, of whom the world has heard much. As Alexei's health continued to improve there was even a little shooting, and a great deal of tennis which the girls, after their long confine-ment to the house, greatly enjoyed. All of us began to be happy again, but one day the Emperor called me into his study and showed me a telegram from his brother, Grand Duke Michail, in which the latter announced his morganatic marriage to the Countess Brassoff, of whom the Emperor strongly disapproved. It was not the marriage itself that so strongly disturbed the Emperor, but that Michail had solemnly given his word of honor that it would never take place. "He broke his word—his word of honor," the Emperor repeated again and again.

Another blow which the Emperor received at this time was the suicide of Admiral Chagin, commandant of the *Standert* and one of the closest friends of the family. The Admiral shot himself on account of an unhappy love affair, and deeply as the Emperor mourned his death he was even more indignant at the manner of it. Russians, I know, are inclined to morbidity, and suicide with them is not an uncommon thing. But Nicholas II always regarded it as an act of dishonor. "Running away from the field of battle," was his characterization of such an act, and when he heard of Chagin's suicide he gave way to a terrible mood of anger and grief. Speaking of both Michail and Chagin he said bitterly: "How, in the midst of the boy's illness and all our trouble, how could they have done such things?" The poor Emperor, to whom every failure of those he loved and trusted came as an utterly unexpected blow, how near was his hour of complete and final disillusionment of nearly all earthly loyalties.

We had a few weeks of peaceful enjoyment before leaving Spala that autumn. The girls, bright and happy once more, rode every morning, the crisp air and the exercise coloring their cheeks and raising their spirits high. The Emperor tramped the woods, sometimes with me as his companion, and on one of these outings we both had a narrow escape from drowning. The Emperor took me for a row on the river which, as I have said, had a very rapid current. Intent on keeping the boat well into the current, the Emperor ran us into a small island, and for a few seconds escape from an ignominious upset seemed impossible. I was thoroughly frightened, the Emperor not a little embarrassed, and ardor for water sports was, for a time, rather lessened in both of us.

On October 21 (Russian Calendar) we celebrated the accession to the throne with high mass and holy communion, and a few days later the doctors decided that Alexei was well enough to be moved to Tsarskoe Selo. The Imperial train was made ready and their Majesties decided that I was to travel on it with the rest of the suite. This was, as a matter of fact, contrary to strict etiquette, and the announcement created among the ladies in waiting much consternation, not to say rancor. There is no question that being a regularly appointed lady in waiting to royalty and having nothing to do when a mere friend of the exalted one happens to be at hand is a bit irritating, so I cannot really blame the Empress's ladies for objecting to me as a traveling companion. The Imperial train, now used, one hears, by the inner circle of the Communists, was composed of a number of luxurious carriages, more like a home than a railway train. In the carriage of the Emperor and Empress the easy chairs and sofas were upholstered in bright chintz and there were books, family photographs, and all sort of familiar trinkets.

The emperor's study was in his favorite green leather, and adjoining their dressing rooms was a large and perfectly equipped bathroom. In this carriage also were rooms for the personal attendants of their Majesties. The Grand Duchesses and their maids had a similar carriage, and Alexei's carriage, which had compartments for the maids of honor and myself, was furnished with every imaginable comfort. The last carriage was the dining wagon with a small anteroom where the inevitable zakouski, the Russian table of *hors d'œuvres*, was served. At the long dining table the Emperor sat with his daughters on either hand, while facing him were Count Fredericks and the ladies in waiting. Throughout the journey of nearly two days the Empress was served in her own room or beside the bed where Alexei lay, very weak, but bright and cheerful once more.

This chapter may well close with one of the opening events of 1913, the Jubilee of the Romanoffs, celebrating the three hundredth anniversary of their reign. In February the Court moved from Tsarskoe Selo to the Winter Palace in Petrograd, a place they disliked because of the vast gloominess of the building and the fact that the only garden was a tiny space hardly large enough for the children to play or to exercise in. On reaching Petrograd the family drove directly across the Neva to Christ's Chapel, the little church of Peter the Great, where is, or was, preserved a miraculous picture of the Christ, very old and highly revered. The public had not been notified that the Imperial Family would first visit this chapel, but their presence quickly became known and they drove back to the Winter Palace through excited, but on the whole undemonstrative, masses of people, a typical Petrograd crowd.

The actual celebration of the Jubilee began with a solemn service in the Cathedral of Our Lady of Kazan, which everyone familiar with Petrograd remembers as one of the most beautiful of Russian churches. The vast building was packed to its utmost capacity, and that means a much larger crowd than in ordinary churches, since in Russia the congregation stands or kneels through the entire service. From my position I had a very good view of both the Emperor and the Tsarevitch, and I was puzzled to see them raise their heads and gaze long at the ceiling, but afterwards they told me that two doves had appeared and had floated for several minutes over their heads. In the religious exaltation of the hour this appeared to the Emperor a symbol that the blessing of God, after three centuries, continued to rest on the House of Romanoff. There followed a long series of functions at the palace, with deputations coming from all over the Empire, the women appearing at receptions and dinners in the beautiful national dress, which were also worn by the Empress and her daughters. The Empress, for all her weariness, was regal in her richly flowing robes and long-veiled, high *kokoshnik*, the Russian national headdress, set with magnificent jewels. She also wore the wide-ribboned order of St. Andrew, which was her sole privilege to wear, and at the most formal of the state dinners she wore the most splendid of all the crown jewels. The young Grand Duchesses were simply but beautifully gowned on all occasions, and they wore the order of Catherine the Great, red ribbons with blazing diamond stars. The crowds were enormous in all the great state rooms, the Imperial Family standing for hours while the multitudes filed past with sweeping curtsies and low bows. So long and fatiguing were these ceremonies that at the end the Empress was literally too fatigued to force a smile. Poor little Alexei also, after being carried through the rooms and obliged to acknowledge a thousand greetings, was taken back to his room in a condition of utter exhaustion.

There were state performances at the theater and the opera, Glinka's "Life for the Tsar" being sung to the usual tumult of applause and adulation, but for all that I felt that there was in the brilliant audience little real enthusiasm, little real loyalty. I saw a cloud over the whole celebration in Petrograd, and this impression, I am almost sure, was shared by the Empress. She told me that she could never feel happy in Petrograd. Everything in the Winter Palace reminded her of earlier years when she and her husband used to go happily to the theater together and returning would have supper in their dressing gowns before the fire talking over the events of the day and evening. "I was so happy then," she said plaintively, "so well and strong. Now I am a wreck."

Much as both she and the Emperor desired to shorten their stay in Petrograd, they were obliged to remain several weeks after the close of the official celebration because Tatiana, who unwisely had drunk the infected water of the capital, fell ill of typhoid and could not for some time be moved. With her lovely brown hair cut short, we finally went back to Tsarskoe Selo, where she made good progress back to health.

In the spring began the celebration of the Jubilee throughout the

THE EMPEROR AND EMPRESS IN OLD SLAVONIC DRESS
1913 JUBILEE.

Empire. The visit to the Volga, especially to Kostrama, the home of the first Romanoff monarch, Michail Feodorovnitch, was a magnificent success, the people actually wading waist deep in the river in order to get nearer the Imperial boat. It was the same through all the surrounding governments, crowds, cheers, acclamations, prayers, and great choruses singing the national hymn, very evidence of love and loyalty. I particularly remember when the cortège reached the town of Pereyaslovl, in the Vladimir Government, because it was from there that my father's family originated, and some of his relatives took part in the day's celebration. The Empress, to my regret, was not present, being confined to her bed on the Imperial train, ill and fatigued, yet under obligation to be ready for special ceremonies in Moscow. It would need a more eloquent pen than mine adequately to describe those days in Moscow, the Holy City of Russia. The weather was perfect, and under the clear sunshine the floating flags and banners, the flower-trimmed buildings, and the numberless decorations made up a spectacle of unforgettable beauty. Leaving his car at some distance from the Kremlin, the Emperor entered the great gate on foot, preceded by chanting priests with waving censers and holy images. Behind the Emperor and his suite came the Empress and Alexei in an open car through crowds that pressed hard against the police lines, while overhead all the bells of Moscow pealed welcome to the Sovereigns. Every day it was the same, demonstrations of love and fealty it seemed that no time or circumstance could ever alter.

THE EMPRESS ON HER BALCONY AT PETERHOF

CHAPTER VIII

NINETEEN-FOURTEEN, that year of fate for all the world, but more than all for my poor country, began its course in Russia, as elsewhere, in apparent peace and tranquillity. With us, as with other civilized people, the tragedy of Sarajevo came as a thrill of horror and surmise. I do not know exactly what we expected to follow that desperate act committed in a distant province of Austria, but certainly not the cataclysm of a World War and the ruin of three of the proudest empires of earth. Very shortly after the assassination of the Austrian heir and his wife the Emperor had gone to Kronstadt, headquarters of the Baltic fleet, to meet French and British squadrons then on cruise in Russian waters.* From Kronstadt he proceeded to Krasnoe, near Petrograd, the great summer central review center of the old Russian Army where the usual military maneuvers were in progress. Returning to Peterhof, the Emperor ordered a hasty departure to Finland because, he said, the political horizon was darkening and he needed a few days of rest and distraction. We sailed on July 6 (Russian Calendar) and had a quiet cruise, the last one we were ever destined to enjoy. Not that we intended it to be our last, for returning to Peterhof, from whence the Emperor hurried again to the reviews, we left nearly all our luggage on the yacht. The Empress, however, in one of her fits of melancholy, told me that she felt that we would never again be together on the *Standert*.

The political skies were indeed darkening. The Serbian murders and the unaccountably arrogant attitude of Austria grew in importance every succeeding day, and for many hours every day the Emperor was closeted in his study with Grand Duke Nicholas, Foreign Minister Sazonoff and other Ministers, all of whom urged on the Emperor the imperative duty of standing by Serbia. During the short intervals of the day when we saw the Emperor he seemed half dazed by the momentous decision he was called upon to make. A few days before mobilization I went to lunch at Krasnoe with a friend whose husband

---

* So little did any of the Allied rulers and statesmen anticipate the World War that in July, 1914, President Poincaré accompanied the French fleet on its cruise to the Baltic. Many festivities were arranged for him, and he was regally entertained by the Emperor. When receiving the ambassadors President Poincaré spoke gravely of the troubled political situation, but he said nothing to indicate that he expected war.

was on the Russian General Staff. In the middle of luncheon this officer, Count Nosstiz, burst into the room exclaiming: "Do you know what the Emperor has done? Can you guess what they have made him do? He has promoted the young men of the Military Academy to be officers, and he has sent the regiments back to their casernes to await orders. All the military attachés are telegraphing their Governments to ask what it means. What can it mean except war?"

From my friend's house I went almost at once back to Peterhof and informed the Empress what I had heard. Her amazement was unbounded, and over and over she repeated that she did not understand, that she could not imagine under what influence the Emperor had acted. He was still at the maneuvers, and although I remained late with the Empress I did not see him that night. The days that followed were full of suspense and anxiety. I spent most of my time playing tennis—very badly—with the girls, but from my occasional contacts with the Empress I knew that she was arguing and pleading against the war which apparently the Emperor felt to be inevitable. In one short talk I had with him on the subject he seemed to find a certain comfort in the thought that war always strengthened national feeling, and in his belief Russia would emerge from a truly righteous war stronger and better than ever. At this time a telegram arrived from Rasputine in Siberia, which plainly irritated the Emperor. Rasputine strongly opposed the war, and predicted that it would result in the destruction of the Empire. But the Emperor refused to believe it and resented what was really an almost unprecedented interference in affairs of state on the part of Rasputine.

I think I have spoken of the Emperor's aversion to the telephone. Up to this time none of his studies were ever fitted with telephones, but now he had wires and instruments installed and spent a great deal of time in conversations with Ministers and members of the military staff. Then came the day of mobilization, the same kind of a day of wild excitement, waving street crowds, weeping women and children, heartrending scenes of parting, that all the warring countries saw and ever will remember. After watching hours of these dreadful scenes in the streets of Peterhof I went to my evening duties with the Empress only to find that she had remained in absolute ignorance of what had been taking place. Mobilization! It was not true, she exclaimed. Certainly armies were moving, but only on the Austrian frontiers. She hurried from the room and I heard her enter the Emperor's study. For half an hour the sound of their excited voices reached my ears. Returning, the Empress dropped on her couch as one overcome by desperate tidings. "War!" She murmured breathlessly. "And I knew nothing of it. This is the end of everything." I could say nothing. I understood as little as she the incomprehensible silence of the Emperor at such an hour, and as always, whatever hurt her hurt me. We sat in silence until eleven when, as usual, the Emperor came in to tea, but he was distraught and gloomy and the tea hour also passed in almost complete silence.

The whole world has read the telegrams sent to Nicholas II by ex-Emperor William in those beginning days of the war. Their purport seemed to be sincere and intimate, begging his old friend and relative to stop mobilization, offering to meet the Emperor for a conference which yet might keep the peace. Historians of the future will have to decide whether those tenders were made in good faith or whether they were part of the sinister diplomacy of that wicked war. Nicholas II did not believe in their good faith, for he replied that he had no right to stop mobilization in Russia when German mobilization was already a matter of fact and that at any hour his frontiers might be crossed by German troops. After this interval the Emperor seemed to be in better spirits. War had come indeed, but even war was better than the threat and the uncertainty of the preceding weeks. The extreme depression of the Empress, however, continued unrelieved. Up to the last moment she hoped against hope, and when the German formal declaration of war was announced she gave way to a perfect passion of weeping, repeating to me through her tears: "This is the end of everything." The state visit of their Majesties to Petrograd soon after the declaration really seemed to justify the Emperor's belief that the war would arouse the national spirit, so long latent, in the Russian people. Never again do I expect to behold such a sight as the streets of Petrograd presented on that day. To say that the streets were crowded, thronged, massed, does not half express it. I do not believe that one single able-bodied person in the whole city remained at home during the hours spent in the capital by the Sovereigns. The streets were almost literally impassable, and the Imperial motor cars, moving at snail's pace from quay to palace through that frenzied sea of people, cheering, singing the national hymn, calling down blessings on the Emperor, was something that will live forever in the memories of all who witnessed it. The Imperial cortège was able, thanks to the police, to reach the Winter Palace at last, but many of the suite were halted by the crowds at the entrance to the great square in front of the palace and had to enter at a side door opening from the small garden to the west.

Inside the palace the crowd was relatively as great as that on the outside. Apparently every man and woman who had the right to appear at Court were massed in the corridors, the staircases, and the state apartments. Slowly their Majesties made their way to the great *Salle de Nicholas*, the largest hall in the palace, and there for several hours they stood receiving the most extraordinary tokens of homage from thousands of officials, ministers, and members of the *noblesse*, both men and women. Te Deums were sung, cheers and acclamations arose, and as the Emperor and Empress moved slowly through the crowds men and women threw themselves on their knees, kissing the hands of their Sovereigns with tears and fervent expressions of loyalty. Standing with others of the suite in the *Halle de Concert*, I watched this remarkable scene, and I listened to the historic speech of the Emperor which ended with the assurance that never would there be an end to Russian military effort until the last German was expelled from the beloved soil. From the *Salle de Nicholas* the Sovereigns passed to a balcony overlooking the great square. There with the Tsarevitch at their side they faced the wildly exulting people who with one accord dropped to their knees with mute gestures of love and obedience. Then as countless flags waved and dipped there arose from the lips and hearts of that vast assembly the moving strains of our great hymn: "God Save the Tsar."

Thus in a passion of renewed love and patriotism began in Russia the war of 1914. That same day the family returned to Peterhof, the Emperor almost immediately leaving for the casernes to bid farewell to regiments leaving for the front. As for the Empress, she became overnight a changed being. Every bodily ill and weakness forgotten, she began at once an extensive plan for a system of hospitals and sanitary trains for the dreadful roll of wounded which she knew must begin with the first battle. Her projected chain of hospitals and sanitary centers reached from Petrograd and Moscow to Charkoff and Odessa in the extreme south of Russia. The center of her personal activity was fixed in a large group of evacuation hospitals in and around Tsarskoe Selo, and there, after bidding farewell to my only brother, who immediately left for the southern front, I joined the Empress. Already her plans were so far matured that ten sanitary trains, bearing her name and the children's, were in active service, and something like eighty-five hospitals were open, or preparing to open, in Tsarskoe Selo, Peterhof, Pavlovsk, Louga, Sablino, and neighboring towns. The Empress, her two older daughters, and myself immediately enrolled under a competent woman surgeon, Dr. Gedroiz, as student nurses, spending two hours of every afternoon under theoretical instruction, and the entire hours of the morning in ward work in the hospitals. For the benefit of those who imagine that the work of a royal nurse is more or less in the nature of play I will describe the average routine of one of those mornings in which I was privileged to assist the Empress Alexandra Feodorovna and the Grand Duchesses Olga and Tatiana, the two last-named girls of nineteen and seventeen. Please remember that we were then only nurses in training. Arriving at the hospital shortly after nine in the morning we went directly to the receiving wards where the men were brought in after having first-aid treatment in the trenches and field hospitals. They had traveled far and were usually disgustingly dirty as well as blood-stained and suffering. Our hands scrubbed in antiseptic solutions we began the work of washing, cleaning, and bandaging maimed bodies, mangled faces, blinded eyes, all the indescribable mutilations of what is called civilized warfare. These we did under the orders and the direction of trained nurses who had the skill to do the things our lack of experience prevented us from doing. As we became accustomed to the work, and as both the Empress and Tatiana had extraordinary ability as nurses, we were given more important work. I speak of the Empress and Tatiana especially because Olga within two months was almost too exhausted and too unnerved to continue, and my abilities proved to be more in the executive and organizing than in the nursing end of hospital work. I have seen the Empress of Russia in the operating room of a hospital holding ether cones, handling sterilized instruments, assisting in the most difficult operations, taking from the hands of the busy surgeons amputated legs and arms, removing bloody and even vermin-infected dressings, enduring all the sights and smells and agonies of that most dreadful of all places, a military hospital in the midst of war. She did her work with the humility and the gentle tirelessness of one dedicated by God to a life of ministration. Tatiana was almost as skillful and quite as devoted as her mother, and complained only that on account of her youth she was spared some of the more trying cases. The Empress was spared nothing, nor did she wish to be. I think I never saw her happier than on the day, at the end of our two months' intensive training, she marched at the head of the procession of nurses to receive the red cross and the diploma of a certificated war nurse.

From that time on our days were literally devoted to toil. We rose at seven in the morning and very often it was an hour or two after midnight before we sought our beds. The Empress, after a morning in the operating room of one hospital, snatched a hasty luncheon and spent the rest of the day in a round of inspection of other hospitals. Every morning early I met her in the little Church of Our Lady of Znamenie, where we went for prayers, driving afterwards to the hospitals. On the days when the sanitary trains arrived with their ghastly loads of wounded we often worked from nine until three without stopping for food or rest. The Empress literally shirked nothing. Sometimes when an unfortunate soldier was told by the surgeons that he must suffer an amputation or undergo an operation which might be fatal, he turned in his bed calling out her name in anguished appeal. "Tsaritsa! Stand near me. Hold my hand that I may have courage." Were the man an officer or a simple peasant boy she always answered the appeal. With her arm under his head she would speak words of comfort and encouragement, praying with him while preparations for the operation were in progress, her own hands assisting in the merciful work of anesthesia. The men idolized her, watched for her coming, reached out bandaged hands to touch her as she passed, smiling happily as she bent over their pillows. Even the dying smiled as she knelt beside their beds murmuring last words of prayer and consolation.

In the last days of November, 1914, the Empress left Tsarskoe Selo for an informal inspection of hospitals within the radius of her especially chosen district. Dressed in the gray uniform of a nursing sister, accompanied by her older daughters, myself, and a small suite, she went to towns surrounding Tsarskoe Selo and southward as far as Pskoff, staff headquarters, where the younger Grand Duchess Marie Pavlovna was a hospital nurse. From there she proceeded to Vilna, Kovno, and Grodno, in which city she met the Emperor and with him went on to Dvinsk. The enthusiasm and affection with which the Empress was met in all these places and in stations along the route beggars description. A hundred incidents of the journey crowd my memory, each one worth the telling had I space to include them in this narrative. I remember, for example, the remarkable scene in the big fortress of Kovno, where acres of hospital beds were assembled and where the tall figure of the Empress, moving through those interminable aisles, was greeted like the visit of an angel. I never recall that journey without remembering the hospital at Grodno, where a gallant young officer lay dying of his wounds. Hearing that the Empress was on her way to the hospital, he rallied unexpectedly and declared to his nurses that he was determined to live until she came. Sheer will power kept life in the man's body until the Empress arrived, and when, at the door of the hospital, she was told of his dying wish to see her she hurried first to his bedside, kneeling beside it and receiving his last smile, his last gasping words of greeting and farewell.

After one very fatiguing day our train passed a sanitary train of the Union of Zemstvos moving south. The Empress, who should have been resting in bed at the time, ordered her train stopped that she might visit, to the surprise and delight of the doctors, this splendidly equipped rolling hospital. Another surprise visit was to the estate of Prince Tichkevitch, whose family supported on their own lands a very efficient hospital unit. It was impossible to avoid noticing how in the towns visited by the Empress, dressed as a simple sister of mercy, the love of the people was most manifest. In Grodno, Dvinsk, and other cities where she appeared with the Emperor there was plenty of enthusiasm, but on those occasions etiquette obliged her to lay aside her uniform and to dress as the wife of the Emperor. Much better the people loved her when she went among them in her nurse's dress, their devoted friend and sister. Etiquette forgotten, they crowded around her, talked to her freely, claimed her as their own.

Soon after returning from this visit of inspection the Empress accompanied by Grand Duchesses Olga and Tatiana, General Racine, Commander of the Palace Guards, a maid of honor and myself, set off on a journey to Moscow, where to my extreme sorrow and dismay I perceived for the first time unmistakable evidences of a spreading intrigue against the Imperial Family. At the station in Moscow the Empress was met by her sister, the Grand Duchess Serge and the latter's intimate friend and the executive of her convent, Mme. Gardieve. Welcome from the people there was none, as General Djounkovsky, Governor of Moscow, had announced, without any authority whatsoever, that the Empress was in the city incognito and did not wish to meet anyone. In con-sequence of this order we drove to the Kremlin through almost empty streets. Nevertheless the Empress began at once the inspection of hospitals, accompanied by General Racine and her maid of honor, Baroness Boukshoevden, daughter of the Russian Ambassador in Denmark. During our stay in Moscow I was not as constantly with the Empress as usual, our rooms in the Kremlin being far apart. However, General Odoevsky, the fine old Governor of the Kremlin, installed a telephone between our rooms, and on her free evenings the Empress often summoned me to sit with her in her dressing room, hung with light blue draperies and looking out over the river and the ancient roofs of Moscow. I lunched and dined with others of the suite in an old part of the immense palace known as the Granovita Palata, and here occurred one night a disagreeable scene in which General Racine, in the presence of the whole company, administered a stinging rebuke to General Djounkovsky, Governor of Moscow, for his responsibility for the cold welcome accorded her Majesty. The Governor turned very pale but made no answer to the accusation of General Racine. Already my mind was in a tumult of trouble, more and more conscious of the atmosphere of intrigue, plots, and conspiracies, the end of which I could not see. In the coldness of the Grand Duchess Serge, in my childhood such a friend to me and to my family, her chilly refusal to listen to her sister's denial of preposterous tales of the political influence exerted by Rasputine, by the general animosity towards myself, I began dimly to realize that there was a plot to strike at her Majesty through Rasputine and myself. There was absolutely nothing I could do, and I had to watch with tearless grief the breach between the sisters grow wider and deeper until their association was robbed of most of its old intimacy. I knew well enough, or I was convinced that I knew, that the dismissed maid of honor, Mlle. Tutcheff, was at the bottom of the whole affair, her family being among the most prominent in Moscow. But I could say nothing, do nothing.

With great relief we saw our train leave Moscow for a round of visits in surrounding territory, and here again the enthusiasm with which the people welcomed the Empress was unbounded. In the town of Toula, for example, and a little farther on in Orel, the people were so tumultuous in their greeting, they crowded so closely around their adored Empress, that our party could scarcely make our way to church and hospital. Once, following the Empress out of a church, carrying in my hands an ikon which had been presented to her, I was fairly overthrown by the crowding multitude and fell halfway down the high flight of steps before friendly hands could get me to my feet. I did not mind this, being only too rejoiced at evidences of love and devotion which the simple people of Russia felt for their Empress. In one town where there were no modern carriages she was dragged along in an old coach of state such as a medieval bishop might have used, the coach being quite covered with flowers and branches. In the town of Charkoff hundreds of students met the train bearing aloft portraits of her Majesty. In the small town of Belgorod, where the Empress wished to stop in order to visit a very sacred monastery, I shall never forget the joy with which the sleepy ischvostiks hurried through the darkness of the night to drive us the three or four versts from the railway to the monastery. Nor can I forget the arrival at the monastery, the sudden flare of lights as the monks hastened out to meet and greet their Sovereign Empress. These were the people, the plain people of Russia, and the difference between them and the plotting officials we had left behind in Moscow was a sad and a terrible contrast.

On December 6 (Russian Calendar), the birthday of the Emperor, we met his train at Voronezh, where our parties joined in visits to Tambov, Riasan, and other towns where the people gave their Majesties wonderful greetings. In Tambov the Emperor and Empress visited and had tea with a charming woman of advanced age, Mme. Alexandra Narishkin, friend of Alexander III and of many distinguished men of her time. Mme. Narishkin, horrible to relate, was afterwards murdered by the Bolsheviki, neither her liberal mind nor her long services to her country, and especially to her humble friends in Tambov, sparing her from the blood lust of the destroyers of Russia.

The journey of their Majesties terminated at Moscow, where the younger children of the family awaited them. I can still see the slim, erect figure of Alexei standing at salute on the station platform, and the rosy, eager faces of Marie and Anastasie welcoming their parents after their long separation. The united family drove to the Kremlin, this time not quite so inhospitably received. In the days following the Moscow hospitals and military organizations were visited in turn, and we included in these visits out of town activities of the Moscow Zemstvo (county council), canteens, etc. In one of these centers our host was Prince Lvoff, afterwards active in demanding the abdication of the Tsar, and I remember with what deference he received their Majesties, and the especial attention he paid to the Tsarevitch, whose autograph he begged for the visitors' book. Before we left

Moscow the Empress paid two visits, one to the old Countess Apraxin, sister of the former first lady in waiting, Princess Galatzine and, with the Emperor, to the Metropolitan Makari, a good man, but mercilessly persecuted during the Revolution.

There was one small but significant incident which happened after our return to Tsarskoe Selo, near the end of the year 1914. It failed of its intended effect, but had it not failed it might have had a far-reaching influence on world events at that time. Looking back on it now, I sometimes wonder exactly what lay back of the plot, and who was responsible for its inception. One evening late in the year I received a visit from two war nurses lately released from a German prison where they had been taken with a portion of a captured Russian regiment. In much perturbation of spirit these nurses told me of a third nurse who had been captured and imprisoned with them. This woman they had come to distrust as she had been accorded many special favors by the Germans. She had been given good food and even champagne, and when the nurses were released she alone was conveyed to the frontier in a motor car, the others going on foot. While in prison this woman had boasted that she expected to be received by the Emperor, to whom she proposed to present the flag of the captured regiment. The other nurses declared that in their opinion his Majesty should be warned of the woman's dubious character.

Hardly knowing what to think of such an extraordinary story, I thought it my duty to lay the matter before General Voyeikoff, Chief Commander of the Palace Guards, and when I learned from him that the Emperor had consented to receive the nurse I begged that the woman be investigated before being allowed to enter the palace. The Emperor showed some vexation, but he consented. When General Voyeikoff examined the woman she made a display of great frankness, handing him a revolver which she said it had been necessary for her to carry at the front. General Voyeikoff, thinking it strange that the weapon had not been taken away from her by the Germans, immediately ordered a search of her effects. In the handbag which she would certainly have carried with her to the palace were found two more loaded revolvers. The woman was, of course, arrested, and although I cannot explain why, her arrest caused great indignation among certain members of the aristocracy who previously had received her at their homes. The whole onus of her arrest was placed on me, although the Emperor declared his belief that she was a German spy sent to assassinate him. That she was a spy I have never doubted, but in my own mind I have never even tried to guess from whence she came.

CHAPTER IX

A VERY few days after the events chronicled in the last chapter I became the victim of a railroad accident which brought me to the threshold of death and for many months made it impossible for me to follow the events of the war, or the growing conspiracy against the Sovereigns. At a little past five o'clock of the afternoon of January 2, 1915, I took the train at Tsarskoe for a short visit to my parents in Petrograd. With me in my carriage was Mme. Shiff, a sister of a distinguished officer of Cuirassiers. We sat talking the usual commonplaces of travel when suddenly, without a moment's notice, there came a tremendous shock and a deafening crash, and I felt myself thrown violently forward, my head towards the roof of the carriage, and both legs held as in a vise in the coils of the steam-heating apparatus. The overturned carriage lurched and broke in two like an eggshell and I felt the bones of my left leg snap sharply. So intense was the pain that I momentarily lost consciousness. Too soon my senses returned to me and I found myself firmly wedged in the wreckage of wood and iron, a great bar of steel crushing my face, and my mouth so choked with blood that I could not utter a sound. All I could do in my agony was silently to pray that God would give me the relief of a quick death, for I could not believe that any human being could endure such pain and live.

After what seemed to me an interminable length of time I felt the pressure on my face removed and a kind voice asked: "Who lies here?" As I managed to breathe my name the rescuers exclaimed in astonishment and alarm, and immediately began to endeavor to extricate me from my agonizing position. By means of ropes passed under my arms and using great care and gentleness they ultimately got me free and laid me on the grass. In a moment's flash I recognized one as a Cossack of the Emperor's special guard, an excellent man named Lichatchieff, and the other as a soldier of the railway battalion. Then I fainted. Ripping loose one of the doors of the railway carriage, the men placed me on it and carried me to a nearby hut already crowded with wounded and dying. Regaining consciousness for a moment, I begged in whispers that Lichatchieff would telephone my parents in Petrograd and their Majesties at the palace. This the good fellow did without delay, and he also brought to my corner one of the surgeons summoned to the wreck. The man gave me a rapid examination and said briefly: "Do not disturb her. She is dying." He left to attend to more hopeful cases, but the faithful soldiers still knelt beside me, straightening my crushed and broken legs and wiping the blood from my lips. In about two hours another doctor, this time the surgeon Gedroiz, under whom the Empress, her daughters, and myself had taken our nurses' training, approached the corner where I lay. I looked with a kind of terror into the face of this woman, for I knew her to be no friend of mine. Simply giving my wounded head a superficial examination she said carelessly that I was a hopeless case, and left me without the slightest attempt to soothe my pain. Not until ten o'clock that night, four hours after the collision which had wrecked two trains, did any help reach me. At that hour arrived General Racine from the palace with orders from their Majesties to do everything possible in my behalf. At his imperative commands I was again placed on a stretcher and carried to a relief train made up of cattle cars. At the moment my poor father and mother arrived from Petrograd and the last things I remember were their sobs and a teaspoonful of brandy mercifully poured down my throat.

At the end of the journey to Tsarskoe Selo I dimly recognized the Empress and the four Grand Duchesses who had come to the station to meet the train. Their faces were full of sympathy and grief, and as they bent over me I found strength to whisper to them: "I am dying." I believed it because the doctors had said so, and because my pain was so great. Then came the ordeal of being lifted into the ambulance and the half-consciousness that the Empress was there too, holding my head on her knees and begging me to have courage. After that came an interval of darkness out of which I awoke in bed and almost free from pain. The Empress who, with my parents, remained near me, asked me if I would like to see the Emperor. Of course I replied that I would, and when he came I pressed the hand he gave me. Dr. Gedroiz, who was in charge of the ward, told everyone coldly to take leave of me as I could not possibly live until morning. "Is it so hopeless?" asked the Emperor. "She still has some strength in her hand."

Later on, I do not know exactly when, I opened my eyes quite clearly, and saw standing beside my bed the tall, gaunt form of Rasputine. He looked at me fixedly and said in a calm voice: "She will live, but will always be a cripple." A prediction which was literally fulfilled, for to this day I can walk only slowly and with the aid of a stout stick. I have been told that Rasputine recalled me from unconsciousness, but of his words I know only what I have recorded.

The next morning I was operated on and for the six weeks following I suppose I suffered as greatly as one can and live. My left leg which had sustained a double fracture, troubled me less than my back and my right leg which had been horribly wrenched and lacerated. My head wounds were also intensely painful and for a time I suffered from inflammation of the brain. My parents, the Empress, and the children came every day to see me, but despite their presence the neglect and unkindness of Dr. Gedroiz continued. The suggestion of the Empress that her trusted physician, Dr. Federoff, be brought into consultation was rudely repulsed by this woman, of whom I may finally say that she is now in high favor with the Bolsheviki whose ranks she joined in the autumn of 1917. Waited upon by none but the most inexperienced nurses, I do not know what might have become of me had not my mother brought to the hospital an old family nurse whom she absolutely insisted should take charge of me. Things went a little better after this, but happy was I when at the end of the sixth week, against the will of Dr. Gedroiz, I left that wretched hospital and was removed to my own home. There in the peace and security of my comfortable bedroom I enjoyed for the first time since my accident quiet and refreshing sleep.

It seems strange that the hostile and envious Court circle had deeply resented the daily visits of the Emperor and Empress to my bedside. To placate the gossipers the Emperor, before visiting me, used to make the rounds of all the wards. In spite of it all I had many visitors and many daily inquiries from the Empress Dowager and others. Very soon after my arrival home I was examined by skillful surgeons, among them Drs. Federoff and Gagentorn, who pronounced my crushed right leg to be in a very bad condition and placed it in a plaster cast, where it remained for two months. The Empress visited me daily, but the Emperor I seldom saw because, as I learned indirectly, the War was going very badly on the Russian front, and the Emperor was almost constantly with the armies. In the last week before Lent he came to my bedside with the Empress, in accordance with an old Russian custom, before confession, to beg my forgiveness for possible wrongs done me during the year past. Their pious humility and also the white and careworn face of the Emperor filled me with emotion which later events served only to increase, for very momentous and trying hours were even then crowding the destiny of Nicholas II, Tsar of all the Russias.

A soldier of the sanitary corps, a man named Jouk, had been assigned to duty at my house, and as soon as I was able to leave my bed he took me daily in a wheeled chair to church, and to the palace. This was the summer of 1915, a time of great tribulation for the Russian Army, as every student of the World War is aware. Grand Duke Nicholai Nicholaievitch was pursuing a policy which rightly disturbed the Emperor, who constantly complained that the commander in chief of his armies sent the men forward without proper ammunition, without artillery support, and with no adequate preparations for safe retreat. Disaster after disaster confirmed the Emperor's fears. Fortress after fortress fell to the Germans. Kovno fell. Novogeorgiesk fell, and finally Warsaw itself fell. It was a terrible day when the Emperor, white and trembling, brought this news to the Empress as we sat at tea on her balcony in the warm autumn air. The Emperor was fairly overcome with grief and humiliation as he finished his tale. "It cannot go on any longer like this," he exclaimed bitterly, and then he went on to declare that in spite of ministerial opposition he was determined to take personal command of the army himself. Only that day Krivosheim, Minister of Agriculture, had addressed him on the impossible condition of Russian internal affairs. Nicholai Nicholaievitch, not content with military supremacy, had assumed almost complete authority over all the business of the Empire. There were in fact two governments in Russia, orders being constantly issued from military headquarters without the knowledge, much less the consent, of the Emperor.

Very soon after the fall of Warsaw it became clear to the Emperor that if he were to retain any dignity whatever he would have to depose Nicholai Nicholaievitch, and I wish here to state, without any reservation whatever, that this decision was reached by the Emperor without advice from Rasputine, myself, or any other person. Even the Empress, although she approved her husband's resolution, had no part in forming it. M. Gilliard has written that the Emperor was forced to his action by bad advisers, especially the Empress and Rasputine, but in this he is absolutely mistaken. M. Gilliard writes that the Emperor was told that Grand Duke Nicholai Nicholaievitch was plotting to confine his Sovereign in a monastery. I do not believe for a moment that Rasputine ever made such a statement, but he did, in my presence, warn the Emperor to watch Nicholai Nicholaievitch and his wife who, he alleged, were at their old practices of table-tipping and spiritism, which he thought to be a highly dangerous way to conduct a war against the Germans. As for me, I repeat that never once did I say or do anything to influence the Emperor in state affairs. I wish I could here reproduce a letter written to my father by the Emperor in which all the reasons for taking the step he did were explained. The letter, alas! was taken from me by the Bolsheviki after my father's death, and I suppose was destroyed.

On the evening when the Emperor met his ministers to announce his great decision I dined at the palace, and I was deeply impressed with the firmness of the Emperor's decision not to be overborne by arguments or vain fears on the part of timid statesmen. As he arose to go to the council chamber the Emperor begged us to pray for him that his resolution should not falter. "You do not know how hard it has been for me to refrain from taking an active part in the command of my beloved army," he said at parting. Overcome and speechless, I pressed into his hand a tiny ikon which I had always worn around my neck, and during the long council which followed the Empress and I prayed fervently for the Emperor and for our distracted country.

As the time passed the Empress's anxiety grew so great that, throwing a cloak around her shoulders and beckoning me to follow, she went out on the balcony, one end of which gave on the council room. Through the lace of the window curtains we could see the Emperor sitting very upright, surrounded by his ministers, one of whom was on his feet speaking earnestly. Our eleven o'clock tea was served long before the Emperor, entirely exhausted, returned from the conference. Throwing himself in an armchair, he stretched himself out like a man spent after extreme exertion, and I could see that his brow and hands were wet with perspiration.

"They did not move me," he said in a low, tense voice. "I listened to all their long, dull speeches, and when all had finished I said: 'Gentlemen, in two days from now I leave for the Stavka.'" As he repeated the words his face lightened, his shoulders straightened, and he appeared like a man whose strength was suddenly renewed.

Yet one more struggle was before him. The Empress Dowager, whom the Emperor visited immediately after the ministerial conference, was by this time thoroughly imbued with the German-spy mania in which the Empress and Rasputine, not to mention myself, were involved. She believed the whole preposterous tissue of lies which had been built up and with all her might she struggled against the Emperor's decision to assume supreme command of the army. For over two hours a painful scene was enacted in the Empress Dowager's gardens, he trying to show her that utter disaster threatened the army and the Empire under existing conditions, and she repeating over and over again the wicked slanders of German plots which she insisted that he was furthering. In the end the Emperor left, terribly shaken, but with his resolution as strong as ever.

Before leaving for staff headquarters the Emperor and his family took communion together at the Feodorovsky Cathedral and at their last meal together he showed himself calm and collected as he had not been for some time; in fact, not since the beginning of the last disastrous campaign. From headquarters the Emperor wrote full accounts of the scenes which took place when he assumed personal command, and of the furious anger, not only of the deposed Nicholai Nicholaievitch but of all his staff, "Every one of whom," wrote the Emperor, "has the ambition himself to govern Russia."

I am not attempting to write a military history of those years, and I am quite aware of the fact that most published accounts of the Russian Army represent Nicholai Nicholaievitch as the devoted friend of the Allies and the Emperor as the pliant tool of German influences. It is undeniable, however, that almost as soon as Nicholai Nicholaievitch had been sent to the Caucasus and the Emperor took command of the Western Army a marked improvement in the general morale became apparent. Retreat at various points was stopped, the whole front strengthened, and a new spirit of loyalty to the Empire was manifest.

I wish to interpolate here, in connection with the Emperor's personal command of the army, a word on the immense service he rendered it at the beginning of the War in suppressing the manufacture and sale of vodka, the curse of the Russian peasantry. The Emperor did this entirely on his own initiative, without advice from his ministers or the Grand Dukes. The Emperor said at the time: "At least by this I will be remembered," and he was, because the condition of the peasants, the town workers, and of course the army became at once immeasurably better. In the midst of war-time privations the savings-banks accounts of the people increased enormously, and in the army there was none of the hideous debauchery which disgraced Russia in the Russo-Japanese War. As an eminent French correspondent long afterwards wrote: "It is to the dethroned Emperor Nicholas that we must accord the honor of having effected the greatest of all internal reforms in war-time Russia, the suppression of alcoholism."

In October the Emperor came to Tsarskoe Selo for a brief visit, and on his return he took with him to the Stavka the young Tsarevitch. This is the first time he had ever separated the boy from his mother, and the Empress was never happy except in the few minutes each day when she was reading the child's daily letter. At nine o'clock at night she went up to his bedroom exactly as though he were there and she was listening to his evening prayers. By day the Empress continued her tireless work in the hospitals from which, by reason of my accident, I had long been excluded. However, at this time, I received from the railroad as compensation for my injuries the considerable sum of eighty thousand rubles, and with the money I established a hospital for convalescent soldiers in which maimed and wounded men received training in various useful trades. This, it is needless to say, became a great source of happiness to me, since I knew as well as the soldiers what it meant to be crippled and helpless. From the first my hospital training school was a most gratifying success, and my personal interest in it never ceased until the Revolution, after which all my efforts at usefulness and service ended in imprisonment and persecution.

Not this action of mine, patriotic though it must have appeared, no amount of devotion of the Empress to the wounded, sufficed to check the rapidly growing propaganda which sought to convict the Imperial Family and all its friends of being German spies. The fact that in England the Empress's brother-in-law, Prince Louis of Battenberg, German-born but a loyal Briton, was forced to resign his command in the British Navy was used with effect against the Empress Alexandra Feodorovna. She knew and resented keenly this insane delusion, and she did everything in her power to overcome it. I remember a day when the Empress received a letter from her brother Ernest, Grand Duke of Hesse, in which he implored her to do something to improve the barbarous conditions of German prisoners in Russia. With streaming tears the Empress owned herself powerless to do anything at all in behalf of the unhappy captives. She had organized a committee for the relief of Russian prisoners in Germany, but this had been fiercely attacked, especially in the columns of *Novy Vremya,* an influential organ of the Constitutional Democratic Party. In this newspaper and in general society the Empress's committee was accused of being a mere camouflage gotten up to shield her real purpose of helping the Germans. Against such attacks the Empress had no defense. Her secretary, Count Rostovseff, indeed tried to refute the story concerning the Empress's prison-camp committee, but the editors of *Novy Vremya* insolently refused to publish his letter of explanation.

The German-spy mania was extended from the palace to almost every Russian who had the misfortune to possess a name that sounded at all German. Count Fredericks and Minister Sturmer were among those who suffered calumny, although neither spoke a single German sentence. But the greatest sufferers were those barons of the Baltic Provinces whose ancestors had bequeathed them names of quite certain German origin. Many of these men were arrested and sent to die, or to suffer worse than death in exile. The sons and relatives of many of these very Baltic proprietors were at the time fighting loyally in the Russian Army. That there were German spies at work in Russia all during the War I have no reason to doubt, but they were the men who after 1917 invited in and exalted Lenine and Trotzky, and not the Empress and her friends, nor yet the persecuted estate owners of the Baltic Provinces. Did the Emperor's family call upon the Germans to rescue them from Siberia? Did any of the Baltic Provinces at Versailles ask to be united to Germany?

The army and navy still remained loyal to the Sovereigns. On one of his home visits to Tsarskoe Selo the Emperor brought with him as a proof of this the Cross of the Order of St. George, the highest of all Russian military decorations, which none could bestow except the Emperor, or the chief command of one of the armies in the field. In this case it was the gallant Southern Army which had voted to bestow it on the Emperor, and his pride and joy in it were humbly great.

* * *

CHAPTER X

TO one who has always held the honor and faith of the Russian people very dear, who has never doubted that after the last hideous phase of revolution and anarchism has passed, the Russian nation will emerge stronger and better than ever before, the writing of these next chapters is a duty inexpressibly painful. I must tell the truth, otherwise it would have been better for me never to have written at all. Yet to picture in anything like its true colors the decadence of Petrograd society from 1914 onward is a task from which any loyal Russian must shrink. Without a knowledge of these conditions, however, students of the Russian Revolution will never be able to understand why the fabric of government slipped so easily from the feeble hands of the Provisional Government to the ruthless and bloody grasp of the Bolshevists.

During the entire winter of 1915, when the War was being waged on all fronts with such disaster to the Allies, when millions of men, Russians, Frenchmen, Belgians, Englishmen, were giving up their lives in the cause of freedom, the aristocracy of the Russian capital was indulging in a reckless orgy of dancing, sports, dining, yes, and wining also in spite of the Emperor's edict against alcohol, spending enormous sums for gowns and jewels, and in every way ignoring the terrible fact that the world was on fire and that civilization was battling for its very life. In the palace the most frugal régime had been adopted. Meals were simple almost to parsimony, no money was spent except for absolute necessities, and the Empress and her daughters spent practically every waking hour working and praying for the soldiers. But society, when it was not otherwise amusing itself, was indulging in a new and madly exciting game of intrigue against the throne. To spread slanders about the Empress, to inflame the simple minds of workmen against the state was the most popular diversion of the aristocracy. A typical instance of this mania was related to me by my sister, who one morning was surprised by an unexpected visit from her sister-in-law, daughter of a very great lady of the aristocracy. Bursting into the room, this woman exclaimed delightedly: "What do you think we are doing now? Spreading stories through all the factories that the Empress is keeping the Emperor constantly drunk. Everybody believes it." I mention this story as typical because the woman involved afterwards became very prominent in the Grand Ducal cabal that forced the abdication, and she was also one of two women present in the Yusupoff Palace on the night of Rasputine's assassination.

Every possible circumstance, no matter how inconsequential, was eagerly seized as capital by these plotters. A former lady in waiting, Marie Vassilchikoff, long retired from Court and living on her Austrian estates, came to Petrograd, I know not how, and asked for an audience with the Empress. Since Russia was at war with Austria this audience could not be granted, nor did the Empress even remotely desire it. Yet as the story was circulated Marie Vassilchikoff was represented as having been sent for by the Empress to negotiate a separate peace with Austria, and that this treachery was frustrated only by the vigorous intervention of the Grand Duchess Serge.

These stories were spread not only by Court and society people, but were made into a regular propaganda in the army, especially among the higher command. The propaganda was chiefly in the hands of members of the Union of Zemstvos, its most successful agent being the infamous Goutchkoff, who now, it is gratifying to know, has earned the contempt of every Russian political group, even including the Bolshevists. Thus in a whirl of heartless gaiety and an organized campaign against the Sovereigns and against the Empire passed the winter of 1915, the dark prelude of darker years to come.

In the spring of that year, my health being still very precarious, their Majesties sent me in charge of a sanitary train filled with invalid soldiers and officers to the soft climate of the Crimea. With me went a sister of mercy and the sanitary-corps man Jouk, of whom I have spoken. On the same train journeyed also three members of the secret police, ostensibly to protect, but really, as I well understood, to spy upon me. Their presence the Empress, who came in the pouring rain to see the train off from the station, was powerless to forbid, as she herself was constantly under the surveillance of the dread Okhrana. Our train traveled slowly, taking five days from Petrograd to the Black Sea. But this we did not mind as we were very comfortable, the weather became beautiful, and our frequent stops at Moscow and towns farther south were full of interest. Our destination was Evpatoria on the eastern shore of the Black Sea, and here all of us were cordially received, M. Duvan, the head man of the city, giving me for a residence his own flower-hung villa overlooking the sea. Here I spent two peaceful months, finding the mud baths wonderfully restoring, and meeting some unusually interesting people. I am sure that few people outside of Russia have ever heard of the Karaim, a racial group among the most ancient in the world and of whom, even then, a bare ten thousand existed. They were not Jews, although they worshipped in synagogues, because they acknowledged Christ as God, or at least a special prophet of God. They were, and are, if they still exist, a strange mixture of pious Jews and early Christians, left-overs from the days of the decaying Roman Empire when Judaism and Christianity were trying to unite in one faith. The head of the Karaim in Evpatoria was a fine black-bearded patriarch named Gaham, and with him I formed an almost immediate friendship. Dressed in the long black robe of his office, he used to sit with me for hours reading and reciting the legends of his people, many reaching back into the dim twilight of civilization. I liked the patriarch, not only for his simplicity and his kindness to me, but for his evident love and loyalty to the Imperial Family, a loyalty shared by all the people of the Karaim.

A telegram from the Empress told me that she was then leaving for the Stavka, from which she and the Emperor and the whole Imperial Family would proceed to the Crimea for an important military and naval review. Obeying her instructions I motored from Evpatoria to Sevastopol, through an enchanting landscape of hills and plains, the latter being literally carpeted with scarlet poppies. Arriving at Sevastopol, I had some difficulty in passing the guard, but the Empress's telegram, marked "Imperial," I had brought with me, and this proved the open sesame to the Emperor's special train. I lunched with the Empress and the Grand Duchesses, meeting the Emperor and Alexei when they came from the reviews at six o'clock. I spent that night in town, and the next day returned to Evpatoria, their Majesties promising to visit me within a few days. On May 16 they arrived and received a most enthusiastic welcome, not only from the townspeople but from the Tartars, who came in from the hills by thousands, from the people of the Karaim, and others as strange and as picturesque. The huge square before the cathedral was strewn with fragrant roses over which the Imperial Family walked to service. The next few hours were spent in a round of visits to churches, hospitals, and sanatoriums, and it was to a late luncheon at my villa that they finally arrived. After luncheon we walked and sat on the beach, but the gathering crowd became so large and so curious that the poor Emperor, who had looked forward to a sea bath and a swim, had to relinquish both. Alexei enjoyed the day, boy fashion, without regard to the crowds, playing on the beach and building a big sand fortress, which the schoolboys of the town next day surrounded by a high wall of stones to protect it from the ravages of the tide. We had tea in the garden, the Empress greatly enjoying the Oriental sweets sent her by the Tartars. In the evening I dined on the Imperial train and traveled with it a short distance on its way back to Petrograd.

In June I returned to Tsarskoe and resumed work in my beloved hospital training school. The weather was unusually hot but the Empress continued her constant duties in the hospitals and operating rooms. Often I accompanied her on her rounds, and it came to me as a painful shock that the surgeons and some of the wounded officers no longer regarded her, as before, with respect and veneration. Too often an officer would assume in her presence a careless and indifferent manner which even a professional nurse would have resented. The Empress never did. She must have noticed evidences of disrespect but no word of complaint ever passed her lips. When I ventured to suggest to her that it might be well to go less frequently to her hospital, she rewarded me with a look of reproach. Whatever other people did, whatever their attitude towards the War, Royalty knew its duty and would perform it faithfully to the end.

Both the Emperor and the Empress during all this rising tide of disaffection persisted in underestimating its importance. The Emperor especially treated the whole movement with the contempt which no doubt it merited but which as a national menace it was far too dangerous to ignore. I realized it keenly, but knowing how impossible it was to make their Majesties understand that everything that was said against me, against Rasputine, against the Ministers, was actually directed against themselves, I was obliged to keep my lips closed. My parents realized as well as I did what was going on. They had good reason, in fact, for my mother had received two most insulting letters, one from Princess Galatzine, sister of Mme. Rodzianko, whose husband was President of the Duma, and another from Mme. Timasheff, a woman of the highest aristocracy, letters which indicated a certain collusion between the writers. In them my mother was brutally informed that neither of the women desired any further acquaintanceship or association with her as she too undoubtedly belonged to the German-spy party. My parents at the time were living quietly in the little seaside town of Terioke, near Petrograd, and were studiously avoiding the vulgar orgies and intrigues of society.

In the midst of all these heart-breaking events I sought distraction in the enlargement and perfecting of my occupational hospital which was rapidly becoming overcrowded with invalids. I bought an additional piece of land and arranged for four portable houses to be brought from Finland. Two of these arrived duly, and I spent hours of absorbing interest watching them being put together on the newly acquired land. All these days I was constantly being bothered by people who, perhaps believing that the money I was investing in hospitals was another proof of my power over the Imperial treasury, tormented me with petitions of every kind and description, but all of them alike in the selfishness of their character. With cold hatred in their eyes, but with hypocritical words on their lips, these people besought my good offices with their Majesties on behalf of their sons, husbands, and relatives, all of whom were alleged to be worthy of promotions and of lucrative positions under the State. One woman of good social position invaded my hospital one day and treated me to a disgraceful scene because I had assured her that I was powerless to further her ambition to see her husband appointed head of a certain Government. Naturally it happened that some petitioners were poor and needy, and these, to the best of my ability, but without any political influence whatever, I did endeavor to help. I know now, after witnessing true sympathy and kindness to prisoners and persecuted, like myself in later days, that I never did half what I might have done in the time of my prosperity. If better days come to Russia in my lifetime God help me to devote all that remains of my years to the poor and especially to prisoners. Now that I have tasted poverty, now that I have known the hopelessness of captivity, I know better than I did what can be done for the lowly and unfortunate.

A number of very disquieting events occurred to us during the summer. On very hot days it was the custom of the Empress and the children to drive through the woods and shaded roads to Pavlovsk, a few versts from Tsarskoe Selo. One stifling afternoon we started out as usual in two carriages, the Empress and myself leading the way. The horses were magnificent animals, apparently in the very pink of condition, but suddenly one of the horses uttered a piercing scream and dropped dead in his harness. The other horse plunged sidewise in terror and for a few minutes it was all the coachman could do to avoid an overturn. The Empress, pale, but as always courageous, got out of the carriage and helped me, who was still on crutches, to alight. The carriage of the children drove up, and getting in, we returned without further incident to the palace. Whatever caused the sudden death of that horse, or what was the object of that carriage accident—if indeed it was an accident—we never knew, but it left behind in my mind, and I think also in the mind of the Empress, a strangely sinister impression. The Empress nevertheless went steadfastly on with her hospital work, arranging in the convalescent wards concerts and entertainments for the pleasure of the wounded. The best singers, the most accomplished musicians, were secured for these concerts, and the men seemed appreciative of them. Yet over the head of the Empress Alexandra Feodorovna drifted darker and darker the shadow of impending doom. The things I dared not say to her began to reach her from others. In August came from the Crimea the head man of the Karaim, of whom I have spoken. From the first he made an agreeable im-pression on the Empress and the children, especially upon Alexei, who never tired of listening to his stories. But Gaham had not made the journey from the Crimea to relate legends and tales. He had previously been connected with the Ministry of Foreign Affairs, serving in Persia and the East, and his acute mind was still occupied with the foreign affairs of the Empire on which he kept himself well informed.

Determined, if possible, to force the Empress to understand the gravity of the situation, he told her a number of extraordinary things which had come to his knowledge, among them an organized plot against the throne which was being carried on by near relatives of the Tsar in the seclusion of an allied foreign embassy in Petrograd. His story, involving, as it did, the ambassador of a friendly power, the trusted representative of an own cousin of the Emperor, seemed to the Empress too preposterous to be credited. Horrified, she ended the conversation, and a few days later she went, taking me with her, to visit the Emperor at the Stavka. What he had to comment on her report of an alleged ambassadorial plot against him I never knew, but I soon became aware that representatives of other foreign countries were undeniably hostile. At the Stavka were military commissions of practically every allied country, among them General Williams and his staff from Great Britain, General Janin from France, General Rikkel from Belgium, and high officers from Italy, Serbia, Rumania, Japan, and other countries, all accompanied by subordinate officers. One afternoon when the gardens were quite crowded by these men and men of our own army, and while the

Empress was making her customary circle, I chanced to overhear a conversation among officers of the foreign military missions, in which the most slanderous words against her Majesty were uttered. "She has come again, it appears," said one of these men, "to see her husband and give him the latest orders of Rasputine." "The suite hate to hear her arrival announced," said another officer. "They know it means changes."

Worse things were said, but without waiting to listen I managed to make my way to the Empress, and that night inviting, as I was well aware, her irritation and disbelief, I related something of what I had overheard. I went further and reminded her of what we both knew, the increasing demoralization of the Emperor's staff. The Grand Dukes and the commanding officers were, as a matter of course, invited each day to lunch with the Emperor, but with insolence and audacity hitherto unheard of, many of the Emperor's near kinsmen declined these invitations. They gave the most trivial and transparent excuses for their absence—headaches, fatigue, previous engagements, alleged duties. The Empress listened to what I said, silent and distraught. She knew, and I also knew, that nothing she could say to the Emperor would make the slightest impression. His eyes and ears were still closed to the gathering tempest.

General Alexieff, Chief of Staff, and undoubtedly a valuable officer, had, I soon learned, been drawn into the plot. The Emperor suspected him to be in correspondence with the traitor Goutchkoff, but when questioned General Alexieff denied this vehemently. He was soon, however, to prove his treachery to the Emperor. There was in attendance on his Majesty at the Stavka an old officer, General Ivanoff, a St. George Cross man, who formerly had held command of the Army of the South. This devoted and loyal old soldier General Alexieff knew he must get rid of, and this, had he been honest, he might have done by pleading age or decreased usefulness. Instead, he merely summoned General Ivanoff and informed him that to the regret of the whole staff he was removed. The Chief of Staff was not responsible for this, he declared, the order having come from the Empress and her accomplices, Rasputine and Mme. Virubova. What General Alexieff said to the Emperor on the subject I do not know, but when next the two met the Emperor turned his head aside. This sudden coldness on the part of the Emperor, whom old General Ivanoff loved dearly, made it impossible for him to seek an audience, and yet the general was valiantly determined not to leave the Stavka without presenting his case to the Sovereign. Calling on me that same day, he repeated to me, while tears rolled down his white beard, the lying words of General Alexieff against the Empress. Feeling it against reason and justice that the Emperor should remain in ignorance of this insult to his wife, I promised to speak to him about it, and this I did, but to little purpose. The Emperor's wrath against Alexieff was indeed kindled but he evidently felt that he could not, at that critical hour, dismiss an officer whose services were so urgently in demand. After-wards, however, his manner towards old General Ivanoff became conspicuously kind.

We remained for some time after this at the Stavka, days to me of such sad remembrance that I can scarcely endure the task of recording them. The Empress and her suite, the Grand Duchesses, and myself lived on board the Imperial train, motor cars coming each day at one o'clock to take us to staff headquarters to luncheon. Headquarters were in an ancient villa of the Governor of the Province, a rather old-fashioned and uncomfortable place. Even the huge dining room where the Emperor and Empress, the staff and the officers of the foreign missions met each day was a dull and gloomy room. When the weather became very warm this dismal apartment was abandoned, and luncheon was served in a large tent in a shady part of the grounds overlooking the town and farther away still the flowing tide of the mighty Dnieper. The only really bright circumstance of the time was the growing health and strength of the Tsarevitch. He was developing marvelously through the summer, both in bodily vigor and in gaiety of spirits. With his tutors, M. Gilliard and Petroff, he romped and played as though illness were a thing to him unknown. With, several of the allied officers, notably with the Belgian General Rikkel, he was also on the best of terms.

Every day after luncheon the maids came from the train with what gowns and other apparel we needed for the remaining functions of the day. There was little room in the house in which to change, but we managed to appropriate a few nooks and corners, and to make ourselves as presentable as possible in the circumstances. In the Emperor's scant hours of leisure he loved to walk with his family in the woods along the river brink, and sometimes when I saw the Empress sitting on the grass talking informally with the peasant women who crowded around her, I took comfort, believing then, as

I still believe, that the great mass of the Russian people were to the end faithful to their Sovereigns. As for the suite, most of them became increasingly indifferent, bound up in their foolish personal affairs, diverting themselves with whispered gossip and laughter, apparently quite indifferent to the calamitous progress of the War. People to whom religion is still in these cynical days a real refuge will understand me when I tell them what comfort I found in an ancient convent in the neighborhood, and in the poor little church which adjoined it. The one treasure of this church was an old and highly revered image of Our Lady of Mogiloff and almost every day of that distressful summer I managed to spend a few minutes on my knees before her dark and mystic image. One day, feeling in my heart the imminence of a danger I dared not name even to myself, I took off my diamond earrings and laid them at the foot of the shrine where I had sought and received peace of mind. I hope my poor offering was received with grace by the saint, who of course did not need it, but whose helpless ones always do. A little later the monks presented me with a small replica of the image, and strangely enough this was the one ikon I was permitted to take with me when I was sent to the Fortress of Peter and Paul.

Of that unhappy summer of 1916 I have only one or two more incidents to relate. One of these was a visit to the Stavka of the Princess Paley, wife of Grand Duke Paul. Coming from Kiev, where the Empress Dowager and the Grand Duke Nicholai Michailovitch were in residence, it appeared ominous to me that they too, all of them, seemed to be inoculated with the delusion of the German spy and the Rasputine influence. Neither the Princess nor the Grand Duke were in the least tactful in the expression of their opinions on the subject. Another visitor to the Stavka was Rodzianko, who came to demand the instant dismissal of Protopopoff, Minister of the Interior, once his friend and confidant, but now accused by the President of the Duma of being a lunatic. The Emperor received Rodzianko coldly, and did not even invite him to lunch. At tea that afternoon the Emperor said that the interview had angered him intensely as he knew quite well that Rodzianko's representations and motives were wholly insincere. Almost everything at the Stavka was growing worse and worse, the Grand Dukes being more insolent than ever and continually annoying General Voyeikoff by ordering trains and motors for themselves without any regard to the requirements of the Emperor. It was with feelings of unspeakable relief that in November, 1916, we left the Stavka for Tsarskoe Selo. In the Imperial train with us traveled young Grand Duke Dmitri Pavlovitch who even then was probably involved in a deadly plot against their Majesties. Yet this young man was able to keep up a pretense of friendship with the Empress, sitting beside her couch and entertaining her by the hour with amusing gossip and stories. Hearing the laughter the Emperor often opened his study door to listen and to join in the conversation. It was a merry journey home, yet within a few days after we arrived troubles again began to multiply. Entering the Empress's door one day, I found her in a passion of indignation and grief. As soon as she could speak she told me that the Emperor had sent her a letter from Nicholai Michailovitch, in which the Empress was specifically charged with the most mischievous political machinations. "Unless this is stopped," the letter concluded, "murders will certainly begin."*

Nicholai Michailovitch, it appears, had gone to the Stavka from the group in Kiev, with the express object of delivering this letter. Every member of the staff knew his errand and expected him to be ignominiously ejected from the Emperor's study. Nothing of the kind happened, and the Grand Duke stayed to luncheon in the most friendly manner. I do not know what he said to the Emperor, but I do know that the letter was laid on the Emperor's desk. Nothing was said or done to avenge this deadly insult to the wife of Nicholas II whom undoubtedly he loved dearer than his own life. The only explanation I can think of was the Emperor's complete absorption in the War, and in his unshaken conviction that the plotters' gossip was entirely harmless. He had the kind of mind which could concentrate on only one thing at a time, and at this period his whole heart and soul was with the fighting armies. I well remember scraps of conversation with him during those days which indicated that in the back of his mind were many plans for future internal reforms. He spoke of important social changes which must come after the War, social and constitutional reforms. "I will do everything necessary afterwards," he said in more than one of these conversations. "But I cannot act now. I cannot do more than one thing at a time."

The Empress, I think, for all her sensitiveness to the abominable

* Previous to the War and the impending revolution the Empress had had very little to do with politics, but it is true that when affairs became desperate she did what she rightly could to advise her husband.

accusations brought against her, tried to preserve the same waiting state of mind. Most disagreeable incidents she kept to herself, yet one day she showed me a letter written directly to her by a Princess Vassilchikoff, a letter so insulting that the Emperor was aroused to order the Princess and her husband, a member of the Duma, to their country estates. This letter was written on small scraps of paper evidently torn from a cheap writing tablet. "At least," said the Empress with faint sarcasm, "she might have used the stationery of a lady when addressing her Sovereign."

What had taken possession of Petrograd society? I often asked myself. Was it a mob delusion, contagious, like certain diseases? Was it a madness born of the War similar to other strange hysterias which arose during some of the wars of the Middle Ages? That the delusion was confined to Petrograd and a few other towns frequented by the aristocracy was perfectly apparent. In the last days of 1916 the Empress with Olga, Tatiana, and General Racine paid a brief visit to Novgorod to inspect military hospitals and to pray in the monastery and church of Sofisky Sobor, one of the oldest churches in Russia. Her visit was opposed, quite senselessly, by Petrograd society, which accused her of going for some bad purpose, God knows what. But at Novgorod the people poured out in throngs to greet her with peals of bells, music, and cheers. Before leaving the city the Empress paid a visit to a very old woman who had spent forty helpless years in bed, still wearing the heavy chains of penitence which as a pilgrim she had, almost a lifetime before, assumed. As her Majesty entered the old woman's cell a feeble voice uttered these words: "Here comes the martyred Empress, Alexandra Feodorovna." What could this aged and bedridden recluse have known or guessed of events which were to come?

CHAPTER XI

IN preceding chapters I have mentioned the name of Rasputine, that strange and ill-starred being about whom almost nothing is known to the multitude but against whom such horrible accusations have been made that he is universally classed with such monsters of iniquity as Cain, Nero, and Judas Iscariot. Even H. G. Wells, in whose "Outline of History" Joan of Arc and Abraham Lincoln are disposed of in a line, sacrifices valuable space to state as an established fact that in 1917 the Russian Court was "dominated by a religious impostor, Rasputin, whose cult was one of unspeakable foulness, a reeking scandal in the face of the world." I have no desire in this book to attempt an exoneration of Rasputine, for I am not so ambitious as to believe that I can change the collective mind of the world on any point. In the interests of historical truth, however, I believe it to be my simple duty to record the plain tale of how and why Rasputine came to be a factor in the lives of Nicholas II and of Alexandra Feodorovna, his wife, and exactly to what extent he did, or rather, did not, dominate the Russian Court. Those who expect from me secret and sensational disclosures will, I fear, be disappointed, for Rasputine's every movement for years was known to the Russian police, and the most sensational fact of his whole career, his assassination, has been described by practically every writer of the events of the Russian Revolution.

I will first explain the exact status of the man, for this does not appear to be generally understood. He has been called a priest, more often still a monk, but the truth is he was not in holy orders at all. He belonged to a curious species of roving religious peasant which in Russia were called *Stranniki*, the nearest English translation of the word being pilgrims. These wandering peasants, common sights in the old Russia, were accustomed to travel from one end of the Empire to the other, often walking with heavy chains on their bodies to make their progress more painful and difficult. They went from church to church, shrine to shrine, monastery to monastery, praying, fasting, mortifying the flesh, and their prayers were, by a very considerable population, eagerly sought and devoutly believed in. Once in a while a *Strannik* appeared who, by virtue of his extreme piety, gift of speech, or strong personality, acquired more than local reputation. Churchmen of high rank, estate owners, and even members of the nobility invited these men to their houses, listened with interest to their discourses, and asked for their prayers. Such a *Strannik* was Gregory Rasputine, who from the humblest beginnings in a remote Siberian village became known all over the Empire as a man of almost superhuman endowment.

Of the type of Russians to whom the *Stranniki* made a genuine appeal the Emperor and Empress undoubtedly belonged. The Emperor, like several of his near ancestors, was a born mystic, and the soul of Alexandra Feodorovna, either from natural inclination or from close association with him whom she so dearly loved, leaned also towards mysticism. By this I do not mean that the Emperor and the Empress were at all interested in spiritualism, table-tipping, or alleged materializations from the world beyond. Far from it. In the earliest days of my acquaintance with the Empress, as far back as 1905, she gave me a special warning against these things, telling me that if I wished for her friendship never to have anything to do with so-called spiritism. Both the Emperor and the Empress were profoundly interested in the religious life and expressions of the whole human race. They read with sympathy and understanding the religious literature not only of Christendom but of India, Persia, and the countries of the Far East. I remember in connection with the Empress's first warning against spiritism that she gave me a book, an obscure fourteenth-century missal called "*Les Amis des Dieu*" which, in spite of her warm recommendation, I found great difficulty in reading. This interest in religion and the life of the spirit was actually what constituted what Mr. Wells calls the "crazy pietism" of Nicholas II. It was simple Christianity lived and not merely subscribed to as a theory. They believed that prophecy, in the Biblical sense of the word, still existed in certain highly gifted and spiritually minded persons. They believed that it was possible outside the church and without the aid of regularly ordained bishops and priests to hold communion with God and with His Spirit. Before I came to Court there was a Frenchman, Dr. Philippe, in whom they reposed the greatest confidence, believing him to be one in whom the gift of prophecy existed. I never knew Dr. Philippe, hence I can speak of him only as a sort of a forerunner of Rasputine, because, as the Empress told me, his coming was foretold by Dr. Philippe. Very shortly before his death the French mystic told them that they would have another friend authorized to speak to them from God, and when Rasputine appeared he was accepted as that friend.

Rasputine, although very poor and humble and almost entirely illiterate, had acquired a great reputation as a preacher, and had especially attracted the attention of Bishop Theofan, a churchman of renown in Petrograd. Bishop Theofan introduced the *Strannik* to the wife of Grand Duke Nicholas, who immediately conceived a warm admiration for him, and began to speak to her friends of his marvelous piety and spiritual insight. At that time the Emperor was on very friendly terms with the Grand Duke Nicholas, or rather with his wife and her sister, two princesses of Montenegro who had married, not quite in conformity with the rules of the Orthodox Church, the brothers, Grand Dukes Nicholas and Peter. One of these sisters, Princess Melitza, Grand Duchess Peter, had something of a reputation as a mystic, and it was at her house that the Emperor and Empress met first Dr. Philippe and later Rasputine. In one of my first conversations with the Empress she told me this, and told me also how deeply the conversation of the Siberian peasant had interested both her husband and herself. In fact Rasputine, at that period, interested and impressed almost everyone with whom he came in contact. When the house of Stolypine was blown up by terrorist bombs and, among others, his beloved daughter was grievously wounded, it was Rasputine whom the famous statesman summoned to her bedside for prayer and supplication. I am aware that the public generally believes that it was I who introduced Rasputine into the Russian Court, but truth compels me to declare that he was well known to the Sovereigns and to most of the Court long before I ever saw him.

It was about a month before my marriage in 1907 that the Empress asked Grand Duchess Peter to make me acquainted with Rasputine. I had heard that the Grand Duchess was very clever and well read, and I was glad of the opportunity of meeting her in her palace on the English Quay in Petrograd. Interesting as I found her, I was nevertheless thrilled with excitement when a servant announ-ced the arrival of Rasputine. Before his entrance the Grand Duchess said to me: "Do not be astonished if I greet him peasant fashion," that is, with three kisses on the cheek. She did so greet him and then she presented us to each other. I saw an elderly peasant, thin, with a pale face, long hair, an uncared-for beard, and the most extraordinary eyes, large, light, brilliant, and apparently capable of seeing into the very mind and soul of the person with whom he held converse. He wore a long peasant coat, black and rather shabby from hard wear and much travel. We talked and the Grand Duchess, speaking in French, bade me ask him to pray for some special desire of mine. Timidly I begged him to pray that God would permit me to spend my whole life serving their Majesties. To this he replied: "Your whole life will be thus spent." We parted then, but shortly afterwards, just before my wedding day, when my heart was in a tumult of doubt and anxiety, I wrote to the Grand Duchess Peter and asked her to seek Rasputine's counsel in my behalf. His word to me was that I would marry as I had planned but that I should not find happiness in my marriage. It will be seen how little I regarded him as a prophet at this time since I paid no attention to his warning. A full year after my marriage I saw Rasputine for the second time. It was on a train going from Petrograd to Tsarskoe Selo, he being on his way there to visit friends who were in no way connected with the Court.

But, asks the bewildered reader, when and how did Rasputine acquire the dreadful, almost unprintable reputation which classes him with the arch-fiend himself? To answer the question satisfactorily I should have to reveal at great length the strangely abnormal and hysterical mentality of the Russian people of that epoch. I shall try to do this as I go farther, but here I shall give, as a sort of illustration of the lunacy of the hour, a little experience of my own. It was on the first occasion after my arrest by Kerensky in the spring of 1917, when I was brought before the High Commission of Justice of the Provisional Government. Weak and ill from my long imprisonment in the gloomy Fortress of Peter and Paul, I found myself facing an imposing group of something like forty judges, all learned in the law and clothed in such dignity of office that I gazed at them in a kind of awe. In my distracted mind I asked myself what questions these grave magistrates would ask me, and in what pro-found language would their questions be clothed. My heart almost stopped beating while I waited for the words of the chief judge. And this is what was said, in a deep and solemn voice: "Tell me, who was it at Court that Rasputine called a flower?" Sheer amazement held me speechless, but even had I been given time I could not have answered the question because there was no such person. The judges whispered together for a moment and then the same man, handing me a piece of cardboard, demanded impressively: "What is the meaning of this secret card which was found in your house by the soldiers?"

I took the piece of cardboard and almost instantly recognized it as a menu card of the yacht *Standert*, dated 1908. On the reverse side were written the names of war vessels present at that date at a naval review held near Kronstadt, Russian vessels all, among which the position of the Imperial yacht was marked by a crown. I handed the menu card back to the judge saying merely: "Look at it, and look at the date." He looked at it and in some confusion muttered: "It is true." One more question those giant intellects found to ask me. "Is it a fact that the Empress could not live without you?" To which I replied as any sensible person would have done: "Why should a happy wife and mother be unable to live without a mere friend?" The inquiry was then hastily closed and I was ordered back to prison, to be watched more closely than ever, *because I would not answer to judgment.*

This is a perfectly fair sample of the madness and confusion of the Russian mind, or rather the Petrograd mind, before and after the Revolution. That this madness, this unreasoning mania for the destruction of all institutions might have something to justify itself in the public mind, it was absolutely necessary to find and to persecute individuals who typified, in popular imagination, the things which were so bitterly hated. Rasputine, more than any one other individual in the Empire, did typify old and unpopular institutions, and I can readily see why some intelligent and fair-minded persons thus accepted him. Dillon, for example, in his book, "The Eclipse of Russia," says: "It is my belief that although his friends were influential Rasputine was a symbol."

Russia, like eighteenth-century France, passed through a period of acute insanity from which it is only now beginning to emerge in remorse and pain. This insanity was by no means confined to the ranks of the so-called Revolutionists. It pervaded the Duma, the highest ranks of society, Royalty itself, all as guilty of Russia's ruin as the most blood-thirsty terrorist. What had happened in these dark years between 1917 and 1923 is simply the punishment of God for the sins of a whole people. When His avenging hand has so plainly been laid upon all of the Russian people how dare any of us lay the calamity entirely at the doors of the Bolsheviki? We Russians look on the appalling condition of our once great country, we behold the famishing millions on the Volga and in the Ukraine, we count the fearful roll of the murdered, the imprisoned, the exiled, and we cry weakly that the Tsar was guilty, Rasputine was guilty, this man and that woman were guilty, but never do we admit that we were all guilty, guilty of blackest treason to our God, our Emperor, our country. Yet not until we cease to accuse others and repent our own sins will the white dawn of God's mercy rise over the starved and barren desert that was once mighty Russia.

Rasputine, it seems to be generally assumed, having been introduced to the Imperial Family, took up his residence in the palace of the Romanoffs and thereafter held in his hands the reins of government. Those who do not literally believe this are nevertheless persuaded that Rasputine lived very near their Majesties, saw them constantly, was consulted and obeyed by the Ministers, and with the aid and connivance of adoring women attached to the Court, ruled by fear and superstition the whole governing class of the Empire. If I denied that Rasputine ever lived at Court, ever had the smallest influence over governmental policies, ever ruled through adoring and superstitious women, I should not hope to be believed. I will then simply call attention to the fact that every move of Rasputine from the hour when he began to frequent the palaces of the Grand Dukes, especially from the day he met the Emperor and Empress in the drawing room of the Grand Duchess Melitza, to the midnight when he met his death in the Yusupoff Palace on the Moika Canal in Petrograd, is a matter of the most minute police record. The police know how many days of each year Rasputine spent in Petrograd and how much of his time was lived in Siberia. They know exactly how many times he called at the palace at Tsarskoe Selo, how long he stayed and who was present. They know when and under exactly the circumstances Rasputine came to my house, and who else came to the house at the same time. The police know more about Rasputine than all the journalists and the historians put together, and their records show that he spent most of his time in Siberia, and that when he visited Petrograd he lived in rather humble lodgings in an unfashionable street, 54 Gorochovaia. Rasputine never lived in the palace, seldom visited it, saw the Emperor less frequently than the Empress, and had among the women of the Court more enemies than friends.

The English-speaking reader may doubt the completeness and the accuracy of police records, knowing that in his own country only criminals and people of the underworld are really watched by the police. To know what police surveillance can mean it is necessary to have known Russia before 1917. I do not speak of the Bolshevik police. It is fairly well known what they are, but after all their methods, if not their motives, are founded on the Okhrana of the old days.

To give an idea of the ever-open and searching eye of the old Russian police I will describe what the situation was in the Imperial palace itself. In connection with the palace, or any of the Imperial residences, the persons of the Emperor and his family, the police force was organized in three sections. There were the palace police, a Cossack *convoi*, and a regiment of Guards known as the *Svodny Polk*. Besides the ranking officers of these organizations there was, over them all, a palace commandant, in the latest days of the Empire, General Voyeikoff. It was impossible for anyone to approach the palace, much less to be received by one of their Majesties, without the fact being known to scores of these police guards. Every soldier, every guard, in uniform or out, kept a notebook in which he was obliged to write down for inspection by his superiors the movements of all persons who entered the palace and even those who passed its walls. Moreover, they were obliged to communicate by telephone with their superior officers every event, however trivial, of which they were witness. This vigilance was extended even to the persons of the Emperor and his family. If the Empress ordered her carriage for two o'clock in the afternoon, the lackey receiving the order immediately informed the nearest police guard of the fact. The guard telephoned the news to the palace commandant's office and from there the information went by telephone to the offices of the separate police organizations: "Her Majesty's carriage has been ordered for two o'clock." This meant that from the time the Empress and her companion, or her children, drove from the palace doors to the hour when they re-turned the roads were lined with police, ready with their notebooks to record every single incident of the drive. Should the Empress stop her carriage to speak to an acquaintance, that unhappy individual would afterwards be approached by a guard standing in the road or behind trees or shrubbery, who would demand: "What is your name, and for what reason had you conversation with her Majesty?" With all her heart the Empress detested this system of police espionage, but it was one of the Russian ironclad traditions which neither she nor the Emperor could alter or abolish.

If the Imperial Family was thus subject to police surveillance the reader can easily imagine how closely the ordinary citizen and especially citizens of eminence were watched. I would not venture to declare on my own unsupported authority that Rasputine rarely visited the palace, at first two or three times a year, and but little oftener at the last, but I can state that these facts are on record in the police annals of Petrograd and Tsarskoe Selo. In the year of his death, 1916, Rasputine saw the Emperor exactly twice. There is one unfortunate fact in connection with these visits. I write it regretfully but it is true, and I can see how that circumstance served with some people to put a false emphasis on the visits of Rasputine to the Imperial household. In spite of the well-known fact that every visit of Rasputine was necessarily a public appearance, in full limelight, as it were, the Emperor and Empress attempted to throw over his visits a certain veil of secrecy. They had done the same thing with Dr. Philippe, and I suppose from the same motives. Every human being craves a little personal privacy. In the most loving family circle who does not at times want to be alone with his thoughts or his prayers behind closed doors? Thus it was with their Majesties. Rasputine represented to them hopes and aspirations far removed from earthly power and glory, and from earthly pain and suffering. They knew that he was a simple peasant and that many people of rank in official circles thought it strange, some even thought it undignified, for their Majesties of great Russia to listen to the counsels of so lowly and ignorant a man. For this reason, I know of no other, the Emperor and Empress vainly tried to make the visits of Rasputine as inconspicuous as possible. He was admitted into a side entrance instead of the main doorway; he went upstairs by a small staircase; he was received in the private apartments and never in the public drawing rooms. It was the same in Tsarskoe Selo and in the Crimea, in which latter place a day's visit served for a year's gossip throughout the entire estate. More than once I pointed out to the Empress the futility of the course pursued. "You know that before he reaches the palace, much less your boudoir, he has been written down at least forty times," I reminded her. The Empress always agreed. She knew that the police were everywhere, inside and outside the palace, in every corridor, at every door. She knew that there could be no secrets in the palace, and the Emperor knew it as well as she did, yet they persisted in trying to shield Rasputine from the publicity they knew to be inevitable for everyone.

It was generally in the evening that he was received, not because the eternal police vigilance was relaxed at that time, but because it was only in the evening that the Emperor found leisure for his personal friends. In the hour following dinner it sometimes happened that little Alexei came downstairs in his blue nightgown to talk with his father a few minutes before going to bed. When on these occasions Rasputine was present, the boy and his parents and any intimate friend who happened to be in the room would listen fascinated while the *Strannik* talked of Siberia and its peasants, of his wanderings through remote corners of Russia, and of his sojourn in the Holy Lands. His speech was simple, but strangely eloquent and uplifting. Their Majesties talked gladly to him of whatever happened to be on their minds, the ill health of their only son, principally, and he seemed to know how to comfort and to give them hope. They were always lighter of heart after his visits, and even had I conspired with him to gain their friendship the effort would have been quite useless and unnecessary. They liked him so well that when gossip or newspaper accusations of Rasputine's drunkenness and debauchery were brought to their attention they said only: "He is hated because we love him." And that ended the matter.

I will say for the Empress that although she had the fullest confidence in Rasputine's integrity she thought it worth while to make some inquiries into his private life in Siberia, where most of his time was spent. On two occasions she sent me, with others, to his distant village of Pokrovskoe to visit him. I wished then, and I do now, that she had selected someone wiser and more critical than myself. Of detective ability I possess not a trace. With me it is always, what I have seen I have seen. In company with Mme. Orloff, mother of General Orloff, and with two other women and our maids, I made the long journey to Siberia leaving the railroad at the little town of Toumean. Here Rasputine met us with a clumsy peasant cart drawn by two farm horses. In this springless vehicle we drove eighty versts across the steppes to the village where Rasputine dwelt with his old wife, his three children, and two aged spinsters who helped in the housework and in the care of the fields and the cattle. The household was almost Biblical in its bare simplicity, all the guests sleeping in an upper chamber on straw mattresses laid on the rough board floor. Except for the beds the rooms were practically without furniture, although on the walls were ikons before which faint tapers burned. We ate our plain meals in the common room downstairs, and in the evening there usually came four peasant men, devoted friends of Rasputine, who were called "the brothers." Sitting around the table they sang prayers and psalms with rustic faith and fervor. Almost every day we went down to the river to watch Rasputine and the brothers, fishermen all, draw in their nets, and often we ate our dinner by the river, cooking fish over little campfires on the shore, sharing in common our raisins, bread, nuts, and perhaps a little pastry. The season being Lent we had no meat, no milk, nor butter.

On my return to Tsarskoe Selo I described this pastoral existence to the Empress, and I had to add to my observations only that the clergy of the village seemed to dislike Rasputine, while the majority of the villagers merely took him for granted as one they had long been accustomed to. In a later year I was again sent to Siberia, this time with Mme. Julia (Lili) Dehn, wife of a naval officer on the yacht *Standert*, and several others, and a man servant as my special assistant as I was then very lame from the railroad accident which I have described. This time we went by boat from Toumean to Tobolsk on the River Toura, to view the relics of the Metropolitan John of Tobolsk, a sainted man of the time of Peter the Great. While in Tobolsk we were entertained in the house of the Governor of the Department, the same house where in the first days of their Siberian exile the Imperial Family were lodged. It was a large, very well furnished house on the river, but one could see that in winter it must have been extremely cold. On our way back we stopped for two days at Pokrovskoe, visiting Rasputine and finding him exactly as before, the old wife and the serving maids still occupied with household tasks and with field labor. I may add that in both of these visits I went to the famous monastery of Verchotourie, on the Ural River, where are kept some deeply venerated relics of St. Simeon. In the forests surrounding the monastery are many tiny wooden huts in which dwell solitary monks or anchorites, and among these was a celebrated old monk known as Father Makari. This aged and pious monk apparently held Rasputine in higher respect than did the village clergy, and they talked together like equals and friends, while we listened silently but with deep interest.

The wave of popular opposition against Rasputine began, I should say, in the last two and a half years of his life. Long after it began, long after his name was reviled and execrated in the press and in society, his lodgings in Petrograd, where he began to spend longer and longer intervals, were constantly crowded with beggars and petitioners. These were people of all stations who believed that whether he were good or evil his influence at Court was limitless. Every kind of petty official, every sort of poverty-stricken aspirant and grafting politician, and, of course, a whole crew of revolutionary agents, spies, and secret police haunted the place, pressing on Rasputine papers and petitions to be presented to the Emperor. To do Rasputine strict justice, he was forever telling the petitioners that it would be no good at all for him to present their papers, but he did not seem to have strength of mind to refuse point-blank to receive them. Often in pity for those who were sick and poor, or as he thought deserving, he would send them to one or another of his rich and influential acquaintances with a note saying: "Please, dear friend, receive him." It is very sad to reflect that his recommendation was the worst possible introduction a poor wretch could bear with him.

One of the hardest tasks which the Empress imposed upon me was the taking of messages, usually about the health of Alexei, to these crowded lodgings of Rasputine. As often as I appeared the people overwhelmed me with demands for money, positions, advancement, pardons, and what not. It was of no use to assure the people that I neither possessed nor desired to possess the kind of influence they believed to be mine. It was equally useless to assure them that their petitions, if I took them, would not be read by the Empress, but would merely be referred to her secretary, Count Rostovseff. Sometimes I encountered a case of great distress which if possible I tried privately to relieve. One day I met on the staircase a very poor young student who asked me if I could help him to a warm coat. I knew where I could get such a coat and I sent it to the student. Months afterwards when I was a prisoner in the fortress I received a note from this young man, telling me that he prayed daily for my safety and release. This almost unique instance of gratitude remains in my mind among memories much less agreeable of my visits to the lodgings of Rasputine.

CHAPTER XII

THERE is a photograph which, in the last days of the Empire, was published all over Russia, and was, I am informed, also published in western Europe and in America. It represents Rasputine sitting like an oracle in his lodgings, surrounded by ladies of the aristocracy. This photograph is supposed to illustrate the enormous hold which Rasputine possessed on the affections of the women of the Court. In plain language it is assumed to be a repre-sentation of Rasputine sitting in the midst of his harem. There has been no account published which, as far as I know, does not dwell on this phase of the Rasputine story, and there have been books published in which the most erotic letters, purporting to have been written him by the Empress herself and even by the innocent young Grand Duchesses, have been included, the publishers apparently never having inquired into their authenticity. Knowing that my evidence will be considered of little worth, I still have the temerity to state without any qualification whatsoever that these stories are without the slightest foundation. Rasputine had no harem at Court. In fact, I cannot remotely imagine a woman of education and refine-ment being attracted to him in a personal way. I never knew of one being so attracted, and although accusations of secret debauchery with women of the lower classes were made against him by agents of the Okhrana, the special inquiry instituted by the Commission of the Provisional Government failed to produce any evidence in support of the charges. The police were never able to bring forward a single woman of any class whom they could accuse with Rasputine.

The photograph, however, is authentic. I figure in it myself, therefore I am in a position to explain it. It shows a group of women and men who after attending early Mass sometimes gathered around Rasputine for religious discourse, for advice on all manner of things, and probably on the part of some for the gratification of idle curiosity. I do not know whether or not in western countries religion produces in the neurotic and shallow-minded a kind of emotional excitement which they mistake for faith, but in Russia there was a time when this was so. For the most part, however, it was really serious people, men and women, who went after Mass to listen to the discourses of Rasputine. He was, as I have said, an unlettered man, but he knew the Scriptures and his interpretations were so keen and so original that highly educated people, even learned churchmen, liked to listen to them. In matters of faith and doctrine he could never be confused or confounded. Moreover, his sympathy and his charity were so wide and tender that he attracted women of narrow lives whose small troubles might have been dismissed as trivial by ordinary confessors. For example, many lovelorn women (men too) used to go to those morning meetings to beg his prayers on their heart's behalf. He knew that unsatisfied love is a very real trouble, and he was always gentle and patient with such people, that is, if their souls were innocent. For irregular love affairs he had no patience whatever, and in this connection I remember an incident which illustrates this point, and also his remarkable powers of divination, or if you prefer, his keen intuition. A young married woman, harmless enough in her intentions, but rather frivolous nevertheless, came one morning to Rasputine's lodgings en route to a rendezvous with a handsome young officer who at the moment strongly attracted her. It was her idea to ask Rasputine's prayers in behalf of her special desire, but before she could say a word to him he gave her a keen glance and said: "I am going to relate to you a story. Once when I was traveling in Siberia I entered a small railroad station and beheld at a table a monk who recognized me and begged me to join him in a glass of tea. As I approached the table I saw him hastily conceal a bottle under the folds of his soutaine. He said: 'You are called a saint. Will you not help me to understand some of the troubled problems of my life?' I replied 'Ah! You call me a saint. But why do you at the time of asking me to help your troubled soul try to hide that bottle under your robe?" The young woman turned deathly pale and without a word rose hastily and left the room.

This is only one of many similar incidents. Once at Kiev a Government functionary approached Rasputine and asked his prayers for one lying very ill. Rasputine's amazing eyes gazed into the eyes of the other and he said calmly: "I advise you to beseech not my prayers but those of Ste. Xenia." The functionary completely taken aback exclaimed: "How could you know that her name was Xenia?" I could relate many other such instances which can, of course, be attributed to intuition, thought transference, anything you like. But of true predictions of future events made by Rasputine what explanation can be given? What of his mysterious powers over the sick?

In behalf of the suffering little Tsarevitch the Emperor and Empress constantly asked the prayers of Rasputine, and the incident which I shall now relate will appeal to any mother or father of a suffering child and will render less childlike the faith of the afflicted parents of the heir to the throne. One day during the War the Emperor left Tsarskoe Selo for general headquarters, taking with him as usual the Tsarevitch. The child seemed to be in good condition, but a few hours after leaving the palace he was taken with a nosebleed. This is ordinarily a harmless enough manifestation, but in one suffering from Alexei's incurable malady it was a very serious thing. The doctors tried every known remedy, but the hemorrhage became steadily worse until death by exhaustion and loss of blood was threatened. I was with the Empress when the telegram came announcing the return of the Emperor and the boy to Tsarskoe Selo, and I can never forget the anguish of mind with which the poor mother awaited the arrival of her sick, perhaps her dying child. Nor can I ever forget the waxen, gravelike pallor of the little pointed face as the boy with infinite care was borne into the palace and laid on his little white bed. Above the blood-soaked bandages his large blue eyes gazed at us with pathos unspeakable, and it seemed to all around the bed that the last hour of the unhappy child was at hand. The physicians kept up their ministrations, exhausting every means known to science to stop the incessant bleeding. In despair the Empress sent for Rasputine. He came into the room, made the sign of the cross over the bed and, looking intently at the almost moribund child, said quietly to the kneeling parents: "Don't be alarmed. Nothing will happen." Then he walked out of the room and out of the palace.

THE THREE CHILDREN OF RASPUTINE BEFORE THEIR HOUSE IN SIBERIA.

THE GUEST ROOM (THE ONLY LARGE ROOM) IN RASPUTINE'S HOUSE IN SIBERIA.

That was all. The child fell asleep, and the next day was so well that the Emperor left for his interrupted visit to the Stavka. Dr. Derevanko and Professor Fedoroff told me afterwards that they did not even attempt to explain the cure. It was simply a fact. For this and for other like services Rasputine never received any money from the Emperor or the Empress. Indeed he was never given any money by their Majesties except an occasional one-hundred-ruble note to pay cab fares and traveling expenses when he was sent for. In the last two years of his life the rent of his modest lodgings in Petrograd was paid. What money he had was received from petitioners who hoped through him to benefit in high quarters. Rasputine took this money, but he gave most of it to the poor, so that when he died his family was left practically penniless. That Rasputine, whatever his faults, was no mercenary is the simple truth. As far back as 1913 Kokovseff, Minister of Finance, who disliked and distrusted Rasputine, offered him 200,000 rubles if he would leave Petrograd and never return. Two hundred thousand rubles was a fortune beyond the dream of avarice to a Russian peasant, but Rasputine declined it, saying that he was not to be bought by anybody. "If their Majesties wish me to leave Petrograd," he said, "I will go at once, and for no money at all."

I know of many cases of illness where the prayers of Rasputine were asked, and had he been so minded he might have demanded and been given vast sums of money. But the fact is he often showed himself extremely reluctant to exert whatever strange power he possessed. In some instances where sick children were involved he would even object, saying: "If God takes him now it is perhaps to save him from future sins."

This indifference to money on the part of Rasputine was all the more conspicuous in a country where almost every hand was stretched out for reward, graft, or blackmail. The episode of one of Rasputine's bitterest enemies, the "mad" monk Illiador, is illuminating. Illiador was a person altogether disreputable, an unfrocked monk, and in my opinion a man mentally as well as morally irresponsible. He made friends with certain ministers, among them Chvostoff, one of several who, after the death of Stolypine, held for a time the portfolio of Minister of the Interior. Between Chvostoff and Illiador was concocted a plot to assassinate Rasputine. This was not successful because Illiador made the mistake of sending his wife to Petrograd with incriminating documents. But he was able to send a woman to Siberia, and she dealt Rasputine a knife wound from which he with difficulty recovered. This was in 1914.

After Rasputine the object of Illiador's greatest hatred was the Empress. His plot against Rasputine failing, he wrote against the Empress one of the most scurrilous and obscene books imaginable, but before attempting to publish it he sent her word that he would sell her the manuscript for sixty thousand rubles. Publishers in America, he wrote, would pay him a much higher price for the book, but he was willing to sacrifice something to save a woman's reputation. To this low blackmailer the indignant Empress returned no answer at all. Illiador lives in Russia now, a great favorite with the

Bolsheviki because of his bitter attacks on the clergy. But whether or not they permitted him to retain his profits on the book against the Empress I do not know.

But what of Rasputine's political influence, his treason with the Germans? The excuse for his murder was that he was leading the Emperor and Empress into the German net, persuading them to betray the Allies by making a separate peace. If I knew or suspected this to be true I would not hesitate to record it here. I would not dare to suppress such important historical evidence, if I had it, because all that I am writing in this book is for the future, not the present; for history, not for the ephemeral journalism of the day. Ministers, politicians, churchmen haunted the lodgings of Rasputine, and if any man ever had an opportunity to mingle in secret diplomacy he was that man. As a matter of plain justice to him, I do not believe such matters ever interested him. On two occasions of which I have knowledge he did give the Emperor political advice, and very shrewd advice, although it was received with irritation and resentment by his Majesty. One of these occasions was in 1912 when Grand Duke Nicholas, whose wife it will be remembered was a Montenegran, tried his every power of persuasion to bring Russia into the Balkan Wars. Rasputine implored the Emperor not to listen to this counsel. Only enemies of Russia, he declared, wanted to involve their country in that struggle, the inevitable outcome of which would be disaster to the Empire and to the house of Romanoff.

Rasputine always dreaded war, predicting that it would surely bring ruin to Russia and the monarchy. At the beginning of the World War he was lying wounded by Illiador's assassin in Siberia, but he sent a long telegram to the Emperor begging him to preserve peace. The Emperor, believing intervention in Serbia a point of honor, tore up the telegram and for a time appeared rather cold towards Rasputine. But as the War progressed they became friends again, for after it became inevitable Rasputine wanted the War fought through to a victorious end. The last time the Emperor saw him, about a month before his assassination, he gave a signal proof of this. The meeting took place in my house, and I heard every word of the conversation. The Emperor was depressed and pessimistic. Owing to heavy storms and lack of transportation facilities there had been difficulty in getting foodstuffs into Petrograd, and even some army battalions were lacking certain necessities. Nature itself, said the Emperor, seemed to be working against Russia's success in the War, to which Rasputine replied strongly advising the Emperor never, on any account, to be tempted to give up the struggle. The country that held out the longest against adverse circumstances, he said, would certainly win the War.

As Rasputine was leaving the house the Emperor asked him, as usual, for his blessing, but Rasputine replied: "This time it is for you to bless me, not I you." Finally at parting he humbly begged the Emperor to do everything he could in behalf of the wounded and of war orphans, reminding him that all Russia was giving its nearest and dearest for his sake. Did Rasputine on this day have a premonition of the fate that was so soon to overtake him? I cannot answer that question. It is impossible for me to know with any certainty whether or not this strange man was actually gifted with the spirit of prophecy or whether his frequent forecastings of truth were simply fruits of a mind more than normally keen and observant. All I can do, all I have attempted to do, is to picture Rasputine as I knew him. I never once saw him otherwise than I have described. I knew that he was reputed to drink and to indulge in other reprehensible practices. I heard, I suppose, every wild tale that was told of him. But no one ever presented to the Imperial Family or to myself any evidence, any facts in support of these accusations. It is a matter of record, and this the historians of the future will stress, that this man was called a criminal, but that he was never meted out the common justice which is supposed to be the right of the most abandoned criminal. He was accused of nameless crimes and he was executed for those crimes. But he was denied even the rough justice of a trial by his self-appointed judges. Did "Tsarist" Russia ever do such a thing to a man caught red-handed in the murder of an Emperor?

I have added as an appendix to this book a document which has been published in Russian and French, but which I believe appears here for the first time in English. It is the statement of Vladimir Michailovitch Roudneff, a judge of a superior court in Ekaterinoslav, one of a number of distinguished jurists appointed by Kerensky, when Minister of Justice in the Provisional Government, to a special High Commission of Inquiry and Investigation into the Acts of the Sovereigns and other prominent personages before the Revolution of 1917. Judge Roudneff, with great courage and honesty, made an effort to sift the evidence against Rasputine and to separate truth from mere rumor. That he was unable to treat the matter in a mood of perfect judicial calm, although he earnestly wished to do so, is proof enough of the madness of the Russian mind in that time of turmoil and bewilderment. Anyone at all familiar with rules of evidence will perceive how, with the best intentions, Judge Roudneff often offers opinion where facts alone are called for. A great many of his statements, if given in a court of justice, would in any civilized country be challenged and probably ruled out. However, the statement is valuable because it is the unique attempt of a justice-loving individual to escape from the mob mind of 1917 Russia and to present impartially the known facts about Rasputine. For his honesty in insisting that the facts be made public Judge Roudneff was ignominiously removed from the commission by its president, Judge Mouravieff. As far as I know and believe, none of the other members of the commission attempted to publish their findings.

I shall always feel that it was a great pity that Rasputine was not arrested, tried in the presence of his accusers and of all available witnesses, and if found guilty punished to the very limit of the law. As it was he was merely lynched and the question of his guilt or innocence will ever remain unsolved. Latest accounts certainly absolve the Empress of Russia from being his tool and his guilty partner, and death, whether by assassination or at the hand of public justice, has the same end, the righteous judgment of God, and from that perfect justice not the worst enemy of the man could bar the soul of Rasputine.

One thing more I deeply regret and that is that Judge Roudneff could not have tried Rasputine in person as he did try me. I appeared before him no less than fifteen times and I always found him studious at getting at the truth, separating facts from hysterical gossip, all in the interests of justice and of historical records. In his reports concerning me there are some errors, but not serious ones, some confusion of dates, but nothing important, and once or twice some trifling injustice for which I bear not the slightest malice. Judge Roudneff, for example, accuses me of loquacity, and in my testimony of jumping irrelevantly from one thought to another. I cannot help wondering if even a learned judge, after weeks of imprisonment, accompanied by inhuman insults and bodily injuries, and for the first time given an opportunity for explanation and self-defense, would have spoken in quite a calm and normal manner. However, I do not complain of anything Judge Roudneff says of me. I am grateful to the only Russian in a position of authority who has had the chivalry to give me the benefit of a reasonable doubt.

All others, including members of the Romanoff family who have known me from my earliest childhood, who in youth danced and chatted with me at Court balls, who knew my mother and my father, with his long and honorable record, have assailed me without a shred of mercy. They have represented me as a common upstart, an outsider in society who managed through unworthy schemes to worm her way into the confidence of the Empress. They have represented me as an abandoned woman, a criminal, a would-be poisoner of the Tsarevitch. They have been so loud in their denunciations of one defenseless woman that they have succeeded in concealing the fact of their own participation in events for which the Sovereigns were brought to ruin. They have thrown a blind before their responsibility for bringing Rasputine to the Court of Russia. Never do they allow it to be remembered that it was the Grand Dukes Nicholas and Peter and their Montenegran wives, Stana and Melitza, who introduced the Emperor and Empress to the poor peasant pilgrim who, had he never been taken up by these aristocrats, might have lived out an obscure, and perhaps valuable, existence in far Siberia. It was easier for these powerful ones, these sheltered women, these noble gentlemen, to avoid explanation of their part in the Russian tragedy and to take refuge behind the skirts of a woman who, after the overthrow of the Imperial Family, had not a friend on earth to defend or to protect her.

CHAPTER XIII

TWO days after the return of the Empress from her visit to Novgorod, in the earliest hours of December 17 (December 31, Western Calendar) was struck the first blow of the "bloodless" Russian Revolution, the assassination of Rasputine. On the afternoon of December 16 (December 30) I was sent by the Empress on an errand, entirely non-political, to Rasputine's lodgings. I went, as always, reluctantly, because I knew the evil construction which would be placed on my errand by any of the conspirators who happened to see me. Yet, as in duty bound, I went. I stayed the shortest possible time, but in that brief interval I heard Rasputine say that he expected to pay a late evening visit to the Yusupoff Palace to meet Grand Duchess Irene, wife of Prince Felix Yusupoff. Although I knew that

Felix had often visited Rasputine it struck me as odd that he should go to their house for the first time at such an unseemly hour. But to my question Rasputine replied that Felix did not wish his parents to know of his visit. As I was leaving the place Rasputine said a strange thing to me. "What more do you want?" he asked in a low voice. "Already you have received all." All that his prayers could give me? Did he mean that?

That evening in the Empress's boudoir I mentioned this proposed midnight visit, and the Empress said in some surprise: "But there must be some mistake. Irene is in the Crimea, and neither of the older Yusupoffs are in town." Once again she repeated thoughtfully: "There is surely a mistake," and then we began to talk of other things. The next morning soon after breakfast I was called on the telephone by one of the daughters of Rasputine, both of whom were being educated in Petrograd. In some anxiety the young girl told me that her father had gone out the night before in the Yusupoff motor car and had not returned. I was startled, of course, and even a little frightened, but I did not then guess the real significance of her news. When I reached the palace I gave the message to the Empress, who listened with a grave face but with little comment. A few minutes later there came a telephone call from Protopopoff in Petrograd. The police, he said, had reported to him that some time after the last midnight a patrolman standing near the entrance of the Yusupoff Palace had been startled by the report of a pistol. Ringing the doorbell, he was met by a Duma member named Puritchkevitch who appeared to be in an advanced stage of intoxication. In answer to the policeman's inquiry as to whether there was trouble in the house the drunken Puritchkevitch said in a jocular tone that it was nothing, nothing at all, only they had just killed Rasputine. The policeman, probably a none too intelligent specimen, took it as a casual joke of one of the high-born. They were always joking about Rasputine. The man moved on, but somewhat later he decided that he ought to report the matter to headquarters, which he did, but even then his superiors appear to have been too incredulous to act at once.

Protopopoff's message, however, so disquieted the Empress that she asked me to summon another of her trusted friends, Mme. Dehn, whose name I have mentioned before. Mme. Dehn came and we talked over the mystery together, but still without conviction that Puritchkevitch's reckless statement contained any real truth. Later in the day, however, came a telephone message from Grand

Duke Dmitri Pavlovitch, asking to be allowed to take tea with the Empress that afternoon at five. The message was conveyed to the Empress, who, pale and reflective, answered formally that she did not care just then to receive his Highness. Dmitri took the reply in bad grace, insisting that he must see the Empress as he had something special to tell her. Again the Empress refused, this time even more curtly. Almost immediately afterwards, almost as if the two men were in the same room, there came a telephone message from Felix Yusupoff asking if I would see him at tea, or later in the day if I so preferred. I answered that the Empress did not wish me to receive any visitors that day, whereupon Felix demanded an audience with the Empress that he might give her a true account of what had occurred. Her Majesty's reply was: "If Felix has anything to say let him write to me." Several times before the day ended telephone messages came from Felix to me, but none of these would the Empress allow me to answer.

Felix finally wrote a letter to the Empress. I cannot quote this letter verbatim, but I remember exactly its contents. By the honor of his house Prince Felix Yusupoff swore to his Sovereign Empress that the rumor of Rasputine's visit to his home was without any foundation whatever. He had indeed seen Rasputine in the interests of Irene's health, but he had never decoyed the man to his palace, as charged. There had been a party there, on the night in question, just a few friends, including Dmitri, to celebrate the opening of Felix's new apartments. All, he confessed, became drunk, and some foolish and reckless things were said and done. By chance, on leaving the house, one of the guests had shot a dog in the courtyard. That was absolutely all. This letter was not answered, but was turned over to the Minister of Justice.

Thoroughly aroused, the Empress now ordered Protopopoff to make an investigation of the whole affair. She called into council also Minister of War Belaieff, a good man, afterwards murdered by the Bolsheviki. The police, at their commands, went to the deserted Yusupoff palace, first searching for and finding the body of the dog which Felix said they had shot. But the bullet hole in the dog's head had let out little blood, and when the men entered the palace they found it a veritable shambles of blood and disorder. Evidences of a terrific struggle were found in the downstairs study of Prince Felix, on the stairs leading to an upper room, and in the room itself. Then, indeed, the whole power of the police was invoked, and somebody was found to testify that in the dead of night a motor car without any lights was seen leaving the Yusupoff Palace and disappearing in the direction of the Neva. Winter nights in Russia are very dark, as everyone knows, and the car was soon swallowed up in the shadows. The river was next searched, and by a hole in the ice, not far from Krestovsky Island, the police found a man's golosh. By Protopopoff's orders divers immediately searched the hole in the ice, and from it was soon dragged the frozen body of Rasputine. Arms and legs were tightly bound with cords, but the unfortunate man had managed to work loose his right hand which was frozen in a last attempt to make the sign of the cross. The body was taken to the Chesma Hospital, where an autopsy was performed. Although there were bullet holes in the back and innumerable cuts and wounds all over the body, the lungs were full of water, proving that they had thrown him alive into the icy river, and that death had occurred by drowning.

As soon as the news became public all Petrograd burst into a wild orgy of rejoicing. The "beast" was slain, the "evil genius" had disappeared never to return. There was no limit to the wild hysteria of the hour. In the midst of these demonstrations came a telephone message from Protopopoff asking the Empress's advice as to an immediate burial place for the murdered man. Ultimately the body would be sent to his Siberian village, but in the present circumstances the Minister of the Interior thought a postponement of this advisable. The Empress agreed, and she replied that a temporary interment might be arranged at Tsarskoe Selo. On December 29 (January 12) the coffin, accompanied by a kind-hearted sister of mercy, arrived at Tsarskoe. That same day the Emperor came home from the front, and in the presence of the Imperial Family and myself the briefest of services were held. On the dead man's breast had been laid an ikon from Novgorod, signed on the reverse by the Empress and her daughters as a last token of respect. The coffin was not even buried in consecrated ground, but in a corner of the palace park, and as it was being lowered a few prayers were said by Father Alexander, priest of the Imperial chapel. This is a true account of the burial of Rasputine, about which so many fantastic tales have been embroidered.

The horror and shock caused by this lynching, for it can be called by no other name, completely shattered the nerves of the family. The Emperor was affected less by the deed itself than by the fact that it was the work of members of his own family. "Before all

Russia," he exclaimed, "I am filled with shame that the hands of my kinsmen are stained with the blood of a simple peasant." Before this he had often shown disgust at the excesses of the Grand Dukes and their followers, but now he expressed himself as being entirely through with them all.

THE EMPRESS AND YOUNG GRAND DUKE DMITRI,
AFTERWARDS ONE OF RASPUTINE'S ASSASSINS.

But Yusupoff and the others were by no means through with the Rasputine affair. Now that they had murdered and were applauded for the deed by all society, it seemed to them that they were in a position to claim full legal immunity. Grand Duke Alexander Michailovitch, the Emperor's brother-in-law, went to Dobrovolsky, Minister of Justice, and with a good deal of swagger told him that it was the will of the family—that is, of the Grand Dukes—that the whole matter should be quietly dropped. The next day, December 21 (January 5), Alexander Michailovitch drove with his oldest son to Tsarskoe Selo and, without the slightest assumption of deference or respect, entered the Emperor's study, demanding, in the name of the family, that no further investigation of the manner of Rasputine's death be made. In a voice that could easily be heard in the corridor outside the Grand Duke shouted that should the Emperor refuse this demand the throne itself would fall. The Emperor's answer to this insolence was an order of banishment to their estates of Nicholai Michailovitch, Felix, and Dmitri. At this the wrath of the Grand Dukes knew no bounds. A letter blazing with anger and impudence, signed by the whole family, was rushed to the Emperor, but his only comment was a single sentence written on the margin:

MINISTER OF COURT COUNT FREDERICKS, THE EMPRESS IN HER RECLINING CHAIR, AND GRAND DUCHESS TATIANA TAKING TEA IN THE WOODS IN FINLAND, 1911.

Nobody has a right to commit murder." Following this came a cringing letter from Dmitri who, like Felix, tried to lie himself out of all complicity in the crime. On his sacred honor, he declared he had had nothing to do with it. If the Emperor would only consent to see him he promised to establish his innocence. But the Emperor would not consent to see Dmitri. Pale and stern he moved through the rooms or sat so darkly plunged in thought that none of us ventured to disturb or even to speak to him. Into this troubled atmosphere a letter was brought to the Emperor by the Minister of the Interior, who had a right to seize suspicious mail matter. It was a letter written by the Princess Yusupoff to the Grand Duchess Xenia, sister of the Tsar and mother of Felix Yusupoff's wife. It was a most indiscreet letter to be sent at such a time, for it was a clear admission of the guilt of all the plotters. Although as a mother (she wrote) she felt deeply her son's position, she congratulated the Grand Duchess Xenia on her husband's conduct in the affair.

Sandro, she said, had saved the whole situation, evidently meaning that his demand for immunity for all concerned would have to be granted. *She was only sorry that the principals had not been able to bring their enterprise to its desired end.* However, there remained only the task of confining *Her.* Before the affair was finally concluded, she feared, they might send Nicholai Nicholaievitch and Stana to their estates. How stupid to have sent away Nicholai Michailovitch!

This was by no means the end of letters and telegrams seized by the police and brought to the palace. Many were written by relatives and close friends, people of the highest rank, and they all revealed a depth of callousness and treachery undreamed of before by the unhappy Sovereigns. When the Empress read these communications and realized that her nearest and dearest connections were in the ranks of her enemies, her head sank on her breast, her eyes grew dark with sorrow, and her whole countenance seemed to wither and grow old. A few days later the Grand Duchess Serge sent her sister several sacred ikons from the shrine of Saratoff. The Empress, without even looking at them, ordered them sent back to the convent of the Grand Duchess in Moscow.

I should add that from the day of the assassination of Rasputine my mail was full of anonymous letters threatening me with death. The Empress, perhaps more than any of us, instinctively aware of the endless ramifications of the Rasputine affair, commanded me in terms that admitted of no argument to leave my house and to take up residence in the palace. Sad as I was to leave the peace of my little home, I had no alternative than to obey, and with my maid I moved into two rooms in the Grand Ducal wing of the palace, occupied also by maids of honor and reached by the fourth large entrance to the palace. From that day, by command of their Majesties, every movement of mine was closely guarded. The soldier Jouk was assigned to my service and without him I never left the palace even to visit my hospital. When in the February following my only brother was married I was not allowed to attend the wedding.

Little by little, in spite of fears, the palace took on a certain air of tranquillity. In the evenings we sat in the mauve boudoir of the Empress; and as of old, the Emperor read aloud. At Christmas their Majesties saw that the customary trees and gifts were sent to the hospitals and that the usual presents were distributed to the servants. The children too had their Christmas celebration, but over us all hung a cloud of sorrow and of disillusionment. Never had the Emperor and Empress of Russia, rulers of nearly two hundred million souls, seemed so lonely or so helpless. Deserted and betrayed by their relatives, calumniated by men who, in the eyes of the outside world, seemed to represent the Russian people, they had no one left except a few faithful friends, and the Emperor's chosen ministers every one of whom was under the ban of popular obloquy. Most of them were accused of being the appointees of Rasputine, but this at least I am in a position to deny.

Sturmer, Minister of the Interior, and afterwards Prime Minister, was, according to Witte, recommended to the Tsar after the assassination of Pleve. The well-known fact that Sturmer was head of the nobility in the Government of Tver, that he was possessed of enormous estates, and that he had held several important positions at Court, ought to be sufficient proof that he needed no help from Rasputine or any other man. Sturmer was an old man, not brilliant perhaps, but certainly a man of high principles. He was arrested by the Provisional Government, and in the fortress suffered such frightful hardships that he died within a day after the Government, unable to fasten on him the slightest guilt, released him from prison. The Social Revolutionary Sokoloff, a just man, if wrong-headed, has declared publicly that had any Constitutional Assembly been held in Russia, the responsibility of Sturmer's death would have been laid upon Milukoff personally.

As for Protopopoff, he was appointed by the Emperor mainly on his record as a confidential agent of the Duma, and as a personal representative of Rodzianko, President of the Fourth Duma. After Protopopoff's return from an important foreign mission on behalf of the Duma he was presented to the Emperor at G. H. Q., and in a letter to the Empress a few days later, he expressed himself as delighted with the man. The appointment was made in one of those moments of impulse characteristic of Nicholas II, yet it must have been the result of some reflection, as it was the Emperor's expressed desire at this time to name a Minister of the Interior who could work in harmony with the Duma. Protopopoff, who, aside from his relations with Rodzianko, had for many years been a delegate from his own Zemstvo to the Union of Zemstvos, naturally appealed to the Emperor as an ideal popular candidate. No one could have been more astonished than he when, almost immediately after his appointment, Rodzianko and almost the entire majority party in the Duma joined in a clamor for Protopopoff's removal. The only charge I ever heard against him was that his mind had suddenly failed. Protopopoff, who was a man of high breeding, was nevertheless exceedingly nervous, and I always thought, somewhat weak-willed. He was not the infirm old man he has generally been represented, being about sixty-four years of age with white hair and mustache and young, bright black eyes. That he had plenty of physical and moral courage was proved by his conduct after the Revolution. Walking to the door of the council chamber of the Duma he announced himself thus: "I am Protopopoff. Arrest me if you like." He was arrested by orders of Rodzianko, but was released later, only to meet death by the bullets of the Bolsheviki. That Protopopoff was on friendly terms with Rasputine is true, but that Rasputine had anything to do with his appointment, or with his retention in office after the attack by the Duma, is simply absurd.

Maklakoff, Minister of the Interior before Protopopoff, was a former governor of Chernigoff. The Emperor met him in the course of a journey to the famous fête of Poltava, a jubilee of the wars of Peter the Great. The acquaintance was made in the leisure of a boat trip, and the Emperor, in another of his fits of impulsiveness, decided that he had found an ideal Minister of the Interior. Their friendship deepened with time, and the Emperor found great satisfaction in his new minister's reports, which he declared reflected his own point of view. Nothing against the administration of Maklakoff was ever even whispered until late in 1914, when Nicholai Nicholaievitch, as supreme commander of the Russian forces in the field, suddenly demanded his demission. Grand Duke Nicholas, it must be said, continually interfered with the affairs of the interior government, with which as military chief he had nothing whatever to do, but in the early days of the War the Emperor seemed to think it the part of wisdom to suffer this irregularity. Reluctantly he yielded to the request for Maklakoff's demission, saying to him with genuine regret: "They demand it, and at such a time I cannot stand against them."

In the place of Maklakoff was named Tcherbatkoff, a friend and protégé of Nicholai Nicholaievitch, a man whose former office had been head of the remount department of the State. Doubtless he knew a great deal about horses, but of the interior affairs of State he knew so little that even the influence of Grand Duke Nicholas was powerless to retain him in office longer than two months.

Tcherbatkoff was followed by Khvostoff who, previous to his appointment, was an entire stranger to Rasputine. Khvostoff had made a record as governor of Nizjni Novgorod, and afterwards as a vigorous anti-German orator in the Duma. He was also supposed to be a devoted friend of the Imperial Family. Soon after his appointment Khvostoff began sedulously to cultivate the friendship of Rasputine, and it is a matter of police record that this Minister of the Interior frequently played on Rasputine's unfortunate weakness for drink. Possibly he thought that by getting the poor man intoxicated he could worm from him the many Court secrets he was supposed to possess. Failing in this Khvostoff began, with the help of Chief of Police Belezky, a plot against Rasputine which nearly succeeded in the latter's assassination. This being discovered the demission of Khvostoff became imperative.

Soukhomlinoff, who when I knew him was an old man of seventy-five, was a former military governor of Kiev, and before his appointment as Minister of War, had been a great favorite of the Emperor. That he showed brilliant ability in the mobilization of the Russian Army in 1914 was admitted by the Allied Governments, and in fact no intrigue against him developed until some time after the beginning of the War. His principal enemies were Grand Duke Nicholas, General Polivanoff, and the notorious Goutchkoff. In my opinion their propaganda against him was instigated solely with the object of impairing the prestige of the Emperor. The crimes laid at the door of Soukhomlinoff were almost countless. He was accused of withholding ammunition from the armies, of harboring German spies in his house, and in general of being completely incapable of performing his duties of office. Of him the English historian Wilton says that time alone will prove whether the odium of the Russian war scandals rested on Soukhomlinoff or on Grand Duke Nicholas. At all events it was poor old Soukhomlinoff who was arrested, tried before a tribunal of the Provisional Government, and sentenced to life imprisonment. His young wife, who was arrested with him, occupied a cell next to mine in the Fortress of Peter and Paul, and without regard to the charges brought against her, I had reason constantly to admire the courage and self-possession with which she bore the hardships of prison life. So great was her dignity and self-command that she became universally respected by the soldiers, and I am confident that this alone saved us both from far worse indignities than those which we were called upon to bear. In prison Mme. Soukhomlinoff managed to keep herself constantly occupied. She wrote and read whenever writing materials and books were procurable, and her clever fingers fashioned out of scraps of the miserable prison bread really beautiful sprays of flowers. For coloring matter she used the paint from a moldering blue stripe on the walls of her cell, and scraps of red paper in which tea was wrapped. After months of imprisonment, bravely endured, Mme. Soukhomlinoff was brought to trial before a court of the Provisional Government. Her examination was of the most searching character, but at its close she left the courtroom fully acquitted, to the applause of the numerous spectators. Taking advantage of an amnesty pronounced some time later Mme. Soukhomlinoff got her aged husband released from prison and saw him safely to Finland. It is rather an anticlimax to the story that after so many trials borne together the marriage of the Soukhomlinoffs was dissolved, Mme. Soukhomlinoff marrying a young Georgian officer with whom she later perished under the Bolshevist terror.

One more person of whom I can speak with knowledge was, although not a minister, falsely alleged to be an appointee of Rasputine. This was the Metropolitan Pitirim, a man of impeccable honesty and very liberal views regarding Church administration. The Emperor met him in late 1914 on one of his visits to the Caucasus, Pitirim then being Exarch of Georgia. Not only the Emperor but his entire suite were enchanted by the charming manners, the piety, and learning of the Exarch, and when, a little later, the Empress met the

Emperor at Veronesh, he told her that he had Pitirim in mind for Metropolitan of Petrograd. Almost immediately after his appointment the propagandists began to connect his elevation with the Rasputine influence, but the truth is that the two men were never at any time on terms of more than formal acquaintanceship. As for their Majesties, they liked and respected Pitirim but he never was an intimate member of their household. Practically all their conversations which I overheard concerned the state of the Church in Georgia, which Pitirim insisted was lower than in other parts of the Empire. The Church of Georgia, Pitirim alleged, received too little support from the State, although it deserved as much if not more than others, because Georgian Christianity is the oldest in all Russia. According to tradition this Church was established by the Holy Virgin herself who, after a shipwreck off Mount Athos, visited Georgia, converted its chiefs and established the first Christian temple. Pitirim was essentially a churchman, yet he always advocated a certain separation of Church and State. That is, he desired the establishment of a parish system whereby the support of the Church should be the responsibility of the people rather than of the Imperial Government. Unworldly to the last degree, he nevertheless came in for his full share of slander and abuse. After my arrest by the Provisional Government my mother visited Kerensky in my behalf, and was astounded when he brutally told her that one of the charges against me was that all my diamonds were gifts from Pitirim, the inference being that we were on unduly intimate terms.

Another high personage to whom I wish to pay the tribute of just appreciation is Count Fredericks, chief minister of the Court. This honorable gentleman had spent almost his entire life in the service of the Imperial Family, having first been attached to the person of Alexander III. Nicholas II and his family he served with ability, discretion, and rare devotion. In virtue of his office he had to deal personally with the affairs of the Grand Dukes, their complicated financial transactions, their morganatic marriages, and other confidential affairs. Everyone, except those of the Grand Dukes who with reason had earned his contempt, loved this charming man whom their Majesties usually spoke of as "our old man." Count Fredericks, in his turn, always called them "*mes enfants.*" His house was to me for many years a second home, his daughters, the elder Mme. Voyeikoff, and the younger one, Emma, being among my dearest friends. Emma, who suffered a painful curvature of the spine, had the compensation of a rarely beautiful singing voice with which she often charmed the Emperor and Empress. Count Fredericks was arrested by the Provisional Government, but owing to his great age, was afterwards released.

The charge has often been brought against Nicholas II that he surrounded himself with inferior men. The fact of the case is that in the beginning of his reign he chose as his chief advisers men of ability and integrity who had been friends of his father, Alexander III. Later he chose men who in his opinion were the best ones available, and it must be admitted that there were few men of first-class ability among whom he could choose. The events of the War and the Revolution prove this, for neither of these two terrible emergencies produced in Russia a single man of conspicuous merit. Not one real leader appeared then nor in the years which have since elapsed. Truly has a distinguished American writer pointed out that never could Bolshevism and its insane philosophy have taken such strong roots in Russia, had not the soil been previously so well prepared. Every Russian who really loved his country must admit the truth of this statement. Too many exiled Russians, however, still cling to the delusion that some outside influence was the cause of their country's downfall. Let them acknowledge the truth that it was Russians themselves, especially Russians of the privileged classes, who principally are responsible for the catastrophe. For years before the Revolution the national spirit was in a state of decline. Few men or women cherished ideals of duty for duty's sake. Patriotism was practically extinct. Family life was weakened, and in the last days, the morale of the whole people was lower than in almost any other country of the civilized world.

May the blood of the thousands of innocents who have perished in War and Revolution wipe out the sins of the old hard-hearted and decadent Russia. May the millions still living, in exile and under Communist oppression, learn that only by repentance and by toleration of others' weaknesses can there be any possibility of a restoration of national life. Not by any outside help but by our own efforts, by loyal Russians coming together, not as political groups but as compatriots, can great Russia rise again out of her shame and desolation and become once more a nation among the nations of the earth.

* * *

CHAPTER XIV

FOR two months after the assassination of Rasputine the Emperor remained at Tsarskoe Selo, but he was by no means idle. In fact his whole heart and mind were occupied, not so much with the scandal that had reached its tragic climax in the Yusupoff Palace, but with the War which at that moment seemed to favor Russian arms. According to our advices the food shortage in Germany and in Turkey had become acute, and the Emperor believed that a vigorous spring offensive might bring the War to a speedy close. In his billiard room were spread out a large number of military maps which no one of the household, not even the Empress, was invited to inspect. The Emperor spent hours over these maps and his plan of a spring campaign, and when he left the billiard room he locked the door and put the key in his pocket. I had never seen him more completely the soldier, the commander in chief of a great army. All this time, from December, 1916, to February, 1917, the Russian front was comparatively quiet, furious snowstorms preventing the advance either of our own or the enemy's forces. Alas! The storms interfered also with railroad transport and Petrograd and Moscow were beginning to feel the pinch of hunger, a fact that gave their Majesties constant concern.

Meanwhile the Grand Duke Alexander Michailovitch persisted in his demand for an interview with the Empress, and as his letters to her failed of their object he began to write to the Grand Duchess Olga. The Empress, whose courage was great enough to enable her to ignore any possible danger to herself, decided to see the man and once for all let him have his say. In this decision the Emperor concurred, but he stipulated that he should be present in case the conversation should become unduly disagreeable. The Emperor's aide-de-camp for the day happened to be a spirited young officer, Lieutenant Linevitch, who after luncheon on the day set for the audience, lingered in the palace, apparently occupied in an amusing puzzle game with Tatiana. Afterwards Linevitch told me that so well did he know the extent of the Grand Ducal cabal, and especially the character of Alexander Michailovitch, that he had remained on purpose and that his sword had been ready at any moment to rescue the Empress from insult or from attempted assassination. As we expected the Grand Duke had nothing new to say to the Empress, but merely reiterated in more than usually violent terms the demand for Protopopoff's dismissal and for a constitutional form of government. The answer to these demands was as usual—everything necessary after the War, no fundamentally dangerous changes while the Germans remained on our soil. The Grand Duke, purple with anger, rushed out of the Empress's sitting room, but instead of leaving the palace, as he was expected to do, he entered the library, ordered pens and paper and began to write a letter to the Emperor's brother, Michail Alexandrovitch. No sooner had he begun his epistle than he perceived standing respectfully in the room the aide-de-camp Linevitch, whom, after a more or less civil greeting, he tried to dismiss. "You may go now," he said, coldly polite, but the astute Linevitch replied with ceremony: "No, your Highness, I am on service today and as long as your Highness is here it is not permitted for me to leave." In a fury Alexander Michailovitch got up and left the palace.

Men like Linevitch and many others, as faithful as ever to their Majesties, saw the threatening tempest more clearly than those within palace walls could possibly see it. The day after the visit of Alexander Michailovitch I received a call from one of the finest of the Romanoff connections, Duke Alexander of Luchtenberg. Pain-fully agitated, the Duke told me that he wanted me to help him to induce the Emperor to take a remarkable, indeed an unprecedented step. At the time of his accession to the throne every member of the family, it is well known, must make a solemn vow of fealty to the Tsar, and the Duke of Luchtenberg now begged me to persuade the Emperor, through the Empress, to exact from all the family a renewal of this vow. For the lives and safety of the Imperial Family the Duke believed this to be absolutely essential. "None of them are loyal, not one," he said earnestly. "And if the Emperor values the lives of his wife and children he must force the Grand Dukes and their families to declare themselves." Quite staggered, I replied that it was impossible for me to make such a proposition to their Majesties, but I added that the Duke himself, as a member of the family, might with entire propriety do so, and thus the matter was decided. Of the details of the conversation between the Emperor and his kinsman I know nothing, but I know that the conversation took place, because later the Emperor remarked in my hearing that "Sandro" Luchtenberg, in the kindness of his heart, had made a great matter out of a trifle, and he added, "Of course I could not ask of my own family the thing he suggested."

As one more indication of the gathering storm there came to me at my hospital from Saratoff an old man so feeble and so deaf that he had to bring with him a woman relative who through long familiarity was able to act as an interpreter in his conversations. This old man represented an organization known as the Union of the Russian People, a large group devoted to the Empire and to the persons of their Majesties. With intense emotion he told me that his organization had incontestable proofs of most treacherous propaganda which was being circulated by the Union of Zemstvos and Towns, under the personal direction of Goutchkoff and Rodzianko. He had brought with him documentary proofs of his assertions and he implored me to help him lay his proofs before the Emperor. I communicated his message to the Emperor, but as he was that day importantly engaged he suggested that the Empress might receive him instead. This she consented to do, but after an hour's conversation she sent the old man away, touched by his devotion but unconvinced of the gravity of the situation as he presented it.

To relieve somewhat the dullness and gloom that had settled on the palace we organized in those early winter days of 1917 a series of chamber-music recitals, the performers being Rumanian musicians who had been playing very beautifully in the convalescent wards of the Tsarskoe Selo hospitals. At the request of the Empress I arranged for performances in my own apartments in the palace, inviting, with their Majesties' approval, the Duke of Luchtenberg, Mme. Dehn, Count Fredericks, his daughters, my sister and her husband, and a few other intimate friends. The concerts were delightful, greatly cheering us all, including the somewhat lonely young Grand Duchesses and the much harassed Emperor. But something in the music, perhaps its wild and mournful tzigane numbers, moved the Empress to the depths of her sensitive soul. Her beautiful eyes became more than ever filled with melancholy and her heart seemed heavy with premonitions of disaster.

Partly because of her increased melancholy and partly moved by just anger against the propagandist press in which our innocent concerts were described as "palace orgies," the Emperor for the first time was awakened to consciousness that the safety of his family was indeed threatened. At least he became aware of the fact that despite the dangerous unrest of the times, Tsarskoe Selo and even Petrograd remained practically ungarrisoned. The capital was guarded by only a few regiments of reserves, while Tsarskoe Selo, the residence of the Imperial Family, had no regiments at all outside its peace-time quota of soldier and Cossack guards. At the command of the Emperor several additional regiments which had served for some time at the front were ordered to Tsarskoe for rest and recuperation, and, although naturally nothing of this was mentioned in the order, to augment if necessary the inadequate military force at hand. The first order was given for a strong detachment of naval guards, but after these men were actually entrained for Tsarskoe they were stopped by a counter order from General Gourko, who in the illness of General Alexieff was in command at G. H. Q. This counter order being at once communicated to the Emperor, he exercised his supreme authority and the regiment once more started for Tsarskoe Selo. But the audacity of General Gourko had not yet reached its limit. When the military train reached the station at Tsarskoe it was met by a telegram from General Gourko to the officer in command, ordering the regiment back to the front. The bewildered officer for a few moments was at a loss what to do, but fortunately news of his dilemma was telephoned to the palace, and the regiment, under the peremptory command of the Emperor, left the train and went into garrison at Tsarskoe. The Emperor next commanded that one of his favorite regiments of Varsovie Lancers be sent to Tsarskoe, but instead General Gourko left headquarters for the palace, where a long interview between the Emperor and the commander took place. By arguments of which I have no knowledge the Emperor was persuaded that the Lancers could not, for the time being, be spared from their front-line position, and he recalled his order.

However, it was clear that the Emperor was at last awake to the appalling menace of disaffection which was closing in like black cloud banks on every hand. The War was going badly, as every student of the times must remember. Brusiloff's brilliant offensive of the summer and autumn of 1916 had indeed made it plain that Russia was by no means out of the struggle, but although this famous drive had netted the Russians a gain of territory even larger than that which was yielded in the great Battle of the Somme, it had finally stopped leaving us with much lost territory still unredeemed. The Emperor knew this and it tormented his heart and soul. The intriguers knew it and resolved to use it as a weapon to get the Tsar away from his capital and from his family. It was on the 19th or 20th of February (Russian Calendar) that the Emperor's brother, Grand Duke Michail Alexandrovitch, visited the palace and told the Emperor that it was his immediate duty to return to the Stavka because of grave threats of mutiny in the army. Very reluctantly the Emperor consented to go. Mutiny in the army was a serious enough matter and demanded the presence of the commander in chief. But other things were at the same time occurring to cause keen anxiety. The Empress had acquainted me with the nature of these dis-quieting events, but because of the international character of the most serious I dislike even now to put them in writing. However, I am here repeating only what was then told me and I have no firsthand information to offer in verification of their truth. Their Majesties had been informed and finally from a source which they believed to be absolutely reliable, that the center of intrigue against the throne was not in any secret garret of disaffected workingmen but in the British Embassy, where the Ambassador, Sir George Buchanan, was personally aiding the Grand Dukes to overthrow Nicholas II and to replace him by his cousin Grand Duke Cyril Vladimirovitch. Sir George Buchanan's main purpose, it was said, was not so much to further the ambitions of the Grand Dukes as it was to weaken Russia as a factor in the future peace conference. Unable fully to believe that an ambassador of one of the Allied Powers would dare to meddle maliciously in the internal affairs of the Empire, the Tsar had nevertheless decided to communicate his information in a personal letter to his cousin King George of England. The Empress, deeply indignant, advised a demand on King George for the Ambassador's recall, but the Emperor replied that he dared not, at such a critical time, make public his distrust of an Ally's representative. Whether or not the Emperor ever wrote his letter to King George I never knew, but that his anxiety and depression of spirits persisted I can well testify. On the evening of February 29, the day before the Emperor's departure, I gave a small dinner to some intimate friends among the officers of the Naval Guard, Mme. Dehn helping me in my duties as hostess. A note from the Empress summoned us all to spend the end of the evening in her sitting room, and as soon as I saw the Emperor I knew that he was seriously upset. During the tea hour he spoke little, and when I tried to catch his eye he turned his head aside. The Empress murmured in my ear that all his instincts warned him against leaving Tsarskoe Selo at that time, and as this coincided exactly with my own judgment I ventured to tell him, on saying good night, that I should hope to the last moment that he would not go away until the worst of the uncertainties in Petrograd were removed. At this he smiled, almost cheerfully, and said that I must not allow myself to be frightened by wild rumors and idle gossip. Go he must, but within ten days he expected to be able to return.

The next morning I went to the door and watched his motor car drive out of the palace grounds, the Empress and the children going with it as far as the station. As usual on such occasions, there was a display of flags, of guards standing at salute, and bells from the churches pealing their farewell. Everything appeared the same, yet in that hour the flags, the soldiers, the pealing bells were speeding the Tsar of all the Russias to his doom.

I felt ill that morning, ill physically as well as mentally, yet as in duty bound I went to my hospital, where a soldier in whose case I took a special interest was to undergo an operation which he dreaded and at which he had implored me to be present. While the anesthetic was being administered I stood beside the poor man holding his hand, but at the same time I realized that I was becoming feverish and that my headache was almost unbearably increasing. Returning to the palace, I lay down in my bedroom, after writing a line to the Empress excusing myself from tea. An hour later Tatiana came in, sympathetic as usual, but troubled because both Olga and Alexei were in bed with high temperatures and the doctors suspected that they might be coming down with measles. A week or two before some small cadets from the military school had spent the afternoon playing with Alexei, and one of these boys had a cough and such a flushed face that the Empress had called the attention of M. Gilliard to the child, fearing illness. The next day we heard that he was ill with measles, but because our minds were so troubled with many other things none of us thought much of the danger of contagion. As for me, even after Tatiana had told me that Olga and Alexei were suspected cases, it did not at once occur to me that I was going to be ill. Still my temperature went on rising and my headache was unrelieved. I lay in bed all the next day until the dinner hour when Mme. Dehn came in and I made a futile effort to get up and dress. Mme. Dehn made me lie down again, and looking me over carefully she said: "You look very badly to me. I think you will have to have the doctor." The next instant, so it seemed to me, the doctor was in the room and I heard him say: "Measles. A bad case." Then I drifted off into sleep or unconsciousness.

That same day Tatiana fell ill, and now the Empress had four of us on her hands. Putting on her nurse's uniform, she spent all the succeeding days between her children's rooms and mine. Half conscious, I felt gratefully her capable hands arranging my pillows, smoothing my burning forehead, and holding to my lips medicines and cooling drinks. Already, as I heard vaguely, Marie and Anastasie had begun to cough, but this news disturbed me only as a passing dream. I was conscious of the presence of my mother and father and of my younger sister, and still as in a kind of nightmare I understood that they and the Empress spoke in hurried whispers of riots and disorders in Petrograd. But of the first days of Revolution, the strikes in Petrograd and Moscow, the revolt of the mobs and the hesitancy of the half-disciplined reserves to restore order, I know nothing except what was afterwards related to me. I do know, however, that through it all the Empress of Russia was completely calm and courageous, and that when my sister, hurrying to the palace after witnessing the wild scenes in Petrograd, had cried out to the Empress that the end had come, her fears were quieted by brave and reassuring words.

It was the devoted old Grand Duke Paul, as the Empress afterwards told me, who brought her the first official tidings, and made her understand that that most calamitous of all blunders, a political revolution in the midst of world war, had been accomplished. Even then she lost none of her marvelous courage. She did not call upon the Ministers or upon the Allied Ambassadors to protect her and her children. With dignity, unmoved she witnessed day by day the cowardly desertion of men who for years had lived at Court and who had enjoyed the faith and friendship of the Imperial Family. One by one they went, General Racine, Count Apraxine, officers and men of the bodyguard, servants the oldest and the most trusted, all with smooth excuses and apologies which translated meant only *sauve qui peut.*

One night came the noise of rioting and the sharp staccato of machine guns apparently approaching nearer and nearer the palace. It was about eleven o'clock and the Empress was sitting for a few minutes' rest on the edge of my bed. Getting up hastily and wrapping herself in a white shawl, she beckoned Marie, the last of the children on her feet, and went out of the palace into the icy air to face whatever threatened. The Naval Guard and the Konvoi Cossacks still remained on duty, although even then they were preparing to desert. It is altogether possible that they would have gone over to the rioters that night had it not been for the unexpected appearance of the Empress and her daughter. From one guard to another they passed, the stately woman and the courageous young girl, undaunted both in the face of deadly danger, speaking words of encouragement, and most of all of simple faith and confidence. This alone held the men at their posts during that dreadful night and prevented the rioters from attacking the palace. The next day the guards disappeared. The Naval Guards, led by Grand Duke Cyril Vladimirovitch,* marched with red flags to the Duma and presented themselves to Rodzianko as joyful revolutionists. The very men who in the previous midnight had hailed the Empress with the traditional greeting, "*Zdravie Jelaim Vashie Imperatorskoe Velichestvo!*" Health and long life to your Majesty! So loud had been their greeting that the Empress, not wishing me to know that she had left the palace, sent a servant to tell me that the Guards were waiting to meet the Emperor.

There was now in or about the palace practically no one to defend the Imperial Family in case the mob decided to attack. Still the Empress remained calm, saying only that she hoped no blood would have to be shed in their defense. A telegram from the Emperor revealed that the crisis had become known to him, for he implored the Empress to join him with the children at headquarters. At the same hour came an astounding message to the Empress from Rodzianko, now head of the Provisional Government, notifying her that she and her whole family must vacate the palace at once. Her answer to both messages was that she could not leave because all five of the children were dangerously ill. Rodzianko's reply to this appeal of an anguished mother was: "When the house is on fire it is time for everything to be thrown out." Desperately the Empress consulted doctors and nurses. Could the children possibly be moved? Could Anna? What was to be done in case the Provisional Government proved altogether pitiless?

Into this soul-racking dilemma of the mother came to the wife of the Emperor the terrible news of his abdication. I could not be with her in that hour of woe, nor did I even see her until the following morning. It was my parents who broke the news to me, almost too ill and too cloudy of mind to comprehend it. Mme. Dehn, who was with the Empress on the evening when Grand Duke Paul arrived with with the fatal tidings, has described the scene when the broken-hearted

* This is the same Cyril Vladimirovitch who has recently proclaimed himself "Head of the Romanoff Family and Guardian of the Throne."

Empress left the Grand Duke and returned to her own room.

"Her face was distorted with agony, her eyes were full of tears. She tottered rather than walked, and I rushed forward and supported her until she reached the writing table between the windows. She leaned heavily against it, and taking my hands in hers she said brokenly: '*Abdiqué!*'

"I could hardly believe my ears. I waited for her next words. They were scarcely audible. At last [still speaking in French, for Mme. Dehn spoke no English] 'Poor darling—alone there and suffering—My God! What he must have suffered!'"

In that hour of supreme agony there was not a word spoken of the loss of a throne. Alexandra Feodorovna's whole heart was with her husband, her sole fears that he might be in danger and that their boy might be taken from them. At once she began to send frantic telegrams to the Emperor begging him to come home as soon as possible. With the refinement of cruelty which marked the whole conduct of the Provisional Government in those days these telegrams were returned to the Empress marked in blue pencil: "Address of person mentioned unknown."

Not even this insolence nor all her fears broke the sublime courage of the Empress. When next morning she entered my sickroom and saw by my tear-drenched face that I knew what had happened her only visible emotion was a slight irritation that other lips than her own had brought me the news. "They should have known that I preferred to tell you myself," she said. It was only when gone her rounds of the palace and was alone in her own bedroom that she finally gave way to her grief. "Mama cried terribly," little Grand Duchess Marie told me. "I cried too, but not more than I could help, for poor Mama's sake." Never in my life, I am certain, shall I behold such proud fortitude as was shown all through those days of wreck and disaster by the Empress and her children. Not one single word of bitterness or resentment passed their lips. "You know, Annia," said the Empress gently, "all is finished for our Russia. But we must not blame the people or the soldiers for what has happened." Too well we knew on whose shoulders the burden of responsibility really rested.

By this time Olga and Alexei were decidedly better, but Tatiana and Anastasie were still very ill and Marie was in the first serious stage of the disease. The Empress in her hospital uniform moved tirelessly from one bed to another. Perceiving that from my floor of the palace practically every servant had fled, even my nurses and my once devoted Jouk having yielded to the general panic, she found people to move my bed upstairs to the old nursery of the Emperor. We were now almost alone in the palace. My father's resignation having been demanded and of course given, my parents were detained in Petrograd.

Days passed and still no word came from the Emperor. The Empress's endurance had almost reached its breaking point when there came to the palace a young woman, the wife of an obscure officer, who threw herself at the feet of the Empress and begged to be allowed the dangerous task of getting a letter through to the Emperor. Gratefully indeed did the Empress accept the offer, and within an hour the brave woman was on her way to Mogiloff. How she managed to reach headquarters, how she passed the cordon of soldiers and finally succeeded in delivering to the captive Emperor his wife's letter we never knew, but all honor to this heroic woman, she did it.

The palace was now full of Revolutionary soldiers, quite drunk with their new liberty. Their heavy boots tramped through all the rooms and corridors, and groups of dirty, unshaven men were constantly pushing their way into the nurseries bawling out hoarsely: "Show us Alexei!" For it was the heir who most of all aroused the interest and curiosity of the mob. Meanwhile, behind closed doors and anxiously awaiting the arrival of the Emperor, the Empress and her few faithful friends were at work forestalling the coming of Kerensky by burning and destroying letters and diaries, intimate personal records too precious to be allowed to fall into the ruthless hands of enemies.

CHAPTER XV

IN anxiety almost unbearable we waited until the morning of March 9 (Russian) the arrival of the Emperor. I was still confined to my bed and Dr. Botkine was making me his first visit of the day when my door flew open and Mme. Dehn, pale with excitement, rushed to my bedside exclaiming breathlessly: "He has come!" As soon as she could command words she described the arrival of the Emperor, not as of yore attended, but guarded like a prisoner by armed soldiers. The Empress was with Alexei when the motor cars drove into the palace grounds, and Mme. Dehn told how she sprang to her feet overjoyed and ran like a schoolgirl down the stairs and through the long corridors to meet her husband. For a time at least the happiness of reunion blotted out the suspense of the past and the gloomy uncertainty of the future. But afterwards, alone, behind their own closed doors, the emotion of the betrayed and deserted Emperor completely overcame his self-control and he sobbed like a child on the breast of his wife. It was four o'clock in the afternoon before she could come to me, and when she came I read in her white, drawn face the whole story of the ordeal through which she had passed. With prideful composure she related the events of the day. I tried to match her in courage but I am afraid I failed. I, who in all the twelve years of my life in the palace had but three times seen tears in the eyes of the Emperor, was entirely overwhelmed at her recital.

"He will not break down a second time," she said with a brave smile. "He is walking in the garden now. Come to the window and see." She helped me to the window and herself pulled aside the curtain. Never, never while I live shall I forget what we saw, we two, clinging together in shame and sorrow for our disgraced country. Below in the garden of the palace which had been his home for twenty years stood the man who until a few days before had been Tsar of all the Russias. With him was his faithful friend Prince Dolgorouky, and surrounding them were six soldiers, say rather six hooligans, armed with rifles. With their fists and with the butts of their guns they pushed the Emperor this way and that as though he were some wretched vagrant they were baiting in a country road. "You can't go there, Gospodin Polkovnik (Mr. Colonel)." "We don't permit you to walk in that direction, Gospodin Polkovnik." "Stand back when you are commanded, Gospodin Polkovnik." The Emperor, apparently unmoved, looked from one of these coarse brutes to another and with great dignity turned and walked back towards the palace. I had been a very sick woman, and I was now hardly fit to stand on my feet. The light went out suddenly and I fainted. But the Empress did not faint. She got me back to my bed, fetched cold water, and when I awoke it was to feel her cool hand bathing my head. From her calm and detached manner no one could have guessed that the scene we had just witnessed was part also of her own tragedy. Before leaving me she said as to a child: "If you will promise to be very good and not cry he shall come to see you this evening."

After dinner they came, the Emperor and Empress with our friend Lili Dehn. The two women sat down at a table with their needlework leaving the Emperor free to sit by my bed and talk to me privately. I have tried to show Nicholas II as a human person, with human emotions, and I have no desire now to represent him, in the hour of his humiliation, as other than a man feeling keenly and acutely the bitterness of his position. I had been unable until the day of his return to realize with any degree of clarity the full extent of his calamity. It was to me almost unbelievable that his enemies, who had so long plotted and schemed for his overthrow, had at last succeeded. It was beyond reason that the Emperor, the finest and best of the whole Romanoff family, should be allowed to fall under the feet of his decadent, treacherous kinsmen and subjects. But the Emperor, his eyes hard and glistening, told me that it was indeed true. And he added: "If all Russia came to me now on their knees I would never return."

With tears in his voice he spoke of the men, his most trusted relations and friends, who had turned against him and caused his downfall. He read me telegrams from Brusiloff, Alexieff, and other of his generals, others from members of the family, including a message from Nicholai Nicholaievitch, in which the writers "on their knees" begged his Imperial Majesty, for the salvation of Russia, to abdicate. In whose favor did they wish him to abdicate? The weak and ineffectual Duma? The great untaught masses of the people? No, to their own blind and self-seeking oligarchy, which, under a regent of its own choosing, would rule the boy Alexei and through him the people and the uncounted wealth of Russia. But this at least the Emperor could and did prevent. Both his heart and his mind forbade him to abdicate in favor of the Tsarevitch. "My boy I will not give to them," he said feelingly. "Let them get some one else, Michail, if he thinks he is strong enough."

I regret that I cannot remember every word the Emperor told me of the scenes in his train when the deputation from the Duma came to demand his abdication. I was trying too hard to obey the Empress's injunction to "be good and not cry." But I remember his telling me how arrogant and vain the deputies, especially Goutchkoff and Shoulgin, showed themselves. On their departure the Emperor's first words were addressed to the two tall Cossacks who stood guard at his door. "It is time now for you to tear my initials from your shoulder straps," he told them. The Cossacks saluted and one of them said: "Please your Imperial Majesty, please allow us to kill them." But the Emperor replied: "It is too late to do that now."

Of his mother, who hurried from Kiev, accompanied by Grand Duke Alexander Michailovitch, to see him, he said that he was vastly comforted to have her near him, but that the sight of the Grand Duke was unendurable. Driving away from the train with the Empress Dowager, the Emperor had been much moved to see the people along the whole distance of two versts fall on their knees to bid him farewell. There was a group of schoolgirls from the institute at Mogiloff who forced their way past the guards and surrounded their Sovereign, begging his handkerchief, his autograph on bits of paper, the buttons from his uniform, anything for a last souvenir. The Emperor's face grew sharply lined when he spoke of those brave girls and the kneeling people. "Why did you not appeal to them?" I asked. "Why did you not appeal to the soldiers?" But the Emperor answered gently: "The people knew themselves powerless, and as for appealing to the soldiers, how could I? Already I had heard threats of murdering my family." His wife and children, he said, were all on earth he had left to live for now. Their happiness and well-being were all his soul desired. As for the Empress, more than himself the real object of malice, only over his body should any hand be raised to injure her. Giving way once more for a brief moment to his grief the Emperor murmured half to himself: "But there is no justice, no justice on earth." Then as if in apology he said: "It has shaken me badly, as you see. For the first few days I was so little myself that I could not even write my diary."

As we talked it came over me for the first time in full force that all was indeed finished for Russia. The army was disrupted, the nation fallen. I could foresee, to some extent at least, the horrors we should have to meet, but in a kind of desperate hope I asked the Emperor if he did not think that the riots and strikes would now be put down. He shook his head. "Not for two years at least," he predicted. But what did he think was to become of him, of the Empress and the children? He did not know, but there was one prayer he should not be too proud to make to his enemies, and that was that they should not send him out of Russia. "Let me live here in my own country, as the humblest and most obscure proprietor, tilling the land and earning the poorest living," he exclaimed. "Send us to any distant corner of Russia, but only let us stay."

This was the only time I ever saw the Emperor in the least degree unmanned, or overcome with the bitterness of grief which I knew must have filled his spirit. After that first day in the palace gardens he gave his jailers no opportunity of insulting him. With Prince Dolgorouky he walked out daily but only along near pathways to the palace doors. The snow was heavy on the ground and the two men vigorously exercised themselves shoveling it from paths and roadways. Often the Emperor would look up from this strenuous work to wave a hand to those of us who were watching from the windows. In the solitude of my sick chamber I tormented myself with thoughts of what might be in store for the Emperor and the beloved family whose happiness and well-being were more to him than the most exalted throne. They were all prisoners of the Duma now, and what dark and hapless fate was the ruthless, irresponsible Duma preparing for them? Not a comforting question to haunt the mind of one ill in body and soul. From my first waking moment on I lived in anticipation of the daily visit of the Empress. She who had all at stake still kept her wonderful courage alive. She came in tall and stately, a smile on her gentle, melancholy face, bringing me the news of the nurseries, messages from the children, making me work, doing everything possible to cheer and to lighten my mind. In the evening the Emperor usually came, wheeling his wife in her invalid's chair, for by night her strength had all but gone. They stayed with me for an hour and then went on to say good night to the suite in the drawing room. Sadly diminished in numbers was that suite, but unchanged in fealty and affection for fallen majesty. Among those devoted friends who appeared almost like the survivors of a shipwreck were Count Benkendorff, brother of the former Russian ambassador to Great Britain, and his wife, who had boldly arrived at the palace when it was first surrounded by mutinous soldiers; two maids of honor, Baroness Buxhoevden and Countess Hendrikoff; the faithful Miss Schneider ("Trina"), Mme. Dehn, Count Fredericks, General Voyeikoff and the Hussar officer, General Groten. The two devoted aides-de-camp, Lieutenant Linevitch and Count Zamirsky, who had flown to the palace to be near the Empress after the abdication, had been forced to leave, or they too would have remained to the end. Of the household M. Gilliard and Mr. Gibbs, the French and English tutors of Alexei, had elected to remain. Madeleine, and several other personal attendants, including three nurses, also stayed. "In good times we served the family," said these honest souls, "never will we forsake them now."

Not once, after the very first of our conversations, and not at any time I believe to others in the palace did the Emperor or the Empress make the smallest complaint of their captivity. They seemed to suffer for Russia rather than for themselves, for they knew, and said so, that the army, suddenly in the midst of war released from all discipline, would soon cease to fight efficiently, or perhaps to obey orders at all. This of course the world knows is precisely what did happen. The Emperor, I must admit, sometimes betrayed a gruesome kind of humor over the fantastic blunders of the self-styled statesmen who were so rapidly making general shipwreck of their revolution. In every way they showed their weakness and bewilderment. Whether or not they feared to trust old officers of the Empire with the custody of the Imperial Family I cannot be sure, but the men they sent to Tsarskoe were a constant source of ironic mirth to the suite. Most of these men were young, raw, underbred, and inexperienced, the best of them being junior officers promoted since 1914. One day one of the guard officers, just to show how democratic Russia had become, swaggered up to the Emperor and offered to shake hands with him. Unfortunately, as he afterwards told me, the Emperor was so busy shoveling snow that he could not take advantage of the man's condescension.

The newly appointed commandant of the palace was a young man named Paul Kotzebou, before the War an officer of the lancers, but for some piece of misconduct cashiered from the service. I had long known Kotzebou and aside from his doubtful army record I was not sorry to see him in the palace, for I knew that if weak of character he was at least kind of heart. Kind indeed he proved himself, for he visited my sickroom in friendly fashion, risked arrest by consenting to smuggle letters to my parents in Petrograd, and was the first to warn me that the Provisional Government was contemplating my arrest. Many of the old friends and advisers of the Emperor were already in prison, but the proposal to arrest a woman whose sole crime had been devotion to the Empress and her children gave us all an uncomfortable, premonitory shock. The distress of the Empress was greater almost than her pride. The mercy she would have scorned to ask for herself she was ready to beg for me, and she did most earnestly implore Kotzebou to intercede in my behalf. "What possible good will it do them to arrest one helpless woman?"

she urged. "Parting with her would be like losing one of my own children." Kotzebou, whatever his feelings, could only reply: "If I could, Madame—but there is nothing I can do, nothing."

The Emperor alone refused to believe my arrest at all probable, but the others were badly frightened at the prospect. The sister of mercy who had worked in my hospital and was taking care of me, almost went on her knees to the Emperor and Empress. "Now is the time to show your real love for Anna Alexandrovna," she cried. "Take her into the rooms of your own children and never let anybody touch her." Cooler counsel came from Count Benkendorff, who advised the Emperor and Empress not to oppose my arrest if it were ordered. The only result of opposition, he pointed out, would be more arrests and perhaps increased hardship for the Empress. "I do not think they will detain her, unless it is in one of the rooms of the Tauride," he said, meaning that I might only be isolated for a time in the palace where the Duma held its sessions. Count Benkendorff was later to learn what kind of justice was being prepared by the criminal lunatics who were at Russia's throat.

One morning towards the 20th of March I had a hurried note from the Empress, the contents of which were enough to make me forget all my own troubles. Marie, who had been very ill and who now she feared was dying, was calling constantly for me. The servant who brought the note told me that Anastasie also was in a critical condition, lungs and ears being in a sad state of inflammation. Oxygen alone was keeping the children alive. Kotzebou was calling on me at the time, and as I sat up in bed wildly demanding to be dressed, he begged me not to leave my room. "They are only waiting until you are well enough to be arrested," he assured me. But though I feared arrest I feared still more letting the child I loved die with one single wish unfulfilled, and as soon as I could be sufficiently clothed it was Kotzebou himself who wheeled my chair through the long corridors to the nurseries. It was the first time in weeks that I had seen the children and our meeting was full of tears. We wept in each other's arms and then without wasting any time I went on into Marie's room. The child indeed seemed to be at the point of death, but when she saw me the suffering in her eyes turned to something like joy. Her weak hands fluttered on the bedclothes and with a feeble cry, "Annia, Annia," she began to weep. Long I sat beside her holding her hot and wasted body in my arms, and when I left her she was asleep. Shaken though I was with that experience, I had one more agony to bear. When my chair was being wheeled back along the corridor I passed the open door of Alexei's room, and this is what I saw. Lying sprawled in a chair was the sailor Derevanko, for many years the personal attendant of the Tsarevitch, and on whom the family had bestowed every kindness, every material benefit. Bitten by the mania of revolution, this man was now displaying his gratitude for all their favors. Insolently he bawled at the boy whom he had formerly loved and cherished, to bring him this or that, to perform any menial service his mean lackey's brain could think of. Dazed and apparently only half conscious of what he was being forced to do, the child moved about trying to obey. It was too much to bear. Hiding my face in my hands, I begged them to take me away from the sickening spectacle.

The next day, my last in the palace, I went again to the children, and for a few hours at least was a little bit happy. The Emperor and Empress had luncheon served in the nurseries, and we were all able to eat in some comfort because both Marie and Anastasie were showing signs of improvement. Still we were troubled because Kotzebou, as a reward for his too kindly treatment of the captives, had that morning been removed from the palace, and the doctors when they came brought with them newspapers, fair samples of the new "free" press of Russia, bristling with frightful stories, especially about me. For the first time I began to realize, with a sick heart, what an arrest might mean, what grotesque charges I might be called upon to face. For the first time, in these newspapers I read the amazing tale of how I had conspired with Dr. Badmieff to poison the Emperor and the Tsarevitch. Dr. Badmieff, that half mad old Siberian root and herb doctor, who never in his life had been admitted to the palace as a physician or even as a friend! It was too absurd to resent. Even the Empress who at first had shown anger, burst into mocking laughter. "Here, Annia," she cried, "keep this story for your collection."

The next day I was arrested. I awoke in a morning of storm and howling wind and in my soul a feeling of dread and foreboding. Immediately after my coffee I wrote a note to the Empress asking her not to wait until afternoon to see me. Her reply was kind and cheering, but she was busy in the nurseries and could not leave until after the arrival of the doctors. With luncheon came Lili Dehn, and scarcely had we finished the meal when we were aware of great noise and confusion in the corridor outside. An icy hand seemed to seize my heart. "They are coming," I whispered, and Mme. Dehn, springing from her chair cried: "Impossible. No—no—" and panic-struck fled the room. The door flew open to admit a frightened servant with a note from the Empress. "Kerensky is going through our rooms. Do not be frightened. God is with us." Hardly had the man retired when again the door opened and another frightened servant, a palace messenger in a feathered cap, announced in a drowned voice the arrival of Kerensky. In a moment the room seemed to fill up with men and walking arrogantly before them I beheld a small, clean-shaven, theatrical person whose essentially weak face was disguised in a Napoleonic frown. Standing over me in his characteristic attitude, right hand thrust into the bosom of his jacket, the man boomed out: "I am the Minister of Justice. You are to dress and go at once to Petrograd." I answered not a word but lay still on my pillows looking him straight in the face. This seemed to disconcert him somewhat for he turned to one of his officers and said nervously: "Ask the doctors if she is fit to go. Otherwise she must be arrested and isolated in the palace." Count Benkendorff, who stood in the back of the room near the door, volunteered to see the doctor, and when he returned it was with the message that Dr. Botkine gave them permission to take me. Afterwards I learned that the Empress reproached the doctor bitterly, saying over and over through her tears: "How can you? How can you? You who have children of your own." But Dr. Botkine was by this time a victim of craven fear, and he was incapable of refusing any request of the Provisional Government.

They gave me time to dress warmly, and I had a moment in which to reply briefly to a note from the Emperor and Empress, in which they enclosed small pictures of Christ and the Virgin, signed with their Majesties' initials, N. and A. When at last I was ready to go it suddenly surged over me that this might be the end of my long association with these dearly loved friends, my Sovereigns, whose intimate lives I had shared for twelve years. Ready to fall on my knees before him if necessary I made a final appeal to Colonel Korovitchinko, the new commandant of the palace, begging him to let me see them for one moment, just long enough to say good-bye. Colonel Korovitchinko, who afterwards died a cruel death at the hands of the Bolsheviki, at first refused, but moved by my tears he relented a little. The Emperor, he said, was outside and could not be summoned, but he would exert his authority far enough to send me under guard to say good-bye to the Empress. Under escort of two officers I was taken to the apartment of Mlle. Schneider, and very soon the pale Empress was wheeled into the room by her devoted attendant Volkov. We had time for only one long embrace and the hurried exchange of two rings. Then Tatiana, who came with her mother, embraced me, weeping, and as she too begged for a last memory gift I gave her the only thing I had to give, my wedding ring. Then the soldiers tore us apart but I saw that the man who gave the order did it with tears in his eyes. The last I remember was the white hand of the Empress pointing upward and her voice: "There we are always together." Volkov, weeping, cried out courageously: "Anna Alexandrovna, God will surely help."

They carried me downstairs to the motor, for I could neither walk nor stand, even with the help of my crutches. At the door stood several soldiers and Court servants, visibly distressed, but by this time I felt nothing, heard nothing. I was turned to stone. When I was lifted into the car I was startled to see there another woman, like myself swathed in wraps and veils. It was Lili Dehn, whose arrest had not before this day even been threatened. Dazed as I was, it was some comfort to hear her whisper that we were to travel to Petrograd together. I recovered myself a little, enough at least to recognize the frightened face of the servant who closed the door of the car. Killed a few months later, this good man had been for a long time a sailor on the Imperial yacht. "Take care of their Majesties," I managed to say to him. Then the motor car shot forward, and I left the palace at Tsarskoe Selo forever. Both Lili and I pressed our faces to the glass in a last effort to see those beloved we were leaving behind, and through the mist and rain we could just discern a group of white-clad figures crowded close to the nursery windows to see us go. In a moment of time the picture was blotted out and we saw only the wet landscape, the storm-bent trees, the rapidly creeping twilight. In another few moments we were at the station, the dear, familiar station of Tsarskoe, where so many, many times I had waited to greet or to say a short farewell to the Emperor and Empress. Ready for us was one of the small Imperial trains, now the special train of Kerensky. Our guards hurried us into a carriage, and the train immediately began to move. At the same time our carriage was invaded by Kerensky and a group of soldiers. Without even a pretense of decent politeness the new Minister of Justice began to shout at us: "Give your family names," and because we did not speak quickly enough the little man became insulted. "You will learn that when *I* ask a question you must answer promptly." We gave our names and Kerensky, turning triumphantly to the soldiers, ejaculated: "Well! Are you convinced now?" Apparently some of the men had expressed doubts as to whether they had bagged the right criminals. Sick and half fainting, I sank back into the cushions and closed my eyes on their departing figures. Lili bent over me with her salts bottle and soon I was able to sit up with some show of courage. It was the first time I had left the house since my illness and I was still very weak.

Arrived in Petrograd, Kerensky paraded us before his officers like barbarian captives of some Roman emperor, but this did not affect us seriously. Our eyes were busy gazing at the changed aspect of Petrograd, soldiers swanking around the streets proud of their slovenly appearance, the badge of their new freedom; mobs of people running aimlessly about, or pausing to listen to street-corner orators; and everywhere on walls and buildings masses of dirty red flags. An old-fashioned coach belong to the Imperial stables had been sent for us and still closely guarded we drove to the Ministry of Justice. There we climbed a long and very steep staircase—how I did it on my crutches I do not yet understand—and were shown into a room on the third floor, empty even of a wooden chair. Silently we stood and waited, and after a time men came in carrying two sofas. On one of these Lili sat down and on the other I lay prone. Again we waited, no one near us save the unkempt soldier who guarded the door. The evening lengthened and finally Kerensky honored us with another brief visit. He did not look at me at all but asked Lili if they had built us a fire. It was an unnecessary question, for he must have felt the icy chill of the room. A few minutes later, however, a servant did build a fire in the tiled stove, and another brought in a tray with eggs and tea. Left alone with the unkempt soldier, the man suddenly amazed us by breaking into a volley of speech in which he cursed most eloquently the new order of things. Nothing good would come of it, nothing, was his opinion. Somewhat reassured because we had a guard who was not at heart a Revolutionist, we lay down, but the night brought to neither of us any anodyne of sleep and rest.

* * *

CHAPTER XVI

MORNING dawned cold and gray, and so exhausted was I with sleeplessness and the discomfort of a hard bed without linen or blankets, that Lili was alarmed and when the tea arrived she begged the soldier who brought it to have a doctor sent me. But Kerensky replied that the doctor was engaged with War Minister Goutchkoff and could not be approached at present. Within a short time I was to be removed to a hospital, and as for Mme. Dehn, she might expect good news soon. As a matter of fact Mme. Dehn was released from custody the next day. Feeling confident that she would be let go, I gave her what jewels I had brought with me, asking her to turn them over to my mother. In return Lili gave me a few necessaries, including a pair of stockings for which later I was extremely grateful because the prison stockings were so coarse and heavy that they hurt my injured leg.

About three o'clock in the afternoon Colonel Peretz, who afterwards wrote a book on the Revolution, came into the room with a group of young boys, former cadets of the military academy, now commissioned officers of the new army. "Say good-bye to your friend and come along," I was ordered, and after a quick embrace I parted with Mme. Dehn, my last link with the past, and followed the men downstairs, where a large motor car was waiting. We all got in, the men's rifles considerably reducing the carrying capacity of the seats. As we drove off the colonel began a long and insulting monologue to which I tried not to listen. "Ah! You and your Grichka (Gregory)," I heard him saying, "what a monument you both deserve for helping us to bring about the Revolution." But all that I wanted to learn from him was my destination, and as if in answer to the unspoken question he said: "All night we were discussing the most appropriate lodgings for you, and we decided on the Troubetskoy Bastion in the fortress." At this point we passed a church and, after the invariable custom, I made the sign of the cross. Colonel Peretz flamed into anger at this. "Don't dare cross your-self," he cried with emphasis on the last word. "Rather pray for the souls of the martyrs of the Revolution." Then as I made no response he exclaimed: "Why don't you answer when I speak to you?" I replied coldly that I had nothing whatever to say to him, whereupon he began to revile the Emperor and Empress in coarsest terms, ending with the words:

"No doubt they are in hysterics over what has happened to them." Then I did speak. "If you knew with what dignity they are enduring what has happened you would not dare say what you have said." After which the monologue was for a moment or two halted.

Turning into the Liteiny, a street in which many barracks and ministries are located, the car stopped and Colonel Peretz dispatched one of the cadet officers on an errand into a Government building. On his return the colonel delayed matters long enough to make a bombastic speech on the great services to the Revolution performed by the cadets, and again we drove on. Realizing that we were not proceeding in the direction of the Fortress of Peter and Paul, I allowed my feminine curiosity to get the better of my pride and I asked whither we were bound. "To the Duma first," was the grim answer. "To the fortress afterwards." Arrived at the Tauride Palace we alighted at what is known as the Ministers' Pavilion and immediately went into the building. What a sight! Crowding the rooms and the corridors, men and women of all ages and conditions, prisoners of the Provisional Government! Looking about, I saw many people of my own class, among them Mme. Soukhomlinoff who for all her manner betrayed might have been a guest rather than a prisoner. We exchanged cheerful greetings and she introduced the two women beside her, Mme. Polouboiarenoff and Mme. Riman, wife of a well-known general. Mme. Polouboiarenoff, of whom I had heard as a brilliant writer on a conservative newspaper (murdered for this later by the Bolsheviki), was quite self-possessed, but Mme. Riman's face was wet with constantly flowing tears. A young girl student, a typical Revolutionist who seemed to be in some kind of authority, passed us in a hurry, pausing to say to Mme. Riman: "What are you crying about? You are going to be set free while these two"—Mme. Soukhomlinoff and myself—"are going to the fortress." Poor Mme. Riman was crying because her husband was already in prison, but the revolutionary student could not be expected to sympathize with that.

It really is easier to be calm over one's own than over another's fate, as I learned when I found myself, with Mme. Soukhomlinoff, once more in a motor car bound for that mysterious prison on the left bank of the Neva, directly opposite the Winter Palace, the Fortress of Peter and Paul. As we left the Tauride the girl student, who after all had some natural feelings, asked me for my father's telephone number that she might notify my parents where I had been sent. "No need to bother about that," broke in the chivalrous Colonel Peretz. "The newspapers will have a full report." "All the better," I rejoined, "for then many more will pray for me."

Rolling into the vast enclosure of the fortress, we stopped at the entrance of the Troubetskoy Bastion. A group of soldiers, dirty and wolfish of demeanor, rushed to meet us. "Now I am bringing you two very desperate political prisoners," shouted the colonel, as the men closed around us. But a stout Cossack, much more human than the rest, assumed authority saying that he was that day acting in place of the governor of the fortress. Preceded by this man, we traversed a long series of narrow, winding stone passages, so dark that I could see only a few feet ahead. Suddenly I was halted, hinges creaked, and I was roughly pushed into a pitch-dark cell the door of which was instantly bolted behind me.

No one who has not been a prisoner can possibly know the sickening sensation which possessed me, standing there in that dark hole, afraid to take a step forward, unable to touch with my groping hands either walls or furniture. My heart leaped and pounded in my breast and I clung desperately to my crutches lest I should fall into that unfathomed darkness. A few minutes of wild terror and then as my eyes grew accustomed to the dark I saw ahead of me a narrow iron cot towards which I moved with infinite caution. In my progress towards the bed my feet sank into pools of stagnant water which covered the floor, and soon I perceived that the walls of the cell were also dripping with moisture. The tiny window, high in the farthest wall, admitted little air, and the whole place was foul with dampness and the odor of years. It reeked with even worse smells as I quickly discovered, for close to the bed was an uncovered toilet connected with archaic plumbing. The bed was hard and lumpy and I do not think that the thin mattress had ever been cleaned or aired. However, that mattress was not to afflict me long. Within a few minutes my cell door was thrown open and several uniformed men entered. At their head was a black-bearded ruffian who told me that he was Koutzmine, representative of the Minister of Justice, and was authorized to arrange the régime of all prisoners. At his orders the soldiers tore from under me the ill-smelling mattress and the hard little pillow, leaving me only a rough bed of planks. Under his orders they tore off my rings and jerked loose a gold chain from which were suspended several precious relics. They hurt me and I cried out in protest, whereupon the soldiers spat at me, struck me with their fists and left, noisily clanging the iron door behind them. Wrapping my cloak around me, I crouched down on the bed shivering from head to foot and filled with such an agony of loathing and disgust and desolation that I thought I should die. Not a particle of food was brought me that day, and nothing broke the monotony of the dragging hours save now and again when the small grating in the door of my cell was pushed aside and a gaping soldier looked in. Then came night, hardly darker than the day, but more silent. Weak with hunger, spent with pain I clutched my aching head with my hands and asked God if He had forgotten me. At that moment of extreme misery I was startled and at the same time strangely comforted by a sudden low but distinct rapping on the other side of the wall. Instinctively I knew that it was Mme. Soukhomlinoff who was trying to speak to me in the only language prisoners have. I rapped back, almost happily, for I felt that with a friend so near I was not entirely deserted.

I must have slept after that, for the next thing I remember was a man entering the cell with a pot of hot water and a small piece of black bread which he placed on an iron shelf near the bed. "As soon as your money arrives you can have tea," he announced briefly. Tea would have been a priceless blessing in that cold place, but I was so thirsty that I drank every drop of the hot water and was thankful. I suppose I ate the black bread too, bad as it was, for I was very hungry.

How to describe the days that followed, slow-paced, monotonous, yet each one filled with its special meed of suffering? On one of the first days a grim woman came in and stripped me of my underclothes, substituting coarse and unclean garments marked with the number of my cell, which was 70. No prison dress seemed to be provided, so I was allowed to keep my own. But in the process of undressing the woman discovered a slender gold bracelet which I had worn day and night for many years and which was locked on my arm. She called Koutzmine and his guard of soldiers and they, indignant that they had overlooked a single article of value, began to force the bracelet over my hand. As the little circlet was not intended to go over my hand their efforts caused me such pain that I screamed in spite of myself. Touched, or perhaps merely annoyed at this, Koutzmine suggested to the soldiers that if I would promise not to give the bracelet to anyone I might be allowed to keep it. But his suggestion met with no sympathy and the bracelet was finally forced over my bruised hand.

The awful food and the still more awful solitude were daily afflictions, and I think they were really the worst of all. Twice a day a soldier brought in a nauseous dish, a kind of soup made of the bones and skin of fish, none too fresh. Sometimes, if the soldier happened to be in an especially vicious mood, he spat in the soup before giving it to me, and more than once I found small pieces of glass among the bones. Yet so ravenous was my hunger that I actually swallowed enough of the vile stuff to keep myself alive. Only by holding my nose with my fingers was I able to get a few spoonfuls down my throat. What was left I was careful to pour into the filthy toilet, for I had been told that unless I ate what was given me I would be left to starve. Hot water and black bread continued to be doled out in small quantities, but there was never any tea. No food was allowed to be given the prisoners even when it was brought to the fortress by relatives and friends. Neither was any kind of occupation given the wretched captives. We were not even allowed to clean our own cells, a soldier coming in once a week to wipe up the wet and slimy floors. When I begged the privilege of doing this myself the soldier replied: "A prisoner who works is not a prisoner at all." It is true that when he has absolutely nothing to do he is worse than a prisoner, he is a living corpse.

Actual death being too merciful for political prisoners, we were taken out, one by one, for ten minutes every day. The exercise ground was a small grassy court where a few shrubs and trees gave promise of green leaves later on. No words can describe the relief, the blessed joy that those few moments of light and air and the sight of the blue sky brought to my heart. It seemed to me that I lived only for those moments. Of course the walled court was well guarded by armed soldiers and never once did their fierce eyes ever leave me. Still it was a bit of God's beautiful world, a breath of His sweet air, and I breathed it deep into my soul, keeping it there for hope and comfort until the next day came. In the center of the court was a small and dingy bath house where, on Fridays and Saturdays, the prisoners were treated to a sort of a bath. On those days we were not permitted to walk, but I for one did not complain of this. Any respite from the gravelike existence of the cells was a blessing. It was still very cold and when I lay down for the night I never removed my clothes. I had two woolen handkerchiefs, or rather, head kerchiefs, and one of these I tied over my head and the other I wrapped around my shoulders for warmth. Usually I slept until about four o'clock when the bells of a church hard by broke into my slumbers. After that I tried to doze, but very soon came the tramp of boots on the stones of the corridors and the crash of wood which the soldiers brought in each day for their stoves. I always woke up shivering and my first move was towards a corner of my cell where the stones were dry and a little warm from the stove outside. Here I huddled and shook until the hot water and the black bread were thrust in. I had never fully recovered from my illness and the cold and damp brought on first a pleurisy and afterwards a racking cough. I was so weak that sometimes in crossing from the bed to what I called the warm corner I slipped and fell and lay on the wet floor unable to rise. The soldier who thus found me, if he were of the half decent sort, would pick me up and throw me on the plank bed. Otherwise he would merely kick me.

For the first two weeks I spent in the Troubetskoy Bastion the only attendants were men. The soldiers had the keys to the cells and the complete freedom of the corridors. The first lot were men of the 3rd Rifle Regiment of Petrograd, but within a few days some of them were shifted and their places were taken by a miscellaneous force from one of the most unruly of the mutinous reserves. Riots and fights between the two bands became an almost daily occurrence and the nerves of the prisoners were tortured by the yells and blows of the battle. My only comfort, aside from the ten minutes' respite of the exercise ground, was in the wall-tapping between my cell and Mme. Soukhomlinoff's. This had developed into a regular code and we managed to carry on, by alternately long and short taps, quite lucid conversations. Once to our fright the Governor of the bastion, Chkoni, caught us at this forbidden game and threatened us, if it happened again, with the dark cell, a place of unknown horrors, as we knew, for we had listened to the groans and cries of the former police chief Belezky while he suffered there. After the warning of Chkoni Mme. Soukhomlinoff and I communicated with each other only in the middle of the night when the snores of the soldiers in the corridors guaranteed a degree of safety. Without these cautiously tapped-out conversations I really do not know how I should have lived and kept sane.

The cough which had been afflicting me grew worse rather than better and the only relief that was offered me was a primitive kind of cupping which did the cough no good but covered my chest with black and blue bruises. Finally, at the request of the sanitary soldier who had done the cupping, the prison doctor was sent for. This man, whose name was Serebrianikoff, was one of the most dreadful persons I ever came in contact with. He had a red, malicious face, his clothes and person were revoltingly dirty, and to increase their effect he wore on his bulging waistcoat a huge red bow, emblem of his revolutionary ardor. When he came into my cell he literally tore the clothes from my back in a pretended examination, then turning to the soldiers in the doorway he shouted: "This woman is the worst of the whole lot; an absolute idiot from a life of vice." Slapping me on one cheek and then on the other, he began to ask me questions which I cannot repeat here of my alleged orgies with Rasputine, with Nicholas and "Alice" as he called the Empress. Even the soldiers looked disgusted and I shuddered away from him sick with repulsion. That night I was so far gone physically and mentally that I could not answer Mme. Soukhomlinoff when she tapped on the wall. All I could do was to cough and shiver and in an incoherent, half mad fashion pray: "My God, my God, hast Thou forsaken me?"

The next morning the soldier who brought my hot water and bread thought me dying and insisted in sending again for the unspeakable Serebrianikoff, although I begged him not to. "Send a woman, I implore you," I whispered. But there was no woman to send, and the prison doctor came instead. Declaring that I was merely shamming, this brute again struck me in the face and left saying: "I'll punish you for this. There'll be no exercise for you for two weeks after you think yourself well enough to go out." He kept his word, and for two weeks after I ceased to be acutely ill I remained all day in my cell weeping for the clean air and a sight of the blue sky. Little trickles of pale sunlight were beginning to steal through my barred windows, the cold was less intense and I knew that outside, in the world of freedom, the spring had come.

One little bit of good news came at this time. Women wardresses had been appointed to look after the special needs of the women prisoners. Two attendants from a women's prison were the first to arrive, but they were so shocked at the conditions they found in the fortress that they refused to stay. They were replaced by others, one a saucy young person whose sole energies went into flirtations with the soldiers, and an older woman with melancholy dark eyes and the best and kindest of hearts. I cannot tell her name because if she is still alive and in Russia she must be in the employ of the Bolsheviki.

I will call her simply the Woman. Her kindness to me I can never repay, but at least I shall never forget it, especially since I knew that every kind act she did was at her own personal risk. The Woman was on duty only until nine o'clock at night and was never allowed to enter my cell alone. Yet she often managed cleverly to follow slowly when she and the guard left the cell, and she frequently dropped on the floor behind her little pieces of sausage, chocolate, or bread nearly white. In the cell we dared not talk, but when she took me to the bath house we exchanged whispered conversations, and through her I got a little news of the exciting events of the time. The Provisional Government was tottering and the star of Kerensky was rising rapidly. The Imperial Family were still at Tsarskoe Selo, prisoners but alive, and that knowledge gave me a new impulse to live.

I must record one especially kind act my new friend did in my behalf. Easter Sunday came, and sitting on my hard bed I ventured to sing softly a verse or two of a well-remembered Easter hymn. On the Good Friday preceding we had been allowed to leave our cells one by one under guard and to confess to a good old priest, whose distress at our sorry plight so moved him that he heard our confessions with great tears in his eyes. Earnestly this old priest had begged Kerensky to allow him to visit prisoners in their cells and do what he could for their comfort, but Kerensky curtly refused.

I was thinking of him on this Easter morning. The soldiers had been running through the corridors calling to one another, perhaps in jest, perhaps as a matter of habit, the Russian greeting: "Kristos Voskrese," Christ is risen, to which the response is: "Voistino Voskrese," He is risen indeed. I could see that the soldiers had plates of the sugary cheese which everybody eats at Easter and which some of the prisoners received. Not I, because I was considered too wicked, too vile. Nevertheless, because of the trickle of sunshine that stole through the bars of my window, and because the old priest had really given me great comfort, I began to sing. Instantly the soldiers outside commanded me rudely to keep silent. It was too much. I laid my head down on the rags that formed my pillow and began to cry miserably. Then my hand strayed under the pillow, touching something. It was a little red Easter egg left there by the Woman, to make me feel that even in that place I was not entirely friendless. Never did a gift come as such a joyful surprise. I hugged it to my heart, kissed it and thanked God.

I was not forsaken. Indeed the worst was already passed for me, for the next day I was told that on every Friday after I was to receive a visit from my parents, whom I had feared I was never to see again on earth.

CHAPTER XVII

VISITORS in prison! Who but one who has spent days and nights of anguished loneliness behind bolted doors can possibly imagine the joy of such anticipation? I looked forward, almost as toward freedom itself, to the first Friday when I should see my beloved parents. I pictured myself running forward to embrace them, I could see my father's kind and loving smile, my mother's blue eyes full of happy tears. How we would sit, hand in hand, and talk over all that had happened since our parting! They would bring me news, messages, perhaps even letters from those other captives in Tsarskoe Selo. I should hear that the children were well again and the Empress's deepest anxieties were removed.

Alas! the harsh reality of my foolish dreams. When the day came I limped, between armed soldiers, through the long, gray corridors to the visitors' room, and there at the end of a long wooden table which divided us like an impassable gulf I saw my mother. There was no embrace allowed, not even a touch of hands. My mother tried to smile, tried to look at me with the love I craved, but in spite of herself her face paled and an expression of horror congealed her features. I stood there before her white with the pasty whiteness of prison, my uncombed, unkempt hair hanging about my shoulders, my dress dirty and wrinkled and an unhealed cut ploughing a bloody furrow across my forehead. To the question she dared not ask I touched the ugly wound and told her it was nothing, nothing. I could have told her that a soldier named Izotov, in a fit of animal temper, had knocked me against the edge of the cell door, and that the cut had received absolutely no attention since. Had we been alone I should have wept the whole story out on her breast, but we were not alone. Standing over us like inquisitors were the Procureur of Petrograd and the terrible Chkoni, governor of the Troubetskoy Bastion, and afterwards governor of the fortress itself. Ten minutes only were allowed us, and at the end of eight fleeting minutes Chkoni, watch in hand, roared out: "Two minutes left. Finish your talk." But we had no talk. Sobs choked our words, the few commonplace words that in such circumstances can be spoken. We could only bid each other be brave and trust in God's mercy. We could but gaze and gaze at each other through streaming tears. Then they separated us.

When the next Friday came I resolved to make myself a little more presentable. I had no mirror but I begged the Woman to loan me a small, cracked fragment. They had taken away all my toilet articles and every single hairpin, but the Woman gave me two hairpins of her own and, combing my hair with my fingers I arranged it more or less neatly. Every day I washed and cared for the cut on my forehead and when the visiting hour at last arrived I fancied that I looked rather more like myself. This time the precious ten minutes were spent with my father, and because he had been prepared in advance for the wretched object his daughter had become our brief interview was less emotional than that of the preceding Friday. Brave and erect my father held himself before those brutal jailers, and my heart glowed with love and pride to see him. We managed to exchange a few sentences and my father told me that he had obtained permission to send me money to buy tea and a few other comforts. He told me that he and my mother had waited three hours to see me and because it had been ruled that they could not both be admitted on the same day that my mother was standing close to the door of the next room just to catch the faint sound of my voice. These words roused Chkoni to a perfect fury. "So!" He fairly yelled. "But I'll spoil that game," and rushing out he slammed the door between the two rooms. My father flushed crimson but he spoke no word nor, of course, did I. A single protest might have meant punishment for me, and for us all no more visits.

I saw my father only three times, my mother a little oftener, as her health was the better of the two. The money my father sent me did not reach me except in very minute sums. By far the greater part of it was kept by the jailers, and gambled away. Not satisfied with that, the men warned my father that nothing except payment to the prison heads would save me from death, or worse still from assault by the soldiers. My father had long ago been deprived of his income, but he and my mother sold some valuables and gave it to the blackmailers who wanted it only for more gambling. Their sacrifice gave my parents a little peace of mind, but it did not save me from three of the most horrible nights I spent in the fortress. On each of these nights my cell was invaded by drunken soldiers who threatened me with unspeakable things. On the first occasion I simply groveled on the wet floor and prayed the man, in the name of his mother and mine, to let me alone, and, drunk as he was, my words actually penetrated his dark soul and shamed it. The next men were less drunk but were far more bestial. At the sight of them I threw myself against the wall and pounded frantically, screaming at the top of my lungs. Mme. Soukhomlinoff heard and understood. She screamed too, frightfully, and with all her might shook the heavy door of her cell. This brought the guard and once more I was saved. The third time I was so paralyzed with fright that I could not scream. I simply fell on my knees, holding up my little ikon, and begged like a trapped animal. The man hesitated a moment, spat on me contemptuously, and left. The next day, half dead with shame and fear, I managed to tell the Woman all that had passed. Indignantly she went to the Governor of the fortress, and after that even I, "the worst woman in prison," was spared the ultimate insult.

Although we could not know it, things were gradually changing for the better in the fortress. A little physical improvement was apparent. The cold had lessened and in our short walks in the prison yard we could see that lovely spring, with its fresh green leaves and springing flowers, had come to stay. I remember one day seeing in the grass a little yellow flower. It may have been a buttercup or a dandelion or something else we ordinarily call weeds, but to my eyes it was an exquisite thing. Audaciously I stooped and picked it, hiding it quickly in the bosom of my dress. The next visiting day I showed it to my father and dropped it on the table. On leaving the room he contrived to get hold of it and after his death in 1918 I found it, carefully preserved among his private papers. I never picked another flower in that prison yard, although once I tried. But this time a guard caught me, and struck the flower from my hand with the end of his rifle.

Things were improving under the surface, but aside from the welcome change in the weather conditions seemed for a time no better. In the cell adjoining that of Mme. Soukhomlinoff was my old friend General Voyeikoff, who was tortured almost as pitilessly as myself. My heart ached for him. In cell 69 was for some time the police detective Manouiloff, but when he was removed to another prison the writer Kolichko was placed in the cell. Kolichko, poor wretch, was so overcome by his arrest and imprisonment that during the first nights he sobbed so long and bitterly that I found it impossible to sleep. I was so unhappy that I began to pray for death, and once I even resolved to end my life. I had no weapon but a rusty needle which I had picked up and carefully concealed, but I had heard somewhere that there was a spot at the base of the brain which if punctured ever so little would cause death. Before seeking that spot I felt that I must say adieu to my brave little friend Mme. Soukhomlinoff, and so softly I rapped out a farewell message on the wall. Her quick mind instantly divined my intention and without losing any time she sent for the Woman and my rusty needle was taken away from me.

It began to be sultry in the Troubetskoy Bastion and the air in the cells became thick and foul. My small window, which looked out on a narrow court and a high wall, admitted little light and no breeze at all. I used to climb painfully up on the iron shelf which did duty for a table and pressing my face close to the bars I breathed in all the air possible. Instead of seeking the warm corner of my cell I now sat for hours together with my body against the wettest and coldest stones. My despondency increased every day, and I almost ceased to pray or to believe that the universe held any God to whom the prayers of captives could ascend. Yet all the time God was sending me help.

One day a soldier came to my cell and roughly bade me get up and go with two guards for examination. Not knowing exactly what that meant, I rose from my cot and followed the men to a room in the fortress where the High Commission of Inquiry appointed by Kerensky was then in session. Bewildered by the sudden transition from the bastion to a room full of comfortable furniture, and almost blinded by the brilliant light and sunshine, I had all I could do to answer their few inconsequential questions. I have described this first examination in another chapter, and I shall not repeat it here. It was so foolish that afterwards in my hot and ill-smelling cell I actually found myself laughing, and it had been a long time since I had laughed. Judge Roudneff, the only one of the commission who showed himself fair-minded or even capable of just judgment, was present at the inquiry, but I do not think he said a word. Afterwards he was charged with full responsibility of my case, and I appeared before him no less than fifteen times. At the close of the first of these personal interviews I thanked Judge Roudneff warmly. Astonished, he asked: "For what do you thank me?" And I answered: "For the happiness of four whole hours of sitting in a room with a window, and through it a glimpse of green trees." He did not reply except with a kind and sympathetic look, but I knew that his heart was touched, and that he received a new conception of what life meant to a prisoner.

Better things still were to come. Without our being aware of it the revolutionary mania had begun to subside a little and those men among our guards who had once been clean and decent were now getting back to their normal state of mind. Poor soldiers! Never let me forget that they were not to blame for the torments they inflicted on me and other prisoners. It was not they who invented the black calumnies that made me seem a creature undeserving of mercy or any clemency. It was not they who fashioned the cross on which I was crucified. The soldiers did only what they were incited to do by men and women far above them, people who conspired to crush me that they might crush the Empress. The soldiers I forgive, but I cannot yet forgive those others. The fate of the Imperial Family, the ruin of Russia, is on their souls. For what they did they have never shown any penitence, but those rough soldiers in the fortress repented and did what they could in atonement. One of the head guards was a man, handsome in a rustic sort of fashion, who at first had treated me with great insolence. One morning this man opened my door, hesitated for a moment, and then said in a low voice: "I am very sorry for you. Please take this," and vanished. "This" was an apple and a small piece of white bread. Another morning the soldier who brought my breakfast spoke in a grumbling aside but loudly enough for me to hear: "What idiocy to keep a poor sick woman in this place." One night the window in my cell door was pushed aside and in a trembling voice someone begged me to give him my hand. Tears fell on it while the unseen friend told me that he was a boy from Samara, and that it broke his heart to see women caged like beasts in such holes. He must have had a good mother, that boy. Perhaps they all had, for it became almost a habit for men passing through my corridor to slip me bits of bread, sausage, or sugar.

The most wonderful piece of good fortune came through the soldier in charge of the prison library. This man visited my cell one day, and after giving me a keen look which I could not understand he laid the library catalogue on my cot and went out. I had little interest in the dull books at our disposal, but when one sits hours in utter idleness he makes occupation out of almost nothing. I opened the catalogue and turned the leaves. To my astonishment out fell a folded paper. Cautiously I opened it and read these words: "Dear Anushka, I am sorry for you. If you have five rubles I can get a letter to your mother." For a long time after the incriminating paper had been destroyed I sat trembling in doubt and foreboding. I had barely five rubles, and if I gave them would they be gambled away? Was the letter a trap? Was it merely an effort to get me into trouble? I did not know, but on a bit of blank paper left in the catalogue I wrote with my stub of a pencil: "I have suffered so much already that I cannot believe that you wish to do me any more harm." Folding the five rubles and the paper into a tiny note, I tucked it into the catalogue and waited. After a while the librarian returned, and this time I read in his silent gaze that he was asking for my confidence. The next day he came back and again left the catalogue on my bed. This time I seized it eagerly and shook its leaves. A letter from my mother dropped out, a short letter, for she had been given only a few minutes to write, but I read and reread it until I knew every word by heart.

Then began a smuggled correspondence with my father and mother, they gladly giving money to the men who risked their own liberty by carrying the letters back and forth. The letters reached me in prison books, in the sheets of my bed, under the tin basin which held my food, and once even in a soldier's sock dropped carelessly on the floor. In this sock was concealed a note from Lili Dehn, free now and in correspondence with the family at Tsarskoe Selo. There was a slip of paper enclosed with a tiny white flower glued to it, and in the Empress's handwriting: "God keep you." Another precious souvenir of the Empress sent me by my mother was a little moonstone ring long ago given me at Tsarskoe. Tearing a rag from the lining of my coat, I made a bag for this jewel, and begging a safety pin from the Woman, I pinned it inside my dress. The poor librarian. This was the last favor he ever did me, for falling under the suspicion of the Governor, he was abruptly discharged. The letters, however, had done me so much good that I was in every way better and more cheerful. I felt in touch with the world again. I knew in a general way what was going on, and though not all the news was pleasant it gave me a sense of being alive and not altogether hopeless. I knew now what tireless efforts were being made in my behalf, and I felt that in the end something must come of them.

My parents had done everything humanly possible to move Kerensky but without any definite success. The first appointment with him was made through his secretary Chalpern, and although my parents were naturally exactly on time Kerensky kept them waiting for two hours. When at last they were received my parents were told that the Empress Alexandra Feodorovna, Rasputine, and Viroubova were responsible for the Revolution and would have to suffer for it. My parents had heard this before, but it was new to them to hear from Kerensky that he knew that I had had a great many diamonds from the Archbishop Pitirim and for that and other reasons nothing could be done for me. Later he softened a little and ended the interview by promising that my whole affair would be investigated. My parents then contrived an interview with the minister of Justice, Pereverzeff. They made two appointments in fact, for the first one Pereverzeff deliberately broke, going out for the day while my parents sat waiting in an ante-room. The next time my mother went to the Ministry she was received and was civilly treated. Pereverzeff also promised that a fair investigation would be made. By this time the Special Commission of Inquiry was sitting and my mother managed to see the president, Mouravieff. She took with her a letter from his brother to me before the abdication of the Emperor. In this letter I was warned of plots against me and was advised to leave the palace. I had replied to this letter, and my mother had a copy of my reply. I had written that I would never leave the Empress. My conscience was clean before God and man and I would remain to the end where God had placed me. I was astonished that a soldier should advise me to run away from a battlefield. Mouravieff who at first had been very harsh, changed after reading the letters. He even asked my mother to allow him to read them to the commission. They were significant, he said. As soon as my case had been referred to Judge Roudneff he called my parents to the Winter Palace, where he had his office, and talked with them, asking a great many questions, for nearly four hours. In this examination, for it was really that, my father and mother were allowed for the first time to defend me, to make explanations of obscure charges, to tell my life story to the man who was to judge me. No one else gave them such an opportunity, not even the Georgian deputy Cheidze, then very prominent in the Petrograd Soviet. Cheidze was kind and said that he would do anything in his power to help me to get justice, but I do not think he ever did anything. Members of the Provisional Government, Rodzianko and Lvoff, to whom, while they were still in power, my parents had written begging to be received, never even replied to the letters.

One day, sitting in my cell and remembering what had been written me in the smuggled letters, another wonderful thing happened. In the noon meal of fish soup which I must eat or starve I found a large piece of really decent meat. I ate it greedily, of course, and the next day I ate another piece which had mysteriously arrived. I took the first opportunity to ask the Woman where the food came from, and she told me that it was a cook, a poor man whose duty it was to carry food to our bastion. He too pitied me, she said, and she thought he might be willing to run almost any risk for me. So almost at once I was again in correspondence with my parents. This cook did more than carry letters, the brave man. He brought me food, chocolates, clean clothes, linen, stockings, and even a fresh frock. Growing bolder, he ventured regularly to take away my soiled linen and to replace it with clean things. All during those months in the fortress I had washed my linen and stockings in cold water, without soap, and in the night had hung them up in the warm corner on a hook improvised from a broken hairpin. Of course they were never clean, nor even, when I put them on, very dry, and now they were stiff with dirt. Can anyone imagine what it was to me to feel a clean, soft, smooth chemise against my skin?

I am sure the cook could never have done so much for me had not the guards closed their eyes to his activities. They were nearly all friendly now, and used to talk with me through the window in my door. In spring a number of pigeons flocked around the fortress and their constant sobbing voices got on my nerves. I spoke of this to one soldier who expressed surprise. "I was shut up here once," he said, "under the old Government, and I didn't find the birds bad at all. I used to feed them through the window." "You had a window in your cell," I exclaimed. "Then it couldn't have been as bad as this." And he assured me that it wasn't as bad under the Autocracy as under the beneficent Provisional Government and the Soviet. The prisoners had much better food and they could exercise two hours a day in the open.

Another prisoner of the Tsar's government, a non-commissioned officer named Diki, who had been very harsh to me in the beginning, now showed me kindness. Instead of robbing me, as of old, of every little privilege, he began to allow me an extra five minutes or so in the courtyard, he, too, saying that in the old days prisoners were better treated. Another of the guards in the courtyards, a man whom I had bitterly hated, and with cause, told the Woman that he wanted to speak to me. Afterwards while walking he approached me and I looked into his coarse face, deeply pitted with smallpox, and listened in fear at what he might have to say. Stammeringly he told me that he had just returned from a leave spent in his home in the Government of Saratoff. Visiting his sister's house, he was amazed to see, hanging under the ikon in the corner of the room, a photograph of me. "What!" he had exclaimed. "Do you have that shameless woman's picture in your house?" Whereupon his brother-in-law retorted: "Never dare to speak against her who was like a mother to me for two years in Tsarskoe. I was in her own hospital in the end, and it was like Heaven." The brother-in-law had charged the guard with all kinds of messages to me, telling him that they prayed for me daily in his family and hoped for my release. "Forgive me for being unjust to you," said the poor soldier, and offered me his hand. This was the first news I had of my hospital, and I learned with joy that the Provisional Government had not closed it.

Later I heard that the Government had not only carried on my work but had added five new buildings. None of my nurses or orderlies had left, though their openly expressed faith in me might easily have secured their dismissal. Some of the invalids had petitioned the Duma for my release, and another group, indignant because a revolutionary newspaper declined to publish their letter refuting the usual slanders about me, wanted to leave the hospital long enough to blow up the office building! They were good at heart, those misguided Russian soldiers, those poor ignorant children. I know them, and whatever they have been forced to do in these years of horror, I still believe them sound and good of soul. In the last days of my imprisonment in Peter and Paul the guards did not even lock my cell door. They used to linger and talk, and sometimes they brought paper and pencils that I might make sketches of them to take home. I was rather clever with a pencil in those days.

* * *

CHAPTER XVIII

THE prison had changed, and except for an occasional riot or a fight between two drinking soldiers, it was almost peaceful. For now there was a man attached to the fortress, a man so brave and kind, and above all so commanding that terrors fled before him—Dr. Ivan Manouchine. The gratitude and respect with which I write his name cannot be expressed in words. It was on the 23rd of April, the name day of the Empress, ever a day of memories to me, that this good man came into the house of pain where lay the prisoners of the Provisional Government. A few weeks before this the soldiers, gradually recovering from their first revolutionary blood lust, had begun to revolt against the needless brutality of the prison doctor, Serebrianikoff, and had finally sent in to the all powerful Kerensky a request for his demission. In those days Kerensky, whose ambition to be at the head of the government was maturing, made a special point of granting soldiers' petitions, and he really consented to replace Serebrianikoff with a physician of reputation. From the point of view of the Duma Dr. Manouchine was entirely a safe man to be appointed. He was a republican in politics, and he conformed to the popular superstition of "dark forces" surrounding the court. But what the Duma did not know about Dr. Manouchine was that he had a heart of gold and a mind that was ruled not by any political party but by principles of right and justice.

When the new prison doctor first came into my cell, accompanied by the retiring man looking frightened and ill at ease, I was lying on my cot in a mood of unusual rebellion. In a quiet, professional voice he asked me how I felt, and when he examined my poor chest and saw it black and blue and swollen from the clumsy cupping it had received, he frowned with displeasure. He gave some quick directions for my relief and in a gentle tone assured me that he intended to visit the bastion every day. It was the first time in many long weeks that I had been spoken to by the type of man we call a gentleman, and after the door closed behind him something in my frozen heart seemed to melt like icicles in the sun. Almost with the faith of childhood I fell on my knees and prayed, and after that I lay down and slept for several hours.

Every day soon after the booming of the noonday gun he came and every one among us stood up as close as possible to the cell doors, waiting to catch the first sound of his voice as he came down the corridor. At every door he stopped and asked the health of the prisoner. To him they were not prisoners but patients, and he treated them with all the skill and, above all, the courtesy he would have accorded the richest and most powerful of his patients. He examined our food and pronounced it entirely unsuited to our needs. He did not stop there, but in the end succeeded in greatly improving the ration and supplementing it for the sick with milk and eggs. How he did it in the Russia of those days I cannot imagine. I only know that Dr. Manouchine had a will of steel, and against that will and the staunch uprightness of his character malice and fanaticism broke like waves against a rock.

Little by little Dr. Manouchine instituted other reforms. The prisoners now received at least a part of the money furnished by their friends outside, and once a week the non-commissioned officer Diki went through the prison answering requests for such necessities as soap, tooth powder, and paper on which petitions to the Governor of the fortress might be written. Often when a prisoner lacked money to pay for these things the doctor supplied it out of his own pocket.

Meanwhile my examinations under the stern but just commissioner Roudneff were going on. Weary under the long and apparently pointless inquisition, I asked Dr. Manouchine one day how much longer he thought they intended to torment me. His reply was grave. "Not long, I think. But before it is over you may have to undergo a still more trying ordeal." A few day later he came to my cell alone; that is, he resolutely closed the door between us and his usual escort of soldiers, and told me in his kindest manner that the Special Commission of Inquiry had almost concluded that the charges against me were without foundation. One more proof, however, was necessary, a physician's sworn statement that the hideous accusations of vice made by enemies of the Emperor and Empress and their closest friends were false. Would I, for my own sake, for the sake of the Imperial Family, submit to a medical examination? Without at all knowing what was implied I gave an instant but rather frightened consent to any examination he thought necessary. It was a terrible ordeal for a woman to live through. Most of the questions asked me were of a nature which appalled me, and yet were beyond my understanding. I cannot here repeat even the least of them. I can only say that they opened up to me an abyss of wickedness and sin which I had not dreamed existed in the human soul. At the end of an hour— or many hours—of trial, I lay on my bed, hands clasped over my eyes, spent, exhausted, utterly incapable of speech. Up to the very end Dr. Manouchine's manner had been that of a physician, but now that it was over it was a friend beyond anything human and sympathetic who laid his hand on my quivering shoulder and said: "This clears you absolutely. They will take my word for it."

Towards the end of May, a hot and wearying season, the fortress was visited by the head of the Provisional Government's Commission of Inquiry, a pompous man, yet in his cautious way, rather kindly. Pausing before my cell, he told me that no crime had been fastened upon me and that I might hope soon to be transferred to a better place. Hope gave me new life momentarily, but as the days dragged on my hope gave way to bitter unbelief. My health always since my arrest indifferent, now began to decline and I could see that the doctor was seriously concerned for me. He came to the prison only four times a week now, and what ages seemed to elapse between his visits. All I had left of courage his voice and ministrations gave me.

One hot June day I was aroused from my sick lethargy by the tramping of heavy boots on the stones of the corridor. The heavy cell door swung open and I saw a crowd of strange men, several of whom unceremoniously invaded my cell and began an examination of my poor effects. Frightened, I watched them as they disdainfully picked up and threw aside the few rags a prisoner is allowed, but my fears were allayed when I saw in the background the tall figure of the doctor. "Do not be afraid, Anna Alexandrovna," he said. "This is only a committee of revision of prisoners." Later I heard him say to the committee: "This woman may have only a few days to live. If you are willing you may take on yourselves the responsibility of her death. As a physician I refuse to do so."

The next day he whispered to me that he was confident that I would be taken away, but that my release might be delayed a little because of renewed riots among the prison guards. He did not know where I was to be taken, and I feared it would be the Women's Prison, which the Woman had told me was almost as bad as the Troubetskoy Bastion. But soon I was relieved of that nightmare, for the doctor came again bringing me the good news that I should probably be taken to the House of Detention in a pleasant neighborhood on the other side of the river. In groups the friendly soldiers came to say good-bye and to assure me that even should the mutinous guards oppose my going they would see to it that I got safely way. Days went by, sleepless nights, and still no order of release arrived. I became almost hysterical with suspense. I gave way to dreadful fits of weeping until even the doctor grew stern and bade me control myself. I felt like a mouse under the teasing claws of a cat, and control was difficult even after I learned that the doctor had persuaded some members of the central committee of the Petrograd Soviet to visit the fortress and to reason with the mutinous guards.

Almost the last day of June, at six in the evening, I was standing barefooted and half dressed against the cool, wet wall of my cell thinking of my mother who, the day before, had visited me. Her face was brighter than usual and she had said to me: "The next time we meet it may be in better circumstances." At the moment my door opened and the hated Chkoni appeared. "Well," he said, with his usual sneer, "did you have hysterics after seeing your mother?" "Certainly not," I replied coldly. "No?" he commented, "I thought you might because to-morrow or the next day they may take you away." I fell against the wall too overcome to speak, too blind to see the hands of the guard pressing my limp hand in congratulation. Tomorrow or next day! The words repeated themselves in my brain countless times. But I was not even to wait until to-morrow, though Chkoni evidently wished me to think so. I heard the voice of the younger and less familiar wardress: "Dress yourself quickly. The doctor is bringing a deputation from the Soviet." I had nothing to put on except my ragged shoes and a torn gray woolen jacket, but these I rapidly seized while the wardress picked up and made a bundle of my small belongings.

On the opposite wall I heard brave Mme. Soukhomlinoff rapping out a farewell message to which I responded as well as I could. Then the deputation arrived, and the doctor. There was some confused talk. I cannot remember a word. I felt myself picked up and carried down the winding corridors. The great door of the bastion rolled open and we passed out into the cool, delicious evening air. There was a motor car into which I was lifted, another car into which the doctor climbed, there were soldiers, some friendly, some seemingly determined that the cars should not leave the courtyard. I remember very little until we drove out of the gates and over the Troizky Bridge. The wind, the brilliant twilight, the sight of water and the blue sky, blinded me so that I had to cover my face with both hands.

Within a short time the cars stopped at the Detention House in the Fourshkatskaia Ulitza, and I was carried into the office of the commissioner. He was an officer, rather short in stature, but dignified and efficient. Offering me his hand, he asked me if I would be seated while he made out the necessary papers. I had time to see that the House of Detention promised to be quite different from a prison. Indeed the soldiers of this house would not even permit the entrance of the fortress guards who had come with me. As if he divined that I was too weak to walk upstairs the commissioner gave orders that I was to be carried. It was into a large, light, clean room that they took me, and at my exclamation of joy at sight of windows the soldiers laughed heartily. But the doctor silenced them. "Go," he said, "see that her parents are telephoned, and send a woman to bathe and dress her." His own arms lifted me from the chair on which I half sat, half lay. On a bed softer and cooler than even existed in my memory he laid me, said good night, and gently left the room.

CHAPTER XIX

I SPENT a happy and peaceful month in the Detention House, the only disturbing event being the so-called July Revolution, the first serious attempt of Lenine's party to seize the government. The Soviet already transcended in power the old Provisional Government, most of whose original members had by this time disappeared from politics. Kerensky was premier, nominally, but only because a remnant of the Russian Army still resisted the separate peace propaganda and remained on duty at the front.

Persons in the Detention House were prisoners in the sense that they were under guard and were not allowed to leave the house. The guards were complacent, though, and visiting between the rooms was permitted. I soon found that I was the only woman in the place, and that some of the men there had suffered greater tortures than I. There were between eighty and ninety officers, almost the last remnant of the garrison of Kronstadt where in the first days of the Revolution the soldiers went quite mad and murdered, in ways too horrible to relate, a great many officers, and even young naval cadets against whom they could have had no possible grudge. The officers in the Detention House were in a sad state of body and mind. We talked together sometimes in the dining room, and learning that they longed for the consolation of Holy Communion, I remembered that my hospital in Tsarskoe Selo possessed a movable altar and holy vessels. With the consent of Nadjaroff, commandant of the Detention House, the altar and my own priest were brought from Tsarskoe and the sacred ceremony was twice celebrated, the last time on July 29, my birthday.

I ought to say of the commandant Nadjaroff that he was an excellent man, kind to the prisoners, and conscientious in his work. The poor man had one fatal weakness, gambling. So strong a hold had this vice on an otherwise good man that when his money ran short he was not above borrowing and even begging from the prisoners and their friends. It seems almost too bad to record this blot on the character of a man who was kind and courteous to me, but I am trying to give the psychology as well as to portray the events of the Russian Revolution, and I must emphasize the fact that it was the weakness and self-indulgence of the people themselves that made the Revolution and its frightful aftermath possible.

From my first day in the Detention House I began to recover my health and my self-control. My windows were not barred, and through the open casement I feasted my eyes on the beauty of grass and trees, on the familiar little church of Sts. Kosma and Damian which stood almost opposite, and, strangest of all to me, of people walking or driving through the streets below. It took a few days for me to get used to a normal state of life, and at first, when night grew near, I was seized with such nervousness that they had to let a maid sleep in the room with me. As the fresh air and sunshine began to bring color to my face and I felt strength returning to my limbs I forgot my fears, and became something like the woman I had been before I was caged like a beast in the Fortress of Peter and Paul. Visitors were admitted both morning and afternoon, and I had the happiness of talking privately with my father and mother and with friends who still remained faithful. They brought me clothes, toilet articles, books, flowers, writing materials, and, best of all, news of what had happened during the months of my imprisonment. I learned of the rapid disintegration of the army under the weak and ineffectual Provisional Government, the tottering state of Kerensky's régime, and the threatening domination of the Soviets. What was in store for Russia no one knew, happily for Russians. Of the fall of the

Soviets and the rise of Bolshevism no one yet had any premonition. The radical element was already in control, and there was a great deal of threatening talk of shooting the Emperor. However, the Imperial Family was still alive and in Tsarskoe Selo, which was as much as I had dared to hope.

Of the events of the July Revolution, the forerunner of the Bolshevist triumph of November, 1917, I know rather less than others who were at full liberty during that terrible week. It was about the 18th of the month, a brilliant summer day, when I was startled by long-continued shouting and bellowing of soldiers in a caserne not far from the house. In great excitement the men were running in and out of the yard calling on the *tovarishi* to arm themselves and join the uprising. As if by magic the streets filled with rough-looking people, singing wild songs, waving their arms, and forming processions behind huge scarlet banners on which I could read such inscriptions as "Down with the War!" "Down with the Provisional Government!" An endless line of these paraders passed and repassed, dirty, disorderly soldiers, equally dirty factory workers, yelling like crazed animals. Once in a while a gray motor truck would dash through the street, laden with shouting men and boys, rifles, and machine guns. In the distance we could hear shots and the ripping noise of the machine guns.

Of course we were all horribly frightened, especially the officers from Kronstadt, who knew that in case of invasion not one of them would be left alive. We were all advised to leave our rooms and take refuge in the corridors, as at any time the rioters might begin firing through the windows. But we were not out of danger even there because many of the guards openly sympathized with the rioters, and the head guard was so jubilant over the course of events that he went around boasting that he was quite prepared to surrender the house and all its inmates at the first demand of the Revolutionists. Some of the guards were better than this man, and one of them, a wearer of the St. George cross, said that in case of trouble he would try to get me to his sister's house, where I would be perfectly safe. For two nights nobody slept or even undressed. In the room next to mine was lodged old General Belaieff, former War Minister, whom imprisonment had left a sad wreck. He, like the other officers, fully expected death, and I found myself in the novel rôle of a cool and collected comforter. I, who had lately been afraid to sleep in a room by myself, now went from one old soldier to another urging them to keep up hope. The days passed, and the firing came no nearer, and within a week troops summoned from the front took possession of the city.

GRAND DUCHESSES OLGA, TATIANA, ANASTASIE, AND MARIE, PRISONERS AT TSARSKOE SELO, 1917.

ANNA VIROUBOVA.
A Photograph Taken Shortly after Her Release from the
Fortress of Peter and Paul, Petrograd.

My examination under the High Commissioner Roudneff not being entirely finished, he came once or twice to the Detention House bringing with him on one occasion Korinsky, Procurator of Petrograd, a courteous gentleman, who at parting expressed a hope that I would soon be free. A few days later, August 5, if I remember correctly, M. Korinsky himself telephoned that if my parents would call at his office they would be given my warrant of release. Alas, my parents happened to be in Terioke that day, but too impatient to wait until the morrow I telephoned my uncle Lachkereff, who immediately hastened to the Procurator's office for the coveted warrant. Trembling with excitement, I stood at my window with several of my good friends waiting the result of his errand. At six o'clock we heard a drosky driven at great speed over the cobbles, and as it came in sight we saw my uncle standing up and wildly waving the papers in his hand. "Free!" he called out. "Anna Alexandrovna, you are free!" The rest is confusion in my mind. There were laughter and sobs. People kissed and embraced me. I was in the drosky driving through Petrograd streets. I was in my uncle's house. The tea table was spread. It was like a dream.

After prison one gets used to freedom by slow degrees. It seems strange at first to be allowed to move about freely, to go to church, to walk, to drive, to go wherever one desires, through woods, along leafy country roads. Not that I was entirely free to go where I liked. I could not safely go to Tsarskoe Selo, even to my own house, which after my arrest had been taken over by the police,, and not only ransacked for evidence against me, but looted of every valuable. It was my faithful old servant Berchik who gave me the details of the search. He, honest soul, who had been forty-five years in the service of my family, was offered ten thousand rubles if he would testify against the Empress and myself. On his indignant refusal the police arrested him, while they tore up the carpets and even the floors of my rooms, demanding of Berchik the whereabouts of secret passages to the palace, the private telegraph and telephone wires to Berlin, my hidden writing desks, and all sorts of nonsense. Especially were they anxious to discover my wine cellar, and when they found that I possessed none they were angry indeed. They took possession of all the letters and papers they could find, and at the end of the search ordered my cook to prepare them an elaborate supper. Then they left taking with them the silverware.

If I could not visit Tsarskoe and those whom I loved and longed to see, I could at least, and I did, hear from the Empress. Just before the family were sent to their exile one of the maids smuggled out a letter which reached me safely and which I quote here, suppressing only the most intimate and affectionate passages.

"I cannot write much," the letter began, "my heart is too full. I love you, we love you, thank you, bless you, kiss the wound on your forehead. . . . I cannot find words. . . . I know what will be your anguish with this great distance between us. They do not tell us where we go (we shall learn only on the train), nor for how long, but we think it is where you were last" (Tobolsk). "Beloved, the misery of leaving! Everything packed up, empty rooms, such pain, the home of twenty-three years. Yet you have suffered far more. Farewell. Somehow let me know you received this. We prayed long before the Virgin of Znomenia, and I remembered the last time it was on your bed. My heart and soul are torn to go so far from home and from you. To be for months without news is terrible. But God is merciful. He won't forsake you, and will bring us together again in sunny times. I fully believe it."

With the letter the Empress sent me a box of my jewels which she had carefully guarded, and I heard a fairly full account of how the summer had been spent. For a time she and the Emperor had been kept apart, being allowed to speak to each other only at table and in the presence of guards. Revolutionary agents tried every possible means of incriminating the Empress, whom they hated even more than the Emperor, but finally failing in their efforts they allowed the family to be together once more. The day after they were sent to Siberia the maid visited me again with the story of their departure. Kerensky personally arranged every detail, and intruded his presence for hours together on the unhappy family. Under his orders everything was made ready for a midnight journey but actually they did not leave the palace until six o'clock in the morning. All night the prisoners sat in their traveling clothes and wraps in the round hall of the palace. At five a courageous servant brought them fresh tea, which gave them a little comfort, especially Alexei, who stood the night badly. They drove away from the palace with perfect serenity as if going on a holiday to Finland or the Crimea. Even the Revolutionary newspapers, with grudging admiration, had to admit this.

A day or two later Mr. Gibbs, Alexei's English tutor, came to see me, and he told me that although he was not permitted to accompany the Imperial Family with the other tutors, M. Gilliard and M. Petroff, he intended to follow them to Tobolsk. He took a photograph of me for the Empress, who was anxious to see for herself if the long imprisonment had impaired my health. As a matter of fact I was not very well just then, as I had something very like jaundice, so I am afraid my photograph was none too reassuring. At this time I was staying in the home of my sister's husband who was attached to the British Military Commission in Petrograd. It was a cool and comfortable apartment, and I should have been contented to stay on indefinitely. But one day my brother-in-law, in deep embarrassment, showed me a letter from his sister, who was expected on a visit. This lady expressed herself unwilling to live under the same roof with a person as notorious as myself, and I, equally unwilling to associate with her, moved back to my uncle's hospitable home. But even there I found no serenity. I had been acquitted of all the crimes charged against me by the Provisional Government,* but now the Government of Kerensky found new accusations to make of me. This time I was a counter-Revolutionist, and as papers served on me in the middle of the night of August 24 (Russian) ordered, I had to leave for an unknown destination within twenty-four hours. As I was without money and was really in need of a physician's care, my relatives began at once to petition every authority for a delay of at least twenty-four hours more. This was finally allowed, but two soldiers were immediately placed before my door and I was a prisoner in my uncle's apartment. Meanwhile my parents and friends continued to make every preparation for my comfort in exile, and two of my hospital staff, the director and a nurse, volunteered to go with me. The night before I left my poor parents stayed with me, none of us going to bed. Very early on a rainy morning two motor cars filled with police came for us. They were kind enough to let my parents accompany me almost to the Finnish side, and they explained that they had come so early because they feared street demonstrations.

At the station we found a miscellaneous company of alleged counter-Revolutionists including a few old acquaintances. Among these was former detective Manouiloff, a tall officer named Groten, the editor, Tanchevsky, and the curious little Siberian doctor Badmieff, with his equally curious wife and child and a young maid named Erika whom I came to know very well. Badmieff was the herb doctor who, it will be remembered, was supposed to purvey the deadly poisons which I was alleged to feed to the Tsarevitch. He was a small, round, shriveled man, excessively old—over a hundred, they said—and in appearance resembled a quaint carved Buddha out of an antiquarian shop. He had the smallest, blackest eyes imagi-nable, set in a face yellow and wrinkled, and his long, scraggly beard was as white as cotton. His wife, many years his junior, and his funny little child, Aida, were as Mongolian in appearance as himself. The maid, Erika, a girl of about eighteen, was not uncomely with her with her bright eyes and short, curly hair. All the "counter-Rev-olutionists" were herded together in one carriage, the one farthest from the engine, and in charge of us was a Jewish official of the Kerensky

---

* See Appendix B.

Government. At Terioke I parted with my father and mother, the train moving on quickly to the Finnish town of Belieovstrov. Here we were met by an enormous crowd of soldiers and working people, all hostile, demanding to see the dangerous counter-Revolutionists. Especially they demanded to see me, but I shrank back in my seat, fearing every moment that the shower of stones against the carriage would break the windows. But quickly the conductor's whistle was blown and the train moved beyond the reach of the mob.

Worse was to come. When we reached Rikimeaki we found waiting us a larger and a still more furious crowd. Our carriage was unfastened from the train and the mob rushed in yelling that we must all be given up and killed. "Give us the Grand Dukes!" they shouted. "Give us Gourko!" I sat with my face buried in the shoulder of my nursing sister fearing that my end had come. My fears were not imaginary, for several ruffians pitched on me shouting that they had found Gourko in women's clothes. Frantically the sister explained that I was not General Gourko but only a woman ill and lame. Refusing to believe her, they demanded that I be stripped, and I have no doubt that this would have happened had not a motor car opportunely dashed up carrying a sailor deputation from the Helsingfors Soviet. These men pushed their way into the carriage, and without ceremony booted the invaders out. One man, a tall, slender youth named Antonoff, made a speech at the top of his voice, commanding the mob to disperse and to leave things in the hands of the Soviet. So authoritatively did he speak that the crowd obeyed him and allowed our carriage to be attached to another train bound for Helsingfors. Antonoff remained with us, and in the friendliest fashion sat down beside me and bade me to be of good cheer. He did not know why we had been sent away from Petrograd, but the Soviet at Helsingfors, of which he was a member, had received a telegram, he thought directly from Kerensky, saying that we were being sent on, and when we arrived were to be placed under arrest. Doubtless there would be explanations, and after that we would surely be released. To my mind the thing seemed not quite so simple. Kerensky had sent us from Petrograd, but not to be imprisoned in Helsingfors. What he desired was that the mobs, notified of our arrival from his office, would kill us before we ever reached Helsingfors at all. No doubt he hoped at the same time to dispose of General Gourko and the Grand Dukes left in Petrograd.

But Gourko was too clever for Kerensky, and made good his escape to Archangel, where he took refuge with the British Occupational Force. As for the Grand Dukes, they were, for some reason, at this time left undisturbed by the Revolutionists.

It was night when we reached Helsingfors and we found the station practically deserted. The main body of the prisoners were taken away into the darkness, but Antonoff said that I and the nurse should spend the night in a hospital adjoining the station. We climbed several flights of steep stairs and passed through wards crowded with blue-gowned sick soldiers and sailors, not one of whom offered us the slightest rudeness. A skilled Finnish nurse undressed me and put me to bed, but unhappily not for long. Scarcely had I composed myself to sleep when the door opened, the lights flashed up, and Antonoff, red and very angry, entered the room. He had gone to the Soviet authorities, confident that he could persuade them to let me remain in the hospital, at least until word came from Petrograd of our exact status. But they refused his request and ordered him to take me at once to the ship on which the other prisoners were confined. There being no appeal I dressed and limped down the long stairs to the street where a dense mob had assembled, shouting, threatening, crowding dangerously around the motor car. It is a horrible thing to hear a mob shrieking for one's blood. One feels like a cornered hare in the face of yelping hounds. With the strength of desperation I clung to the arm of Antonoff, who for all I knew might yield suddenly and throw me to the crowd. Unworthy thought, for the man held me firmly, all the time demanding that the people give room and let us reach the car. When they saw me in the car their fury seemed to redouble. "Daughter of the Romanoffs," they yelled, "how dare she ride in a motor car? Let her get out and walk." Standing up in the car Antonoff repeated his commands that the mob disperse, and slowly at first and then more rapidly we got away. We reached the distant water front, and I was taken from the car to a ship. Picture my astonishment when I found myself standing on the deck of the *Polar Star*, the light and beautiful yacht on which I had so often sailed in Finnish waters with the Imperial Family. With all the Imperial property the *Polar Star* had been confiscated by the Provisional Government, and it was but another sign of the changing times that the yacht had later been taken away from the Provisional Government and was now the property of the Soviets, being the *Zentrobalt*, or headquarters of the

Baltic fleet.

From the deck I was hurried past the open door of the main dining salon, once a place of ceremony and good living, now a dingy, disordered apartment where crowds of illiterate workmen gathered to dispose of the rest of Russia's ruined fleet and the future of our unhappy country.* At least a hundred of these men were in the salon when I passed it first, and during the five days I spent on the yacht their voices seemed to go on in endless orations, ceaseless wrangling, twenty-four hours at a stretch. It was like nothing I can describe, like an ill-disciplined lunatic asylum. I was herded with the other "counter-Revolutionists" far below decks in what I conjectured had been the stokers' quarters. The stifling little cabins were filthy, like all the rest of the yacht, and they simply swarmed with vermin. It was so dark that night and day the electric lights burned, and I was thankful for that because somehow the bright light seemed to be a kind of protection against the swarm of grimacing, obscene sailors who infested the place, amusing themselves with discussions as to when and how we were likely to be killed. During the whole of the first night Antonoff stood guard over us and warned the sailors that no murder could be done without authority from the Soviet. Over and over again they suggested that he leave the place, but he always replied firmly that he was responsible for the prisoners and could not go. Finally towards morning the sailors left, and afterwards we learned that their blood lust towards us was not merely simulated. They had gone directly from the yacht to the *Petropavlovsk*, the flagship of the fleet, and had killed every one of the old officers left on board.

Antonoff left us early in the morning, left us expecting to return, but he never did return nor did we ever see or hear of him again. Such sudden disappearances were common enough even in those early days of the Russian Revolution, before murder became the fine art into which it has since developed. Five days we remained on the *Polar Star*, very miserable in our vermin-infested quarters below decks, but mercifully allowed part of each day in the open air. They might have allowed us longer time on deck had it not been for the hostile crowds that constantly thronged the quays. My time was spent in the shelter of the deckhouse near the main salon, a spot where in the old days the Empress and I loved to sit with our books

---

* Finland had not then separated from the old Russian Empire.

and work. Here five years before, when the Empress Dowager visited the yacht, I had taken a photograph of her with her arm around the shoulders of the Emperor, both smiling and happy in the sparkling light of the fjord. Every corner of the yacht had been exquisitely clean and white in those days. Dirty as the yacht's present crew appeared, I cannot say they starved their prisoners or were cruel to them. We had soup, meat, bread, and tea, luxurious fare compared to Peter and Paul. Our worst condition was suspense of mind as to our ultimate fate. At every change of guard we begged news from Petrograd, but always we received the same answer. The Kerensky Government gave no reason or justification for our arrest. Two of the sailors were especially friendly to me because, as they explained, they came from Rojdestino, our family estate near Moscow. "If we had known that you were going to be brought here," they said, "we might have done something. But now it is too late." That night I found in my cabin a tiny note, ill-spelled and badly written, warning me that all of us were about to be transferred to the Fortress of Sveaborg in the Bay of Helsingfors. "We are so sorry," the note concluded. Although it was unsigned, I knew the note must have been sent in kindness by one of the men from my old home. But at the prospect of another imprisonment my heart turned sick with dread.

Next evening came Ostrovsky, head of the Helsingfors Okhrana, accompanied by several members of the main committee of the Soviet. Ostrovsky was a very young man, scarcely eighteen I should judge, but he had fierce eyes and all the assurance of a born leader. Turning to my nurse, to Mme. Badmieff, Erika the maid, and her little Mongolian charge Aida, he said roughly that they were free but that all the rest would be taken at once to the fortress. In a sudden panic of alarm I threw myself into the arms of my nursing sister and begged her to accompany me. But she too was fear-stricken and drew back while all the men laughed heartlessly. "What's the difference?" asked Ostrovsky brutally. "You're all going to be shot anyhow." At which the dauntless Erika, putting Aida into her mother's arms, came over to me and tucking her hand under my arms said: "I'm not afraid. I'm going wherever the doctor goes and I'll stand by you both." I gave the trembling nurse a small box containing all the trinkets I had brought with me, gave her messages to my father and mother, and followed my fellow unfortunates to the deck, down a slippery gangplank to waiting motor boats on which we traveled the half hour's journey from the yacht to the fortress.

CHAPTER XX

SVEABORG before the War was one of three principal naval stations of the Russian Empire, the other two being Kronstadt and Reval. Sveaborg occupies a number of small islands in the Bay of Helsingfors. The bay itself, shaped like a rather narrow half moon, is so enclosed by these wooded islands that in winter the salt water freezes solidly. In summer the islands are green and lovely and a few of them, not under military control, are used by the Finns as pleasure resorts. Even in the darkness and in the unfortuitous circumstances of our arrival I could see that the main island might be a very attractive place. Up a steep hill we panted, past a white church surrounded with trees, and at last reached the place of our confinement, a long, dingy, one-storied stronghold. A young officer and several very dirty soldiers took our records, and Erika and I were pushed into a small cell with two wooden bunks covered with dust and alas, nothing else. The place smelled as only old prisons do smell, and the only air came in through a small window high in one of the walls. Wrapping ourselves in our coats, we lay down on the hard planks and tried to sleep. In the early dawn we got up, our backs aching and our throats choked with dust, but the irrepressible Erika laughed so heartily and sneezed so comically that I found it impossible to lament our surroundings. The place was a dreadful hole just the same, no proper toilet facilities at hand, and of course no opportunity of washing, to say nothing of bathing. We had to pay for our food at the rate of about ten rubles a day, at that time no small amount of money. The food was not very bad except that Stepan, the commissary, used to wipe our plates with a disgustingly dirty towel which he wore around his neck, the same towel being used in a laudable attempt to wipe the dust from our bunks.

Climbing on the bunks, we had a view through the window of a new building going up, the workmen being women as well as men. At the same time we got a glimpse of the detective Manouiloff who, ever pessimistic, held up three fingers as an expression of his belief that we had only that many days to live. We, however, ventured the guess that we would not remain at Sveaborg more than a month. It was a mere hazard but it turned out a fortunate one. We remained just about a month. It was a queer life we lived during that month, surrounded by tipsy and irresponsible men whose officers seemed to fear them too much to insist upon discipline. The officers, especially one fine young man, did everything they dared to make us comfortable. After the first ten days our plank beds were furnished with green leather cushions which might have made sleep a comfort if they had not persisted in slipping from under us about as soon as we dozed off. Somewhat later, a week perhaps before our liberation, these cushions were replaced by real mattresses stuffed with seaweed, wonderfully luxurious by comparison with the bare boards. The prisoners were exercised every day in the open under Sveaborg guards and the gaze of a crowd of Finnish Bolshevists. These people seemed at first immensely diverted by the pomposity of the Siberian doctor Badmieff who, in his long white robe, tall cap, and white gloves was certainly a curious spectacle. Soon they tired of him and turned their stolid, expressionless eyes on the other prisoners with what intentions we could only conjecture. Badmieff continued to be a center of interest in the prison. Erika, his faithful disciple, demanded the privilege of attending him, and this was granted. Every day he sat cross-legged like the Buddha he so much resembled, dictating endless medical treatises to Erika. In the evenings he used to put his lamp on the floor at the foot of his bunk, strew around it flowers and leaves brought from outside, burn some kind of ill-smelling herbs for incense, and generally create what I assumed to be the occult atmosphere of his beloved Thibet. Erika, scantily clad, always attended these séances and gradually they appeared to hypnotize the sailors, who thought highly of the doctor's professional powers. Indeed towards the end I often heard them swearing that whoever left the fortress, they would at least keep their highly esteemed *tovarish* Badmieff and his Siberian-Thibetan lore.

In sad contrast to the condition of Dr. Badmieff was that of the poor editor, Glinka Janchevsky, who being without money was treated with the utmost contempt. Housed in a wretched cell covered with obscene drawings, the miserable man spent most of his time lying on his wooden bed wrapped up, head and all, in his overcoat. He used to creep to our cell door with a glass of hot water in his hand begging for a pinch of tea and, if we had it, a little sugar. Every day he used to ask pathetically: "When do you think we shall be let go?" Like all journalists, he was famished for news, and whenever I got hold of a stray newspaper I used to read it to him from the first column to the last.

The vacillating conduct of the Bolshevist sailors toward the prisoners of Kerensky I can only ascribe to the increasingly bitter conflict going on between the weak Provisional Government and the Bolsheviki. The sailors hated us because we were "bourgeois," but they spared us because Kerensky desired our destruction. The officers good-naturedly brought me flowers from outside, an occasional newspaper, and even letters from people in Helsingfors who knew my history and pitied my fate. Sometimes I was even invited to tea with the officers, and twice I was taken out of prison, ostensibly for examination, but really to attend services at the little white church on the island. The guards were rough and kind by turns, sometimes uttering horrible threats against all the prisoners, sometimes bringing me a handful of the wild flowers they knew I loved to have near me. Discipline was lax, and we never knew from one day to another what might befall. For example, the padlock to my cell got lost and for several nights the door was left unlocked. One can imagine how I slept! On one of these unguarded nights the cell was invaded by a group of drunken and lustful men. Erika and I fought them, screaming at the top of our lungs, until a few sober and better-minded sailors came to the rescue. A day or two later, when a rumor spread that we were all to be hanged, I among the first, I for one felt less terror than relief. Anything, even hanging, seemed better than this lunatic prison where the guards drank, played cards, and wrangled all night, and where the men's attitude towards Erika and myself, the only women, was by turns dangerously savage and dangerously friendly.

Besides the Kerensky prisoners the fortress sheltered eight or nine prisoners charged with crimes ranging from theft to murder. Some of these whom we encountered in the exercise yard looked like very decent men, shining perhaps by contrast with the rowdy Revolutionists I had seen in the course of two imprisonments. For these unfortunates and for the guards we bought cigarettes, thus establishing more cordial relations. Nobody knew or could guess what was going to happen to us. One day appeared the president of the Helsingfors Soviet, a black-eyed Jew named Sheiman, who assured us that we were to be sent back to Petrograd, and that we might as well have our things ready by nine o'clock that night. Nothing happened that night, nor did we, for some reason, expect anything. The next day Sheiman came again with his bodyguard of soldiers and sailors, and told us that his Soviet refused for a time to release us. It appeared that telegrams had arrived from Kerensky and from Cheidze, the Georgian leader in the Petrograd Soviet, urgently demanding our return. The Helsingfors Soviet might have obliged Cheidze, but they would not honor any demand of Kerensky's, so there we were. The Provisional Government and the Petrograd Soviet sent over several deputies, Kaplan, a small, black-bearded man, who smilingly told us that there was no possible hope for us; Sokoloff, the famous, or rather infamous, author in the first instance of Order No. 1 which was principally responsible for the break-up of the army; and Joffe, the little Jew, who, a few years later, became influential enough to be included among the delegates to the Genoa Conference. After their visit, I don't know why, prison discipline became still further relaxed. We had visitors and the attention of physicians if we needed it. We were informed that henceforth we would not be regarded as prisoners at all, but only as persons temporarily detained. Two hours a day after this we were allowed in the open air, and I became very friendly with the Finnish women carpenters at work on the new building on our island. These good souls brought me bottles of delicious milk, and one day the building foreman, a Moscow Russian, invited me to his house to tea, and here I, a poor prisoner, was treated with such deference that I was actually embarrassed. Not one of the family would eat with me or even sit down in my presence.

At this time Erika and I were given a more commodious cell furnished with the seaweed mattresses of which I have spoken. But to our horror we found the walls covered with the most frightful scrawls and pictures. The sailor guards, however, brought water and sponges and with many apologies washed off the disgusting records as well as they could. I was thankful for this a few days later when all unexpectedly I received a visit from my dear mother. It had been some days after our parting at the frontier before she and my father learned that I was in prison. Immediately they had gone to Helsingfors to appeal to General Stachovitch, the Governor of Finland. But he advised them to avoid trouble for themselves, perhaps for me also, by going quietly back to Petrograd. My parents gave him money for me, which I never received, and despite the Governor's advice they stayed on in Helsingfors in faint hope of seeing me. Dr. Manouchine, my mother told me, had returned from a long visit in the Caucasus and was doing what he could to get me released. My mother also gave me news of the last struggle to maintain the army, the conflict between Korniloff and Kerensky, ending, as everyone knows, in the death of Korniloff. These two were about equally hated by the

Sveaborg sailors who would gladly have murdered them both. They had begun to speak with unbounded admiration of Lenine and Trotzky, especially of Lenine, who they declared was the coming saviour of Russia.

Bolshevism was in the air, and for a moment it assumed a really benevolent aspect. I remember a deputation of Kronstadt Bolshevists who came to Sveaborg to inspect us and to review our entire case. Some of these men were very civil to me, asking many questions about the Imperial Family and the life of the Court. At parting one said to me naïvely: "You are quite different from what I thought you'd be, and I shall tell the comrades so." The very next day another deputation came and, characteristic of the confused state of the public mind, these men were as brutal as the others had been kind. They stormed down the prison corridors roaring: "Where is Viroubova? Show us Viroubova!" I cowered in my cell, but when the guard came and admonished me, for my own safety, to show myself to the men I gathered courage to speak to them. Totally unprepared to see the terrible Viroubova merely a crippled woman in a shabby frock, the men suddenly quieted down and made civil response to my words. "We didn't know that you were ill," said one of the men as they prepared to move on.

Although we did not know it at the time, our fate really hung on the outcome of a Congress of Soviets which was then being held in Petrograd, and to which both Sheiman and Ostrovsky were delegates. Sheiman returned to Helsingfors and visiting my cell told me that both Trotzky and Lounacharsky were insistent on the release of Kerensky's prisoners. That evening, he said, would be held a secret session of the executives of the Helsingfors Soviet at which he would urge the recommendation of Trotzky and Lounacharsky. If the executives agreed the question would then be referred to the entire Soviet, made up principally of sailors of the old Baltic fleet. That evening I was invited to tea in the officers' quarters, and while sitting there the telephone rang. "It is for you," said the officer who answered the call. I picked up the receiver and heard Sheiman's voice saying briefly: "The executive has voted unanimously for the release of the prisoners."

There was little sleep for me that night, but tired as I was by morning, I greeted happily the unkempt cook and his messy breakfast plate. All day I waited with the dumb patience only prisoners know, and at early evening I was rewarded by the appearance of Sheiman and Ostrovsky. "Put on your coat and follow me," said Sheiman. "I have resolved to take you, on my own responsibility, to the hospital." To my nursing sister, who had spent the afternoon with me, he gave orders to go to Helsingfors and wait for further directions. At the prison gate Sheiman signed the necessary papers, and hurrying me past two gaping Bolshevist soldiers, he led the way down a bypath to the water. Boarding a small motor launch manned by a single sailor, we started off at high speed for Helsingfors. There was one bad moment when we approached a low bridge occupied by a strong guard, but at Sheiman's directions, uttered in a short whisper, I lay down flat in the launch and we passed unchallenged. The first stars were shining in the clear autumn sky as we reached the military quay of the town. We ran in under the lee of a huge warship and stepped ashore. There was a motor car waiting and the chauffeur, who evidently knew his business, started his engine without a word or even a turn of his head.

Sheiman spoke only one sentence. "Tovarish Nicholai, drive to—" naming a street and number. At once we were off, my head fairly swimming at the sight of electric lights, shaded streets, and people walking up and down. Turning into a quiet street we left the car, all three of us shaking hands with the discreet driver. Bidding Ostrovsky find my nurse and my small luggage, Sheiman conducted me to the door of the hospital where a nice clean Finnish nurse took me in charge and put me to bed in one of the freshest, airiest, most comfortable rooms I have ever occupied. "Take good care of this lady," were the last words of the President of the Helsingfors Soviet, "and let no one intrude on her." His words and the assured smile of the nurse were good soporifics and I fell almost instantly into a deep sleep.

Two days later, September 30 (Russian), Sheiman came to see me with the news that Trotzky had ordered all the Kerensky prisoners back to Petrograd, and that he, Sheiman, had personally seen to it that my nurse and my aunt, who was at that time in Helsingfors, were to accompany me. Sheiman himself, and also Ostrovsky, who was unfortunately very drunk, went with us in the train which left Helsingfors that same night about half past ten. It was an unpleasant journey, the prisoners being in a state of wild excitement, and many of the red-badged officers more or less tipsy. With my aunt and the nurse I sat in a corner of a dirty compartment praying for the day to come. At nine in the morning we reached Petrograd, and Sheiman, still solicitous of my welfare, escorted the three of us to the Smolny Institute, once an aristocratic school for girls, now the headquarters of the Petrograd Soviet. Here I had the happiness once more to embrace my mother, who, with relatives of other prisoners, waited our arrival. Many Soviet authorities were in the place, among others Kameneff, a small red-bearded man, and his wife, a sister of the renowned Trotzky. Both of the Kameneffs were extremely kind to us, seeing that my companions and I had tea and food, and expressing the hope that I should soon be out of trouble. Kameneff telephoned Kerensky's headquarters asking leave to send us home, but as it was a holiday nobody answered the call. "Well, go home anyhow," said Kameneff, leaving the telephone, but Sokolov stopped us long enough to make us understand that the prisoners all had to appear the next day before the High Commission in the Winter Palace. I never saw the Kameneffs again even to thank them for their kindness, but I read in the Kerensky news-papers that I was on terms of intimacy with them and was therefore a Bolshevist. It was even stated that I was a close friend of the afterwards notorious woman commissar Kolantai, whom I have never seen, and that Trotzky was a familiar visitor in my house.

Thus ended my second term of imprisonment. First I was arrested as a German spy and intrigant, next as a counter-Revolutionary. Now I was accused of being a Bolshevist and the name of Trotzky instead of Rasputine was linked with mine. Hardly knowing what next was in store for me, I reported at once to the High Commission. Here I was told that their inquiries concerning me were finished, and that I had better see the Minister of the Interior. At this ministry I was informed that I was in no immediate danger but that I would remain under police surveillance. I asked why, but got no satisfactory answer. Later I learned that the tottering Provisional Government wanted to send me and all the "counter-Revolutionists" to Archangel, but this move Dr. Manouchine, who was still very influential, was determined to prevent.

From my uncle's house, where I had first taken refuge, I moved to a discreet lodging in the heart of the city and from this place I never once in daylight ventured out. This was in late October, 1917, and the Bolshevist revolution had begun in deadly earnest. Day after day I sat listening to the sound of rifle shots and the putter of machine guns, the pounding of armored cars over the stone pavements, and the tramp, tramp, tramp of soldiers. Russia was getting ready for the long promised constitutional convention which turned out to be a

Communist *coup d'état.* Once in a while the husband of my landlady, a naval man, came to my lodgings, and it was he who gave me news of the arrest of the Provisional Government, the siege of the Winter Palace, and the ignominious collapse of Kerensky while women soldiers fought and died to hide his flight! The scenes in the streets, as they were described to me, were appalling, and soon it was decided that my retreat was too near the center of hostilities to be at all safe. About the end of October I was taken by night to a distant quarter of the town to the tiny apartment of an old woman, formerly a masseuse in my hospital. Here came our old servant Berchik, keen to protect me from danger, and here we stayed for a month, when my mother found me a still safer lodging on the sixth floor of a house in the Fourtchkatskaia, a cozy little apartment whose windows gave a pleasant view of roofs and church steeples. There for eight months I lived like a recluse, once in a great while venturing to go to church, well guarded by Berchik and the nurse. The Bolshevik Government seemed successfully established, and its policy of blood and terror and extermination was well under way. Yet in my hidden retreat it seemed to me that, for a time at least, I was forgotten, and my troubles were all over.

CHAPTER XXI

PARADOXICAL though it may appear, the last months of 1917 and the winter of 1918, spent in a hidden lodging in turbulent Petrograd, were more peaceful than any period I had known since the Revolution began. I knew that the city and the country were in the hands of fanatic Bolshevists and that under their ruthless theory of government no human life was at all secure. Food and fuel were scarce and dear, and there was no doubt that things were destined to grow worse long before they could, in any imaginable circumstances, grow better. The wreck of the army was complete, and while the war still waged in western Europe we, who had had so much to do with defiance of German militarism, were completely out of the final struggle. The peace of my soul was partly born of ignorance, I suppose, the ignorance of events shared by everyone not immediately in contact with the world catastrophe. I was free, I lived in a comfortable apartment, my dear father and mother came daily to see me, and two of my faithful old servants lived with me and were ready to protect me from all enemies.

Also, because the mind cannot fully realize the worst, I believed that the Russian chaos was a temporary manifestation. I thought I saw signs of a reaction in favor of the exiled Emperor. In this I was certainly encouraged by two of the oldest and most prominent Revolutionists known to the outside world, Bourtseff, a leader among the old Social Revolutionaries, and the novelist Gorky. It was in December, 1917, if I remember correctly, that I learned that Gorky was anxious to meet me, and as I preferred to keep my small corner of safety as free from visitors as possible, I made an appointment with the novelist in his own home, a modest apartment on the Petrograd side of the Neva, not far from the fortress. Gorky, whose gaunt features are familiar to all readers, is said to be a sufferer from tuberculosis, but as he has lived many years since the first rumors of this disease were circulated, there may be some reason to doubt his affliction. That he is a sick man none can doubt, for his high cheek bones seem almost to pierce his colorless skin and his darkly luminous eyes are deeply sunken in his head. For two hours of this first interview I sat in conversation with Gorky, strange creature, who at times seems to be heart and soul a Bolshevist and at other times openly expresses his loathing and disgust of their insane and destructive policies. To me Gorky was gentle and sympathetic, and what he said about the Emperor and Empress filled my heart with encouragement and hope. They were, he declared, the poor scapegoats of the Revolution, martyrs to the fanaticism of the time. He had examined with care the private apartments of the palace and he saw clearly that these unhappy ones were not even what are called aristocrats, but merely a bourgeois family devoted to each other and to their children, as well as to their ideals of righteous living. He expressed himself as bitterly disappointed in the Revolution and in the character of the Russian proletariat. Earnestly he advised me to live as quietly as possible, never reminding the Bolshevist authorities or any strangers of my existence. My duty, he told me, was to live and to devote myself to writing the true story of the lives of the Emperor and Empress. "You owe this to Russia," he said, "for what you can write may help to bring peace between the Emperor and the people."

Twice afterwards I saw and talked with Gorky, showing him a few pages of my reminiscences. He urged me to go on writing, suppressing nothing of the truth, and he even offered to help me with my work. But writing in Russia was at that time too dangerous a trade to be followed with any degree of confidence, and it was not until I was safely beyond the frontiers that I dared begin writing freely and at length. I wish to say, however, that it was principally due to Gorky's encouragement and to the encouragement of an American literary friend, Rheta Childe Dorr, that I ventured to attempt authorship, or rather that I undertook to present to the world, as they really were, my Sovereigns and my best beloved friends. My casual acquaintanceship with Gorky was naturally seized upon by certain foreign journalists as evidence that I had gone over to the Bolsheviki, and much abuse and scorn were hurled against me. How little those writers knew of Gorky and his half-hearted support of the Lenine policies! He held an important office under the Communists, it is true, and his wife, a former actress, was in the commissariat of theatricals and entertainments. But no man in Bolshevist Russia has ever been permitted more freedom of thought and speech than Gorky. He has done things which would have brought almost any other man to torture and death. I know, for example, that he sheltered under his roof at least one of the Romanoffs, and that the man was finally assisted by him across the Finnish frontier. Gorky interested himself also in the fate of several of the Grand Dukes, Nicholai Michailovitch, Paul and George, who were arrested and later shot to death in Peter and Paul. Gorky did everything in his power to save these men, in whom personally he had no interest whatever. He simply believed their murder to be unjustified, and it is said that he actually induced Lenine to sign an order for their release and deportation, but the order was signed too late, and the men were brutally executed.

At Christmas, 1917, I had a great happiness, nothing less than letters and a parcel of food from the exiles in Tobolsk. There were two parcels in fact, one containing flour, sugar, macaroni, and sausage, wonderful luxuries, and the other a pair of stockings knit by the Empress's own hands, a warm scarf, and some pretty Christmas cards illuminated in her well-remembered style. I made myself a tiny Christmas tree decorated with bits of tinsel and holly berries and hung with these precious tokens of affection and remembrance. Nor was this the only Christmas joy vouchsafed me after a year of sorrow and suffering. Under the escort of my good old servant Berchik I ventured to attend mass in the big church near the Nicholai station, a church built to commemorate the three hundredth anniversary of the Romanoff succession. After the service an old monk approached me and invited me to accompany him into the *réfectoire* of his monastery. I followed him, a little unwillingly, for one never knew what might happen. Entering I saw, to my astonishment, about two hundred factory women who almost filled the bare and lofty room. The old monk introduced me to the women, and to my bewilderment their leader came forward bowing, and holding in her outstretched hands a clean white towel on which reposed a silver ikon. It was an image of Our Lady of Unexpected Joy, and the kind woman told me that she and her fellow workers felt that after all that I had unjustly suffered in the fortress I ought to have from those who sympathized with me an expression of confidence and goodwill. She added that were I again in trouble I might feel myself free to take refuge in the lodgings of any one of them. Overcome with emotion, I could utter only a few stammering words of thanks. I kissed the good woman heartily, and all who could approached and embraced me. Knowing that I longed for more tangible expressions of gratitude, the good old monk pressed into my hands a number of sacred pictures and these I gave away, as long as they lasted, to my new friends. No words can tell how deeply I felt the kindness of these working women who, out of their scanty wages, bought a silver ikon to give to a woman of whom they knew nothing except that she had, as they believed, been persecuted for others' sake.

I needed the assurance that in the cruel world around me there were those who wished me well, for in the first months of the new year came one of the bitterest sorrows of my life, the death of my deeply loved and revered father. He died very suddenly, and without any pain, on January 25, 1918, leaving the world bereft of one of the kindest, most gifted, and sympathetic men of his generation in Russia. I have described my father as a musician and a composer, as well as a lifelong friend and functionary of the Imperial Family. His years of service as keeper of the privy purse might have made him a rich man, but so utterly honest was he that he accepted nothing except his moderate salary and he died leaving almost nothing, nothing but an unfading memory and the deep affection of my friends, including scores of poor students whose musical education and advancement he had furthered. At his funeral his own compositions were sung by volunteer choirs of his musician friends, and these followed his coffin in long procession the length of the Nevski Prospekt to the cemetery of the Alexandra Nevskaia Lavra, a monastic burial place where many of our greatest lie in everlasting repose. My mother came to live with me in my obscure lodgings, and together we faced our desolate future.

One thing alone lightened the darkness of those days. This was a correspondence daringly undertaken with my beloved friends in Siberia. Even now, and at this distance from Russia I cannot divulge the names of those brave and devoted ones who smuggled the letters and parcels to and from the house in Tobolsk, and got them to me and to the small group of faithful men and women in Petrograd. The two chiefly concerned, a man and a woman, of course lived in constant peril of discovery and death. Yet they gladly risked their lives that their Sovereigns might have the happiness of private communication with their friends. At this time their Majesties were permitted to write and receive a few letters, but every line was read by their jailers, and their list of correspondents was rigidly censored. Even in the letters smuggled out from Tobolsk the utmost precautions had to be observed, and the reader can see with what veiled and discreet phrases the sentences are couched.

I give these letters exactly as they were written, suppressing only certain messages of affection too intimate to make public. Most of the letters were written by the Empress, but one at least came from the Emperor, and a number are from the children. To me these letters are infinitely precious, not only as personal messages, but as proofs of the dauntless courage and deep religious faith of these martyrs of the Russian Revolution. Their patriotism and their love of country never faltered for a single moment, nor did they ever utter a complaint or a reproach against those who had so heartlessly betrayed them. It seems to me impossible that anyone, reading these letters, intended only for my own eyes, can continue to misjudge the lives and the characters of Nicholas II and the Empress Alexandra Feodorovna. What they reveal is their secret selves, unknown except to those who knew them best and knowing them loved them as they deserved to be loved.

The first communication to reach me was a brief message from the Empress, dated October 14, 1917, a short time after the news of my liberation from the fortress reached her in Siberia.

* * *

My darling: We are thinking constantly of you and of all the suffering you have had to endure. God help you in the future. How are your weak heart and your poor legs? We hope to go to Communion as usual if we are to be allowed. Lessons have begun again with Mr. Gibbs also. So glad, at last. We are all well. It is beautifully sunny. I sit behind this wall in the yard and work. Greetings to the doctors, the priest, and the nurses in your hospital. I kiss you and pray God to keep you.

A week later the Empress wrote me a long letter in which she ventures a few details of life in Tobolsk.

October 21, 1917.

My darling: I was inexpressibly glad to get news of you, and I kiss you fondly for all your loving thoughts of me. There are no real barriers between souls who really understand each other, but still it is natural for hearts to crave expressions of love. I wrote to you on the 14th, and now will try to send this to the same address, but I don't know how long you will remain. I wonder if you got my letter. I had hoped so much that you would see Zina and find comfort in her friendship. The expression in the eyes in the photograph which was brought me* has impressed me deeply, and I wept freely as I looked at it. Ah, God! Still He is merciful and will never forget His own. Great will be their reward in Heaven. The more we suffer here the fairer it will be on that other shore where so many dear ones await us. How are our Friend's† dear children, how well does the boy learn, and where do they live?

Dear little Owl, I kiss you tenderly. You are in all our hearts. We pray for you and often talk of you. In God's hands lie all things. From this great distance it is a difficult thing to help and comfort a loved one who is suffering. We hope tomorrow to go to Holy Communion, but neither today nor yesterday were we allowed to go to church. We have had services at home, last night prayers for the dead, tonight confession and evening prayer. You are ever with us, a kindred soul. How many things I long to say and to ask of you. It is strange to be in this house and to sleep in the dark bedroom.‡ I have heard nothing from Lili D. for some time. We are all well. I have been suffering from neuralgia in the head but now Dr. Kostritzky has come to treat me. We have spoken often of you.

They say that life in the Crimea is dreadful now. Still Olga A. is happy with her little Tichon whom she is nursing herself. They have no servants

---

* The snapshot taken of me by Mr. Gibbs soon after I was released from the fortress.
† Rasputine.
‡ This was the house and the room I occupied in my stay in Tobolsk on my second visit to Siberia.

so she and N. A. look after everything. Dobiasgin, we hear, has died of cancer. The needlework you sent me was the only token we have received from any of our friends. Where is poor Catherine? We suffer so for all, and we pray for all of you. That is all we can do. The weather is bad these last few days, and I never venture out because my heart is not behaving very well. I get a great deal of consolation reading the Bible. I often read it to the children, and I am sure that you also read it. Write soon again. We all kiss and bless you. May God sustain and keep you. My heart is full, but words are feeble things.

Yours, A.

The jacket warms and comforts me. I am surrounded by your dear presents, the blue dressing gown, red slippers, silver tray and spoon, the stick, etc. The ikon I wear. I do not remember the people you are living with now. Did you see the regimental priest from Peterhof? Ask the prayers of O. Hovari for us. God be with you. Love to your parents. Madeleine and Anna are still in Petrograd.

Card from Alexei, November 24, 1917.

I remember you often and am very sad. I remember your little house. We cut wood in the daytime for our baths. The days pass very quickly. Greetings to all.

On the same day the Empress wrote me a short letter in English.

Yesterday I received your letter dated November 6, and I thank you for it from my heart. It was such a joy to hear from you and to think how merciful is God to have given you this compensation. Your life in town must be more than unpleasant, confined in stuffy rooms, steep stairs to climb, no lovely walks possible, horrors all around you. Poor child! You know that in heart and soul I am near you, sharing all your pain and sorrow and praying for you fervently. Every day I read in the book you gave me seven years ago, "Day by Day," and like it very much. There are lovely passages in it.

The weather is very changeable, frost, sunshine, then darkness and thawings. Desperately dull for those who enjoy long walks and are deprived of them. Lessons continue as usual. Mother and daughters work and knit a great deal, making Christmas presents. How time flies! In two weeks more it will be eight months since I saw you last. And you, my little one, so far away in loneliness and sorrow. But you know where to seek consolation and strength, and you know that God will never forsake you. His love is over all.

On the whole we are all well, since I do not count chills and colds. Alexei's knee and arm swell from time to time, but happily without any pain. My heart has not been behaving very well. I read much, and live in the past, which is so full of rich memories. I have full trust in a brighter future. He will never forsake those who love and trust in His infinite mercy, and when we least expect it He will send help, and will save our unhappy country. Patience, faith and truth.

How did you like the two little colored cards? I have not heard from Lili Dehn for three months. It is hard to be cut off from all one's dear friends. I am so glad that your old servant and Nastia are with you, but where are the maids, Zina and Mainia? So Father Makari has left us. But he is really nearer than he was before.

Our thoughts will be very close together next month. You remember our last journey and what followed. After this anniversary it seems to me that God will show mercy. Kiss Praskovia and the children for me. The maid Liza and the girls have not come yet. All of us send tenderest love, blessings and kisses. God bless you, dearest friend. Keep a brave heart.

P. S. I should like to send you a little food, some macaroni for instance.

Up to this time, nearly the end of the year 1917, the Imperial Family in exile were treated with a certain degree of consideration. They had plenty of food and a limited freedom. In the next letter I received from the Empress, dated December 8, she speaks with gratitude of the fact that some of her favorite books were permitted to be retained by her, as a little later she overflows with gratitude to one of the Bolshevist Commissars who sent her a few familiar pictures and trinkets from the old home in Tsarskoe Selo. Little by little, however, privileges were taken from the family, and their status became that of criminal prisoners. I leave this to be shown in the letters which follow. On December 8, 1917, the Empress wrote me, in Russian, a letter which shows how poignantly she and the Emperor felt the desperate situation in Russia.

My darling: In thoughts and prayers we are always together. Still it is hard not to see each other. My heart is so full, there is so much I would like to know, so many thoughts I should like to share with you. But we hope the time will come when we shall see each other, and all the old friends who now are scattered in different parts of the world.

I am sorry you have had a misunderstanding with one of your best friends. That should never happen. This is no time to judge one's friends, every one of us being on such an unnatural strain.

We here live far from everybody and life is quiet, but we read of all the horrors that are going on. But I shall not speak of them. You live in their very center, and that is enough for you to bear. Petty troubles surround us. The maids have been in Tobolsk four days and yet they are not allowed to come to our house, although it was promised that they should. How pitiful this everlasting suspicion and fear. I suppose it will be the same with Isa.* Nobody is now allowed to approach us, but I hope they will soon see how stupid and brutal and unfair it is to keep them (the maids) waiting.

It is very cold—24 degrees of frost. We shiver in the rooms, and there is always a strong draught from the windows. Your pretty jacket is so useful. We all have chilblains on our fingers. (You remember how you suffered from them in your cold little house?) I am writing this while resting before dinner. Little Jimmy lies near me while his mistress plays the piano. On the 6th Alexei, Marie, and Gilik (M. Gilliard) acted a little play for us. The others are committing to memory scenes from French plays. Excellent distraction, and good for the memory. The evenings we spend together. He reads aloud to us, and I embroider. I am very busy all day preparing Christmas presents; painting ribbons for book markers, and cards as of old. I also have lessons with the children, as the priest is no longer permitted to come. But I like these lessons very much. So many things come back to my mind. I am reading with pleasure the works of Archbishop Wissky. I did not have them formerly. Lately also I have read Tichon Zadonsky. In spite of everything I was able to bring some of my favorite books with me. Do you read the Bible I gave you? Do you know that there is now a much more complete edition? I have given one to the children, and I have managed to get a large one for myself. There are some beautiful passages in the Proverbs of Solomon. The Psalms also give me peace. Dear, we understand each other. I thank you for everything, and in memory I live over again our happy past.

One of our former wounded men, Pr. Eristoff, is in hospital again. I don't know the reason. If possible give hearty greetings to him from us all. Give sincere thanks and greetings to Madame S. and her husband. God bless and comfort him.

Where are Serge (Mme. Viroubova's brother) and his wife? I received a touching letter from Zina. I know the past is all done with, but I thank God for all that we have received, and I live in the memory that cannot be taken from me. Still I worry often for my dearly loved, far distant, foolish little friend. I am glad that you have resumed your maiden name. Give greetings to Emma F., the English Red Cross nurse, and to your dear parents.

On the 6th we had service at home, not being allowed to go to church on account of some kind of a disturbance. I have not been out in the fresh

*Baroness Buxhoevden, lady in waiting.

air for four weeks. I can't go out in such bitter weather because of my heart. Nevertheless church draws me almost irresistibly.

I showed your photographs to Valia and Gilik. I did not want to show them to the ladies, your face is too dear and precious to me. Nastinka is too distant. She is very sweet, but she does not seem near to me. All my dear ones are far away. But I am surrounded by their photographs and gifts—jackets, dressing gowns, slippers, silver dish, spoons, and ikons. How I would like to send you something, but I fear it would get lost. I kiss you tenderly, love, and bless you. We all kiss you. He was touched by your letter of congratulation. We pray for you, and we think of you, not always without tears.

Yours.

The next day the Empress wrote again.

This is the feast day of the Virgin of Unexpected Joy. I always read the day's service, and I know that you, dear, do the same. It is the anniversary of our last journey together, to Saratoff. Do you remember how lovely it was? The old holy woman is dead now, but I keep her ikon always near me. Yesterday it was nine months since we were taken into captivity, and more than four months since we came here. Which of the English nurses was it who wrote to me? I am surprised to hear that Nini Voyeikoff and her family did not receive the ikons I sent them before leaving. Give kind regards to your faithful old servant and Nastia. This year I cannot give them anything for their Christmas tree. How sad. My dear, you are splendid. Christ be with you. Give my thanks to Fathers John and Dosifei for their remembrance. I am writing this morning in bed. Jimmy is sleeping nearly under my nose and interfering with my writing. Ortipo lies on my feet and keeps them warm.

Fancy that the kind Kommissar Makaroff sent me my pictures two months ago, St. Simeon Nesterofts, the little Annunciation from the bedroom, four small prints from my mauve room, five pastels of Kaulbach, four enlarged snapshots from Livadia; Tatiania and me, Alexei as sentry, Alexander III, Nicholas I, and also a small carpet from my bedroom.

My wicker lounge chair too is standing in my bedroom now. Among the other cushions is the one filled with rose leave given me by the Tartar women. It has been with me all the way. At the last moment of the night at Tsarskoe I took it with me, slept on it on the train and on the boat, and the lovely smell refreshed me. Have you had any news of Gaham (Chief of the Karaim)? Write to him and give him my regards. One of our former wounded, Sirobojarski, has visited him. There are 22 degrees of frost today, but bright sunshine. Do you remember the sister of mercy K. M. Bitner? She is giving the children lessons. What luck! The days fly. It is

Saturday again, and we shall have evening service at nine. A corner of the drawing room has been arranged with our ikons and lamps. It is homelike—but not church. I got so used to going almost daily for three years to the church of Znamenia before going on to the hospitals at Tsarskoe.

I advise you to write to M. Gilliard. (Now I have refilled my fountain pen.) Would you like some macaroni and coffee? I hope soon to send you some. It is so difficult for me here to take the vegetables out of the soup without eating any of it.* It is easy for me to fast and to do without fresh air but I sleep badly. Yet I hardly feel any of the ills of the flesh. My heart is better, as I live such a quiet life, almost without exercise. I have been very thin but it is less noticeable now, although my gowns are like sacks. I am quite gray too.

The spirits of the whole family are good. God is very near us, we feel His support, and are often amazed that we can endure events and separations which once might have killed us. Although we suffer horribly still there is peace in our souls. I suffer most for Russia, and I suffer for you too, but I know that ultimately all will be for the best. Only I don't understand anything any longer. Everyone seems to have gone mad. I think of you daily and love you dearly. You are splendid and I know how wonderfully you have grown. Do you remember the picture by Nesteroffs, Christ's Bride? Does the convent still attract you in spite of your new friend? God will direct everything. I want to believe that I shall see your buildings (my hospital) in the style of a convent. Where are the sisters of mercy Mary and Tatiana? What has become of Princess Chakoffskaia, and has she married her friend? Old Madame Orloff has written me that her grandson John was killed in the War, and that his fiancée killed herself from grief. Now they are buried beside his father.

My regards to my dear Lancers, to Jakoleff, Father John, and others. Pray for them all. I am sure that God will have mercy on our Russia. Has she not atoned for her awful sins?

My love, burn my letters. It is better. I have kept nothing of the dear past. We all kiss you tenderly and bless you. God is great and will not forsake those encircled by His love. Dear child, I shall be thinking of you especially

During that December I had the happiness of receiving letters from the Emperor, Alexei, and the Grand Duchesses Tatiana, Olga, during Christmas. I hope that we will meet again, but where and how is in His hands. We must leave it all to Him who knows all better than we. and Anastasie. The Emperor wrote acknowledging a note of mine written on his name day.

* The Empress Alexandra Feodorovna was always a strict vegetarian.

Tobolsk, 10 December, 1917.

Thank you so much for your kind wishes on my name day. Our thoughts and prayers are *always* with you, poor suffering creature. Her Majesty reads to us all your lines. Horrid to think all you had to go through. We are all right here. It is quite quiet. Pity you are not with us. Kisses and blessings without end from your loving friend, N.

Give my best love to your parents.

The children's letters were devoured because they gave so many details of the family life in Tobolsk. On December 9 Tatiana wrote:

My darling: I often think and pray for you, and we are always remembering and speaking of you. It is hard that we cannot see each other, but God will surely help us, and we will meet again in better times. We wear the frocks your kind friends sent us, and your little gifts are always with us, reminding us of you. We live quietly and peacefully. The days pass quickly. In the morning we have lessons, walk from eleven to twelve before the house in a place surrounded for us by a high board fence. We lunch together downstairs, sometimes Mamma and Alexei with us, but generally they lunch upstairs alone in Papa's study. In the after-noon we go out again for half an hour if it is not too cold. Tea upstairs, and then we read or write. Sometimes Papa reads aloud, and so goes by every day. On Saturdays we have evening service in the big hall at nine o'clock. Until that hour the priest has to serve in the church. On Sundays, when we are allowed, we go to a near-by church at eight o'clock in the morning. We go on foot through a garden, the soldiers who came here with us standing all around. They serve mass for us separately, and then have a mass for everybody. On holidays, alas, we have to have small service at home. We had to have home service on the 6th (St. Nicholas' day), and it was sad on such a big holiday not to be in church, but one can't have everything one wants, can one? I hope you at least can go to church. How are your heart and your poor legs? Do you see the doctor of your hospital? You remember how we used to tease you. Greetings to your old servants. Where are your brother and his wife? Have they got a baby? God bless you, my darling beloved. All our letters (permitted letters) go through the Kommissar. I am glad that the parents of Eristoff are kind to you. Him I remember well, but I never saw the parents. Isa has not come yet. Has she been to see you? I kiss you tenderly and love you.

Your T.

My darling dear Annia, How happy I was to hear from you. Thank you for the letter and the things. I wrote to you yesterday. It is so strange to be staying in the house where you stayed. Remember that we are sending this parcel secretly, so don't mention it. It is the only time probably that we can do it. Yesterday's letter I sent through the Kommissar. I am always thinking of you, my darling. We speak much of you among ourselves and also to Gilik, Valia, Prince Dolgorouky, and Mr. Gibbs. I wear your bracelet and never take it off, the one you gave me on January 12, my name day. You remember that cozy evening by the fireside? How nice it was. Did you ever see Groten and Linevitch?* Well, good-bye, my darling Annia. I kiss you tenderly and love you.

Your T.

From the Grand Duke Alexei, December 10, 1917.

My darling, I hope you got my postcard. Thank you very, very much for the little mushroom. Your perfumes remind us so much of you. Every day I pray God we shall live together again. God bless you.

Yours, A.

From the Grand Duchess Olga on the same date.

My darling, what joy it was to see your dear handwriting, and all the little things. Thanks awfully for all. Your perfumes reminded us so of you, your cabin on board, etc. It was very sad. I remember you often, kiss and love you. We four live in the corner blue room, arranged all quite cozily. Opposite to us in the little room is Papa's dressing room and Alexei's, then comes his room with Nagori. The brown room is Papa's and Mamma's bedroom. Then the sitting room, big hall, and beyond Papa's study. When there are big frosts it is very cold, and draughts blow from all the windows. We were today in church. Well, I wish you a peaceful and sunny Christmas. God bless you, darling. I kiss you over and over again.

Ever your own Olga.

From the Grand Duchess Anastasie.

My darling and dear: Thank you tenderly for your little gift. It was so nice to have it, reminding me especially of you. We remember and speak of you often, and in our prayers we are always together. The little dog you gave is always with us and is very nice. We have arranged our rooms comfortably and all four live together. We often sit in the windows looking at the people passing, and this gives us distraction. We have acted little plays for amusement. We walk in the garden behind high planks. God bless you.

AN.

* Groten and Linevitch were the two aides-de-camp who were so devoted to the family during the trying period before the Revolution. Afterwards they were denied entrance to the palace.

From the Empress.

My own precious child: It seems strange writing in English after nine weary months. We are doing a risky thing sending this parcel, but we profit through — who is still on the outside. Only promise to burn all we write as it could do you endless harm if they discovered that you were still in contact with us. Therefore don't judge those who are afraid to visit you, just leave time for people to quiet down. You cannot imagine the joy of getting your sweet letters. I have read and reread them over and over to myself and to the others. We all share the anguish, and the misery, and the joy to know that you are free at last. I won't speak of what you have gone through. Forget it, with the old name you have thrown away. Now live again.

One has so much to say that one ends by saying nothing. I am unaccustomed to writing anything of consequence, just short letters or cards, nothing of consequence. Your perfume quite overcame us. It went the round of our tea table, and we all saw you quite clearly before us. I have no "white rose" to send you, and could only scent the shawl with vervaine. Thanks for your own mauve bottle, the lovely blue silk jacket, and the excellent pastilles. The children and Father were so touched with the things you sent, which we remember so well, and packed up at Tsarskoe. We have none of such things with us, so alas, we have nothing to send you. I hope you got the food through — and Mme. —. I have sent you at least five painted cards, always to be recognized by my signature. I have always to be imagining new things!

Yes, God is wonderful and has sent you (as always) in great sorrow, a new friend. I bless him for all that he has done for you, and I cannot refrain from sending him an image, as to all who are kind to you. Excuse this bad writing, but my pen is bad, and my fingers are stiff from cold. We had the blessing of going to church at eight o'clock this morning. They don't always allow us to go. The maids are not yet let in as they have no papers, so the odious commandant doesn't admit them. The soldiers think we already have too many people with us. Well, thanks to all this we can still write to you. Something good always comes out of everything.

Many things are very hard . . . our hearts are ready to burst at times. Happily there is nothing in this place that reminds us of you. This is better than it was at home where every corner was full of you. Ah, child, I am proud of you. Hard lessons, hard school, but you have passed your examinations so well. Thanks, child, for all you have said for us, for standing up for us, and for having borne all for our own and for Russia's sake. God alone can recompense you, for if He has let you see horrors He has permitted you to gaze a little into yonder world. Our souls are nearer now than before. I feel especially near you when I am reading the Bible. The children also are always finding texts suiting you. I am so contented with their souls. I hope God will bless my lessons with Baby. The ground is rich, but is the seed ripe enough? I do try my utmost, for all my life lies in this.

Dear, I carry you always with me. I never am separated from your ring, but at night I wear it on my bracelet as it is so loose on my finger. After we received our Friend's cross we got also this cross to bear. God knows it is painful being cut off from the lives of those dear to us, after being accustomed for years to share every thought. But my child has grown self-dependent with time. In your love we are always together. I wish we were so in fact, but God knows best. One learns to forget personal desires. God is merciful and will never forsake His children who trust Him.

I do hope this letter and parcel will reach you safely, only you had better write and tell — that you get everything safely. Nobody here must dream that we evade them, otherwise it would injure the kind commandant and they might remove him.

I keep myself occupied ceaselessly. Lessons begin at nine (in bed). Up at noon for religious lessons with Tatiana, Marie, Anastasie, and Alexei. I have a German lesson three times a week with Tatiana and once with Marie, besides reading with Tatiana. Also I sew, embroider, and paint, with spectacles on because my eyes have become too weak to do without them. I read "good books" a great deal, love the Bible, and from time to time read novels. I am so sad because they are allowed no walks except before the house and behind a high fence. But at least they have fresh air, and we are grateful for anything. He is simply marvelous. Such meekness while all the time suffering intensely for the country. A real marvel. The others are all good and brave and uncomplaining, and Alexei is an angel. He and I dine *à deux* and generally lunch so, but sometimes downstairs with the others.

They don't allow the priest to come to us for lessons, and even during services officers, commandant and Kommissar, stand near by to prevent any conversation between us. Strangely enough Germogene is Bishop here, but at present he is in Moscow. We have had no news from my old home or from England. All are well, we hear, in the Crimea, but the Empress Dowager has grown old and very sad and tearful. As for me my heart is better as I lead such a quiet life. I feel utter trust and faith that all will be well, that this is the worst, and that soon the sun will be shining brightly. But oh, the victims, and the innocent blood yet to be shed! We fear that Baby's other little friend from Mogiloff who was at M. has been killed, as his name was included among cadets killed at Moscow. Oh, God, save Russia! That is the cry of one's soul, morning, noon and night. Only not that shameless peace.*

I hope you got yesterday's letter through Mme. ——'s son-in-law. How

* Brest-Litovsk.

nice that you have him in charge of your affairs. Today my mind is full of Novgorod and the awful 17th.* Russia must suffer for that murder too. Dear, I am glad you see me in your dreams. I have seen you only twice, vaguely, but some day we shall be together again. When? I do not ask. He alone knows. How can one ask more? We simply give thanks for every day safely ended. I hope nobody will ever see these letters, as the smallest thing makes them react upon us with severity. That is to say we get no church services outside or in. The suite and the maids may leave the house only if guarded by soldiers, so of course they avoid going. Some of the soldiers are kind, others horrid.

Forgive this mess, but I am in a hurry and the table is crowded with painting materials. So glad you liked my old blue book. I have not a line of yours—all the past is a dream. One keeps only tears and grateful memories. One by one all earthly things slip away, houses and possessions ruined, friends vanished. One lives from day to day. But God is in all, and nature never changes. I can see all around me churches (long to go to them), and hills, the lovely world. Wolkoff wheels me in my chair to church across the street from the public garden. Some of the people bow and bless us, but others don't dare. All our letters and parcels are examined, but this one today is contraband. Father and Alexei are sad to think they have nothing to send you, and I can only clasp my weary child in my arms and hold her there as of old. I feel old, oh, so old, but I am still the mother of this country, and I suffer its pains as my own child's pains, and I love it in spite of all its sins and horrors. No one can tear a child from its mother's heart, and neither can you tear away one's country, although Russia's black ingratitude to the Emperor breaks my heart. Not that it is the *whole* country, though. God have mercy and save Russia.

Little friend, Christmas without me—up in the sixth story! My beloved child, long ago I took you to hold in my heart and never to be separated. In my heart is love and forgiveness for everything, though at times I am not as patient as I ought to be. I get angry when people are dishonest, or when they unnecessarily hurt and offend those I love. Father, on the other hand, bears everything. He wrote to you of his own accord. I did not ask him. Please thank everybody who wrote to us in English. But the less *they* know we correspond the better, otherwise they may stop all letters.

Ever your own, A.

The increasing poverty and hardships which surrounded the exiles, to say nothing of the lonely desolation of their lives, could not be kept out of the Empress's letters, although she tried to write cheerfully. I could read, in the growing discursiveness of her contra-

---

* Anniversary of Rasputine's assassination.

band letters, the disturbed and abnormal condition of her usual keen and concise mind. On December 15, 1917, she wrote:

> Dearest little one: Again I am writing to you, and you must thank — and reply carefully. My maids are not yet allowed to come to me, although they have been here eleven days. I don't know how it will come out. Isa (Baroness Buxhoevden, lady in waiting) is ill again. I hear that she will be allowed in when she arrives, as she has a *permis*, but I doubt it. I understand your wounded feelings when she did not go to see you, but does she know your address? She is timid, and her conscience in regard to you is not quite clear. She remembers perhaps my words to her last Autumn that there might come a time when she too would be taken from me and not allowed to return. She lives in the Gorochovaia with a niece. Zizi Narishkine (a former lady in waiting) lives in the Sergievskja, 54.
>
> I hope you will receive the things we sent for Christmas. Anna and Wolkoff helped me to send the parcels, the others I sent through —, so I make use of the opportunity to write to you. Be sure to write when you receive them. I make a note in my book whenever I write. I have drawn some postcards. Did you receive them? One of these days I shall send you some flour.
>
> It is bright sunshine and everything glitters with hoar frost. There are such moonlight nights, it must be ideal on the hills. But my poor unfortunates can only pace up and down the narrow yard. How I long to take Communion. We took it last on October 22, but now it is so awkward, one has to ask permission before doing the least thing. I am reading Solomon and the writings of St. Seraph, every time finding something new. How glad I am that none of your things got lost, the albums I left with mine in the trunk. It is dreary without them, but still better so, for it would hurt to look at them and remember. Some thoughts one is obliged to drive away, they are too poignant, too fresh in one's memory. All things for us are in the past, and what the future holds I cannot guess, but God knows, and I have given everything into His keeping. Pray for us and for those we love, and especially for Russia when you are at the shrine of the "All-Hearing Virgin." I love her beautiful face. I have asked Chemoduroff to take out a prayer (slip of paper with names of you all) on Sunday.
>
> Where is your poor old Grandmamma? I often think of her in her loneliness, and of your stories after you had been to see her. Who will wish you a happy Christmas on the telephone? Where is Serge and his wife? Where is Alexander Pavlovitch? Did you know that Linewitch had married, and Groten also, straight from the Fortress? Have you seen Mania Rebinder? This Summer they were still at Pavlovskoie, but since we left we have heard nothing of them. Where are Bishops Isidor and

Melchisedek? Is it true that Protopopoff has creeping paralysis? Poor old man, I understand that he has not been able to write anything yet, his experiences being too near. Strange are our lives, are they not? One could write volumes.

Zinaida Tolstoaia and her husband have been in Odessa for some time. They write frequently, dear people. Rita Hitrovo is staying with them, but she scarcely writes at all. They are expecting Lili Dehn soon, but I have heard nothing from her for four months. One of our wounded, Sedloff, is also in Odessa. Do you know anything of Malama?* Did Eristoff give you Tatiana's letter? Baida Apraxin and the whole family except the husband are in Yalta. He is in Moscow at the church conference. Professor Serge Petrovitch is also in Moscow. Petroff was, and Konrad is, in Tsarskoe. There too is Marie Rudiger Belaieff. Constadious, our old general, is dead. I try to give you news of all, though you probably know more than I do.

The children wear the brooches that Mme. Soukhomlinoff sent them. Mine I hung over a frame. Do you ever see old Mme. Orloff? Her grandson John was killed, and her Alexei is far away. It is sad for the poor old woman.

I am knitting stockings for the small one (Alexei). He asked for a pair as all his are in holes. Mine are warm and thick like the ones I gave the wounded, do you remember? I make everything now. Father's trousers are torn and darned, the girls' under-linen in rags. Dreadful, is it not? I have grown quite gray. Anastasie, to her despair, is now very fat, as Marie was, round and fat to the waist, with short legs. I do hope she will grow. Olga and Tatiana are both thin, but their hair grows beautifully so that they can go without scarfs. Fancy that the papers say that Prince Volodia Troubetskoy has joined Kaledin with all his men. Splendid! I am sure that N. D.† will take part also now that he is serving in Odessa. I find myself writing in English, I don't know why. Be sure to burn all these letters as at any time your house may be searched again.

---

* A wounded officer and friend.
† A well-known marine officer.

CHAPTER XXII

THROUGH the winter and spring of 1918 I continued to receive letters and parcels, mostly contraband, from my friends in Siberia. I wish I dared to tell how and through whom these precious messages reached me, for it all belongs in the story of Revolutionary Russia. It illustrates the truth, often demonstrated, that tyranny and oppression can never kill the spirit of freedom in human beings. There are always a minority of people who hold their lives cheap by comparison with liberty, and in such people lives deathlessly the inspiration of fidelity to those they love, no matter how relentlessly the loved ones are persecuted. Poor as I was, poor as was the small group of friends who worked with me to communicate with the Imperial Family, we managed to get to them the necessities they lacked. Dangerous and difficult as travel was in those days, every traveler being almost certain to be searched several times along the way, there were three, two officers and a young girl, who at the risk of imprisonment and death by the most unspeakable tortures, calmly and fearlessly acted as emmissaries back and forth between Petrograd and remote Tobolsk. They had friends along the way, of course, but how they managed, through months of constant peril, to carry on their work is one of those mysteries which, to my mind, are not wholly earthly.

On January 9, 1918, I received the following Christmas letter from the Empress.

Thank you, darling, for all your letters which were a great joy to me and to us all. On Christmas Eve I received the letter and the perfume, then more scent by little ——. I regret not having seen her. Did you receive the parcels sent through the several friends, flour, coffee, tea, and lapscha (a kind of macaroni)? The letters and the snapshots sent through ——, did you get them? I am worried as I hear that all parcels containing food are opened. I begin today to number my letters, and you must keep account of them. Your cards, the small silver dish, and Lili's tiny silver bell I have not yet been able to receive.

We all congratulate you on your name day. May God bless, comfort, strengthen you, and give you joy. Believe, dear, that God will yet save our beloved country. He will not be unforgiving. Think of the Old Testament and the sufferings of the Children of Israel for their sins. And now it is we who have forgotten God, and that is why they* cannot bring any happiness. How I prayed on the 6th that God would send the spirit of good judgment and the fear of the Lord. Everyone apparently have lost their heads. The reign of terror is not yet over, and it is the sufferings of the innocent which nearly kills us. What do people live on now that everything is taken from them, their homes, their incomes, their money? We must have sinned terribly for our Father in Heaven to punish so frightfully. But I firmly and unfalteringly believe that in the end He will save us. The strange thing about the Russian character is that it can so suddenly change to evil, cruelty, and unreason, and can as suddenly change back again. This is in fact simply want of character. Russians are in reality big, ignorant children. However it is well known that during long wars all bad passions flame up. What is happening is awful, the murders, the persecutions, the imprisonments, but all of it must be suffered if we are to be cleansed, new born.

Forgive me, darling, that I write to you so sadly. I often wear your jackets, the blue and the mauve, as it is fearfully cold in the house. Outside the frosts are not often severe, and sometimes I go out and even sit on the balcony. The children are just recovering from scarletina, except Anastasie, who did not catch it. The elder ones began the new year by being in bed, Marie, of course, having a temperature of 39.5. Their hair is growing well. Lessons have begun again. Yesterday I gave three. Today I am free, and am therefore writing. On the 2nd of January I thought of you and sent a candle to be set before the Holy Seraphim. I have asked that prayers may be said in the cathedral where the relics lie, for all our dear ones. You remember the old pilgrim who came to Tsarskoe Selo. Fancy that he has been here. He wandered in with his big staff, and sent me a prosvera (holy bread).

I have begun your books. The style is quite different from the others. I have got myself some good books, too, but have not much time for reading. I embroider, knit, draw, and give lessons, but my eyes are getting weaker so that I can no longer work without glasses. You will see me quite an old woman! Did you know that the marine officer Nicolai Demenkoff has appendicitis? He is in Odessa. One of our wounded, Oroborjarsky, was operated on there a month ago. He is so sad and homesick, so far away. I correspond with his mother, a gentle, good, and really Christian soul. Lili Dehn went to see her.

I trust you received the painted cards that I put in the parcel of provisions. Not all were successful. If you receive my letters just write, thanks for No. I, etc. My three maids and Isa are still not allowed to come to us, and they are very much distressed, just sitting idle. But — is of better use on the outside. Little one, where are your brother Serge and his wife?

* Presumably the Soviet Government. (from previous page)

I know nothing of them. Your poor sister Alya, I hope she is not too sad; she has friends, but her husband, has he not become too sad away from her? How are the sweet children? Miss Ida is with her still, I hope. Did you know that sister Grekova is to be married soon to Baron Taube? How glad I am that you have seen A. P. Did he not seem strange out of uniform, and what did he say about his brother? Ah, all is past, and will never return. We must begin a new life and forget self. I must finish, my dear little soul. Christ be with you. Greetings to all. I kiss your mother. I congratulate you again. I want quickly to finish the small painting, and get it to you. I fear you are again passing through fearful days. Reports filter through of murders of officers in Sevastopol. Rodionoff and his brother are there.

Your own, A.

On the 16th of January the Empress wrote me a letter in Old Slavonic style to congratulate me on my name day. In this she addresses me as "Sister Seraphine." I should explain that my hospital in Tsarskoe Selo bore the name of that saint, because it was on her day that I suffered the terrible railway accident which left me lamed for life, but which gave me, in damages, the funds for founding the hospital.

Dearly beloved Sister Seraphine:

From a full heart I wish you well on your name day! God send you many blessings, good health, fortitude, meekness, strength to bear all punishments and sorrows sent by God, and gladness of soul. May the sun lighten the path you tread through life, warm all by your love, and let your light shine forth these sad, gloomy days. Do not despair, suffering sister, God will hear your prayers, all in good time. Also we pray for thee, sister chosen of the Lord. We have thee in fond remembrance. Your little corner is far away from us. All who love thee in this place send greetings. Do not misjudge the bad writing of thy sister. She is illiterate, an ailing lay sister. I am learning the writing of prayers, but weakness of sight prevents my striving. I read the works of Bishop Gr. Nissky, but he writes too much of the creation of the world. From our sister Zinaida I have received news, so much good will in every word, breathing peace of the soul.

The family known to thee are in good health, the children have suffered from the usual ills of the young, but are now restored to health. The youngest ill, but in good spirits however, and without suffering. The Lord has blessed the weather, beautiful and soft. Thy sister walks out and enjoys the sun, but when there is more frost she hides in her cell, takes a stocking, puts on her spectacles, and knits. Sister Sophia,* not long since arrived, has not been granted admittance, those in authority having refused it. She has found hospitality at the priest's with her old woman. The other sisters are all in different places. Dearly loved sister, art thou not weary reading this letter? All the others have gone to dinner. I remain on guard by the sick Anastasia. In the cells next to ours is sister Catherina† giving a lesson. We are embroidering for church, Sisters Tatiana and Maria with great zeal. Our father Nicholas gathers us around him in the evenings, and reads to us while we pass the time with needlework. With his meekness and good health he does not disdain to saw and chop wood for our needs, cleans the roads, too, with the children. Our mother Alexandra greets thee, sister, and sends her motherly blessings and hopes, sister, that thou livest in the Spirit of Christ. Life is hard but the spirit is strong. Dear sister Seraphine, may God keep thee. I beg for your prayers. Christ be with thee.

            The Sinful sister F<small>EODORA</small>.

 Prayers!

16ᵒ Января 1918 г. + 51.

"Милая, дорогая, возлюбленная
Сестрица Серафима!

Отъ нѣжнолюбящаго сердца поздравляю Васъ многолюбивая страдалъница моя съ праздникомъ Вашимъ. Да ниспошлетъ Вамъ Господь Богъ всякихъ благъ — добраго здоровья, крѣпость духа, кротость, терпѣніе, силы перенести всѣ обиды и гоненіе, душевную радость. Да освѣтитъ лучъ солнца ярко и ясно путь Вашъ жизненный. Сами погрѣйте всѣхъ любовью Вашей. Да свѣтитъ свѣтъ Вашъ въ отихъ темныхъ, неясныхъ дняхъ. Не унывай, родимая скорбящая сестра! Господь услышитъ твои молитвы. Все въ свое время. Молимся и мы за Васъ Богомъ зъ данную сестру, всѣми наемъ Васъ. Уголокъ Вашъ убогій да ленъ отъ насъ. Всѣ любящіе

ONE OF THE EMPRESS'S LAST LETTERS, WRITTEN IN OLD SLAVONIC TO MME. VIROUBOVA IN 1918.

* Isa, Baroness Buxhoevden, lady in waiting.
† Miss Schneider.

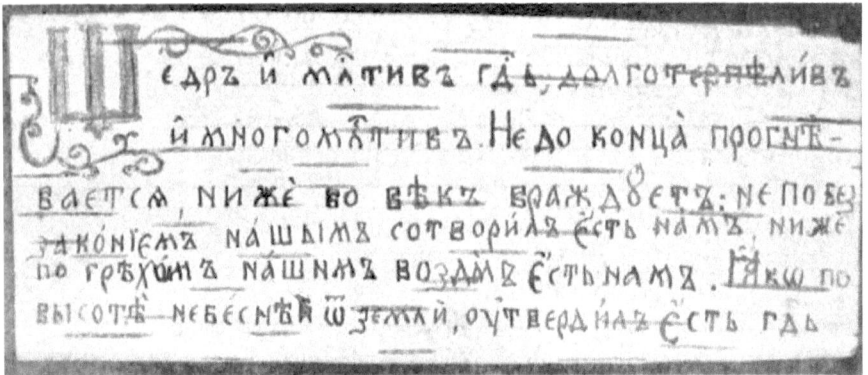

SMUGGLED LETTER FROM THE EMPRESS TO MME. VIROUBOVA WRITTEN IN OLD SLAVONIC ON BIRCH-BARK AFTER PAPER GAVE OUT.

22 of January.

So unexpectedly I received the letter of the 1st and the card of the 10th. I hasten to reply. Tenderly we thank through you Karochinsky. Really it is touching that even now we are not forgotten. God grant that his estates should be spared. God bless him. I am sending you some food but I do not know if it will ever reach you. Often we think of you. I wrote to you on the 16th through the hospital, on the 17th a card by Mr. Gibbs, and on the 9th two letters by ——. There! I have dropped my favorite pen and broken it. How provoking! It is fearfully cold, 29 degrees, 7 in the bathroom, and blowing in from everywhere. Such a wind, but they are all out. We hope to see the officer Tamarov if only from a distance. So glad you received everything. I hope you wear the gray shawl, and that it smells of vervaine, a well-remembered scent. Kind Zinoschka found it in Odessa, and sent it to me.

I am so surprised you have made the acquaintance of Gorky. He was awful formerly. Disgusting and immoral books and plays he wrote. Can it be the same man? How he fought against father and Russia when he lived in Italy. Be careful, my love. I am so glad you can go to church. To us it is forbidden, so service is at home, and a new priest serves. How glad I am that all is well with Serge. With Tina it will be difficult, but God will help her. It is true what they say about Marie Rebinder's husband? She wrote me, through Isa, that they are still in Petrograd, and that they threatened to kill him. It is difficult to understand people now. Sometimes they are with the Bolshevists outwardly, but in their hearts they are against them.

The cross we hung over the children's beds during their illness but during church service it lies on the table. Bishop Gerogene serves special prayers daily for father and mother—he is quite on their side, which is strange. I must hurry as one waits to take this letter. I am sending you a prayer I wrote on a piece of birchbark we cut. I can't draw much as my eyes are so bad, also my fingers are quite stiff from cold. Such a wind, and it blows so in the rooms. I am sending you a little image of the Holy Virgin. Thanks for the lovely prayer. I wear often the jackets you gave me. I send you all my soul-prayers and love. I believe firmly so I am quite calm. We are all your own and kiss you tenderly.

On the same day Grand Duchess Olga wrote a brief note.

Dearest, we were so glad to hear from you. How cold it is these days, and what a strong wind. We have just come back from a walk. On our window it is written—"Anna darling—" I wonder who wrote it. God bless you, dear. Be well.

Your OLGA.

Give my love to all who remember me.

Two other notes from Olga followed in February and just before Easter.

Darling, with all my loving heart I am with you these hard days for you. God help and comfort you, my darling. On Mamma's table stands the mauve bottle you sent her and which reminds us so much of you. There is much sun, but great frosts also and winds, and very cold in the rooms, especially in our corner room, where we live as before. All are well, and we walk much in the yard. There are many churches around here, so we are always hearing bells ringing. God bless you, darling. How sad your brother and sister are not with you.

Your own OLGA.

We all congratulate you tenderly with the coming Easter, and wish you to spend it as peacefully as anyone can now. I always think of you when they sing during mass the prayer we used to sing together on the yacht. I kiss you.

OLGA.

The other children also wrote me at this time. Grand Duchess Tatiana wrote two short but characteristic notes, the first one on my name day, January 12. In all these letters it will be seen how confidently the family looked forward to a future of freedom and happiness. This constant optimism in the midst of ever-increasing surveillance and cruelty is my excuse for including notes of slight general interest.

Tatiana wrote first:

"You remember the cozy evenings by the fireside? How nice it was. Did you again see Groten and Linevitch? (the faithful aides-de-camp). Well, good-bye, my darling Annia. God bless you. Good-bye—till when?

Your T.

Also—

My beloved darling. How happy we are to get news from you. I hope you got my letters. I think often of you and pray God to keep you from all harm and help you. I am glad you know the Eristoffs now. We get such good letters from Zina, she writes so well. There are many sadnesses in these days. God be with you. It is very cold. Papa wears his Cossack uniform and we remember how much you liked it. I kiss you tenderly, and love you, and congratulate you on your dear name day.

T.

From the Grand Duchess Marie Nicolaevna.

Good morning, my darling! What a long time since I have written to you, and how glad I was to get your little letter. It is very sad we don't see each other, but God will arrange for us to meet, and what joy it will be then. We live in the house where you have been. Do you remember the rooms? They are quite comfortable when a little arranged. We walk out twice every day. Some of the people here are kind. Every day I remember you, and love you very much. Mr. Gibbs gave us photographs he made of you—it was so nice to have them. Your perfumes remind us so much of you. I wish you every blessing from God, and kiss you tenderly. Don't be sad. Love to all yours.

Your loving MARIE.

My darling beloved, how are you? We are all well, walk much in the yard, and have a little hill down which we can slide. There is much frost these days so Mama sits at home. You will probably get this in February, so I congratulate you on your name day. God help you in future and bless you. We always remember and speak of you. May God guard all your ways. Don't be sad, dear. All will be well, and we shall be together again. I kiss you tenderly.

MARIE.

Alexei wrote that same month of January, 1918:

My darling Annia. We are so glad to have news from you, and to hear that you got all our things. Today there are 29 degrees of frost, a strong wind, and sunshine. We walked, and I went on skees in the yard. Yesterday I acted with Tatiana and Gilik a French piece. We are now preparing another piece. We have a few good soldiers with whom I play games in their rooms. Kolia Deravenko comes to me on holidays. Nagorini, the sailor, sleeps with me. As servants we have Wolkoff, Sednoff, Troup, and Chemoduroff. It is time to go to lunch. I kiss and embrace you. God bless you.

ALEXEI.

The remaining letters from the Empress, dating from the end of January to the last days of April, 1918, are uncomplaining, yet are full of suffering and the prescience of tragic events to come. I do not believe that the Empress ever lost faith in the ultimate happiness of her beloved family, but her keen mind fully comprehended the terrible march of events in the torn Empire, and she knew that trials and still greater trials had to be faced by the Emperor and herself. Her courage in the face of this certain conviction is beyond any praise of mine.

On the 23rd of January she wrote:

My precious child: There is a possibility of writing to you now as —— leaves here on the 26th. I only hope no one robs him on the way. He takes you two pounds of macaroni, three pounds of rice, and a little ham. It is so well —— does not live with us. I have knitted stockings, and have knitted you a pair. They are men's size but they will do under valenki and when it is cold in the rooms. Here we have 29 degrees of frost, and 6 in the big room. It is blowing terribly. I was keenly touched by the money you sent, but do not send any more as for the present we have all we need. There have been days when we did not know what to do. I wonder what you are living on. The little money you had I put in the box with your jewels. (My fingers are so stiff I can hardly hold my pen.) I am glad your rooms are so comfortable and so light, but it must be difficult for you to climb the long staircase. How are your poor back and legs?

I know nothing about Lili Dehn, and from my two sisters and my brother I have heard nothing for a year. Only one letter from my sister Elizabeth (Grand Duchess Serge) last summer. Olga Alexandrovna* writes long letters to the children all about her boy whom she adores and nurses herself. The grandmamma I think is getting very old, and is very sad.

Tudles has four in her room. They say that Marie P.† lives well in

---

* Sister of the Emperor.
† Grand Duchess Marie Pavlovna.

Kisslowdsk, both her sons are with her and she receives all the *beau monde* from Petrograd. Merika* lives there also and is expecting a baby. Marianna Ratkova has bought a house there, and receives on Thursdays. Mr. Gibbs asks often about you, also Tudles, and my big Niouta Demidoff. The little doggy lies on my knees and warms them. It is mortally cold, but in Petrograd there is probably worse darkness, hunger, and cold. God help you all to bear it patiently. The worse here the better in yonder world.

It hurts to think how much bloodshed will have to be before better days come. Darling, I send you all my love, and am so sad I can send you little else. I embroider for the church when my eyes allow me, otherwise I knit, but soon I shall have no more wool. We can't get any here—too dear, and very bad. I have had a letter from Shoura Petrovskaia, who is taking care of her brother's children. She sews boots and sells them. In October the children got a letter from their old nurse in England—the first one from there. What rot they publish about Tatiana in the newspapers! Do you see your new friend and saviour often? How is he? Love to your kind parents. I would love to write you certain things of interest, but just now there are many things one can't put in a letter. The little one has put on a sweater, and the girls wear valenki in their rooms. I know how sad you would feel.

The kind servant Sednoff has just brought me a cup of cocoa to warm me up. How do you pray with the rosary, and what prayers do you say on every tenth? I generally say Our Father and to the Holy Virgin, but should one say the same prayer to the end? I looked for it in the books but did not get any information. I long so to go to church but they allow us that only on great holidays (feasts). So we hope to go on the 2nd of February, and on the 3rd I shall order prayers at the relics for you. How is poor old Soukhomlinoff? Where is Sacha? I suppose one may completely trust the little officer you sent. I asked him to make the acquaintance of the priest who served us before, a most devoted and energetic man, a real fighting priest—more than spiritual perhaps—yet with a charming face, and a constantly sweet smile, very thin, long gray beard, and clever eyes. His feeling for us is known all over the country now by the good ones, therefore they took him away from us, but perhaps better so, as he can do more now. The Bishop is quite for father and mother, and so is the Patriarch in Moscow, and it seems most of the clergy. Only you must be careful what sort of people come to you. I am so anxious about your seeing Gorky. Be prudent, and don't have any serious conversations with him. People will try to get around you as before. I don't mean real friends, honest-meaning people, but others who for personal reasons will use you as their shield. Then you will have the brutes after you again.

I am racking my brains what to send you, as one can get nothing here at

* Princess Galatzine.

all. Our Christmas presents were all the work of our own hands, and now I must give my eyes a rest. How pleased I was that Princess Eristoff has spoken so kindly of us. Give her and also her son our love. Where does he serve now? The people here are very friendly—lots of Kirghise. When I sit in the window they bow to me, if the soldiers are not looking.

What dreadful news about the robbing of the sacristy in the Winter Palace. There were so many precious relics and many of our own ikons. They say it has been the same in the church of Gatchina. Did you know that the portraits of my parents and of father have been utterly destroyed? Also my Russian Court dresses and all the others as well? But the destruction of the churches is the worst of all. They say it was the soldiers from the hospital in the Winter Palace who did it. We hear that the soldiers in Smolny have seized all available food, and are quite indifferent to the prospect of the people starving. Why was money sent to us rather than having been given to the poor? True, there were for us some very difficult times when we could not pay any bills, and when for four months the servants had to go without any wages. The soldiers here were not paid, so they simply took our money to keep them quiet. All this is petty, but it makes great trouble for the commandant. The Hofmarshall Chancelerie is still in existence, but when they abolish it I really don't know what we shall do. Well, God will help, and we still have what we need.

I think often of Livadia and what may be happening there. They say that many former political prisoners are stationed there. Where is our dear yacht, the *Standert*? I am afraid to inquire about it. My God! How I suffered when I heard that you were imprisoned on the *Polar Star*. I cannot think of the yacht. It hurts too much.

It is said that our Kommissar is about to be removed, and we are so rejoiced. His assistant will leave with him. They are both terrible men, Siberian convicts formerly. The Kommissar was in prison for fifteen years. The soldiers have decided to send them away, but thank God they have left us our commandant. The soldiers manage absolutely everything here.

I am lying down, as it is six o'clock. There is a fire burning but it barely warms the room. Soon the little one will be coming in for a lesson. I am teaching the children the Divine Service. May God help me to teach it to them so that it will remain with them through their whole lives, and develop their souls. It is a big responsibility. It is such a blessing to live all together, and be so near to one another. Still you must know what I have to endure, having no news from my brother, nor any idea of what lies in the future. My poor brother also knows nothing of us. If I thought my own little old home and the family would have to suffer what we have—it is awful! Then it might begin also in England. However you remember that our Friend said that no harm would come to my old home.* I try to suppress all these thoughts that my soul may not be overwhelmed with despair. I trust all my dear ones to the Holy Virgin. May she shield them from all evil. I still have much to thank God for; you are well, and I can write to you; I am not separated from our own darlings. Thank God we are still in Russia (this is the chief thing), and we are near the relics of the Metropolitan John, and we have peace. Good-bye, my little daughter.

Old friends continued to be very dear to the exiled Empress, and she kept up her interest in all their affairs. Of my sister-in-law who had her first child while her husband was fighting on the Rumanian front the Empress wrote:

How much better it would have been if Tina could have gone to Odessa to have her baby, not far from Serge, and where kind Zinotchka could have looked after her and arranged everything. But now that the Rumanians have taken Kichineff Serge has probably left, and they are together again. Sharing hardships will cause their love to increase and strengthen. How is Alyas's (my sister) health? Was it Mariana's former husband, Derfelden, who was killed in the south? Her mother and family live in Boris's house.

I sometimes see Isa in the street (*i.e.* from the window). The sister of mercy Tatiana Andrievna is now in Petrograd taking care of her sister. Later she will return to Moscow. She seems rather nervous. Give our greetings to our confessor, father Afanasi, father Alexander, and my poor old Zio. I don't know anything about my second servant Kondratieff. What has become of our chauffeurs and the coachman Konkoff? Is old General Schwedoff still alive?

Holy Virgin, keep my daughter from all danger, bless and console her!

5th of February, 1918.

My own darling little one, How terribly sad I am for you about the death of your dear father, and that I could not be with you to help and console you in your great sorrow. You know that I am with you in my prayers. May Christ and the Holy Virgin comfort you, and wipe the tears from your eyes. May God receive his soul in peace. Tomorrow morning I will ask Anoushka to go and order service for him for forty days near the relics. Alas we can pray only at home. In him we both lost a true friend of many years. Father and the children suffer with you, tenderly kiss you, and know all that your sensitive heart feels.

As your telegram went by post I don't know what day God took him to

---

* (previous page) Rasputine foresaw this correctly and the Grand Duke of Hesse retains his old home in peace.

himself. Is it possible it was the same day you wrote to me? I am so glad you saw him daily, but how did it happen, your poor father? For himself one must thank God—so many hardships to live through—no home, and everything so bad. I remember how it was foretold to us (by Rasputine) that he would die when Serge married. And you two women are all alone now. I wonder if your brother-in-law was there to help you, or your kind uncle. I shall try to write to his address a long letter, and also to your mother. Tell her I kiss her tenderly, and how much we have always loved her and honored your father. He was a rare man. Don't cry. He is happy now, rests and prays for you at the Throne of God.

I am glad that you received my two letters. Now you will get two more. What your little messenger will tell you about your dear ones is for yourself alone. What horrors go on at Yalta and Massandra—My God! Where is the salvation for us all and for the poor officers? All the churches being ruined—nothing held sacred any more—it will finish in some terrible earthquake, or something like it as the chastisement of God. May He have mercy on our beloved country. How I pray for Russia.

They say that the Japanese are in Tomsk and keep good order there. I hope you got our little parcel. As we have no sugar I shall send you a little honey which you can eat during Lent. We live still by the old style, but probably shall have to change. Only I don't know how it will be then with Lent and all the services (festivals and fasts). The people may be very angry if two weeks are thrown out. That is why it was never done before.

The sun shines and even warms us in the day times. I feel that God will not forsake but will save us, though all is so dark and tears are flowing everywhere. My little one, don't suffer too much. All this had to be. Only My God, how sorry I am for the innocent ones killed everywhere. I can't write any more. Ask your mother to forgive the mistakes I shall make in writing to her in Russian, and that I cannot express myself as warmly as I would like to. Good-bye, my darling. I am sending you letters from father and the children.

2nd of March, 1918.

Darling child: Thanks for all from father, mother and the children. How you spoil us all by your dear letters and gifts. I was very anxious going so long without news from you, especially as rumors came that you were gone. Alas, I can't write you as I could wish for fear that this may fall into other hands. We have not yet received all that you have sent (contraband). It comes to us little by little. Dear child, do be careful of the people who come to see you. The way is so slippery, and it is so easy to fall. Sometimes a road is cleared through the snow on which one's true friends are to walk—and then the road becomes still more slippery!

We are all right, and I am now a real mistress of a household, going over accounts with M. Gilliard. New work and very practical. The weather is sunny—they are even sunburned, and even when the frost comes back it is warmer in the sun. I have sat twice on the balcony and sometimes sit in the yard. My heart has been much better, but for a week I have had great pains in it again. I worry so much. My God! How Russia suffers. You know that I love it even more than you do, miserable country, demolished from within, and by the Germans from without. Since the Revolution they have conquered a great deal of it without even a battle. If they created order now in Russia how dreadful would be the country's debasement—to have to be grateful to the enemy. They must never dare to attempt any conversations with father or mother.

We hope to go to Communion next week, if they allow us to go to church. We have not been since the 6th of January. I shall pray to the rosary you have written. Kiss your poor mother. I am glad you took some of your things from the hospital. Best love to poor G. Soukhomlinoff. What terrible times you are all living through. On the whole we are better off than you. Soon spring is coming to rejoice our hearts. The way of the cross first—then joy and gladness. It will soon be a year since we parted, but what is time? Life here is nothing—eternity is everything, and what we are doing is preparing our souls for the Kingdom of Heaven. Thus nothing, after all, is terrible, and if they do take everything from us they cannot take our souls. Have patience, and these days of suffering will end, we shall forget all the anguish and thank God. God help those who see only the bad, and don't try to understand that all this will pass. It cannot be otherwise. I cannot write all that fills my soul, but you, my little martyr, understand it better than I. You are farther on than I. We live here on earth but we are already half gone to the next world. We see with different eyes, and that makes it often difficult to associate with people who call themselves, and really are religious. My greatest sin is my irritability. The endless stupidity of my maid, for instance—she can't help being stupid, she is so often untruthful, or else she begins to sermonize like a preacher and then I burst—you know how hot-tempered I am. It is not difficult to bear great trials, but these little buzzing mosquitoes are so trying. I want to be a better woman, and I try. For long periods I am really patient, and then breaks out again my bad temper. We are to have a new confessor, the second in these seven months. I beg your forgiveness, too, darling. Day after tomorrow is the Sunday before Lent when one asks forgiveness for all one's faults. Forgive the past, and pray for me. Yesterday we had prayers for the dead, and we did not forget your father. A few days ago was the twenty-sixth anniversary of my father's death. I long to warm and to comfort others—but alas, I do not feel drawn to those around me here. I am cold towards them, and this, too, is wrong of me.

The cowardly yielding of the Bolshevist government to the triumphant Germans was a source of constant suffering to the Empress. In subsequent letters written me that spring she speaks almost indifferently of the cold and privations suffered in the house in Tobolsk, but she becomes passionate when she writes of the German invasion.

What a nightmare it is that it is Germans who are saving Russia (from Communism) and are restoring order. What could be more humiliating for us? With one hand the Germans give, and with the other they take away. Already they have seized an enormous territory. God help and save this unhappy country. Probably He wills us to endure all these insults, but that we must take them from the Germans almost kills me. During a war one can understand these things happening, but not during a revolution. Now Batoum has been taken—our country is disintegrating into bits. I cannot think calmly about it. Such hideous pain in heart and soul. Yet I am sure God will not leave it like this. He will send wisdom and save Russia I am sure.

It will always be to me an immense gratification that in the midst of her great pain and sorrow for Russia's piteous plight our small group of friends in Petrograd, and those brave souls who dared to risk their lives as message bearers, were able to get to the forlorn family in desolate Siberia at least the necessities of life of which a cruel and inefficient government deprived them. The Empress who all her life had but to command what she wanted for herself and her children was grateful, pathetically grateful, for the simple garments, the cheap little luxuries, even the materials for needlework we were able to convey to them. She thanks me almost effusively for the jackets and sweaters we sent her and the girls in their cold rooms. The wool was so soft and nice, but the linen, she feared, was almost too fine. This was early in March, but spring was already creeping across the steppes.

The weather is so fine that I have been sitting out on the balcony writing music for the Lenten prayers, as we have no printed notes. We had to sing this morning without any preparation, but it went—well, not too badly. God helped. After service we tried to sing some new prayers with the new deacon, and I hope it will go better tonight.*

On Wednesday, Friday and Saturday mornings we were allowed to go to the eight o'clock morning service in church—imagine the joy and comfort! The other days we five women will sing during the home service. It reminds me of Livadia and Oreanda. This week we shall spend the evenings alone with the children, as we want to read together. I know of nothing new. My heart is troubled but my soul remains tranquil as I feel God always near. Yet what are they deciding on in Moscow? God help us.

"Peace and yet the Germans continue to advance farther and farther in," wrote the Empress on March 13 (Russian). "When will it all finish? When God allows. How I love my country, with all its faults. It grows dearer and dearer to me, and I thank God daily that He allowed us to remain here and did not send us farther away. Believe in the people, darling. The nation is strong, and young, and as soft as wax. Just now it is in bad hands, and darkness and anarchy reigns. But the King of Glory will come and will save, strengthen, and give wisdom to the people who are now deceived."

For some reason the Empress seemed to feel that the Lenten season of 1918 was destined to end in an Easter resurrection of the torn and distracted country. At least so her letters indicate. In a mood of fitful kindness and mercy the Bolshevist soldiers in authority in Tobolsk allowed their captives to go rather often to church and to Communion during this season, and the Empress was very happy in consequence. Her letters were full of prayers for the country, in which the whole family joined, and they appeared to look forward to Easter as the day when God would give some token that the sins of the Russian people, for which they were suffering, were forgiven. Yet never once did she speak of regaining power or the throne. All that was over and forgotten. Neither the Emperor nor the Empress ever indicated in any syllable that they expected to be returned to their former eminence. In fact they never spoke of what might actually happen to the Russian Empire, but they believed that God would hold it together and restore its people to wisdom and strength. For themselves they seemed to look forward to nothing better than an obscure existence with other Russian people. How uncomplainingly they accepted the hard terms of their lives, how grateful they were for the love of distant friends whom they might never see again, is shown in all the last letters I received from the

---

* (previous page) Western readers perhaps do not know how indispensable is vocal music in Russian church services where no organ is permitted. All priests are trained musicians, and there is much congregational singing.

Empress during March, 1918. After receiving one of our parcels of clothing she wrote me:

We are endlessly touched by all your love and thoughtfulness. Thank everybody for us, please, but really it is too bad to spoil us so, for you are among so many difficulties and we have not many privations, I assure you. We have enough to eat, and in many respects are rich compared with you. The children put on yesterday your lovely blouses. The hats also are very useful, as we have none of this sort. The pink jacket is far too pretty for an old woman like me, but the hat is all right for my gray hair. What a lot of things! The books I have already begun to read, and for all the rest such tender thanks. He was so pleased by the military suit, vest, and trousers you sent him, and all the lovely things. From whom came the ancient image? I love it.

Our last gifts to you, including the Easter eggs, will get off today. I can't get much here except a little flour. Just now we are completely shut off from the south, but we did get, a short time ago, letters from Odessa. What they have gone through there is quite terrible. Lili is alone in the country with her grandmother and our godchild, surrounded by the enemy. The big Princess Bariatinsky and Mme. Tolstoy were in prison in Yalta, the former merely because she took the part of the Tartars. Babia Apraxine with her mother and children live upstairs in their house, the lower floor being occupied by soldiers. Grand Duchess Xenia with her husband, children, and mother are living in Dülburg. Olga Alexandrovna (the Emperor's sister) lives in Haraks in a small house because if she had remained in Aitodor she would have had to pay for the house. What the Germans are doing! Keeping order in the towns but taking everything. All the wheat is in their hands, and it is said that they take seed-corn, coal, former Russian soldiers—everything. The Germans are now in Bierki and in Charkoff, Poltava Government. Batoum is in the hands of the Turks.

Sunbeam (Alexei) has been ill in bed for the past week. I don't know whether coughing brought on the attack, or whether he picked up something heavy, but he had an awful internal hemorrhage and suffered fearfully. He is better now, but sleeps badly and the pains, though less severe, have not entirely ceased. He is frightfully thin and yellow, reminding me of Spala. Do you remember? But yesterday he began to eat a little, and Dr. Derevanko is satisfied with his progress. The child has to lie on his back without moving, and he gets so tired. I sit all day beside him, holding his aching legs, and I have grown almost as thin as he. It is certain now that we shall celebrate Easter at home because it will be better for him if we have a service together. I try to hope that this attack will pass more quickly than usual. It must, since all Winter he was so well.

I have not been outside the house for a week. I am no longer permitted to sit on the balcony, and I avoid going downstairs. I am sorry that your heart is bad again, but I can understand it. Be sure and let me know well in advance if you move again. Everyone, we hear, has been sent away from Tsarskoe. Poor Tsarskoe, who will take care of the rooms now? What do they mean when they speak of an "état de siège" there? . . .

Darling "Sister Seraphine":

I want to talk to you again, knowing how anxious you will be for Sunbeam. The blood recedes quickly—that is why today he again had very severe pains. Yesterday for the first time he smiled and talked with us, even played cards, and slept two hours during the day. He is frightfully thin, with enormous eyes, just as at Spala. He likes to be read to, eats little—no appetite at all in fact. I am with him the whole day, Tatiana or Mr. Gilliard relieving me at intervals. Mr. Gilliard reads to him tirelessly, or warms his legs with the Fohn apparatus. Today it is snowing again but the snow melts rapidly, and it is very muddy. I have not been out for a week and a half, as I am so tired that I don't dare to risk the stairs. So I sit with Alexei. A great number of new troops have come from everywhere. A new Kommissar has arrived from Moscow, a man named Jakovleff, and today we shall have to make his acquaintance. It gets very hot in this town in Summer, is frightfully dusty, and at times very humid. We are begging to be transferred for the hot months to some convent. I know that you too are longing for fresh air, and I trust that by God's mercy it may become possible for us all.

They are always hinting to us that we shall have to travel either very far away, or to the center (of Siberia), but we hope that this will not happen, as it would be dreadful at this season. How nice it would be if your brother could settle himself in Odessa. We are quite cut off from the south, never hear from anybody. The little officer will tell you—he saw me apart from the others.* I am so afraid that false rumors will reach your ears—people lie so frantically. Probably the little one's illness was reported as something different, as an excuse for our not being moved.† Well, all is God's will. The deeper you look the more you understand that this is so. All sorrows are sent us to free us from our sins or as a test of our faith, an example to others. It requires good food to make plants grow strong and beautiful, and the gardener walking through his garden wants to be pleased with his flowers. If they do not grow properly he takes his pruning knife and cuts,

---

* By this the Empress meant that the secret messenger would give me particulars she dared not write in her letter.
† To a convent as they desired.

waiting for the sunshine to coax them into growth again. I should like to be a painter, and make a picture of this beautiful garden and all that grows in it. I remember English gardens, and at Livadia you saw an illustrated book I had of them, so you will understand.

Just now eleven men have passed on horseback, good faces, mere boys—this I have not seen the like of for a long time. They are the guard of the new Kommissar. Sometimes we see men with the most awful faces. I would not include them in my garden picture. The only place for them would be outside where the merciful sunshine could reach them and make them clean from all the dirt and evil with which they are covered.

God bless you, darling child. Our prayers and blessings surround you. I was so pleased with the little mauve Easter egg, and all the rest. But I wish I could send you back the money I know you need for yourself. May the Holy Virgin guard you from all danger. Kiss your dear mother for me. Greetings to your old servant, the doctors, and Fathers John and Dosifei. I have seen the new Kommissar, and he really hasn't a bad face. Today is Sacha's (Count Voronzeff, aide-de-camp) birthday.

March 21.

Darling child, we thank you for all your gifts, the little eggs, the cards, and the chocolate for the little one. Thank your mother for the books. Father was delighted with the cigarettes, which he found so good, and also with the sweets. Snow has fallen again, although the sunshine is bright. The little one's leg is gradually getting better, he suffers less, and had a really good sleep last night. Today we are expecting to be searched—very agreeable! I don't know how it will be later about sending letters. I only hope it will be possible, and I pray for help. The atmosphere around us is fairly electrified. We feel that a storm is approaching, but we know that God is merciful, and will care for us. Things are growing very anguishing. Today we shall have a small service at home, for which we are thankful, but it is hard, nevertheless, not to be allowed to go to church. You under-stand how that is, my little martyr.

I shall not send this, as ordinarily, through ——, as she too is going to be searched. It was so nice of you to send her a dress. I add my thanks to hers. Today is the twenty-fourth anniversary of our engagement. How sad it is to remember that we had to burn all our letters, yours too, and others as dear.* (*see footnote on next page*) But what was to be done? One must not attach one's soul to earthly things, but words written by beloved hands penetrate the very heart, become a part of life itself.

I wish I had something sweet to send you, but I haven't anything. Why did you not keep that chocolate for yourself? You need it more than the children do. We are allowed one and a half pounds of sugar every month, but more is always given us by kind-hearted people here. I never touch sugar during Lent, but that does not seem to be a deprivation now. I was so sorry to hear that my poor lancer Ossorgine had been killed, and so many others besides. What a lot of misery and useless sacrifice! But they are all happier now in the other world. Though we know that the storm is coming nearer and nearer, our souls are at peace. Whatever happens will be through God's will. Thank God, at least, the little one is better.

May I send the money back to you? I am sure you will need it if you have to move again. God guard you. I bless and kiss you, and carry you always in my heart. Keep well and brave. Greetings to all from your ever loving.
A.

This letter, written near the end of March, 1918, was the last I ever received written by her Majesty's own hand. A little later in the spring of that year she and the Emperor were hurriedly removed to Ekaterinaburg—the last place from which the world has received tidings of them. The children and most of the suite were left behind in Tobolsk, the poor little Alexei still ill and suffering, and cruelly deprived of the solace of his mother's love and devotion. In May I received a brief letter from Grand Duchess Olga who with difficulty managed to get me news of her parents and the family.

Darling, I take the first opportunity to write you the latest news we have had from ours in Ekaterinaburg. They wrote on the 23rd of April that the journey over the rough roads was terrible, but that in spite of great weariness they are well. They live in three rooms and eat the same food as the soldiers. The little one is better but is still in bed. As soon as he is well enough to be moved we shall join them. We have had letters from Zina but none from Lili. Have Alya and your brother written? The weather has become milder, the ice is out of the river Irtish, but nothing is green yet. Darling, you must know how dreadful it all is. We kiss and embrace you. God bless you.

OLGA.

(previous page)
* All purely personal letters were burned in the palace at Tsarskoe Selo as soon as the news of the Emperor's abdication reached us, the Empress being determined that her most sacred possessions should not be made public by the Provisional Government. She never recovered from the grief of destroying her youthful love letters, which were more to her than the most costly jewels she possessed, the richest of any sovereign in Europe. To me this is a singular revelation of the real character of the Empress.

After this short letter from Olga came a card from Ekaterinaburg written by one of the Empress's maids at her dictation. It contained a few loving words, and the news that they were recovering from the fatigue of their terrible journey. They were living in two rooms—probably, although this is not stated, under great privations. She hoped, but could not tell yet, that our correspondence could be continued. It never was. I had a card a little later from Mr. Gibbs saying that he and M. Gilliard had brought the children from Tobolsk to Ekaterinaburg and that the family was again united. The card was written from the train where he and M. Gilliard were living, not having been allowed to join the family in their stockaded house. Mr. Gibbs had an intuition that both of these devoted tutors were soon to be sent out of the country and such proved to be the case. This was my last news of my Empress and of my Sovereigns, best of all earthly friends.

In July short paragraphs appeared in the Bolshevist newspapers saying that by order of the Soviet at Ekaterinaburg the Emperor had been shot but that the Empress and the children had been removed to a place of safety. The announcement horrified me, yet left me without any exact conviction of its truth. Soviet newspapers published what they were ordered to publish without any regard whatever to facts. Thus when a little later it was announced that the whole family had been murdered—executed, as they phrased it—imagine "executing" five perfectly innocent children!—I could not make myself believe it. Yet little by little the public began to believe it, and it is certain that Nicholas II and his family have disappeared behind one of the world's greatest and most tragic mysteries. With them disappeared all of the suite and the servants who were permitted to accompany them to the house in Ekaterinaburg. My reason tells me that it is probable that they were all foully murdered, that they are dead and beyond the sorrows of this life forever. But reason is not always amenable. There are many of us in Russia and in exile who, knowing the vastness of the enormous empire, the remoteness of its communications with the outside world, know well the possibilities of imprisonment in monasteries, in mines, in deep forests from which no news can penetrate. We hope. That is all I can say. It is said, although I have no firsthand information on the subject, that the Empress Dowager has never believed that either of her sons was killed. The Soviet newspapers published accounts of the "execution" of Grand Duke Michail, and strong evidence has been presented that he was murdered in Siberia with others of the family, including the Grand Duchess Serge. These same newspapers, however, officially stated that Grand Duke Michail had been assisted to escape by English officers.

The most fantastic contradictions concerning all these alleged murders have from time to time cropped up. When I was in prison in the autumn of 1919 a fellow prisoner of the Chekha, the wife of an aide-de-camp of Grand Duke Michail, told me positively that she had received a letter from the Emperor's brother, safe and well in England.

Perhaps the strangest incident of the kind happened to me when I was hiding from the Chekha after my last imprisonment and my narrow escape from a Kronstadt firing squad. A woman unknown to me approached me and calling me by my name, which of course I did not acknowledge, showed me a photograph of a woman in nun's robes standing between two men, priests or monks. "This," she said mysteriously and in a whisper, "is one you know well. She sent it to you by my hands and asks you to write her a message that you are well, and also to give your address that she may write you a letter."

I looked long at the photograph—a poor print—and I could not deny to myself that there was something of a likeness in the face, and especially in the long, delicate hands. But the Empress had always been slender, and after her ill health became almost emaciated. This woman was stout. I might, had I had the slightest assurance of safety, have taken the risk of writing my name and address for this stranger. But no one in Russia takes such risks. The net of the Chekha is too far flung.

I have one word more to say about these letters of the Empress Alexandra Feodorovna. I have translated them as faithfully and as literally as possible, leaving out absolutely nothing except a few messages of affection and some religious expressions which seem to me too intimate to make public, and which might appear exaggerated to western readers. I have included letters which may be thought trivial in subject, but I have done it purposely because I yearned to present the Empress as she was, simple, self-sacrificing, a devoted wife, mother, and friend, an intense patriot, deeply and consistently religious. She had her human faults and failings, as she freely admits. Some of these traits can be described, as the French express it, as "the faults of her quality." Thus her great love for her husband, which never ceased to be romantic and youthful, caused her at times cruel heart pangs. Because this has nothing to do with her life or her story I should not allude to the one cloud that ever came between us—jealousy. I should leave that painful, fleeting episode alone, knowing that she would wish it forgotten, except that in certain letters which have been published she herself has spoken of it so bitterly that were I to omit mention of it entirely I might be accused of suppressing facts.

I have, I think, spoken frankly of the preference of the Emperor for my society at times, in long walks, in tennis, in conversation. In the early part of 1914 the Empress was ill, very low-spirited, and full of morbid reflections. She was much alone, as the Emperor was occupied many hours every day, and the children were busy with their lessons. In the Emperor's leisure moments he developed a more than ordinary desire for my companionship, perhaps only because I was an entirely healthy, normal woman, heart and soul devoted to the family, and one from whom it was never necessary to keep anything secret. We were much together in those days, and before either of us realized it the Empress became mortally jealous and suspicious of every movement of her husband and of myself. In letters written during this period, especially from the Crimea during the spring of 1914, the Empress said some very unkind and cruel things of me, or at least I should consider them cruel if they had not been rooted in illness, and in physical and mental misery. Of course the Court knew of the estrangement between us, and I regret to say that there were many who delighted in it and did what they could to make it permanent. My only real friends were Count Fredericks, Minister of the Court, and his two daughters, who stood by me loyally and kept me in courage.

That this illusion of jealousy was entirely dissipated, that the Empress finally realized that my love and devotion for her precluded any possibility of the things she feared, her letters to me from Siberia amply demonstrate. Our friendship became more deeply cemented than before, and nothing but death can ever sever the bond between us.

Other letters written by the Empress to her husband between 1914 and 1916 have within this past year found publication by a Russian firm in Berlin. Some of them have been reproduced in the London *Times*, and I have no doubt that they will also be published in America. These letters reveal the character of the Empress exactly as I knew her. It is balm to my bruised heart to read in the London *Times* that whatever has been said of her betrayal, or attempted betrayal of Russia during the war, must be abandoned as a legend without the least foundation. So must also be discarded accusations against her of any but spiritual relations with Rasputine. That she believed in him as a man sent of God is true, but that his influence on her, and through her on the Emperor's policies, had any political importance I must steadfastly deny. Both the Empress and Rasputine liked Protopopoff and trusted him. But that had nothing to do with his ministerial tenure. The Empress, and I think also Rasputine, disliked and distrusted Grand Duke Nicholas. But that had nothing to do with his demission. In these affairs the Emperor made his own decisions, as I have stated. The strongest proof of what I have written will be found in the letters of the Empress, those she wrote to the Emperor, to her relations in Germany and England, and those included in this volume. Nothing contradictory, nothing inconsistent has ever been discovered, despite the efforts of the Empress's bitter enemies, the Provisional Government and the Bolshevists. Before all the world, before the historians of the future, Alexandra Feodorovna, Empress of Russia, stands absolved.

CHAPTER XXIII

TOWARDS the close of the summer of 1918 life in Russia became almost indescribably chaotic and miserable. Most of the shops were closed, and only the few who could pay fantastic prices were able to buy food. There was a little bread, a very little butter, some meat, and a few farm products. Tea and coffee had completely disappeared, dried leaves taking their places, but even these substitutes were frightfully dear and very difficult to find. The trouble was that the Bolshevist authorities forbade the peasants to bring any food into Petrograd, and soldiers were kept on guard at the railway stations to confiscate any stocks that tried to run the blockade. Frequently the market stalls were raided, and what food was there was seized, and the merchants arrested. Food smuggling went on on a fairly large scale, and if one had money he could at least avoid starvation. Most people of our class lived by selling, one by one, jewels, furs, pictures, art objects, an enterprising class of Jewish dealers having sprung up as by magic to take advantage of the opportunity. There was also a new kind of merchant class, people of the intelligentsia, who knew the value of lace, furs, old china and embroideries, who dealt with us with more courtesy and rather less avarice than the Jews.

My mother and I fell into dire poverty. A home we had, and even a few valuable jewels, but we clung to everything we had as shipwrecked sailors to their life belts. We could not look far ahead, and we viewed complete bankruptcy with fear and dread. I recall one bitter day in that summer sitting down on a park bench weary and desolate as any pauper, for I had not in my pocket money enough to go home in a tram. I do not remember how I got home, but I remember that in that dark hour a former banker whom we had long known called at our lodgings and told us that he had a little money which he was about to smuggle to the Imperial Family in Siberia. He wanted us to accept twenty thousand rubles of this for our immediate needs, and gladly we did accept it. Very soon afterwards the banker suddenly and mysteriously disappeared, and his fate remains to this day a profound mystery. I do not even know if he succeeded in getting the money to Siberia. However, with the hope he inspired in me I began to think of possible resources which I might turn to account. My hospital in Tsarskoe Selo had been closed by the Bolsheviki, but its expensive equipment of furniture, instruments, horses and carriages still remained, and I employed a lawyer to go over the books and to estimate what money I could realize from a sale of the whole property. To my dismay I learned that the place with everything in it had been seized by my director and head nurse who, under the Bolshevist policy of confiscation, claimed all, ostensibly as state property but really as their own, for they had become ardent Bolshevists. I made a personal appeal to these old employees of mine to let me have at least one cow for my mother who, be1ing very frail, needed milk. They simply laughed at me. My lawyer took steps to protect my rights, and the result of this rash action was that the former director denounced me to the Chekha as a counter-Revolutionist, and in the middle of an October night our home was invaded by armed men who arrested me and my nursing sister, and looted our rooms of everything that caught their fancy. Among other things they took was a letter from the Emperor to my father explaining the conditions which led him to assume supreme command of the army. This letter, treasured by me, seemed to them somehow very incriminating.

Driven ahead of the soldiers, I went downstairs and climbed into a motor truck which conveyed us to the headquarters of the Chekha in Gorohvaia Street. After my name had been taken by a slovenly official I followed the guard to one of two large rooms which formed the women's ward of the prison. There must have been close to two hundred women crowded in these rooms. They slept sometimes three to a narrow bed, they lay on the tables and even on the bare floor. The air of the place was, of course, utterly foul, for many of the women were of the class that never washes. Some were of gentle birth and breeding, accused of no particular offense, but held, according to Bolshevist custom, as hostages and possible witnesses for others who were under examination or who were wanted and could not be found. In the early morning all the prisoners got up from their narrow beds or the hard floor and made their way under soldier escort to a toilet where they washed their faces and hands. As I sat miserably on the edge of my bed a woman came up to me introducing herself as Mlle. Shoulgine, the oldest inhabitant of the place, and therefore a kind of a monitor. It was her business, she said, to see that each prisoner received food and to handle any letters or petitions the women might desire to send out. I told her that I desired to send a petition to the head of the Chekha, or to whatever committee was in charge of the prison, asking the nature of the charges against me, and begging for an early trial. This petition was duly dispatched, and very soon after a very large man, a Jew, came to see me and promised that my affair would be promptly investigated. The soldiers on guard spoke to me kindly and offered, if I had money, to carry letters back and forth from my home. I gave them money and was comforted to hear from my mother that Dr. Manouchine was once more working for my release. Although not a Bolshevist, the doctor's skill was greatly respected by the Communists, who had appointed him head physician of the old Detention House. There was a student doctor attached to our prison, and merely because he was a friend of Dr. Manouchine and knew that I was also, he was courteous and attentive to me. So potent is the influence of a truly great character.

The five days I spent in that filthy, crowded cell will never leave my memory. Every moment was a nightmare. Twice a day they served us with bowls of so-called soup, hot water with a little grease and a few wilted vegetables. This with small pieces of sour black bread was all the food vouchsafed us. Some of the prisoners got additional food from outside, and usually these fortunate ones divided what they had with the others. There was one beautiful woman of the half-world who daily received from some source ample food, and like most of the women of her class she was generous. I was told that she had been arrested because she had hidden and helped her lover, a White officer, to escape, and that she felt proud to be suffering for his sake. Perhaps it was from friends of his that she received the food, yet women of her kind, God knows, very seldom meet with gratitude even from those who owe it most.

Although I was accused of no crime and had no idea what accusations could be brought against me, I lived as all the others lived, in a state of constant anxiety and fear. All day and all night we heard the sound of motors and of motor horns, we saw prisoners brought in, and from our windows we could see great quantities of loot which the Bolshevist soldiers had collected, silver, pictures, rich wearing apparel, everything that appealed to them as valuable. In the courtyard we could see the men fighting like wolves over their spoils. It was like living in a pirates' den rather than a prison, and yet we were often enough reminded that we were prisoners. One day all the women in my room were roughly ordered into a larger room literally heaped with archives of the Imperial Government. With soldiers standing over us we set to work like charwomen to sort the papers and tie them up in neat bundles. Very often in the night when we were sleeping exhausted in our cell rooms the electric lights would suddenly be turned on, guards would call out names, and half a dozen frightened women would get up, gather their rags about them, and go out. Some returned, some disappeared. No one knew whose turn would come next or what her fate would be.

The name of my nursing sister was called before mine, and within a short time she returned smiling to say that she was to be sent home at once and that I should soon follow. Two hours later soldiers appeared at the grating and one called out my surname: "Tanieva, to Viborg Prison." I had spirit enough to demand the papers consigning me to this dread women's prison, but the soldiers merely pushed me back with the butts of their guns and bade me lose no time in obeying orders. I still had a little money with which I paid for a cab instead of walking the long distance to the prison, and I begged the soldiers to stop on the way and let me see my mother.

For this privilege I offered all the money remaining in my purse, which the soldiers took, also bargaining for the ring I wore on my hand. This I declined to give so they philosophically said: "Oh, well, why not?" And stopped the cab at the door of my mother's lodgings. Of course my poor mother was overjoyed to see me, even for a moment, and so was old Berchik, now almost at the end of his life. Both assured me that everything was being done in my behalf and that at the Viborg prison I would be in less danger of death than at the Chekha headquarters. I might even hope to be admitted to the prison hospital.

A little heartened in spite of myself I went on to Viborg, which lies in a far quarter of the town of what is known as the Viborg side of the Neva. A rather pretty Bolshevist girl was in charge of the receiving office, and when I pleaded ill health and asked to be sent to the hospital she promised to see what could be done. Viborg prison was one of many which during the first frenzied days of the Revolution were thrown open, the prisoners released, and the wardresses murdered. I do not know how other women were induced to take their places, but I do know that the women in whose charge I was placed were so kind and considerate that had any attempt been made against them the prisoners themselves would have fought in their defense. The wardress who locked me in my cell stopped to say a comforting word, and because she saw that I was shivering with cold as well as nervousness, she brought me bread and a little hot soup.

After some hours I had another visitor, Princess Kakouatoff, accused of being the ringleader of an anti-Bolshevist plot, who had been six months in Viborg and was regarded as a "trusty." Among other privileges she had the right to telephone friends of new prisoners, and at my request she telephoned messages to friends who could be of use to my mother if not to me. The princess brought me a little portion of fish which I ate hungrily, and I think she was also instrumental in finally getting me into the prison hospital. This was after I had fainted on the floor of my cell, and everyone in authority, including the prison doctor, knew that I was in no condition to endure the noisy confusion of the huge cell house. The hospital was a little cleaner than the rest of the prison, but it was a pretty dreadful place just the same. For nurses we had good-conduct prisoners, women of low type who stole food and everything else they could lay hands on. They stripped me of my clothes, substituting the prison chemise and blue dressing gown, and took away all my hairpins. I was given a bed in a room with six other women, one of them a particularly awful syphilis case, and two others, very dirty, who spent most of their time going over each other's heads for vermin. I stayed in this ghastly place a very short time, a woman doctor and a prisoner of my own class, Baroness Rosen, succeeding in getting me transferred to a better ward. Nevertheless the whole prison hospital was horrible. The trusties in charge of the wards were in the habit of eating the meat out of the prisoners' bowls, and fighting for food among prisoners throughout the institution was a daily occurrence. I can describe Viborg prison and most of its inmates in one word—beastly. Many of the women were syphilitic, most were verminous, some were half mad. One who slept near me had murdered her husband and burned his body. Nearly all sang the most obscene songs and held unrepeatable conversations. Mostly they were so depraved that the doctor in his rounds showed that he was afraid of them. Yet there were among them a few women who, like myself, had led sheltered and religious lives, and who were only now learning that such abandoned specimens of womanhood existed on the earth. There was no attempt at reforming the women. Once there had been a church attached to the prison, but this the Bolsheviki had closed, substituting a cinema to which on special occasions some of the prisoners were admitted. Not many political prisoners had this privilege because they were treated much more rigorously than common criminals. It was the common criminals also, the thieves, murderers, prostitutes, who were released in advance of "counter-Revolutionists," those accused, however vaguely, of political activities.

All the prisons of Petrograd by this time were so crowded with so-called political prisoners that even the women's prison was obliged to receive an overflow of sick men prisoners. This wholesale imprisonment of anti-Bolshevists naturally led to the shooting of thousands of citizens, shooting being simpler than feeding and housing, and in addition an economy of effort on the part of those charged with the mockery of trials. Later the Chekha dispensed with this mockery, but in those days prisoners were given the pretense of a hearing. I can testify to their futility, because I went through more than half a dozen trials and in no case was I accused of any crime, tried for any definite offense, or given anything like a fair hearing. On September 10, 1918, word was brought to the Viborg prison that on the next morning I was to be taken away not to return. This seemed to be a death sentence, and all that night I lay awake thinking of my poor mother and wondering what would become of her alone in the midst of the Bolshevist inferno. Silently and long I prayed for her and for the peaceful release of my own tried soul.

Very early in the morning I was summoned, my own clothes were given me, and I was led to the receiving office of the prison. Here two soldiers waited, and I was taken out between them and marched to the headquarters of the Chekha. In a small, dirty room I underwent an examination by two Jewish Communists, one of whom, Vladimirov—nearly all Jewish Communists assume Russian names—being prominent in the councils of the Communist central committee. For fully an hour these men did everything they could to terrorize me. They accused me of being a spy, of plotting against the Chekha, of being a dangerous counter-Revolutionist. They told me that I was to be shot at once and that they intended to shoot all the intellectuals and the "Bourju," leaving the proletariat in full possession of Russia. They continued this bluster until from sheer weariness they stopped, then one of the men leaned his elbows on the table and with a smile that was meant to be ingratiating said confidentially: "I tell you what. You relate the *true* story of Rasputine and perhaps we won't have you shot, at least not today." I assured the man that I knew no more about Rasputine than they did, perhaps not as much, since I had no access to police records and they had. Then they wanted to know all about the Czar and the life of the Court. As well as I could I satisfied their curiosity, which was that of ignorant children, and at the end of an exhausting interrogation they actually sent me, not to a wall and a firing squad, but back to the filthy cell in the Viborg prison. I dropped on my dirty bed, swallowed a little food brought me by a sympathetic fellow prisoner, and resigned myself for what next might happen to me. What happened was astonishing. A soldier came to the door and called out: "Tanieva, with your things to go home."

Within a short time I stood trembling and weak on the pavement in front of the prison. I could not have walked to my lodgings, in fact I felt incapable of walking at all, but a strange woman observing me and my piteous condition approached, put her arm around me, and helped me into a drosky. I had a little money, perhaps fifty rubles, and I gave it all to the ischvostik to drive me home. Here I found an amazing state of affairs, the general immorality and demoralization into which Bolshevism was driving the people having penetrated our own place. Everyone was turning thief, and my nursing sister, who had been with me since 1905, whom my mother had treated like a daughter, had become inoculated with the virus of evil. The woman had not only appropriated almost all the clothes I possessed, but had stolen all the trinkets and bits of jewelry she could lay hands on. She had even taken the carpets from the floors and stored them in her room. Not daring to attempt to regain any of this property I asked the nurse to please take what she wanted and leave the apartment. "Not at all," she replied. "This place suits me very well and as long as I choose I shall remain." She had embraced Bolshevism, not I am sure from principle, but as the safest policy, and in time she became rich in jewels, finery, and miscellaneous loot. It was months before we finally induced her to leave, and after her departure I have reason to believe that she did everything she could to keep me in trouble with the Bolshevists.

By this time the Communist régime was fully organized. The whole town was divided into districts, each one under command of a group of soldiers who had full license to search—and rob—houses, and to make arrests. Every night the search went on. At seven o'clock all electric lights were turned off, and when, two or three hours later, they suddenly flashed up again, every soul in the district was seized with fear, knowing that this was the signal for the invasion. Often women were included in the searching parties, terrible women dressed in silks and strung with jewelry, stolen of course from the hated "Bourju." Seven times our home was raided, once on the authority of an anonymous letter charging that we were in possession of firearms. Once more I was dragged off to an interminable examination, this time before the staff of the Red Army in a house in Gogol Street. The close connection between the Chekha and the Red Army was apparent because in the two hours during which I sat in the ante-chamber waiting examination a Lettish official of the Chekha passed freely in and out of the committee room, occasionally throwing me a reassuring word. My case would be settled favorably, he said, and it was, for the committee after bullying me for a length of time, dropped the subject of concealed firearms, assumed the snobbish and half cringing air with which I was becoming familiar to the point of nausea, and began asking questions about the Imperial household. They produced a large album of photographs and made me go through it and identify each picture. Finally the head inquisitor told me magnanimously that I could go home, cleared by the highest authority, but that soldiers would go with me and make sure that there were no revolvers or pistols in the house. The search was made anew, and then the men left, obviously disappointed that practically nothing worth stealing had come to light.

Two things of importance were happening in those days. The White Army was approaching Petrograd, and in all the streets soldiers were drilling in anticipation of a battle. Airplanes whirred overhead, and once in so often a shell screamed over the housetops. We prayed for the coming of the White Army, and at the same time dreaded the massacres we knew would precede its entry into the town. The second thing that marked this date was the Communist system of public feeding, free food being furnished by cards distributed according to the status of the individual. The Bolshevist authorities and the soldiers of course had the most food and the best. Next came the proletariat, so-called, and last of all the "Bourju" was provided for. These of the lowest strata in society got hardly anything at all and would have starved, most of them, had it not been for the food smuggling which constantly went on, the peasants from out of town boldly bringing in bulky parcels, and taking back in return for their food, not Bolshevist money, which they disdained, but everything they could accumulate in the way of furniture or dress materials. They even accepted window curtains and table linen, anything, in fact, that could be fashioned into clothing. These same peasants before the Revolution had been expert spinners and weavers, but now they scorned such plebeian occupations because it was easier to barter grains, milk, vegetables, and other produce for the last possessions of the townspeople.

We went on living, somehow, parting with clothing and furniture, burning boxes and even chairs for fuel, walking miles for stray bits of wood, praying for the success of the White forces, praying for protection against what must happen before that success could be achieved. My mother all these days was very ill with dysentery, which was rife in Petrograd, and I had that additional suffering, for I knew that it would take little to bring her frail life to an end.

* * *

CHAPTER XXIV

ON September 22 (October 6, New Style) I went in the evening to a lecture in a church. At that time every non-Bolshevist spent as many hours every day as possible in the churches, praying or listening to words of hope and comfort from the priests. The church was, in fact, the only home of peace and rest in the whole of the distracted country. That particular night in church I met some old friends who invited me to go home with them rather than walk the long and dreary, even the dangerous way back to my lodgings. I stayed with my friends that night, and the next morning early I went to mass in the little church where Father John of Kronstadt lies buried. I reached home about midday, and found the place in the possession of soldiers, two of whom had waited the entire night to arrest me, this time as a hostage, the White Army being reported within a few miles of Petrograd. My sick mother prepared me a little food, made a parcel of my scanty linen, and once more we bade each other the despairing farewell of two who knew that they might never meet again on earth. I was quickly conveyed to the headquarters of the Chekha where I was greeted with the exultant welcome: "Aha! Here we have the bird who has dared to stay out a whole night."

Thrust into the old filthy, ill-smelling cell room I found a spot near a dirty window from which I could get a far glimpse of the golden dome of St. Isaac's Cathedral. During my whole term in this place I kept my eyes and my whole mind on that golden dome, trying to forget the hell that whirled around me. The woman in charge of the room was a Finnish girl who had committed the crime of trying to run away to Finland. She was a stenographer and clerk, and the Chekha used her by night as an office assistant. Whether by nature or by association she had become as hard and as ruthless as her captors, and her imprisonment had many mitigations. It was her pleasant duty to make out the lists of those who, twice a week, were taken to Kronstadt to be shot, and her reports on the subject which she confided regularly to her chosen comrade, a Georgian dancer named Menabde, were enough to sicken even those of us who had become accustomed to wholesale slaughter of unoffending human beings. We heard little else except death and threats of death in this place. There was an official named Boze in the prison, and often we heard him screeching through the telephone to his wife that he would be late to dinner that night because he had a load of "game" to get off to Kronstadt. Under such conditions pity and sympathy become strangely dulled. On occasions when I was sent to the kitchens for hot water I used to get glimpses of the "game," huddled wretchedly in their seats or restlessly pacing their cells—waiting. Often when I returned with the water I found the seats and the cells empty, and although my heart sank and my senses swam, I never felt the screaming horror a normal person would have felt. This dulling of the emotions, I suppose, is nature's way of keeping the mind from giving way entirely. Of course nature took away all human dignity and self-respect, this, too, in mercy. Any prisoner who went to the kitchens was greeted with jeers and foul abuse from the cooks who threw us handfuls of potato parings and withered cabbage leaves, quite as one would throw bones to dogs. Like dogs we eagerly snatched at these leavings, because the prisoners' regular rations were nothing half as palatable, being mostly wormy dried fish and a disgusting substitute for bread.

One day I was called up for examination, and this time a real surprise awaited me. My judge was an Esthonian named Otto, not altogether a brutal man, as it turned out. As I approached his desk he regarded me grimly and without a word handed me a letter, unsigned, and reading about as follows: "To the Lady in Waiting, Anna Viroubova. You are the only one who can save us from this terrible Bolshevik administration, as you are at the head of a great organization fully equipped with guns and ammunition." Sternly the Esthonian judge commanded me to tell him the truth about the organization of which I was the head. Of course I told him that the whole thing was an invention, and he astonished me by saying that although the letter had been posted to my address he had very much doubted its verity. Then he asked, almost gently: "Are you very hungry?" Taken off my guard as much by the kindness as by the prospect of food, I fell against the desk murmuring only half aloud: "Hungry? Yes, oh, yes." Whereupon he opened a drawer of his desk and handed me a large piece of fresh, sweet bread. "Go now," he said, "and I will discuss your case with my colleague Vikman. In the evening we will see you again."

At eleven that night I was again summoned, this time before the two men. The Esthonian, still kind and courteous, gave me a glass of steaming tea, which did much to lend me courage. Both he and Vikman then put me through a searching examination especially about my relations, real and assumed, with the Imperial Family and with persons of the Court. At three in the morning they released me, more dead than alive with fatigue, Otto telling me heartily that he thought I would be set free within a few days. Vikman, however, declared that my case would have to be referred to Moscow and that I need not expect an early release. I went back to my evil cage expecting nothing. I knew, that the threat of the White Army advance filled with terror the whole Bolshevist population, and that in case of actual battle no life outside the slim Communist ranks would be worth the smallest scrap of their worthless paper money.

Very shortly after my return to the cell room I began to hear my name whispered from one wretched woman to another, and I accepted this without much emotion as a prelude to a boat journey to Kronstadt. Early on a certain morning a soldier approached the door and bawled out: "Tanieva, you to Moscow." I happened to be exceedingly ill that day, but mechanically I picked up my little handkerchief containing my few possessions, including a Bible, and followed the escort of two soldiers down the steep steps, as I believed, to my death. Perhaps they had orders to take me to Kronstadt, I cannot be sure of that, but I do know that the route we followed did not lead to the Moscow station. We had walked but a short distance when one of the soldiers said to the other: "What's the good of two of us bothering with one lame woman? I'll take care of her and you can go along. It will soon be over anyway." Nothing loath the other soldier, glad to get out of anything resembling work, took himself off while I, in charge of one armed man, mounted the crowded tram and rode on toward an unknown destination. At a certain point we had to change trams, and here occurred an incident so extraordinary that I almost hesitate to strain the credulity of a non-Russian reader by relating it. The second tram had been delayed for some reason, and a considerable crowd of passengers was waiting for it on the street corner. My soldier stood at my side waiting with the rest, but soon he became impatient. Ordering me not to move an inch in his absence, he ran down the street a short distance to see if the tram were in sight. As soon as he turned his back, people in the crowd began to speak to me. A girl in whom I recognized a former acquaintance asked me where I was going, and when I told her she took a bracelet I gave her and promised to carry it, with news of my fate, to my poor mother. An officer of the old army came up to me saying: "Are you not Anna Alexandrovna?" And when I said yes, he too asked me where I was being taken.

"Kronstadt, I think," I answered, but he said: "Who knows?" and pressed into my hands a roll of bills saying that they might be of use to me.

Other people surrounded me, mostly strangers, but two of them women whom I had often seen at mass in the small church of Father John. They said: "Why should you be shot? The soldier has not come back. Run while the chance is yours. Father John will surely help you." Encouraged by their sympathy, yet hardly knowing what I was doing, I limped off on my crutch much faster than I could have believed possible, the whole street-corner crowd spreading out to shield my flight. I limped and stumbled down Michel Street as far as the Nevski Prospekt weeping and praying all the time: "God save me! God save me!" until I reached the old shopping arcade known as the Gostiny Dvor. Here I caught sight of my soldier running in frantic pursuit of his escaped prisoner. It seemed all over with me then but I crouched in a corner of the deserted building and miraculously the soldier ran on without seeing me. As soon as I thought it at all safe I crept out of the old arcade and turned into the Zagorodny Prospekt, where I found a solitary cab. "Take me quickly," I cried to the ischvostik. "My mother is dying." The man replied indifferently that he had a fare waiting, but I thrust into his hands the entire roll of bills given me by the friendly officer, at the same time climbing into the drosky.

Said the ischvostik, "Where shall I drive you?" I gasped out the address of a friend in the suburbs of the city, and the man lashed his half-starved animal into a walk. After what seemed to me many hours we reached the place, I rang the doorbell and fell across the threshold in a dead faint.

My friend and her husband courageously took me in, fed, warmed me, and put me to bed. They even dared to send word to my mother that I was for the moment safe from pursuit, but they warned her not to come near the house as soldiers would certainly be watching her every movement. As a matter of fact my mother was visited by Red soldiers, arrested in her bed, and closely guarded for three weeks. Our maid also was arrested, as was everyone who came to the house. The old Berchick who had spent almost his entire lifetime in the service of our family was taken ill during this period and died. For five days his body lay uncoffined in the house, the Bolshevist authorities refusing him a burial permit. It was for my mother an interval of utter despair, since in addition to the death of

Berchick she lived in constant fear of my rearrest. In the opinion of the Bolshevist soldiers, however, I had escaped to the White Army, and photographs of me were posted conspicuously in all the railway stations.

The kind friends who had taken me in dared not for their lives keep me long, and wishing them nothing of harm I set out on a dark night without a kopeck in my pockets and with no certain idea where I could find a bed. I had in mind a religious hostel, a place where a few students, men and women, lived under the chaperonage of an old nun. There I went, begging them for Christ's sake to take me in, and there I was hidden for five perilous days. A girl student volunteered to go to see my mother, and go she did, but when hours passed, a day passed, and she did not return, a panic of fear seized all of us, and rather than expose these kind people to risk of imprisonment and death I voluntarily left the place. What else could I do?

How shall I describe the horrors of the next few months? Like a hunted animal I crept from one shelter to another, always leaving when it seemed at all possible that my protectors might be punished for their charity. Four nights I spent in the cell of an old nun whom I knew, but pitying her fears I put on the black head kerchief of a peasant woman and started in a cab, on borrowed money, for the house of a friend near the Alexandra Lavra on the outskirts of the town. All unknown to me a decree had that day been issued that no one could ride in a cab without written permission from the authorities. Consequently before we had traveled half the journey the cab was stopped by two women police, fierce creatures armed with rifles, who called out to the ischvostik: "Halt! We arrest you and your passenger." Hastily I crammed all the money I had into the ischvostik's hand and begged the women to let me go as I had just been discharged from hospital and knew nothing of the new rule. Oddly enough they let us drive on, but very soon the ischvostik, sick with terror, stopped his horse and told me that he would take me no further. I got out and staggered on through the muddy snow, for it was now late in the autumn of 1919. A former officer whom I had once known well met and recognizing me asked if he might not accompany me to my destination. "No, no," I cried. "It would be madness for you to be seen with me. I cannot explain, only go, go, as fast as you can." I staggered on, dripping with rain until I reached my friend's house. To my now customary greeting: "I am running away. Will you hide me?" she replied: "Come in. I have two others." Thus did brave Russians in those days risk their lives to save those of others. Under her protection I lived ten days, and in her house I met a woman, a servant in one of the Communist kitchens, who having access to food and supplies, afterwards more than once saved me from starvation.

From one such kindly haven to another I fled in the dead of night. Once I was received in the home of an English woman who out of her scanty stores gave me warm stockings, gloves, and a sweater. Another day or two I spent in the rooms of a dressmaker whose husband was an unwilling soldier in the Red Army. Once I ventured back to the student hostel, where they welcomed me and fed me well, one of their number having just returned from the country with a stock of smuggled food. Here I had news from my dear mother from the girl who had gone to her on my behalf, and had, after ten days' detention by the Chekha, got back to the hostel. Some members of the Chekha, she informed me, looked forward to shooting me instantly when I was caught, but others said that it was certain that I was with the White Army and would never be caught.

From the hostel I sought a paid lodging with the family of a former member of the orchestra of the Imperial Theater. These people, however, were very mercenary and would receive me only on advance payment of a large sum of money. Almost everything my mother and I had owned had been sold long before, but I retained a pendant of aquamarines and diamonds, a wedding present from the Empress, safely hidden in the house of a friend. This I had sold for fifty thousand rubles, giving half the money to the musician's wife in return for a few days' shelter in a wretchedly dirty, unheated room. Here I had to cut my hair short to get rid of vermin, and feeling unable to endure the hole I left it. Yet finding my next lodgings even worse, I returned, and here in the midst of discomfort and bitter cold, I had the joy of meeting my mother and also my aunt Lashkeroff, who brought me the welcome news that they thought they had at last found me a permanently safe retreat. It was miles from where I was staying, and I had to walk every step of the way, but when I arrived I found my hostess a lovely woman belonging to the Salvation Army. Gladly would I have stayed with her indefinitely but that was impossible as I had no passport and the police began to haunt the neighborhood. She did not abandon me for all that, but got me a new shelter in the home of a good priest and his wife. From here I was handed on from one to another of the priest's parishioners to whom he confided the story of my harried career. Once an Esthonian woman told me that her sister had found a Finnish woman who, for a good price, was willing to take fugitives over the frontier, and she strongly advised me to attempt the flight. Some instinct forbade, and it turned out a good instinct, for the Finnish woman, after taking the money, had abandoned the Esthonian's poor sister in the midst of a wood, from which she had to return, empty of purse and in deadly peril of arrest.

Cutting the story of my fugitive existence short, I finally found something like a permanent abode in the tiny and happily obscure woodland cottage of a working engineer, who kindly offered to take me in to his bachelor quarters a mile or two outside of Petrograd. Here I became once more the happy possessor of a passport, true not in my own name but perfectly legal otherwise. In Russia when a girl marries she gives up her passport to the priest, receiving a new one in the name of her husband. My kind old priest gave one of these maiden passports to the engineer, at the same time reporting to the Commissar of his neighborhood that such a passport had been lost. This was to prevent any possible trouble or inquiry. The Commissar obligingly gave the priest a duplicate, signed and sealed by Bolshevist authority. Now again I was a human being, for no one in Russia can be said to have any identity unless he is in possession of a passport. Mine described me as a teacher, and as such I was henceforth entitled to the Communist rations. For the time being I was less a teacher than an unskilled household servant, for naturally I wanted to do everything possible to repay the good engineer for affording me a safe shelter. I knew nothing whatever of cooking or housework, yet I attempted to do both. The engineer himself was absent all day, but when he returned at night he carried in wood enough to last twenty-four hours, and also water which had to be brought from a great distance. Food, of course, was very scarce. My mother and the friendly priest brought all they could, but even so I would often have suffered had it not been for my old acquaintance, the woman who worked in the Communist kitchen. And here I have to tell another incident which may seem impossible to some readers. One day I was sitting in the little house in the wood, feeling as secure as an escaped prisoner can feel, when I heard a sudden loud knocking at the door. There was no possible place where I could hide, but I sat absolutely still in my chair, hardly breathing for fear of disclosing the fact that the house was not empty. Again came the knocking at the door, this time louder and more peremptory than before. Realizing that it was useless to resist, I arose and with a prayer on my lips, I went to the door and opened it. No one was there. Nothing was in sight save the wintry trees and the frozen path that led to the highway. But yes! There almost at the end of the path stood the shivering figure of a little girl, the daughter of the woman in the Communist kitchen.

"Oh!" she cried, seeing me in the doorway. "I have been looking everywhere for your house and I could not find it."

"But you knocked," I said.

"No, I didn't," declared the child. "I haven't been near the house. I just this minute turned into the pathway to get out of the wind. I'm so glad I've found you. Mother has sent you something."

Who knocked at my door twice? The wind? It never did before or afterwards. If you believe in Providence, as I do, you may agree with me that God did not intend me at that time to starve in the depths of a desolate forest. If you prefer another explanation seek it.

In January, 1920, my kind friend the engineer told me reluctantly that he was about to marry and that the tiny room I occupied would have to be given up. I had not the remotest idea where I was to go. Above all things I desired to embrace a religious life, but in those perilous days no convent in Petrograd dared receive me. The convents were constantly being raided, and the younger nuns were frequently taken out and forced to work on the streets. No religious house could shelter a fugitive even though she possessed a false passport. Again I became a vagrant, spending a night here, a day there, sleeping in any refuge that opened to me. Towards the end of March I again found a home in the house of a priest and his wife who were as parents to me, and to whom I owe a lifetime of gratitude. Here I found not only safety but work, that blessed anodyne against all trouble. My passport, as I have said, described me as a teacher, and a teacher I now became, thanks to my new friends, who found me plenty of pupils among the working-class children of the neighborhood. I taught them the simple elements, and to children of the more intellectual classes languages and music. My pay was in food, but food in the Bolshevist paradise is worth much more than money, so I was completely satisfied.

By this time my appearance was so changed that I lost all fear of the police or the Chekha. One day when I was slowly walking the long distance across the river to my favorite church, the resting place of Father John, a motor car stopped in my path and I recognized as its occupant the Chekha inquisitor Boze, the man who had several times been my brutal jailer. "Grazhdanka (Citizeness)," he addressed me, "please tell me where to find —" he named a street and number whither he was bound, doubtless on some errand of terror. Giving him the direction, I moved on as fast as my crippled legs could carry me, but I need not have been afraid for he did not know me at all.

So went the year 1920, my mother and I and the good priest's family often discussing the possibilities of escape from the increasing starvation, death, and terror which everywhere surrounded us. People did escape, we knew, but how were we to do it—two women, one old and the other lame? It seemed altogether impossible. Besides, we had almost nothing with which to buy our way out of the country. My only shoes were homemade affairs of carpet, and I was so careful of them that often when walking I took them off and carried them in my hands to preserve them. Another thing, beset with dangers as we were in Russia we were no longer hungry, because I had an increasing number of pupils, and each one meant a tiny portion of food and firewood for my mother, my friends, and myself. But here is a strange and a universally human thing. Food and warmth do not bring content to prisoners, they create courage, and when one day in late October we received a letter from my sister, safe in a near-by country which I may not name, the flame of adventure blazed up in the soul of my brave little mother and in my own heart. My sister suggested the possibility of our getting out by one of the ways that persist in flourishing in spite of Bolshevism and the Chekha, and she offered us, if we succeeded in escaping, the shelter of her own home. I cannot reveal any detail of those secret ways of escape, because they still exist, and must not in any way be placed in jeopardy. Enough it is to say that Petrograd is separated from Finland by only a few versts of land, carefully guarded, and by a narrow arm of the Baltic Sea which cannot be quite as successfully guarded. In winter this water freezes, not as unsalted water freezes, smooth and thick and safe for passage, but in rough and treacherous hummocks of mixed ice and snow, with unexpected gaps of half-frozen water opening here and there between the ice masses. Still, the icy Baltic does at times admit of sledge passage, and there are men who make a business of taking over—for a price far beyond what most Russians can afford—refugees who have friends waiting for them in Finland or in countries to the west and south. Sometimes Red soldiers have to be bribed, and often they sell out the people whose money they accept. Sometimes also the men who contract to take refugees over the ice betray their passengers to the Bolshevik guards. Any way you look at it, escape from Bolshevik Russia is about as perilous as going unarmed into a tiger's cage. Yet people dare it, and we did.

It was about the first of December in our calendar, in the year 1920, when we received a second smuggled letter from my sister: "Be ready whenever we send for you." For that promised summons we waited in desperate suspense until two days after Christmas. Then to my mother's lodging came a fisherman and his little boy with the whispered news that we were to go with them on the day following. My mother found means of sending the news to our friend the priest, and he brought it to me. "Tomorrow at four o'clock you go abroad."

The next day at the appointed hour my mother and I, two shivering creatures facing death, but ready, met at a small railway station leading along the Baltic shores. The fisherman's son was also at the station, but obeying instructions, we did not notice him but simply followed wherever he led. Our train journey was short, and at five o'clock, pitch dark in the Russian winter, we alighted at a poor village, following the boy who carried on his back a bag of potatoes. Alas! In the darkness and confusion we lost him, and stood in the icy cold like lost souls, not knowing where to turn. Suddenly out of the shadows a peasant woman approached us. "Are you looking for a boy with a bag of potatoes?" she said in a low voice, and to our frightened assent she murmured: "Follow me." We followed, although, for all we knew, it was to a Chekha prison. Anybody in Russia may be Chekha, the friend who invites you to dinner, the man who buys your last jewel, the woman who offers to guide you over an unknown road. You can trust no one, consequently, when you must, you trust anyone. We followed the peasant woman into a dim hut, and there we found two fishermen who assured us that they were ready that night to take us across the frozen Baltic to a village on the Finnish side. Their horses and sledges, they told us, were safely hidden, but they would be ready to take us and three other fugitives, a lady, a child, and a maid, as soon as we could safely venture to leave the village. As luck would have it there was a festival and a dance going on that night, and we had to sit in that stifling hut in complete silence until two o'clock. Also we had to pay for our shelter and escape one hundred thousand rubles, which my mother had secured by selling her last treasure, a pearl necklace.

When the last peasant had gone to bed and silence wrapped the village, we stole out through the mud and the snow, and got into the rough sledge. Hardly had we struck the rough ice of the Baltic when the sledge overturned, waking the child who, silent before, now began to cry and to beg to go home. The little thing spoke only French and I can still hear him repeating over and over again in a high baby voice which he did not know imperiled the lives of all of us: "Maman, Maman, à la maison, à la maison." For six hours we drove thus, slowly and cautiously over the rotten ice, one of the men driving, and the other running ahead with a long pole testing the ice for a safe pathway. Often we stopped to listen for possible sentinels, and once in the neighborhood of Kronstadt we had such a fright that I wonder the men dared go farther. Plainly to our ears came the grinding of machinery, and we knew that where there was machinery there were men. We stopped long and listened, until our driver suddenly remembered that the noise was that of an ice breaker several miles out of our highway. By this time I was so stiff and drowsy with cold, so nearly frozen, in fact, that I hardly cared what happened to us. Seeing my wretched state, one of the men took off an extra pair of woolen socks he wore and slipped them on my feet. The unknown lady who accompanied us also spared me a warm wrap, and by rubbing and holding me close to their bodies they kept me alive. At eight o'clock of a pale winter morning they lifted me out of the sledge and with the others I stood trembling on the snowy shores of Finland.

"Now you are out of Sovdepia" (Soviet land), said the fishermen cheerfully, "but we are not safe yet, for the Finnish police may catch us and send us back." Hurriedly we climbed the hill to the cottage of one of the smugglers. Here we met his wife, who, gray with fear, came out to meet her husband after his night of peril on the ice. The woman gave us hot coffee, bread, and cheese, but she would not keep us long in her house. We knew that we must report as soon as possible at the quarantine station, and we knew, besides, that the sorely tried Finnish authorities would not be any too glad to see us coming. Do not blame the Finns for this. Every Russian refugee is a burden on their slender resources, and too often a pretended refugee is merely a Bolshevik agent sent to stir up trouble among disaffected workmen. However, on this occasion the Finns received our wretched group with infinite kindness, and made us comfortable during the required period we spent in the quarantine station. Then we went to our separate destinations, all of us to poverty, obscurity, homesickness, to that sunless clime which waits the exile wherever he may go. In the country where my mother and I finally arrived we found my sister, happier than ourselves, because she left Russia before the great horror began, thus saving part of her fortune. My sister gave us food, clothing, a lodging. Except for her bounty we had lost everything we ever owned, home, friends, possessions, country, for Russians now have no country, no flag, no place in the wide world. The best any of us can hope for is an obscure corner in some foreign land where we can earn enough to buy our daily bread, and a quiet place in which to pray every day of our lives: "God save Russia."

I am told, although I can hardly believe it, that in other lands, even in free America, there are beings so deluded that they wish to bring about revolution and Bolshevism. I do not wish for any of them the long nightmare of suffering that I, one of millions, have suffered under revolution and Bolshevism. I pray only that there may be revealed to them the fate of the betrayed who have died and are dying under the criminal administration of the Provisional Government and, later, of Lenine and his fanatical followers. If they can be made to know only in part what my poor, ravished country is today, they will forget their delusions and pray with the exiles: "God save Russia."

APPENDIX A

THE TRUTH CONCERNING THE RUSSIAN IMPERIAL FAMILY

Statement of Vladimir Michailovitch Roudneff, appointed by Minister of Justice Kerensky Special High Commissioner for Revision and Investigation of the actions of Ministers and other High Personages of the Imperial Government.

"I was acting as Procureur of the Court of Assizes of Ekaterinoslav when I received orders from Minister of Justice Kerensky to become a member of the High Commission of Inquiry charged with an examination of the acts and abuses of ministers and other high personages of the former Government. While working with this Commission in Petrograd I was especially assigned to examination of sources of secret influences at Court which were known as Dark Forces. My work with the Commission lasted until August, 1917, when I was forced to leave because the President, Mourvavieff, insisted upon my making reports of a plainly prejud-icial character.

"As an Attorney General (*juge d'instruction*) I had access to all documents, and the right to be present at the examination of all witnesses, with the view of establishing impartially the part played by persons accused by society and the public press of exerting influence on foreign and domestic politics. I was assigned to read all the papers and letters found in the Winter Palace, the palace at Tsarskoe Selo, and at Peterhof, especially the personal correspondence of the Emperor and Empress, certain of the Grand Dukes, and also the correspondence seized in the course of examination of the house of Archbishop Varnava, also of Countess S. S. Ignatieff, Dr. Badmaeff, Voyeikoff, and Anna Viroubova, and also to the relations existing between the Imperial family and the German Imperial family. Being aware of the importance of my inquiry in throwing light on historical events preceding and following the Revolution, I made copies of all documents and letters, *dossiers*, and statements of witnesses. In leaving Petrograd I took with me all these copies, concealing them in my home in Ekaterinoslav, but it is probable that these documents were destroyed when the Bolsheviki raided my house. If by happy chance I find that they still exist I shall certainly publish them in full, without any comments of my own.

"In the meantime I consider it my duty to write a short account of the principal persons who were accused of being Dark Forces. I must, however, warn the reader that as I write from memory some details may escape my mind. When I went to Petrograd to begin my work with the High Commission I admit that I was influenced by all the pamphlets and newspaper articles on the subject of the Rasputine influence, and other rumors and gossip, and I began my work under the domination of preconceived prejudices. But careful and impartial investigation soon forced me to the opinion that these rumors and newspaper accounts were based on slender foundations.

"The most interesting person charged with exercising a malign influence on political affairs was Gregory Rasputine, therefore this person was the central figure of my investigations. The account of the surveillance under which he lived, up to the very day of his death, is of great importance. This surveillance was exercised by the ordinary as well as the secret police, special agents noting all his goings and comings, some of these agents being disguised as policemen or as servants. Everything concerning the movements of Rasputine was carefully recorded every day. If he left his house, even for an hour or two, the moment of his departure and his return was noted, and also every person he met on the road.

"The secret agents kept strict account of all people he met and of all who visited him. In cases where the names of these persons were not known their full descriptions were taken. After having read all papers and examined many witnesses I reached the conclusion that Rasputine was a person more complex and less comprehensible than had been previously represented. In studying his personality I naturally paid attention to the chronological order of circumstances which finally opened to the man the doors of the Tsar's palace, and I discovered that the first preliminary was his acquaintance with the well known, pious, and learned churchmen Bishops Theofan and Hermogen. I noted also that it was afterwards due to the influence of Rasputine that these two great pillars of the Orthodox Church fell into disfavor. He was the cause of the relegation of Hermogen to the Monastery of Saratoff, and of the disgrace (demotion) of Theofan, after these two archbishops, discovering Rasputine's low instincts, openly turned against him. All the evidence pointed to the conclusion that in the inner life of Rasputine, a simple peasant of the Government of Tobolsk, there occurred suddenly a complete change transforming him and turning him toward Christ. Only in this way can I explain to myself his intimacy with these two remarkable bishops. This hypothesis is moreover confirmed by Rasputine's story of his journey to the Holy Land. This book is marked by extreme naïveté, simplicity, and sincerity. On the recommendation of the exalted churchmen mentioned, Rasputine was received by the Grand Duchesses Anastasie Nicholaevna and Melitza Nicholaevna, and it was through them that he made the acquaintance of Mme. Viroubova, *née* Tanieff, then maid of honor. He made a deep impression on this very religiously inclined woman, and gained at last an entry to the Imperial Palace. It was then that awoke in him his worst instincts, hitherto repressed, and it was then that he began adroitly to exploit the religious fervor possessed by very high personages. It must be admitted that he played his part with astonishing cleverness. Correspondence bearing on the subject and the testimony of various witnesses prove that Rasputine refused all subsidies, gratuities, and even honors which were freely offered him by their Majesties, indicating thus his integrity, his disinterestedness, and his profound devotion to the Throne, insisting that he was an intercessor for the Imperial family before God's throne. He alleged that everyone envied him his position, that he was surrounded by intriguers and slanderers, and that therefore evil reports concerning him were unworthy of belief. The only favor he accepted was the rental of his lodgings, paid by the personal Chancellor of his Majesty. He also accepted presents made by the hands of the Imperial family, such as shirts, waist-bands, etc.

"Rasputine had free entry to the apartments of the Emperor, saying prayers, addressing the Emperor and Empress with the familiar 'thou,' and greeting them in the Siberian peasant manner (with a kiss). It is known that he warned the Emperor, 'My death shall be thine also,' and that at Court he was regarded as a man gifted with the power of forecasting events. His predictions were couched in mysterious phrases like those of the Pythons of antiquity.

"Rasputine's income was derived from numerous persons who desired positions and money, and used Rasputine as their intermediary with the Emperor. Rasputine asked favors for his clients, promising, if these were granted, all kinds of blessings to the

Imperial family and to Russia.

"To this must be added that Rasputine possessed within himself a strange power by which he was able to exercise hypnotic suggestion. I have been able to establish the fact that he cured by hypnotism the disease of St. Vitus Dance which afflicted the son of one of his friends, Simanovitch. The young man was a student in the College of Commerce, and his malady completely disappeared after two séances in which Rasputine plunged the patient into hypnotic slumbers.

"Another case establishing the hypnotic power of Rasputine may be noted. During the winter of 1914-15 he was called to the house of the superintendent of railways in Tsarskoe Selo where lay, entirely unconscious, Anna Alexandrovna Viroubova, who had been seriously injured in a railroad accident. She was suffering from broken legs and a fracture of the skull. Their Majesties were in the room when Rasputine arrived, and he, simply raising his arms, said to the unconscious woman: 'Anushka, open your eyes,' which she instantly did, looking intelligently around her. This naturally made a deep impression on everyone present, including their Majesties, and it served to increase the prestige of Rasputine. Although Rasputine could barely read and write, he was far from being an inferior person. He had a keen and observant intellect, and a rare faculty of reading the character of any person with whom he came in contact. The rudeness and exaggerated simplicity of his bearing, which lent him the appearance of a common peasant, served to remind observers of his humble origin and his lack of culture.

"As so much was bruited in the public press about the immorality of Rasputine, the closest attention was given to this phase of his question. From the reports of the secret police it was proved that his love affairs consisted solely in night orgies with music-hall singers and an occasional petitioner. It is on record that when he was drunk he sometimes hinted of intimacies in higher circles, especially in those circles through which he had risen to power, but of his relations with women of high society nothing was established, either by police records or by information acquired by the commission. In the papers of the Bishop Varnava was found a telegram from Rasputine as follows: 'My dear, I cannot come, my silly women are shedding tears and won't let me go.' As for the accusation that in Siberia Rasputine was accustomed to bathe in company with women, and that he was affiliated with the 'Khlysty' sect, the Extraordinary Commission referred these charges to Gramoglassoff, professor in the Ecclesiastical Academy (of Moscow), who after examination of all the evidence, testified that among peasants of many parts of Siberia the common bath was a usual custom, and that he found no evidence in the writings or preachings of Rasputine of any affiliation with the 'Khlysty' doctrines.

"Rasputine was a man of large heart. He kept open house, and his lodgings were always crowded with a curiously mixed company living at his expense. To acquire the aureole of a benefactor, to follow the precepts of the Gospels according to which the generous hand is always filled, Rasputine took the money offered by his petitioners, but he gave generously to the poor and to people of the lower classes who begged his assistance. Thus he built up a reputation of being at once a generous and a disinterested man. Besides these alms Rasputine spent large sums in restaurants, cafés, music halls, and in the streets, so that when he died he left practically nothing. The investigation disclosed an immense amount of evidence concerning the petitions carried by Rasputine to Court, but all these, as has been said, referred merely to applications for positions, favors, railway concessions, and the like. Notwithstanding his great influence at Court not a single indication of Rasputine's political activity was disclosed.

"Many proofs of his influence were found in the papers of General Voyeikoff, Commandant of the Palace, as for example the following: 'My dear, Arrange this affair. Gregory.' These letters were annotated by Voyeikoff, with the names and addresses of the petitioners, the nature of their demands, the results of their applications, and the date of the replies. Many letters of the same kind were found among the papers of President of the Council of Ministers, Sturmer, and of other high personages. All the letters concerned themselves exclusively with favors and protection for the people in whom Rasputine interested himself. He had special names for various persons with whom he was in frequent contact. Sturmer was called 'The Old Man,' Archbishop Varnava 'Butterfly,' the Emperor 'Papa,' and the Empress 'Mama.' The nickname of Varnava, 'Butterfly,' was found in a letter to Mme. Viroubova.

"The inquiry into the influence of Rasputine on the Imperial family was intensive, but it was definitely established that that influence had its source in the profound religious sentiments of their Majesties, joined to their conviction that Rasputine was a saint, and was the sole intermediary between God and the Emperor, as well as of all Russia. The Imperial family believed that they saw proofs of his sanctity in his psychic power over certain persons of the Court, such as bringing back to life and consciousness the desperately injured Mme. Viroubova, whose case has been described; also in his undoubtedly benign influence on the health of the heir, and on a whole series of fulfilled forecasting of events.

"It is evident that sly and unscrupulous people did everything in their power to profit by Rasputine's influence on the Imperial family, thus waking up in the man his worst instincts. This is particularly true of the former Minister of the Interior, A. N. Khvostoff and of Belezky, Director of the Police Department. To consolidate their position at Court they came to an understanding with Rasputine whereby they agreed to pay him, out of the private funds of the Police Department, the sum of three thousand rubles monthly, besides other sums, that he might require, provided he helped them to place candidates agreeable to them. Rasputine accepted these conditions, and for three months filled his engagements, but finding that the arrangement was not advantageous to himself, returned to his independent manner of work. Khvostoff, fearing that Rasputine would betray him, began openly to oppose him. He knew that he stood well with the Imperial family, and he counted also on the coöperation of the Duma, of which he was a member, and in which Rasputine was cordially hated. This put Belezky in a difficult position, because he doubted Khvostoff's power at Court, and he had no doubt at all concerning Rasputine's power. Belezky decided therefore to betray his chief, and range himself on the side of Rasputine. His object was, to use the words of Rasputine himself, to throw down the Khvostoff ministry. The struggle between these two officials culminated in the famous plot against the life of Rasputine, which created such a sensation in the press during the year 1916. The plot was laid by Belezky in the following manner. An engineer named Heine, owner of several private gambling houses in Petrograd, was hired to go to Christiania to meet the unfrocked monk Illiador Troufanoff, a former friend of Rasputine. The result of this journey was a series of telegrams addressed to Heine and signed by Illiador covertly alluding to a conspiracy against the life of Rasputine. In one of these telegrams it was stated that the forty men engaged in the conspiracy were dissatisfied to wait longer, and it was necessary to send them immediately thirty thousand rubles. These telegrams, coming in war time from a neutral country, were delivered to the police, only after having been read being passed on to the person addressed. Finally, after receiving all the telegrams, Heine presented himself to Rasputine in the guise of a repentant sinner, giving him full details of the plot, in which he owned himself concerned, but which he vowed Khvostoff to be the leading spirit. The result was that Rasputine took the story to the Imperial family, and the dismissal of Khvostoff quickly followed. It is an interesting fact that Heine's telegrams from Christiania mentioned a number of names of persons living in Tsaritzine, former friends of Illiador, who were supposed to be in Christiania busy with the details of the plot. The evidence given at the inquiry proved beyond doubt that the persons concerned had never left their homes.

"Personally the official Khvostoff was highly esteemed by both the Emperor and the Empress, they believing him to be sincerely religious, and devoted to the interests of the Imperial family and to Russia, but the evidence shows that he was really devoted only to his personal interests. He once invited the head of the Gendarmerie, General Komissaroff, to go with him in civilian dress, and to introduce Rasputine to the Metropolitan Pitirim. They were received by a novice who went to the Metropolitan's study to announce them. When the Metropolitan appeared Rasputine introduced General Komissaroff, and disagreeable as it was to see a gendarme officer in his house, his Eminence invited the men to follow him into his study. There they discovered Khvostoff sitting on a sofa. Seeing Rasputine Khvostoff laughed rather nervously, but continued his conversation with the Metropolitan, then, rising to take his departure, asked General Komissaroff to drive home with him. Komissaroff found himself in an awkward position, and when Khvostoff suddenly asked him if he understood the affair he answered in the negative. 'Well,' said Khvostoff, 'it is now clear in what relation Pitirim stands with Rasputine. When you were announced he was just telling me that he had nothing in common with Rasputine, and that the person who was waiting to see him was an eminent Georgian. "Permit me," he said, "to leave you for a few minutes." Now we see who the "eminent Georgian" really was.' This was testified to by Komissaroff himself.

"Of all the ministers Khvostoff was the closest to Rasputine. Rumors of the intimate relations between Sturmer and Rasputine were found to be without foundation. There was between them, it is true, a friendship. Sturmer understood Rasputine's great influence, and did what he could to advance the interests of his clients. He sent fruit, wine, and delicacies to Rasputine, but there is no evidence that he allowed him to influence political affairs. The relations between Rasputine and Protopopoff, who, for some reason, Rasputine called 'Kalinine' were no more intimate, although Protopopoff liked Rasputine, and it is certain that Rasputine defended Protopopoff when the position of the latter was menaced. This was done usually in the absence of the Sovereigns, Rasputine addressing himself to the Empress, at the same time uttering predictions.

"Protopopoff distinguished himself by an extraordinary lack of will power, representing at different times quite opposing organizations. He was even at one time elected vice-president of the Duma. Protopopoff has publicly been accused of initiating and carrying out an attempt to put down the popular uprising of the first days of the Revolution. He is accused of having placed machine guns on the roofs of houses to shoot down the armed insurgents. However, the *juge d'instruction* Jousvik-Kompaneitz, after having interrogated many witnesses, and examining all the machine guns found in the streets of Petrograd in the first days of the Revolution, has testified that all the machine guns belonged to different regiments, and none, not even those found on the roofs of houses, to the police. Generally speaking, there were no machine guns on roofs, except those placed there at the beginning of the war as a defense against airplane attacks. It must be said that during the critical days of February, 1917, Protopopoff showed a complete incapacity, and from the legal point of view, his absolutely criminal weakness. Among his papers were found intimate and even affectionate letters from Rasputine, but not one letter contained anything more than recommendations in favor of his protégés. Nor in the papers of any other high personages were found letters of different tenor signed by Rasputine. Both press and public seem to have been persuaded that Rasputine was very intimate with two political adventurers, Dr. Badmaeff and Prince Andronnikoff, and that through him these men were able to exercise wide political influence. Evidence has established, however, that these rumors were without any foundation. The two adventurers were, in fact, nothing more than the hangers-on of Rasputine, glad to gather up the crumbs from his table, and falsely representing to their clients that they had influence over Rasputine, and through him influence at Court."

(Here follows at some length the result of the High Commission's inquiry into the activities of Dr. Badmaeff and Prince Andronnikoff, but as they have nothing whatever to do with this history they are omitted. A. V.)

"Badmaeff was the physician of Minister Protopopoff, but the Imperial family had no confidence in his methods—any more than had Rasputine—and in an examination of the servants of the Imperial household, it was demonstrated clearly that the Thibetan doctor had never been called in his professional capacity to the apartments of the Emperor's children.

"General Voyeikoff, Commandant of the Palace, I examined many times in the Fortress of Petropavlosk where he was imprisoned. He did not play a very powerful rôle at Court, but according to letters from his wife, daughter of Court Minister Fredericks, covering the years 1914-15, and found in his house, he was esteemed by the Imperial family as a man devoted to the throne, an impression which I, after several interviews with him, did not share. From letters of Voyeikoff to his wife it is plain that he was hostile to Rasputine. In certain of the letters he calls Rasputine the evil genius of the Imperial family and of Russia, and he believed that his intimacy at Court discredited the throne and gave strength to humors and opinions and slanderous stories by which the anti-Government party profited. Nevertheless he took full advantage of the influence of Rasputine. He had not the courage to reject his petitions, which is proved by the annotations in his handwriting on the letters of Rasputine."

(High Commissioner Roudneff adds that, in his opinion, Voyeikoff thought badly of Rasputine, and that his wife hated the man, but that neither of them communicated their views to the Imperial family. A. V.)

"Having heard a great deal of the exceptional influence at Court of Mme. Viroubova, and of her relations with Rasputine, and having read and believed what was said about her in society and the press, I must admit that when I went to examine her in the Fortress of Petropavlosk I was frankly prejudiced against her. This hostility remained with me up to the moment of her entrance into the office of the Fortress under the escort of two soldiers. As she entered the room I was struck with the expression of her eyes, an expression of more than earthly gentleness and meekness. This first impression was confirmed in all my subsequent interviews with her. From the first conversation which I had with her I became convinced that, given her individuality and her character, she could never have had any influence on politics either foreign or domestic. I believe this in the first place because of the essentially feminine point of view shown by her on all political matters of which we talked, and in the second place because of her loquacity and her complete incapacity to keep secret even facts which might reflect on herself. I became convinced that to ask Mme. Viroubova to keep anything a secret was equivalent to proclaiming it from the housetops, because anything that she thought important she felt impelled to communicate, not only to friends but to possible foes. Noting these two characteristics of Mme. Viroubova, I asked myself two questions—why she stood in close relations with Rasputine, and what was the secret of her intimacy with the Imperial family.

"I found the answer to the first question in conversations with the parents of Mme. Viroubova, M. Tanieff, chief of the private Chancellory of his Majesty, and his wife, *née* Countess Tolstoy. From them I learned of an episode in the life of their daughter which, in my opinion, explained why Rasputine obtained later such an influence over the will of the young woman. At the age of thirteen Mme. Viroubova fell gravely ill of typhus, the illness being complicated with peritonitis, and her condition, according to the physicians, was desperate. Her parents called to her bedside the famous priest, Father John of Kronstadt. Following his prayers the illness took a favorable turn, and the young girl was soon pronounced out of danger. This made a deep impression on her mind, and thereafter strongly inclined her to a religious life.

"Mme. Viroubova first met Rasputine in the house of the Grand Duchess Melitza Nicholaevna (wife of Grand Duke Peter), and that meeting was not a happy event. The Grand Duchess had prepared Mme. Viroubova for the meeting by conversations on the subject of religion, and had given her certain French books on occult subjects. Later the Grand Duchess invited Mme. Viroubova to her house, promising to introduce her to a great intercessor before God in favor of Russia, a man who possessed gifts of prophecy, and the faculty of curing the sick. This interview by Mme. Viroubova, then Mlle. Tanieff, made a great impression on the young woman who was then on the eve of marriage with Lieutenant Viroubova. Rasputine spoke only on religious subjects, and when the young girl asked him if he approved her marriage he answered allegorically saying that the pathway of life was strewn not only with roses but with thorns, and that man progressed towards perfection only through sufferings and trials.

"The marriage of Mme. Viroubova was from the first unhappy. According to the testimony of Mme. Tanieff, the man was completely impotent, addicted to perverted practices and saddistic habits, causing her daughter the most frightful moral sufferings and physical disgust. Nevertheless, believing in the Biblical injunction 'Whom God hath joined let no man put asunder,' Mme. Viroubova for a time kept her sufferings a secret even from her parents, and only after she had been nearly killed by her husband did she reveal to them the tragedy of her marriage. The result was, of course, a divorce. The testimony of Mme. Tanieff concerning the moral character of her son-in-law was confirmed by a medical examination of Mme. Viroubova, ordered by the Commission of Inquiry, and by which was established the virginity of the young woman. This examination was held in May, 1917. In consequence of her shocking marital experience the religious inclinations of Mme. Viroubova were increased and were developed into something approaching religious mania. She became the purest and most sincere admirer of Rasputine, who, up to the last day of his life, she considered a holy man, and one completely disinterested from every worldly point of view.

"In regard to the question of the intimacy of Mme. Viroubova with the Imperial family, I concluded that it had its roots in the wholly different mentalities of the Empress and Mme. Viroubova, that attraction of opposites which so often seems necessary to complete a balance. The two women were entirely different, and yet they had many things in common. Both, for example, were devotedly fond of music, and as the Empress possessed an agreeable contralto voice and Mme. Viroubova a good soprano, they occupied many leisure hours singing duets.

"Such were the conditions which produced in the minds of persons ignorant of the nature of the intimacy between the Empress and Mme. Viroubova, belief in the exceptional influence of Mme. Viroubova on Court affairs. As has been said, Mme. Viroubova possessed no such influence, nor could she have possessed it. The Empress dominated the intelligence and the will of Mme. Viroubova, but the attachment between the two women was very strong. The religious instincts deeply rooted in their two natures explains the tragedy of their veneration of Rasputine. The relations between the

Empress and Mme. Viroubova could be likened to those of a mother and daughter, nothing more.

"My opinions regarding the moral qualities of Mme. Viroubova, resulting from interviews with her in the Fortress of Petropavlosk and in the Winter Palace were entirely confirmed by the forgiving and Christian spirit displayed by her towards those who had caused her, in the course of her imprisonment, the most horrible suffering. Of the insults and tortures to which she was subjected in the Fortress I did not learn, in the first instance, from Mme. Viroubova herself, but from her mother. Only on direct examination did Mme. Viroubova confirm her mother's testimony, and even then she spoke calmly and with astonishing meekness, saying that her persecutors should not be blamed too severely because they did not realize what they were doing. These tortures of the prison guards, such as spitting in her face, dealing her blows on the head and body, accusing her of being the mistress of the Emperor and of Rasputine, tearing off her clothes and threatening to murder a sick woman who could walk only with the aid of crutches, caused the Commission of Inquiry to transfer the prisoner to a house formerly occupied by the Director of the Gendarmerie (House of Detention). The testimony of Mme. Viroubova presented a complete contrast to that of Prince Andronnikoff. Her statements were all candid and sincere, and their truth was subsequently established beyond doubt by documentary evidence. The only fault I found with Mme. Viroubova was her tendency to wordiness, and her amazing habit of skipping from one subject to another, without regard to the fact that she might be hurting her own cause. Mme. Viroubova appears to have interceded at Court for various persons, but her petitions were received with a certain distrust because of her known goodness and her simplicity of mind.

"The character of the Empress Alexandra was shown clearly in her correspondence with the Emperor and with Mme. Viroubova. This correspondence, in French and English, is filled with sentiments of affection for her husband and children. The Empress occupied herself personally with the education of her children, and she often indicates in her letters that it is desirable not to spoil them or to give them habits of luxury. The correspondence reveals also the deep piety of the Empress. In her letters to her husband she often describes her emotions during religious services, and speaks of the peace and tranquillity of her soul after prayer. Hardly ever, in the course of this long correspondence, are any allusions made to politics. The letters concern intimate and family affairs only. In passages in which Rasputine is mentioned she speaks of him as 'that holy man,' and shows that she considers him one sent of God, a prophet, and a man who prays sincerely for the Imperial family. Through the whole correspondence, which covers a period of ten years, I found not one single letter written in German. According to the testimony of Court adherents I have proof that before the War German was never spoken at Court. Because of public rumors of the sympathy of the Empress for Germany and of the existence in the Palace at Tsarskoe Selo of private wires to Berlin, I made a careful examination of the apartments of the Imperial family, and I found no indications at all of communications between the Imperial household of Russia and the Imperial household of Germany. I also examined the rumors concerning the beneficence of the Empress towards the German wounded and prisoners of War, and I found that the Empress showed compassion for the sufferings of Germans and Russians alike, without distinction, desiring to fulfill the injunction of Christ who said that whoever visited the sick and suffering also visited Himself.

"For these reasons, and above all on account of the frail health of the Empress, who suffered from a disease of the heart, the Imperial family led a very retired life, which favored the development, especially in the Empress, of extreme piety. Inspired by her devotion the Empress introduced into certain churches attached to the Court a régime of monastic services, and followed with delight, in spite of her ill health, up to the very end, masses which lasted for hours on end. This same excessive religious zeal was the foundation for her admiration for Gregory Rasputine, who, possessing an extraordinary power of suggestion, exercised an undeniably salutary effect on the invalid Tsarevitch. Because of her extreme piety the Empress was in no proper state of mind to understand the real source of the amazing influence of Rasputine on the health of the Heir, and she believed the explanation to be due, not at all to hypnotism, but to the celestial gifts which Rasputine owed to the sanctity of his life.

"A year and a half before the Revolution of 1917, the former monk, Illiador Troufanoff, sent his wife from Christiania to Petrograd with the proposal that the Imperial family purchase the manuscript of his book, which later appeared under the title of 'The Holy Devil,' in which the relations of the Imperial family with Rasputine were scandalously represented. The Police Department interested itself in the matter, and at its own imminent risk entered into negotiations with the wife of Illiador concerning the purchase of the manuscript for which Illiador demanded, I am assured, sixty thousand rubles. The affair was finally submitted to the Empress Alexandra who repudiated with indignation the vile proposition of Illiador, saying that 'white could never be made black, and that an innocent person could never be assoiled.'

"In terminating this inquiry I believe it necessary to repeat that Bishops Theofan and Hermogen contributed importantly to the introduction of Rasputine at Court. It was because of their recommendations that the Empress, in the beginning, received Rasputine cordially and confidently. Her sentiments towards him were fortified only by the reasons indicated in the course of this document."

APPENDIX B

Copy of certificate of acquittal of Anna Viroubova issued by the High Commission of Inquiry, August, 1917.

Ministry of Justice	*Testimonial*
The High Commission of Inquiry into the acts and abuses of Ministers and other High Personages of the Former Government.	This testimonial delivered to Anna Alexandrovna Viroubova at the end of the investigation of the High Commission of Inquiry, certifies that she was found not guilty and that she will not again be called to judgment. This statement is given under the signature and seal of the President of the High Commission.
25th of August, 1917.	
No. 3285	
Petrograd	
Winter Palace	
Tel. 1-38-20 and 186.	
(Seal)	(*Signed*) N. MOURVAVIEFF.

THE LAST PHOTOGRAPH TAKEN OF THE EMPRESS AND HER
DAUGHTERS, OLGA AND TATIANA, 1918

END OF BOOK THREE

LIST OF ILLUSTRATIONS

All the images used for this volume are rights free, i.e. in the public domain, and were sourced from either Wikimedia or Yandex LLC.

Empress Alexandra Feodorovna with Alexander Leonide, 1909. Lili Dehn's son born 9 August 1908, affectionately called 'Titi'.

PAGE

Cover C. Radziwill; L. Dehn; A. Viroubova
17 Book One cover and author Catherine Radziwill
20 Book I frontispiece portrait of Alexandra Feodorovna
42 Shoulder portrait of Princess Alix of Hesse and by Rhine
46 Shoulder portrait of Dowager Maria Feodorovna
66 Shoulder portrait of Grand Duchess Marie Pawlowna
73 Shoulder portrait of the Czar Nicholas II
94 Shoulder portrait of Grand Duke Nicholas Nikolaevich
105 General Orloff and Anna Viroubova with Czar on Standart

128 The Palace of Tsarskoye Selo (i.e. Catherine Palace)
151 Portrait of Raspoutine
157 Portrait of Peter Badmaieff
160 Full portrait in uniform of Cesarewitsch Alexei
170 Shoulder portrait of Alexander Protopopoff
176 Portrait of Mikhail Rodzianlo
182 Poster for La Grande Duchesse De Gérolstein
186 Royal Family portrait
193 Book Two shoulder portrait of author Lili Dehn
207 Portrait of Alexandra Feodorovna and son Alexei
217 Empress Alexandra Feodorovna doing needle work
219 Inset: Anna Viroubova
219 Standing portrait of Anna Viroubova
250 H.I.M. Nicholas II on Standart portrait with officers
250 Empress Alexandra Feodorovna aboard Standart
250 The Emperor with Tsarevitch on Tender
285 Thumbnail portrait of royal family
290 Shoulder portrait of Doctor Direvanko
291 Emperor out in the field with Lieutenant Dehn
291 The Tsarevitch at attention at G.H.Q.
291 Tsarevitch and his dog 'Joy'
308 The Emperor with Tsarevitch Alexei on the balcony
308 Empress Alexandra Feodorovna sitting with flowers
322 Drawing of Empress's note
339 Drawing of part of Empress's letter
340 Drawing of Empress's letter to Lily Dehn
345 Drawing of part of letter 30th July 1917
346 Drawing of Christmas card made by the Empress
350 Drawing of letter from Empress to Lily Dehn
354 Book Three full portrait of Anna Viroubova in habit
355 Sitting portrait of Empress Alexandra Feodorovna
364 Empress Alexandra on pony chaise
364 Empress and Tatiana in bed
365 Side portrait of Alexander Tannieff
382 Emperor and Empress relaxing on deck of Standart
382 Empress on deck of Standart handing gifts to sailors
393 Royal Family on jetty alongside Standart, in Yalta
394 Nicholas II, with Mdm Viroubova walking in Hamburg

ILLUSTRATIONS

407 Shoulder portrait of Mlle Sofia Tutcheff
412 Emperor and Tsarevitch in naval uniforms on Standart
413 Tsarevich Alexei with his minder Dr. Derevanko
413 The Emperor, Empress and Tsarevich in the gardens
427 Emperor and Empress in Slavic dress at ball of 1903
428 A sickly Empress on the Peterhof balcony
471 Rasputin's three children
472 Rasputin's guestroom
481 Empress with Grand Duke Dmitri
482 Empress Alexandra taking tea in the woods of Finland
534 The four Grand Duchesses (Princesses)
535 Shoulder portrait of Anna Viroubova
571 Drawing of last letter from Empress to Anna Viroubova
572 Drawing Smuggle letter from Empress to Anna Viroubova
625 Last known photograph of Empress and daughters, 1918
626 The Empress holding young Tatiana, 1909
628 Princess Victoria Melita

PRINCESS VICTORIA MELITA
Of Saxe-Coburg and Gotha

INDEX OF NAMES

A
Alexander II, 84, 177, 201, 289, 359
Alexander III, 4, 6, 23, 25-31, 34-35, 44, 51-53, 59, 61, 68, 134, 141, 177, 179, 372-373, 386, 406, 410, 419, 437, 488-489, 559
Alexandra, Feodorovna, *passim*
Alexis Michaelovitch, (Tsar), 363
Anastasie, Grand Duchess (aka Anastasia), 211, 223, 238-239, 242-243, 252, 282, 284-285, 287-289, 300, 305, 316, 343, 373, 411-412, 437, 496, 498, 505-506, 560, 562, 564, 567, 569, 571, 613
Antoinette, Marie, 5, 9, 23, 45, 47, 91, 245
Antonoff, 539-541
Appraxin (aka Apraxine), Count, 290
Apraxin, Countess Baida, 438, 567

B
Badmaieff (aka Badmieff), 156-157, 506, 538, 542, 544
Bariatinsky, Princess, 68, 228, 240, 583
Belaieff, (Minister of War), 479, 533, 567
Beletsky, General, 257
Benckendorff, Count, 284, 287, 295, 304, 317-318, 324
Berchik, 536, 550, 553, 594
Birileff, Admiral, 370
Botkin (aka Botkine), Dr. 234, 289, 344, 385, 499
Bouvier, Caroline Lee, 6
Brassoff, Countess, 423
Brisac, Mme., 414
Buchanan, Sir George (Ambassador), 494
Buxhoevden, Baroness (aka Buxhoeveden), 503, 558, 566, 571

C
Catherine the Great, 45, 127, 153, 165, 215, 249, 366, 398, 426
Chagin, Admiral, 370, 423-424
Cheidze, Deputy, 524, 545-546
Chemoduroff, 410, 566, 575
Cherevin, Lieutenant-General Peter Alexander Aleksandrovich, 4
Chkoni, 515, 518-519, 530
Clementine, Princess (of Coburg), 271

D
Dehn Charles, 211, 213-214, 221, 270, 273, 277, 291
Dehn, Madame – 5, 9-11, 14-15, 222, 286, 298, 325, 334-337, 341, 467, 478, 492, 494-495, 497-501, 503, 506-508, 510, 523, 557, 567, 569, 575
Demenkoff, Nikolai, 569
Demidoff, Anna (aka Niouta), 410, 576
Derevanko (aka Direvenko), Kolia, 00
Direvenko (aka Derevanko), Dr, 289-290, 378, 415-416, 422, 472, 506, 583
Djounkovsky, General (Governor of Moscow), 435-436
Dobiasgin, 556
Dolgorouky, Prince, 190, 500, 503, 562
Dolgorouky, Princess, 201,
Dorr, Rheta Childe, 552
Duvan, M., 448

E
Edward VII, 32, 246
Elidor, 249, 253, 258, 264
Elizabeth Feodorovna, 360, 362, 369, 391, 401, 435-436, 448, 575, 588
Etiquette, Louise of Battenberg (see Princess Louise)

F
Fedoroff, Professor, 313, 422, 472
Feodorovna, Tsaritsa Alexandra (aka Alix of Hesse and by Rhine) – See Alexandra Feodorovna
Feodorovna, GD Elizabeth (aka GD Serge) – See Elizabeth Feodorovna
Feodorovna, Maria (aka Marie Feodorowna) – See Marie Dowager-Empress
Feodorovnitch, Michail (First Tsar), 427

INDEX

Ferdinand, King (of Bulgaria), 129-130, 271
Fredericks, Count (Minister of the Court), 221-222

G

Gagentorn, Dr., 441
Galitzyne (aka Golitzin), Princess, 35, 151, 212-213
Gapone, (priest), 108
Gardieve, Mme., 435
Gedroiz, Dr., 433, 440-441
Gendrinkoff, Countess, 296
General:
  Aléxieieff (aka Alexieff), 167, 175, 181, 453-454, 493, 501
  Belaieff, 479, 533, 567
  Bogdanovitch, 402
  Gourko, 278, 493, 539-540
  Groten, 503, 538, 562, 566, 574
  Ivanoff, 453-454, 486
  Januchevitch, 144
  Komissaroff, 617
  Korniloff, 181, 187, 304, 546
  Mannerheim, 423
  Odoevsky, 436
  Poole, 541
  Polivanoff, 486
  Racine, 435-436, 440, 457, 496
  Rikkel, 452, 454
  Tcherewine, 26, 30
  Williams, 452
  Woyeikoff, 173, 175
George V, (of Great Britain) 221, 243, 315-316, 494
Germogen (see Hermogen)
Gibbs, Mr. (English tutor), 241, 300, 408, 503, 537, 555, 562, 572, 574, 576, 587
Gilliard, M. Pierre (French tutor), 14, 238, 241, 300, 408-409, 423, 442-443, 454, 495, 503, 537, 558, 560, 580, 584, 587
Golovina, Mary, 264
Gorémykine, Count (Prime Minister), 147
Gorky, (novelist), 551-552, 572, 576
Goutchkoff, M. (Minister of War), 302-303, 313, 448, 453, 486, 492, 501, 510
Gramoglassoff, professor, 614
Grancy, Mme (hofmistress of the Court of Hesse), 375, 395

Grand Duchesses:
  Anastasia Nicholaiewna (see Anastasie)
  Elizabeth (Elizabeth Feodorovna) of Gerolstein, 182
  Marie Alexandrowna of Coburg, 27
  Olga of Oldenburg, 80
  Olga Nicholaiewna, 42
  Marie (aka Maria) Nicholaiewna, *passim*
  Marie Paul, 315
  Melitza Nicholaevna, 389, 460, 463, 477, 613, 620
  Tatiana Nicholaiewna, 237, 239-240, 282, 288, 323, 325, 348, 360, 364, 388-389, 411, 414, 420, 433, 482, 495, 498, 561, 564, 567, 571, 573-576, 578, 584
  Xenia Alexandrowna, 37, 80, 371-372, 470, 483
Grand Duke:
  Alexander Michaylovitch, 80, 96
  Alexis, Tsarevich, 100-101, 103, 114, 117, 126, 155, 157, 166, 242, 282, 313
  Cyril, Vladimirovitch, 83-85, 216, 292, 494, 497
  Dmitri Pavlovitch, 379, 456, 479, 481-483
  Ernest, of Hesse, 391, 395, 406
  George Alexandrovich, 386, 389, 552
  George of Leuchtenberg, 40, 70
  Michael, 40, 53, 85, 125, 180, 305
  Nicholas (Nicholai) Nicholaievitch, 71-73, 76-77, 79, 87, 139, 142-145, 442-444, 455-456, 483, 486, 501
  Nikolai Michailovich, 482, 552-553
  Louis, (aka Prince Louis of Battenberg), 55, 445
  Paul, Alexandrowitch, 81-81, 84, 172, 180, 264, 282-283, 286-287, 293, 302-303, 379, 418, 455, 496-497, 552
  Sergius, 39-40, 44, 49, 57, 97
Grotten (aka Groten), Colonel, 276, 278, 282, 284, 503, 538, 562, 566, 574

H

Hélène of Orléans, Princess, 27
Hendrikoff, Countess, 503
Hermogen, Bishop (aka Germogen, Germogene, Gerogene), 249, 253, 564, 572, 612, 624
Hitrowo, Rita, 293

INDEX

Hohenlohe, Princess, (wife of Imperial Chancellor), 41
Horvat, Colonel, 197-198, 208
Hvostchinsky, Captain, 282

I

Ignatieff, Countess Sophy S., 111, 611
Illiador, 473-474, 616-617, 623-624
Irene, Princess, (of Prussia -formerly of Hesse, aka Princess Henry of Prussia), 135, 366, 368-369, 373, 395, 416, 422

J

Janchevsky, Glinka, 544
John, Father (of Kronstadt), 362, 560, 599, 602, 607, 620
Joseph, Francis, 50, 132

K

Kapnist, Count, 276
Karloff, Count, 379
Katoff, 410
Keller, Count, 313, 346, 348
Kennedy, Jaqueline, 7
Kerensky, Alexander Feodorovitch, 322-325, 327-329, 332-335, 337-338, 342, 352, 461, 475, 488, 499, 507-510, 517, 521, 524, 527, 531-532, 537, 540, 542, 544-550, 611
Kerr, Miss, 395
Khvostoff, A. N. (Minister of the Interior), 486, 616-617
Kitchener, Lord, 225
Kobilinsky, Commandant, 339-339, 341-342, 344
Kolantai, Mme. (Commisar), 549
Kolémine, Madame, 55-57, 60
Kolichko, (writer), 521
Korinsky, M., 535
Kontaisoff, Count, 359
Korovichenko (aka Korovitchinko), Colonel, 324
Kostritzky, Dr., 555
Kotzebue (aka Kotzebou), Colonel Paul, 278, 311, 315, 317-318, 320, 321, 504-506
Kotzebue-Pilar, Countess, 278

Koutousoff, Prince (Field Marshal), Goleniktcheff, 198, 359
Kouzmine, Lieutenant, 292
Krivosheim, (Minister of Agriculture), 442
Krzesinska, Mlle (Polish dancer), 28, 67, 69-70, 88

L

Laptinsky, Akilina, 262, 267
Lamsdorff, Count, 75
Leopold, (QV's youngest son), 366
Lenin (aka Lenine), 199, 352, 446, 531, 547, 552, 610
Lichatchieff, Mr, 439-440
Linavitch, 276, 283
Linevitch, Lieutenant, 490-491, 503, 562, 574
Lounacharsky, 547
Louis XVI, 5, 45, 47, 174, 179, 189, 245
Lvoff, Prince, 335, 437, 525

M

Makari, (priest), 346, 438, 467, 557
Makharoff, Admiral, 96
Malzoff, Mme., 406
Manassavitch-Maniuloff, GD Wladimir, 86, 118, 121-122, 124, 131, 138, 142, 147-148, 150, 162
Manouchine, Dr., 527-529, 546, 549, 592
Manouiloff, Detective, 520, 538, 543
Margaret of Prussia, Princess, 27
Marie, Dowager-Empress, (aka Maria Feodorovna, Feodorowna) 12, 34-35, 37-38, 45-46, 62-65, 102
Markoff, Lieutenant, 297
Mary, Queen (of England), 217, 232, 260
Melita, Princess Victoria, (of Saxe-Coburg and Gotha) 628
Menabde, (dancer), 599
Miasocdoff-Ivanof, 292
Miliukoff, Professor, 150, 185
Mourawieff (aka Mouravieff), Judge (Minister for Foreign Affairs), 75, 190

N

Nagorini, 575
Narishkin, Mme. Alexandra, 437

Narishkine, Zizi, 437, 566
Nicholai Michailovitch, 455
Nicholas II, 442, 456, 458-459, 485, 488-489, 494, 501, 554, 587
Nissky, Bishop, 570
Nosstiz, Count, 430

O

Olga, Grand Duchess (Alexandrovna), 81
Olga, Grand Duchess (Nicholaiewna), 42, 236-237, 239, 242, 281-282, 285, 288-289, 306, 323, 325-326, 345, 348, 360, 386, 388-389, 392, 394, 411, 414, 418, 420, 433, 435, 457, 490, 495, 498, 555, 560, 562, 567, 573, 575, 586-587, 625
Olga, Grand Duchess (of Oldenburg), 80
Orbelliany, Princess, 299
Orchard, Miss, 324, 384
Orianda, 209, 210
Orloff, General (aka Colonel) Alexander, 90-93, 95-106, 114, 116-118, 121, 127, 137, 144, 156, 178, 188, 218, 252, 258, 378-379, 383
Orloff, Princess Olga, 258

P

Paul I, 87, 276, 289, 359
Pavlovitch, Alexander, 566
Pavlovitch (Pawlowitch), GD Dmitry, 155, 456, 479
Pawlowna, Princess Marie (wife of GD Wladimir – aunt to Emperor), 31, 63-64, 66
Peretz, Colonel, 510-512
Pereverzeff, Judge, 524
Peter the Great, 152, 158, 182, 425, 467, 485
Petroff, M., 408, 454, 537, 567
Petrovskaia, Shoura, 576
Philippe, M., 72, 74-80, 119, 459-460, 465
Pistolkors, Madame Allie, 82, 84, 282-283
Pitirim, Archbishop, 163, 487-488, 524, 617
Pleve, von (aka Plehwe) (Minister of the Interior), 97, 118, 484
Pobedonostsev, Konstantin Petrovich, 4
Poincaré, President (of France), 131, 429
Polouboiarenoff, Mme., 511

Potsdam, Lord of, 41, 109
Pourtalès, Count, (German Ambassador to Russia), 131
Prince:
 Andrew, Prince (of Greece), 395
 Andronnikoff, 618-619, 622
 Boris, 418, 578
 Carol (of Rumania), 418
 Dolgoroukoff, 185
 George, Prince (of Greece), 395
 George Shrinsky-Shihmatoff, 341
 Lobanoff, 50
 Radolin, 41
 Stanislaw Albrecht Radziwill, 6
 Troubetskoy, Volodia, 190, 510, 512, 515, 518, 529, 567
Princess:
 Alice of Great Britain, 5, 51, 57-58, 69, 234, 372, 395
 Bariatinsky, Marie, 68, 228, 240, 583
 Eleanor of Sohmslich, 372, 375, 391, 395
 Kakouatoff, 594
 Louise, (of Battenberg - daughter of Victoria Battenberg), 375, 395
 Marie (of Greece), 389
 Oblensky, 372, 402, 406
 Orbeliani, 12, 234, 367, 368-369
 Scnkovsky, 369
 Youriewsky, 38
Protopopoff, Alexander Dmitrievich, (Minister of the Interior), 86, 148-150, 155, 159, 162-163, 165-170, 172-173, 263, 266, 275, 279, 455, 478-480, 485, 491, 567, 590, 618-619
Puchkine, Miss (Head Nurse), 404
Puritchkevitch, M., 478
Putiata, Bishop Vladimir, 401-402

Q

Queen Louise of Denmark, (formerly Louise of Hesse-Kassel), 51
Queen Alexandra of Great Britain, 34, 316, 419

R

Rabindar, Maria (Marie) 276
Rasputin (aka Raspoutine), 5, 10-16, 212, 218,

225, 233, 237-238, 248-249, 251-273, 275, 329, 331-332, 352, 354, 359, 379, 401-402, 416, 422, 430, 441-444, 448, 450, 453, 455, 457-488, 490, 516, 524, 549, 579, 590, 596, 612-624
Raswosoff, Admiral, 343
Ratief, Prince, 297, 410, 578
Rauchfuss, Dr., 404, 422
Resin, General, 282, 292-293, 297
Retief, Prince, 302
Rheta, (American writer), 552
Riman, Mme., 511
Ripe, Miss, 208
Rodzianko (aka Rodziansko), M., 171-172, 176, 296, 314, 455, 485, 492, 497, 525
Rodzianko, Mme., 450
Rostovseff, Count, (Empress's secretary), 396, 446, 468
Roudneff, Judge, 13, 475-476, 521-522, 524, 528, 535, 611, 619
Rousky, General, 313-314

S

Sablin, M., 281, 286-287, 433
Sandro, (husband to GD Xenia), 483, 491
Sazonoff, Mr (Foreign Minister), 138, 156, 429
Schabelsky, (priest), 141
Schneider, Mlle, 228, 286, 370, 408, 503, 508, 571
Schweinitz, General von, 30
Sednoff, 573
Shiff, Mme., 539
Shoulenbourg, Colonel, 405
Shoulgine, Mme., 313, 592
Shrinsky-Shihmatoff, Prince, 341
Sokoloff, M., 546
Soukhomlinoff, General, 274, 486-487, 576, 580
Soukhomlinoff, Mme., 487, 511, 515-516, 576 520-521, 530
Stackelberg, Baron, 313-314
Stolypine, Mr, 123-125, 416, 460, 473
Stopford, A., 315
Sturmer, Mr, 86, 137, 140-142, 144, 147-148-150, 155, 159, 162-163, 165-166, 168-169, 173, 446, 484, 615, 617

T

Tanieff, Madame (aka Tanieva - later Viroubova), (see Virouboff, Madame Anna)
Tanieff (aka Tanieiew), General Alexander Sergievitch, 85, 282, 359, 365, 620
Tanchevsky, 538
Tcherbatkoff, M., 486
Theofan, Bishop, 459, 612, 624
Tikhon, Patriarch, 402
Timasheff, Mme., 450
Tolstoaia, Zinaida, 567, 570
Tolstoy, Count (General), 359, 370,
Tolstoy, Countess, 583, 620
Toutelberg, Louise, 231
Trepoff, Mr (Head of Cabinet), 150
Tretskaia, Mme, 377
Trotzky, Leon, 446, 547-549
Troup, 575
Tutcheff, Mlle Sophie, 14, 237-238, 401-402, 407, 436

V

Varnava, Bishop, 259, 611, 614-615
Vasiltchikoff, Princess, 276
Vassilchikoff, Mme. (Lady in waiting), 448, 457
Vechniakoff, Marie (Head Nurse), 410, 415, 423
Velepolsky, Count, 421
Victoria, Princess (of Battenberg), 40, 135, 374-375, 395
Victoria, Queen, 5-6, 29, 32, 51, 54-57, 135, 197, 217, 327, 234-235, 249, 306, 352, 366, 372
Virouboff, Alexander, 218, 251-252, 378
Virouboff, Madame Anna, (aka Wyrubewa, Viroubova), *passim*
Volkoff (aka Wolkoff), 294, 300, 302-303, 309-310
Voronzoff (Voronzeff), Countess, 372

W

Wilhelm II, Kaiser, (aka William II), 6, 27, 29-30, 40-42, 50, 59, 130-131, 133, 135-138, 146-148, 150, 162, 165, 169, 184-185
Wissky, Archbishop, 558

Witte, Count Alexander, 109, 147, 371, 376, 484
Worontzoff-Daschkoff, Count, 145

Y
Yousopoff (yusupoff), Prince Felix, 201, 264, 269
Yousopoff (yusupoff), Princess Irene, 477-479

Z
Zadonsky, Tichin, 558

BOOK INFORMATION

65 Illustrations

Word Count

Introduction:	5,734
Book I:	63,854
Book II:	62,095
Book III:	115,098
Total word count:	251,831

Comparisons:	Ulysses	(265, 222)
	Pride and Prejudice	(122,685)

Volume II editions
Black & White images

Ebook   ISBN: 978-1-80517-208-6
Paperback ISBN: 978-1-80517-078-5 (cream paper, matt cover)
Hardback ISBN: 978-1-80517-207-9 (cream paper, gloss cover)
Hardback ISBN: 978-1-80517-079-2 (groundwood paper with dust jacket)

Series editions

Nicholas II – Tsar to Saint
The Memories of a Russian Yesteryear Volume 1
The Memories of a Russian Yesteryear Volume 2
The Memories of a Russian Yesteryear Volume 3

OTHER BOOKS BY THIS AUTHOR

NICHOLAS II – TSAR TO SAINT
THE RULER THAT LOST A DYNASTY

ebook
ISBN: 978-1-80352-908-0

Paperback
B&W on Groundwood paper
ISBN: 978-1-80352-799-4

Paperback
B&W on Cream paper
ISBN: 979-8-85465-243-8

Hardback
B&W on Groundwood paper
with dust jacket
ISBN: 978-1-80352-911-0

Hardback
B&W on Cream paper
ISBN: 979-8-85221-513-0

Pages: 546 / Illustrations: 203

From the back Cover:

Why was Russia's Imperial Family murdered? What part did they play in the revolution that gave rise to the Bolsheviks and transformed Russian Orthodoxy and State in to the Soviet Union? Tony Abbott takes us back to the pivotal moment in 1894 when Nicholas Alexandrovich Romanov became Tsar and there existed a real opportunity for Russia to modernise and become an industrial power and world leader. This is an incredible story of two rulers very much in love, who unwittingly created the circumstances that collapsed their dynasty.

Through first hand commentaries and with over 200 images, the events around the twenty-three year reign of Nicholas II are presented with clear and acute observations. What emerges is a fascinating insight of the man who made history by helping to bring about the revolution of an empire.

www.ingramcontent.com/pod-product-compliance
Lightning Source LLC
Chambersburg PA
CBHW020727220426
43209CB00082B/23